Contemporary European Politics

In this important new introductory textbook, José Magone provides an accessible and comprehensive introduction to contemporary European politics.

The unification of the European continent since the Fall of the Berlin Wall in 1989 and the collapse of communist regimes in Central and Eastern Europe has changed the nature of European politics. This book seeks to address the new European politics that emerged out of this coming together of West and East.

Utilising a pan-European comparative approach, the book:

- covers key topics, with chapters on the history, theory, institutions, parties and party systems, interest groups, systems of interest intermediation and civil society, the impact of European public policy and the emergence of a European common and foreign policy;
- provides detailed comparisons of the national political systems across Europe, including Central and Eastern Europe and the Balkans;
- contextualises national politics in the growing importance of European integration;
- examines the European Union multilevel governance system approach, highlighting relationships and interactions between the global, supranational, national, regional and local levels;
- analyses th change from modern politics, in which the nation-state was still in command of domestic politics and its own borders, to postmodern politics in which de-territorialisation, de-nationalisation and internationalisation processes have transformed the national politics of European states;
- facilitates learning through a wide range of pedagogical features, including chapter summaries, guides to further reading, questions for revision and extensive use of maps, figures, case studies and tables.

Richly illustrated throughout, this work is an indispensable resource for all students and academics of European politics.

José M. Magone is Professor in Regional and Global Governance at the Berlin School of Economics. He was previously Reader in European Politics at the University of Hull. Among his publications are *Politics of Southern Europe* (2003), *The Developing Place of Portugal in the European Union* (2004), *The New World Architecture* (2006) and *Contemporary Spanish Politics* (Second Edition, 2009).

Contemporary European Politics

A comparative introduction

José M. Magone

Routledge
Taylor & Francis Group

LONDON AND NEW YORK

First published 2011
by Routledge
2 Park Square, Milton Park, Abingdon, Oxon, OX14 4RN

Simultaneously published in the USA and Canada
by Routledge
711 Third Avenue, New York, NY 10017

Routledge is an imprint of the Taylor & Francis Group, an informa business

Typeset in Sabon and Futura by
Florence Production Ltd, Stoodleigh, Devon
Printed and bound in Great Britain by
TJI Digital, Padstow, Cornwall

British Library Cataloguing in Publication Data
A catalogue record for this book is available from the British Library

Library of Congress Cataloging in Publication Data
Magone, José M.
   Contemporary European politics: a comparative introduction/
   José M. Magone.
       p. cm.
   1. Europe – Politics and government.   2. European Union countries –
   Politics and government.   I. Title.
   JN12.M345 2011
   320.94—dc22   2010005146

ISBN: 978–0–415–41892–8 (hbk)
ISBN: 978–0–415–41893–5 (pbk)
ISBN: 978–0–203–84639–1 (ebk)

**For my dear nephew Leo
A great champion of life**

A nation without the means of reform is without the means of survival.

Edmund Burke (1729–97)

La démocratie a donc deux excès à eviter: l'esprit d'inegalité, qui la mène à l'aristocratie, ou au gouvernement d'un seul; et l'esprit d'égalité extreme, qui la conduit au despotisme d'un seul, comme le despotisme d'un seul finit par la conquête.

Montesquieu (1689–1755)

Seele des Menschen,
Wie gleichst Du dem Wasser!
Schicksal des Menschen,
Wie gleichst Du Dem Wind!

Johan Wolfgang Goethe (1749–1832)
(Extract from *Gesang der Geister über den Wasser!*)

Contents

CONTENTS

CONTENTS

Figures

Tables

Boxes

BOXES

Preface

This book is based on my extensive research on European politics, both for comparative publications and for my fifteen years of teaching in this area. Two teaching modules that I delivered in the Department of Politics and International Studies, entitled 'Conflict and Consensus in European Politics' and 'Diversity and Convergence in European Politics', provide the basis for this book. Many of these topics were included in lectures and tutorials. I also had the opportunity to continue to teach aspects of European and European Union politics at my new position in Berlin. The two academic environments have enhanced my understanding of European politics. In Hull, I had the privilege of teaching students in a variety of different fields, such as Politics, European Studies, Business Studies, History, Law and Economics. Owing to the success of the two modules on which this book has been based, I also developed a lighter-weight free elective called 'Comparative European Politics' for students from other faculties in Hull. Many of these students' ideas have been included in this book. I was very privileged to gain such an insight from students in both Hull and Berlin. I want to thank all my students for contributing to exciting discussions about European politics, particularly in the dynamic tutorials.

This book profited immensely from the Brynmor Jones Library in Hull and the Staatsbibliothek at the Potsdamer Platz in Berlin. Both libraries have facilitated my work; for European politics it is essential that libraries are up to date because of the richness and diversity of the continent itself, a continent that is constantly reinventing itself and in which each country provides a wealth of different experiences. A pan-European academic community is contributing to our better knowledge of European countries, and this book attempts to give a comparative overview of European countries from a pan-European perspective. It takes into account the growing importance of the European Union, and that national sovereignty is being replaced by post-sovereign forms of cooperation and integration. This book can only be a modest introduction to the richness and diversity of European politics and I take full responsibility for any errors or omissions in the book. In spite of this, I hope it can offer a interesting and absorbing introduction to students of European politics, and inspire further innovative research in this area.

I would like to thank my colleagues from my former Department of Politics and International Relations at the University of Hull. Special thanks go to Rudi Wurzel and Cristina Leston-Bandeira who belonged to the same teaching cluster of European politics and with whom I worked closely over fourteen years. I was also privileged to work with *eminence grise* Jack Hayward. His vast knowledge and passion for European politics was and will remain a source of inspiration that also had its impact on this book.

I also benefited from the various international research projects I took part in over the past fifteen years. These collective projects led to excellent edited monographs that I was able to use extensively when writing this book. I would like to thank all those who invited me to take part in these projects, in which I learned a great deal about other countries and regions. A special thank you goes to the many people I have worked with or with whom I have had academic exchanges, particularly Nancy Bermeo, José Ramón Montero, John Loughlin, Juliet Lodge, Jens Borchert David Hanley, Peter Mair, my university teacher Wolfgang C. Muller, Patrick Dumont, Luca Verzichelli, Michael Edinger, Thomas Saalfeld, Tanja Börzel, Paul G. Lewis, Andris Runcis, Liewen de Winter, Ian Manners, Alasdair Young, Chad Damro and Feliciana Rajewska.

I particularly would like to thank Attila Ågh of the Centre for Democracy Studies at the Corvinus University in Budapest for the many books on Hungary, Central and Eastern Europe that he gave me at European and international conferences and that were used extensively in some chapters. Needless to say, these books form a cherished treasure in my library. Three sources of inspiration for this book are Gordon Smith, who died recently, Samuel E. Finer and Klaus von Beyme. I would like to thank all three for having published so many books based in excellent research and scholarship.

I especially would like to thank especially Senior Publisher Craig Fowlie for supporting this project and for so patiently waiting for the manuscript. I also extend my thanks to his assistant, Nicola Parkin, who has been very supportive during the writing and completion processes. Moreover, I am very grateful to copy-editor Jane Fieldsend who, in a very interactive dialogue, considerably improved the quality of the text. Furthermore, I would like to thank the production team at Florence Production, particularly Sue Leaper, Fiona Isaac and Julia Mitchell for their hard work and commitment. Their teamwork was instrumental in transforming the manuscript into what, I would say personally, is a beautiful book.

Last, but not least, I want to thank very much my Mom for her enthusiasm and support during the process of writing.

Berlin, June 2010

Abbreviations

ABVV/FGTB	Algemeen Vaksverbond – Fédération Général du Travail de Belgique – General Federation of Labour of Belgium
ACLVB/CGSLB	Algemene Centrale der Liberale Vakbonden van België/ Centrale Générale des Syndicats Liberaux de Belgique – ACLVB/CGSLB
ACV	Algemeen Christenlijk Vaksverbond/Confédération des syndicats chrétiens en Belgique – ACV–CSC
AEBR	Association of European Border Regions
AER	Association of European Regions
AN	Alleanza Nazionale – National Alliance
AWPL	Akcja Wyborcza Polaków na Litwie (AWPL) – Electoral Action of Poles in Lithuania (Polish minority)
BDA	Bund der Deutschen Arbeitgeber– Association of German Employers
BDI	Bund der Deutschen Industrie – Association of German Industry
BNG	Bloque Nacionalista Galego – Nationalist Galician Block
BNP	British National Party
BRWG	Better Regulation Working Group
BSP	Bălgarska Socialističeska Partija – Bulgarian Socialist Party
BUSINESSEUROPE	Union of Employers and Business Organisations in Europe
BZÖ	Bündnis für die Zukunft Österreichs – Union for the Future of Austria
CAF	Common Assessment Framework
CAP	Common Agricultural Policy
CARCE	Comisión de Asuntos Relacionados con la Comunidad Europea – Committee on European Community Affairs
CBI	Confederation of British Industry
CCOO	Comisiones Obreras –Workers' Commissions

CDA	Christen Democratisch Appel –Christian Democratic Appeal
CDC	Centro Cristiano Democratico – Democratic Christian Centre
CDH	Centre Démocratie Humaniste – Democratic Humanist Centre
CDR	Comissão de Desenvolvimento Regional – Commission of Regional Development
CDS-PP	Centro Democratico Social–Partido Popular – Democratic Social Centre–People's Party
CDU	Christlich-Demokratische Union – Christian Democratic Union
CD&V	Christen-Democratisch en Vlaams-Christian – Democratic and Flemish
CEAC/COSAC	Committee of European Affairs Committees
CEEP	Centre Européen des Entreprises à Participation Public d'Intérêt Économique Général – European Centre of Enterprises Providing Public Services
CEMR	Council of European Municipalities and Regions
CEOE	Confederación Española de Organizaciones Empresariales – Spanish Confederation of Enterpreneurial Organisations
CEPYME	Confederación Española de Pequeñas y Medianas Empresas – Spanish Confederation of Small and Middle Sized Enterprises
CFDT	Confédération Française Démocratique du Travail – French Democratic Confederation of Work
CFTC	Confédération Française des Travailleurs Chrétiens – French Confederation of Christian Workers
CGE–CGC	Confédération Général de l'Encadrement – Confédération Generale de Cadres – General Confederation of Cadres
CGIL	Confederazione Generale Italiana del Lavoro – Italian General Confederation of Labour
CGPJ	Consejo General del Poder Judicial – General Council of the Judiciary Power
CGT	Confédération Générale du Travail – General Confederation of Labour
CGTP	Confederação Geral dos Trabalhadores Portugueses – General Confederation of Portuguese Workers
CGPME	Confédération Général des Petites et Moyennes Entreprises et du Patronat – General Confederation of Small and Middle Enterprises and Employers
CIP	Confederação da Industria Portuguesa – Confederation of Portuguese Industry
CISL	Confederazione dei Sindacati dei Lavoratori – Confederation of Trade Unions of the Workers
CiU	Convergencia i Unió – Convergence and Union
CNV	Christelijk Nationaal Vakverbond – Christian National Trade Unions
Comecon/CMEA	Council for Mutual Economic Assistance

Cominform	Communist Information Bureau
Comintern	Third Communist International
CONFINDUSTRIA	Confederazione di Industria – Confederation of Industry
COR	Committee of the Regions
COREPER	Committee of Permanent Representatives
CPLP	Comunidade de Paises de Lingua Portuguesa – Community of Portuguese Speaking Countries
CPI	Corruption Perception Index
CPMR	Conference of Peripheral and Maritime Regions
CSCE	Conference for Security and Cooperation in Europe
CSF	Common Support Framework
CSFP	Common Foreign Security Policy
CSM	Conseil Superieur de la Magistrature – Higher Council of the Judiciary
CSM	Conselho Superior da Magistratura
CSM	Consiglio Superiore de la Magistratura – Higher Council of the Judiciary
ČSSD	Česká strana sociálně demokratická – Czech Social Democratic Party
CSU	Christlich Soziale Union – Christian Social Union
CSV	Chrestlich Social Vollekspartei – Christian Social People's Party
CVP	Christiliche Volkspartei – Christian People's Party
CVP/PSC	Christen-Demokratisch Volkspartij – Parti Social Christien – Christian Democratic People's Party – Christian Social Party
DC	Democrazia Cristiana – Christian Democracy
DeSus	Demokratična Stranka Upokojencev Slovenije – Democratic Pensioners' Party of Slovenia
DF	Dansk Folke Parti – Danish People's Party
DGB	Deutsche Gewerkschaftsbund
DP	Darbo Partija – Labour Party
DPS	Dviženie za Prava i Svobodi – Movement for Rights and Freedoms
DUP	Democratic Unionist Party
DVU	Deutsche Volksunion – German People's Union
EAGGF	European Agricultural Guidance and Guarantee Fund
EAP	Environmental Action Plan
EC	European Community
ECHR	European Court of Human Rights
ECJ	European Court of Justice
ECOFIN	European Council of Finance Ministers of the European Union
ECSC	European Community for Steel and Coal
EDA	European Defence Agency
EEA	European Economic Area
EEC	European Economic Community
EFQM	European Framework for Quality Management
EFTA	European Free Trade Area

eGWG	e-Government Group
EHAK	Partido Comunista de las Tierras Bascas – Communist Party of the Basque Country
EIPA	European Institute for Public Administration
ELDR	European Liberal, Democratic and Reform Party
EMS	European Monetary System
EMU	European Monetary Union
ENA	École Nationale D'Administration – National School of Administration
ENM	École Nationale de Magistrature – National School of Magistrates
ENP	European Neighbourhood Policy
EPP–ED	European People's Party–European Democrats
ER	Eestimaa Rohelised Estonian Greens
ERC	Ezquerra Republicana de Catalunya – Republican Left of Catalonia
ERDF	European Regional Development Fund
ERL	Eestimaa Rahvaliit – Estonian People's Union
ERM	Exchange Rate Mechanism
ERP	European Recovery Plan
ESDP	European Security and Defence Policy
ESF	European Social Fund
ETA	Euskadi ta Askatasuna – Basque Country and Freedom
ETUC	European Trade Union Confederation
EU	European Union
EUL–NGL	European United Left–Nordic Green Left Group
EUMC	European Union Military Committee
EUMS	European Military Staff Committee
EUPAN	European Union Public Administration Network
Euratom	European Atomic Community
EUSC	European Satellite Centre
FDP	Freie Demokratische Partei – Free Democratic Party
FDP–PRD	Freisinnig-Demokratische Partei der Schweiz – Parti radical-démocratique suisse
Fidesz–MPS	Fidesz–Magyar Polgári Szövetség – Fidesz–Hungarian Citizen's Federation
FN	Front National – National Front
FNV	Federatie Nederlandse Vakbeweging – Dutch Federation of Trade Unions
FO	Force Ouvrière – Workers'Force
FPÖ	Freiheitliche Partei Österreichs – Freedom Party of Austria
GDP	Gross Domestic Product
GERB	Grajdani za evropeisko razvitie na Bulgarija – Citizens for the European Development of Bulgaria
GNI	Gross National Income
HMCS	Her Majesty's Court Service
HRMG	Human Resources Management Group
ICTU	Irish Congress of Trade Unions

IPSG	Innovative Public Services
IRL	Isamaa ja Res Publica Liit – Pro Patria and Res Publica
ISS-EU	Institute for Security Studies of the European Union
IU	Izquierda Unida – United Left
IV	Industriellenvereinigung – Industrial Association
JL	Jaunais Laiks – New Era
K	Eesti Keskerakond – Estonian Centre Party
KD	Kristendemokraterna – Christian Democrats
KDH	Kresťanskodemokratické hnutie – Christian Democratic Union
KDNP	Kereszténydemokrata Néppárt – Christian Democratic People's Party
KDU–CSL	Křesťansko-demokratická unie–Československá strana lidová – Christian Democratic Union–Czechoslovak People's Party
KFP	Konservative Folkepartiet – Conservative People's Party
KFP	Kristellig Folkeparti – Christian People's Party
KKE	Kommunistiko Komma Ellada – Communist Party of Greece
KOK	Kansallinen Kokoomus – National Coalition Party
KSČM	Komunistická strana Čech a Moravy – Communist Party of Bohemia and Moravia
KVP	Katholieke Volkspartij – Catholic People's Party
KWNS	Keynesian Welfare National State
KZP	Katholische Zentrumspartei
LDS	Liberalna Demokracija Slovenije – Liberal Democracy of Slovenia
LiCS	Liberalų ir Centro Sąjunga – Liberal and Centre Union
LN	Lega Nord per l'independenza di Padania – Northern League for the independence of Padania
LO	Landesorganisationen – Trade Union Confederation in Sweden, Denmark and Norway
LPP–LC	Latvijas Pirmā Partija–Latvijas Ceļš
LPR	Liga Polskich Rodzin – League of Polish Families
LRLS	Lietuvos Respublikos Liberalų Sąjūdis – Lithuanian Republic Liberal Movement
LSDP	Lietuvos socialdemocratu partija – Lithuanian Social Democratic Party
LS–HZDS	Ľudová strana–Hnutie za demokratické Slovensko
LVLS	Lietuvos Valstiečių Liaudininkų Sąjunga – Lithuanian Peasant Popular Union
LZS	Centriska Partija–Latvijas Zemnieku Savienība – Centre Party–Latvian Peasants Union
MDF	Hungarian Democratic Forum
MEDEF	Movement des Entrepreneurs Français – Movement of French Entrepreneurs
MoDem	Mouvement Democrat – Democratic Movement
MR	Mouvement Reformateur – Reforming Movement

MSI	Movimento Sociale Italiano – Italian Social Movement
MSZP	Magyar Szocialista Párt – Hungarian Socialist Party
NAF	Norges Arbeidsgiverforening – Norwegian Employers' Organisation
NATO	North Atlantic Treaty Organisation
ND	Nea Dimokratia – New Democracy
NDSV	Nacionalno Dviženie za Stabilnost i Văzhod – National Movement for Stability and Progress
NGO	Non-Governmental Organisation
NHS	National Health Service
NKV	Nederlands Katholieke Vakverbond – Dutch Catholic Trade Union Confederation
NPD	Nationaldemokratische Partei Deutschlands – National Democratic Party of Germany
NPM	New Public Management
NS	Naujoji Sąjunga–Socialliberalai – New Union–Social Liberals
NSDAP	Nationalsozialististische Deutsche Arbeiterpartei – German National Socialist Workers' Party
NSI	Nova Slovenija–Krščanska Ljudska Stranka – New Slovenia–Christian People's Party
NVV	Nederlands Verbond van Vakbewegingen – Dutch Union of Trade Unions
ODS	Občanská demokratická strana – Democratic Civic Party
OECD	Organisation for Economic Cooperation and Development
OEEC	Organisation for European Economic Cooperation
ÖGB	Österreichischer Gewerkschaftsbund – Austrian Trade Union Confederation
OMC	Open Method of Coordination
OPEC	Organisation of Petroleum Exporting Countries
OSCE	Organisation for Security and Cooperation in Europe
ÖVP	Österreichische Volkspartei – Austrian People's Party
PASOK	Panneliniko Sosialistiko Kinima – Panhellenic Socialist Movement
PCE	Partido Comunista Español – Spanish Communist Party
PCF	Parti Comuniste Français – French Communist Party
PCI	Partito Comunista Italiano – Italian Communist Party
PCP	Partido Comunista Português – Portuguese Communist Party
PCTVL	Par Cilvēka Tiesībām Vienotā Latvijā – For Human Rights in United Latvia
PD	Partidul Democrat – Democratic Party
PD	Partito Democratico – Democratic Party
PdL	Partito delle Libertá
PDS	Partei des Demokratischen Sozialismus – Party of Democratic Socialism
PDS	Partito Democratico della Sinistra – Democratic Party of the Left

PES	Party of European Socialists
PiS	Prawo i Sprawiedliwość – Law and Justice
PL	Popolo della Libertà – People of Freedom
PLD	Partidul Liberal Democrat – Liberal Democratic Party
PLI	Partito Liberale Italiano – Italian Liberal Party
PNF	Partito Nazionale Fascista – National Fascist Party
PNL	Partidul National Liberal – National Liberal Party
PNV	Partido Nacionalista Vasco – Basque Nationalist Party
PO	Platforma Obywatelska – Civic Platform
POB	Parti Ouvrier Belge – Belgian Workers' Party
PP	Partido Popular – People's Party
PPI	Partito Populare Italiano – Italian People's Pary
PRACE	Programa de Reestruturação da Administração Central do Estado – Programme for the Restructuring of the Central State Administration
PRC	Partito della Rifondazione Comunista – Party of Communist Refoundation
PRI	Partito Republicano Italiano – Italian Republican Party
PRM	Partidul Romania Mare – Great Romania Party
PS	Partido Socialista – Socialist Party
PS	Parti Socialiste – Socialist Party
PSC	Political and Security Committee
PSD	Partido Socialdemocrata – Social Democratic Party
PSD	Partidul Social Democrat – Social Democratic Party
PSDI	Partito Socialdemocratico Italiano – Italian Social Democratic Party
PSI	Partito Socialista Italiano – PSI
PSL	Polskie Stronnictwo Ludowe – Polish People's Party
PSOE	Partido Socialista Obrero Español – Spanish Socialist Workers Party
PvdA	Partij van der Arbeid – Labour Party
RE	Eesti Reformierakond – Estonian Reform Party
RKSP	Roomisch Katholieke Staatspartij – Roman Catholic State Party
SAP	Sveriges Socialdemokratiska Arbetareparti – Swedish Social Democratic Workers' Party
SD	Socialni Demokrati – Social Democrats
SDE	Sotsiaaldemokraatlik Erakond – Social Democratic Party
SDKU–DS	Slovenská demokratická a kresťanská únia–Demokratická strana – Slovakian Democratic and Christian Union–Democratic Party
SDL	Sojusz Lewicy Demokratycznej – Democratic Left Alliance
SDLP	Social Democratic and Labour Party
SDS	Slovenska Demokratska Stranka – Slovenian Democratic Party
SDS	Săjuz na Demokratični Sili – Union of Democratic Forces
SEA	Single European Act

SEM	Single European Market
SF	Sinn Fein – We, ourselves
SF/RK	Svenska folkspartiet/Ruotsalainen kansanpuolue – Swedish People's Party
SFP	Socialistisk Folkeparti – Socialist People's Party
SCP	Stability and Convergence Programme
SGP	Stability and Growth Pact
SIGMA	Support for Improvement and Governance and Management in Central and Eastern European Countries
SKL	Suomen Kristilinen Liitto – Finnish Christian Party
SLS	Slovenska Ljudska Stranka – Slovenian People's Party
SMER–SD	Smer–Sociálna Demokracia-Direction – Social Democracy
SMK	Strana maďarskej koalície–Magyar Koalíció Pártja – Party of the Hungarian Coalition
SNP	Scottish National Party
SNS	Slovenska Nacionalna Stranka – Slovenian National Party (Nationalist)
SNS	Slovenská Národná Strana-Slovak National Party (Nationalist)
SP.A	Socialistische Partij – Anders – Socialist Party – Different
SPD	Sozialdemokratische Partei Deutschlands – Social Democratic Party of Germany
SPÖ	Sozialdemokratisches Partei Österreichs – Social Democratic Party of Austria
SRB	Samoobrona Rzeczpospolitei Polskiei – Self-defence of Republic of Poland
SV	Socialistisk Venstreparti – Socialist Left Party
SVP	Schweizerische Volkspartei – Swiss People's Party
SWPR	Schumpeterian Workfare Post-national Regime
SYN/SYRIZA	Synaspismos tis Rizospastikis Aristeras (SYRIZA) – Coalition of Radical Left
SzDSz	Szabad Demokraták Szövetsége – Union of Free Democrats
TA	Treaty of Amsterdam
TEU	Treaty of the European Union/Treaty of Maastricht
TP	Tautas Partija – People's Party
TPP	Tautos Prisikėlimo Partija – National Revival Party
TS-LKD	Tėvynės Sąjunga–Lietuvos Krikščionys Demokratai – Homeland Union–Lithuanian Christian Democrats
TT	Tvarka ir Teisingumas – Order and Justice
TUC	Trade Union Congress
UDF	Union de la Democratie Française – Union of French Democracy
UDMR	Uniunea Democratică Maghiară din România – Hungarian Democratic Union in Romania
UEN	Union of European Nations
UGT	União Geral dos Trabalhadores – General Union of Workers

UGT	Union General de Trabajadores – General Union of Workers
UIL	Unione Italiana del Lavoro – Italian Union of Labour
UK	United Kingdom
UMP	Union pour le Mouvement Populaire – Union for the People's Movement
UN	United Nations
UNAPL	Union National des Professions Liberales – National Union of Liberal Professions
UPA	Union Professionelle Artisanale – Crafts Union
USA	United States of America
USSR	Union of Socialist Soviet Republics
UUP	Ulster Unionist Party
VB	Vlaams Belang – Flemish Interest
VBO-FEB	Verbond van Belgische Ondernemingen – Fédération des Employeurs de Belgique
VLD	Vlaamse Liberalen en Democraten – Flemish Liberals and Democrats
VVD	Volkspartij voor Vrijheid en Democratie – People's Party for Freedom and Democracy
WASG	Wahlgruppe für Arbeit und soziale Gerechtigkeit – Electoral Group for Work and Social Justice
Z	Zares – For Real

Introduction to contemporary European politics

- The rationale of the book: the emergence of new European politics
- A comparative approach: cross-country differences, similarities and convergences
- Reducing complexity through the use of regional clusters
- The 'great transformation' of the late twentieth century
- The growing importance of the European integration process
- Constitutions and constitutionalism
  - The origins of European constitutions
  - The structure of European constitutions
- The structure of this book

SUMMARY OF CHAPTER 1

This chapter explains why it is important to study European politics comparatively. The past four decades saw major changes in European politics. Social, economic, political, cultural and international change has led to new conditions for national political institutions and actors. The chapter gives an initial outline of the differences between some of the larger regions of Europe.

The chapter also gives an introduction to the growing role of the European Union in shaping national politics. Additionally, there is an introduction to the constitutions and constitutionalism of European countries, including a discussion of the main principles, rights, duties and defined institutional order.

The chapter concludes with an overview of the book chapters as a whole.

The rationale of the book: the emergence of new European politics

The unification of the European continent since the fall of the Berlin Wall in 1989 and the collapse of communist regimes in Central and Eastern Europe has changed the nature of European politics. This book seeks to address the new European politics that emerged out of this coming together of West and East. Accordingly, a pan-European approach towards contemporary politics is used in order to understand better the political, social and economic dynamics of Europe.

Although we focus on comparing the national political systems across Europe, this is contextualised within the overarching and growing importance of European integration. The European Union multilevel governance system approach will be used to show the relationships and interactions between the supranational, national, regional and local levels. Some references will also be made to the relationship between the European Union and global governance (see below and also Chapters 4 and 13).

In this book we argue that European politics has changed since the 1970s from modern politics, in which the nation-state was still in command of domestic politics, to postmodern politics, in which de-territorialisation, de-nationalisation and internationalisation have considerably changed the national politics of individual member states. The individualisation of societies and the plurality of living forms have also led to changes to party systems and electoral politics. Moreover, the policies related to the Single European Market have 'hollowed out' considerably the capabilities and choices of national governments.

The decline of the industrial sector and the increasing importance of the services sector have also lead to a change in political culture in most European countries. The change in values and mentalities in the new Europe is central to the transformation of European politics. Christian Welzel's and Ronald Inglehart's thesis that we are embedded in a cultural transition from survival values linked to the industrial society to self-expressive values in the post-industrial society will be central to the present book (Inglehart and Welzel, 2005).

A comparative approach: cross-country differences, similarities and convergences

Since Aristotle's book *Politics*, the comparative approach has been an excellent way to identify – out of the uniqueness of each political system, groups or 'families' of countries – a method that clearly helps us to reduce the complexity of analysing all the political systems of Europe. The main aim of the comparative approach is not only to reduce complexity by showing similarities and differences, but also to identify patterns of behaviour within institutions such as political parties, parliaments, governments and the judiciary (Finer, 1970: 38–9).

If we take membership of the Council of Europe – the largest intergovernmental organisation in Europe, not to be confused with the European Union, a much smaller supranational institution – there are 47 European countries. This number includes Turkey, Russia, Ukraine, Moldavia, Georgia, Armenia and Azerbaijan. Only Belarus, which is the only dictatorship in Europe and which does not comply with the minimum standards of democratic order, is excluded from membership. A more restricted definition of Europe includes: the 27 members of the European Union; the Balkan states (expected to become members at some stage in the future); and the European Economic Area countries of Iceland, Norway and Liechtenstein. Meanwhile, Iceland has also become a potential candidate country for joining the European Union (*Euractiv*, 27 July 2009). This would lead to a total of 36 countries. Kosovo remains in a limbo situation due to the split in the international community about its recognition; 54 out of 192 countries have recognised Kosovo, including 22 of the EU member states. Within the EU, Greece, Spain, Romania, Slovakia and Cyprus are against Kosovo becoming a member (*BBC News*, 17 February 2009) and only the future will show whether there can be a solution to this problem. The present Serbian government seems to be taking a more pragmatic approach, due to its intention to join the European Union.

We have excluded an in-depth consideration of Russia, Ukraine, Moldavia, Turkey, Georgia, Armenia and Azerbaijan. However, in some chapters we still make reference to those countries. One of the main reasons is that they represent different 'families', more on the sidelines of European politics. Russia and Ukraine have semi-presidential systems in which many problems with democracy still persist, in terms of elections, oppression of civil society and the press (Ross, 2004; Boeckh and Völkl, 2007). Turkey has made substantial progress towards democracy, but there are still problems with regard to the role of the military in the political system, human rights abuses and the role of women in society. The electoral system is also quite restrictive – with a 12 per cent threshold, which may prevent fragmentation but also allows a considerable sector of society to be excluded (Altunişik and Tür, 2005). The Caucasus democracies, even Georgia, are still far from meeting the minimum democratic standards established by the European Union. Moreover, these former Soviet republics have yet to deal with many unresolved disputes over territories in which minorities from other neighbouring countries live. The conflict between Georgia and Russia during the summer of 2008 over Abkhazia and South Ossetia and the ongoing situation between Azerbaijan and Armenia since 1991 over Nagorno-Karabakh are examples of such conflicts (Opitz, 2009).

> **Box 1.1 Why compare European countries?**
>
> - In order to understand the main features of European politics it is important to reduce complexity.
> - The main task is to group countries into 'families' and compare these families so that comparison of 37 European countries becomes manageable.
> - The comparative method allows us to classify, describe and analyse not only individual countries but also 'families' of countries using a vast number of political variables.
> - The comparison of different political systems contributes to a better understanding of how institutions and processes work and helps identify which similarities and differences one can find between the various 'families' of countries.

In order to gain broader insights into contemporary European politics, we focus on the 37 countries, which clearly represent different patterns of European politics (Table 1.1). The least developed region in terms of democracy and human rights is the Balkans, nevertheless it is expected that the continuing support of the European Union will lead to considerable improvements for this region in the future. Probably, the most problematic country is Bosnia-Herzegovina, which is made up from three different ethnic groups and where reconciliation, imposed mainly by the international community, has been difficult to achieve.

In this book, we follow Samuel E. Finer's interpretation of the comparative approach. The main task is to group institutions, political systems or processes into 'families' or 'types' that are close to each other. Grouping countries that resemble each other into families and contrasting the countries both within the families and in relation to the countries within the other families helps us to understand why and how differences and similarities exist between countries. The main questions in this book are: *why* European political systems, or at least families of countries, are different from or similar to each other; and *how* these differences and similarities are demonstrated (Finer, 1974: 38–39). In responding to these questions, we are able to learn a lot about some of the positive and negative aspects of institutions and processes, as well as understand why some political systems are performing better or worse than others. This process also allows the uniqueness of some political systems or ill-conceived institutional transfers from one country to another to be identified. Therefore, the book will mainly describe, classify and analyse comparatively the diverse political systems of Europe. In the end, comparing European politics depends very much on what the researcher believes is important to compare. Samuel Finer claimed that:

> the problem is to establish categories that are neither so numerous as to make comparisons impossible nor so few as to make contrasts impossible. And how many categories there should be, and of what type, depends upon the initial criteria we select. But what one observer thinks an important or significant criterion of comparison and contrast may be trivial to another.
>
> (Finer, 1974: 39)

One characteristic of this book is that it attempts to compare, at the least, all 37 countries of Europe (although subject to how much information exists). In this sense, this reveals an ambition to overcome the bias of most comparative books on Europe, which focus only on the larger countries plus, on occasion, the Netherlands. We have combined the comparative approach with detailed information about each of the European countries. Of course, such an enterprise will be stronger in some sections than others, but we considered it important to be distinctive from most comparative studies on European politics. In this book, both larger and smaller countries have been covered extensively in order to achieve a more balanced approach to the reality of European politics.

Reducing complexity through the use of regional clusters

In order to reduce the complexity of individually analysing all thirty-six countries, we grouped them into regional clusters. This allowed us to simplify the comparing of countries (see Table 1.1), although we also kept some flexibility in using these regional clusters. Other categories at times superseded the importance of regional political cultures – for example, if countries clearly belong to a particular type such as majoritarian versus consensus democracies, weak or strong parliaments, federal or unitary states, then these regional clusters were only partially used or completely discarded. We differentiated at least twelve regions, some of them, such as France and Turkey, consisting of one country only.

The **Benelux countries:** Belgium, the Netherlands and Luxembourg have a common history. Belgium became independent from the Netherlands in 1830. Luxembourg became independent after the Vienna Congress, though it has strong historical links with both Belgium and the Netherlands. The union known as the Benelux was formed after 1944.

Germanic/Drei-Sat Europe: This comprises Germany, Austria, Switzerland and Lichtenstein. 'Germanic' is clearly a difficult label, but it refers to the common language of the three/four countries. In the case of Switzerland, there is also francophone Switzerland, influenced more by France; however, the vast majority of the population in Switzerland is German-speaking. There is a common television channel called 3Sat, established in 1984 by the public televisions of Austria (ORF), Switzerland (SRG) and Germany (ZDF, ARD) that broadcasts in all three countries.

Nordic Europe: This comprises the Scandinavian countries – Norway, Sweden and Denmark. Additionally Finland and Iceland are also included. The cooperation between the Nordic countries is intense, so that this region has a strong common identity.

British Isles: This includes the United Kingdom and the Republic of Ireland. Although the UK is a monarchy and the Republic of Ireland is a republic, the historical legacy and the common language makes it sensible to group these two countries together. There is also the issue of Northern Ireland that has led to joint efforts by the two countries to achieve a settlement. There are considerable political institutionalised channels between the two countries.

Table 1.1 Data on territory and population of countries in Europe, according to regional clusters

Regional clusters	Countries	Area in square kilometers	Population in millions (2005)	Urban population
Benelux	Belgium	32,545	10.479	97
	Luxembourg	2,586	0.457	83
	Netherlands	41,526	16.320	80
Germanic Europe	Austria	83,871	8.233	66
	Germany	357,093	82.469	85
	Switzerland	41,285	7.437	75
Nordic Europe	Denmark	43,098	5.416	86
	Finland	338,144	5.246	61
	Iceland	103,000	0.297	93
	Norway	323,759	4.623	77
	Sweden	449,964	9.024	84
British Isles	Ireland	70,273	4.159	61
	United Kingdom	242,910	60.550	90
Southern Europe	Greece	131,957	11.104	59
	Italy	301,336	58.607	68
	Portugal	92,345	10.549	58
	Spain	504,645	43.398	77
France	France	543,965	60.873	77
Mediterranean islands	Cyprus	9,251	0.758	69
	Malta	316	0.404	95
Baltic Europe	Estonia	45,227	1.346	69
	Latvia	64,589	2.301	68
	Lithuania	65,301	3.414	67
Central Europe	Czech Republic	78,866	10.234	74
	Hungary	93,030	10.087	66
	Poland	312,685	38.165	62
	Slovakia	49,034	5.387	56
	Slovenia	20,253	2.001	51
Eastern Europe	Bulgaria	110,194	7.740	70
	Romania	238,391	21.634	54
Balkan Europe	Albania	28,748	3.13	45
	Bosnia-Herzegovina	51,129	3.907	46
	Croatia	56,542	4.443	57
	Macedonia	25,713	2.034	69
	Serbia	88,361	9.863	52
	Montenegro	13,812	0.608	52
Turkey	Turkey	779,452	72.065	67

Source: Data from Fischer Taschenbuch Verlag (2008: 522–5)

Southern Europe: This comprises Portugal, Spain, Greece and Italy. There are many common features in the politics of these four countries: the longevity of authoritarian dictatorships in Portugal (1926–74), Spain (1939–75) and Italy (1922–45), and the right-wing democracy in Greece (1952–67) is one such common feature. Other features have included the difficulties of all four countries to move towards a more qualitative form of democracy. Civil society is still quite weak in Portugal, Spain and Greece.

France: The uniqueness of France deserves a special place in the typology.

Mediterranean islands: The island status of Malta and Cyprus located in the Mediterranean is ideal for grouping them together.

Baltic Europe: The three former Soviet republics of Estonia, Latvia and Lithuania gained independence in 1990–91. They work together through Baltic institutions and all of them were independent between 1918 and 1939. They are also small democracies with small populations, which is clearly a good reason to group them together.

(East) Central Europe: According to Attila Ågh, a Hungarian political scientist, there are considerable differences in both development and political culture between the east Central European countries and the Eastern European ones. The Central European countries are Hungary, the Czech Republic, Slovakia, Poland and Slovenia. Although Slovenia belongs geographically to the western Balkans, in terms of political culture and development it leans more towards East Central Europe.

Eastern Europe: This comprises Bulgaria and Romania. In comparison to East Central Europe, they are less developed and their political systems are still being consolidated. Political corruption has been a major problem for both countries.

Balkan Europe: This comprises most of the republics of former Yugoslavia and Albania. The countries are Serbia, Croatia, Bosnia-Herzegovina, Macedonia, Montenegro and Kosovo. Kosovo is acknowledged by most European countries (exceptions being Greece, Spain, Romania, Slovakia and Cyprus), and internationally by some countries, for example the USA, however it is not recognised by Russia or China.

Turkey: Some authors include Turkey as part of Southern Europe, others tend to exclude it. In this book we have left it out because thirty-seven countries are already being discussed. Adding Turkey would have complicated this comparative enterprise (see Table 1.1 and Figure 1.1).

One particular issue is that the socioeconomic living standards of the different regional clusters still show many disparities (Figure 1.2). While Nordic countries, Benelux and Germanic Europe have high living standards with the highest human development index of the world and a favourable structure of opportunities for the participation and empowerment of women, such standards are not reached in Southern Europe.

If we look at Central and Eastern European countries and the Balkans we can see that living conditions are even worse than in the other two groups. Last but not least, Turkey is still way behind the more developed European democracies, particularly in relation to the Gender Empowerment Measure (GEM) that consists of leading positions taken up by women in politics, the economy and society (Table 1.2).

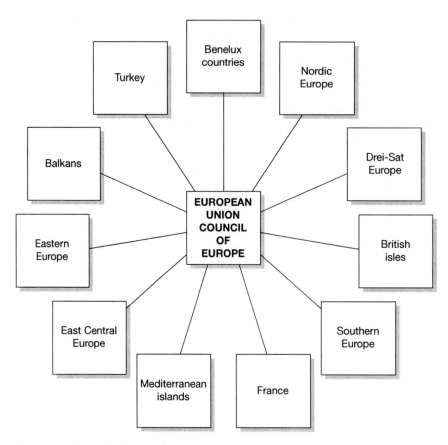

Figure 1.1 Regional clusters of Europe

In order to get a first quantitative overview of the differences between the regional clusters, we use here the well-established human development index and the gender empowerment measurement developed by the United Nations. These two indexes are quite useful, owing to their universal acceptance, but also because the United Nations collects data from all countries of the world. In spite of this, there are missing data for some countries in the Balkans such as Serbia, Montenegro, Albania and Bosnia-Herzegovina. The graph in Figure 1.3 shows that economic prosperity is highest in the Nordic countries, Benelux, the Drei-Sat countries, France and the British Isles. The lowest is to be found in the Balkans, Eastern Europe, Baltic Europe and Turkey. In-between, we can see Southern and Central Europe and the Mediterranean islands. This leads to a similar differentiation in terms of human development index and gender empowerment measurement (Figure 1.4). The latter measures gender equality. As a rule of thumb, one could dare to assert that the greater gender equality, the more democratic is a society. The Nordic countries are known for a very lively participating civil society in a consensus-seeking and building political system. In contrast, the Balkans, Eastern Europe and Turkey still have a long way to go in order to achieve greater gender equality

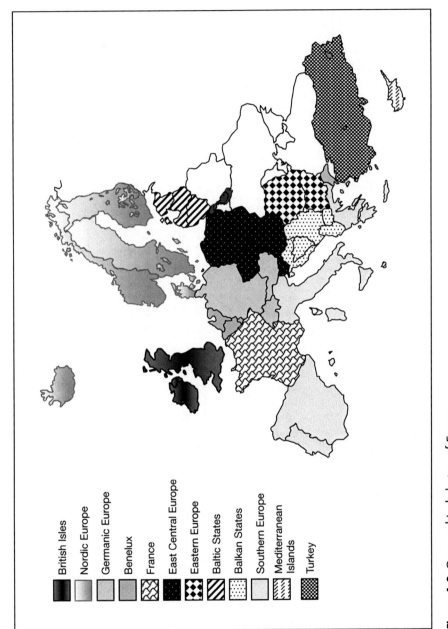

British Isles
Nordic Europe
Germanic Europe
Benelux
France
East Central Europe
Eastern Europe
Baltic States
Balkan States
Southern Europe
Mediterranean
Islands
Turkey

Figure 1.2 Geographical clusters of Europe

Table 1.2 Socioeconomic data on European countries

Regional clusters	Countries	GDP/per capita (2005) US$ PPP	Human development index (HDI)	Gender empowerment measure (GEM) 2007
Benelux	Belgium	32,119	0.946	0.850
	Luxembourg	60,228	0.944	
	Netherlands	32,684	0.953	0.859
Germanic Europe	Austria	33,700	0.948	0.788
	Germany	29,461	0.935	0.831
	Switzerland	35,633	0.955	0.660
Nordic Europe	Denmark	33,973	0.949	0.875
	Finland	32,153	0.952	0.887
	Iceland	36,500	0.968	0.862
	Norway	41,420	0.968	0.910
	Sweden	32,525	0.956	
British Isles	Ireland	38,505	0.959	0.699
	United Kingdom	33,238	0.946	0.783
Southern Europe	Greece	23,381	0.926	0.622
	Italy	28,529	0.941	0.693
	Portugal	20,410	0.897	0.692
	Spain	27,169	0.949	0.794
France	France	30,386	0.952	0.718
Mediterranean islands	Cyprus	22,699	0.903	0.580
	Malta	19,189	0.878	0.514
Baltic Europe	Estonia	15,478	0.860	0.637
	Latvia	13,646	0.855	0.619
	Lithuania	14,494	0.862	0.669
Central Europe	Czech Republic	20,538	0.891	0.627
	Hungary	17,887	0.874	0.569
	Poland	13,847	0.870	0.614
	Slovakia	15,871	0.863	0.630
	Slovenia	22,273	0.917	0.622
Eastern Europe	Bulgaria	9,032	0.824	0.606
	Romania	9,060	0.813	0.497
Balkan Europe	Albania	5,316	0.801	–
	Bosnia-Herzegovina	7,032	0.803	–
	Croatia	13,042	0.850	0.612
	Macedonia	7,200	0.801	0.649
	Serbia	–	–	
	Montenegro	–	–	
Turkey	Turkey	8,407	0.775	0.298

Source: Data from United Nations, Human Development Report 2007–8 (New York 2007)

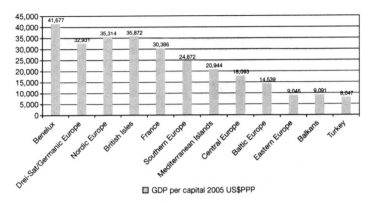

Figure 1.3 Gross Domestic Product per capita, 2005 in US dollars, according to purchasing power parity (PPP)

Source: Based on data from United Nations Human Development Report 2007–8 (New York 2007)

and therefore a more democratic society. Such gender equality is still lagging behind in Southern, Central and Baltic Europe. Similar index levels to the Nordic countries can be found in the British Isles, France, the Drei-Sat countries and the Benelux.

In spite of these figures giving only a snapshot of the different regional clusters, they immediately show how diverse Europe still is. It is the aim of this book to look through all political aspects of European politics in order to compare the similarities, differences and tendencies towards convergence between the countries.

The 'great transformation' of the late twentieth century

Since the early 1970s European politics has changed considerably. Apart from the growing impact of globalisation and Europeanisation processes, one can observe change in the social structure of European societies in this major transformation. In the transition from the nineteenth to the twentieth centuries, the industrial revolution had already led to major changes and transformations in society, politics and the economy. Economic historian Karl Polanyi called this the 'great transformation' (Polanyi, 1944). Similarly, in the late twentieth century, particularly since the 1970s, a major 'great transformation' took place that has affected politics, the economy and society. Chapter 3 deals more in detail with these transformations. In this first introductory chapter it suffices to describe superficially which main changes have taken place in European politics (see Figure 1.5).

State: One of the crucial features of the modern state is its internal and external sovereignty. Over the past three decades it has been experiencing a decline of both kinds of sovereignty. Since the 1990s, particularly resulting from the European integration process, most European countries have shared sovereignty in many policy areas, for example the environment, justice and home affairs, economic and monetary policy, and trade policy. Pooling sovereignty together at European Union level allows for more leverage and influence (for further detail see Chapters 7 and 13).

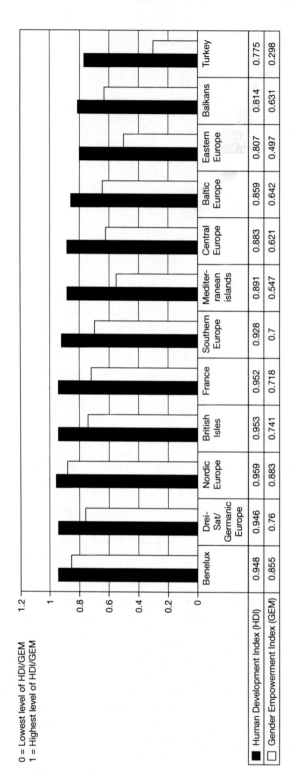

0 = Lowest level of HDI/GEM
1 = Highest level of HDI/GEM

	Benelux	Drei-Sat/ Germanic Europe	Nordic Europe	British Isles	France	Southern Europe	Mediter- ranean islands	Central Europe	Baltic Europe	Eastern Europe	Balkans	Turkey
■ Human Development Index (HDI)	0.948	0.946	0.959	0.953	0.952	0.928	0.891	0.883	0.859	0.807	0.814	0.775
□ Gender Empowerment Index (GEM)	0.855	0.76	0.883	0.741	0.718	0.7	0.547	0.621	0.642	0.497	0.631	0.298

Figure 1.4 Human development index (HDI) and gender empowerment index (GEM), according to regional clusters in Europe, 2007

Source: Based on data from United Nations, Human Development Report 2007–8 (New York 2007), author's own computation and graph

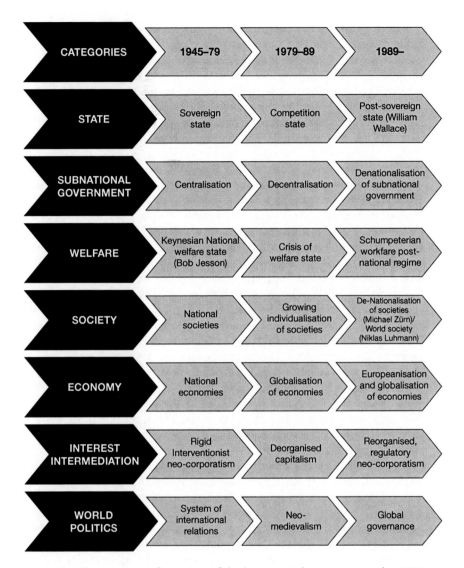

CATEGORIES	1945–79	1979–89	1989–
STATE	Sovereign state	Competition state	Post-sovereign state (William Wallace)
SUBNATIONAL GOVERNMENT	Centralisation	Decentralisation	Denationalisation of subnational government
WELFARE	Keynesian National welfare state (Bob Jesson)	Crisis of welfare state	Schumpeterian workfare post-national regime
SOCIETY	National societies	Growing individualisation of societies	De-Nationalisation of societies (Michael Zürn)/ World society (Niklas Luhmann)
ECONOMY	National economies	Globalisation of economies	Europeanisation and globalisation of economies
INTEREST INTERMEDIATION	Rigid Interventionist neo-corporatism	Deorganised capitalism	Reorganised, regulatory neo-corporatism
WORLD POLITICS	System of international relations	Neo-medievalism	Global governance

Figure 1.5 The 'great transformation' of the late twentieth century since the 1970s

Subnational government: Until the late 1960s most European countries were highly centralised, the exceptions being the federal states of West Germany, Switzerland and Austria. This changed considerably during the 1980s and 1990s. The regions became more self-conscious and practised their own para-diplomacy, bypassing the main gatekeeper of central government. Many countries such as the United Kingdom, Italy, Spain, Belgium, Poland, the Czech Republic and Slovakia moved to decentralised subnational government structures. Other countries such as Sweden, Finland, Denmark and the Netherlands adjusted to more flexible structures in order to deal with the emerging EU multilevel governance systems.

Exceptions to this decentralisation process have so far been Portugal, Spain, Bulgaria, Romania and Ireland. Such centralisation has not been very positive for the development of these countries (see Chapter 8).

Welfare: In the 1970s, the post-war economies stopped growing economically. Stagflation – stagnation of the economy mixed with high levels of inflation – created problems for the competitiveness of West European economies (Scharpf, 1999), and the economic situation was no better in Eastern Europe. The state was becoming quite inefficient, mainly owing to increasing welfare costs. Since the 1980s, national governments have tried to reduce welfare costs with limited success. In the United Kingdom, Prime Minister Margaret Thatcher championed the retreat of the state from the economy and society. However, even her government was not able to substantially reduce the costs of the welfare state between 1979 and 1990. Since the beginning of the millennium, a more instrumental approach called flexicurity has been adopted. Flexicurity means greater flexibility in labour markets accompanied by strong welfare systems to help people return to work with new qualifications as soon as possible. It is quite an expensive system that was devised in Denmark and is widespread in the Nordic countries; however, such a transfer to *all* European countries may have quite different results, particularly in the Southern, Central and Eastern European countries, which have weaker welfare states. This may then create more flexibility in labour markets, by making dismissal by employers easier, but will fail to upgrade the welfare state. There is a thrust in most European countries towards increased flexibility in the labour markets supported by welfare states. Social benefits are increasingly linked to employment policies. Activation policies in the labour market determine whether someone is entitled to benefits or not. This transition from 'welfare' to 'workfare' thus represents a cultural shift in the understanding of the welfare state (Chapters 4 and 13).

Society: Many populations (for example, in Germany and France) are still adjusting to this new reality. The fairly homogeneous national societies of the 1950s and 1960s have been replaced by more heterogeneous ones, where immigrants have integrated or live in European societies. 'Multicultural' societies have emerged in the United Kingdom, France, Spain, Belgium, the Netherlands and Germany. However, each country has developed different immigration policies. The European integration process is pushing countries to make an effort to integrate the immigrant population. This is important, because European societies are currently being affected by a major demographic change arising from a low birth rate and an ageing population. Immigration is the only way to sustain the economic development that these societies have enjoyed until now. Moreover, societies have been undergoing de-nationalisation owing to the increasing processes of globalisation. The traditional national European societies no longer exist (see Chapter 3).

Economy: The booming economies of Western Europe up to the late 1960s were replaced by a period of stagflation. Most European economies were challenged by competition coming from 'Asian tigers' and other industrialising countries. Liberalisation policies, initiated originally in the UK under Prime Minister Margaret Thatcher, spread across Europe and became an important part of the agenda of the European Community during the presidency of the Commission by French politician Jacques Delors between 1985 and 1995. The Single European Market programme developed by Commissioner Lord Cockfield put member states of the EC/EU under pressure to liberalise their economies. National market economies were being replaced by a European economy, in order to enable global competition. This of course led to a decline in the steering ability of member states. Economic and Monetary Union (EMU) and the introduction of the euro in twelve countries further reduced the powers of national governments. The financial crisis of 2008–9 showed how interconnected and vulnerable are European economies to global events and processes (see Chapters 4 and 13).

Interest intermediation: After 1945 most Western European countries were very keen to integrate the social partners, employers' and workers' organisations, in economic and social policy-making. The main aim was to achieve a high level of social peace and economic stability. In the boom periods of the 1950s and 1960s, with an expanding welfare state and the improving conditions of the vast majority of the population, which was strongly organised in trade union organisations, such social peace and economic stability could be preserved. However, when stagflation set in and the economy became inefficient, the new liberalisation thrusts led to a decline of such neo-corporatist arrangements. In the 1980s, one has to speak of 'disorganised capitalism', of which the British example under Prime Minister Margaret Thatcher became the most radical expression. In 1984, she won a battle with the coal miners' trade unions, led by radical Arthur Scargill, that changed the nature of interest intermediation in the United Kingdom. However, since the 1990s there has been a return of cooperation with social partners in order to achieve support for regulatory policies in the economy (Schmitter and Grote, 1997). Thus, at supranational level, the social partners have become more involved in the legislative process in the areas of employment and social policy (Chapter 12).

World politics: In the past four decades there has also been also a shift from a system of international relations in which states act according to their interests and are the only actors, and fight each other according to their national interest (the realist school), to a more complex global governance system in which other actors have emerged and been able to influence world politics, for example international Non-Governmental Organisations (NGOs), supra-national organisations such as the EU and also subnational actors such as the regions. Hedley Bull characterised this transition as 'neo-medievalism' in direct reference to the medieval period, when nation-states were still loose entities, frequently unable to control their borders, and the Catholic Church was able to fight against kings and, particularly, the German emperor (see Chapter 2). The growing importance of transnational corporations and their corporate social responsibility policies has changed the role of the state in world politics (Bull, 2003: 245–6) (see Chapter 14).

The growing importance of the European integration process

European integration has been taking place since the second half of the 1940s. However, only after Jacques Delors became the president of the European Commission in 1985 did the European integration process gain new dynamics. Within a decade, Delors transformed an almost invisible supranational organisation into a world economic and political power. This transformation was not easy, as there was a continuing resistance on the part of the member states to transfer more powers to the EU. In spite of this, the achievements of European integration since 1985 have been remarkable. In twenty-five years, the EU now has a common currency, the euro, has progressed considerably in the creation of a Single European Market (SEM), has developed long-term strategies to gain more influence over the world economy, has expanded its common foreign and security policy, has a common trade policy and is a world leader in the global climate change debate. The visionary strategic approach of Jacques Delors has transformed the EU into what it is today. Although a lot has been achieved, efforts continue on account of pressure from globalisation processes.

This book also intends to show that there is a growing intertwinedness between the national and supranational policy-making of the EU. In reality, the member states of the EU have become part of a new political system *sui generis* (Hix, 2005; Schmidt, 2005). This means that member states are no longer completely sovereign over all their policies and politics. On the contrary, they increasingly work more closely together in order to move towards a European dimension of policy-making, such as the construction of the Single European Market or the Economic and Monetary Union (EMU). Local, regional, national and supranational institutions interact with each other and with market and civil society actors in a multilevel governance system, which means that policy-making and politics have become fairly complex. The best example is the Economic and Monetary Union, which was established in three phases during the 1990s. Originally, only eleven countries (later this increased to twelve) were able to qualify for the first wave of membership; however today there are sixteen members. This Euro group have built an inner core of policy-making, adopting the euro and developing their own policies for the benefit of their economies. Other EU member states that are not part of the eurozone have only observer status. The EMU has also established a strong European Central Bank that now has monopoly over monetary issues. This is paralleled by the broad guidelines on economic policy set up by the Council of Finance Ministers (ECOFIN) of the EU. These guidelines have become increasingly strict over time. All EU member states have to comply with the Maastricht criteria, which put restrictions on budget deficits (not more than 3 per cent of Gross Domestic Product (GDP)), on public debt (not more than 60 per cent of GDP) and on inflation (not more than 2 per cent of the country with the lowest inflation)

The financial crisis of 2008–9 has shown how vulnerable small states are to changes in the world economy. The economy of Iceland collapsed as a result of the speculative behaviour of US banks, and this quickly led for calls within Iceland to join the EU as soon as possible. Such a fast-track path towards full membership has been possible, because Iceland was already part of the European Economic Area (EEA), along with Norway and Lichtenstein. This has meant that Iceland set about adopting most EU legislation without having any decision-making power. Two weeks after Iceland submitted its application for EU membership, the Council of the European Union welcomed it (on 27 July 2009), and the European Commission was invited to issue an opinion on the merits of the application. This is in contrast to the more difficult negotiations with Central and Eastern European countries (which have lasted more than a decade), and those currently with the Balkan countries and Turkey.

In Chapter 4, the growing importance of Europeanisation processes leading up to a new multilevel governance system will be discussed thoroughly. More generally, most chapters also deal with this European dimension, demonstrating that the local, regional, national and supranational levels are becoming increasingly intertwined.

Such processes have led (and continue to lead) to further changes in society, culture, politics and the economy. Eurosceptic left-wing and right-wing parties have emerged in the past two decades raising awareness of the loss of national sovereignty. The transfer of competences to the supranational level can be regarded as a danger to national traditions and culture and these smaller parties are able to attract a considerable share of the vote in elections. Moreover, the populations of the member states can have difficulty in regarding themselves as part of the European Union. There is a general feeling of disconnection on the part of many European citizens from what is happening in Brussels, where most EU institutions are located. In the European Parliament elections of 4–7 June 2009, only 43 per cent of EU citizens cast their vote. Such low turnout allows the smaller parties to mobilise their supporters. In different countries new or extreme right-wing parties that campaigned against the European Union have been able to gain representation. For example, the Party of Freedom under the leadership of Geert Wilders in the Netherlands was able to achieve 17 per cent in its first election, the British National Party under the leadership of Nick Griffin has two seats in the European Parliament, and the emergence of the Movement for a Better Hungary (JOBBIK) under the leadership of Gabor Vona gained 14.7 per cent of the vote and three seats (European Parliament, 2010).

Constitutions and constitutionalism

The origins of European constitutions

In spite of the European integration process, for each individual country the national constitution remains the most important document (Figure 1.6, Box 1.2). The failure to adopt a Constitutional Treaty in 2005, following negative referenda in both France and the Netherlands in May and June respectively, shows the reluctance of most populations to reduce the importance of their own national constitutions. Although it is fair to say that other factors played a role in the two referenda, there is clearly also concern about loss of national sovereignty. In this section, we give some first comparative insights into constitutions and constitutionalism that will help the reader throughout the book to understand which principles, rights, duties and institutional orders are common to all European countries. The role of the Council of Europe and the European Union in framing national constitutional orders cannot be emphasised enough.

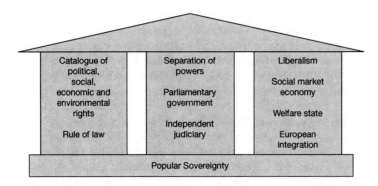

Figure 1.6 Constitutions in Europe

Any modern democratic political system needs some kind of code of practice setting out the rules of the game for institutional interaction and for the involvement of the population. European constitutionalism emerged as a reaction to the arbitrary absolutist monarchies of the early modern period. Authors such as John Locke (*Two Treatises of Government*) and Montesquieu (*The Spirit of Laws*), who advocated a more accountable form of government, gave primacy to parliament or to a system of laws. Constitutionalism is a crucial part of democratic political systems and normally frames the way in which institutions are run in a particular country. In most countries the constitutional settlement in a Constituent Assembly is an important cross-party forum for drafting the laws. Such a constituent process goes back to the first constitution during the French Revolution. Since then, most European countries have experienced several processes taking them towards either creating or adjusting a constitutional order. It is very important that legislators get this founding document right, in order that the constitutional practice achieves

---

Box 1.2 Constitutions and constitutionalism

- The constitution is the most important document in a democratic country.
- It is the source of the 'rule of law' of a country, so that arbitrariness in civil, political, economic, social and cultural life is prevented.
- First constitutions were drafted against arbitrary absolutist monarchies of the eighteenth century.
- In Europe almost all constitutions are 'written' codified documents.
- The United Kingdom has an 'unwritten' constitution that is based on several historical documents and political convention.
- Although the separation of powers – executive, legislative and judicial – is well enshrined in most constitutions, the reality in most European countries is one of close cooperation between executive and legislative power.

political stability in the political system. Moreover, this genetic code will frame national life. The German Basic Law (*Grundgesetz*) of 1949 and the Spanish constitution of 1978 can be regarded as positive examples of such consensualism. In both cases, the historical legacy of Nazi Germany (1933–45) and the Francoist authoritarian regime (1939–75) played a role in moderating the positions of the different political parties and enhancing the propensity to consensualism. Originally, constitutions were very rigid and change was quite difficult, but the acceleration of international change and European integration has led to several amendments to European constitutions. The Finnish, Swiss and German constitutions are good examples in this respect.

One factor that may determine a higher level of democratic culture in any one particular country is the longevity of the constitution. In the Nordic countries the longevity of the constitution is quite great, going back to the early nineteenth century, while other countries such as France, Spain, Portugal and the eastern Balkans are characterised by a discontinuous history of constitutionalism. Probably, one of the oldest constitutions in Europe is the Norwegian Eidsvoll constitution of 17 May 1814, which became a symbol of collective resistance against the Swedish occupation. Norway was granted a quite considerable level of autonomy throughout the nineteenth century that allowed for the establishment of a strong nationalist movement leading to independence in 1905. Although the Swedish and Norwegian constitutions may be regarded as the oldest, they were subject to many revisions and amendments throughout their histories. The Swedish constitution was changed considerably in 1975 and consists now of several documents that perform different functions. The Instrument of Government is the actual constitution, but it is complemented by the Act of Succession and the Freedom of Press Act.

In contrast, the Central and Eastern European countries got new constitutions in the 1990s. In Poland, in 1992, a round table led to a compromise between the communist elites and the new democratic opposition (called the 'small constitution'). Many negative aspects related to this constitution were changed in 1997, particularly by reducing the powers of the directly elected president in the political system. In Hungary, the old socialist constitution of 1949 was amended and restructured in 1989, so that it became compatible with liberal democracy. Both Hungarians and Poles took some devices from the German constitution, for example the constructive motion of censure, which ensures that before the opposition can challenge an incumbent government it has to provide an alternative candidate and a new programme. In a similar way to Germany and Austria, Hungary has been characterised as a chancellor's democracy (Schiemann, 2004: 131). Other countries, for example Bulgaria, Romania, Croatia, the Czech Republic and Slovakia, have established new constitutions. In the case of the 'velvet divorce' of Czechoslovakia, the original agreed constitution of 1992 remained unchanged in the Czech Republic, other than some minor revisions, whereas it was replaced with a new one in Slovakia.

Some countries, for example Austria and Latvia, have constitutions that, in spite of interruption by the Nazi and Soviet periods respectively, emphasise the continuity of historical legacy. The Austrian constitution of 1920–29 was taken over by the Second Republic after 1945. In contrast to the First Republic, the new Republic was characterised by the Allied occupation until 1955. The rise of Nikita Khrushchev in the Soviet Union during this period led to the state treaty (*Staastsvertrag*) that allowed Austria to become independent and simultaneously adopt neutrality. Although the constitution is the same for the two periods, the Second Republic is characterised by consensus and cooperation and is completely different from the First Republic in which paramilitary movements attached to the political parties dictated the polarised violent climate. This led to the emergence of Austrofascism (1934–38) and, later, the occupation by Nazi Germany.

In Latvia, the democratic constitution of 1922 was taken over, subject to some amendments and changes, when the country regained independence in 1992. The constitution and the political culture were very keen to emphasise the continuity of the regime, in spite of the long period of Soviet rule between 1940 and 1992.

According to Richard Rose (1995), one can identify at least four roads taken by European countries towards today's constitutions: evolution (e.g. the UK, the Nordic countries), gradual independence from tutelage (e.g. Malta, Cyprus), discontinuous regime (e.g. France, Southern European countries) and defeat/occupation/liberation (e.g. Germany, France and Central and Eastern European countries) (see Table 1.3). Some constitutions are characterised by evolution, others emerge after revolutionary periods or historical junctures. Moreover, some changes take place internally, while in other countries external factors play a major role in the emergence of a constitution.

After more than two hundred years of European constitutionalism, constitutions have become very similar to each other. In contrast to the evolutionary unwritten non-codified constitution of the United Kingdom, all other European constitutions are written and codified. Although the United Kingdom can be distinguished in this respect, there have been calls for a modernisation of the constitution in order to overcome uncertainties for some issues. The New Labour government that came to power in 1997 pushed forward an ambitious agenda of constitutional reform that was intended to bring the United Kingdom closer to other European countries. Moreover, where European Union law supersedes national law, it has become instrumental in changing important parts of the

Table 1.3 Paths to constitutionalism in contemporary Europe

		Primary pressure	
		Internal	External
Tempo	Gradual	Evolution e.g., UK, Nordic countries, Netherlands	Tutelage e.g., Benign Empire, Malta, Cyprus
	Abrupt	Discontinuity regime Vacuum e.g., Southern Europe, 5th French Republic	Defeat and occupation e.g., Germany, France after 1945, CEECs after 1989

Source: Adapted from Rose, 1995: 74

unwritten UK constitution. Furthermore, the European Convention on Human Rights monitored closely by the European Court of Human Rights (ECHR) attached to the Council of Europe has been used by several citizens of the United Kingdom to challenge national legislation.

The structure of European constitutions

European constitutions have similar structures. Most of them have adjusted the model of the American and French revolutionary constitutions to modern times. Most constitutions start with a preamble related to the historical legacy or the moment of the constitutional settlement and are then followed by different sections defining the 'rules of the game'. The first section normally includes the human and political rights of citizens or the definition of what constitutes a particular state and what is its nature. One of the best examples of a constitution in which human and political rights are particularly emphasised is probably Germany's Basic Law. Nazi rule and its barbarism led to a strong emphasis on human dignity (article 1), in contrast to the constitution of the Weimar Republic, where civil and political rights were in the second main part, starting with article 109. Article 1 of Germany's Basic Law states as follows:

Article 1 [Human dignity]
1   Human dignity shall be inviolable. To respect and protect it shall be the duty of all state authority.
2   The German people therefore acknowledge inviolable and inalienable human rights as the basis of every community, of peace and of justice in the world.
3   The following basic rights shall bind the legislature, the executive, and the judiciary as directly applicable law.

In many constitutions, for example the Italian constitution, the catalogue of rights is extended to the social sphere. In some countries, rights are also extended to quality of life and the environment indicating that the catalogue of rights has been increased over time. This makes the protection of such rights and duties quite a complex task for any European state.

A further section of the constitution defines the main institutions and their relationships to each other. This is an important core aspect of constitutions, because members of a constituent assembly have to get this right in order to prevent the failure of the constitution. Using the historical legacy, as in the cases of Spain, Germany, France and Bosnia-Herzegovina, is a good way to avoid ill-designed institutions. This was particularly the case for Bosnia-Herzegovina: in order to accommodate the three different ethnic groups – Bosniak-Muslims, Croats and Serbs – Bosnia-Herzegovina had to create a rotating system at presidential level and provide equal representation for all ethnic groups in the bicameral parliament. However, today Bosnia-Herzegovina is still split between the Bosnian-Croatian Federation and the Serbian Republic (Republika Srpska). Tensions between the ethnic groups still exist.

European constitutions will also define the political structure of the territory. According to John Loughlin, four main forms of organising territory can be recognised in Europe: federal, regionalised unitary, decentralised unitary and centralised unitary systems (Loughlin, 2000: 26–7).

1   *The federal model* (Belgium, Germany and Austria) allows for a very decentralised political structure with elected subnational units.
2   *The regionalised unitary system* (France, Italy, Poland, the Czech Republic, United Kingdom and Spain) has become closer to the federal model, but the centre still keeps many important decisions under control. Within this form, there are differences in the degree of decentralisation: Spain is quite decentralised, while in France, Poland and the Czech Republic the centre has a stronger position vis-à-vis the subnational units.
3   The third form of territorial organisation is the *decentralised unitary state* (for example, the Netherlands, Denmark, Sweden and Finland). Denmark has decentralised most of its public administration. Now, only about 20 per cent of all civil services are based in the centre and fulfil merely coordinating tasks.

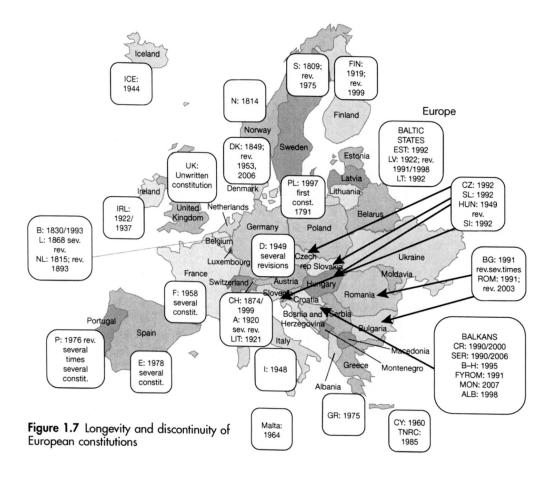

Figure 1.7 Longevity and discontinuity of European constitutions

4   The fourth form of political territorial organisation is the *centralised unitary state*. Here, there are also degrees of centralisation. Among the most centralised countries in the European Union are Portugal and Greece, in spite of attempts by the European Union and the political elites to change this tendency.

A constitution normally ends with the description of procedures for special situations, such as the institutional requirements for constitutional revision and the state of emergency and other important aspects related to individual institutions. A list of contents of an average European constitution is presented in Figure 1.7.

In sum, constitutionalism in Europe is in permanent evolution. Globalisation and Europeanisation are important factors putting the existing constitutions under pressure and constitutions have to be updated and revised. In this sense, constitutions are no longer sacred documents drafted for eternity. They are human products and therefore need to be adjusted to meet new challenges. This means that we are experiencing a growing flexibility of the constitutional order, so that global and European trends can be taken into account. Moreover, the emergence of a constitutionalisation process at European level has also challenged the aspect of national sovereignty in many European countries. The European Convention that drafted the Constitutional Treaty in 2002–3 and was then rejected by the French and Dutch referenda in 2005 was probably just the first step towards this process of constitutionalisation (Wessels, 2002, 2008) (see Chapters 4 and 13).

In the following chapters we seek to compare all these countries and try to find commonalities and differences between not only the different regions but also between the countries within a region.

The structure of this book

- In Chapter 2 we address the historical legacy of European political systems. We emphasise the most important historical junctures of such development of European politics.
- Chapter 3 discusses the main theoretical framework for the analysis of European politics developed by Stein Rokkan. The past three decades have considerably changed the theoretical foundations upon which Rokkan developed his ideas on European politics. The chapter provides discussion of some important issues of contemporary European politics.
- Chapter 4 looks at the way national politics now have to take into account the Europeanisation processes coming from the supranational level (a change stemming from the presidency of Jacques Delors between 1985 and 1995). The incrementalism of European policies has put the member states of the EU under considerable pressure. This first introductory chapter will be followed up by sections on European integration in many of the subsequent chapters. Moreover, Chapters 13 and 14 deal with the impact of European public policy-making on member states and the intertwinedness of national and European foreign and defence policies respectively.

- Chapters 5–8 deal with the core institutions, public administration reform and the judiciary respectively.
- In Chapter 9, the differences in territorial governance are compared.
- This is followed by Chapters 10, 11 and 12 on political parties, elections and party systems, and interest groups and systems of interest intermediation.
- Chapters 13 and 14 discuss the impact of the European Union on national public policy and the foreign and defence policies
- Some final concluding remarks about reinventing European politics are expressed in Chapter 15.

Selected references

Comparative approach

Finer, Samuel E. (1970), *Comparative Government*. London: Penguin Press.

Landmann, Todd (2003), *Issues and Methods in Comparative Politics: An Introduction*. London: Routledge.

Smith, Gordon (1976), *The Politics of Western Europe*. London: Heinemann.

Constitutions and constitutionalism

Bellamy, Richard (ed.) (2007), *Constitutionalism and Democracy*. Dartmouth: Ashgate.

Bellamy, Richard and Dario Castiglione (eds) (1996), Constitutionalism in Transformation: European and Theoretical Perspectives, special issue of *Political Studies Association*, 44(3).

Bogdanor, Vernon (ed.) (1988), *Constitutions in Democratic Politics*. Aldershot: Gower.

International Comparative Law, www.verfassungsvergleich.de/
    Database of all European and non-European constitutions in English, regularly updated.

QUESTIONS FOR REVISION

- What are the main principles of European constitutionalism?
- Compare the strengths and weaknesses of the German 'Basic Law' and the French constitution of the Fifth Republic.
- What are the main features of the British unwritten constitution? Compare it with written constitutions in Europe.
- How successful has the constitutional settlement and consolidation in Central and Eastern Europe been so far?
- Explain constitutional developments in Spain and Belgium since the 1970s.

Chapter 2

The historical development of European politics

- The emergence of European politics in the Late Middle Ages
- The Reformation, wars of religion and the European state system
- The French Revolution and the emergence of the national state
- The Democratic Revolution of 1848 and the rise of liberal democracy
- Industrialisation, the proletariat and the social question
- The new imperialism, new militarism, and the First World War (1914–18)
- The Russian Revolution and the expansion of communism (1917–89)
- The politics of totalitarianism: fascism, national socialism and Stalinism
- Reconstruction, consensus and division of Europe after 1945
- Jean Monnet, Robert Schuman and the beginnings of European integration
- The oil crisis of the 1970s and the silent post-materialist revolution
- The Fall of the Berlin Wall and the emergence of a new European era
- European integration and Euro-scepticism
- Conclusions: European politics as a kaleidoscope of experiment, innovation and tradition

SUMMARY OF CHAPTER 2

European politics can only be understood through its history. This chapter summarises the main developments of European politics since the Middle Ages.

The chapter starts with the emergence of European politics in the Late Middle Ages. It then discusses the main junctures of European politics during:

- the Reformation and Counter-Reformation;
- the French Revolution of 1789;
- the Democratic Revolution of 1848;
- the Industrial Revolution of the eighteenth and nineteenth centuries;
- the Russian Revolution of 1917;
- the totalitarian dictatorships of the inter-war period;
- the reconstruction of Europe after 1945;
- the beginnings of European integration in the 1970s;
- the crisis of the 1970s;
- the politics after the Fall of the Berlin Wall.

The main objective of the chapter is to make students acquainted with the most important historical junctures of European politics. This is quite important, because today's European politics were shaped by those events and led to distinctive features in different countries. In order to understand these differences, it is important to have a good knowledge of the transformations that have taken place since the late Middle Ages.

The emergence of European politics in the Late Middle Ages

European politics emerged out of the Late Middle Ages in the thirteenth and fourteenth centuries. The Middle Ages that spans the period between the ninth and fourteenth centuries was a period of melancholy and intense sadness. It was also characterised by pessimism. This was a reflection of the life that people had to endure, which was marked by human insecurity, wars and the subsequent devastation they caused, and the very rapid spread of disease, including the plague. Moreover, political institutional development was ad hoc and without purpose, based on opportunistic use of existing structures and legal frameworks (Huizinga, 1955: 30, 36).

The political world of the Middle Ages was intrinsically linked to Christian religion and the powerful Church. The attitude of the population and elites was very much oriented towards the end of the world. Therefore, the main form of historical interpretation are the world chronicles divided into seven ages, according to the seven days during which God created the world. Particularly, during the year 1000 the population believed that the end of the world was coming and that humanity had to prepare for it. The universal Christian Church provided the moral basis for the universal unity of mankind. The will of God permeated all aspects of life. Nevertheless, there was a general acknowledgment of the twofold nature of man, spiritual and temporal, that, according to interpretation, allowed for challenges against the hegemony of the Church to be made by powerful rulers. Indeed, one of the main disputes of the Middle Ages was between the Church and the German emperor about the Church's hegemony over the temporal world. The climax was the fight of German Emperor Frederick I (Barbarossa, 1123–90) against Eugenius III and Adrian IV in order to restore the power of previous emperors. Frederick I became German emperor in 1152, succeeding his uncle Conrad III. After his succession he organised the German princes in order to challenge the temporal authority of the papacy. The climax was the non-recognition of Alexander III (1105–81) and the support of anti-popes to challenge him. Alexander III, who was elected in 1159 to succeed Adrian IV, was forced into exile by Frederick I in 1162 and had to live in France for most of the period of his pontificate. However, the northern Italian cities (organised in the Lombard League) rallied to the cause of Pope Alexander III and put an army together to fend off the incursions of Frederick I. In 1176, the army of Frederick I was defeated by the Lombard League in Legnano in Lombardy. Frederick I had to acknowledge Alexander III and sign the Peace Treaty of Venice (1177) (Davis, 1988: 303–17). In spite of this victory of the papacy, the conflict between spiritual and temporal power continued throughout the Middle Ages. At the end of the Late Middle Ages several states had emerged in Europe, including France, England and Spain, which continued to be part of the Christian world, but also became strong enough to have temporal power and even some power of appointment over ecclesiastic positions within their territories.

Feudalism was the main social structure during the Middle Ages, becoming an intrinsic part of the emerging nation-states of Europe. According to François Ganshof, a former eminent specialist on feudalism, the main features of feudalism were:

- a society based on a widespread, hierarchical and static system of relationships of personal dependency;
- with a specialised military class occupying the higher levels in the social grade system of rights over land created by this subdivision; and
- corresponding in broad outline to the grades of personal dependence just referred to; and
- dispersal of political authority amongst a hierarchy of persons who exercise in their own interest powers normally attributed to the State and which are often, in fact, derived from its break-up.

(Ganshof, 1964: xv)

The last feature, related to the dispersal of political authority among a hierarchy of persons, had at its top the king or emperor. However, the autonomy of the individual lords in relation to their vassals was quite wide-reaching. Feudalism originated in France after the break-up of the Carolingian Empire (set up by Charlemagne (742–814), the first German emperor). It was an ad hoc system created in response to the lack of political institutions. In most countries, the monarchy had to share power with its vassals, but in the Late Middle Ages France, Spain, Portugal and England were able to establish more advanced political structures that allowed the establishment of a fledgling nation-state. It is probable that the most centralised feudal system could be found in England, because at that time, following the Norman invasion by William the Conqueror in 1066, all land belonged to the king, and so all lords were vassals of the monarchy.

Feudalism spread to all parts of Europe; nevertheless, the more mature forms could be found in Western Europe. The social structure of feudalism was based on three estates: the knights, the Church, and the intellectuals, although, according to Johan Huizinga, there were in reality twelve estates (Huizinga, 1955: 17). The establishment of assemblies that allowed the most important estates to be represented can be regarded as the origins of parliamentarianism in Europe. The most developed such assembly was likely to have been the English parliament (Finer, 1999: 1336).

The system of justice was also ad hoc, fragmented and based on customary law. It was separated from the feudal structure, although the respective lords and vassals sat in these courts. The structures became more sophisticated at the end of the Middle Ages. In France, the Parlement de Paris and other regional branches were established throughout the thirteenth century, replacing the ad hoc structures created at the peak of feudalism. Nevertheless, a unified valid legal system across the country did not exist until the seventeenth century. Similarly, in England the reintroduction of Roman Law allowed for a more systematic and organised record of judgements and administrative decisions. Samuel E. Finer assessed the English Royal Justice System as quite costly, but it was perceived as being fair in sorting out legal disputes (Finer, 1999: 905–9). Similarly, other countries developed more complex judiciary systems with the progression of the Middle Ages, but all remained fragmented and divided. As already mentioned, the rediscovery of Roman Law, which was derived from the Digest of Roman Law, developed under the auspices of the Roman Emperor Justinian (483–565), was an important turning point for a more sophisticated approach to law. Roman Law was rediscovered in Italy and taught in the main universities, such as Bologna and Salerno, before it found its way into other parts of Europe. Its dissemination was very uneven across Europe, being more successful in Western Europe and slower in Germany and in the east of the continent (Gierke, 1996: xiii). The growing importance of law in Europe was a sign that government was becoming more complex with time and both the respective rulers and the population desired a higher level of predictability and regularity (Koenigsberger, 1987: 232–3).

Towards the end of the Middle Ages, in the thirteenth and fourteenth centuries, most of Europe had reached a high level of stability. According to Koenigsberger, the different nation-states of Europe began to emerge and slowly overcome the fluid political territorial organisation, which until then had been regionalised and compartmentalised (Koenigsberger, 1987: 230). An interstate system began to emerge that became characteristic of Europe and was later exported to other parts of the world (Finer, 1999: 1298–306). Around 1500, the interstate system comprised more or less several stable states. In the south-west, there were Portugal and Spain (after the Reconquista against the Islamic caliphate Al Andalus in both countries), in the north-west there were England (which integrated Wales in the thirteenth century), Scotland and Ireland. In the west, there was France. And in Central Europe, there was the Roman German Empire, which consisted of several statelets. One could also see the slow emergence of the Austrian Empire.

In the east, things were more fluid, both in the Balkans with Serbia and the Albanian principality, Croatia and Bosnia, and also in Hungary, Moldavia and Bulgaria. The emergence of the Ottoman Empire after the fall of Constantinople in 1450 became a major threat to these south-eastern countries. Pockets of feudalism and feudal structure survived until the eighteenth and nineteenth centuries, but at the end of the Middle Ages one could already see the emergence of pockets of capitalism in the urban centres, particularly in the northern city states of Italy and the Netherlands. A new, more self-confident, *Zeitgeist* was replacing the sad melancholic world of the Middle Ages.

The Reformation, wars of religion and the European state system

This new era is referred to as the Renaissance, in which a paradigm change took place from a society that was largely theocentric and geocentric, to one that was anthropocentric and heliocentric. This meant that the unity of the universal Church and the political world, which believed the planet Earth to be the centre of the universe, was replaced by a growing conflict between the two. A turning point was the scientific revolution, the centre of which was the discovery that the Earth rotates around the sun and not the other way round. One of the main frustrations for historians of the Middle Ages was the lack of individual traits in paintings and other forms of art. Everything remained very abstract in order to underpin the ideology of the time. In contrast, the Renaissance is a celebration of individualism and individual contributions to the particular period in time (Huizinga, 1955: 217, 267–8).

This paradigm shift is certainly sustained by the expansion of capitalism as an alternative economic system. At the end of the Middle Ages, the bourgeoisie, in the form of businessmen who lived in the dynamic urban centres between the Netherlands and northern Italy, were an important social group undermining the previous feudal and stratified society. The embryonic characteristics of capitalism expanded considerably during the fifteenth and sixteenth centuries, transforming pockets of trade and industry into an overall system. One could experience the rise of an industrial proletariat, the establishment of 'a complex system of international credit and exchange, and even to some extent a division of labour and some form of specialisation'. Investment in new projects linked to the establishment of the first European colonies further contributed to the expansion of the new capitalist spirit (Green, 1974: 21–2; Wallerstein, 1974).

In contrast to the Middle Ages, the Renaissance was an optimistic and future-oriented age. Although elements of modern European politics could be found in the Late Middle Ages, it was only in the fifteenth and sixteenth centuries that politics expanded and became consolidated. Several factors led to the formation of this new era.

First of all, the existing nation-states of Western Europe increased their ability to control and expand their territory. They created the principle of territorial sovereignty that is intrinsically the principle of the reason of state (*raison d'état*). This suggested that the rulers of the different national countries had to do everything in their power to further the interests of the state by whatever means

(Meinecke, 1998). Second, France, England, Spain and Portugal became absolutist states, meaning that the king was chosen by God and therefore became the direct divine intermediary in their own territory. The most developed form of such absolutism could be found in the sixteenth and seventeenth centuries in France during the reigns of Louis XIII and Louis XIV. The absolutist state had a future-oriented purpose to expand the territory and increase the power of the country in relation to other countries (Friedrich, 1952: 197–245).

Third, the rise of the nation-state was paralleled by the decline of the papacy. Corruption, the selling of offices and indulgence selling (which allowed sins to be forgiven in exchange for cash in order to finance the building of St Peter's) were major factors in undermining both the spiritual and temporal authority of the Church. The once united political and spiritual world of the Middle Ages became fragmented and divided. The rise of the nation-state and the *raison d'état* strengthened the position of monarchs in relation to the national churches (Meinecke, 1998). The growing importance of individualism contributed to the intellectual challenge and criticism of the Church. Already at the beginning of the fifteenth century, the Bohemian reformer Jan Hus (1372–1415) dared to criticise the Church and all negative aspects, and, in the Council of Constance, he was condemned and burned at the stake. His death led to the Hussite wars in Bohemia, which today are regarded as one of the important moments of Czech nationalism, particularly after Sigismund I, the German emperor, also became king of Bohemia following King Wenceslas' death. One century later, Martin Luther (1483–1546) emerged as one of the first protagonists of the Reformation of the Church. He had been a professor of Theology at the University of Wittenberg since 1508 and spent most of his time studying, praying and teaching. Indeed, he was an ascetic friar until 1517. On All Saints' Eve he nailed up his Ninety-five Theses at the Castle Chapel of Wittenberg against indulgence selling. Luther's Ninety-five Theses were written in Latin, but the act itself gained such a good reputation that they were translated into German. After attempts to get Luther to change his views failed, he was banned from the Empire by the Edict of Worms in 1521. He fled and hid in Wartburg Castle. There, he made the major contribution of translating the Bible from Greek into German, which became an important foundation of the modern German language.

Luther returned the same year to Wittenberg and helped to sort out the growing conflict between his adherents and other groups of the community. He was also engaged in stopping the Peasants' Wars, which erupted between 1524 and 1526 and which were based on false arguments derived from his writings. Luther remained a prolific writer throughout his life and an established figure in German history (Green, 1974: 109–25). One of the consequences of Martin Luther's Reformation is that the different states and statelets of the German Empire accepted either the Lutheran confession or the Catholic one. Each state would make a choice about confession to be adopted across its territory. In the end, the Augsburg Peace settled this issue in 1555. The adopted formula was *cuius regio, eius religio* (each region, the respective religion), meaning that each state and statelet had the right to choose a religious confession that was valid for the whole territory. This consensual formula and the mechanisms of reconciliation in Augsburg were characterised by Gerhard Lehmbruch as one of the sources of consociationalism in what he called West Central Europe, comprising Germany, Switzerland, Austria, the Netherlands and Belgium (Lehmbruch, 2002). The Reformation expanded to other parts of Europe through Ulrich Zwingli (1484–1531) in Zurich and John Calvin (1509–64) in Geneva, and through the Huguenots in France in the second half of the sixteenth century and to the Nordic countries. From the efforts of these different reformers there emerged different groups, which tended to interpret their teachings in either a more moderate or a more radical form. Among the most influential reformers was John Calvin, who emphasised predestination theory, which acknowledged that, in spite of man's free will, man is not created equal, but is either granted eternal life or eternal damnation. For Max Weber this predestination theory became an important cultural frame of mind for the emergence of the bourgeoisie and capitalism, and was to become a major source of dispute between different academics. Indeed, even today, his theory is still a major source of discussion (Weber, 1934).

In France, the spread of Protestantism throughout the second half of the sixteenth and early seventeenth centuries led to a civil war that culminated in the St Bartholomew's Massacre of Huguenot leaders by King Charles IX and his mother Catherine de Médicis during August 1572. After a lengthy and bloody civil war between the two confessions, in 1598 King Henry IV finally declared the Edict of Nantes, which allowed Huguenots complete religious freedom. However, the growth of Protestantism in France led to a less tolerant approach by the subsequent King Louis XIII and King Louis XIV. Further wars against the Huguenots led to their persecution and the revocation of the Edict of Nantes in 1685 by Louis XIV. Between 400,000 and one million Huguenots fled the country to Prussia, England, the Swiss Confederation and other countries. Today one can still find vestiges of such emigration in the French names of many Germans in Berlin.

Throughout the first half of the seventeenth century these political–religious wars dominated the European continent. Religious adherence and nation-building became intrinsic processes. In England, Henry VIII (1491–1547) established the Anglican Church by proclaiming the First Act of Succession and the Act of Supremacy in 1534. The origins of the split with Rome were the divorce of Henry VIII from Catherine of Aragón and his marriage to his second wife Anne Boleyn, a marriage that was condemned by Rome. The break with Rome was supported by Parliament.

The Thirty Years' War (1618–48) led to the intervention of all European powers and to several wars on German soil. It led to the devastation of the country and the continuing fragmentation of the German Empire. The main powers – France, Austria, Sweden and the German states – aligned alongside the Catholic and Protestant confessions. In the end, the peace treaties of Westphalia in Münster and Osnabrück in 1648 established the first European interstate system and a central juncture of modern European politics (Friedrich, 1952: 161–97; Green, 1974: 293–313) (Box 2.1).

One of the characteristics of the absolutist state was the permanent condition of being at war with both its neighbours and also with countries in other continents. The climax of such wars was in the sixteenth and seventeenth centuries. According to V.H. Green, commercial issues also became causes for war in the sixteenth and seventeenth centuries. In both centuries, only four years were without wars (1548, 1549, 1550, 1610) (Green, 1974: 386). The Thirty Years' War (1618–48) and subsequent peace treaties established the first interstate

---

Box 2.1 Historical junctures of European politics

1648: The peace of Westphalia

- After the Thirty Years' War (1618–48) between Catholic and Protestant states in Germany and Bohemia, in which Denmark, Sweden and France intervened on behalf of one of the parties, a peace treaty was signed in the Westphalian city of Münster.
- One of the major consequences of the peace of Westphalia was the official establishment of a European interstate system, in which France emerged as the dominant power of the continent.
- The Thirty Years' War was conducted mainly in Germany, which lost one-fifth of its population and suffered the devastation of the country as a consequence.

---

system, one that was to remain the main feature of modern European politics up to the present day, despite efforts towards European integration. The Seven Years' War (1756–63) between France and England could really be called 'the first world war', because it expanded as far as the extra-European colonial empires of these two powers. It led to overlapping wars in which European powers, such as the emerging Prussia, Russia, Austria, France and Sweden, became involved (Dorn, 1963: 318–64). According to Charles Tilly, war was an important factor leading to the establishment of the modern state. The development of new technologies allowed for ever-growing possibilities to expand and control territories. The establishment of standing armies led to drill and discipline that enhanced the efficiency of military action (Tilly, 1990). Apart from France, Prussia was an emerging power in which such military discipline continued to dominate society and politics until the end of the second German Empire in 1918. This naturally was paralleled by a civilising process among the more affluent classes of European societies that slowly trickled down to the lower classes. The civilising process introduced a whole etiquette of manners at table and other aspects of life, which created standardised ways of behaviour inculcated from early childhood among the whole population, but particularly among the aristocratic and bourgeois elites (Elias, 1976).

Last but not least, the Enlightenment of the eighteenth century influenced some monarchs, for example Empress Maria Theresa and Emperor Joseph II of Austria, to introduce compulsory education for the population and regard this as a benefit for the overall economy (Anderson, 1963: 125–7; Williams, 1999: 411–12, 431–2).

The economic rationale became more important throughout the eighteenth century. Mercantilism tended to strengthen the economic power of a nation. Therefore, mercantilists postulated that such strength was to be achieved by protection of industry and trade. Moreover, a country should export more than it imports and hence be able to accumulate gold and silver reserves. Mercantilism was an important doctrine for the emerging nation-state, because it fitted within the framework of *raison d'état*. Nevertheless, in the eighteenth century the physiocrats (supporters of the rule of natural law) criticised mercantilism as undermining the course of natural economic processes. The most prominent representative was François Quesnay, who was against the mercantilist notion of accumulation of silver and gold, and who advocated the principles of laissez-faire and laissez-passer of economic processes. At the centre of the new doctrine was the belief that only agriculture was able to produce wealth. The physiocrats can be regarded as the predecessors of the first theorists of capitalism as we know them today. Adam Smith (1723–90) in his book the *Wealth of Nations* advocated the free market economy based on trade – the idea of an 'invisible hand' that regulated such economic processes – and based his theory on the anthropological benevolent nature of man (Anderson, 1963: 74–80).

The emergence and spread of the capitalist spirit put some nations in an advantageous position in relation to others. The power of a country stemmed from a mix of promoting capitalist enterprise in trade and industry, a powerful army and navy and, of course, its colonies. After the wars against the Hapsburg Spanish Empire that lasted almost a century between 1566 and 1648, Spain's influence in the European state system and in the emerging race for overseas colonies began to decline. In the process, England supported the insurgencies in the late sixteenth century, leading to the defeat of the Spanish Armada in the English Channel in 1588. The Dutch Republic of the United Provinces became established and could be considered the first 'superpower'. Such political, economic and military power had been established during the sixteenth century, but became more visible in the seventeenth century. The power of the Netherlands was only eclipsed at the beginning of the eighteenth century, when England formed a personal union with Scotland creating the United Kingdom of Great Britain through the Act of Union in 1707, adopting the new principles of free market capitalism across the country and in relation to the colonies, something that had previously been denied to the Scottish population (Israel, 1998).

On the eve of the French Revolution, the European interstate system created by the Peace of Westphalia became more or less stable (see Figure 2.1). Most West European powers were shifting their wars to other parts of the world, while in the east the continuing strength of the Ottoman Empire dominated the Balkans and was challenging the eastern parts of Hungary and Austria. Finally in 1683, Polish King Johan Sobieski and his troops were able to fight back the Ottoman troops. Nevertheless, the territorial integrity of Poland was undermined by the increasing corruption of the nobility in the Sejm (parliament). Polish kings were normally elected by the nobility, but corruption allowed the powers of the region – Russia, Prussia and Austria – to partition the territory in 1772, 1793 and 1795 with the result that Poland ceased to exist. Although Germany was fragmented into different kingdoms and statelets, Prussia was nonetheless able to establish itself as a regional power. In the west, Portugal, Spain, France, Switzerland and the United Kingdom including Ireland were independent countries. The Netherlands was for a short period in personal union with the United Kingdom between 1689 and 1702 through King William of Orange. Italy was still divided into small kingdoms and republics in the north, dominated by the Church state in middle Italy, and, from 1735, controlled by the Spanish Bourbons in the south, because the southern Kingdom of Naples and Kingdom of Sicily were united through royal personal union.

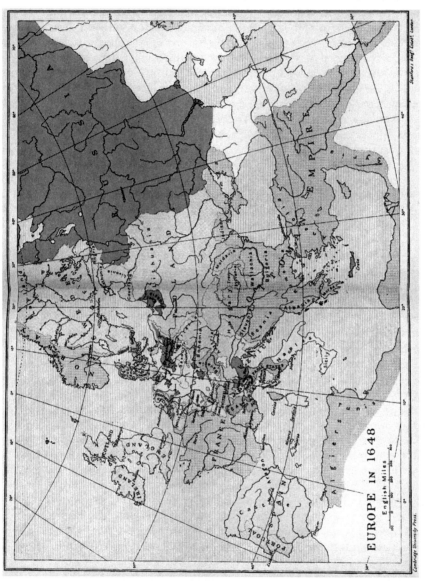

Figure 2.1 Europe after the Peace of Westphalia, 1648

Source: Reprinted from A.W. Ward, G.W. Prothero, Stanley Leathes and E.A. Benians (eds) (1912), *The Cambridge Modern History Atlas*. Oxford: Oxford University Press, map 41 with permission of Cambridge University Press (this is an old large map, therefore the folding line is visible)

Through the Kalmar Union of 1397, Norway became a province of Denmark. Finland was part of Sweden; nevertheless, the Northern War (1700–21) against Russia led to territorial concessions. The Finnish independence movement began to emerge in the late eighteenth century and was to become important throughout the nineteenth century. In the east, the kingdom of Hungary was dominated by the Hapsburg monarchy. In spite of growing conflict with the Russian Empire, the Ottoman Empire was able to hold on to most of south-east Europe.

The French Revolution and the emergence of the national state

After the Peace of Westphalia of 1648, the French Revolution of 1789 should probably be considered the most important event for modern European politics. The year 1789 represents a shift from the remnants of a feudal world towards a modern one. The revolutionary period lasted from 1789 to 1799. The main reason for the French Revolution was the deterioration in the finances of the French monarchy. Mismanagement, the heavy costs of wars in Europe and around the world, and the effects of systemic corruption led to a growing demand for convening the parliament of estates, the Estates-General (*États-Généraux*). They met on 5 May 1789 in Versailles. Nevertheless, the privileged estates' clergy and nobility were against the introduction of a simple majority vote, because the Third Estate was the strongest group. This led eventually to the proclamation of a National Assembly by the Third Estate against the will of the king. On 27 June King Louis XVI capitulated and accepted the National Constituent Assembly and the drafting of a new constitution. The climax of the revolution was the storming of the Bastille, where political prisoners were held, on 14 July 1789, the present national holiday in France.

In spite of certain measures by the king, such as the reinstatement of Jacques Necker, a popular finance minister, the radicalisation of the revolutionary process became inevitable (Rudé, 1980: 83–105) (Figure 2.2, Box 2.2).

The new constitution was only ratified in 1792 and was fairly radical. Also important was the Bill of Rights enshrined in the preamble of the constitution. Throughout this period new radical groups such as the Jacobins and the Cordeliers pushed the pace of the revolutionary process. The new Legislative Assembly, which consisted of 750 members, convened on 1 October 1791. Soon, it became evident that there were different opinions about what should happen to the king and the monarchy. For the first time in the history of European politics, different political parties began to emerge. They would sit in the Assembly from right to left. On the right, the Feuillants wanted to preserve the monarchy and the king and were regarded as the conservatives of the Assembly. In the middle, the majority of MPs were moderate and without any concrete position in relation to the monarchy. Last but not least, on the left one could find the Girondins and the Montagnards (Jacobins and Cordeliers). Both groups wanted a republic, the difference being only that the former advocated federalism and the latter a unitary state (Brinton, 1934: 88–116).

The radicalisation of the French Revolution and the hostility towards the king led to a growing alliance of other European monarchs, particularly Austria's Leopold II, against France. The 'French revolutionary wars', as they are often called, started in 1792 and lasted until 1815. The initial defeats of the French army led

---

Box 2.2 Historical junctures of European politics

1789: The French Revolution

- The demand of the *Tiers État* (Third Estate of the emerging bourgeoisie) for proper representation in relation to the nobility and clergy in the *États Généraux* (General Estates, national parliament).
- Dependency of the king on the General Estates resulting from his catastrophic financial situation.
- The most famous event was the storming of the Bastille (the prison where political prisoners were held) on 14 July 1789.
- Some achievements:
  - the institutionalisation of written constitutions;
  - the roots of nationalism across Europe;
  - the establishment of modern political parties based on a left–right ideological spectrum;
  - the establishment of the Napoleonic Code, exported to other European countries such as Spain, Portugal, Italy and Belgium;
  - the establishment of national education systems.
- Some negative aspects:
  - the radicalisation of revolutionary processes leading to totalitarian regimes;
  - 'La Terreur': the persecution of all opponents to the regime in the climax of radicalisation of the Revolution under Robespierre.

---

to further radicalisation of the government. The government was taken over by the Montagnards under the leadership of George Danton. Soon the fortunes of the French army changed, particularly after the victory of Valmy over the Prussian troops on 20 September 1792. This led to the proclamation of the Republic and the condemnation of the king to the death penalty: he was executed on 21 January 1793. The growing anti-revolutionary coalition in Europe led to declarations of war against England, Spain and the Netherlands and meant that the French government had to use a *levée en masse* (mass conscription of soldiers) for a national army. An army of over 300,000 men was created to fight against the other European powers; one year later this was expanded to 750,000 men who took fast-track training courses and were then sent to the front (Brinton, 1934: 164–89; Thomson, 1972).

Furthermore, more radical elements pushed the boundaries of the revolutionary process. A Committee of Public Safety was established, a new more radical constitution adopted, a new religion called the 'Cult of Reason' created, and a new Republican calendar (based on the year that the Republic was proclaimed) replaced the Gregorian one. This was exacerbated by a reign of terror, from April 1793 to July 1794, in which potential enemies of the Revolution were identified and executed by the guillotine. The main protagonist of the policies of the Committee of Public Safety, which was in principle accountable to the National Assembly, but in reality became an arbitrary government, was Maximilien Robespierre. He used and abused his power to crush opposition in the name of potential counter-revolutionary coups. The re-emerging success of the French army against the Austrian Netherlands led to growing dissatisfaction with Robespierre and his supporters. They were imprisoned and condemned to death, by guillotine, on 27 July 1794 (also called the 9 Thermidor II after the Republican calendar) (Rudé, 1980: 142–59; Brinton, 1934: 142–63, 190–211).

The reign of terror is today regarded by political scientists as the origin of totalitarian democracy. Many comparisons to the Russian Revolution and other revolutions of the twentieth century were drawn by political scientists. Among the major features of totalitarian democracy is the dominance of a self-proclaimed elite, such as the Committee of Public Safety, that is allegedly in possession of the absolute truth and abuses its powers to crush alternatives. Moreover, it will typically use a sophisticated police system to control the population. The killing and intimidating of the opposition is regarded as a control mechanism. It was reported that over 40,000 people across France were executed during the period of terror. Additionally, there is also a strong ideological commitment to a model of society (in this case the Republican model of virtue) and socialisation (in this case mainly through the Cult of Reason). The Cult of Reason led to the decapitation of all Christian figures from churches and the removal of all Christian symbols. They were replaced by symbols related to the 'Supreme Being', based on the principles of Deism and the Enlightenment. Such totalitarian movements as national socialism, fascism and communism (see below) emerged in the early twentieth century, playing, and continuing to play, a major role in European politics (Talmon, 1955; Brinton, 1952).

The fall of Robespierre and the radical Jacobins led to the establishment of a more moderate Committee of Public Safety, with the excesses of the Revolution being reversed. In October 1795, a new more moderate constitution was drafted giving power to the Directory of five. This third constitution lasted until Napoleon imposed his own constitution in November 1799. Between 1795 and 1799, the new French political system was increasingly dominated by the external wars being conducted against several powers. This was the main source of the rising popularity of Napoleon Bonaparte, who became one of the main protagonists in these wars outside France. Despite these external warfare successes, the social and economic crisis deepened and the Directory became fairly unpopular, leading to the collapse of the radical majority in elections in 1797, 1798 and 1799. During an expedition in Egypt, Napoleon returned to France and, with Directors Paul de Barras and Emmanuel Joseph Sieyès, carried out a successful *coup d'état* on 9 November 1799 (18th Brumaire VII). He replaced the 1795 constitution with a new one, giving himself strong powers. He became the First Consul supported by two subordinate consuls. Moreover, the new constitution envisaged the establishment of a nominated state council and senate (Thomson, 1972: 42–8). Externally, France had also established six satellite republics in the Netherlands (Batavian Republic), in Switzerland (Helvetic Republic) and in Italy (Cisalpine Republic, Roman Republic, Parthenopean Republic and Ligurian Republic). Belgium, the former Spanish Netherlands, became annexed (Thomson, 1972: 52–3).

Napoleon's new constitutional framework was in reality a military dictatorship. After declaring himself First Consul for life in 1803, he decided to transform

France into an empire one year later. In 1804, Napoleon was crowned by Pope Pius VII in Paris. Despite this authoritarian streak in Napoleon, it should be acknowledged that he introduced major reforms that would continue for most of the European continent. The most important reform was probably the codification of French law based on the principles of Roman law. The French Napoleonic Code was designed to create greater security and stability in human relations in France. The Napoleonic Code, consisting of 2,287 articles, was completed in 1804. A further reform area was education, in which the creation of a centralised Ministry of Public Education, in turn leading to the first attempts to form a national education policy, was undertaken. Although primary education was neglected, a secondary school network was established in order to train future soldiers. Napoleon was also able to reform the finance and monetary system in order to create economic stability. Last, but not least, he strengthened and reformed public administration in order to have stronger control of public policies, taxation and the citizens. Napoleon's Empire was controlled by a sophisticated police system, which removed opposition to his military dictatorship. After 1806, such repressive policies became tighter (Thomson, 1972: 56–63).

Although Napoleon controlled most of Europe, Great Britain and Russia were the two powers that were able to resist his incursions. Holding a war on two fronts finally sealed his fate. Military defeat in Russia and the alliance of Great Britain, Prussia and Austria from 1813 onwards led to the collapse of the empire. At the end of 1813, following the severe defeat of Napoleon at Leipzig, France was invaded and finally capitulated on 7 April 1814, with Napoleon abdicating as Emperor of the French. He retired, as sovereign ruler, to Elba. Nevertheless in March 1815 he returned to France and tried again to rally the troops against the other European powers. The defeat at the battle of Waterloo led to his second abdication in June 1815 and he was deported to the Atlantic island of St Helena (Thomson, 1972: 72–6).

The significance of the French Revolution and the Napoleonic Wars cannot be emphasised enough. First of all, it spread innovation and the modernisation of law and public administration through the adoption of the Napoleonic Code in many countries. Second, French nationalism led to reactive nationalism on the parts of the invaded countries and territories. Most of this nationalism then continued as a part of the national politics of each country (Hobsbawn, 2000; Thomson, 1972: 70–1). Third, it led to the spread of written constitutionalism, which was regarded as an important means of constraining arbitrary power. Such constitutionalism could be hijacked, in the same way as Napoleon's consulate, but it remained one of the founding stones of the new era of democratic politics. Such a democratisation process lasted right up to the 1990s, when most Central and Eastern European countries were finally able to establish definitive democratic regimes.

The Democratic Revolution of 1848 and the rise of liberal democracy

After the end of the Napoleonic Wars a period of restoration of the former absolutist monarchies took place. The Congress of Vienna of 1815 created a first system of coordination between the different emerging nation-states in order to prevent the return of revolutionary tendencies. The 'Concert of Europe' re-established a conservative monarchistic Europe based on principles of absolutism. The re-established monarchies of the European continent wanted to preserve a balance of power between the different main countries (Holsti, 2000). This Concert of Europe was pushed through particularly strongly by the Austrian foreign minister, Prince Klemens von Metternich (1773–1859), who, after the revolutionary process, wanted to restore order in the European continent. He was able to gain hegemony in the German system of states and also attempted to do so in Italy but with mixed success. The domestic policies of the Austrian Empire, established in 1808, were of a repressive nature. Secret police became an important tool to control opposition throughout the first half of the nineteenth century. The policies of law and order were conducive to the emergence of a bourgeoisie that clearly contributed to the economic well-being of the countries (Vocelka, 2002: 174–8). In spite of the policies of the Concert of Europe the containment of the revolutionary spirit was only partly possible.

Therefore, after the Westphalian Peace of 1648 and the French Revolution of 1789 the third major juncture of European politics is the year 1848, when democratic revolutions took place in different European countries and started a pan-continental transition to mass politics (Figure 2.3). However, the process towards such revolutions had already started during the first half of the nineteenth century. Depending on the nature of the regime, democratisation processes were either evolutionary and peaceful or revolutionary.

The United Kingdom and the Nordic countries: early democratisation

In contrast to most continental European democracies, the United Kingdom and the Nordic countries evolved slowly by the way of reform to full democracy.

In the United Kingdom, an evolutionary process towards democratisation started at the end of the seventeenth century after the 'Glorious Revolution' of 1688, which led to the forced abdication of the Catholic king, James II, and his replacement by the Dutch William of Orange. The role of parliament was considerably enhanced after this seemingly 'peaceful' *coup d'état*. This event marks the introduction of a 'limited monarchy' in which parliament made the decisions about taxation and other issues of national relevance (including the army). In spite of this parliamentarisation, the British political system, like any other in Europe, was still dominated by a high level of political corruption, particularly in the appointment of offices. Nevertheless, in the nineteenth century voting rights were expanded to more parts of the population. In 1832, the Reform Act was passed, following a conflict between the more conservative Tories and the more liberal Whigs under Lord Grey. In the end, the passing of the bill was only possible after William IV appointed a large number of Whigs to the House of Lords in order to offset the blocking Conservative majority. The reform itself got rid of the rotten and pocket (dominated by a single powerful landowner) boroughs that had lost population and importance during the ongoing industrial revolution, and enhanced the position of cities such as Manchester, Birmingham and Bradford. In the 1840s,

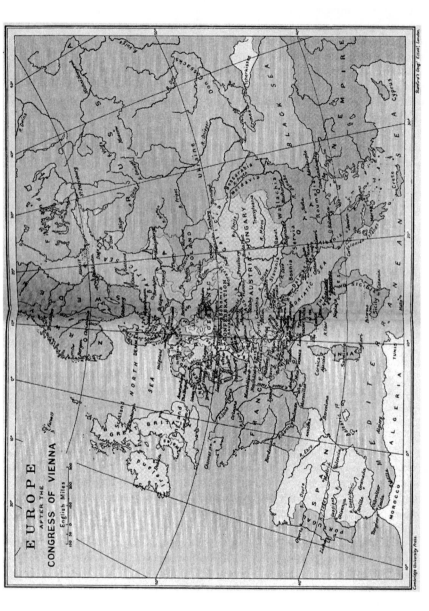

Figure 2.2 Europe after the Vienna Congress, 1815

Source: Reprinted from A.W. Ward, G.W. Prothero, Stanley Leathes and E.A. Benians (eds) (1912) *The Cambridge Modern History Atlas*. Oxford: Oxford University Press, map 102 with permission of Cambridge University Press (this is an old large map, therefore the folding line is visible)

the Chartist movement, based on a People's Charter signed by workers across England, clearly wanted to introduce universal male suffrage. However, this was rejected by parliament. In spite of this, further reform bills allowed the steady integration of the vast part of the population into democratic politics. Throughout the nineteenth century universal suffrage was extended and the constitutional monarchy responded to major social and economic changes. In the early twentieth century, male universal suffrage was introduced in 1918 and the female vote in 1928 (Harvey and Bather, 1982: 44–52).

Development towards democracy in Scandinavia evolved evolutionarily as well. Sweden moved to a liberal democracy at a very early stage. After defeat against Russia during the Napoleonic Wars, Gustav Adolph IV was deposed by the army and the Riksdag proclaimed a constitution that remained in force until 1975. After the Congress of Vienna, Sweden's king was a foreigner from the Bernadotte family, Charles XIV John (1818–44). Although the constitution of 1809 was the document of reference for politics in Sweden, in reality the king controlled both politics and policy. Liberal opposition throughout the century led to reforms in order to make the political system more democratic. By mid century, Sweden had moved towards being one of the most democratic political systems in Europe. In 1865–66 a bicameral chamber was established, which abolished the representation by estates and introduced a directly elected lower chamber. Further reforms in 1907 and 1917 led to the granting of male and female universal suffrage respectively.

After 1848, Denmark became a constitutional monarchy and also started a process of evolutionary democratisation and social legislation. The emergence of a social democratic party in the 1880s contributed to the inclusion of the working class into the new democratic political system. Throughout the early twentieth century, particularly in 1901 and 1915, further reforms were undertaken to consolidate the parliamentary regime. Finally in 1918, universal suffrage was introduced.

In 1814, Sweden attacked Norway and created a union between the two countries. In spite of Swedish control of Norway, domestic politics became increasingly influenced by a strong Norwegian nationalism. At the centre of this nationalism was the Storting, the unicameral parliament, that found itself in opposition to Sweden on several occasions. The 1814 Eidsvoll constitution gave strong powers to the Storting that allowed the assembly to resist Swedish attempts to curtail autonomy. Norwegian nationalists became more demanding and self-confident after 1848. Throughout the second half of the century, there was permanent conflict with the institutions of the union. Finally, in 1905 the Norwegian government unilaterally declared independence from Sweden, later confirmed through negotiations and the signing of the Treaty of Karlstad. The democratisation process since 1914 reached its peak with the granting of the right to vote to women in 1913 (Arter, 1999: 30–6).

Similarly to Norway, Finland was granted autonomy within the Russian Empire. Despite attempts by Russian nationalists to curtail such autonomy in the second half of the nineteenth century, Finnish nationalism and pragmatism prevailed. The Bolshevik Revolution in 1917 was an important catalyst for the independence of Finland, and one year later it became an independent country. In spite of a short civil war between communists and nationalists, the country was able to progress to a republican constitution. In terms of democratisation, in 1906 Finland made the transition from one of the most autocratic and undemocratic representative systems to being a fully-fledged democracy based on universal suffrage (Kirby, 2006: 104–64).

France: discontinuous democratisation process

On the continent, after 15 years of a return of absolutist rulers, new democratic movements began to emerge.

By 1830, a new revolution in France forced the ultra-conservative King Charles X to resign, and he was replaced by Louis Philippe, a member of the younger branch of the Bourbons. After 1815, France became a constitutional monarchy, but with a very restricted suffrage of 100,000 property owners. Nevertheless, the prospect that the revolutionary achievements could be reversed by an ultra-conservative monarch was a major worry for both the bourgeoisie and the wider population. Louis Philippe became known as the citizens' king. Economically, France profited from the newly found political stability, in spite of the fact that the regime was dominated by the well-to-do classes. Education policy concentrated on the establishment of a national network of primary schools in all communes (Cobban, 1963: 123–5).

Discontent with King Louis Philippe and his prime minister, François Guizot, led to protests in France in February 1848. One of the main reasons for this was that France was facing an economic depression and King Louis Philippe resisted the new political demands being made. Repressive policies against the opposition led to the proclamation of the Second Republic. Nevertheless, it became clear in the autumn elections for the National Assembly that the radical Republicans were a minority in relation to the moderate forces. Moreover, the victory of the nephew of Napoleon Bonaparte, Louis Bonaparte, in the presidential elections led to a difficult coalition between the conservative monarchist government and the president. The continuing threat of radical revolution was used by Louis Bonaparte to undertake a *coup d'état* in early December 1851, establishing the Second Empire and his self-proclamation to Emperor Napoleon III, before the scheduled legitimate presidential elections of 1852. Despite that, the Second Empire, which lasted until 1871 (the year of defeat in the Franco-Prussian wars), was a period of economic growth, political reform and stability. Failure in foreign policy and several wars contributed to the establishment of the Third Republic that was to last until 1940, when France was occupied by German troops and a dictatorship was established in the southern part of France called Vichy France (Cobban, 1963: 196–210).

The emergence of Belgium

In August 1830, the former Spanish Lowlands (which were an integral part of the kingdom of the Netherlands after the Congress of Vienna of 1815), influenced by events in France, staged an uprising that led to its independence and the foundation of the Belgian state. One of the main reasons for this uprising was the fact that Belgium was predominantly Catholic and resented being under the rule of a Protestant king, William I of the Netherlands. The new independent state created one of the most advanced constitutions in Europe. The new king, Leopold I, was astute about pushing forward Belgian interests and enhancing the position of the country within Europe. Later on, Belgium became a model for Central and Eastern European countries such as Bulgaria and Romania (Witte *et al.*, 2000: 18–23).

The Democratic Revolution of 1848: Italy, Germany, the Austrian Empire and Hungary

In 1848, several revolutions took place across Europe. In Italy, Germany and Hungary they became embryonic movements of nationalism and unification. In Italy, the two key figures were Giuseppe Mazzini and Giuseppe Garibaldi who were major protagonists of the Italian unification movement. The Kingdom of Piedmont, Sardinia and Savoy under King Charles Albert represented the Italian nation against the continuing dominance of the Austrian Hapsburgs in the north of Italy. The reawakening of Italian nationalism (*Risorgimento*) was to continue until 1870, when the Church state in the middle of Italy was reduced to the Vatican within the city of Rome. The main thrusts towards reunification came during the premiership of Count Camillo Cavour (1810–61) in the Kingdom of Sardinia after 1852. He was to be instrumental in pushing forward the unification of the country through alliances with the superpowers, enabling increases in territory throughout the 1850s. In 1861, King Victor Emmanuel II was proclaimed king of Italy. Within a decade, the Risorgimento ('resurgence') led to the unification of Italy. The former Church state in the middle of Italy was annexed by the Italian state, and reduced to just the Vatican city (Di Scala, 1995: 75–117).

In Germany, the year 1848 led also to early attempts to achieve national integration. The Constituent Assembly of Frankfurt am Main that convened in May and was to discuss a German constitution during the course of one year, led to a major rift between the supporters of a Germany under Prussian leadership (*Kleindeutsche Lösung*) and those who backed leadership under the Austrian Empire (*Grossdeutsche Lösung*). The rift also brought to the fore the religious differences between Protestant states and representatives supporting leadership of Prussia and Catholic states under the leadership of the Austrian Empire. In the end, 1848 sealed the hegemony of Prussia over a still very fragmented Germany (Behnen, 2002: 471) (Box 2.3).

When Emperor Franz-Joseph II came to power in 1848, after the resignation of Ferdinand I, he pursued repressive policies in order to crush the revolutionary movement in Austria. Nevertheless, by 1859 he had started a process of democratisation with a limited constitution and census electoral system. It evolved towards a fully-fledged constitutional monarchy and the introduction of universal male suffrage in 1907 (Vocelka, 2002: 198–220).

Moreover, in other parts of the empire, particularly Hungary and northern Italy, there were strong nationalist developments. In Hungary, Lajos Kossuth (1802–94) became an important national figure, pushing for the independence of the country. Throughout 1848–49, a nationalist liberation and democratic movement emerged in Hungary. It was influenced by the democratic revolution in Paris in February 1848. The climax was Lajos Kossuth's dictatorship in the country during April and August 1849. Already, in 1848 as a finance minister, Kossuth

---

Box 2.3 Historical junctures of European politics

1848: The Democratic Revolution

- A series of revolutions in different countries such as Germany, Italy, the Austrian Empire and Hungary undertaken by elites and social groups excluded from power and wanting political liberalisation and democratisation.
- A first wave took place in 1830–2 in the Benelux countries and France.
- It was a reaction against the conservative 'Concert of Europe' orchestrated by the Holy Alliance, dominated by the Austrian foreign minister and later Chancellor Prince Metternich.
- It led to similar revolutionary processes throughout the second half of the nineteenth century, combined with an independence struggle as in Bulgaria and Romania in 1878.

---

had shown dictatorial tendencies combined with strong nationalism. After the intervention of the Russian army, which was part of the conservative alliance with Austria–Hungary, the latter again gained overall control over the country, and Kossuth went into exile.

Despite this setback, Hungary was to gain equal status after the *Ausgleich* (compromise) of 1867 proclaimed by Emperor Franz-Joseph II. Hungary obtained its own constitution and had an almost independent status in the dual empire. Both concessions of Franz-Joseph II were consequences of defeats in Italy in 1859, when the Kingdom of Piedmont was able to expel the Habsburgs from Italy, and in July 1866, when Austria lost in the decisive battle of Koniggrätz against the Prussian troops under Helmuth von Moltke. In a similar way to the Italian case, Prussia achieved an end to the influence of the Austrian Empire in Germany. In 1871, twenty-two principalities agreed to establish the Second German Empire under the leadership of Prussia. William I became German Emperor and Otto von Bismarck became his Chancellor. Although this German Empire had a constitution, parliament and democracy were very limited. In order to counteract the growing socialist movement, Bismarck introduced the first embryonic welfare state, which was to remain a major feature of the German political system up to the present day. The Second German Empire ended after defeat in the First World War in 1918 (Behnen, 2002: 513–17; Düllfer, 2002: 546–7).

Ireland: the struggle for independence

In Ireland, a national movement against British rule was always present throughout the eighteenth and nineteenth centuries. In spite of representation of Ireland in the House of Commons, the movement in Southern Ireland gained momentum shortly before the First World War, leading to independence in 1922 through the Anglo-Irish Act. The Anglo-Irish Act allowed the establishment of the Irish Free State which would be integrated into the Commonwealth. This was to end when a new constitution was proclaimed by President Eamon De Valera in 1937 and the Republic of Ireland in April 1949 (Coakley, 2000).

The Baltic states and Russia

The dominance of the Russian Empire prevented the Baltic states from becoming independent in the nineteenth century. Nevertheless, the February Revolution and the Bolshevik October Revolution in Russia presented opportunities for all three Baltic states to become independent. All three Baltic states, Estonia, Latvia and Lithuania, were able to break away between 1918 and 1920 and move towards independent democracies.

Iberian democratisation: Spain and Portugal

In Southern Europe, the year 1848 also had impact when the cause of liberalism against the conservative forces of the different regimes was pushed forward. In the Iberian peninsula, both Portugal and Spain were characterised by a discontinuous process towards democracy. Periods of restricted democracy were either interrupted by military coup attempts or authoritarian periods of rule. Nevertheless, in both countries after 1871 liberal constitutional monarchies were established. Portuguese *rotativismo* and Spanish *turno pacifico* were based on the regular alternation of power of a two-party system. Owing to the small electorate, the two political parties were able to rig elections through clientelism and patronage. During the early twentieth century the whole political system degenerated into systemic corruption that was accompanied by a high level of political violence. In Portugal, the Republican movement was able to overthrow the monarchy in 1910, but this new regime also degenerated into systemic corruption in its quest to prevent the monarchists from returning to power. By mid 1926, the new republican regime was overthrown by a military *coup d'état*. In Spain, the high level of political violence, the growing anarchist movement, and systemic corruption further undermined the regime. In 1923, General Miguel Primo de Rivera established a development dictatorship, based on the principle of creating law and order (Magone, 2003: 21–63).

The Ottoman Empire and the independence of the Balkan countries

The Ottoman Empire dominated south-eastern Europe until the eighteenth century, but the inability of reform and the growing disintegration of the peripheral parts of the empire allowed for the emergence of nationalist movements in different parts of the western and eastern Balkans.

In the western Balkans, Serbian nationalism became the major expression of this newly found self-confidence in relation to the Ottoman Empire. The growing influence of Russia in this region protected Serbia from being dominated by the Ottoman Empire. What was probably the most influential independence movement was undertaken by the Greek nationalist elites between 1807 and 1830. In the end, a constitutional monarchy was established during the nineteenth century and it continued until 1974, in spite of different constitutions. Similarly to Portugal and Spain, a two-party system based on a small electorate was established, although by the 1920s it had degenerated into corruption. In the same way as in the other Southern European countries, periods of democracy were interrupted by attempts to establish authoritarian rule such as those by General Theodoros Pangalos in 1925–26 and General Ioannis Metaxas between 1936 and 1941. The main challenger to several conservative monarchs was Eleftherios Venizelos, who became prime minister several times in the inter-war period, but was constantly challenged by coup attempts of the military. Greece was also engaged in a policy of uniting (*einosis*) all Greek-speaking territories including Cyprus, which led to tension with its neighbours, in particular Turkey (Clogg, 1998).

In the eastern Balkans, Bulgaria and Romania were also influenced by the revolutions of 1848. Nationalist movements began to emerge at the end of the eighteenth century and continued throughout the nineteenth century. They led to national independence in Romania in 1859 and Bulgaria in 1878. In both cases, as already mentioned, West European liberal constitutions, which closely followed that of Belgium in 1831, were adopted. In both countries, the British model of a two-party system of conservatives and liberals was established, but the impact was different in the two countries. Romania, which comprised Walachia and Moldavia, was able to profit from a restricted democracy that was to last beyond the First World War. After the First World War, the peace treaty of Trianon in 1920 led to the expansion of Romanian territory at the cost of former Hungarian territory, and also led to a doubling of the population. In Bulgaria, the two-party system soon collapsed into more parties and led to systemic corruption. Moreover, democracy was interrupted by short periods of authoritarian dictatorship that undermined a continuous democratisation process. In contrast to Romania, Bulgaria joined the Central Powers and suffered a reduction of territory in the conference at Neuilly on 27 November 1919.

In conclusion, 1848 has directly or indirectly been a major juncture of European politics. The revolutions and social movements emerging before, during and after 1848 led to the expansion of universal suffrage and the establishment of a model of liberal democracy that was interpreted in each country in a different manner. This provided the conditions for the diversity of European democratic politics that we know today. Apart from democratisation, 1848 was an important catalyst, or at least, reinforced the activity of movements of independence in the Balkans, Italy, Germany and Hungary.

Industrialisation, the proletariat and the social question

The democratisation process was intrinsically linked to the industrial revolution, which was not just a point in time but a process that lasted for more than a century. The industrial revolution transformed European semi-feudal societies into modern dynamic ones. The economic historian Karl Polanyi called it the 'great transformation' (1944). It emerged from the use of new technologies, for example the spinning wheel, steam engines applied to trains and ships, and the blast furnaces in the steel industry. Among the most important aspects of the industrial revolution were the invention and expansion on a mass scale of the railway and the telegraph. All this allowed for the establishment of modern administrative apparatus, which was able to provide a very full overview of the citizens within a territory. The expansion of democratisation had an important impact on government. Public bureaucracies, which were increasingly subject to systems of law in order to avoid arbitrary decisions, increased considerably throughout the nineteenth and early twentieth centuries. The rule of law and the neutrality of the judiciary became important aspects of the new modern democratic state (Silberman, 1993; Finer, 1949: 710).

One of the main reasons for the growth of public bureaucracies was that industrialisation led to a more complex society in which capitalism became the main economic model. The high level of demand for manufactured goods led to a thrust towards integration of global markets. One of the consequences was the mass migration of the rural population to urban areas, where they lived in appalling conditions. A detailed report by Friedrich Engels in 1844 of the working conditions of workers in England gave rise to the term 'Manchester capitalism', named after the city that was the centre of the textile industry in the United Kingdom. Among the negative aspects of 'Manchester capitalism' were unregulated labour leading to accidents, the exploitation of child labour in the textile industry, and both women and men having to work more than twelve hours a day. In addition, there was a 'truck system' set up by employers that allowed further exploitation of workers. This system provided workers with accommodation in overcrowded places and with the basic articles for survival through the employer's shop, with a consequence of debt dependency. Over time, workers accumulated debts that they were unable to repay within their lifetime. They became more or less slaves of the factory system (Engels, 1974). This was one of the conditions for the establishment of a rich bourgeoisie, who could make large profits from their various enterprises. The more or less peaceful nineteenth century also allowed for the prediction of trade arrangements and commitments that further fostered the economies of most European states. At the centre of the 'age of capital' was the United Kingdom of Great Britain. Early industrialisation in Britain created a first national mass market, something that was emulated in other countries. By the end of the nineteenth century, it became clear that economic development in Europe would decide the influence of a country in the world as a whole. While Britain, France, and the German and Austrian empires were at the centre of this industrial revolution and consequently at the centre of economic development in Europe, the southern, south-eastern and eastern countries, including Russia, became economically peripheral (Hobsbawn, 1984; Ferguson, 2007).

In the second half of the nineteenth century, there was a growing concern with the social conditions of the working classes leading to the emergence of new political parties that were keen to improve these conditions. Among the most important critical thinkers were Friedrich Engels and Karl Marx. Friedrich Engels wrote one of the first major criticisms of Manchester capitalism in his *The Condition of the Working Class in England* (1844) (see above) and proposed social reform in order to improve the situation of the working classes. He teamed with Karl Marx and during the 1848 revolutionary period they published the *Communist Manifesto*, which was to remain the founding document of social democracy and communism. When they wrote the *Communist Manifesto*, the working class was increasing, but still small in terms of creating a political movement. Nevertheless, the social democratic and communist ideologies were able to mobilise a large part of the working class at the end of the nineteenth and beginning of the early twentieth centuries. One of the factors was that while industrialisation was creating a huge proletariat, the structure of opportunities for social democratic parties increased considerably owing to the extension of suffrage. In 1864, a First International Working Mens' Association was founded in London under the leadership of Karl Marx. However, he had to deal with criticisms of his approach, strategy and leadership style from Russian anarchist Mikhail Bakunin. The divisions and other wrong decisions led to the end of the International in 1876, although nonetheless the seeds of a revolutionary movement of fundamental importance had now been sown.

After Marx's death in 1883, social democratic parties emerged in most European countries. Marxism became the foundation of social democracy so that a Second International was established in 1889. The Second International created a new organisation based on national membership. It led to the development of many national parties, which now leaned towards reformist policies and abandoned revolutionary politics. Among the best known protagonists of this reformism was Eduard Bernstein from the German social democratic party. Bernsteinianism advocated that the social democratic parties should take part in elections and gain influence through the representative system. For hardline Marxists this was regarded as betrayal of the working class. Many futile discussions between revolutionaries and revisionists took place during the late nineteenth and early twentieth centuries. Probably, the most famous schism was that of Russian social democracy in 1905, between the Mensheviks under Georgy Plekhanov and the Bolsheviks under Ivan Illitsch Lenin, the former representing a reformist wing of the party, and the latter pushing for revolutionary politics. In October 1917, the Bolshevik revolution led to the victory of the radicals and the establishment of a Communist International (Ulam, 1998: 493–514).

The emerging social democratic parties in Western Europe followed a reformist approach. The German, Belgian, Dutch, Austrian and Nordic social democrats were engaged in alleviating the fate of the working classes by creating tailored institutions for their benefit, such as libraries, community centres, health centres and sports facilities. Through this network of institutions they created a subculture that voted en masse for these social democratic parties. This encapsulation of the working class electorate remained an important factor for the stability of electorates after 1885 (Bartolini and Mair, 1990; Bartolini, 2000) (see Chapter 3).

The growth in complexity, the extension of suffrage and the emergence of new social democratic parties led to pre-emptive attempts by conservative governments to neutralise the revolutionary potential of the social question, which might in the long run have destroyed the political, social and economic stability that late nineteenth- and early twentieth-century nation-states were enjoying. The best example was in the German Empire under Chancellor Otto von Bismarck. After consultation, he introduced the first elements of a welfare state with initial measures of social protection for the working class. Although the Bismarckian welfare state was rudimentary, it nonetheless showed clear results. The main idea was to bind the working class to a benevolent state. The social legislation introduced health insurance (1883), accident insurance (1884) and old age and invalidity insurance (1889) for workers. In spite of some initial success, Bismarck's attempts to reduce the power of the social democratic movement was not realistic. The benefit system was too rudimentary and basic, so that the working class tended to support the Social Democratic Workers Party (SDAP) for further reforms. Similar rudimentary welfare states emerged across Europe (Düllfer, 2002: 546–7).

Although the social democratic party was forbidden in 1878, through the *Sozialistengesetze* (Laws against socialist activity), after Bismarck's resignation in 1890, the party was able to operate freely and quite successfully (Düllfer, 2002: 543–7). Last but not least, political Catholicism emerged as a reaction to centralised nation-states and the social democratic parties. Christian democratic parties developed social policies after Pope Leo XIII published the encyclical *Rerum Novarum* (1891), which clearly allowed such parties to be more fully engaged in the social question and act politically in different countries. In the case of Germany, Bismarck was very keen to reduce the power of Catholicism in the German Empire. The *Kulturkampf* was the fight of the lay state to gain complete supremacy over the powerful spiritual religious confessions, in particular Catholicism. *Kulturkampf* became less relevant after 1875 because Bismarck looked for conservative partners, among them the emerging Catholic-inspired party, which was against social democracy. The Zentrums Partei, which had close relations to the Vatican, became an important ally of Bismarck against what was perceived to be the main enemy of the empire: social democracy (Düllfer, 2002: 524–5). In the late nineteenth and early twentieth centuries Christian democratic parties emerged in Belgium, the Netherlands, Germany, Austria, Switzerland and Italy (after 1919).

In conclusion, industrialisation transformed European societies. A new large working class and the expansion of universal suffrage led to the emergence of mass politics. The social question became a permanent important issue of European politics, and even today it still remains an important part of the political agenda. Furthermore, the growing importance of the state and public bureaucracies in designing and implementing social and other public policies created a more intrusive state, which also began to develop the first statistical databases (Finer, 1949: 48).

The new imperialism, new militarism and the First World War (1914–18)

The industrial revolution further increased the integration of regional markets into one large one. This had consequences for the categories of world politics and geography. The best example of this was the acceptance of Greenwich time in an interstate conference of twenty-five countries that convened on 22 October 1884 in Washington, DC. The supremacy of the British Empire on the world political stage was reflected in the fact that, by 1883, 72 per cent of the world's shipping used charts drawn to the Greenwich meridian and only 8 per cent to the Parisian meridian (Schaeffer, 1982: 76–9).

This was relevant because, at the end of the nineteenth century, the new-found belief in progress led to a race to create large colonial empires outside Europe. Several European powers emulated Britain in establishing colonies that sustained the demand for manufactured products. While Britain had expanded her colonial influence to all parts of the world, Germany and France competed for colonies in Asia and Africa. Even Belgium established a colony in the Congo, which in 1885 was acquired privately by King Leopold II and led to the brutal exploitation of the indigenous population. Between 1898 and 1908 it was taken over by the Belgian state, which was backed by the strong, globally influential, Belgian financial bourgeois elites (Witte *et al.*, 2000: 99–100).

In contrast, former colonial powers such as Portugal and Spain became extremely vulnerable to the economic strength of the other powers. In Spain, the catastrophic year of 1898 led to the loss of Cuba, the Philippines and Puerto Rico in the Spanish–American war, leading to a major identity and cultural crisis in the country (Carr, 1999). In 1908, Portugal tried to create a corridor between Mozambique and Angola, situated on the south-eastern and south-western African coasts, respectively, which led to an ultimatum by the British government to refrain from this. The main reason for the ultimatum was that the corridor would interrupt the ambitions of the British Empire to have a vertical corridor between Cairo and Cape Town. Owing to

Figure 2.3 Europe before the First World War, 1914

the military and economic weakness of the country, the Portuguese government had to back down to the British demands (Oliveira Marques, 1983: 206–11).

While France and Britain were established powers, Germany, Italy and Belgium emerged as powers symbolising the new imperialism that was strongly linked to the globalisation of capitalism. While Germany laid claims in 1885 and 1886 to South West Africa (Namibia), Togo, Zanzibar and Cameroon, Italy pushed for a colonisation of Libya. At this time, strange theories related to imperialism emerged, such as that by Enrico Corradini, a prolific Italian writer. Corradini developed the idea that Italy had to compensate for the lack of economic power by diverting the growing immigration of a large part of the population from South America to new colonies to be found in Africa, including Libya. He characterised Italy as a 'proletarian' nation that was taking its place in the imperialist race in relation to the 'bourgeois' rich nations such as Britain, France and Germany (De Grand, 1978).

This new imperialism was supported by a new militarism that, during the early twentieth century, was to spill over into the First World War (Figure 2.3).

Figure 2.4 Europe after the First World War, 1919

Although the murder of Crown Prince Ferdinand in Sarajevo in July 1914 is regarded as the trigger leading up to the First World War, there was a general atmosphere that was somehow conducive to this belligerent attitude. The network of alliances between the different superpowers was set in motion after the ultimatum on Serbia ran out (Tuchman, 1962). After a long peaceful nineteenth century with only small regional wars outside or on the periphery of Europe, most armies went into war believing that they would be home within a couple months. Instead, the First World War lasted for four years until November 1918. The war led to major transformations in Europe. Apart from the fact that the Austrian, German, Russian and Ottoman Empires collapsed and led to the emergence of new nation-states, the Russian Bolshevik Revolution transformed European politics completely. The establishment of a communist country in Russia was to shape the order of Europe until the Fall of the Berlin Wall in 1989 (Figure 2.5).

In 1919–20, as a consequence of the Peace Treaties in Versailles, Trianon and Neuilly, Europe consisted of a lot of new states in the east (Figure 2.4). Apart from the present configuration in the western Balkans, most Central and Eastern countries gained their independence and some of them territory and population.

The Russian Revolution and the expansion of communism (1917–89)

The Russian Bolshevik Revolution of October 1917 was certainly one of the most important junctures of European politics (Box 2.4). Originally, Ivan Illitsch Lenin did not believe that the revolution in Russia, the weakest link in the chain of capitalism, would be able to survive without a simultaneous revolution in Germany. During the Spartacus revolt in Munich in 1919, Russian troops were stationed in Poland, so that they could help the Germans to stage the revolution. However, this did not happen. In the end the Russian Revolution remained restricted to Russia. One of the reasons for the Russian Revolution was that Czar Nicholas II had conducted a disastrous campaign in the First World War. Apart from defeat on various fronts, the economic and social situation was extremely precarious. The February Revolution of 1917 established a provisional government that also had difficulties controlling the problems caused by the war and Czarist policies. Among the more charismatic politicians was Aleksandr Kerensky who became prime minister in July. Despite his attempts to create greater stability, the situation continued to worsen. A *coup d'état* organised by Lenin and the Bolsheviks in October (November 7, according to the Gregorian calendar) 1917 led to the establishment of a communist regime. A civil war (1918–21) broke out between the Bolsheviks (who created a Red Army) and the anti-communist monarchists (also known as the Whites). Throughout the 1920s, the new regime introduced a planned economy with unsatisfactory success. After victory in the civil war, Lenin decided to change course by adopting in 1921 the New Economic Policy (NEP), which lasted until 1928. The NEP allowed for a restricted entrepreneurial market for consumer and light industry goods, while heavy industry and other goods were controlled by the state. The death of Lenin, following three strokes, led to internal infighting. In the course of this internal infighting, Josef Stalin prevailed and

---

Box 2.4 Historical junctures of European politics

1917: The Russian Revolution

- The catastrophic running of the First World War, combined with a disastrous economic and social situation, led to the Russian Revolution in 1917.
- A first revolution took place in March 1917 owing to shortage of bread. The revolutionary situation led to the abdication from the throne by Czar Nicholas II. A provisional government introduced democratic institutions and liberalisation, but was not willing to give up the war effort.
- A second revolution undertaken by Ivan Illitsch Lenin and the Bolsheviks (in reality a successful *coup d'état*) took place on 26 October (Gregorian calendar 7 November). The 'October Revolution' led to the establishment of the first Communist regime, which became quite influential in European politics.
- The October Revolution led to the establishment of the Third Communist International that became an extended arm of Russian foreign policy. This became clear under Josef Stalin, who contributed with his expansionary policies in Central and Eastern Europe to the division of Europe between 1947 and 1989.

---

further reinforced the existing repressive policies of the Soviet regime. He decided on a return to a planned economy and, furthermore, forced collectivisation of the agricultural sector. What became known as Stalinism was labelled by political scientists as belonging to the totalitarian pattern of regimes.

One of the most important instruments of communist expansion was the Communist International (*Comintern*), founded in 1920 and based on twenty-one principles – principles that Moscow forced all parties to adhere to, which included total discipline and complete allegiance to the Soviet leadership. During Stalin's time the Comintern was used to protect the first socialist nation, the Soviet Union. It became an integral part of Soviet foreign policy. Communist parties were founded across Europe, among which the Italian and French were the strongest. These new Communist parties were at the centre of resistance movements against authoritarian regimes that emerged in Southern, Central and Eastern Europe. Western powers tried to contain the expansion of communism through a *cordon sanitaire* consisting of the countries of southern and south-eastern Europe, but their efforts failed when the Second World War broke out. After the war, Stalin's Soviet Union was able to control most of Central and Eastern Europe by establishing people's democracies dominated by communist parties. It led to the division of Europe and the beginning of the cold war that was to last until the Fall of the Berlin Wall in 1989.

The politics of totalitarianism: fascism, national socialism and Stalinism

After the First World War, Europe consisted of many new democracies. Universal suffrage was becoming a reality in many countries, but overall the picture was quite uneven from country to country. As already mentioned, many Western European countries moved to universal suffrage by the end of the 1920s, among them the United Kingdom, Ireland, the Nordic countries, Belgium, the Netherlands, Germany and Austria. However, the picture in the rest of Europe was more uneven. Southern and south-eastern Europe still had restricted or manipulated electoral systems. In some cases, countries just introduced authoritarian dictatorships in order to deal with the political and economic instability of emerging democratisation. The inter-war period was characterised by many economic problems that, after a golden period in the 1920s, were exacerbated by an economic depression in 1929. The crash of the Stock Exchange in New York and other countries had devastating consequences for these newly emerging democracies. Authoritarian regimes were regarded as a third way, avoiding the dangers of communist revolution and the instability of liberal democracy.

Italian fascism was regarded as the prototype of such regimes. After the war, Italy was affected by a severe economic and social crisis. Although universal male suffrage was granted in 1919, the phenomenon of mass politics was too new, and new political parties too inexperienced, to achieve a stability of the political system. Giovanni Giolitti, the main architect of the pre-war Italian system based on clientelism and patronage, tried to apply the same methods of control that he had used in the pre-1918 constitutional monarchy, for example clientelism, patronage, corruption and co-optation of anti-systemic parties into the political system, but without success (Salomone, 1960; Hentze, 1939). In Turin, the main factories became centres of socialist revolution. The 'Red Biennium' of 1918–20 was influenced by events in the Soviet Union.

New moderate mass parties, such as the new Christian democratic Italian People's Party (Partito Popolare Italiano, PPI) and the Italian Socialist Party (Partito Socialista Italiano, PSI) emerged in post-war Italy. Nevertheless the National Fascist Party (Partito Nazionale Fascista, PNF), which derived its ideology from the Italian nationalism of the pre-war and revolutionary politics of the socialist parties, pushed for an authoritarian solution in order to not only restore law and order but also to restore the glory of the Roman Empire. Romanness (*Romanitá*) was part of the liturgy of the Italian Fascist Party, and fulfilled the function of a substitute religion, a so-called civil religion (Polanyi, 1944: 241). The strategy of the fascist party under the leadership of Benito Mussolini was to destabilise further the vulnerable post-war Italian party system and seize power by presenting itself as the only alternative to liberal democracy. Mussolini could rely on a vast number of people who were discontented with the existing liberal democratic political system. He created the *Fasci di Combattimento* (fighting bands) in order to achieve a change of regime. Fascist squads terrorised the left-wing politicians and local government authorities. After issuing an ultimatum, Benito Mussolini marched on Rome on 31 October 1922, and was then invited by King Vittorio Emmanuele III to form a government. In 1924, after successful legislative elections in which an electoral coalition led by the PNF was able to get over 60 per cent of votes and seats, Mussolini began to restructure the liberal democratic political system into a dictatorship. New laws led to the establishment of an authoritarian state based on a new corporatist organisation of the economy. Corporatism drew some inspiration from the social doctrine of Catholicism and was presented as a third way between capitalism and communism. In the essence, corporatism wanted to restore an idealised harmony between labour and employers' organisations, which was perceived to have existed in the Middle Ages, and avoided both the negative aspects of competition and the restrictions of a planned economy. At the centre of the ideology of fascism were three principles – the glorification of the nation, the paternalist family and harmony with the Church. Mussolini was able to settle the longstanding conflict between the Italian state and the Catholic Church through the signing of the Lateran Treaty, which stipulated that the Vatican recognise the sovereignty of Italy and vice versa. Moreover, it regulated state-Catholic Church relations.

Although it was Mussolini who developed the idea of the *stato totalitario* (totalitarian state) geared towards fulfilling the destiny of the Italian nation, fascism never managed to fully indoctrinate and control the population. Despite totalitarian pretensions, it degenerated in the 1930s and early 1940s to an authoritarian state. This assessment is also valid for Italian imperialism, which led to the control of Libya and invasion of Ethiopia in 1936. Nevertheless, in the late 1930s, Mussolini became an increasingly junior partner of the Berlin–Rome axis. Italy's entrance into the Second World War led to catastrophic results, and ultimately to the downfall of the regime after 1943.

More ruthless than Mussolini's semi-totalitarian regime, was the national socialist state in Germany. One of the main distinctive characteristics was the xenophobic thrust in the overall ideology of national socialism. In the same way as in Italy, the national socialist strategy was based on destabilisation of the liberal democratic regime of the Weimar Republic. The economic depression of 1929 badly affected the German economy. Unemployment was quite high. Adolf Hitler and the German National Socialist Workers Party (Nationalsozialistische Deutsche Arbeiterpartei, NSDAP) used political violence and scare tactics to come to power. The NSDAP came to power in 1933, because no party was able to achieve the absolute majority needed in the elections to the Reichstag. Franz von Papen, an ultra-conservative leader of the Catholic Centre Party, a successor of the Zentrumspartei of the nineteenth century, supported Adolf Hitler in his bid to become German chancellor, in order to undermine the efforts of his own rival, Kurt von Schleicher, to come to power. In the end, this mistake by von Papen led to the establishment of a totalitarian dictatorship. The institutions enshrined in the constitution were suspended and replaced by new national socialist bodies. The militaristic indoctrination through the total mobilisation of the population created a totalitarian state, which in turn led to the Second World War. Moreover, a new militaristic liturgy of mass rallies and other devices created a similar civil religion around the glorification of the German nation and its reconstructed past and future (Michalka, 2002: 694–715).

Among the most perfidious aspects of national socialism was the xenophobic racist theory attached to it. The glorification of the German nation was interpreted in racist terms, meaning that only Aryan Germans belonged to it. It meant that any other groups that were not able to produce proof through blood of their 'aryan-ness', were excluded from society. Although the main targeted group was the German Jewish population, other groups, such as gypsies, homosexuals and mentally ill or physically handicapped people, were also excluded from society. These groups were sent to concentration camps. In 1941, such exclusion turned into policies of extermination, the so-called final solution (*Endlösung*). The holocaust, the systematic killing of an estimated six million Jews in the 1940s by the national socialist regime, became a major tragedy for European politics. Even today, the holocaust and the consequences of it are felt deeply in the way Europeans conduct politics. Although the German and Austrian governments have established funds to compensate victims of the holocaust, the tragedy remains a reminder of how human beings can easily fall into barbarianism (Michalka, 2002: 715–19, 750–4).

National socialism was also characterised by a very aggressive foreign policy, which finally led to the Second World War. The trigger for the Second World War was the invasion of Poland on 1 September 1939; nevertheless, before that Hitler had invaded Czechoslovakia and Austria. One of the driving forces for the expansionist policies was *Lebensraumpolitik* (policy of living space) (Michalka, 2002: 720–5).

Fascism, national socialism and Stalinism are regarded as three forms of totalitarian rule that became widespread in the twentieth century. As already mentioned, the origins of totalitarian rule could be found in the French Revolution and became more sophisticated in the early decades of mass politics. The complete control of all activities within a regime by the state is referred to as totalitarianism. Fascist Italy, Nazi Germany and Stalin's Soviet Union were characterised by several common features such as:

1   a one-party system;
2   the blurring of the state and party bureaucracies;
3   the total indoctrination of the population through an ideology (communism, national socialism, fascism);
4   the creation of social and political structures for the total mobilisation of the population;
5   the use of secret police to control the population;
6   an expansionist and aggressive foreign policy (Friedrich, 1966).

During the inter-war period, only a few countries were able to resist the totalitarian or authoritarian temptation. Regimes emulating fascism were established in most countries in Europe. Some of them could count on the support of national socialist Germany, particularly during the Second World War (for example, the Croatian Ustaše regime). Many of these regimes crumbled during the Second World War, some of them, particularly in Central and Eastern Europe, became totalitarian people's democracies between 1944 and 1989. Nevertheless, in Portugal and Spain such regimes survived until 1974 and 1975 respectively. Only a few democracies survived the totalitarian/authoritarian temptation of the 1920s and 1930s, among them the United Kingdom, France, Belgium, the Netherlands, Czechoslovakia and the Scandinavian countries.

The Second World War changed all this; the aggressive policies of the Third Reich led to the division of Europe into two large blocks, the Allies, comprising the United Kingdom, the United States and the Soviet Union, and the Axis powers comprising Nazi Germany, Italy and Japan. Many countries in Central and Eastern Europe, Nordic Europe and western Central Europe became annexed by Germany; and friendly regimes such as the Quisling government in Norway, the Vichy regime in southern France and the Ustaša regime in Croatia were established to run day-to-day business. The collapse of the Third Reich and, later on, the Japanese Empire in 1945 created the conditions for a more democratic and united Europe.

Reconstruction, consensus and the division of Europe after 1945

After the victory of the Allied forces over the Axis powers, the devastated economies of Europe were the starting point for a period of more than sixty years of peace. The First and Second World Wars left a strong imprint on the culture of the European countries. The dark history of the holocaust should remind us forever of the way Europeans could behave towards each other and minorities within their countries. The end of 'Europe's Civil War' (this term describes the First and Second World Wars and the inter-war period) was an important turning point in the organisation of society (Mazower, 1998). The post-Second World War period was one of social democratic consensus. On the one hand, conservative or Christian democratic parties and, on the other, social democratic parties, converged towards consensus in terms of social and economic policies. The devastating consequences of the free-fall liberalism of the late 1920s led to a stronger engagement of the state in providing the population with basic social needs. Austria, Germany, the Benelux countries, France and the Nordic countries are good examples in this respect. Particularly the Nordic countries had already established a strong reputation during the inter-war period (Esping-Andersen, 1985), one which was emulated by other countries such as Austria, Germany and the Benelux countries. The reconstruction of the economies of these countries was paralleled by the establishment of a generous welfare system that expanded considerably up to the mid 1970s. In the case of West Germany, social policies were regarded as an important bulwark against a return of populism and national socialism (movements that were able to profit from the large armies of unemployment of the early 1930s). Of all the OECD countries, West Germany spent the most in social expenditure in the 1960s. In 1942, during the Second World War, Sir William Beveridge chaired a United Kingdom commission in charge of dealing with the reform of social legislation. The outcome was a comprehensive social policy plan based on principles of social citizenship that comprised health care, an unemployment scheme, social benefits and a pension system.

The difficult social situation in the inter-war period, during which unemployment was extremely high, led to the wish of the political elites to improve conditions after the Second World War. In the 1945 legislative elections, Labour won against the Conservatives under Winston Churchill. This demonstrated the general support of the population for the introduction of welfare policies. The Clement Attlee cabinet introduced major social reforms. Among them the introduction of the National Health Service (NHS) under the leadership of the state secretary for health, Aneurin Bevan, in 1948. Today, the NHS still represents a symbolic foundation stone of Labour politics, and it was also embraced by the Conservatives as part of the social democratic consensus. By the 1960s, all West European democracies had thriving economies; even the economies of the last two authoritarian dictatorships, Spain and Portugal, were able to profit from accelerated economic growth.

The Southern European countries (Italy, Portugal, Spain and Greece) were also to establish such welfare states at a later stage, owing to their delayed economic development. The accelerated economic growth of Italy, the 'Italian miracle', started in the mid 1950s, but only in the late 1960s was there a genuine demand by Italian workers for some of the benefits of economic success (Ginsborg, 1990).

The economic recovery of Western Europe was not possible without American help. The destroyed economies of Europe were a major problem for the United States. This was the largest market for their goods and therefore there was a need to support reconstruction efforts in order to recreate demand in Europe. The European Recovery Programme (ERP, or Marshall Plan) was devised by US State Secretary George Catlett Marshall in order to help reconstruct the economies of Europe. Originally, the Central and Eastern European countries including the Soviet Union were invited to take part in the ERP. Nevertheless, the growing tensions between the USA and the Soviet Union, arising from the satellisation of most Central and Eastern European countries by the latter, led to the rejection to take part in such invitation. Therefore, the Marshall Plan became caught up in the ideological war between the USA and the Soviet Union and was used in its later phases to boost the defence policies of West Germany and the other Allies. Between 1947 and 1952, the Marshall Plan disbursed about US$ 13 billion, most of which went to the United Kingdom (24.3 per cent), France (20.2 per cent), Italy (11 per cent), West Germany (10 per cent) and the Netherlands (8.5 per cent). In total fifteen countries profited from the American funds, including Turkey and the authoritarian dictatorships of Portugal and Spain. The funding was spent through the Organisation for European Economic Cooperation (OEEC). The overall idea of the American administration was to push for a single European market, because this would be much easier and cheaper for American firms to distribute their goods. Instead, European rivalries and concerns about sovereignty prevented such innovative integration of Europe to take place. There was some American desire to transform the OEEC into a supranational organisation that would create such a single European market, but this plan was resisted by several countries, in particular France (Milward, 1992).

The ideologisation of the Marshall Plan was inevitable. The growing hold of the Soviet Union on the countries of Central and Eastern Europe between 1945 and 1949 led to the emergence of the cold war. It became an important instrument among others of the overall doctrine of President Harry S. Truman on 12 March 1947. Similarly, the Soviet Union presented their own doctrine of the inevitable war between the imperialist camp (the United States and its allies) and the anti-imperialist camp (the Soviet Union and the new people's democracies) by Foreign Minister Andrej Shdanov. At the end of September 1947 in Szklarska Poreba, Poland, the Communist Information Bureau (Cominform) was founded by eight communist parties of Central and Eastern Europe (Poland, Czechoslovakia, Hungary, Romania, Bulgaria, Yugoslavia and the Soviet Union), France and Italy. Although the Cominform was just a network of information exchanges, the Western allies regarded this as a possible resurrection of the Comintern of the 1920s and 1930s. Throughout this period, the Soviet Union was trying to rein in the Yugoslav Communist Party to no avail. The successful liberation of the western Balkans from Nazi Germany by the communist partisans under the leadership of Josip Broz Tito, without the help of the Soviet Union, gave them enough self-confidence to resist Soviet control of the country. Between March 1948 and September 1949 there was a growing tension between the two countries until finally there was a break in the relationship. In response to this defiance of

Soviet dominance, the United States was generous in providing 'aid without strings', which was used to finance the entire Yugoslav budget until the death of Stalin in 1953, when, finally, normal relations between the two countries resumed (Halperin, 1957: 178). Similarly, the Cominform was an important mechanism to control the communist parties in France and Italy, whose leadership had been in exile in the Soviet Union. From the point of view of the allies, the closeness of the French and Italian communist parties to Stalin's Soviet Union was regarded as a threat to these democracies.

The division of Europe goes back to the Yalta (4–11 February 1945) and Potsdam conferences (17 July and 2 August 1945). In particular, Yalta had allegedly led to a secret agreement, scribbled on a piece of scrap paper, to divide Europe into spheres of influence. The division of Europe led to a nuclear arms race that was used as a deterrent by both the West and the East against each other. The result was a 'cold war' that led to thousands of troops being deployed permanently along the Iron Curtain. The military North Atlantic Treaty Organisation (NATO) was founded in 1949, comprising West European countries, Greece, Turkey and the two Iberian dictatorships. And the Warsaw Pact was established in 1955, comprising the Central and Eastern European communist countries.

The occupation of most Central and Eastern European countries (apart from Yugoslavia) led to the establishment of popular front governments, in which the Communist Party gained the upper hand, step by step. This process became known as 'salami tactics', referring to the fact that, little by little, members of the popular government and the opposition were either absorbed by the communist-led coalition or got rid of. Despite the success of the communist parties in Central and Eastern Europe, to achieve control over the respective countries, the Stalin–Tito controversy led to major purges of alleged nationalists or supporters of Tito. These show trials conducted in all people's democracies reinforced the image of totalitarianism in these countries (Crampton, 2002: 26–37).

Among the most famous show trials were: Laszlo Rajk in Hungary (condemned to the death penalty); Wladislaw Gomulka in Poland (condemned to house arrest); and Traicho Kostov in Bulgaria (sentenced to death) (Brzezinski, 1965: 91–7).

The people's democracies established during the second half of the 1940s emulated the Soviet model, but were considered to be less advanced than the motherland of socialism. To counteract the Marshall Plan, the Soviet Union and the Central and Eastern European countries founded the Council for Mutual Economic Assistance (Comecon, CMEA) in January 1949 in Moscow. Its main intention was to assist and coordinate the economic development of its members (Bideleux and Jeffries, 2007a: 463).

By 1949, the division of Europe was a fait accompli. After the Basic Law of Germany was proclaimed in 1949, the German Democratic Republic established itself as a Soviet satellite state. The two Germanies remained at the forefront of the cold war, as the West Berlin blockade of 1948–49 showed. The Allies supplied the western part of the city through an airlift that lasted for eleven months. Moreover, an embargo on strategic goods of the Soviet Union and Central and Eastern European countries contributed to the lifting of the blockade on 30 May 1949 (Wegs and Ladrech, 2006: 17–19).

After Stalin's death, there were signs of rebellion and opposition in most people's democracies (Figure 2.5). In Moscow, a *trojka* took over, however it was

Figure 2.5 The cold war in Europe, 1947–89

afraid of allowing a new dictator like Stalin to emerge. Slowly, Nikita Khrushchev was able to introduce policies of de-Stalinisation that culminated in the condemnation of Stalin and his abuses in a secret report to the twentieth party conference of the Communist Party on 25 February 1956. The new leadership also replaced Zhdanov's doctrine of inevitable war between the imperialist and anti-imperialist camp by the doctrine of 'peaceful coexistence', which envisaged a competitiveness between the communist and capitalist model. The transition period in Moscow was used by the opposition in some Central European countries to rebel against the totalitarian regimes in their countries. On 17 June 1953, an uprising of workers in East Berlin, the capital of the German Democratic Republic, was crushed with brutal force leading to the death of twenty-one people and the arrest of over 1,000 insurgents. Moreover, many people made efforts to leave the GDR for West Germany, in spite of the closed border. By 1961, 3 million had left the country, so that the East German leadership decided to build a concrete wall between West and East Berlin. The GDR became known as one of the most orthodox communist countries (Bideleux and Jeffries, 2007a: 490–1).

Similarly, in Poland, the workers' strike in Poznan in June 1956 led to a major crisis in the relationship between Poland and the Soviet Union. The rehabilitation of the national communist Vladislav Gomulka and his diplomatic skills prevented the intervention of the Soviet troops, which would have intended to crush resistance in Poland. Gomulka promised to remain loyal to the Soviet Union, but introduced reforms towards a Polish way to socialism (Bideleux and Jeffries, 2007a: 476–7).

In July 1953, the Communist Party in Hungary deposed the unpopular leader Mátyás Rákosi and replaced him with Imre Nagy. Despite pressure from Moscow to reinstate Rákosi, and later on his deputy Erno Gerö, Imre Nagy was able to return to power. In 1956, he proclaimed that Hungary was leaving the Warsaw Pact, the intergovernmental military organisation that functioned as a counterpart to NATO. As a response, Soviet troops crushed the Nagy regime and put János Kádár in its place. This ended the honeymoon with Soviet leader Nikita Khrushchev. Kádár became a symbol of betrayal of the Hungarian uprising, but at the same time he introduced major reforms that led to a so-called 'Goulash communism', meaning that the communist leadership allowed some private enterprise in the economy. The result was that, over time, Hungary became one of the less orthodox communist regimes in the Central and Eastern block (Bideleux and Jeffries, 2007a: 477–8).

Soviet leader Leonid Brezhnev emerged as the successor of Khrushchev after 1966. The 'Prague Spring' of 1968 under the leadership of national communist Alexander Dubček was intended to introduce major economic reforms in order to activate the Czechoslovak economy. Several economists supported Dubček. He was also supported by a large number of people in the Party. In the end, troops from the Warsaw Pact invaded the country and replaced the leadership. The intervention of the Warsaw Pact was based on the principle of socialist brotherhood and the new Brezhnev doctrine that regarded such action as legitimate, if there was sufficient evidence to believe that capitalism would be restored in a socialist country (Bideleux, Jeffries, 2007a: 491–3). Czechoslovakia turned out to be one of the most orthodox regimes on the eve of the 1989 Central and Eastern European revolutions.

By the mid 1970s the Iron Curtain was quite entrenched in the minds of Europe on both sides of the fence. Despite the tensions between the two superpowers, a form of coexistence, based on peaceful tolerance, was established between West and East. It led to the Conference of Security and Cooperation in Europe in Helsinki in the summer 1975 and the beginnings of a unification process between the West and East of Europe.

Jean Monnet, Robert Schuman and the beginnings of European integration

After the Second World War, peace was the main item on the agenda of all countries (Box 2.5). After two devastating World Wars, Europe wanted to ensure that such a calamity would not happen again. In the post-war period several plans emerged aimed at achieving a political unification of Europe. The political integration of Europe was regarded as an important project in order to overcome the nationalisms that had led to such devastating results. Despite many attempts, the main European powers, France and the United Kingdom, were not able to agree on the model of such integration. The best example was the Council of Europe, which was originally devised as a supranational organisation, but in the end it was downgraded to an intergovernmental body in order to accommodate the United Kingdom. The Council of Europe was founded on 5 May 1949 by ten West European countries. Its role remained confined to the development of pan-European legal frameworks, among them the European Convention of Human Rights (1950) and the Convention for the Protection of National Minorities (1995). The institution remained dormant until the 1970s, but in the 1980s and 1990s regained new prominence as an ante-chamber for European Union membership. Today, the Council of Europe comprises over forty-three members, including countries of the Caucasus, the Russian Federation and Ukraine. Among the most prestigious institutions is the European Court of Human Rights in Strasbourg, which is the last court of appeal for European countries, when defendants have exhausted all legal routes at a national level. The rulings of the ECHR are of considerable importance for national judicial systems, because they contribute to changes in legislation for particularly difficult issues.

Disappointment with the Council of Europe led to further projects of European integration. Apart from the US-driven OEEC, the reconciliation between France and Germany through the initiative of French foreign minister Robert Schuman was devised by the head of the French Planning Agency, Jean Monnet. It started by creating a European community of steel and coal (ECSC) through the Treaty of Paris in 1951. The ECSC became the first economic supranational organisation consisting of six member states – France, West Germany, the Benelux countries and Italy. At the centre stood the High Authority, presided over by Jean Monnet. This modest approach of one step after another had the ambitious aim of achieving the 'United States of Europe' in the long term. The successful integra-

---

Box 2.5 Historical junctures of European politics

1952/1958/1993: The European integration process

- In spite of continuing resistance of the United Kingdom, French Foreign Minister Robert Schuman, advised by civil servant Jean Monnet, created with West Germany and other European countries (Benelux and Italy) a supra-national European Community of Steel and Coal (ECSC). The main objective was to share the coal resources of the Ruhr, which, in the past, had been a source of political conflict. The United States was an important supporter and promoter of the idea.
- This became known as the 'Schuman Plan' proclaimed by French Foreign Minister Robert Schuman on 9 May 1950.
- After lengthy negotiations, two further communities were created in 1958:
  - The European Economic Community; and
  - Euratom [related to nuclear energy].
- A further milestone was the Treaty of the European Union (TEU), signed in Maastricht and ratified in 1993. It created the legal foundations for Economic and Monetary Union (EMU), Justice and Home Affairs (JHA) and Common Foreign and Security Policy (CFSP).

tion of those two major essential areas of industrial society led, in 1958, to the Treaty of Rome (which founded Euratom, related to atomic energy and the European Economic Community) (Dinan, 2004: 46–82).

Despite its ambition to be a supranational organisation, the European Economic Community was very much dominated by the member states. During the 1960s, the Commission tried to push forward the agreed plan of a single European market. It was instrumental in completing a wide range of legislation in order to achieve the completion of the common market. Between 1959 and 1968 all internal tariffs were removed. Furthermore, on 1 July 1967 the three communities were merged into one, receiving the name of 'European Community'.

In 1962, a common agricultural policy was introduced in order to protect farmers from agricultural imports. The fast progress of European integration was abruptly halted, when the president of France, Charles de Gaulle, was against the transfer of additional financial powers to the Commission and the European Parliament in relation to CAP. Moreover, de Gaulle was against the introduction of majority voting (the treaties of 1958 stipulated that it was to be introduced in 1966). De Gaulle's position was not accepted by the other parties, so France removed its representatives from the Council of Ministers and the Committee of Permanent Representatives. This led to a major crisis in the European Economic Community, which became known as the French Empty Chair Policy. Nevertheless, a narrow victory in the presidential elections against pro-EC François Mitterrand in December 1965, led to a change of mind and to the Luxembourg Compromise of 28–29 January 1966. In this agreement, the discussion about further financial powers of the Commission and the European Parliament were to be delayed and decided at a later point in time, with majority voting continuing to be upheld particularly in matters that were of national interest (Dinan, 2004: 101–19). This naturally reinforced intergovernmentalism against the supranationalism of the Commission. The Luxembourg Compromise is known for having slowed down or even halted the ambitions of the supranational institutions. Indeed, the period between 1966 and 1985 is known as 'Eurosclerosis'. Although there was ambition to push forward a monetary union by the end of the 1970s, as advocated in the Werner report, the deteriorating economic and social situation relating to the oil shock of 1974 and 1979 (see below, p. 66) contributed to the stagnation of the project (Dinan, 2004: 177–8).

Despite this setback, the EC was able to introduce the informal European Council during the French presidency of 1974. Moreover, the introduction of direct elections to the European parliament in 1979 created a new dynamics in this supranational institution. The European parliament received some powers related to the approval of certain parts of the budget and was strongly integrated in the assent procedure relating to the integration of new members (Corbett et al., 2007: 12–14).

Last but not least, after a full decade of delay owing to Charles de Gaulle's veto, the United Kingdom, Ireland and Denmark joined the EC. Until then, the three countries had been members of a competing organisation led by the United Kingdom called European Free Trade Area (EFTA), which was less ambitious than the EC in its aims (Nugent, 2004: 22–7).

In sum, despite all setbacks the western part of the continent was moving slowly but steadily towards economic integration.

The oil crisis of the 1970s and the silent post-materialist revolution

One of the major events of the 1970s in Europe was the almost simultaneous collapse of three authoritarian regimes in Southern Europe: the Carnation Revolution on 25 April 1974 in Portugal; the evolutionary transition to democracy in Spain after the death of dictator General Francisco Franco on 20 November 1975; and, last but not least, the collapse of the military dictatorship of the Colonels in Greece in July 1974. This became known as the beginning of the third wave of democratisation, which also expanded to Latin America, Africa and Asia in the 1980s and 1990s. All three democratic transitions were successful, so that after this point no more authoritarian dictatorships existed in Western Europe. Throughout the 1970s and 1980s these new democracies consolidated and became quite stable politically and economically. One important factor was their integration into the EC in the 1980s. Apart from the consolidation of democracy and stabilisation of the southern flank of NATO in the context of the cold war, the structural funds of the EC were important in strengthening the weak infrastructures of these countries (Huntington, 1991; Pridham, 1985).

In the context of the cold war, the Helsinki Conference for Security and Cooperation in Europe (CSCE) took place in the summer of 1975 and should be regarded as a milestone in the process of European unification. The Helsinki accords signed on 1 August 1975 started a structured dialogue between West and East in order to improve the protection of human rights in Europe. The transitions to democracy in Southern Europe and the emergence of Eurocommunism in Italy, Spain and France were major concerns for the USA. The growing political instability in Southern Europe, particularly in Portugal, was a major concern to NATO, which was afraid that the Soviet Union wanted to gain control over the country (Maxwell, 1995). In spite of these tensions, the highly significant CSCE became an important forum to discuss issues of a pan-European dimension. The dialogue concentrated on four main areas: (1) European security; (2) scientific and economic cooperation; (3) humanitarian and cultural cooperation; and (4) follow-up to the conference. In 1994, the CSCE was transformed from a conference into an organisation with headquarters in the Hofburg building in Vienna.

After decades of sustainable, uninterrupted economic growth, most European countries began to slow down and even stagnate economically. And after decades of the welfare state, the whole economic system was becoming less and less competitive. The growing importance of other economic powers such as Japan, the United States and new emerging economies in Southeast Asia were a major factor in the loss of competitiveness of European economies. The high costs of the welfare state were not only undermining countries and preventing investment in the economy, but were also reducing the profit margins of public and private enterprises, necessary for reinvestment in innovation, research and development. One major problem in most West European countries was that, after the Second World War, they had taken over a huge public sector that, over time, became less and less competitive (Wegs and Ladrech, 2006: 262–4). In many cases, public enterprises accumulated huge losses that had to be financed from the state budget. The best examples were the policies of the Austrian social democratic government under Chancellor Bruno Kreisky. This social democratic leader created one of the most advanced social market economies. It was based on neo-corporatist institutions, such as the *Sozialpartnerschaft* (social partnership) and led to informal decisions being made between the Austrian trade union confederation (Öster-reichischer Gewerkschaftsbund, ÖGB), the Association of Austrian Industries (Industriellenvereinigung, IV) as well as the public chambers for industry, agriculture, commerce and labour in economic and social matters. These decisions were then simply adopted by the government. This consultation with the social partners was a founding stone of political and economic stability in the country. Such policies were summarised in the term 'Austrokeynesianismus'. However, at the end of the 1970s Kreisky abused Keynesian policies by keeping a huge number of public employees despite public firms accumulating huge losses. He was extremely influenced by the dangers of unemployment during the 1920s and 1930s (Vocelka, 2002; Pelinka and Rosenberger, 2003: 41–3). Similar neo-corporatist strategies were followed across Western Europe, particularly in the Benelux and Nordic countries.

Moreover, the Organisation of Oil Producing Countries (OPEC) reacted to the Yom Kippur War of October 1973 in which Israel was attacked by Egypt and Syria. The six-day war led to a complete victory of the Israeli army over the powers of the region leading later to peace agreements. During the Yom Kippur War, OPEC, dominated mainly by Arab states, increased its price by 70 per cent, and two months later it further raised its prices by 130 per cent. The United States and the Netherlands, which both supported Israel, were punished with oil embargos. Until the different countries were able to find alternative oil and energy supplies they were exposed to continuous price rises until end of the decade.

One of the main consequences of higher oil prices was growing inflation that hit consumers hard. The overall macroeconomic policy mix of failing Keynesianism and rising inflation undermined the prospects of a recovery.

In this context, the neo-monetarist policies of British Prime Minister Margaret Thatcher after her election in 1979 became an important model for most European countries. It entailed the control of monetary circulation and major reforms in the public sector and the state, including welfare policies. The policies, known as Thatcherism, aimed at reactivating Britain's market economy after a long period of stagnation caused by social unrest that itself stemmed from intensive trade union activity. Thatcherism in the 1980s led to major changes in order to make the United Kingdom more competitive worldwide. One of the major policies of Thatcherism was privatisation, which led to the restructuring of major public enterprises and resulted in lay-offs on a mass scale in order to make companies not only profitable again but also attractive for potential foreign and domestic investors. This also included the privatisation of public utilities, such as the national railway system, other public transport, telecommunications, water, gas and electricity, allowing. the state to become lighter and more competitive in international terms. Thatcherism successfully propagated the idea of 'people's capitalism' by advocating the idea of share ownership. At the core of the intended social revolution was the facilitation of the private ownership of council houses. Thatcherism also introduced major reforms in the public administration by allowing new public management thinking to modernise the relationship between civil servants and citizens. It allowed the line between the public and the private sectors to become blurred. Today, public–private partnership schemes can be found in schools and hospitals as well as other sectors in Britain. There were negative aspects to the reforms of Margaret Thatcher, such as: the establishment of a two-tier society; sidelining of workers' rights and trade unionism; high unemployment towards the end of the Thatcher period in 1991; and speculation in the housing market leading to many houses being repossessed by banks. Nonetheless, other countries, including the European Communities, took on many of these ideas (Overbeek, 1991).

Apart from Germany, most countries engaged in major reforms. In France, François Mitterrand's victory in the presidential elections of 1981 and that of the Socialist Party in the legislative elections, provided a great opportunity to push through a social democratic agenda. The socialist government started with Keynesian policies towards the public sector; however, unemployment continued to rise quite steadily. The only way out was to begin a process of privatisation in order to reduce the expenditure of the state. The French socialists have done this more humanely than the Thatcher regime; nevertheless, they had to change towards neo-monetarist policies, keeping inflation low in order to stop the vicious circle of hyper-inflation (Elgie, 2003: 25–6).

Reforms were also undertaken in the Netherlands, which was suffering from a major recession. Through cooperation with social partners, major reforms in the public sector and in relation to the economy were undertaken, leading to the Polder socioeconomic model at the beginning of the 1990s (Hendriks, 2001). Under Prime Minister Franz Vranitzky, Austria also began major reforms in the 1980s, leading to privatisation of the huge public sector. Similarly, reforms that reached well into the 1990s were undertaken in other countries, such as Italy and Greece. Last but not least, in Germany a major tax, pensioners' and labour market reform took place during Gerhard Schröder's red–green government between 1998 and 2005 (see Chapter 12).

In the 1980s and 1990s, European countries experienced a transformation of welfare states based on the principles of social redistribution towards a competitive state that has to survive in an increasingly globalised world. The restructuring of the state towards lighter structures and the drive to make policies more efficient changed the socioeconomic dynamics of most European countries (Cerny, 1990).

This period of economic and social restructuring also led to major reforms of the welfare state. According to Bob Jessop, the socioeconomic reforms allowed the transformation of the welfare state into a 'workfare' state to take place – a workfare state being one in which the allocation of social benefits is linked to the willingness of receivers to actively seek employment and to employability (Jessop, 2002: 138–40).

The appointment of Jacques Delors to the presidency of the Commission of the European Communities in 1985 was a crucial turning point for the dynamics of European politics and the economy. His dynamism led to the transformation of the European Communities into the European Union. One of the most important objectives was to push forward the Single European Market and make Europe the most competitive regional economy. The main competitors were the United States and Japan/Southeast Asia. The report of economist Paolo Cecchini showed that the creation of an SEM would considerably reduce production costs through the establishment of economies of scale and, in the long term, lead to an increase in employment. Although Delors was interested in preserving some aspects of the inherited social market economy, he was advocating softer Thatcherite policies at a European level. Moreover, the White Paper on the Single European Market, elaborated by Lord Cockfield in 1985, envisaged its basic implementation by the end of 1992. The Single European Act (SEA) was an important step towards further European integration. This expressed itself in the change to the decision-making process within the Council of Ministers. Until the approval of the SEA, decision-making about any legislative proposal had to be unanimous and each country had veto rights. After the SEA, a qualified majority, consisting of an allocation of votes to each country based on national population, was introduced for all areas related to the Single European Market programme. Moreover, the European Parliament had to be consulted and if a decision of the Council of Ministers was rejected, the latter could only override the elected chamber unanimously. The SEA also strengthened the role of environment policy, social and cohesion policy and the embryonic European foreign and security policy. This last was done through the formalisation of European Political Cooperation – until then this had been an informal network of diplomats from the member states who coordinated their national policies in order to speak on behalf of the EC with one voice on international relations. Another major achievement of Jacques Delors was to integrate the new member states (Greece (1981), Portugal (1986) and Spain (1986)) by achieving a doubling of the EU budget – of which 35 per cent was destined for structural funding in order for them to catch up with the rest of the developed economies and thus create a level playing field (Cecchini *et al.*, 1988; Dinan, 2004).

One of the major consequences of these economic transformations was that society became more post-industrial and individualised. New technologies allowed for a personalisation of consumer goods and also the luxury of nomadism. This had implications for politics. The new information age is more value-oriented than ideology-oriented. Loyalty to social cleavages, which led to translation into political votes for particular parties, became replaced by a de-aligned individualised electorate that voted for parties instrumentally and on a value basis (see Chapter 3).

Last, but not least, these socioeconomic transformations have led to the emergence of new populist parties on the right or left of the political spectrum that may be able to offer simple solutions to the insecurities felt during this period (Mudde, 2004). Among such parties are the Flemish Interest (Vlaams Belang) in Belgium, both the Freedom Party (Freiheitliche Partei Österreichs, FPÖ) and the Union for the Future of Austria (Bündnis für die Zukunft Österreichs, BZÖ) in Austria, the Swiss People's Party(Schweizerische Volkspartei, SVP) in Switzerland, the National Front (Front National, FN) in France and the British National Party (BNP) in the UK.

The Fall of the Berlin Wall and the emergence of a new European era

Throughout the 1970s and 1980s the economies of the Soviet Union and the Central and Eastern European countries were stagnating. They were not able to meet the demand for most consumer goods. The planned economy was too oriented towards heavy industry goods in order to keep up the arms race with the West. In the Soviet Union, the emergence of leader Mikhail Gorbachev was regarded as a possibility for achieving reform. Gorbachev wanted to introduce *perestrojka* (reform) and *glasnost* (transparency) to the Soviet system. He tried to reactivate political institutions and civil society after decades of totalitarian rule. Nevertheless, this led to an explosion of demands and the final demise of the Soviet Union on 25 December 1991. Although Gorbachev does not have a high reputation in Russia, he was instrumental in dismantling the Iron Curtain and paving the way for democratic transition throughout the whole of Central and Eastern Europe (Wegs and Ladrech, 2006: 220–4).

This process began with the withdrawal of support to the repressive policies of Erich Honecker in the GDR. Many East Germans fled to West Germany through Hungary and Austria during the summer and early autumn 1989. The protests continued throughout October until negotiations had to be undertaken to start a process of German reunification. Finally, on 9 November 1989, the Berlin Wall was dismantled by the people themselves (Box 2.6). The process of German reunification ended on 3 October 1990, after lengthy negotiations between the West and East German elites and the four allied powers (the US, the UK, France and the Soviet Union). The speedy reunification was mainly owing to the efforts of West German chancellor Helmut Kohl, who clearly feared a change of mind in Moscow. This is also one of the reasons why the West German Basic Law had just been extended to the territory of the former German Democratic Republic (Vogt, 2002: 920–41).

Between May 1988 and December 1989, other Central and Eastern European countries moved towards democracy. The only country that had opened up considerably and made possible regular exchange with the West was Hungary. Following the 1956 uprising, the reforms of János Kádár had led to tolerance of a private enterprise culture that was able to deliver the market with the necessary consumer goods. 'Goulash communism' was also successful in pushing the boundaries of freedom. In May 1988, János Kádár was forced to resign and was replaced by a collective leadership. The Communist Party was dissolved and

---

Box 2.6 Historical junctures of European politics

1989: The Fall of the Berlin Wall

- Between 1947 and 1989 Europe was divided by the 'Iron Curtain'.
- On 9 November 1989, after the mounting discontent of the East German people, the Berlin Wall dividing Germany and the city was opened, leading to the collapse of communist rule in Central and Eastern Europe.
- After lengthy negotiations, it led to the reunification of Germany on 3 October 1990, a major holiday in the country.
- From November to December, one after another the communist regimes in Central and Eastern Europe were toppled.
- 1989 can be regarded as the start of a new era of European politics.

replaced by the Hungarian Socialist Party. The Hungarian constitution was amended to allow democratic transition. After the first free legislative elections, the Hungarian Democratic Forum (MDF), an umbrella party, won the elections while the re-formed communists got only 10 per cent. In subsequent elections, the re-formed communists were able to recover. A stable two-party system emerged, allowing for alternation between left and right (Wegs and Ladrech, 2006: 228–31; Montgomery, 2006: 412–14).

In Poland, a dialogue between General Jaruzelski and the main opposition group, Solidarnošč, led to restricted legislative elections on 4 June 1989. The elections resulted in a considerable victory for the latter in the free elected seats of the Sejm and all seats of the Senate. The establishment of an all-party government under the leadership of Christian democrat Tadeusz Mazowiecki led to major reforms, directed at the establishment of a liberal democracy and a free market economy. Such democratic transition ended with the adoption of a new constitution in 1997, after the Small constitution of 1993 was regarded as having many flaws. Today, however, the Polish party system is still far from consolidated (Sanford, 2001: 54–83; Taras, 2006: 358–60).

In November 1989, several demonstrations for democratic reform took place in Czechoslovakia, the country with the most orthodox and rigid regime. This led to the establishment of a 'government of national understanding' and the election of Václav Havel as president in December. In the first legislative elections on 10 June 1990, the umbrella Citizens' Forum (OF) won 53 per cent in the Czech Republic and Public against Violence (VPN) won 32 per cent in Slovakia. The federal nature of Czechoslovakia was then contested by Slovak nationalists leading to the 'velvet divorce' of both parts of Czechoslovakia after the June 1992 legislative elections. While the Czech Republic was able to achieve a high level of stability, Slovakia is still haunted by the Movement for a Democratic Slovakia (HZDS) under the leadership of Vladimir Mečiar, who has used a populist–nationalist discourse, particularly against the Hungarian minority. Even more radical has been the Slovak Nationalist Party (Wegs and Ladrech, 2006: 203–6; Vodička, 2005: 43–54).

In 2005, both became part of a coalition government under the direction of Robert Fico's Third Way Social Democratic Party. In spite of all concerns, the coalition has been performing well, leading to the adoption of the euro by the country on 1 January 2009.

In Bulgaria, several demonstrations during 1989 led to the resignation of leader Todor Zhivkov from all offices. A national round table in January to March 1990 started the process towards democratic transition. However, the elections of June 1990 led to the victory of the Bulgarian Socialist Party, the former Communist Party under a new name. The opposition renewed its demonstrations during summer and autumn 1990, forcing a renewed round table in January 1991. On 12 July 1991, a new constitution was approved that led to the first legislative elections in October 1991, leading to the victory of the Union of Democratic Forces (SDS). In spite of this victory, the Bulgarian Socialist Party continues to be an important party in the country. This could not be changed even after the arrival of former King Simeon II and his national movement, Simeon II, in 2001 (Crampton, 2002: 308–14).

The bloodiest revolution was in Romania, leading to the fall of former dictator Nicolaj Ceausescu and his family on 22 December 1989. It was a *coup d'état* of a part of the Communist Party against Ceausescu. Soon after, Ceausescu's entire family was executed, and Ion Iliescu and the Front of National Salvation took over on 26 December. Ion Iliescu was elected as president in 1990 and also in 1992 and 2000. The re-formed communists in the renamed Party of Social Democracy in Romania remain an influential party on the left in the new political system (Crampton, 2002: 324–31).

The failed coup attempt in the Soviet Union in August 1991 also strengthened the independence movements in the Baltic countries. All three countries proclaimed independence in 1990, but Moscow delayed her acknowledgement of independence. There were interventions in Lithuania and Latvia in early 1991, nevertheless by the autumn, the independence of all three Baltic states was recognised (Smith, 2002: 65–93; Pabriks and Purs, 2002: 45–66; Lane, 2002: 87–131).

The recent democratisation processes in Central and Eastern Europe were a major boost for the European integration process. Negotiations between COMECON and the European Communities had started in 1988 (Smith, 2004: 29–35). The 1989 events forced the European Communities to develop a common strategy for all the countries. This process took place between 1989 and 1993. One of the reasons for the delay was that the European Union was dealing with the process of accession of Austria, Sweden, Finland and possibly Norway, due to take place in 1995. After a rejection of EU membership in Norway, only Sweden, Finland and Austria joined the EU. Only afterwards did the European Union devote more attention to the Central and Eastern European democratisation processes.

Box 2.7 Historical junctures of European politics

2004–7: United Europe

- After a decade of negotiations between 1993 and 2002, finally most Central and Eastern European countries joined the European Union on 1 May 2004.
- This was followed by the accession of Bulgaria and Romania on 1 January 2007.
- There are now twenty-seven member states in the European Union, the vast majority of European States.
- It is expected that Iceland, the Balkan countries and eventually Turkey will join the European Union in the next decade.
- Turkey will have most obstacles to overcome such as the Cyprus question, the need for major political, economic and social reforms in the country, and the opposition of the majority in several EU countries, particularly France and Austria, which will conduct national referendums on accession of Turkey to the European Union after negotiations are concluded. Growing opposition of new and extreme right-wing parties against EU membership of Europe (using the slogan 'Against the Islamisation of Europe') has been shaping the debate as well.

Apart from financial and logistical support, major reforms had to be undertaken to comply with what has been labelled the 'Copenhagen criteria', comprising political, economic and administrative issues (Box 2.7). These criteria were agreed during the Danish presidency of the European Union in 1993. Almost a decade later, during the Danish presidency of 2002, most Central and Eastern European countries apart from Bulgaria and Romania (plus the Mediterranean islands of Cyprus and Malta) were allowed to join the EU (Lippert, 2003). By 1 May 2004, the European Union had enlarged to twenty-five members, and Romania and Bulgaria joined on 1 January 2007, increasing the number to twenty-seven (see Figure 2.6).

Figure 2.6 Political Europe, 2010

In spite of this success, the European continent was struck by tragedy. The fratricide wars in former Yugoslavia in the 1990s showed how weak European institutions were in dealing with such conflicts. The nationalist policies of Serbian leader Slobodan Milošević were a major factor in leading to the complete disintegration of Yugoslavia. In 1992, Slovenia was already able to free itself from the federation in spite of threats coming from Belgrade. Afterwards Croatia followed the path of independence leading to a short war between the two sides. Then the main focus of conflict became the multi-ethnic Bosnia-Herzegovina, consisting of Bosnian-Muslims, Croats and Serbs. Ethnic cleansing between the different groups, in particular by Serbs and Croats led to war crimes. The conflict was only stopped after NATO bombardment and the deployment of peacekeeping troops stipulated in the Dayton agreement (also signed by Slobodan Milošević in 1995). Despite this agreement, a reintegration of Bosnia-Herzegovina has been quite a difficult process and only possible because of the presence of both the peacekeeping forces and civilian officers deployed by the international community. In spite of these defeats, Milošević's war against the Kosovo Liberation Army (KLA) in Kosovo led to a further attempt at ethnic cleansing of the Albanian population in 1999. Milošević's policies were very much a response to the attempt by the KLA to intimidate the small Serbian minority in the region. The intervention of NATO under the leadership of Secretary-General Javier Solana, which consisted of bombarding key strategic positions in Serbia, led to the surrender of Milošević. The independence of Macedonia (or correctly Former Republic of Yugoslavia Macedonia) in 1993, did not spare the country from ethnic tensions. Indeed, in July 2001 ethnic tensions led to a major insurgency on the part of the large Albanian minority. This was only diffused when NATO and, later on, European Union peacekeeping troops were deployed (Crampton, 2002: 239–98; Bideleux and Jeffries, 2007b: 451–2).

The independence of Montenegro from Serbia after the referendum of 21 May 2006 led to a further fragmentation of Yugoslavia. Montenegro has only 650,000 inhabitants, who are extremely divided in their loyalties to Serbia (*Neue Zürcher Zeitung*, 14 July 2006: 4). Last, but not least, the recent unilateral declaration of independence of Kosovo from Serbia has led to further tensions and a nationalist backlash in the region (*El Pais*, 23 February 2008: 3–4; *El Pais*, 28 February 2008: 2–3) (Figure 2.6). Many countries with similar problems, such as Russia, China and Spain, refrained from acknowledging the independence of Kosovo, for fear that this may set a precedent for their own territories.

European integration and Euro-scepticism

In the past two decades the European Union has become an important actor in the continent. In the 1990s, several treaties changed the lives of European citizens considerably. The Treaty of the European Union (TEU) signed in Maastricht in 1991 and ratified in 1993 led to the establishment of a route for Economic and Monetary Union. By 2002, twelve countries had introduced the single European currency, the euro, in their countries. Slovenia joined in 2007, Malta and Cyprus in 2008 and Slovakia in 2009; other countries of Central and Eastern Europe may join as soon as they have fulfilled the Maastricht criteria. The Treaty of the European Union strengthened the position of national parliaments in the European Union and allowed social partners to develop framework agreements that could be translated into European law. The TEU also expanded majority voting to more policy areas. Moreover, it introduced new intergovernmental integration pillars, such as Common Foreign and Security Policy (CFSP) and Justice and Home Affairs (JHA). The Amsterdam Treaty signed in 1997 and ratified in 1999 further strengthened the CFSP by creating the High Representative attached to the Council of the European Union. A 'militarisation' of the CFSP has been occurring since the Kosovo War of 1999, in order to avoid future situations whereby Europeans are mere bystanders in such conflicts. The then forthcoming enlargement to Central and Eastern Europe and the Mediterranean islands led to the Nice Treaty that was adopted during the French presidency. This was achieved after hard bargaining between the member states. The compromise was about voting rights allocation in a qualified majority in the Council of Ministers and seats in the European parliament. Although Germany had the largest population, its allocation of voting rights in the Council was capped at the same as the other larger countries; however, it was compensated with the largest number of MEPs. Big winners in the allocation of votes were Spain and Poland, which got almost as many voting rights as the larger countries, although their populations were much smaller. The small countries of about ten million each, such as Portugal, Belgium and Hungary, were those that lost influence in terms of voting rights. Nevertheless, the process of integration came to a halt after the European Convention of 2002–3 when, following the signature of the Constitutional Treaty by representatives of member states in Rome in November 2004, the French and Dutch rejected it in their respective referendums on 29 May and 1 June 2005 respectively. Among the reasons for this is a general feeling of alienation in relation to further enlargement of the European Union. Moreover, fear of 'social dumping' as a result of Central and Eastern European immigration to Western European countries also played a major role in decision-making, owing to the fact that the Single European Market may undermine existing lifestyles.

Euro-scepticism in both its moderate and more radical forms has been more prominent since the Treaty of the European Union. The Portuguese presidency of the European Communities was taken by surprise when the Danes rejected the Treaty of the European Union in 1992. The Danes had to renegotiate and exclude themselves from EMU in order to achieve acceptance of the TEU by the population in a second referendum. A similar incident happened to the Nice Treaty in 2001, following the Irish referendum. The low level of participation led to rejection, however a second referendum in 2002 endorsed it. In some countries, such as the United Kingdom, Denmark, Austria, Switzerland, Poland, France and the Czech Republic, there are parties that either reject some supranational policies or totally reject the European Union. This may be a new socio-political rift that surfaces when European Union issues are discussed. European parliament elections have become such an event in which this socioeconomic cleavage regularly emerges. It means that, at last, the highly elite-driven European Union project has been checked and controlled by more self-confident national populations (Taggart, 1995; Taggart and Szcerbiak, 2004).

Conclusions: European politics as a kaleidoscope of experiment, innovation and tradition

This chapter intended to give an overview of European politics since the Late Middle Ages. In the past five hundred years, European politics has been evolving towards emancipation and self-expressive values (Inglehart and Welzel, 2005). The complexity and diversity of national political systems and political cultures are intrinsically linked to processes of convergence and cooperation. The common heritage in both good and bad times transformed national histories as part of what we call here 'interconnected European politics'. All parts of Europe contributed to the richness and diversity of the political systems that we experience today. The Belgian constitution of 1831 was an important template for the constitutions of the Balkans. The strong French franc of the early 1990s was an emulation of the German Deutschmark. Many two-party systems in Southern Europe of the nineteenth century emulated the British system. Similarly, the Hungarian constitution of 1989 borrowed many devices from the German constitution in order to achieve a stable political system. It is integration based on choices by political elites that has led to European politics through political institutional transfer. These political institutional transfers play out differently in different countries. The historical legacy of European politics helps us to recognise the transformative capacity of institutions and political systems and their interactions with each other. In short, European politics is a changing kaleidoscope of tradition, experiment and innovation, that preserves its vitality and ability to reinvent itself.

Suggested reading

On the Middle Ages

Davies, Norman (1997), *Europe: A History*. London: Pimlico.

Davis, R.H.C. (1970), *A History of Medieval Europe: From Constantine to Saint Louis*. London: Longman.

Koenigsberger, H.G. (1987), *Medieval Europe: 400–1500*. London: Longman.

Huizinga, J. (1924, 1987), *The Waning of the Middle Ages*. London: Penguin Books.

On the Early Modern Age

Green, V.H.H. (1964), *Renaissance and Reformation: A Survey of European History Between 1450 and 1660*. London: Edward Arnold.

Hobsbawn, Eric J. (1990, 2000), *Nations and Nationalism since 1970: Programme, Myth, Reality*. Cambridge: Cambridge University Press.

Kamen, Henry (2000), *Early Modern European Society*. London: Routledge.

Rudé, George (1964, 1980), *Revolutionary Europe 1783–1815*. London: Fontana.

Williams, E.N (1999), *The Ancien Regime in Europe: Government and Society in the Major States 1648–1789*. London: Pimlico.

On the nineteenth century

Ferguson, Niall (2003, 2007), *Empire: How Britain Made the Modern World*. London: Penguin.

Hobsbawn, E.J. (1964), *The Age of Revolution 1789–1848*. London: Cardinal.

—— (1975, 1989), *The Age of Capital 1848–1875*. New York: Meridian.

—— (1987), *The Age of Empire 1875–1914*. London: Weidenfeld & Nicolson.

On the twentieth century and twenty-first century

Bideleux, Robert and Ian Jeffries (2007a), *A History of Eastern Europe: Crisis and Change*. London: Routledge.

—— (2007b), *The Balkans: A Post-Communist History*. London: Routledge.

Hobsbawn, Eric J. (1994), *The Age of Extremes: The Short Twentieth Century 1914–1991*. London: Abacus.

Mazower, Marc (1998), *Dark Continent. Europe's Twentieth Century*. London: Penguin.

Wegs, Robert J. and Robert Ladrech (2006), *Europe Since 1945: A Concise History*. Basingstoke: Palgrave.

QUESTIONS FOR REVISION

- Which main historical events shaped European politics?
- What is the main legacy of the French Revolution?
- What is understood by the 'cold war' after 1945 and what were the implications for Europe?
- Explain the importance of the 1989 Fall of the Berlin Wall.
- What were the main achievements of the European integration process?

Chapter 3

The transformation of European politics

- Towards a new understanding of European politics
- Stein Rokkan's theory of European politics
  - Nation-building and the formation of cleavages
  - The translation of cleavages into stable party systems
  - Rokkan's interest in centre-periphery cleavages
  - Reviewing the criticisms of Stein Rokkan's theory
- The postmodernisation of European politics: the society of individuals and the impact of the new media
  - From the industrial to the post-industrial society
  - From a welfare to a workfare state
  - Towards the post-industrial economy
  - The decline of religious cleavages and religiosity
  - The rise of regional identity and the impact on national political cultures
  - From a homogeneous national to a heterogeneous multicultural society
- Conclusions: the great transformation of the late twentieth century

SUMMARY OF CHAPTER 3

In this chapter, we will discuss the main theory of European politics elaborated by the Norwegian Stein Rokkan. The theory was developed over several decades until his death in 1979. The chapter is divided in four main parts:

- Towards a new understanding of European politics;
- Stein Rokkan theory of European politics;
- The postmodernisation of European politics;
- Conclusions.

The main aim of the chapter is to raise awareness of the theoretical foundations of European politics and its transformation since the 1970s. The second section is dedicated to the pioneering work of Stein Rokkan, the third section analyses the main transformations since his death. The chapter closes with some conclusions.

Towards a new understanding of European politics

During the past thirty years European politics underwent major transformations that we are able to recognise only now, with the benefit of hindsight. Throughout these decades the new transformations were analysed using theoretical instruments of the past. In this sense, students of European politics were confronted with a constant mismatch between theory and reality. The main theoretical edifice for understanding European politics was developed by Stein Rokkan. Many scholars took inspiration from his writings and developed different interpretations that are still important, but no longer reflect the fast changing reality of European politics today.

One of the main problems of Rokkan's theory is that it is embedded in the period 1945–67, which was characterised by a high level of political and economic stability. This does not help us to explain the period following 1967, which is characterised by high levels of political, social and economic change. However, this is not the place to criticise the huge and pioneering work of Stein Rokkan on nation-building, democratisation of national politics and the making of European party systems.

On the contrary, the work of this eminent Norwegian can only be an inspiration for us all. It should be acknowledged that Rokkan's theories have limited validity up to the 1970s, though mainly for Western Europe. His studies were concentrated on specific regions and countries where academic literature and data were available. In this sense, the Iberian countries, the Balkans, Central and Eastern Europe and even France (Guillorel, 1981: 390) are either completely neglected or scarcely covered. In spite of that, Rokkan left us an enormous legacy, a huge data collection and a host of ideas for renewed thinking about European politics.

Therefore, it is important to look at his main theoretical contributions in order to understand what has been happening to European politics since the mid

1970s. In this sense, this chapter is a guiding theoretical framework for understanding the present transformations of European politics without any claims to be comprehensive.

Indeed, one important fact is that the growing importance of processes of globalisation, reinforced by the rhythm and acceleration of new mobile information technologies, has contributed to postmodernisation, or, as we argue in this book, some 'Americanisation' of European politics. The emergence of a new impetus in the European integration process through the active presidency of the European Commission by Jacques Delors between 1985 and 1995 further contributed to this process. However, it is important to make clear that Americanisation does not mean that Europe is becoming a carbon copy of the United States of America. On the contrary, it means rather that certain features of American politics and society are becoming commonplace in European countries and across the world, with the qualification that the way these features are played out in each country depends on the different political cultures. European national political cultures still matter, but they are converging towards standardisation – through national channels, as before, but also, increasingly, through European and global channels as well. This is possible, because the old class-based system of modern industrial society has been replaced by a flexible, individualised, market-oriented one. As this new class system, based on production and control of knowledge, replaces the old industrial class system, the differences between groups become blurred (Esping-Andersen, 1995; Drucker, 2001: 4).

This chapter is divided into three main parts: the first part deals with the main aspects of Stein Rokkan's theoretical contribution. The second part is dedicated to the criticisms to which Rokkan has been subjected since the 1970s. And the third part discusses the main catalysts for change during the past forty years.

Stein Rokkan's theory of European politics

Although there is diversity in Europe and one has to speak of different Europes, the trend towards convergence is largely inevitable. Comparative European politics does still matter, but convergence trends have been more important than actual conflict. Nonetheless, it is argued that, in spite of the tendencies towards convergence, national politics still matter and will not go away in the foreseeable future.

Stein Rokkan is therefore important, because he argued that such a trend from conflict towards consensus and non-violent decision-making of modern societies had been manifesting itself since the Middle Ages.

Rokkan was interested in three main issues:

1   *The nation-building process and the emergence of national politics.* This includes also the process towards inclusive citizenship.
2   *How different subcultures are accommodated through national party systems.* Here, he focused predominantly on studying the different cleavages that emerged through historical legacy.
3   *The the centre-periphery cleavage.* Rokkan's Norwegian background and particularly his origins in the northern part of the country (Lofoten) led to a strong interest in comparing centre-periphery relations across Europe.

If we look at the EU membership referendums held in Norway in 1973 and 1994 we can observe some continuity of opposition against the EU in the northern rural and coastal areas, which can be compared with the pro-European southern urbanised Norway, especially around the capital city of Oslo (Heidar, 1995: 446–7).

Nation-building and the formation of cleavages

It is not Rokkan's studies on nation-building and the emergence of national politics that stirred controversy among scholars. On the contrary, his historical-theoretical work on how citizenship emerged in European countries is well recognised. Today it forms the foundations for many studies on democratisation in Europe and other continents. Indeed, Rokkan's work allowed for differentiation within Europe, for example early democratisation, late democratisation, continuous democratisation and discontinuous democratisation (see Chapter 1, pp. 17–23).

While Rokkan concentrated his studies on Western European countries and was very strong on the analysis of such processes in Northern Europe, the recent democratisation of Southern, Central and Eastern Europe allows us to finally map out the asymmetrical democratisation among European countries (Box 3.1).

Rokkan thoroughly studied transformations related to nation-building and the establishment of national politics in the nineteenth and early twentieth centuries. He was particularly interested in understanding the making and spreading of citizenship in the different European countries. His main aim was to map out the process of democratisation in Europe. Indeed, his ambition was to create a conceptual map of Europe.

Box 3.1 Stein Rokkan (1921–79)

Stein Rokkan was probably the greatest and most influential political scientist in European politics in the post-war period following 1945 until his death.

He was born on 7 July 1921 in the small village of Vågan, in the Lofoten in the northern province of Nordland in Norway. He studied philosophy in Oslo; however, he had a broad range of interests, particularly in the social sciences.

His main work is his conceptual map of Europe, which is based on historical path-dependency in the explanation of state- and nation-building. Furthermore, he was a pioneer in the development of longitudinal and synchronic empirical databases for several European countries for comparative purposes.

Appreciated by his fellow colleagues, his dynamism and hard work made him an invaluable leader in the profession. He took the first steps towards global comparative studies under the auspices of the United Nations. He was also a co-founder of the European Consortium for Political Research, which has existed for almost four decades.

He died on 22 July 1979 in the city of Bergen.

His Norwegian background also gave him the insight that nation-building can be a process that takes place simultaneously with the democratisation process. This, of course, makes the whole process towards national politics in the different countries more diverse.

One particular aspect of his studies was that one cannot conceptualise a democratising nation-state as a homogeneous unit. On the contrary, he emphasised that societies are heterogeneous and characterised by cleavages. In spite of using the concept of cleavages, Rokkan never defined it; he clearly had difficulty in reaching a final definition. Nevertheless, he was very keen to emphasise that cleavage structures already existed before party systems emerged (Flora, 1999: 34). He was extremely influenced by a book written by Eugen Weber, called *Making Peasants into Frenchmen*, which showed this process of nationalisation of the masses and the creation of citizenship. Weber's historical masterpiece shows how rural France became increasingly integrated into mass politics between 1860 and 1914 and hence how the social fabric in the countryside became less stable, more porous and dominated by the rhythm coming from the urban centres (Weber, 1977).

Stefano Bartolini and Peter Mair endeavoured to come to a workable definition of the concept of cleavage. According to them, a cleavage is created through a process of closure that includes several factors. This closure is organised through marriage, common educational institutions, the spatial setting of the population, religious practices and social customs. In this cultural distinctiveness there is a high level of social homogeneity. This cultural distinctiveness leads to the establishment of social and political institutions in order to defend the way of life of the community. Cultural distinctiveness, social homogeneity and the establishment of dense organisational structures contribute to long-term stable socio-political membership of a subculture and allows for the translation of this membership into party and electoral politics (Bartolini and Mair, 1990: 225). According to Bartolini and Mair these three factors lead to the stability of electorates in the long run. They represent them as a three-dimensional cube (Figure 3.1).

One of the big achievements of Rokkan was to make a connection between the socio-political processes and critical junctures of European politics. By critical

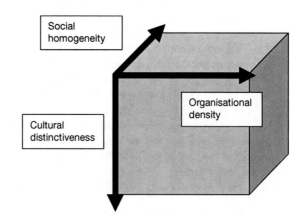

Figure 3.1
The dimensions of Rokkan's cleavage, according to Stefano Bartolini and Peter Mair

Source: Bartolini and Mair, 1991: 225.
Reproduced by permission of Cambridge University Press

junctures, he meant crucial European events that had a greater or smaller impact on all European countries (see Chapter 2). The three main junctures leading to cleavages were:

1   first, during the *Reformation* – the struggle for the control of the ecclesiastical organisations within the national territory;
2   second, in the wake of the *'Democratic Revolution' after 1789* – the conflict over the control of the vast machineries of mass education to be built up by the mobilising nation-states;
3   finally, during the early phases of the *Industrial Revolution* – the opposition between landed interests and claims of the rising commercial and industrial leadership in cities and towns.

(Lipset and Rokkan, 1967: 36–7)

In a more reflective way, with the hindsight of having read through all the manuscripts of Stein Rokkan, Peter Flora identified four cleavages:

•   **Cleavage I**: Opposition against centralisation after the French Revolution in 1789;
•   **Cleavage II**: State–Church conflicts over control over education since the eighteenth century;
•   **Cleavage III**: The rural–urban conflict that emerged during the industrial revolution since the late eighteenth century;
•   **Cleavage IV**: The workers–employers conflict that emerged as a consequence of the industrial revolution since the late eighteenth century: the so-called 'class cleavage'.

(The above is the author's summary, taken from Rokkan, 1980: 121; Flora, 1999: 37–8; Bartolini, 2000. See also Figure 3.2.)

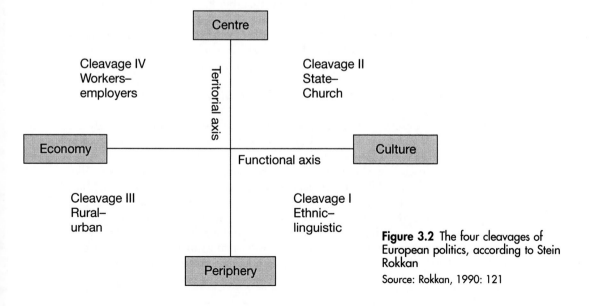

Figure 3.2 The four cleavages of European politics, according to Stein Rokkan
Source: Rokkan, 1990: 121

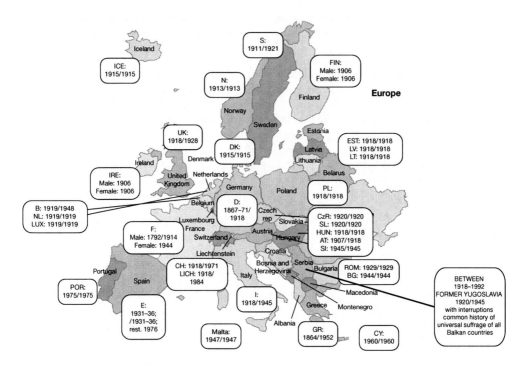

Figure 3.3 Universal suffrage in Europe

Rokkan did not exclude the emergence of new cleavages after these three crucial events, but his theoretical framework was organised around the three critical junctures that produced the four cleavages. He certainly acknowledged that the Russian Revolution of 1917 was a major critical juncture, but he was not sure whether the emergence of new communist parties that followed should be considered to be a new cleavage, distinct from that established earlier by the employers–workers during the nineteenth century (Rokkan, 1999: 305, 310).

The translation of cleavages into stable party systems

Rokkan was extremely interested in using these identified cleavages to study the development towards universal suffrage in a comparative perspective (Rokkan in Flora *et al.*, 1999: 252–3) (see Figure 3.3).

In this sense, he was interested in the incorporation of the masses into national politics. The likely instruments/institutions to achieve this were political parties. The translation of cleavage structures into party systems became the central part of his theoretical work. He was very keen to reduce this process of creating party systems in the different European countries to a model of development. He identified four thresholds for the emergence of a functioning party system that have to be overcome over time, although not necessarily in sequence or in a particular time span:

- **Legitimation**: level of acceptance of protest within the political system;
- **Incorporation**: denial or granting of political citizenship status in the political system;
- **Representation**: movement's ability to achieve representation in the political system;
- **Majority power**: the definition of electoral rules agreed between the main political actors of the political system.

(The above is the author's summary, taken from Lipset and Rokkan, 1967: 27–32)

Legitimation: This should be considered as an important threshold because, without legitimation, a political system will be dealing with an increasing number of protest movements. Opening up the political system for political activism will, of course, strengthen the establishment of political parties that channel the protests of their constituencies into mainstream politics and therefore help to legitimise the political system through its participation.

Incorporation: This refers to the acknowledgement of political rights for a vast majority of the population. The denial of political citizenship may put the political system under pressure. The extension of universal suffrage in stages allowed for an ordered process towards democracy as experienced in the United Kingdom and Scandinavia. In many continental countries, such as in Southern, Central and Eastern Europe, the process of incorporation was quite conflictive.

Representation: Another major aspect is the ability to achieve representation in the political system. This threshold is important because it further legitimises the political system and translates incorporation into concrete influence. The emergence of working-class parties in the late nineteenth and early twentieth centuries and their representation in national parties can be regarded as an important process in overcoming this threshold. The manipulation of the representative system, for example through the rigging of elections, as in Spain from 1870 until 1923, may lead to the emergence of political violence and even terrorist activity.

Majority power: The definition of the rules of the game in electoral politics is essential for the successful integration of political cleavages in the political system. It is important that all relevant social groups feel properly represented through their parties. A positive example of this is the Dutch policy of pacification during and after the First World War. This allowed the establishment of a proportional representation system, in which all relevant political groups could find a place in the new political system. Other issues that were important to different cleavages, such as the funding of faith-based private schools, were solved through this settlement (Lijphart, 1975: 70–2).

According to Rokkan there is an interconnection between these four thresholds. They all put each other under pressure, not necessarily in a sequential order, but nevertheless in some kind of relationship. These interrelated pressures will lead to political parties that are able to structure the cleavages and contribute to the integration of the political system. The political party is a crucial agent of conflict but also one of integration as well. Political parties fulfil three main functions:

- **Expressive function**: Parties express and structure the way of thinking and the demands of a particular cleavage or subculture inside a country.
- **Instrumental function**: The use of party structures for the achievement of the demands of a particular cleavage or subculture. This may include participation in elections, representative institutions or other forms of participation in which the party functions as a channel.
- **Representative function**: The participation in institutions such as parliament. The representative function allows also for incorporation into the political system and achievement of the demands of a particular constituency through peaceful means.

As Rokkan emphasises, the main role for political parties is to provide channels of integration in order that the democratic state is able to remain stable over time. Competition between parties allows a legitimate system for implementing the demands of different cleavages of society, either through single or coalition government. Lipset and Rokkan summarise as follows:

> A competitive party system protects the nation against the discontents of its citizens: grievances and attacks are deflected from the overall system and directed toward the current set of powerholders . . .
> . . . The establishment of regular channels for the expression of conflicting interests has helped to stabilize the structure of a great number of nation-states. The effective equalization of the status of different denominations has helped to take much of the brunt off the earlier conflicts over religious issues.
> The extension of suffrage and the enforcement of the freedom of political expression also helped to strengthen the legitimacy of the nation-state.
> The opening up of channels of expression of manifest or latent conflicts between the established and the underprivileged classes may have brought many systems out of equilibrium in the earlier phase but tended to strengthen the body politic over time.
> This conflict–integration dialectic is of central concern in current research on the comparative sociology of political parties.
> (Lipset and Rokkan, 1967: 4–5)

One of the most controversial of Stein Rokkan's theses, which he presented with Seymour Martin Lipset, was that most European party systems froze in the inter-war period (Box 3.2). This meant that in the late 1960s citizens were able to choose from the same number of mass parties that existed in the inter-war period. Indeed, his 'freezing hypothesis' generated major criticisms soon after it was published. Party system change in some European countries led to a very high level of volatility in many European countries, in particular Denmark and the Netherlands. Lipset and Rokkan argued that the majority of citizens in Western Europe had been acquainted with the existing parties since their childhood, or at least when they were allowed to vote for the first time. In this sense, they were socialised into particular subcultures that reinforced these cleavages (Lipset and Rokkan, 1967: 50). For the moment it suffices to present Rokkan's freezing hypothesis. We will look at the criticisms of this highly controversial thesis in the next section.

Box 3.2 The freezing hypothesis

Seymour Martin Lipset and Stein Rokkan edited a volume together with the title *Party Systems and Voter Alignments: Cross National Perspectives* (New York: The Free Press, 1967). In the introductory chapter called 'Cleavage structures, party systems and voter alignments: an introduction' (pp. 1–67), they presented a theory about the consolidation and institutionalisation of parties and party systems in Europe. The main thesis was that the party systems of 1967 had not changed particularly since the 1920s. They presented the thesis that the then contemporary party systems in different countries had been frozen since the 1920s. This meant that electorates had tended to vote for the same parties since the 1920s.

This was a daring thesis because, not long after the chapter was published, many countries (for example, the Netherlands and Denmark) had to deal with considerable party change. Supporters of this thesis, such as Peter Mair, argue that it is still valid owing to the low level of volatility from election to election. However, there are also critics of the thesis, for example Stephen Wolinetz and Mogens Pedersen.

Rokkan's interest in centre-periphery cleavages

Although Rokkan was interested in centre-periphery relations and the process of nation-building throughout his life, it is only in the later phase of his distinguished career that we find a more systematic work in relation to it. He teamed up with Derek W. Urwin to present a more organised view of his centre-periphery cleavage research. This work starts with a dominant interest in the periphery or peripherality of regions in relation to the centre. He recognised three features that characterised the periphery in relation to one or more centres.

- First, the periphery was dependent on one or more centres and had not enough resources to overcome this dependency. The best examples of such peripheries are, of course, Galicia in Spain, Wales in the United Kingdom and the regions in southern Italy.
- Second, the periphery had a marginal culture without a proper identity. It may be fragmented and divided.
- Third, its economy was normally quite weak and extremely dependent on the centre. Here again the southern Italian regions, the German Eastern *Länder*, Spanish Andalucia or the Austrian Burgenland can be named as examples. The extreme case is when this periphery is dependent on the exchange of just one commodity. In any case, peripheral economies have always to pay more for any services offered within a territory owing to the distance from the centres. In short, Rokkan counts three features for the ideal type of periphery: distance, political and economic dependency, and difference.

(The above is the author's summary, taken from Rokkan and Urwin, 1983: 2–3.)

Rokkan became interested in the periphery owing to the fact that he himself came from the periphery in Norway (he was born in Vågan in the Lofoten on 7 July 1921, an island off the northern coast of Norway). This interest was reinforced by the fact that regionalism experienced a revival in the late 1960s and early 1970s. He spoke of the 'silent regionalist revolution'. In some ways he regarded this as a revolt of the regions with a stronger subnational identity than with the respective centralised national states. This revived consciousness could be witnessed in many West European countries, in particular in Italy after the introduction of regionalisation, in France, in the United Kingdom and, understandably, in the then authoritarian Spain.

This renaissance of regions could take different forms. For example: the revival of the regional language; the right to use the minority language in education; the establishment of mass media structures; in dealings with government agencies (as could be found in Austria among the Slovenes and Croats in Carinthia); and claims for self-determination (as presented by the Basque nationalists in Spain or the Scottish nationalists in the UK). This revivalism undermined the reified reality of the nation-state, which was very much taken for granted, and which itself was a social construction sustained by national socialisation systems and other ideological devices (for example, a nationalist civil religion) (Rokkan and Urwin, 1983: 118).

In particular, the revival of languages was an important factor in recreating regional peripheral identities. Since the Renaissance, nation-states across Europe had made huge efforts to impose a national language across a circumscribed territory and language is an important factor in fostering a national identity. Three reasons should be mentioned in this context:

1   It is the main element in defining a group. It clearly informs cultural practices. Extinction of language contributes to the extinction of a particular culture.
2   It was also interpreted as an expression of hegemony and 'progress' in the nineteenth century in contrast to tendencies towards tribalism and the fragmentation of territory.
3   It is and was the most efficient instrument of the state for creating a national identity. The sustainability of the nation-state depended on state policies geared towards reinforcing national identity. The socialisation into a national identity through language allowed for a fast mobilisation of citizens at specific moments.

(The above is the author's summary, taken from Schröder, 1993: 28–39; Hobsbawn, 2000: 54–63.)

Throughout the nineteenth and twentieth centuries the larger nation-states pursued language policies nationally and internationally to achieve even more influence. The era of imperialism led to the expansion of the languages of superpowers, for example English, French, German and Russian, across the globe. Smaller, less viable languages and cultures were simply absorbed into the dominant culture (Schröder, 1993: 45). In some cases, new nation-states tried to impose new national languages but without very much success. This was the case of Nynorsk in Norway, which was created for the purpose of overcoming differences across the territory. In spite of this attempt, the more popular Danicised Norwegian was a major impediment for its dissemination and today only about 20 per cent of Norwegians speak Nynorsk. Another attempt was the creation of the artificial Serbo-Croat language in former Yugoslavia. Serbo-Croat was soon replaced by the different languages of the new, independent countries during the 1990s. These examples show that artificial languages implemented at a late stage in the nation-building process may not have the desired success.

In this sense, it is possible to see the development of the centre-periphery cleavage in four main phases, with asymmetrical, synchronic development in different countries.

First phase (1780–1918): National elites created aspirations for national integration in respective countries. Some countries such as France and Spain had already created strong states that were engaged in constructing the nation. Germany and Italy created such nation-states only after the 1870s.

Second phase (1918–45): Nationalisation of the masses. This was a period where mass politics began to emerge in most European countries. Different countries developed different approaches to integration. Successful evolutionary integration could be witnessed in the northern countries, while in Germany, Italy, Portugal, Spain and most Central and Eastern European countries authoritarian and/or totalitarian regimes emerged as a consequence.

Third phase(1945–79): Social democratic consensus. There was a growing cooperation within a European integration framework, but the nation-state remained the main centre of decision-making. The introduction of welfare states further led to the nationalisation and centralisation of the nation-state. Periphery movements were perceived as negative and a threat for the unity of the state.

Fourth phase(1979–): Erosion of national sovereignty owing to globalisation. The difficulty of steering public policy in a globalised accelerated economy has led to the establishment of regimes of shared sovereignty. Simultaneously, the region has become a more flexible unit in the political economy. At the same time, the nation-state has become decentralised, giving greater autonomy to the region (e.g. France in 1983, the UK in 1997, Spain in 1978 and Belgium in 1993). There is also a growing process of de-nationalisation towards supranational and intergovernmental forms of integration, such as the case of the European Union (these four phases are influenced by Hobsbawn, 2000).

One of the findings of Rokkan was that Europe was characterised by two kinds of periphery, which define the incomplete process of nationalisation: the interface peripheries and the external peripheries.

Interface peripheries are located between two countries and can produce a culture that encompasses both languages and cultures. The best example is Alsace-Lorraine, which has been a field of conflict between Germany and France since the sixteenth century. Other examples are Wallonia and Flanders in Belgium and Schleswig-Holstein between Germany and Denmark.

The external peripheries had the opportunities to become national centres themselves owing to their economic prosperity and cultural awareness, but failed to achieve this. Examples are the Basque Country and Catalonia in Spain, Occitania in France, Scotland in the United Kingdom, and Bavaria in Germany. They remain today regions with a strong cultural awareness, but firmly embedded in national states. In some of them we can find strong political movements demanding independence; for example, the moderate Scottish National Party (SNP) in Scotland, the moderate National Basque Party (Partido Nacionalista Vasco, PNV) and the radical Communist Party of the Basque Country (Partido Comunista de las Tierras Bascas, EHAK), and the political arm of the terrorist organisation Basque Country and Freedom (Euskadi ta Askatasuma, ETA) in Spain. Demands for long-term independence have also been voiced by the Catalan Convergence and Union (Convergencia I Unio, CiU) and the Republican Catalan Left (Ezquerra Republicana de Catalunya, ERC) in Spain and the Flemish Interest (Vlaams Belang, VB) in Flanders. It is particularly in these interface and external peripheries that we can still find the strongest pockets of regionalist nationalism, and these continue to have a strong impact on the national politics of the respective countries.

This growing erosion of the nation-state from above and below (Christiansen and Jørgensen, 2000) is one of the features of the great transition of the late twentieth century that demands a reconsideration of the theories of Stein Rokkan. The European nation-states are no longer the main decision-making units and they are interdependently integrated with other European and non-European countries. As a contrast to the rigid structures of government of the nation-state, today there is emerging a more flexible multilevel governance system, which has eroded the boundaries between the public sphere (a monopoly of the state up to the mid 1970s) and the private sphere. Governance allows interaction between the two sectors and even strong cooperation. Many public services, such as national health services and education, are being contracted out to private providers with 'soft' monitoring by regulatory agencies. Governance is very much a product of the neo-liberal revolution introduced during Prime Minister Margaret Thatcher's period (1979–90). Governance is basically a reliance of government on public–private networks. There is also a general belief that these networks will self-organise themselves, closely following the liberal principle of the invisible hand (Rhodes, 1996: 659–65; Rhodes, 1997) (see Chapters 4 and 13 for EU multilevel governance and Chapter 7 for the emergence of the governance concept in public administration).

Reviewing the criticisms of Stein Rokkan's theory

According to Stein Kuhnle, Stein Rokkan's contribution remained restricted to certain aspects of the development of democratic politics. Kuhnle distinguishes between four main phases in the emergence of the modern democratic state:

- *the state-building process*, which took place during and since the fifteenth and sixteenth centuries (policies geared towards establishment of a tax-collecting bureaucracy, the establishment of an army; and protection of the country from a monopoly of violence by establishing a police force);
- *the nation-building process*, which took place in the period following the French revolution of 1789 (policies geared towards homogeneisation of the country);

- *the democratisation and participation process*, which took place between 1789 and 1945 (the emergence of mass democracy);
- *the redistribution process* that took place mainly after 1945 (welfare state).

According to Kuhnle, Rokkan concentrated most of his work on the third phase, relating to the emergence of mass democracy. He also worked on the nation-building process to a certain extent, but he neglected both the violent state-building process and the subsequent redistributive welfare state. This verdict of Kuhnle does not diminish the importance of Rokkan for contemporary European politics, but shows that his hypotheses were very much set around the third phase of the development of the modern democratic state. Rokkan's interest focused on the emergence of mass politics and how political parties were able to structure this new phenomenon (Kuhnle, 1981: 502; see also Ferrera, 2005).

For this reason Charles Tilly, one of the former most important scholars of the European state-building process, criticised Stein Rokkan, because Rokkan studied history from the present time back to the past. This is regarded by Tilly as a problematic approach, owing to the fact that it tends to simplify a much more complicated process, which is characterised by contingencies. According to Tilly, Rokkan's political development studies were embedded in the booming literature of the 1960s and 1970s that tended to ignore war in the whole process of state-building. In this sense, Rokkan's studies would discuss political developments through the lenses of the present, instead of being committed to serious historical research. His retrospective approach does not account for the 'powerful constraints in which all choices operate' and 'obscures the multiple, systematic, unanticipated consequences of the choices made' (Tilly, 1981: 123).

Although Rokkan collected large amounts of data and information, his reading of historical development was very much constrained by his training as a philosopher and social scientist. His hypotheses are very appealing and have some heuristic importance, but it is important to be aware of his limitations as a scholar.

Criticisms of the freezing hypothesis

In spite of this benevolent critique of Charles Tilly, the fiercest criticism came from political scientists. Stein Rokkan and Seymour Martin Lipset's 'freezing hypothesis' became the main target for criticism. One of the foremost reasons for the criticisms was that, shortly after the hypothesis was published, major changes began to occur in most West European party systems. The fragmentation of the Dutch and the Danish party systems, where there was a high level of volatility and therefore party system change, were probably the best examples of these changes. The fragmentation of the Danish party system in the 1970s led to the establishment of over ten parties. Among them were parties that were Euro-sceptic, anti-immigration and anti-taxation (for example, the Progress Party). They reacted against the Danish membership of the EC in 1973 and against the growing migrant population in the country. In the Netherlands, the main Catholic and Protestant parties experienced a decline in support, although in the end, after long negotiations, the Christian-Democratic Appeal (Christen-Democratisch Appél, CDA) was established in 1980 leading to a reversal of fortunes.

The criticisms and qualifications of the 'freezing hypothesis' can be categorised in at least five groups:

1   Aggregated volatility has increased since 1966, challenging the 'freezing hypothesis' (Mogens Pedersen, Stephen Wolinetz).
2   Emerging new parties (such as the green parties, extreme right-wing populist parties or Euro-sceptic parties) are challenging the established ones (Herbert Kitschelt).
3   New social movements, other forms of interest groups and political inter-mediation (e.g. extra-parliamentary opposition and NGOs) are challenging the once monopolistic relationship between parties and society.
4   The individualisation of society and the erosion of cleavages are leading to the emergence of a more flexible 'cartel party' ('light party'), which uses new marketing technologies to attract voters. In order to survive, parties are office-seeking (Richard Katz, Peter Mair).
5   The 'Americanisation' of European politics (e.g. two-party system, primaries, political marketing, light parties, importance of campaign funding) has increased considerably since the 1960s (Klaus von Beyme, Seymour Martin Lipset).

(1) *Increased volatility after 1966.* Among the critics, Mogens Pedersen pointed out that Rokkan's agenda of tracking down the development of mass parties and its emphasis on stability was now being replaced by a new agenda, which emerged in the 1970s and was concerned with the growing party system change in some countries in relation to others. He identified two groups of countries.

•   Group one countries were those that registered a low level of inter-block, intra-block and general volatility – meaning the transfer of votes from one ideological block to another and/or between parties of the same ideological family, for example Austria, Sweden and Switzerland.
•   Group two countries were those of high general volatility, for example France, Italy, Belgium, the Netherlands, the United Kingdom, Finland and Ireland. This growing volatility was evidence that the 'freezing hypothesis' should be questioned (Pedersen, 1979).

As a response, Peter Mair, one of the most prominent supporters of the 'freezing hypothesis' in the 1990s, drew attention to the fact that, in contrast with the inter-war period, the average general volatility of West European party systems was quite low. He presented a figure of 8.1 per cent for the post-1945 period, with inter-block volatility being even lower at around 2.1 per cent (Mair, 1993). Although Pedersen identified a very important trend towards volatility and party system change in most West European countries, Mair's argument was persuasive because, in spite of the erosion of cleavages, the traditional party families seemed to be able to adjust to the new conditions of the electoral market and electoral availability. Even today, many of the parties of the inter-war period are still dominant in most West European democracies. However, the case for Southern, Central and Eastern Europe is quite different: here new party systems have emerged and connections to the existing party systems of the inter-war period are tenuous or non-existent.

(2) *The emergence of new parties.* One major criticism presented by Kitschelt (Kitschelt, 1995; see also Ignazi, 1997) was that, in the 1980s and 1990s, new political parties emerged, which were able to capture a share of the electorate. The best examples are the Green parties, which emerged as social and political environmental movements against, for example, nuclear energy plants, the destruction of natural habitats and the deployment of nuclear warheads. Parts of the peace movement were also integrated in these very heterogeneous movements. In the early 1980s, such movements translated into parties in Germany, Austria, Belgium, the Netherlands and the Scandinavian countries. This was regarded as additional evidence that party systems were changing and cleavages were not frozen (Kitschelt, 1995; Ignazi, 1997). One important and influential international document was the report of the Club of Rome called *The Limits of Growth*. In this document, it was predicted that the main natural energy resources would come to an end within the next sixty years (Meadows, 1972). Today, scientists are more critical of this report, but at the time it had a major impact on the research community. The environmental movements and their translation into viable parties represented the rise of what has been labelled a post-materialist society, with distinctive values that contrasted with those of the industrial society. This new subculture was sceptical of the politics of exponential growth and advocated policies of sustainable growth in which the environment would be protected. Today green issues now form part of the global agenda (for example, the concerns of global climate change, the protection of endangered species and the growing importance of clean, environmentally friendly technologies). The main scholar who has drawn attention to the emergence of a post-materialist society is Ronald Inglehart. His studies are now globally acknowledged and have become part of the regularly held International Social Sciences Survey, which tries to assess the development of individual countries towards this post-materialist society (Inglehart, 1977; 1968; Inglehart and Welzel, 2005).

As well as the green parties, other parties emerged to challenge the established political parties. Among them were what Paul Taggart labelled as the 'new populist' parties, which address several aspects of new politics. New populism emerged in the 1980s in some of the most established democracies, including France, Germany, Belgium, the Netherlands, Germany, Austria and Denmark. Most of these new populist parties could be summed up as 'new right' political groups, because they addressed topics that the established centre-right parties would not dare to put at the top of the agenda (for example, the limits of immigration and issues of law and order. Although most of these parties were positioned on the right (for example the Pim Fortuyn List in the Netherlands and the Danish People's Party in Denmark), there were also examples of such parties on the left. Of these, the best example is the Scottish Socialist Party, which is able to challenge the New Labour Party by being more radical in its demands. Other parties may combine far-right ideology and new politics issues, for example the Front National in France and, until 2004, the Freedom Party in Austria. All these parties were able to achieve substantial electoral results over a fairly lengthy period of time, suggesting that they are signals of party-system change in most countries. Most recently, the Euro-sceptic parties in the United Kingdom (UK Independence Party), Scandinavia (Danish People's Party) and Central and Eastern Europe (Attack in Bulgaria, the Great Romania Party in Romania and the Slovak Nationalist Party in Slovakia) further add to this expression of new populism, which appeals to a wide section of the population (Taggart, 1998, 2000, 2004; Taggart and Sczerbiak, 2004).

(3) *The emergence of civil society organisations.* Another criticism is that in the last sixty years political parties have lost their monopoly in terms of representation of the interests of the population. The emergence of national civil societies, with thousands of interest groups, and non-governmental organisations created new forms of policy influence. The role of civil liberties organisations, environmental associations, consumer groups and think-tanks has made the interaction between parties and the population much more complex. The expansion of education allows citizens to be much better informed about all policy areas. New technologies, such as the internet and television, allow citizens access to a large amount of information and hence form a more balanced view. Moreover, the role of newspapers and investigative journalism increases the level of transparency and accountability, if we exclude the more sensationalist and less serious representatives of the profession. The participation in non-governmental organisations has been increasing since the 1970s. Moreover, non-governmental organisations are now better integrated in multilevel European networks and can cooperate with their counterparts in other countries as well as at the supranational level. Last, but not least, new movements, such as the anti-globalisation European Social Forum, are networked with the Global Social Forum, which emerged in the beginning of the twenty-first century (Della Porta, 2003). While these social movements were able to increase their participation in the last three decades, the membership of political parties has been declining (Katz and Mair, 1992; Mair and van Biezen, 2001).

(4) *The emergence of cartel parties.* A result of these changes was that political parties therefore had to change considerably in order to adapt to these new realities. According to Richard Katz and Peter Mair, a major transformation of political parties is taking place in all European countries. The catch-all party of the 1960s and 1970s is being replaced by the cartel party, which no longer represents an encapsulated 'frozen' subculture/constituency, but is interested in preserving its position of power in the political system. This twenty-first-century political party is electoralist in its nature and prioritises the winning of elections, in order that the majority of its party in office is re-elected. Owing to the fact that, on average, West European parties have lost 25 per cent of their members, the parties have become more dependent on state funding (Mair, 1997: 128–31; Katz and Mair, 2002: 126). Apart from the United Kingdom, the Netherlands and Switzerland, all other European countries introduced systems of public party funding (some more generous than others), which contribute to electoral expenditure according to the number of votes obtained, a subsidy to the parliamentary group over the legislature period, and funding for the central party. Such systems are fairly generous in Germany, Belgium, Portugal, Spain and Austria. The cartel party has become an electoral machine with a lightweight structure. The best examples of the 'party *lite*', which uses new technologies, has a smaller number of functionaries and a small membership, are: the Democrats of the Left (Democratici della Sinistra, DS) until 2007 in Italy; New Labour in the United Kingdom; and the Union for the People's Majority (Union pour la Majorité Populaire, UMP) in France. The late appearance of modern parties in the new democracies that emerged in the 1970s in Southern

Europe (Portugal, Spain and Greece) and in the 1990s in Central and Eastern Europe and the Baltic states prevented an early encapsulation of parts of the electorate, so that they became from the outset cartel parties, highly dependent on state funding and with access to the media, but with low levels of membership (van Biezen, 2003: 36, 40–1) (see also Chapter 6).

(5) *The 'Americanisation' of European politics.* Last, but not least, political parties are now acting in complex electoral markets that require knowledge of political marketing, permanent management of election changes, and optimal use of new technologies, new media and focus groups (Newman, 1999; Mair, Müller and Plasser, 2004). According to Manuel Castells, national politics in all European politics has become Americanised (Castells, 2000: 317–18). Such Americanisation of European politics is leading to the bipolarisation of party systems, similar to the American and British systems, in many countries (for example, Portugal, Spain, Italy, Greece, Austria, Germany and, naturally, France (von Beyme, 1996: 140)). This Americanisation also expresses itself in the transformation of former encapsulated ideologically and socially segmented cleavages, which were reproduced election after election, into a volatile, individualised electoral market. This means that people vote instrumentally for the party that is able to offer them the better deal. This electoral market behaviour of both the political parties and the electorate has also changed attitudes towards politics. One consequence of this de-ideologisation is that charismatic leaders are now dominating the political process. Electoral campaigns are devised around the party leader. According to Richard Katz and Peter Mair, 'The leaders become the party, the party becomes the leaders' (Katz and Mair, 2002: 126). The personalisation of politics has its extreme expression in the presidentialisation of the prime ministerial office in some countries (good examples are the United Kingdom, Germany, Spain and Italy) (Poguntke and Webb, 2005) (see Chapter 5 for presidentialisation of government).

European integration as a new development of political restructuring

Stein Rokkan was a Euro-sceptic scholar who was not convinced that European integration would substantially change the development of European politics. However, Stefano Bartolini tried to develop Rokkan's theory, taking into account the recent thrust of European integration since 1985.

Today we have to include a new phase related to the growing trans-nationalisation of national politics through the policies of the European Union. According to the excellent work of Stefano Bartolini, we may be in a process of reconfiguration of centre formation, system-building and political structuring between the nation-state and the European Union. This means that many Euro-sceptic parties are already sensing this transformation that Bartolini characterises as the sixth developmental trend in European history since the sixteenth century (see Figure 3.4). According to him we are experiencing a further restructuring of European politics, following

1   the processes of state building;
2   capitalist development since the sixteenth century;

3   nation-building since the nineteenth century;
4   democratisation; and
5   welfare state development since the twentieth century.

He analyses the sixth process, related to European integration, as follows:

> Integration, as a sixth powerful phase in the development of the European
> system of states, economies, nations, democracies, and welfares necessarily
> relates to each of the five preceding phases. This process of European
> integration was triggered by two main problem-pressures. On the one hand,
> it was driven by the unbearable costs of rivalries of the state systems in an
> era of war technologies whose destructive power had become dispropor-
> tionate to the stake of the rivalries themselves. On the other, it was driven
> by the growing pressure deriving from the slow but significant economic
> peripheralisation of Europe in the post-Second World War world economy
> and the corresponding perception of the inadequacy of the European state
> as a unit of economic organisation in world competition. European integra-
> tion can therefore be historically interpreted as a response by national elites
> to the weakening of the European state system and to the new pressures
> brought to bear by capitalist world development.
>
> (Bartolini, 2005: 366)

In sum, the contribution of Stein Rokkan for the theory of European politics is
invaluable and a good basis for research. Nevertheless, the transformations that
have taken place since the late 1960s have created a new reality that can only be
understood if we use Rokkan's ideas in a less rigid and doctrinal way, but flexibly
and as an inspiration to understanding present European politics. In the following
pages we will delineate some of the changes that lie behind the transformation of

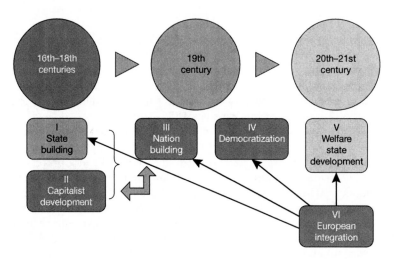

Figure 3.4 The six phases of development of European politics, according to Stefano
Bartolini
Source: Based on a figure by Bartolini, 2005: 366

European politics since the late 1960s. Although these changes have been identified as the most important ones, there is no claim for comprehensiveness. On the one hand, the reality is too complex to be reduced to an identification of some political, social, economic and cultural trends. On the other hand, there is always a need for mapping the main issues of research, in order to get some understanding of these highly interconnected processes.

The postmodernisation of European politics: the society of individuals and the impact of the new media

From the industrial to the post-industrial society

In the past four decades major changes have taken place in national societies in Europe. Among these changes are: the growth of the welfare states after 1945; the technical progress achieved in the last sixty years; different waves of immigration both within and from outside Europe; the decline of religion and religiously based cleavages; the end of class politics as we knew it until the late 1970s; the emergence of civil society; and the rise of subnational consciousness and identity in some European countries. There were two oil shocks in the 1970s. The first, in 1973, related to the Yom Kippur War of Israel with the Arab countries. The second, in 1979, was due to the Iranian revolution. Major strategic decisions made by transnational corporations led to further globalisation in the following years. States became more vulnerable to those globalisation processes and had to adjust accordingly. One of the main consequences was the privatisation of the huge state sector that existed in all European countries. As a response, after 1985 the European integration process gained new momentum through the policies of president Jacques Delors, who strived to protect European economies from globalisation effects by establishing a Single European Market (SEM). The general hope was that the SEM would contribute to the creation of new jobs, mainly through economies of scale, and enhance the competitiveness of Europe with regard to Japan and the United States (Cecchini *et al.*, 1988).

The European integration process played an important role in increasing the networks between national economies, societies and political systems. This process of transformation has strong similarities to what Karl Polanyi identified as the 'great transformation' from the nineteenth to the twentieth century that led to the industrialisation and modernisation of national societies. One of the consequences was the migration of the rural population to the larger cities and the emergence of an industrial working class (Polanyi, 1944). Modernisation can be characterised as a transition from simple agrarian societies to complex differentiated industrial societies (Wolfgang Zapf, quoted in Immerfall, 1995: 41). This process started in England, Belgium and Germany and later expanded to other countries. One of the consequences was the need to integrate the new citizens into the new political system through the extension of suffrage and creation of political parties, this including large parts of the electorate. In some cases, integration led to the emergence of totalitarian regimes (for example, Nazi Germany and Italy as well as in many other European countries) (see above and Chapter 1).

Since the 1970s another great transformation, similar to that of the nineteenth century, has been taking place. The great transformation of the late twentieth century is the transition from a modern class-based society to a postmodern knowledge-based one (see Table 3.1). Classes still exist, but they are less visible today, and are determined not only by profession but also by additional factors, such as marriage, number of children and education. One of the characteristics is the increase of the new middle classes who are employed in the services sector (Esping-Andersen, 1995). Moreover, since 1970 there has been a growing need for governments to control expenditure of welfare policies. The transformation of the welfare state into a workfare state, which links any benefits to employability, allows most of the funding to be shifted to socially excluded people (Jessop, 2002).

While modern society was characterised by a homogeneous national population, since 1945 waves of immigration from other European countries, and also from outside Europe, to the more advanced European economies, have made present postmodern societies more heterogeneous and multicultural. Demographic developments, in which the birth rate is too low to sustain population levels in most European countries, has increased the need for ordered immigration policies (Hohn, 1997), otherwise there would be an imbalance between the older generations (who, as a result of both medical progress and better living conditions, are living much longer), and the younger cohorts working in the labour market and supporting the pension system. Most European countries are reforming their pension systems, so that the solidarity linkage between older and newer cohorts is preserved. Such reforms entail the expansion of the working age, incentives for more savings, and adherence to supplementary private pension schemes. Budgetary policies need to be designed from a long-term perspective in order to preserve their sustainability in the future. The European integration process through Economic and Monetary Union puts constant pressure on national governments to take into account the demographic changes and their long-term effects on pensions (see Chapter 13, section on Economic and Monetary Policy). The necessary increased immigration, reinforcing the heterogeneous multicultural societies, creates more tensions if there are no integration policies to allow immigrants and their families to become part of the society. Such debates and tensions have been quite intense in many countries, for example in Germany, Austria, the Netherlands, Belgium, France and the United Kingdom.

Religion and religiosity declined considerably in the last three decades and modern class-based cleavages have been substantially eroded, being replaced by a society of individuals who act either politically, based on values, or instrumentally, according to the principle of the best deal.

According to Ronald Inglehart and Christian Welzel, most European countries are moving towards a post-materialist society. They conceptualise human development as a transition from modern societies integrated into collective structures (parties, factories, the Church) with materialist survival values of consumption to postmodern societies integrated into flexible tailored structures (e.g. non-governmental organisations) with post-materialist values emphasising human emancipation, gender equality and self-expression (Inglehart and Welzel, 2005: 262). The development is, not surprisingly, quite uneven across Europe. The most developed post-material societies are in Nordic Europe, the Netherlands and Germany, while Southern Europe (particularly Portugal and Greece) and the Central and Eastern European countries lag behind in this process (see Box 3.3 and Figure 3.5).

Table 3.1 The great transformation of the late twentieth century

	Dimensions	Industrial age (1945–79)	Information age (1980s–)
Politics	State	Government, welfare state	Governance, workfare state
	Parties	Catch-all parties and mass parties	Cartel party
	Participation	Monopoly of political parties through encapsulation of cleavages	Pluralisation of participation forms – conventional and unconventional
	Territorial structure	Tendency towards centralised, hierarchical structures	Tendency towards decentralisation and subnationalisation of politics
Economy	Economy	Economy centred around industrial sector	Economy centred around tertiary sector
	Structure of economy	• Fordism, • dominance of huge factories • synchronisation of space and time through assembly line	• post-Fordism • lean production • dominance of small enterprises, • decentralisation and relocation of production to labour-intensive countries
	Labour market objective	Full employment	Employability
	Interest intermediation	Interventionist social democratic neo-corporatism	Regulatory liberal neo-corporatism
Society	Nature of society	Homogeneous national society	Heterogeneous multicultural society
	Social structure	Class-based society Dominant working class	Knowledge-based society New middle classes dominant
	Social mobility	Increase of upward mobility through redistributive welfare policies	Increase of both upward and downward mobility owing to reduction of redistributive welfare policies
	Civil society	Emergence of civil society organised within collective official organisations	Increase in complexity of civil society, non-governmental organisations

Source: Author

> ## Box 3.3 Materialism vs post-materialism
>
> - According to Ronald Inglehart and Christian Welzel in their book *Modernization, Cultural Change and Democracy: The Human Development Sequence* (Cambridge: Cambridge University Press, 2005), a world development is taking place, moving from a materialist society, based on survival values, to a post-materialist society, based on self-expressive values.
> - The materialist society is usually linked to the process of industrialisation and industrial society, but not always.
> - The post-industrial society is usually linked to the information and services society, but not always.
> - Some European countries have a tendency towards post-materialist values, for example the Nordic countries, the Netherlands, Belgium, Luxembourg, Germany, Austria, Switzerland and the UK.
> - Some European countries still have a tendency towards materialist values, for example the Southern, Central and Eastern European countries.

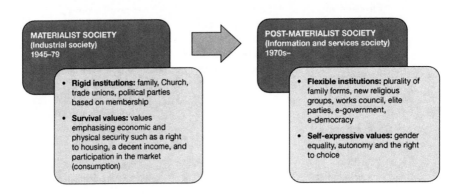

Figure 3.5 From materialist to post-materialist society in Europe

In spite of these cross-regional differences, the European integration process is a major factor in pushing all other parts of Europe towards the Nordic pattern. For example, until the 1970s Portugal and Greece were emigration countries. Most emigrants went to richer northern countries, such as Germany, Belgium, the Netherlands, the United Kingdom and France. After 1974, most of these richer countries began to have major economic problems. And after joining the EC/EU, Southern Europe became an immigration target for people from Africa, Asia and Eastern Europe. One of the main reasons that Southern Europe became an attractive destination for immigration is the fact that their border controls are less stringent and, also, that in the past three decades Southern European countries have become wealthier.

Although over three-quarters of Europeans support the institution of marriage, postmodern society saw the rise of a pluralisation of living styles that had an impact on politics. While in the modern industrial society, the nuclear family of two to three children was the dominant family form, today the number of single households has increased considerably. Moreover, there are more varieties of families, for example single-mother families, bi-nuclear families, two-career families, same-sex families and working parents. This naturally makes politics and policy-making more complex. Family and marriage can be expressed in different ways and politicians have to be aware of it. The social organisation of society has become more fragmented and more complex, not least because the number of divorces has increased considerably – in the United Kingdom as well as certain countries in Nordic Europe it has actually overtaken the number of marriages per year. These developments are uneven across Europe, with the Southern European countries and Ireland (owing to their Catholic traditions) lagging behind in this respect. Apart from cultural constraints, another main reason is the late economic development of these societies (Hopflinger, 1997; Immerfall, 1997: 143; Castells, 2000: 223; Mau and Verwiebe, 2009: 101–4).

All these transformations led to what Zygmunt Bauman calls the 'individualised society', meaning that former encapsulated social and political cleavages are being replaced by a looser, less rigid organisation of society, based on individual freedom, self-expression and choice (Bauman, 2001). This individualised society has major consequences for politics. Political parties can no longer count on the automatic support of political subcultures, but have to compete with other parties for each vote in a very volatile electoral market. As already mentioned, parties act in complex electoral markets in which focus groups, opinion polls, political marketing and use of the media become crucial for electoral success (Mair *et al.*, 2004: 3–9) (see also Chapters 10 and 11 for a fuller discussion on political parties, party systems and elections).

From a welfare to a workfare state

Another major change in many advanced European societies, which is being emulated by the periphery, is the gradual replacement of the welfare states, which existed until the 1970s, by workfare systems (Figure 3.6). The industrial society achieved a high level of stability, because generous welfare states were established that gave way to social peace between the employees' representatives, employers' representatives and the state. One of the main policies of the welfare state was to achieve full employment (meaning unemployment levels at less than 3 per cent of the working population). This meant that in many cases (e.g. in Austria during the Bruno Kreisky premiership in the 1970s) the state would subsidise public sector working places at a loss just to preserve a high level of employment. Most countries had large public sectors that provided employment to a large part of the population. Bob Jessop characterised this as the 'Keynesian welfare national state' (KWNS). He refers to John Maynard Keynes (1883–1946), an eminent British economist, who proposed expansive public works policies to achieve a relaunching of an internal market, which may be in recession. So the full employment demand in most West European countries of the 1970s was a major aspect of the KWNS.

Some of these policies were conducted in periods of expansion, so they then had a negative impact in periods of recession. One important aspect was the fact that KWNS was possible because the level of national autonomy was much higher than in the present post-industrial society. Furthermore, the 'mixed economy', in Germany called the *soziale Marktwirtschaft* (social market economy), was the predominant economic organisation. The state intervened regularly in the economy. This meant that the huge public sector in most West European countries played a role in steering the strategy of the national economy and 'compensating for market failures' (Jessop, 2002: 58–9). The KWNS was particularly expansive in the Scandinavian countries, Germany and Austria. Indeed, Gösta Esping-Andersen developed a typology of three welfare state models: (i) the social democratic Nordic model, which was the most generous one and was geared towards reducing inequalities in society; (ii) the conservative model prominent in Belgium, Austria and Germany, which was more geared towards stability of economic and social relations; and (iii) last, but not least, the liberal welfare state, which was minimalist in its provision (the best example of this being the American welfare system). In Europe the United Kingdom is probably the country that comes closest to this third type (Esping-Andersen, 1990). It is necessary to be cautious about generalisations, because some countries may be hybrid systems – in-between types. Probably Belgium could be more properly placed between the social democratic and the conservative model. The Swiss case is very much influenced by the conservative models of Austria and Germany, but its development is more akin to the liberal model (Armingeon, 2001a,b).

Most recently, Martin Rhodes and Maurizio Ferrera have added the 'Southern' model of the welfare state: it is narrower in scope than the other welfare states in terms of provision and is dominated by elements of clientelism and patronage. The Southern European type comprises Portugal, Spain, Greece and Italy. Furthermore, there is now discussion of the Central and Eastern European welfare state created after 1989. As a result of the recession at the beginning of the 1990s, the welfare provision that existed in the former socialist people's republics declined considerably after the transition from a planned to a liberal market economy, leading to an increase in poverty and unemployment. The new welfare systems in Central and Eastern Europe are too weak to provide adequate support for the population. Aspects of micro-corruption, clientelism and patronage may affect a fair redistribution of social benefits (Ferrera *et. al.*, 2000) (Box 3.4).

The KWNS model began to be replaced at the end of the 1970s by what Jessop calls the 'Schumpeterian workfare post-national regime' (SWPR). Joseph Schumpeter (1883–1950) was an Austro-American political economist who was based for most of his academic life at Harvard University. He developed economic theories based on the importance of innovation and competitiveness. Schumpeterianism emphasises the importance of innovation characteristics, particularly of the knowledge-based economy. SWPR emphasises aspects of employability and there is a clear dominance of economic priorities over the more efficient way of using social policy. The erosion of national autonomy and the adjustment of state structures towards globalisation processes is a further feature of this regime. Furthermore, the role of government is replaced by a self-organising and regulatory governance system to correct market and state failures (Jessop, 2002: 252–3). Governance emerged out of the growing retreat of the state throughout the 1980s and 1990s. It is a non-hierarchical, horizontal complex set of policy networks and is regarded as being differentiated from hierarchies, such as

---

Box 3.4 From three to five worlds of welfare

In 1990, political sociologist Gösta Esping-Andersen wrote his book *Three Worlds of Welfare* (Cambridge: Cambridge University Press) in which he presented a typology of three welfare states:

- the *liberal welfare state* – based on universalistic minimalist coverage funded through the national taxation system (UK, Switzerland, USA, New Zealand, Australia);
- the *social democratic–Nordic welfare state* – based on universal, extensive coverage funded through the national taxation system (Sweden, Norway, Denmark, Finland and Iceland);
- the *conservative–continental welfare state* – based on universal, extensive coverage funded originally through employers' and employees' contributions and increasingly through additional state funding (Germany, Austria, Belgium, Netherlands and France).

In 2000, political scientists Maurizio Ferrera, Anton Hemerijk and Martin Rhodes wrote a book, in Portuguese, entitled *The Future of Social Europe: Recasting Work and Welfare in the New Economy* (Oeiras: Celta), in which they added two more welfare state types to the typology:

- the *Southern European welfare state* with pretensions of universal coverage; however, in reality characterised by particularist–clientelist regimes mixed with a minimal, universal coverage; it combines elements of the liberal and the conservative–continental welfare states (Italy, Portugal, Spain and Greece);
- the *Central and Eastern European welfare state* with pretensions of universal coverage; however, in reality also characterised by micro-corruption and low benefits; depending on the country, a mix of liberal and continental welfare states is also the rule (Hungary, the Czech Republic, Slovakia, Poland, Slovenia, Bulgaria, Romania).

---

government and markets. The state has an overarching 'meta-governance' supervisory capacity to ensure that partial policy regimes of governance are working properly. This transformation from government to governance took place in the 1980s and 1990s, led by the Thatcher governments in the United Kingdom between 1979 and 1990 and the Reagan government in the United States between 1981 and 1992. The reduction of the state, the privatisation of many public services and the huge public sector led to the introduction of market principles in British public administration. Following this, similar public service reforms were introduced in most European countries (Rhodes, 1996, 1997) (see Chapter 7 for more on governance in public administration).

One of the main intentions of workfare states is to reduce the number of people dependent on social benefits. There is also a tendency to introduce market

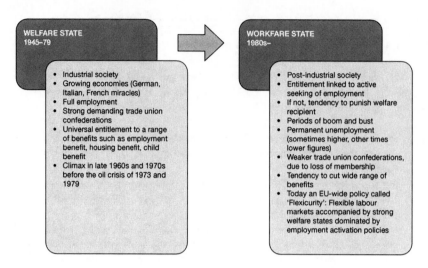

Figure 3.6 From welfare to workfare state

principles in the health and education sectors. Once again, the United Kingdom is at the forefront of such principles. The privatisation of certain services in the National Health Service (NHS) and the creation of business-sponsored city academies are two examples. The welfare state reforms in France, Germany and Sweden show that the British example is being largely emulated, but with each country taking into account its respective national characteristics. In Germany, the Hartz IV reforms in the welfare state helped to modernise the cumbersome state employment agency; nevertheless, the level of opposition has been considerable, particularly in the eastern *Länder* (Kemmerling and Bruttel, 2006). In the first half of 2006, the attempt by Dominique de Villepin to make the labour laws more flexible in order to increase the employment of younger people led to considerable social protest and had to be withdrawn after the intervention of President Jacques Chirac (*The Economist*, 12 April 2006). In the Netherlands, the Balkenende government tried to reform the incapacity benefits system, from which over one million people profited, however it met with considerable social protest from trade unions. Such reforms also took place in other European countries with varying degrees of success (Grünell and van het Kaar, 2003).

Social policy in the workfare state concentrates particularly on bringing people back to work and social exclusion is regarded as an issue that has to be addressed by a positive social policy. This means mainly policies to facilitate inclusion into the labour market.

Towards the post-industrial economy: the end of traditional class politics

Until the 1960s, social democratic and communist parties were able to mobilise large constituencies in the working class. It was the climax of the industrial Fordist age, in which the working class in the industrial sector was the dominant social group.

However, since the 1970s and 1980s such support of the working class for social democratic and communist countries has been declining (for an excellent account of the class cleavage, see Bartolini, 2000 and Kitschelt, 1995). The main reason is the transition from the modern industrial to the postmodern post-industrial society.

One of the main features of postmodern society is the steady decline both of the industrial sector as the largest in terms of Gross Domestic Product (GDP) and in the employment of the majority of the working population. The decline of the industrial and the agricultural sectors has been replaced by an increase in the services sector. The vast majority of the population is now employed in the services sector and this has major consequences for society. The services sector is quite dynamic and volatile. It allows for the emergence of what has been dubbed as the 'new middle classes', with high levels of educational attainment, working in knowledge-based sectors. It means that the traditional industrial society, in which the working class was the dominant group, is being replaced by a new class system based on knowledge-based skills. Education attainment becomes an important element in establishing such a new class system (Immerfall, 1995: 67–72; Haller, 1997: 391–402). Gösta Esping-Andersen labelled this as 'changing classes'. In this process there is an emergence of a new, unskilled underclass, at the bottom of the new class pyramid, which performs all possible jobs. At the top of the pyramid, there are knowledge producers, such as scientists and professionals. All the other groups fall between these two extremes (Esping-Andersen, 1995; Esping-Andersen *et al.*, 1995).

Such de-industrialisation is asymmetrical across Europe. The poorer Southern European countries of Portugal and Greece may be able to attract some of the jobs lost in the more advanced economies, nevertheless a growing challenge comes from cheap labour within the emerging economies (for example, China, India and other developing countries), giving Southern, Central and Eastern Europe only a mid-term advantage. Most of these industries have been reallocated to developing countries, which were able to produce labour-intensive products at a lower cost, with the result that the role of knowledge-based investment has become crucial for the survival of European countries. The investment in knowledge-based innovation has become a major issue for most members of the European Union, who want to create the most competitive knowledge-based economy of the world by 2010 (Tsoukalis, 2005: 232–3).

This target seems to be ambitious, because there are still considerable differences between the different parts of Europe. Competitive behaviour related to performance is one of the main features of post-industrial societies. Labour markets become more flexible but jobs become less secure and, instead of secure employment, employability and mobility are encouraged. The EU policies relating to the creation of the Single European Market are a major factor in reshaping the national economies and labour markets in European societies. A buzz word used in the European Union is 'flexicurity', meaning flexible labour markets supported by strong welfare states. The model was developed in Denmark and other Nordic countries. Certainly, it will be quite difficult to transfer the model to the less wealthy economies in Southern, Central and Eastern Europe (Table 3.2).

This means the traditional class cleavage – based on a more or less homogeneous working class, which worked in large factories over the same period of time and which was protected by strong social legislation and agreed wages through

Table 3.2 The industrial sector in selected European countries

Country	Period of industrial dominance	Climax share of employment in industrial sector	Year	Structure of employment 2006 *2005		
				Agriculture	Industry	Services
Austria	1951–66	42.8	1973	11.4	22.9	65.7
Belgium	1880–1965	49.1	1947	2*	20.6*	77.4*
Denmark	Never	37.8	1969–70	3	20.9	76.1
Finland	Never	36.1	1975	4.9	25.8	69.3
France	1954–59	39.5	1973	3.4	20.4	76.2
Germany	1907–75	48.5	1970	2.2	25.5	72.4
Greece	Never	30.2	1980	14.4	22.9	62.7
Iceland	Never	39	1963			
Ireland	Never	32.6	1974	5.8	27.6	66.6
Italy	1960–65	39.7	1971	4.1	28.4	67.5
Luxembourg	1947–69	46.9	1966	1.3	20.8	77.9
Netherlands	Never	41.1	1965	3.1	17	79.8
Norway	Never	37.5	1971			
Portugal	1982	37.5	1982	11.2	27.4	61.4
Spain	Never	38.4	1975	5	29.6	65.4
Sweden	1940–59	42.8	1965	2.1	22.3	75.7
Switzerland	1888–1970	48.8	1963–64			
UK	1821–1959	52.2	1911	1.7	21.6	76.7

Source: Immerfall, 1995: 69; European Commission, 2007: 286–315; for Portugal data from April 2010, Statistics Portugal, available online at: www.ine.pt/xportal/xmain?xpid=INE&xpgid=ine_publicacoes&PUBLICACOESpub_boui=89811894&PUBLICACOESmodo=2 (accessed 19 June 2010); for the UK, data from 2006 quoted from Mau und Verwiebe, 2009: 144

regular negotiations between employers' and employees' organisations – was eroded after the 1980s (Ebbinghaus and Visser, 1997; Traxler, 2004) (see Chapter 12 on neo-corporatism).

The emergence of new technologies, the rise of the new middle classes and the erosion of the traditional working class led to changes in the parties that relied on the political support of such constituencies. In the 1990s, parties such as the Italian Communist Party (Partito Comunista Italiano, PCI), the Austrian Social Democratic Party (Sozialdemokratisches Partei Österreichs, SPÖ), the Swedish Social Democratic Party (Sveriges Socialdemokratiska Arbetareparti, SAP), the Labour Party in the UK and the Labour Party in the Netherlands (Partij van der Arbeid, PvdA) had to move strategically to the centre and begin to appeal to the new middle classes. In some ways these parties became victims of their own success, particularly as a result of the redistribution policies introduced by generous welfare states. Probably, the most clear transformation was undertaken by the PCI that changed its name to Democratic Party of the Left (Partito Democratico della Sinistra, PDS) in 1991, became a social democratic party and later joined Socialist

International. Later it dropped the word party and became the Democrats of the Left within the Ulivo coalition (1996–98) and the Unione (2006–8), emulating American-style politics. In 2007, it merged with other parties and formed the Democratic Party (Partito Democratico, PD). A painful transition to centre politics was undertaken by the British Labour Party. Under the leadership of Tony Blair and Gordon Brown, the party became less bound to the working-class subculture and had a more socially heterogeneous base (Fielding, 1997; see also Franklin, 1985). New Labour learned a lot from the Conservatives under Margaret Thatcher who were able to stay in power from 1979 to 1997.

This 'bourgeoisification' of the working class forced many social democratic parties to move to the centre and abandon class-based, socially heterogeneous politics. Herbert Kitschelt speaks of a 'transformation of social democracy', resulting from the growing importance of the new middle classes, new politics and post-materialist values. As a consequence, social democratic parties had to develop socially heterogeneous politics in order to appeal to different constituencies simultaneously, which led to less ideological but more pragmatic party strategies (Kitschelt, 1995: 295–301). Indeed, the erosion of closed working-class subcultures with their organisations (trade unions, cultural centres, sports organisations, working men's clubs) contributed to a further 'liberalisation' of national electoral markets. Although principles related to the protection of welfare policies, equality of opportunity and support for public services continue to be crucial elements of social democratic policy, they are no longer related to a particular class. One could say that class voting continues to be relevant in many countries, but traditional class politics, based on encapsulated subcultures, is declining fast. Class voting has also become much more complicated owing to the differentiation of the services sector. There is considerable cultural heterogeneity between groups within the services sector; also the working class has lost its homogeneity and is no longer embedded in a synchronic spatio-temporal context.

According to the index developed by Robert Alford in the 1960s, which measures the level of support of manual workers for left-wing parties by subtracting the share of vote of non-manual workers from all voters to those parties, class voting has been declining (Alford, 1964: 73–86). Paul Nieuwbeerta and Nan Dirk De Graaf have identified three groups of countries in Western Europe in terms of their level of class-voting. In spite of the differences, the countries with the highest level of class voting since 1961 had also the steepest declines according to the Alford Index – in Britain from 38.3 per cent in the decade of 1961–70 to 23.4 per cent in the decade of 1981–90. For the same period in Denmark, the decline was from 52 to 20 per cent; in Finland, from 50.2 to 35.7 per cent; in Norway, from 32 to 20.5 per cent; and, in Sweden, from 40.7 to 32.7 per cent (Nieuwbeerta and De Graaf, 1999: 32). The process of erosion has been quite asymmetrical (Table 3.3 and Figure 3.7).

Class voting is still important in Germany. Traditionally, unionised workers tend to vote for the German Social Democratic Party (Klingemann, 1999: 124). In the 2005 general election, both main parties, in particular the SPD, had to deal with the electoral coalition between the Party of Democratic Socialism (Partei des Demokratischen Sozialismus, PDS), which emerged out of the dominant coalition in the former German Democratic Republic, and the Electoral Group for Work and Social Justice (Wahlgruppe für Arbeit und soziale Gerechtigkeit, WASG),

Table 3.3 A typology of class voting in Western Europe, 1945–90

Low level of class voting	Intermediate level of class voting	High level of class voting
France	Austria	United Kingdom
Greece	Belgium	Denmark
Ireland	Germany	Finland
Italy	Luxembourg	Norway
Netherlands	Sweden	
Portugal		
Spain		
Switzerland		

Source: Based on Nieuwbeerta and De Graaf, 1999: 31

led by Oskar Lafontaine. The party was able to gain substantial numbers of votes from the less advantaged classes, including the unemployed and pensioners (Bundeszentrale für Politische Bildung, 2005). Although the SPD moved towards the centre after the Bad Godesberg party conference of 1958, there was a further shift towards the centre under the leadership of Gerhard Schröder. Die *neue Mitte* (the new centre) was inspired by Tony Blair's introduction of the Third Way in the United Kingdom. The Third Way constitutes an Americanisation of social democratic politics, because it draws strongly on Bill Clinton's Democratic Party politics (Giddens, 1998).

In the Nordic countries, the strong social democratic parties attracted considerable working-class votes. According to Svallfors, welfare policies are still important for both large public and private sector employees (Svallfors, 1999: 206). Protection of the welfare state is certainly a source of support for the SAP. In Norway, both the social democratic party and the socialist left party had to adjust to the process of 'changing classes'. Both parties moved to the centre, appealing to the new middle classes. The socialist left party includes 'green politics' and 'new politics' issues in its programme in order to be able to compete in the electoral market (Ringdal and Hines, 1999: 200–2).

In Southern Europe, class politics was important in the 1970s, but later on all three main social democratic parties – the Spanish Socialist Workers' Party (Partido Socialista Obrero Español, PSOE), the Socialist Party in Portugal (Partido Socialista, PS) and the Panhellenic Socialist Movement (PASOK) had to adjust to the new middle classes and developed socially heterogeneous strategies. The impact of social class on voting declined considerably from the early 1980s to the early 1990s. The highest level for class voting could be found in Spain. The PSOE could rely on a long historical legacy going back to the nineteenth century. In this sense, their victory of 1982 also profited from some historical voting. Since 1979, the PSOE has already introduced a major modernisation of the party programme and removed references to Marxism. In Portugal, the blue-collar workers tended to vote for the Communist Party (Partido Comunista Português, PCP) and the white-collar workers for the Socialist Party (Partido Socialista, PS). While the PCP remained one of the last orthodox communist parties and had to rely on a stagnant ageing electorate, a considerable modernisation of the PS in the 1980s and 1990s made the party more

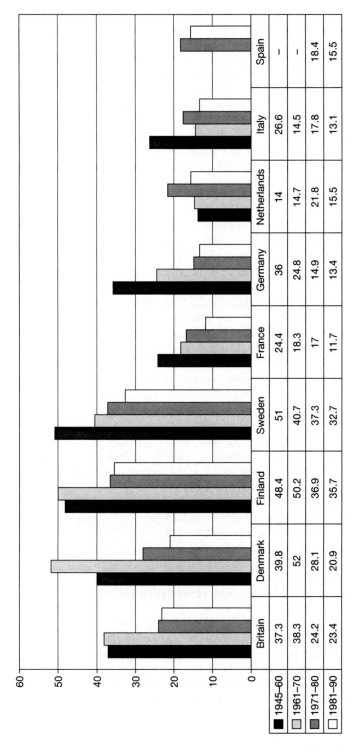

	Britain	Denmark	Finland	Sweden	France	Germany	Netherlands	Italy	Spain
1945–60	37.3	39.8	48.4	51	24.4	36	14	26.6	–
1961–70	38.3	52	50.2	40.7	18.3	24.8	14.7	14.5	–
1971–80	24.2	28.1	36.9	37.3	17	14.9	21.8	17.8	18.4
1981–90	23.4	20.9	35.7	32.7	11.7	13.4	15.5	13.1	15.5

Figure 3.7 Decline of class voting for selected European countries, 1945–90

Source: Author's own graph based on data from Nieuwbeerta, De Graf, 1999: 32

appealing to the new middle classes. It competes mainly with the liberal-modernising Social Democratic Party (Partido Socialdemocrata, PSD). In Greece, the populist nature of PASOK and the conservative ND showed that class is almost irrelevant in Greece (Gunther and Montero, 2001; Gunther, 2002: 44).

While in Western Europe traditional class voting is declining, in the new party systems of Central and Eastern Europe it seems to be increasing. A perceptive study on the Czech Republic brings to the fore that the introduction of a liberal market economy after the collapse of communism led to polarisation between pro-market liberal parties and left-wing parties. This did not become clear in the first election of 1992, in which the Civic Forum (ODS) fared well and the left – the Social Democrats (ČSSD) and the Communist Party – had quite bad results. However, the situation changed considerably in the 1996 elections, in which the ČSSD did well and was a match for the Civic Forum. Mateju *et al.* show that there is some polarised class voting going on between the classes, including the working class (which lost out in the transition to democracy) and the middle classes (Mateju *et al.*, 1999: 240–9). Although it is too early to draw any final conclusions, there is polarisation of the vote: in Hungary between the left-wing block Hungarian Socialist Party (MSZP)/Free Democrats (SzDSz) and the right-wing Hungarian Democratic Forum (MDF)/Federation of Young Democrats (FideSz-MPP); in Poland between the Democratic Left Alliance (SDL)/Union of Labour (UP) and the broad coalition of Law and Justice (PiS)/Samoobroona/League of Polish Families (LPR); and in Bulgaria between the Bulgarian Socialist Party (BSP) and Union of Democratic Forces (SDS)/National Movement of Simeon II (NDSV). Similarly, reformed communist parties such as the Social Democratic Party (PSD) in Romania and the Social Democratic Party (LSDP) in Lithuania have certainly profited from voting by disadvantaged classes in these countries (see also Dalton, 2002: 206–7).

In sum, traditional class voting and class politics, with which we were familiar until the 1960s, have waned, because of the erosion of collective identities around the working class and established middle classes. Instead, a new class structure has emerged that is fragmented and differentiated in terms of categories and not attached to large collective identities. Parties now have to devise socially heterogeneous catch-all strategies to appeal to different constituencies with different lifestyles. This means that the way in which people vote depends on short-term factors and the offers presented by parties in the competitive electoral market. A similar trend has eroded religious collective identities, as the following pages show.

The decline of religious cleavages and religiosity

One of the consequences of the transition from a materialist to post-materialist society is the fact that it leads to reinforced secularisation, meaning there is a decline in participation in traditional religious rites and growing emancipation of the population from the tutelage of Church organisations (see Box 3.5 and Figure 3.8). The religiosity index shows that the northern parts of Europe are more secularised than the south. Moreover, Greek Orthodox and Catholic countries as well as countries with large Muslim populations are more religious than Protestant Christian countries (see Figure 3.9).

Box 3.5 The secularisation of society

The word 'secular' is concerned with the affairs of this world. 'Secularise' means to transfer something from a religious to a non-religious use, or from control by a religious body to control by the state or a lay body. It may also mean the removal of the religious dimension or religious element from something.

Secularisation characterises a societal process, in which the role of religion is replaced by the principles of the 'non-denominational' state. This means particularly the laicisation of civil life and the reduction of the influence of the Church in society. Central to this secularisation is the emergence of the modern state, based on the principle of strict separation of state and Church. Such a process was undertaken by all European countries in the nineteenth and first half of the twentieth centuries.

Probably, the most advanced secularisation processes can be observed in Nordic Europe, Germany, the Netherlands, Britain and France. Less advanced secularisation can be found in the Catholic countries of Southern Europe and Ireland.

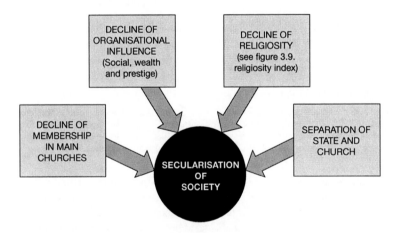

Figure 3.8 The secularisation of society
Source: Adapted, simplified and amended from Giddens, 2000: 486–7

Among the different trends towards secularisation are the decline of church attendance among religious groups and the decline in the belief in God and life after death. The trend has been downwards across Europe, in some regions steeper than others. While secularisation progressed considerably in the Nordic countries and Central and Eastern Europe, apart from Poland, Southern Europe lags behind in this trend. Nevertheless, even in Southern Europe we can recognise a stronger trend of secularisation in Spain while there is greater resistance to it in Italy, Portugal and Greece. Religious voting has been strongest in areas where relations

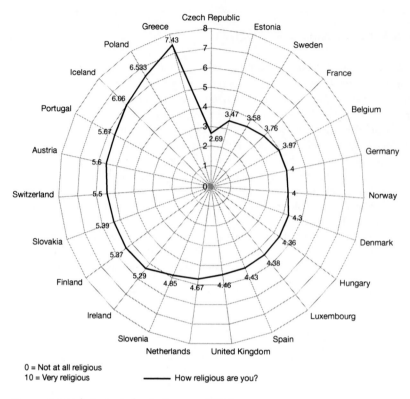

Figure 3.9 Religiosity index in Europe, 2004

Source: *European Social Survey round 2.* R. Jowell and the Central Co-ordinating Team, European Social Survey (2004/2005), *Technical Report,* London: Centre for Comparative Social Surveys, City University (2005) at Norwegian Social Science Data Services (NSD). Available online at: http://ess.nsd.uib.no (accessed 23 January 2009). Author's own interpretation and tabulation

between the Church and the liberal state were tense. This was quite marked before the First World War and during the inter-war period. After the Second World War most Christian democratic parties became catch-all parties in order to counteract the declining subcultural religious voting. Nevertheless, not all countries have the same religious make-up. It is sensible to differentiate between homogeneous Catholic countries (Portugal, Spain, Italy), homogeneous Protestant countries (Sweden, Denmark, Norway), homogeneous Christian Orthodox countries (Greece) and confessionally mixed countries (the Netherlands, Germany and Switzerland). In the Balkans one can find some confessionally mixed countries, for example Bosnia-Herzegovina, which consists of three ethnic minorities: the Bosniak-Muslims, the Catholic Croats and the Greek Orthodox Serbs.

The cleavage based on religion emphasised particularly policy tensions between the Church and the state. Strong subcultural cleavages that translated into electoral voting could be found in countries with strong Catholic minorities, such as the Netherlands and Germany. In the Netherlands, a Catholic subculture persisted in the southern region of South Holland and Limburg. This was the core of the Catholic vote that voted for the traditional Roman Catholic State Party

(Romaan Katholieke Staatspartij, RKSP) founded in 1926 during the inter-war period. After the Second World War, it renamed itself as the Catholic People's Party (Katholieke Volkspartij, KVP). Apart from the Dutch-reformed Protestant confession, other splinter confessions emerged at the end of the nineteenth century. One such was the Anti-Revolutionary Party (ARP), founded in 1889 by Abraham Kuyper and supported by the monarchy under the Orange dynasty against the emerging idea of popular sovereignty introduced by the French Revolution. It was a movement of the lower middle classes (*kleine luyden*) against the growing importance of liberal parties. In 1908, the Christian Historical Union (CHU) split from the ARP and created a more moderate alternative. Splinters remained a regular feature of Christian-inspired parties until the 1970s, however the religious vote became less and less sustainable after 1970. Indeed, the share of the confessional parties declined from over 55 per cent in 1952 to less than 30 per cent in 1998. Therefore, after long negotiations, KVP, ARP and CHU decided to merge and form the catch-all Christian Democratic Appeal (Christen Democratisch Appel, CDA) in 1980. Catholicism has still 28 per cent of adherents, while the share of the Dutch Reformed (11 per cent) and the Calvinists (7 per cent) have been eroding much faster. What is also interesting is the large number – 43 per cent – who declared that they did not adhere to any religious confession. This contrasts heavily with 14.4 per cent in 1930 and 23.6 per cent in 1971. There is a strong de-confessionalisation taking place, meaning that the link between politics and religious belief is becoming more tenuous with time. The religious factor only plays a role among practitioners – about 3–4 per cent in each confession (van Holsteyn and Irwin, 2000: 82–5).

Following the constitution of the German Empire after 1870, the Catholic Centre Party (Katholische Zentrumspartei, KZP) was established to counteract the policies of Chancellor Bismarck against the Catholic Church. It was a resistance party to protect the interests of the Catholic Church and its adherents. The party continued throughout the Weimar Republic. After the Second World War, the Christian Democratic Union–Christian Social Union (Christliche Demokratische Union–Christliche Sozialunion/CDU-CSU) was established as an inter-confessional party of Protestants and Catholics. (The CSU was the sister Bavarian party, which was mainly Catholic.) Although the religious vote eroded substantially in Germany, in comparison with other countries, the CDU/CSU is still able to attract a large part of the religiously motivated vote when issues such as abortion and teaching of religion in public schools emerge (for example, the organisation of a referendum concerning the reintroduction of religion as a subject in school curricula in Berlin in 2009). Indeed, the Catholic religious vote seems to be more resilient than the Protestant vote. Catholics support the CDU/CSU more strongly, while Protestants tend towards the SPD. After *die Wende* and unification of both parts of the country, the GDR government had been successful in eroding the importance of religion in society. In the 1990s, both the Protestant and Catholic Churches had to deal with a considerable decline in membership. Adherents have to pay a Church tax that is delivered by the state to the different confessions and many people have left the Churches in order to avoid such payments (Roberts, 1999: 65–9) (Figure 3.10).

In Switzerland, as in Germany, Catholic cantons resisted becoming a part of federal Switzerland until 1848. Nevertheless, following 1848, the Catholic conservatives and the Protestant liberals created the foundations of a constitutional settlement. Despite this compromise, the eleven Catholic cantons continued to live

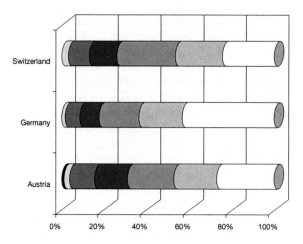

	Austria	Germany	Switzerland
■ Everyday	1.1	0.2	0.3
☐ More than once a week	2.5	1.3	2.7
▨ Once a week	11.7	7.2	9.9
■ At least once a month	15.8	9.1	13.3
▨ Only on special holidays	21.9	18.6	27.3
☐ Less often	19.5	19.8	21.5
☐ Never	27.4	43.7	25

Figure 3.10 Attendance at church in Drei-Sat Europe, 2004

Source: *European Social Survey round 2*. R. Jowell and the Central Co-ordinating Team, European Social Survey (2004/2005), *Technical Report*, London: Centre for Comparative Social Surveys, City University (2005) at Norwegian Social Science Data Services (NSD). Available online at http://ess.nsd.uib.no (accessed on 23 January 2009). Author's own interpretation and tabulation

apart from the mainstream. The *Kulturkampf* taking place in Germany spilled over to Switzerland, leading to a revision of the constitution in 1873–74 with the main aim to remove articles that discriminated against the Catholic population (40 per cent). Thereafter, the Catholic Conservatives changed their name to Christian Democratic People's Party (CVP). The plurality electoral system was a major obstacle for strong representation of the CVP. This was to change after 1918, when a proportional electoral system was introduced, which allowed for the representation of the CVP at government level. The strong continuity of political parties in Switzerland has led to a formula for proportional representation for all parties in the Federal Government (Bundesrat). The CVP was entitled to two out of the seven seats. Nevertheless, in recent years the share of the vote of the CVP has been declining, leading to the loss of one of the two seats traditionally allocated to the party in the Federal Council (Federal Government) to the highly populist Swiss People's Party (SVP). After the legislative elections of 2007, the election of Christoph Blocher, the leader of the SVP, was blocked by the main political parties and therefore the SVP withdrew its representatives from the Federal Council, creating a precedent in a consensus democracy. However, in December 2008, a more moderate representative of the SVP replaced one of the rebels (who had to resign owing to a political scandal), so that the SVP is again part of the Federal Government.

The religious vote, which, according to the multicultural model, has always been moderate, became institutionalised during the first half of the twentieth century, and has been losing its significance since the elections of 1999. The level of volatility has increased considerably, allowing for the populist SVP to gain votes from the CVP. Linder speaks of a neutralisation of the cultural–confessional vote (Linder, 2005: 89–90).

In Italy, Belgium, Austria and Luxembourg, four Catholic homogeneous countries, the religious vote was extremely politicised throughout the nineteenth and twentieth centuries. In Italy, the late establishment of the Italian nation-state led to the annexation of middle Italy, which belonged to the Vatican. The Catholic Church remained restricted to the Vatican state. This led to a policy of intransigency and opposition to the Italian state. In 1868, Catholics were urged to boycott elections in new Italy. This policy was made official in 1874 by Pius IX. It meant that Catholics could not be elected and could not take part in elections (*né eletti, né elettori*). The policy was withdrawn in 1904–5 by Pius X. And finally, in 1919, Benedict XV allowed Don Luigi Sturzo to found the Italian People's Party (Partito Popolare Italiano, PPI). The party was an instant success because it could rely on the large infrastructure of the Church. Fascism led to the end of the PPI in 1922, but many members of the party were to take part in the foundation of Christian democracy (Democrazia Cristiana, DC) in 1943. Christian democracy was able to create a right-centre subcultural cleavage that translated into political voting in elections. DC defined itself in relation to the strong Italian Communist Party (Partito Comunista Italiano, PCI). The decline of religious voting for DC began to happen after 1976. Throughout the 1980s the electoral share declined considerably. Finally, after the elections of 1992, the DC collapsed owing to the Tangentopoli affair ('Kickback city scandal'). Between 1948 and 1992, DC built a network of systemic corruption in order to remain in power and prevent the second largest party coming to power (Guzzini, 1994; Rhodes, 1997). Forza Italia and other small Italian parties (for example, Margherita until 2007) were still catching some of this religious vote. One of the reasons for the decline of DC was the speedy secularisation of Italian society since the 1970s. Indeed, the number of people attending church declined from 69 per cent in 1956 to 30 per cent in the 1970s. The role of the papacy, which is based in the Vatican city, may be one of the main reasons for the high level of church attendance. In spite of the collapse of Christian democracy, religious voting continues to be salient, but now it is tenuous and distributed among several Christian democratic parties, including the former Forza Italia (National Alliance), and now the Party of Freedom (Donovan, 1999: 147).

In Belgium, the dominance until 1965 of the Christian Democratic People's Party/ Christian Social Party (CVP/CSP), which had constituted a subculture against the liberal and socialist parties, began to wane. The process of secularisation, the growing tensions between the Flemish and the Walloons led to the erosion of parties that were dependent on the religious vote. Traditionally, Christian democrats were stronger in Flanders than in Wallonia. The creation of two new regional party systems following the adoption of the new federal constitution in 1993 led further to a decline in voting for both Christian democratic parties and the rise of the liberal parties. Most recently, both parties have changed their names in order to adjust to a more catch-all-based strategy. In Flanders, the Christian Democratic and Flemish Party (Christen-Democratisch & Vlaams, CD&V) now places greater emphasis on ethnic identity in order to compete better within the Flemish regional party system. In Wallonia, the Democratic Humanist Centre (Centre Democrat Humaniste, CDH) dropped the 'Christian' label, so that it is able to attract votes from all religious groups, including those of Islamic faith. The share of both parties together declined from 41.46 per cent in 1961 to 18.3 per cent in 2003. One of the main reasons for this is that, according to the European Social Survey, only 40 per cent of the population declares itself as belonging to a religion, even if 90 per cent declare themselves as being Catholic (see Figure 3.11, Table 3.4).

In Austria, the Austrian People's Party (Österreichisches Volkspartei, ÖVP) is presently one of the strongest parties in Austria. Although the historical legacy of the ÖVP is Christian democracy, the party was able to move towards a right-centre position and become a strong catch-all party. Moreover, religion is still important in Austrian society. The number of people who declare themselves as belonging to a religion is 71 per cent. According to Albert F. Reiterer, the number of atheists was 96,000 (12 per cent) in 2001. This means that, in spite of secularisation, the level of subjective religiosity is still high in comparison to, say, Belgium or the Scandinavian countries. Nevertheless, the erosion of practising Catholics

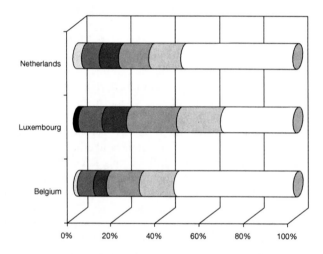

	Belgium	Luxembourg	Netherlands
■ Everyday	0.4	0.1	0.3
□ More than once a week	1.6	2.1	4.1
▨ Once a week	7.4	11.5	8.8
■ At least once a month	6.4	11	8.6
▨ Only on special holidays	14.8	22.8	13.4
▨ Less often	15.5	19.9	14.1
□ Never	54	32.6	50.7

Figure 3.11 Attendance at church in Belgium, the Netherlands and Luxembourg, 2004
Source: *European Social Survey round 2*. R. Jowell and the Central Co-ordinating Team, European Social Survey (2004/2005), *Technical Report*, London: Centre for Comparative Social Surveys, City University (2005) at Norwegian Social Science Data Services (NSD). Available online at http://ess.nsd.uib.no (accessed on 23 January 2009). Author's own interpretation and tabulation

Table 3.4 Religious denomination according to European social survey, 2004

	Roman Catholic	Protestant	Eastern Ortho-dox	Other Christian denom-inations	Jewish	Islam	Eastern religions	Other non-Christian religions
Drei-Sat Europe								
Austria	89.1	4.7	1	1.8	0.1	1.8	1.1	0.4
Germany	43	47.5	1.4	2.9	0	4.1	0.6	0.4
Switzerland	46.8	46.4	1.5	1.7	0.2	2.1	1.4	0.1
BENELUX								
Belgium	87.9	1.4	0.4	1.1	0	7.2	1.1	0.9
Netherlands	50.4	37.8	0.3	6.9	0.0	2.5	0.5	2.2
Luxembourg	72.6	1.1	0.5	21.9	0.4	2.1	0.5	0.9
Nordic Europe								
Denmark	1.8	93.5	0.1	1.5	0.1	2	0.2	0.8
Iceland	0	91.1	0	8.2	0	0	0.4	0.4
Norway	1.9	86.8	0.8	0.5	0	0.1	0	0
Sweden	3.1	87.1	1.5	4	0.2	2.4	0.8	1
British Isles								
United Kingdom	21.5	49.9	0.6	20.3	0.5	5	1.8	0.4
Ireland	95.8	3.4	0	0.6	0	0	0.1	0.1
Southern Europe								
Portugal	96.6	0.5	0	2.4	0.2	0.1	0.1	0.2
Spain	94.3	0.7	0.7	1.5	0	2.1	0.3	0.5
Greece	1.2	0.4	96.5	0.1	0	1.6	0.1	0.1
Central and Eastern Europe								
Czech Republic	87.4	9.6	0.8	1.1	0	0	0	1.2
Poland	98.4	0.3	0.8	0.5	0	0.1	0	0
Estonia	2.7	38.3	51	6.5	0	0.7	0	0.9
Slovenia	93.6	2.6	2.1	0.3	0	1.3	0	0.1
Slovakia	79.4	9.1	1.6	8.3	0.3	0.2	0.2	1

Source: European Social Survey (2004), religious denomination

and Protestants is a continuing process (Reiterer, 2003: 124–5). The same applies to Luxembourg, where the Christian People's Party (Chrestlich Social Vollekspartei, CSV) dominates the party system.

In contrast to these Catholic homogeneous and confessionally mixed countries, secularisation in the Protestant homogeneous countries of Nordic Europe has advanced most quickly. After the Reformation, national churches, which were united with the state, were established in these countries. This is the main reason why the religious cleavage has almost no salience in the Nordic countries. Most Christian democrat parties emerged much later and as a reaction to the secularisation of life. The Christian Democrats in Denmark and the Christian Union in Finland are small parties, but the Christian Democratic People's Party in Norway and the Christian Democrats in Sweden are now larger parties and are able to play a role in possible coalition arrangements. The Christian Democrats in Norway have been able to lead a coalition under Kjell Magne Bondevik between 1998 and 2005, with an interruption in 2000–1. The religious voting seems to be concentrated in certain peripheral regions of the countries and directed against the centre. In Norway, it is this 'Bible Belt' concentrated in the south and west, in Finland the rural parts of the south, in Sweden most of the votes are located in Jonköping in the south, while in Denmark they are concentrated in northern Jutland (Madeley, 2000: 34–8) (see Figure 3.12).

In both the United Kingdom and France religious voting is quite tenuous, but still exists. Neither the United Kingdom nor France have Christian democratic parties, but religious voting may go to the main parties in the political system. In

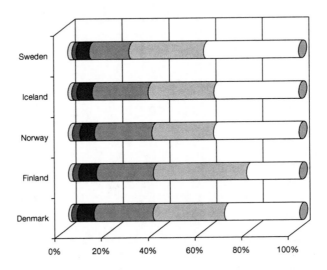

	Denmark	Finland	Norway	Iceland	Sweden
■ Everyday	0.3	0	0.1	0.2	0.1
☐ More than once a week	0.9	1.8	1.6	1.4	1.5
■ Once a week	2	3	3.5	2.5	2.3
■ At least once a month	8.2	7.7	6.6	7.2	5.8
■ Only on special holidays	25.4	24.6	24.6	23.7	16.9
☐ Less often	30.7	39.6	26.5	28.1	32
☐ Never	32.6	23.2	37.1	36.9	41.4

Figure 3.12 Church attendance in Nordic Europe, 2004

Source: *European Social Survey round 2.* R. Jowell and the Central Co-ordinating Team, *European Social Survey (2004/2005), Technical Report,* London: Centre for Comparative Social Surveys, City University (2005) at Norwegian Social Science Data Services (NSD). Available online at http://ess.nsd.uib.no (accessed on 23 January 2009). Author's own interpretation and tabulation

France, it is normally the right-centre parties that attract religiously motivated votes from practising Catholics. The non-practising Catholics may tend towards the left-wing parties, in particular the Socialist Party. The National Front (Front National, FN) is not able to attract the vote of the practising Catholics and most of its votes come from non-religious people.

Similarly, the electoral system leads to a split of the religious vote between the two main parties in Britain. Catholics tend to vote for the Labour Party, while practising Protestants are strong supporters of the Conservative Party. The religious vote is stronger and more salient in Scotland. Secularisation has progressed considerably in both countries, which are closer to the Scandinavian pattern (Roberts, 1999: 68–9; Bréchon, 2000). The conflict in Northern Ireland has perpetuated the cleavage between Catholics, who tend to support nationalism by voting either Sinn Fein or the Social Democratic Liberal Party, and Protestants, who support the Union with the rest of the United Kingdom by voting for the Ulster Unionists and the Unionist Democratic Party. The difficulties in creating a final settlement continued to allow this cleavage to exist. It is expected that the agreed final settlement negotiated in 2007 will lead to a waning of such divisions and create more common ground between the two communities.

Religion plays a major role in the Republic of Ireland, although, in terms of party politics, the main cleavage seems to be related to the struggle for independence. According to Daniele Caramani, the two main parties, Fianna Fail (Soldiers of Destiny) and Fine Gael (Tribe of the Gael) emerged as a response to the treaty signed between Britain and the Irish Free State in 1921. Fianna Fail was against the treaty and Fine Gael was for it. Most supporters of Fianna Fail were in the more agricultural parts of the west of Ireland, while Fine Gael could count on the support of the more urbanised regions of the east. Religion has remained part of the overall identity of the Irish Free State and is not used for party political cleavages. Nevertheless, in such important issues as abortion, same-sex marriages and homosexuality, the Irish Catholic Church has been influential. Along with Portugal, Ireland has still one of the most restricted abortion laws. Fianna Fail tends to profit more from confessionalism paired with nationalism than Fine Gael (Farrell, 1999: 30–6; Caramani, 2004: 260–1) (see Figure 3.13).

In the new democracies of Southern, Central and Eastern Europe the new party systems lack the historical continuity of cleavage-building that is common in the more established democracies. Nevertheless, it seems that the earlier transition to democracy in Southern Europe led to stronger cleavage-building than in Central and Eastern Europe. The strongest example of religious voting is in Portugal, where the small Christian democratic party, Democratic Social Centre (Centro Democratico e Social, CDS), which between 1992 and 2005 turned Euro-sceptic, can rely on a religious voting from the small farmers of the north and the more conservative lower middle classes. The only problem is that the share of small farmers is eroding, as a result of the high level of economic and social development. The party has almost disappeared at local level, but still achieves 8 per cent of the vote nationally. Such a cleavage emerged as a response to the radical left-wing revolutionary transition of 1974–75, when the small farmers felt threatened by the radicalised military and were afraid of losing their small plots of land (Jalali, 2002: 90). In Greece, the Orthodox Church is an important part of the national identity. Its national character neutralises the use of religion for political encapsulation of

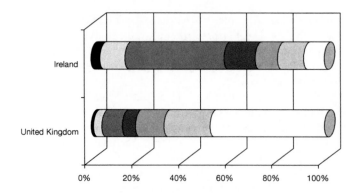

	United Kingdom	Ireland
■ Everyday	1	4.8
☐ More than once a week	3.2	10.7
■ Once a week	9.8	12.7
■ At least once a month	6.3	13.4
▨ Only on special holidays	12.3	9.8
▨ Less often	19.3	10.5
☐ Never	48.2	8.2

Figure 3.13 Church attendance in the United Kingdom and Republic of Ireland, 2004
Source: *European Social Survey round 2*. R. Jowell and the Central Co-ordinating Team, European Social Survey (2004/2005), *Technical Report*, London: Centre for Comparative Social Surveys, City University (2005) at Norwegian Social Science Data Services (NSD). Available online at http://ess.nsd.uib.no (accessed on 23 January 2009). Author's own interpretation and tabulation

the electorate. Greece has one of the highest subjective religiosity values and the Church is among the best-valued institutions. Therefore, religious voting is tenuous, although it tends to go to the conservative New Democracy.

In contrast, secularisation has advanced considerably in Spain, with the process taking place over the last two decades. Democratisation has contributed to the erosion of any religiously motivated voting. According to José Ramon Montero and Kerman Calvo, religious voting is no longer very important in determining electoral behaviour. The hard-core traditional Catholics may vote for the People's Party (PP), but the moderate Catholics may switch between the PP and the Socialist Party (PSOE) (Montero and Calvo, 2005; Montero and Calvo, 2000: 133–4) (see Figure 3.14).

Many of the Central and Eastern European party systems are still unstable and characterised by high levels of volatility. Parties tend to use the media to reach their voters and neglect party organisation, meaning that they are, in effect, catch-all parties. Nevertheless, some tenuous religious voting exists in some countries to varying degrees. In some cases, for example Hungary, the Czech Republic, Slovakia and Slovenia, Christian democratic parties have emerged and been able to gather some support. Whereas in the more fragmented party systems of Slovakia and Slovenia, different Christian democratic parties emerged competing for the religious vote. Religion plays a major role in Poland (one of the most religious countries of

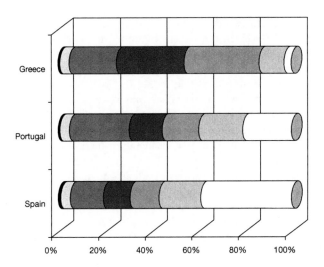

	Spain	Portugal	Greece
■ Everyday	1.6	0.8	0.7
☐ More than once a week	3.4	3.7	3.9
▨ Once a week	14	25.4	19.9
■ At least once a month	11.7	14.1	28.8
▨ Only on special holidays	12.2	15.4	32.2
▨ Less often	17.6	18.3	10.9
☐ Never	39.5	22.2	3.5

Figure 3.14 Church attendance in Southern Europe, 2004

Source: *European Social Survey round 2*. R. Jowell and the Central Co-ordinating Team, European Social Survey (2004/2005), *Technical Report*, London: Centre for Comparative Social Surveys, City University (2005) at Norwegian Social Science Data Services (NSD). Available online at http://ess.nsd.uib.no (accessed on 23 January 2009). Author's own interpretation and tabulation

the world along with the United States), particularly with regard to issues such as abortion. The 2005-elected conservative coalition government consisted of three parties – the Law and Justice (PiS), Self-Defense (Samobroona) and League of Polish Families (LPR) – that all relied very much on conservative religious voting against the reformed communists of the Social Democratic League. In particular, LPR is an extremely conservative, Euro-sceptic party that relies on such votes. In Hungary, a bipolar coalition system has emerged that also polarises the religious vote towards the right-centre parties, opposing the left-centre ones. The Hungarian Democratic Forum (MDF), the Free Democrats (SZDSZ), the Farmers' Party (FKGP) and the Christian Democratic People's Party (KDNP) are all able to attract such religious voting. It is particularly in the last that the religious vote tends to concentrate. Although the KDNP was able to achieve 6.1 per cent in 1990 and 7.2 per cent in 1994, it declined to 2.8 per cent, with no seats, in 1998; and was also not able to achieve a seat in the elections of 2002. Other parties, particularly the Free Democrats have been the main winners of defections from the KDNP. Once again, religious voting is associated with opposition to the former communist regime and particularly the reformed communists of the Social Democratic Party (MZSP) (Eniyedi, 2000: 157–61). In the Czech Republic, the Christian democratic party, People's Party of Czechoslovakia (KDU–CSL), founded in 1918, still plays a major role in coalition politics between the left-wing Social Democrats (ČSSD) and the conservative Civic Forum (ODS) (Figure 3.15).

Religion combined with nationalism played a major role in the Balkan wars and the constitution of the new states. The Catholic Croats, Christian Orthodox Serbians and Bosniak-Muslims conducted war campaigns based on their different ethnic and religious identities. Ethnic cleansing of territory became a well-known tactic to get rid of minorities. Today, Macedonia, Kosovo and Montenegro have still to deal with their large minorities of Albanians and Serbians respectively.

In sum, religious voting still exists across Europe, nevertheless historical traditions, continuity of party systems and the nature of democratic transitions play a major role in sustaining such a vote. The role of post-materialist values, which do not necessarily undermine religiosity, certainly tends to support the movement away from organised religion and towards its privatisation.

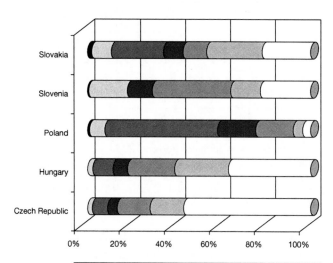

	Czech Republic	Hungary	Poland	Slovenia	Slovakia
■ Everyday	0.4	0.1	0.8	0.5	2
□ More than once a week	1.7	1.9	6.2	2.3	8
▨ Once a week	5.9	8.4	49.7	13.8	22.8
■ At least once a month	4.5	6.8	17.3	11.5	8.9
▨ Only on special holidays	14.3	20.6	16.7	35	10.3
□ Less often	15	23.5	4.3	12.8	24.8
□ Never	58.1	38.6	5.1	24.1	23.2

Figure 3.15 Church attendance in Central and Eastern Europe, 2004

Source: *European Social Survey round 2.* R. Jowell and the Central Co-ordinating Team, European Social Survey (2004/2005), *Technical Report*, London: Centre for Comparative Social Surveys, City University (2005) at Norwegian Social Science Data Services (NSD). Available online at http://ess.nsd.uib.no (accessed on 23 January 2009). Author's own interpretation and tabulation

The rise of regional identity and the impact on national political cultures

The original starting point of Stein Rokkan's research on European politics was the centre-periphery cleavage. As already mentioned, at the end of his life he concentrated his research on the regional awakening of many regions across Europe. In the 1970s the first signs of increased regional awareness and consciousness began to emerge. Two countries in particular led to the strengthening of regional identity in Europe: Spain and Belgium. On one hand, the Spanish constitution of 1978 allowed the re-emergence of regional identities after a long dictatorship in which they were oppressed. Although the autonomy granted in the constitution was originally only intended for the historic regions of Catalonia, the Basque Country and Galicia, other regions were soon able to profit from one of the articles that allowed for a slower route towards autonomy. Between 1979 and 1983, seventeen autonomous communities emerged across Spain, each one with its own political system and some with strong regionalist parties. In spite of this explosion of regionalism, strong centre-periphery cleavages only existed in Catalonia, the Basque Country and Galicia. Throughout the 1980s and 1990s the competences of the seventeen autonomous communities were upgraded and levelled. In spite of that, the historical regions were able to keep more competences than others.

Recently, the autonomy statutes have been reviewed. In Catalonia, a reform of the autonomy statute went through parliament with the support of the Catalan Socialist Party, a regional branch of the Spanish Socialist Workers Party at national level, and the main regionalist–nationalist Catalan party, Convergence and Union. It was confirmed by the population through a referendum, which allowed the inclusion of the highly symbolic word 'nation' when referring to Catalonia. However, the relationship between centre and periphery has become more complex and difficult between the central government and the Basque Country. Basque terrorism, perpetrated by the terrorist organisation Basque Country and Freedom (Euskadi ta Askatasuna, ETA), has led to alienation between Basque nationalists and the rest of Spain. In 2001, former regional president Juan José Ibarretxe proposed a plan for independence of the region from Spain. This entailed the conduct of a referendum on independence of the Basque Country, similar to that achieved by the Parti Quebecois in Quebec in 1995, which ended with the narrow defeat of the independence supporters. The political elites of the main political parties, People's Party (Partido Popular, PP) and the Socialist Party (PSOE) rejected this plan. The Basque Country is divided, and it is believed that only one-quarter to one-third of the population has a nationalist tendency. In the March 2009 Basque elections, the main nationalist party, Basque Nationalist Party, lost a tiny majority and socialist Patxi Lopez became the new regional president. He formed a single-party government with the regional parliamentary support of the People's Party. This has been a turning point for Basque politics because, for the first time, one of the main national parties is governing in the region without the PNV.

In Galicia, the Nationalist Galician Block (Bloque Nacionalista Galego, BNG) was able to make an impact during the presidency of Xosé Manuel Beiras, but internal infighting has led to a decline since the late 1990s. There are about ten regionalist parties represented in the lower chamber of the Spanish Parliament (Congress of Deputies), representing about 10–12 per cent of the electorate, of which the parties achieving more than 1 per cent are from Catalonia and the Basque Country. In the March 2009 elections, the conservative People's Party returned to power, after four years of a Socialist–BNG government (Magone, 2009a: 184).

While Spain remains a regionalised unitary state, Belgium became a federal state after 1993. The regional cleavage between the Francophone Walloons and the Dutch-speaking Flemish has existed since the nineteenth century, but it became particularly acute in the 1960s. Ethnic conflict between the two communities led to a complete separation of administration. The most difficult issue was Brussels itself, which was mixed. Moreover, about 100,000 German-speaking Belgians live close to the German border in Eupen and St Vinth. The ethnic cleavage is now institutionalised through three main regions (Flanders, Wallonia and Brussels) and three cultural communities (Dutch-speaking, French-speaking and German-speaking). The Flemish- and Dutch-speaking communities have merged into one administration. There is no longer a one-party system. Instead, the two parties each receive their seats in the national parliament based on the national share of the vote. In spite of this high level of autonomy, there are calls for independence from some parties, for example the xenophobic Vlaams Belang (Flemish Interest, VB). VB's vote has increased considerably and is particularly strong in Antwerp and the northern cities of the region. VB has been ostracised by all the other mainstream parties, nevertheless this resulted in even more attraction among the electorate (Erk, 2005).

According to Liesbet Hooghe, Belgium is still one country because of the European Union. It seems that the strong pro-European sentiment of Belgians is one way to compensate for the separation of the two main ethnic communities. There have been plans to continue the process towards confederation, meaning that both main regions would become distinctive countries, but still held together by a minimalist confederal structure (Hooghe, 1994).

In Western Europe, regionalism and regionalisation became important in France, the United Kingdom and Italy. In France, the introduction of twenty-six regions in 1983 was designed to achieve a decentralisation of policy-making in order to respond to the pressures of globalisation. The regions are not very strong (in terms of competences) and regional consciousness has not emerged out of these administrative structures (Cole, 1998).

In contrast, following calls for devolution made by Welsh and Scottish nationalists since the 1970s, in 1997 the United Kingdom started a devolution process, which led to a transfer of competences to the Scottish Parliament and the Welsh Assembly. The successful peace process in Northern Ireland has also led to the re-establishment of its Assembly. The UK has completed a decade of devolution and it is to be acknowledged that it has led to a democratic revitalisation in these parts of the country. However, the failure of former Deputy Prime Minister John Prescott to get through a second wave of devolution in England in 2005 has led to an abrupt halt to such constitutional reform. There is also a growing uneasiness among English MPs that Scottish, Welsh and Irish MPs can block legislation that relates solely to England, while they are not allowed to do so in relation to Scottish, Irish and Welsh matters. This 'West Lothian question' continues to be part of the discussion related to devolution (Bogdanor, 1999).

In Italy, administrative regions were included in the constitution of 1948, but they were only implemented in 1970. Regions remained extended arms of the central government until the late 1990s. However, it appears that the more regionally conscious northern regions have been able to profit from the decentralisation process, while the southern regions have continued to stagnate. Throughout the 1990s competences were transferred to regions in order to improve efficiency in policy-making. The growing pressures from the European Union led to the introduction of multilevel governance structures in the Italian political system. The Berlusconi coalition government between 2001 and 2006 tried to introduce a new structure similar to that of Spain, but this was rejected by the population in June 2006 (*The Economist*, 29 June 2006). After a decade of insignificant electoral results, Umberto Bossi was able to create the Northern League (Lega Nord, LN), which was able to achieve about 20–30 per cent in Lombardy and other northern regions, and which translated into 8 per cent of the vote at national level in the 1990s. The LN was able to profit from the collapse of the former *partitocrazia* and became associated with Silvio Berlusconi's Forza Italia. The LN was extremely xenophobic and populist. It started as a movement against the transfer of funds to the southern Italians, who were characterised as lazy. Afterwards, the xenophobic discourse was directed against immigration coming from the Muslim world and Africa. One of the demands of the LN was that the regions north of the river Po should become independent of Italy. This 'Padania' should follow the same example as Slovenia, because it belonged to Europe and was different from the underdeveloped southern regions. After joining the electoral coalition of Silvio Berlusconi in 2001, LN rejected the discourse and asked for a federal structure for Italy (Albertazzi and McDonnell, 2005).

Switzerland remains the ideal model for coexistence of different ethnic groups. It consists of four main ethnic groups: German-speaking (63 per cent), French-speaking (19 per cent), Italian-speaking (7.6 per cent) and Raetoroman-speaking (0.6 per cent). These groups make up the traditional linguistic groups of Switzerland; nevertheless, there is also about 20 per cent of the population made up of foreigners who speak other languages. It seems that the linguistic cleavage does not affect the nature of the party system. On the contrary, the traditional main parties continue to have support across Switzerland. The main problem is that the linguistic communities are living apart and not interacting with each other. For example, each region has its own television service. Additionally, globalisation is undermining the learning of a second language of the country. In an era of globalisation, children learn English, instead of French, German or Italian as their second language. Moreover, in referendums such as on the European Economic Area of 1992 and the bilateral treaties of 2000, a cleavage between pro-European Francophones and Euro-sceptic German-speakers became quite salient (Linder, 2005: 90).

In Finland, the only major ethnic-regional cleavage relates to the Swedish minority living in the Åland islands. The main party representing the Swedish minority is the Swedish People's Party (Svenska Folkspartiet/Ruotsalainen Kansanpuolue, SF/RK). According to Daniele Caramani, the party also has support in Helsinki and Turun-Porin (Caramani, 2004: 134–5). It scores on average about 10–15 per cent and was an important coalition party in both the Anneli Jaatteenmaki and Matti Vanhanen governments (Sundberg, 2004: 1002–3).

Central and Eastern Europe and the Balkans are both complicated. Ethnic minorities have set up their own parties in order to protect their rights. This has led to reactions from nationalist parties. In Romania, the Hungarian Democratic Union of Romania (UDMR) regularly achieves 6–7 per cent in national elections, currently with twenty-two MPs and nine senators in both houses in the Romanian Parliament. The Hungarian minority makes up 6.6 per cent of the population and is mainly based in the western part of the country. The nationalist party, the Greater Romanian Party, under the leadership of Corneliu Vadim Tudor, is one of the major opponents of the UDMR. There are also many other minorities represented in Parliament. In Slovakia, the Hungarian Coalition Party (SMK) has been able to establish itself as the main party representing the interests of the Hungarian minority. It received 11.16 per cent of the vote and twenty seats in the elections of 2002, and became a member of the coalition government of Mikulas Džurinda, the leader of the Democratic and Christian Union (SDKU). The Hungarian vote for SMK is a reaction against the nationalist movement for a democratic Slovakia, led by Vladimir Mečiar and the Slovak Nationalist Party. In Bulgaria, the Movement for Rights and Freedoms (DPS) represents the Turkish minority. It achieves about 7–8 per cent in elections. The Turkish minority is based closer to the Turkish border and is estimated to be about 9.5 per cent of the population. Since 2005, the Turkish minority has had to deal with the new right-wing xenophobic party, Attack, which is directed against the Turkish minority. The large Russian minorities in Latvia and Lithuania have been a major problem for the small endogenous populations. In Latvia, the Russian minority makes up 29.6 per cent of the population and a substantial part does not speak Latvian. Hence, they remain without citizenship: often known as 'denizens'. The main political vehicle for this minority is For Human Rights in United Latvia (PCTVL), which consists of an alliance of parties able to achieve about 18–19 per cent of the vote in a highly fragmented multi-party system and which is still excluded from mainstream politics. In Estonia, the 30 per cent Russian minority is represented mainly by the United People's Party of Estonia (EUPP), which has remained a small party, achieving between 2 and 6 per cent. In Lithuania, there are small Polish (6.74 per cent) and Russian (6.31 per cent) minorities, but they are better integrated into society and politics.

The most positive process was the 'velvet divorce' between the Czech Republic and Slovakia in 1992. After eighteen years it can be acknowledged that the separation has been successful and both countries are profiting from the 2004 accession to the European Union.

The Balkans are still fairly unstable, making a final judgement difficult. The most interesting experiment is probably Bosnia-Herzegovina, which is a confederation of three different ethnic groups – the Serbs of the Serbian Republic, the Bosniak-Croats, and Bosniak-Muslims from the Bosniak–Croatian Federation – with a collective presidency representing the three minorities. The war that took place between 1992 and 1995 nonetheless still affects good relationships between the three communities and the reconciliation process has been slow. Other new nation-states such as Macedonia and Montenegro have to deal with large minorities. Moreover, the special case of Kosovo is still waiting for a settlement. The unilateral declaration of independence by the Kosovo government in February 2008 is a further example of this fragmentation of existing nation-states.

In sum, regional cleavages and even national secession became important in the 1980s and 1990s. This shows that the regional–ethnic cleavage is still an important aspect of European politics, in some, though not all, of the countries. One particular consequence is that there are now many more countries in Europe, some of them quite small (for example, Montenegro). This adds to the diversity and complexity of European politics, and also to the difficulties faced in decision-making processes at European Union level.

From a homogeneous national to a heterogeneous multicultural society

The immigration waves to different European countries since 1945 have led to less homogeneous national societies. Today, most European societies are hetero-geneous and multicultural. There may be some resistance by segments of national populations to this, but the decline or stagnation of growth in most endogenous populations, as well as the parallel process of higher birth rates of immigrant populations, has created new, more ethnically diverse, societies. In this respect, the United Kingdom, Belgium, the Netherlands and France are probably among the best examples of truly multicultural societies (Figure 3.16). The discussion of multiculturalism follows at least two different strands. One is, basically, the Republican 'melting pot', assimilationist model, in which ethnic diversity is acknow-ledged, but overridden by the principles of Republican citizenship based on equal rights for all groups. Religious differences are a private matter and should remain separated from the affairs of the state. This model is common in most European countries, even in the constitutional monarchies of the Netherlands and Belgium. Integration into national society based on egalitarian principles and respect for diversity is central (Figure 3.17).

The other model is the acknowledgment of diversity and its expression. In this model, there is strong autonomy of ethnic groups, which are invited to integrate into society, but there is no overarching ideology of citizenry. Citizenry can be expressed in different ways, without forcing all groups to follow a set of principles. The separation between the private and the public is less clear. This second model is followed in the United Kingdom, where it is not only applied to non-European ethnic groups coming from the Caribbean, India, Pakistan and Africa, but also to the different endogenous groups, such as the Welsh, Scottish and Irish. The principle of tolerance of cultural diversity is central to this model of multiculturalism.

However, the best model probably lies between assimilation and multicultur-alism. It is labelled today as integrationism. It is also the emerging model for European countries (Box 3.6).

Most European societies are either at one end or the other of the spectrum but are moving towards the middle, with levels of tolerance is higher in some societies than in others. In 2002–3, the first European Social Survey, conducted in twenty-one countries, gave a snapshot of how far each different society is from a multicultural society. In some cases, the high level of ethnic homogeneity makes a society insensitive to calls for a multicultural society and these societies do not need to face any problems of integration. In this sense, we have an asymmetrical picture of multiculturalism in Europe. Some societies overwhelmingly advocate an assimilationist approach, for example as in Portugal, Poland and Greece, which are fairly homogeneous, with foreign national populations of below 2–3 per cent. Assimilationism is also strong in the Central and Eastern European countries, which may be related to the fact that all these countries had a late development towards

---

Box 3.6 Assimilationism, multiculturalism and integrationism

European societies are no longer homogeneous nation-states. On the contrary, they have become heterogeneous, incorporating many integrated as well as non-integrated immigrants. Today and in the future, because of the demographic changes of ageing populations and low birth rates, proper integration of immigrants will be a crucially important aspect of government policy. There are different forms of integrating immigrants into society.

- **Assimilationism:** Immigrants have to adjust to the culture of the host country and become part of it, in extreme cases giving up their home culture.
- **Multiculturalism:** Immigrants and other groups in society are able to live according to their cultural values. The danger is that multiculturalism may lead to segregationism and to 'parallel societies', which do not interact with mainstream society. Such examples of 'parallel societies' can be found in the Netherlands, Germany and the United Kingdom, for example, among the Muslim community.
- **Integrationism:** This is the middle way between assimilationism and multi-culturalism. The European Union is pushing for a common active policy of integration of immigrants that includes introductory language and citizenry courses. More active engagement in integrating immigrants into the labour market is also required. The Dutch model has been copied across the EU.

---

nationhood. At the other end of the spectrum are the more industrialised Nordic countries and those of western Central Europe. Switzerland, Germany and Sweden are the most tolerant towards diversity. Switzerland can be regarded as the model of multiculturalism par excellence. As well as the linguistic cleavages between the French-speaking, German-speaking, Italian-speaking and Raetoroman-speaking groups, Switzerland has had to deal with a large immigrant population (about 20 per cent) coming mainly from Southern European countries, such as Portugal, Spain, Italy and Greece. This is confirmed by the multiculturalism indicator that raises questions about tolerance of different religions. This question targets different con-fessions of the same religion (as in Ireland) and also the growing Muslim population in many European countries (such as the United Kingdom, the Netherlands, France, Germany and Spain) (see Figure 3.16).

Although the change of government in Spain on 14 March 2004 led to a different approach towards the Muslim population in the country, in the Nether-lands, the United Kingdom, Germany and France policies of terrorism containment or prevention created a negative atmosphere. In the UK, one year after the London bombings on 7 July 2005, Prime Minister Tony Blair blamed the Muslim com-munity for not being more proactive in helping the authorities to find potential terrorism plots. The general feeling was that there was still a serious lack of dia-logue and cooperation between government authorities and the ethnic communities. The indiscriminate shooting of the Brazilian, Jean Charles de Menezes, on 21 July

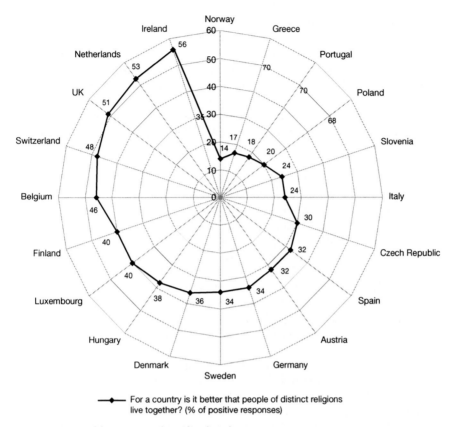

Figure 3.16 Tendency towards multiculturalism, 2002–3
Source: European Social Survey, 2002–3, adapted from Martinez-Herrera, Moualhi, 2005: 347

2005 and the lack of accountability and culpability in this respect was compounded by the police raid on a house in north-east London in which two Muslim brothers lived, one of whom was shot without prior warning. These were major factors that undermined confidence in the police force in the United Kingdom (*The Economist*, 17 June 2006: 32–7; *The Independent*, 18 July 2006: 6; *The Economist*, 8 July 2006: 29–30) and led, in 2008, to the resignation of Metropolitan Police Chief Ian Blair. Finally, in December 2008, after a trial in which the Metropolitan Police were found guilty of the incident, the new police chief had to apologise. Moreover, the greatest shock was that the atrocious London bombings of 2005, which claimed fifty-two victims, were perpetrated by young Muslim men who lived in the north of England and were of British citizenship. This threw a sharp light on the failures of integration for the first and second Muslim generations.

Nonetheless, despite the many failures of integration in the UK, the awareness of racism has been raised and the advantages of multiculturalism have been recognised. There is also recognition that some assimilation and integration has to accompany such multiculturalism and diversity. The ideal is to strike a balance between assimilation and multiculturalism.

The case of France highlights that Republican assimilation policies have failed in relation to the second generation of Muslim immigrants, especially for those living in suburban areas of the major towns. The urban riots of November 2005 and 2007, in which cars and businesses were vandalised, showed that the poorest sectors of the population were not able to become part of French society. On the contrary, the high levels of unemployment in France – between 9 and 10 per cent – has particularly affected the young Muslim population, without proper qualifications, living in the suburban areas of the cities. The negative language of former Interior Minister Nicolas Sarkozy against these sectors only served to inflame the situation. The use of the internet helped to sustain the riots across France over several days, which in turn led to the intervention of the army to prevent an escalation of the situation. Although the French national football team is a symbol of multiculturalism, having a high percentage of players with non-French cultural backgrounds, the concrete reality showed that most second-generation Muslim youths were living with little hope. This strengthened the Front National of Jean Marie Le Pen, which was able to gain support based on a simplistic racist discourse (*The Economist*, 17 November 2005; *The Economist*, 14 December 2005; *The Economist*, 29 November 2007). According to Christian Joppke, since the early 1990s the French have moved towards a less assimilationist and more integrationist approach, in which aspects of citizenship, language learning and understanding of French culture have been central to the socialisation of new immigrants into the country (Joppke, 2007: 9–12).

The model for such an integrationist approach to immigration is the Netherlands. The Netherlands was well known for its extremely tolerant policies towards immigrants and the multicultural approach was dominant there. However, since the 1990s, there has been a movement towards integrationist policies because of the lack of integration of some groups in the major cities of the country, particularly Amsterdam and Rotterdam. The formation of the political party Pim Fortuyn List (Lijst Pim Fortuyn, LPF) in 2002 and the murder of Pim Fortuyn himself, a sociology professor and politician, shortly before the elections by an environmentalist, who disagreed with Fortuyn's negative campaign against the Muslim population, brought these issues of immigration and integration to the fore. The murder of film director Theo van Gogh by Islamic fundamentalists, after the making of a controversial film on women in Islam, further showed the growing tensions in the population. The policies of the Dutch government have become less liberal and tolerant, and today any legal immigrant has to follow successfully a process of civic integration in which they are required to learn the language, have a knowledge of Dutch culture, and be aware of the rights and duties of citizens (Joppke, 2007: 6–9).

As already mentioned, a high level of assimilation tendencies can be found in the Southern and Central and Eastern European countries. In particular, the homogeneous societies of Portugal and Greece have encountered difficulties in coping with the new situation, whereby they are no longer emigration countries but have become immigration countries (see Figure 3.17).

Meanwhile, the Dutch model has become the benchmark and is regarded as best practice. The European Union is moving towards such a common framework of integration. According to Joppke, five aspects are highlighted in integrationist policies:

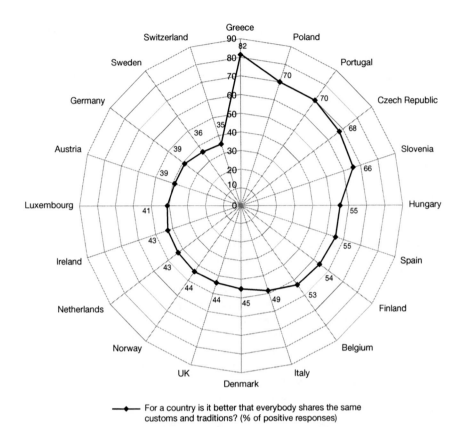

Figure 3.17 Assimilation indicator (European Social Survey, 2002–3)
Source: European Social Survey, 2002–3, adapted from Martinez-Herrera, Moualhi, 2005: 347

1. Integration is a dynamic, two-way process of mutual accommodation by all immigrants and residents of the member states.
2. There are concrete expectations on immigrants: 'Integration implies respect for the basic values of the European Union, the principles of liberty, democracy, respect for human rights and fundamental freedoms, and the rule of law'.
3. Employment is a key part of the integration process: important to provide jobs for the immigration community, so that 'parallel societies' may not emerge which undermine integration.
4. Basic knowledge of the host society's language, history, and institutions is indispensable to integration (compulsory). This was pioneered by the Netherlands in 1990s and has been emulated by Finland, Denmark, Austria, Germany, France and the UK.
5. Access for immigrants to institutions, as well as to public and private goods and services, on a basis equal to national citizens and in a non-discriminatory way, is a critical foundation for better integration.

(Joppke, 2007: 2–5)

Joppke labels this as 'repressive liberalism' owing to the shift from more tolerant to stricter immigration and integration policies. The slow convergence of immigration policy across the EU will certainly contribute increasingly to the consolidation of this common framework, even though different countries may apply these principles to different degrees. It still remains a broad framework that depends on the configuration of political, economic and social forces in each individual country (Joppke, 2007: 14–18).

According to Jeremy Rifkin, Europe will need 50 million immigrants by 2050 in order to compensate for the negative growth of the population. This means that European countries will have to continue the trend towards multicultural integration strategies, if national societies are to rejuvenate and continue to exist. He proposed the integration of Turkey as a solution to the problem, because it has a growing population and is quite young in comparison to most European countries (Rifkin, 2004: 252–7).

A multicultural index shows that Southern, Central and Eastern European countries are still far from the model of a multicultural society. In contrast, Switzerland, Austria, Germany, the UK, Ireland, Sweden, Denmark, Finland and the Benelux countries have all moved towards being multicultural societies. Apart from Finland, most of these countries have been targets for immigration from other European countries or non-European ones for a long time, and so they have had a long period to adjust and develop positive attitudes towards multiculturalism. However, immigration is new in Southern, Central and Eastern Europe. The late creation of nation-states in the eastern part of the European continent is a further factor for strong racist and xenophobic tendencies in these countries. One good example is the recent rise of the Bulgarian xenophobic party, Attack, which principally targets the Turkish ethnic minority in the country. Nevertheless, it has to be acknowledged that in Slovakia, Hungary, Romania, Bulgaria, Latvia, Estonia and Lithuania ethnic minorities have some representation in national parliaments and are actively taking part in government coalitions. In a couple more decades, these countries will probably also have become models of multiculturalism in their own right. Spain and Italy are moving slowly towards multiculturalism. The vast majority of the populations of Central and Eastern Europe still manifest strong assimilationist tendencies, but tolerance for diversity has been growing in recent years. In their pursuit to become members of the European Union, these countries have had to fulfil a set of criteria related to the protection of the human rights of ethnic minorities. Most problems can be found in the Baltic states in relation to the large Russian minorities. In Latvia and Estonia in particular, there is occasional friction with Moscow about the Russian minorities within each country. A major challenge for Europe will be the countries that emerged out of the breakdown of former Yugoslavia. The most complex case is Bosnia-Herzegovina, which consists of Serbs, Croats and Bosniak-Muslims. The Balkan wars have alienated these minorities and it is proving difficult to find a permanent reconciliation.

The other major problem continues to be the case of Kosovo, which was exacerbated after the unilateral declaration of independence by Kosovo. Serbia claims to be an integral part of the country, but this is opposed by the government in Priština. The positive referendum for the independence of Montenegro from Serbia in 2006 can be regarded as encouraging. Only the future will tell whether this small state of 300,000, with its large Serbian minority, will be viable and able to reconcile the wishes of the two ethnic groups. Last, but not least, Macedonia, with its large Albanian population, still needs the presence of EU troops to prevent clashes between the two ethnic minorities. All these countries are supposed to join the EU within the next decade, so their progress in protection of ethnic minorities and consolidation of multicultural cooperation will be of central importance (see Figure 3.18, Table 3.5).

Multiculturalism implies not only the acceptance of ethnic otherness, but also other lifestyles and sexual inclinations, such as homosexuality. Tolerance of diversity has become an important issue in present European societies. Indeed, according to the studies of Ronald Inglehart and Christian Welzel, tolerance of homosexual behaviour is regarded as one of the indicators of a society moving towards post-material self-expression values. In this sense, the most permissive societies are in Nordic Europe, western Central Europe or Spain (Figure 3.19).

As shown in Figure 3.19, out of seventy-seven societies worldwide, only eleven had values below 53 per cent in terms of disapproval of homosexuality, all other societies including the USA (60 per cent) were above. Among the most recent issues related to emancipation of the gay community has been the issue of same-sex

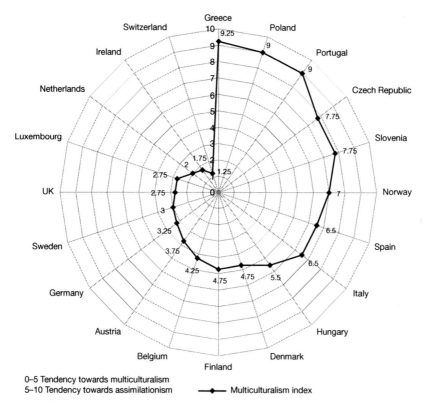

0–5 Tendency towards multiculturalism
5–10 Tendency towards assimilationism   ◆ Multiculturalism index

Figure 3.18 Multiculturalism index, 2002–3

Source: Author's own calculations based on European Social Survey, 2002–3, adapted from Martinez-Herrera, Moualhi, 2005: 347

Table 3.5 Populations and ethnic groups

Regional clusters	Countries	Core national population	Foreign nationals	Large Muslim population
Benelux	Belgium	9,978,681 57.8% Flemish 32.7% Walloon 1.1% German	9.1%	350,000 (3.5%)
	Luxembourg	276,600 (62.7%)	164,700 (37.3%)	–
	Netherlands	16,371,000	4.3%	911,314 (5.7%)
Germanic Europe	Austria	8,065,466	8.9% 4% former Yugoslavia 1.6% Turks 3.3% other	338,750 (4.2%)
	Germany (2003)	82,531,671	8.9%	3,200,000 (3.9%)
	Liechtenstein (2002)	33,863	34.2%	1,388,383 (4.1%)
	Switzerland (2003)	7,367,800	20.5%	316,815 (4.3%)
Nordic Europe	Denmark (2000, 2004)	5,330,020	5%	
	Finland (2000)	5,181,115 92.4% Finns 5.63% Swede-Finns 2% other		
	Iceland	264,922		
	Norway (2001)	4,520,900	4.1%	62,051 (1.4%)
	Sweden (1991,1999)	8,585,907	6.7%	90,000 (1.1%)
British Isles	Ireland (2002)	3,917,336		
	United Kingdom (2001)	58,789,194 80% English 10% Scots 4% Northern Irish 2% Welsh		1.5 million (2.6%)
Southern Europe	Andorra	65,844 36% Catalans 40.6% Spanish 10.2% Portuguese 6.5% French 6.7% other		–
	France (1999)	59,485,000		5 million (8.4%)
	Greece (2001)	10,939,771		

Table 3.5 Continued

Regional clusters	Countries	Core national population	Foreign nationals	Large Muslim population
	Italy (2001)	56,995,744 1.6% Sardinians 1.3% Raetoromans/Friaul 1% other		
	Portugal (2001)	10,318,084	2.2%	
	San Marino	26,941	29.3% 19.3% Italians	
	Spain	40,847,371	5.9%	300,000 (0.7%)
Mediterranean Islands	Cyprus	689,565 (with North Cyprus) 211,191		
	Malta	376,513		–
Baltic Europe	Estonia (2000)	1,356,931 65.3% Estonians 28.1% Russians 2.5% Ukrainians 1.5% Bielorussians 0.9% Finns		
	Latvia (2000)	2,375,339 57.6% Latvians 29.6% Russians 4.1% Bielorussians 2.1% Other		
	Lithuania (2001)	3,490,800 83.45% Lithuanians 6.74% Polish 6.31% Russians 1.23% Bielorussians 0.65% Ukrainians		
Central Europe	Czech Republic	10,292,933 90.3% Czechs 3.7% Marish 1.9% Slovaks 1% Other		
	Hungary	10,197,119 96.6% Hungarians 4.3% Other		
	Poland	36,620,000 12.9% Germans 7.7% Ukrainians 5.2% Bielorussians		

Table 3.5 Continued

Regional clusters	Countries	Core national population	Foreign nationals	Large Muslim population
	Slovakia	5,379,455 85.8% Slovaks 9.7% Hungarians 1.7% Roma 1% Other		
Eastern Europe	Bulgaria	7,973,671 83.5% Bulgarians 9.5% Turks 4.6% Roma 1.5% Other		1,044,550 (13.1%)
	Romania (2002)	21,698,181 89.5% Romanian 6.6% Hungarians 2.5% Roma 1% Other		65,095 (0.3%)
Balkan Europe	Albania (2001)	3,087,159		2,161,011 (70%)
	Bosnia-Herzegovina (2000)	4,364,574 48% Bosniaken 37% Serbian 14% Croatian	–	1,745,830 (40%)
	Croatia (2001)	4,437,460 89.6% Croats 4.5% Serbs 5.9% other		57,687 (1.3%)
	Macedonia (2002)	2,022,547 64.18% Macedonier 25.17% Albanians Roma 1.78% Serbs 0.84% Bosniaks 0.48%	–	608,779 (30.1%)
	Montenegro Serbia	615,035		
	Slovenia (2002)	1,964,036 83.6% Slovenes 2% Serbs 1.8% Croats 1.1% Bosniaks		53,029 (2.7%)
Turkey	Turkey (2000)	67,844,903 70% Turks 20% Kurds 3% other		61,060,413 (90%)

Source: Collected from Fischer Taschenverlag (2008)

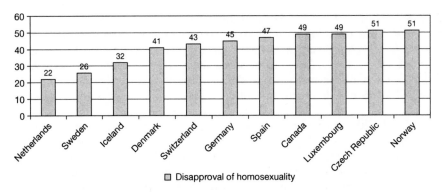

Figure 3.19 Disapproval of homosexuality (World Values Survey, 2000)
Source: World Values Surveys (2000), quoted in Inglehart, Welzel, 2005: 41

marriages, which has led to major splits in many societies. The legalisation of same-sex marriages in the Netherlands, Germany, Canada, France, Spain and the UK is contributing to a more permissive, but also more tolerant, society (Inglehart and Welzel, 2005: 126–9.) In Central and Eastern European countries and the Baltic there is still a strong prejudice against homosexuality. While the summer love parade has become a symbol of gay pride and also an important tourism event in Germany, in Latvia or Russia the gay movement has to face major obstacles from the authorities and the intolerance of society to demonstrate in the streets (Die Presse, 20 July 2006, p. 5). This criterion can be used as an indicator for the level of development of a society towards post-materialist values of self-expression and tolerance towards multiculturalism. Multiculturalism and post-materialist values of emancipation will continue to shape politics and the political culture of most European countries.

In sum, the growing diversity of European societies can only be ordered through the use of well structured, positive immigration policies, which should be combined with an integration policy based on a good mix of assimilationist and multiculturalist measures. Indeed, such a mix strategy may well make European societies richer and stronger in the context of globalisation.

Conclusions: the great transformation of the late twentieth century

In the past three decades politics in Europe were subject to major transformations, which are still ongoing. We started this chapter with a review of Stein Rokkan's theory on European politics and we continued with the main criticisms of Rokkan's theory expressed by several scholars. Following that, the main trends of transformation of the last three decades were outlined.

First, politics in Europe changed considerably as a response to economic and social changes. The traditional collective identities – working class, Catholic sub-culture, Protestant subculture – have been eroded since the 1960s and replaced by a more 'individualised society' (Bauman, 2001), which is also pluralistic in terms of lifestyle.

Second, the traditional cleavages identified by Stein Rokkan were no longer a reliable source of voting for political parties, as a result of the erosion of collective identities. Political parties now have to compete for every vote in a competitive electoral market. They have to use the media and new marketing techniques to reach their different constituencies. Most social democratic and Christian democratic parties have had to move to the centre and appeal to the growing sector of the new middle classes.

Third, although traditional and new class voting may still be happening, political parties tend to use socially heterogeneous strategies based on short-term issue-based campaigns to attract voters. This means that class politics is no longer a viable strategy for the larger parties, but, in the medium term, it may strengthen the position of smaller communist parties or left-wing parties.

Fourth, religious voting has been dwindling in most countries, which have undergone the processes of secularisation, erosion of collective identities and the transition from materialist to post-materialist values, based on emancipation, self-expression values, the questioning of authority and a shift from 'fixed forms of dogmatic religion to individual forms of spiritual religion' (Inglehart and Welzel, 2005: 31).

Fifth, in the last forty years a regional consciousness against the centralising tendencies of the nation-state has been growing. In some countries, such as Spain and Belgium, it has led to a substantial autonomy for subnational units. The new nationalism in Central and Eastern Europe has also led to secession and the creation of new states, contributing considerably to the destabilisation of certain parts of Europe, particularly the Balkans. Furthermore, the multilevel governance approach of the European Commission has had major implications for many countries, such as Italy, Sweden and Finland, in terms of the organisation of policy-making.

Suggested reading

Stein Rokkan theory and party systems

Bartolini, Stefano (2000), *The Political Mobilization of the European Left, 1860–1980: The Class Cleavage*. Cambridge: Cambridge University Press.

—— (2005), *Restructuring Europe: Centre Formation, System Building, and Political Structuring between the Nation State and the European Union*. Oxford: Oxford University Press.

Bartolini, Stefano and Peter Mair (1990), *Identity, Competition, and Electoral Availability: The Stabilisation of European Electorates 1985–1985*. Cambridge: Cambridge University Press.

Broughton, David and Hans-Martien ten Napel (eds) (2000), *Religion and Mass Electoral Behaviour in Europe*. London: Routledge.

Caramani, Daniele (2004), *The Nationalization of Politics: The Formation of National Electorates and Party Systems in Western Europe*. Cambridge: Cambridge University Press.

Flora, Peter (1999), Introduction and Interpretation. In: Peter Flora with Stein Kuhnle and Derek Urwin (eds), *State Formation, Nation-Building and Mass Politics in Europe: The Theory of Stein Rokkan*. Oxford: Clarendon Press, pp. 1–91.

Flora, Peter with Stein Kuhnle and Derek Urwin (eds) (1999), *State Formation, Nation-Building and Mass Politics in Europe. The Theory of Stein Rokkan.* Oxford: Clarendon Press.

Franklin, Mark (1985), *The Decline of Class Voting in Britain: Changes in the Basis of Electoral Choice 1964–1983.* Oxford: Clarendon Press.

Kitschelt, Herbert (1995b), *The Transformation of European Social Democracy.* Cambridge: Cambridge University Press.

Lipset, Seymour Martin and Stein Rokkan (1967), Cleavage Structures, Party Systems and Voter Alignments: An Introduction. In: Seymour Martin Lipset and Stein Rokkan (eds), *Party Systems and Voter Alignments: Cross-National Perspectives.* New York: The Free Press, pp. 1–64.

Mair, Peter (1997), *Party System Change. Approaches and Interpretations.* Oxford: Oxford University Press.

Smith, Gordon (1972), *Politics in Western Europe.* London: Heinemann, Chapter 1.

Van Biezen, Ingrid (2003), *Political Parties in New Democracies: Party Organization in Southern and East-Central Europe.* Basingstoke: Palgrave.

Welfare state and social change

Esping-Andersen, Gösta (1990), *The Three Worlds of Welfare Capitalism.* Princeton, NJ: Princeton University Press.

Esping-Andersen, Gösta (ed.) (1995), *Changing Classes: Stratification and Mobility in Post-Industrial Societies.* London: Sage.

Ferrera, Maurizio (2005), *The Boundaries of Welfare: European Integration and the New Spatial Politics of Social Protection.* Oxford: Oxford University Press.

Inglehart, Ronald and Christian Welzel (2005), *Modernization, Cultural Change and Democracy: The Human Development Sequence.* Cambridge: Cambridge University Press.

Jessop, Bob (2002), *The Future of the Capitalist State.* London: Polity Press.

QUESTIONS FOR REVISION

- Explain what is meant by the 'freezing hypothesis' of party systems and outline the main criticisms?
- Compare the main political cleavages between the Netherlands, Germany and Italy.
- How relevant are historically grown political cleavages in contemporary Europe? Discuss using examples from at least two different regions of Europe.
- Explain what is understood by 'post-materialism' and what impact, if any, it has on European societies.
- Is support and opposition to European integration becoming a new political cleavage?

National politics and the European Union

- The transformation of the European Union since 1985
- National governments and parliaments in the European Union multilevel governance system
  - The Council of Ministers of the European Union
  - National parliaments and the European Union
- Europeanisation of national politics and domestication of European politics
  - Top-down vertical Europeanisation of national politics
  - Horizontal Europeanisation or transnationalisation of politics
  - Bottom-up domestication of European politics
- Conclusions: the intertwinedness of the European Union multilevel governance system

SUMMARY OF CHAPTER 4

This chapter seeks to introduce the growing impact of the European integration process on its member states. In 2010, the European Union currently comprises 27 member states, the vast majority of European countries. It has become a political system *sui generis*, still awaiting its final form. The member states have become part of this EU multilevel governance system comprising the supranational/European, national, regional and local levels.

Many policies, once agreed by the member states in the Council of the European Union and the European Parliament at supranational level, are implemented top-down at the national level. This top-down implementation leads to processes of **vertical Europeanisation**. Good examples of such top-down EU policies are environmental policy and the implementation of structural funds.

In many policy areas processes take place over a longer period of time. Among these policies that are controlled by the member states, but increasingly coordinated at supranational or transnational level, are the employment and social policies and the convergence processes in public administration. This is called **horizontal** or **transnational Europeanisation**.

A third process that can be identified is a bottom-up process. It means that member states can initiate new policy areas or transfer relevant issues such as immigration or constitutional politics to the supranational level. This is called the **domestication of European politics.**

The politics of EU multilevel governance enhanced the role of national actors, such as national parliaments, which try to retain influence within the new structure of opportunities of multilevel governance.

The transformation of the European Union since 1985

The Franco–German reconciliation that has taken place since 1950 has been the major factor leading to European integration. The cooperation between former French Foreign Minister Robert Schuman and German Chancellor Konrad Adenauer has to be regarded as a milestone in European politics and the role of the United States in encouraging the French government to take the first step should not be underestimated. Although, in Zurich in 1945, Winston Churchill spoke about the 'United States of Europe', it was the British inclination not to join any supranational organisation. However, the United States wanted to push forward a supranationalisation project for the continent. The foremost advocate of this approach was George F. Kennan, head of the policy planning staff at the State Department. Encouraged by the United States, Robert Schuman took on this leadership role and announced the 'Schuman plan', which envisaged a communitarisation of the coal resources in the Ruhr region (Clemens *et al.*, 2008: 96–7) (see Box 4.1). This led to the establishment of the European Community for Steel and Coal (ECSC) in 1952, and, later, the European Economic Community (EEC) and Euratom in 1958. Today, these remain the founding treaties of the European

Union. These treaties were only changed through the implementation of the Single European Act in 1987, the Treaty of the European Union in 1993, and the updated and amended versions of the Treaty of Amsterdam in 1997 and the Nice Treaty of 2001. There was an attempt to develop it into a constitutional treaty in 2004–5, but two referendums in France (May 2005) and the Netherlands (June 2005) led to its failure to achieve ratification. A new start was made by Chancellor Angela Merkel in her capacity as president of the Council of the European Union in the first half of 2007. It was followed by the Portuguese prime minister, José Socrates, in the second half. In the referendum in Ireland in 2008, the Lisbon

---

Box 4.1 The founding fathers of the European Union

Robert Schuman (1886–1963)

French foreign minster between 1948 and 1952, on 9 May 1950 Schuman presented the 'Schuman plan', which led to the establishment of the European Community of Steel and Coal (ECSC) in 1952. He began the French–German reconciliation process. He was president of the European Parliament between 1958 and 1960.

Jean Monnet (1888–1979)

Monnet was a French civil servant who developed the 'Schuman plan', which led to the foundation of the ECSC. He also became its first High Commissioner between 1952 and 1955. However, he became disillusioned about the slow pace of integration and founded his own movement called the 'United States of Europe'.

Konrad Adenauer (1876–1967)

German chancellor between 1949 and 1963, Adenauer was the main partner, with Robert Schuman, in the processes of French–German reconciliation and European integration. In 1963, Adenauer signed a Treaty of Friendship with his French counterpart, Charles de Gaulle. This treaty was to institutionalise Franco–German cooperation, which lay at the heart of European integration.

Altiero Di Spinelli (1907–86)

An Italian communist politician, Spinelli was Commissioner of the European Communities between 1970 and 1976. After three years as Member of Parliament in the Italian Parliament, he was elected to the European Parliament in 1979. As Member of the European Parliament he became one of its most active leaders. He also became associated with the draft version of the Treaty of the European Union.

Paul-Henri Spaak (1899–1972)

Spaak was a Belgian foreign minister, and later prime minister, who was an enthusiastic supporter of European integration. He was instrumental in drafting the treaty leading to the formation of European Economic Community and Euratom in 1958.

Treaty was rejected. In spite of this, following negotiations with the Irish government, a second referendum with a much higher turnout (58 per cent compared to 53.3 per cent), led to the adoption of the Lisbon Treaty with 67 per cent of the votes cast (*Irish Times*, 3 October 2009) (see Box 4.2).

Starting in 1985, the new president of the European Commission, Jacques Delors, transformed the role of the European Community within a decade. Until that date, the member states had the pace of the European integration process under control, whereas from 1985 onwards the pace was set by the European Commission. During the incumbency period of Jacques Delors, the number of policy legislative initiatives increased exponentially. This incrementalism of policy-making reached its peak in 1995. but then declined when Delors was succeeded by other, less charismatic, commissioners, such as Jacques Santer, Romano Prodi and Manuel Durão Barroso (Pollack, 1994, 2000).

In the previous chapter, we referred to the recent work of Stefano Bartolini, who identified the European integration process as a new stage of development of European politics. There is a political restructuring process between national political systems and the European Union taking place that is qualitatively transforming European politics. According to Bartolini, the European integration process is the sixth stage in such development, following:

(1)   State building
(2)   Capitalist development
(3)   Nation-building
(4)   Democratisation
(5)   Welfare state development.

(Bartolini, 2005: 366)

The 1980s and 1990s can be identified as an important juncture in this process. The qualitative difference before and after 1985 was that these European policies put member states under permanent pressure to transpose a huge amount of legislation into national law, in order to achieve the completion of the Single European Market (SEM). They also created league tables in which 'leaders' and 'laggards' of EU policy-making implementation were highlighted. In such league

---

Box 4.2 The legal evolution of the European Union

1952	European Community for Coal and Steel (ECSC)
1958	European Economic Community (EEC)
1987	Single European Act (SEA)
1993	Treaty of the European Union (Maastricht)
1999	Treaty of Amsterdam
2003	Treaty of Nice
2004–5	Constitutional treaty (failed to be ratified)
2009	Treaty of Lisbon

tables, Scandinavian countries were, and still are, normally at the top, with Greece and Italy at the bottom (Börzel, 2001). According to Marco Giuliani, majoritarian democracies, such as the United Kingdom, perform better than consensus democracies, such as Austria or Belgium, in the transposition of EC law (Giuliani, 2003: 144). However, territorial organisations seem to play no role in such performance. All this shows is that there is a need for comparative analysis because of the differential impact of European integration on individual member states (see Box 4.3).

This permanent pressure led to the growing importance of the supranational institutions of the European Commission and the European Parliament (Box 4.4). Although the centre of decision-making still lies in the Council of Ministers, the incrementalism of policy-making strengthened the position of the European Commission as the motor of European integration. This triadic relationship has become even closer in the past three decades. The intergovernmental Council of Ministers of the European Union now has only few areas in which the representatives are able to vote by unanimity. Today, the vast majority of policies are shared between the supranational institutions and the member states, and most policy areas are decided by a qualified majority in the Council of Ministers. Since the Treaty of Maastricht, and particularly since the ratification of the Treaty of Amsterdam, the role of the directly elected European Parliament has been enhanced through the

---

Box 4.3 Jacques Delors and the relaunching of the European integration process

Jacques Delors was the president of the European Commission between 1985 and 1995. Between 1966 and 1985, European integration had evolved very slowly, partly because of the fear of member states of losing sovereignty to the supranational institution, and partly because of the economic crisis of the 1970s. High levels of unemployment and difficulties in making European economies more competitive created a structure of opportunities for the new president of the European Commission. Through his 'Russian dolls' approach, he was able to implement a strategic vision of the future of European integration. Within his two terms in office he achieved:

- a schedule and legal framework for the implementation of the Single European Market (SEM) by 1992;
- an expansion of the competences and strengthening of the role of the motor of European integration of the European Commission;
- a doubling of the EU budget – twice, once in 1988 and again in 1992;
- the upgrading of the treaties of the 1950s through the Single European Act (SEA) and the Treaty of the European Union (1993). The latter included a new political architecture for Europe:
  - the creation of Economic and Monetary Union (EMU);
  - the creation of the pillar of Justice and Home Affairs dealing with judiciary and EU-wide security issues;
  - the creation of the Common Foreign and Security Policy (CFSP).

Box 4.4 The institutions of the European Union: the European Commission

The main administrative machinery of the European Union is the European Commission. It is a supranational institution with the aim of progressing the European integration process. Therefore, it is often referred to as the 'motor' of European integration. It has the right to initiate legislation, which is then is forwarded to the Council of Ministers and the European Parliament. It comprises over 30,000 European civil servants who are divided between thirty-seven directorates-general and services (such as the Statistical Office or the Office for Official Publications) and several other agencies (such as the European Foundation for the Improvement of Living Conditions (EUROFOUND), the European Environment Agency (EEA), FRONTEX (for border control coordination), and the European Union Agency for Fundamental Rights (FRA)).

The president of the European Commission is appointed by the Council of Ministers and confirmed by the European Parliament, selecting the cabinet of commissioners based on a list of three candidates nominated by each country. The selected commissioners also have to be confirmed by the European Parliament. They are appointed for five years, a period that now coincides with the European Parliament elections cycle.

After successive enlargements, there are now too many commissioners for the amount of work in the European Commission, so, following 2014, it will be reduced to fifteen members. The selection of the fifteen member states is to be based on a rotation system in order to allow a balanced representation of smaller and larger countries. Member states should not be outside the European Commission for more than one term, and, once confirmed, commissioners should represent the interests of the European Union and cease to be national representatives. In reality, commissioners build bridges to their member states in order to inform the public and promote the idea of European integration.

---

co-decision procedure. In spite of differences, the vast majority of legislation is approved consensually. Difficult legislative bills are discussed in a conciliation committee, consisting of representatives of the Council of Ministers and the European Parliament (Wallace, W., 2005: 49–66; Pollack, 2004). In spite of its low-key presence at national level, the European Parliament has become a central player in the decision-making process and shaping of a European deliberative space (Hix *et al.*, 2007). Furthermore, the institutional triadic is complemented by an independent European Court of Justice that oversees and and makes judgements on the correct implementation of European law. So far, this has been the most innovative part of the European integration process. Over the last sixty years, the EU accumulated a huge quantity of European legal documents as well as decisions based on case work, making European law fairly complex. This process has led to the merging of different European traditions into one overarching legal system, which

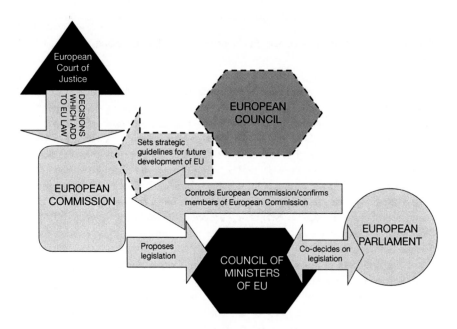

Figure 4.1 The core EU supranational decision-making system (simplified)

is above national law. Today, most national law is, in effect, translated European law, because of the adjustments governments have to make to comply with supranational legislation (Wallace, W., 2005: 69–74) (see Figure 4.1).

The constant top-down pressure has also led to the growing integration of national and European Union political systems. Indeed, Simon Hix speaks of the political system of the European Union: member states are part of a network of formal and informal interactions, which allow stable decision-making and implementation processes. Moreover, citizens are involved in these processes, both through institutions and also through other, less formal, structures. The constant top-down pressures of policy-making coming from the European Commission have led to Europeanisation processes that in turn have given rise to a convergence between the national political systems. Nevertheless, Hix makes clear that the European Union is not a state in the historical sense: it is a supranational organisation (Hix, 2005: 2–9). Sovereignty still lies with the member states, although, as William Wallace asserts, because of the transfer of competences in key policy areas, the EU is a 'post-sovereign polity' based on 'shared pooled sovereignty' (Wallace, W., 2005). Maybe a better explanation for the reluctance of political scientists to call it a state is that the European Union is still not an international legal entity and, more importantly, it has still not achieved a constitutional settlement. Its undefined character between a state and an international organisation makes it difficult to find a final formula to characterise it. The systemic nature of the European Union became clearer after the incrementalism of policy-making during the Delors period. The main reason is that new policies led to changes in the relationship between supranational and national institutions. According to Wolfgang Wessels, Andreas

Maurer and Jürgen Mittag, the process of systemic integration between the different levels of governance, particularly the national and supranational, can be called 'fusion'. Wessels *et al.* define the fusion theory as follows:

> The fusion theory goes beyond the analysis of integration at a given (set of) time(s) and tries to offer tools for understanding the dynamics of the EU system over time. It regards EU institutions and procedures as core channels and instruments by which national governments and administrations, as well as other public and private actors, increasingly pool and share public resources from several levels to attain commonly identified goals. Institutional and procedural growth and differentiation – from the ECSC – signals and reflects a growing participation of several actors from different levels, which is sometimes overshadowed by cyclical ups and downs in the political and public mood. However, each 'up' leads to a ratchet effect by which the level of activities in the valley of day-to-day politics will have moved to a higher plateau of a supranational communitarisation. The major feature of this process is a transfer and a 'fusion' of public instruments from several state levels linked with the respective 'Europeanisation' of national actors and institutions.
>
> (Wessels *et al.*, 2003: 14)

This supranational and national integration of levels is best exemplified by what we can call the 'transnational level' (see Figure 4.2), in which officials from both national and supranational institutions work together, prepare policy-making initiatives and are engaged in decision-making processes. All these processes take place between the supranational and national levels: for example, the 300 working groups and the Committee of the Permanent Representatives (COREPER), which take pre-decisions on behalf of the member states before they come to the Council of Ministers, and the over 300 working groups within the Council of Ministers that deliberate legislation initiatives proposed by the European Commission before a final decision is taken by the higher bodies. Attached to the European Commission is a myriad of advisory, management and regulatory committees, known by the general term 'comitology'. Depending on the nature of the committee, there are national civil servants and or representatives of national interest groups at this level. This allows the European Commission to deliberate on policy proposals before they are submitted to the committees of the Council of Ministers. In 2000, according to Renaud Dehousse, there were 244 committees overseeing the implementation of rules set out by the European institutions, and there were further scientific and consultative ones over and above these (Dehousse, 2003: 800; see also Maurer *et al.*, 2000: 37). In 2005 and 2006 these numbers increased to 250 and 277 respectively, most of them in the areas of enterprise and industry, agriculture and rural development, transport, and energy and environment (European Commission, 2007a: 6).

A large number of officials involved in comitology travel between national capitals (Bach, 1995; Maurer *et al.*, 2000: 41). This has been recently labelled as a form of deliberative democracy, also called 'deliberative supranationalism'. There is also the issue of the socialisation of an emerging transnational European elite, who reinforce and sediment the European integration process (Pollack, 2004:

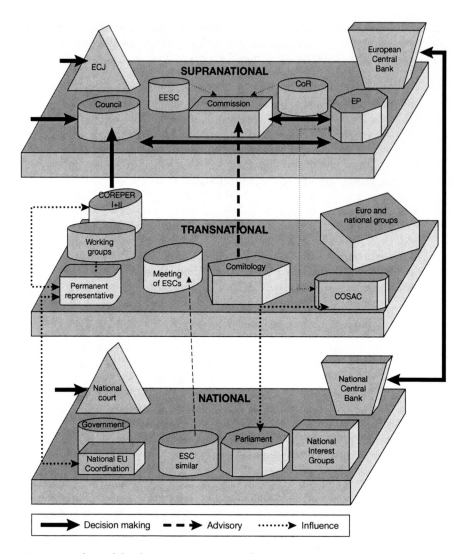

Figure 4.2 The multilevel governance system of the European Union

412; Radaelli, 1999; Quaglia *et al.*, 2008). Moreover, there are also similar intermediate transnational structures at the national parliament levels, the Committee of European Affairs Committees (CEAC/COSAC), among the European constitutional courts and the European Court of Justice, and the Economic and Social Committees of the European Union (Magone, 1999). All this shows that the national political systems have to be studied in this growing integration of national and supranational levels. What is more, this multilevel governance system is even more complex if we take into account the emergence of subnational actors since the 1970s. As already mentioned in the previous chapter, Stein Rokkan had recognised that in this respect there was a silent revolution taking place in Europe.

In this sense, we have to characterise the EU as a multilevel governance system in which subnational, national, transnational and supranational actors are engaged in policy-making processes (Marks, 1993: 410) (see Figure 4.2).

This means that, in order to study contemporary national political systems in Europe, we need to take into account the systemic nature of the European Union. Although diversity between European national political systems persists and will not disappear in the near future, there have also been processes of convergence and institutional adjustments.

National governments and parliaments in the European Union multilevel governance system

The Council of Ministers of the European Union

The governments of the member states are also involved in policy-making at the supranational level. The Council of Ministers of the European Union consists of the Council of Ministers of the individual states. National government ministers of a particular policy area meet with their counterparts regularly in Brussels and Luxembourg. There are nine Council Formations, of which those of the economic and finance ministers and foreign ministers are among the most important. They meet once a month. In contrast, ministers for education and other less central areas meet twice a year. There is a general misperception that the European Union imposes legislation on the member states. In reality, the Council of Ministers is probably the most important institution of the European Union. The governments of the member states are central to decision-making and most decisions are taken by consensus.

The Council of Ministers of the European Union has grown over time. It has a general-secretariat, with roughly 2,500 civil servants, which supports the work of the Council of Ministers (see Box 4.5). The EU legislation is proposed by the European Commission, which sends it to the Council of Ministers (of the European Union) for scrutiny or approval. The legislation is studied by over 250 working groups in which seconded civil servants from the member states take part and negotiate the proposed legislation. Most of the legislation is approved through consensual agreement – only legislative acts in which no agreement could be reached are sent to the Committee of Permanent Representatives (COREPER), which tries to find a solution at ambassadorial level, before sending it to the Council of Ministers. However, if there are legislative acts that do not achieve agreement at COREPER level, then they are still sent to the Council of Ministers. In the agenda, they will appear in part B as unsolved legislative acts, while part A is reserved for legislative acts already agreed at the lower levels (Lewis, 2007: 162–6). The permanent representatives are the ambassadorial heads of the permanent representations of the member states, located in Brussels (near the Robert Schuman roundabout, where the main building of the Council lies: the Justus Lipsius building). Each permanent representation has between 20 (Luxembourg) and 68 (Germany) seconded civil servants who are involved in the working groups (Kassim, 2003: 97).

Box 4.5 The institutions of the European Union: the Council of Ministers of the European Union and the European Council

The Council of Ministers was, until 1987, the main decision-making institution of the then European Community. However, since the Single European Act (SEA) in 1987, the Treaty of the European Union (1993) and subsequent Treaties of Amsterdam (1999) and Nice (2003), it has had to share many decisions with the European Parliament. This 'co-decision' procedure is used in an increasing number of areas. Before 1987, decisions were taken by unanimity which clearly complicated the whole process if a country decided to use their veto. Today, most decisions are taken by qualified majority or consensus, and only very few decisions lead to controversy. The Council of the European Union has a general-secretariat, with roughly 2,500 civil servants, which supports the work of the Council of Ministers. It also houses the Common Foreign and Security Policy (CFSP) machinery (see Chapter 14).

The Council of Ministers consists of the ministers of the different national governments. There have been nine formations since 2002:

- general affairs and external relations (most important formation with prime ministers and foreign ministers);
- economy and finances;
- justice and home affairs;
- employment, social policy, consumers' protection, health;
- competitiveness, internal market, research and industry;
- transport, telecommunications, energy;
- agriculture and fisheries;
- environment;
- education, youth and culture.

The presidency of the Council of Ministers of the European Union rotates every six months according to a plan agreed by the member states. The new Lisbon Treaty introduced the appointment of a president of the European Council by the Council of Ministers for a term of two-and-a-half years, which can be renewed. The first president is the Belgian Herman van Rompuy, who was appointed in November 2009. This would be a major step towards more efficient institutions and would contribute to savings by the member states.

The European Council meets four times a year. It consists of heads of state and prime ministers of the member states. It sets the strategic goals for the future of the European Union and makes 'history-making' decisions (Peterson and Bomberg, 1999: 10–16).

It is important to recognise the extent to which the European legislative process has become very complex. There are over thirty procedures involving the European Parliament in order to decide on legislation. Until 1986, unanimity was the only major procedure that existed, however after that date qualified majority voting was introduced, allowing more flexibility. Most of the discussions in intergovernmental conferences, such as in Nice in 2000 or (relating to the constitutional treaty) during 2003 and 2004, were about the distribution of votes in the Council. Because of the failure to achieve a positive referendum on the constitutional treaty in France and the Netherlands in 2005, the distribution of votes agreed at the Nice European Council is still in force. This led to a formula for a triple majority: a majority of member states (14), which in turn represents at least 62 per cent of the EU population, and a minimum of 255 of the total votes (74 per cent) (Lewis, 2007: 163; Wessels, 2008: 203) (see Figures 4.3 and 4.4).

The Lisbon Treaty changed this provision to a double majority of '55/65' (55 per cent of member states, but at least fifteen member states and 65 per cent of the EU population) (Wessels, 2008: 203) (see Figure 4.5).

The pattern of voting behaviour so far has been consensual and based on negotiated compromise. It takes about one-and-a-half years to decide on any one particular piece of legislation. Also, the involvement of the European Parliament has not changed this situation. About 85 per cent of EU legislation adopted by the co-decision procedure is by consensus and negotiated compromise. The rest of the legislative bills go through the conciliation process, which has also been reasonably successful in solving many of the differences between the institutions (Lewis, 2007: 161). The Council of Ministers voting configurations can also be influenced

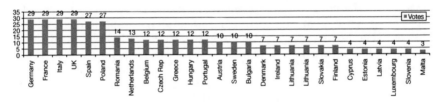

Figure 4.3 The distribution of votes in the Council of Ministers after the Nice Treaty, 2003

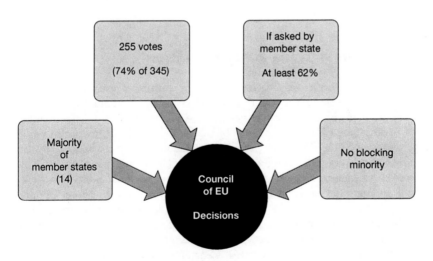

Figure 4.4 Decision-making by qualified majority, according to the Nice Treaty, 2003

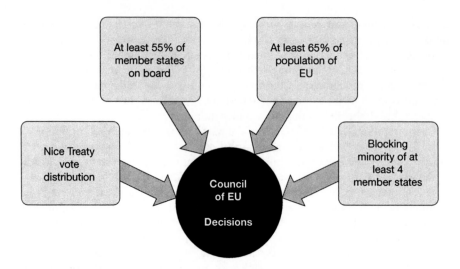

Figure 4.5 Decision-making by the qualified majority, according to the Lisbon Treaty

by party political aspects. The voting behaviour of governments may also be influenced by their attachment to a particular parliamentary group in the European Parliament. The relative majority of the European People's Party in the 1999 European Parliament elections was certainly a major factor in the selection of José Manuel Durão Barroso as president of the European Commission. This means that the first signs of a multilevel governance party political dynamics has begun to emerge at supranational level (Pollack, 2004).

In sum, governments are today working in a multilevel governance environment. The national level is just one of the arenas in which governments are active. Apart from the European Union, there is also growing activity at the international level.

National parliaments and the European Union

Over the last two decades the acceleration of the European integration process contributed to a considerable amount of EU legislation being decided at the supranational level. The thrust for this acceleration was the decision by the member states to create a Single European Market by early 1993. At the centre of this vision was the president of the European Commission, Jacques Delors, who also pushed other policy areas such as Economic and Monetary Union and social policy. This top-down Europeanisation created major pressures on national political systems in general, and national parliaments in particular. Today the *acquis communautaire*, the EU legislation that has to be transposed into national law, has increased to over 80,000 pages. New member states, such as the Central and Eastern European countries, had to implement this *acquis communautaire* within a very short period of time. This meant that, in many cases, Central and Eastern European parliaments (for example, Bulgaria, Romania and Slovenia) were sidelined. In this sense,

John O'Brennan and Tapio Raunio speak of a 'de-parlamentarisation' of national political systems. De-parlamentarisation means that 'the development of European integration led to an erosion of parliamentary control over executive office holders. The argument about de-parlamentarisation is based both on constitutional rules and on the political dynamics of the EU policy process' (O'Brennan and Raunio, 2007: 2). This de-parlamentarisation has been taking place with greater intensity since the early 1990s. The Council of Ministers of the European Union, with all its different configurations, has been extending the number of policy areas by which it decides with a qualified majority since 1986.

Therefore, national parliaments have to respond to a changed environment. In an interesting study, Katrin Auel showed that parliaments develop different strategies to play a role in the new EU multilevel governance system. She studied the French Assemblée Nationale, the German Bundestag, the British Parliament and the Danish Folketing. She differentiated between passive and active Europeanisation. The former means the impact that European integration has on a particular parliament; and the latter means the proactive strategy a national parliament uses to gain influence in the European context (Auel, 2007: 158). This latter meaning of Europeanisation, 'strategic Europeanisation', allows us to see differences between the different parliaments. According to Auel, the British Parliament concentrates on public control of any bills coming from the European Union and keeps the pressure on government both to explain what it is doing and to keep parliament informed at all times. The embarrassment of government ministers in relation to a particular policy can be part of the strategy. There is no attempt by the British to influence the supranational level – it concentrates its efforts on being a gatekeeper with regard to EU legislation.

In contrast, the French National Assembly, which has considerably weaker powers, has stepped up its engagement in the European integration process by being a public deliberation forum. It seeks to be an alternative source of information in relation to the government's position for civil society at large. It became a 'public deliberation' forum and has gained a good reputation for well-written and well-researched information papers. Its engagement concentrates also on the national level. The German Parliament does not regard the supranational level as a threat, but as an extension of its activities. This means that it seeks to informally collaborate and cooperate with the EU institutions. This has to do with the German political culture of the last fifty years, which regards the EU as a part of the German identity. Thus, the German Parliament bypasses the national government and cooperates informally with the EU institutions. Last, but not least, the Danish Folketing works closely with government. The Danish minority or coalition governments are dependent on the majority of the Danish Folketing, in that they always need to get a mandate for the country's position in all EU decisions in the Council of Ministers of the EU. The political culture is quite divided in terms of support for European integration. One half of the country is supportive, but the other half is Euro-sceptic. This means that the Committee of European Affairs receives detailed information with attached explanatory memoranda for all EU documents and that ministers each have to report on their position to the Committee before they go to Brussels. In case the Committee does not favour a decision taken by a minister following negotiations with other countries, it may use its parliamentary reserve (a right to veto any decisions taken by the government on behalf of the country in the EU without its consent) in order to reject it (Auel, 2007: 167–72). In this sense, the Danish Folketing is well integrated in the decision-making process. According to Finn Laursen, in 90 per cent of cases any particular minister keeps to the negotiated mandate, or changes with a view to meeting the support of a majority of the members (Laursen, 2001: 105–10; Jensen, 2007: 221–3).

These four parliaments are probably the more sophisticated in terms of scrutinising EU legislation. The Danish model has been copied by the Swedish Parliament, which established the Committee on European affairs (EU – Nämnden) after 1995 (Hegeland, 2001: 380–6), and by the Finnish Eduskunda, in which the work is shared between the Grand Committee (responsible for EC and Home and Justice affairs) and the Committee of Foreign Affairs (Common Foreign and Security Policy) (Raunio and Tiilikainen, 2003: 79). Among the stronger parliaments in terms of EU scrutiny, the Austrian Parliament should be discussed. Since Austria joined the European Union in 1995, parliamentary powers in relation to EU legislation scrutiny have increased considerably. The Austrian main committee, Hauptschuss, receives over 22,000 documents every year, although only about twenty legislative acts are dealt with in any depth. This main committee and its subcommittee on EU affairs is simply overwhelmed by the sheer volume of documents and constrained by the lack of resources to deal with more. This naturally hinders the position of parliament in relation to the government. Although advice from parliament is binding for the government, the sheer amount of work makes it difficult for parliament to make an important impact (Schefbeck, 2006: 157; Blumel and Neuhold, 2001: 325–31).

Auel's findings are confirmed by a seminal research project under the leadership of Andreas Maurer and Wolfgang Wessels, in which they differentiate between multilevel players (e.g., Denmark), European players (the European Parliament), national players (e.g., the Netherlands) and slow adapters (e.g., Italy). Based on their research, we can adapt their typology to include the Central and Eastern European countries and the Mediterranean islands.

Based on this typology, Maurer and Wessels differentiate between three kinds of parliaments in dealing with EU affairs: strong policy-making, modest policy-influencing and weak parliaments (see Tables 4.1 and 4.2). The scrutiny variables are related to its scope, the time and management of it, and its impact.

According to this typology, and confirmed by empirical evidence, the Southern European parliaments have been fairly inconsistent in terms of EU scrutiny. While Nordic parliaments, the UK and Germany have an *ex ante* (before it is sent to Council of Ministers) right to influence EU policy, the three parliaments in Portugal, Spain and Greece have only *post facto* (after) scrutiny powers, although their activity has increased since 1993. Italy is the only parliament with some *ex ante* powers, which are used to conduct hearings (Magone, 2007a,b). In Italy, the main instrument is the annual community law (*la legge communitaria*), which is submitted by the government, detailing all EU legislative acts that have been transposed into national law. In spite of this improvement, Italy is one of the laggards in terms of transposition of EU legislation into national law. The level of activity of the standing Committee on European Affairs in the Chamber of Deputies and the *Giunta* in the Senate is fairly high. Most work is related to hearings of ministers and civil servants as well as representatives of civil society, allowing parliament to receive orally updated information on major aspects of European integration (Bindi Calussi and Grassi, 2001: 286–90).

Table 4.1 Parliaments as actors in the EU multilevel governance system

PARTICIPATION IN NATIONAL ARENA

STRONG ⟶ WEAK

PARTICIPATION IN THE BRUSSELS/STRASSBOURG ARENA

STRONG

MULTI LEVEL PLAYERS	EUROPEAN PLAYERS
Finland	European Parliament
Denmark	
Sweden	Belgium
Germany	United Kingdom
France	
NATIONAL PLAYERS	SLOW ADAPTERS
Austria	Ireland
Netherlands	Luxembourg
	Italy
	Spain
	Portugal
	Greece
	Hungary
	Czech Republic
	Slovakia
	Poland
	Latvia
	Lithuania
	Estonia
	Bulgaria
	Romania
	Malta
WEAK	Cyprus

Source: Adapted from Maurer and Wessels, 2001: 463. Author's own update included Central and Eastern European Parliaments

In Portugal there is the Committee of European Affairs, which has been fairly hard working, despite the lack of human and financial resources. The intensity and quality of its work depends very much on the chairman (Magone, 2004: 42–5). In the ninth legislature period (2005–), the prominent former commissioner for justice and home affairs, António Vitorino, took over the committee and has created a strong dynamic around it. In Spain, the bicameral committee for European affairs is one of the weakest of all the member states of the EU. It undertakes hearings of government ministers and civil servants, and monitors the work of the government. However, the pro-European political culture among MPs makes scrutiny less necessary than in Euro-sceptic Nordic Europe (Basabe Llorens and Gonzalez Escudero, 2001). Last, but not least, Greece has had major difficulties in establishing a Committee of European Affairs. It meets irregularly and, to date, its contribution has not been very great (Yannis, 2004: 136).

Table 4.2 Parliamentary participation in EC/EU affairs

	Scrutiny variables			
	Scope	Timing and management	Impact	Countries
Weak parliaments	Rather low	Reactive and poor management	Low	• Ireland • Belgium • Luxembourg • Italy • Spain • Portugal • Greece • Hungary • Poland • Czech Republic • Slovakia • Slovenia • Latvia • Estonia • Lithuania • Bulgaria • Romania
Modest policy-influencing parliaments (*able to modify or to reject government proposals*)	Low–high	Reactive but formalised	High	• Germany • Netherlands • UK • France
Strong policy-making parliaments (able to substitute government proposals)	High	Anticipative, proactive and institutionalised	High	• Denmark • Sweden • Finland • Austria

Source: Adapted from Maurer and Wessels, 2001: 462 (author's own update by including Central and Eastern European Parliaments)

The Central and Eastern European parliaments were under considerable pressure to transpose the EU *acquis communautaire* before accession. It remains to be seen whether these new committees of European affairs are able to improve their parliamentary scrutiny. Several studies seem to suggest that Central and Eastern European parliaments may evolve in the same direction as Southern European parliaments. The lack of experience in EU matters, the language barrier and the high turnover of Members of Parliament have been factors undermining the establishment of a more professional way of scrutinising EU legislation. In this sense, Central and Eastern European parliaments are 'overburdened' by the new tasks of Europeanisation, which currently overlap with the ongoing democratisation and professionalisation process (Ågh, 2007: 258–62). Among the more institutionalised committees of European affairs are those in the Hungarian and Polish parliaments. Both were established in the early 1990s. However, there is a big gap between the legal–institutional and the political reality. The over-politicisation of the domestic field in Hungary and populism in Poland, creates major problems for professionalisation in the area of European Union affairs (Győri, 2007: 236; Łazowski, 2007: 203). Similar trends can be found in Bulgaria, where parliament has, thus far, been sidelined (Stoykova, 2007: 266–8). In contrast, the Slovenian parliament was able to achieve a law of cooperation in EU matters, which was a realistic attempt to achieve a minimal standard of scrutiny of EU legislation (Vehar, 2007: 246–51).

Other EU parliaments fall between these two groups of parliaments. The overwhelming support of the population for European integration contributed certainly to the 'light touch' approach of the Irish parliament in relation to its scrutiny of European affairs. However, since 1993, the Committee of European Affairs has become more active, particularly in major issues of European integration (Laffan, 2001: 258–64). In the same way as Ireland and the Southern European countries, Belgium is very supportive of European integration, which explains the lack of a thorough scrutiny of EU legislation (Vandevivere, 2001: 85–6). The Dutch Committee of European Affairs in the Tweede Kamer has been weaker, when compared to Sweden and Finland. There is also a Committee of European Affairs in the Eerste Kamer, although it has not been particularly efficient in scrutinising EU legislation. However, since the ratification of the Treaty of Amsterdam, there has been a move to improve procedures in order to improve its scrutiny of the transposition of EU legislation into national law and so control the government in this respect (Hoetjes, 2001: 348–56).

Last, but not least, it is important to mention the growing importance of the European Parliament in this context. Since its direct election in 1979, the European Parliament has been an important democratic institution in the multilevel governance system. For example, it was the European Parliament that started the first steps towards cooperation of parliaments in Europe in 1989. Today, the national parliaments meet twice a year in the country in which the presidency lies. Also, an informal network, called the Conference of European Affairs Committee (CEAC or COSAC in its French acronym), has been established. Although most of the activities have been informal, they have contributed to the exchange of information and the establishment of databases. Many countries, such as Italy, Germany and France, have a parliamentary office in the European Parliament in order to liaise better with this institution.

The European Parliament is now a co-legislator with the Council of Ministers of the European Union (see Boxes 4.6 and 4.7). Since the Treaty of Maastricht (1993), which was consolidated in the Treaty of Amsterdam (1999), and the Treaty of Nice (2003), the co-decision procedure has allowed the influence of the European Parliament over EU legislation to grow. In this sense, it has constrained the powers of member states to veto legislation. There is a conciliation procedure that allows for the settling of disputes between the two institutions. However, only a minority of legislative acts are actually contentious; the vast majority are approved through compromise and consensus.

Box 4.6 The institutions of the European Union: the European Parliament

The European Parliament has evolved from a mere consultative and appointed assembly to a decision-making legislature that is directly elected. The direct election of the European Parliament was introduced in 1979. Since then, there have been seven elections. The 736 members of the European Parliament are elected by a proportional representation system, which differs in detail between the countries, for a five-year period. They are organised according to parliamentary party groups. Following the 2009 elections there are seven parliamentary party groups:

- European People's Party (Christian democrats, conservatives)
- Progressive Alliance of Socialists and Democrats
- Alliance of Liberals and Democrats in Europe
- Greens/European Free Alliance
- European Conservatives and Reformist Group (British conservatives and Czech conservatives, new formation)
- European United Left/Nordic and Green Left
- Europe of Democracy and Freedom.

The powers of the European Parliament have evolved over time. According to Wolfgang Wessels, in 2002, following the adoption of the Nice Treaty, there is participation of the EP through the co-decision procedure for 17.7 per cent of articles. Other forms of participation are assent (7.8 per cent), consultation (30.7 per cent), cooperation (1.8 per cent) and information (5.1 per cent). However, the EP did not participate in 38.6 per cent of articles related to the legislative process enshrined in the treaties. The Lisbon Treaty would increase the number of articles covered by the co-decision procedure to 38.8 per cent, and reduce the non-participation share to 26.7 per cent (Wessels, 2008: 124).

The EP still has three different seats: Strasbourg, Brussels and Luxembourg. Strasbourg remains the main seat for plenary sessions, while committee meetings and parliamentary group meetings take place in Brussels. Luxembourg holds a large part of the administration of the European Parliament.

Box 4.7 The institutions of the European Union: the European Court of Justice

One of the great achievements of the European Union was the creation of its own supranational European law, which overrides national law. Today, most national legal systems are simply transpositions of European law. The European Court of Justice, based in Luxembourg, has the highest instance of dealing with judicial decisions relating to the internal market, but also, increasingly, it deals with other issues as well. It consists of twenty-seven judges, one for every member state.

Throughout the last six decades, the European Court of Justice emerged as an important player in shaping the European integration process. Many decisions of the ECJ have led to changes in European and national law. Although most of the ECJ's decisions have been to do with the internal market and competitive policy, they have also had, indirectly, political, social and cultural implications.

The ECJ has the First Instance Court to sort out less relevant from more relevant cases, when complicated, because of its increasing workload. Furthermore, the Court for the Civil Service makes decisions about EU internal administrative matters.

The European Commission, member states, corporate organisations and individuals can all file complaints to the ECJ. Decisions by the ECJ are binding, but the enforcement mechanisms are still in the making. It is quite astonishing how decisions of the ECJ are complied with, despite the absence of enforcement mechanisms. In recent years, the ECJ has created a network of judicial authorities at national level in order to increase its efficiency in making decisions (for further information see Chapter 8).

The European Parliament consists of 736 members, with seven parliamentary groups (although see Box 4.6). It has representatives of all the member states. The two main groups are the European People's Party and the Alliance of Socialists and Democrats. They clearly shape the agenda of the chamber and overall culture of parliamentarianism. The most cohesive group is probably the European Socialist Party, while the European People's Party suffers from having a wide range of diverse parties who are unable to find a common programme. Other parliamentary groups are the Liberal and Democratic group, the Greens and Regionalists, the European United Left and Nordic Left group, the Eurosceptic Europe of Democracy and Freedom, and, last but not least, the European Conservative group. In the last three decades, the turnout at European Parliament elections has been low, thus undermining its legitimacy, nonetheless the European Parliament has become a more professional and institutionalised body (Kreppel, 2002; Hix et al., 2007). There is evidence of the emergence of a European political class that seeks to make a career in the European Parliament and is shaping a culture of European parliamentarianism at supranational level (Pasquinucci and Verzichelli, 2004). This became evident when Jacques Santer was forced to resign following allegations of corruption and nepotism based on the report of the Committee of Independent Experts in 1999; and when the newly appointed president of the Commission, José Manuel Durão Barroso, had difficulties getting some of the proposed candidates for the Commission approved.

Europeanisation of national politics and domestication of European politics

The previous section showed that, since 1985, there has been a growing integration between national and supranational politics. This Europeanisation is increasingly complemented by a 'domestication' of European politics, in which national actors try to shape the future and ongoing policies of the European Union. Tanja Börzel and Thomas Risse characterised this as the *uploading* of preferences by national actors to the supranational level (in our language here, the domestication of European politics) and the *downloading* of supranational policies to the national level (in our language, the Europeanisation of national politics) (Börzel and Risse, 2003: 62). Both processes are intertwined and systemic. In another study, Börzel refers to downloading as Europeanisation and uploading as European integration (Börzel, 2005: 46). Although Börzel is right about Europeanisation, I would argue that the uploading process may be better defined as the domestication of European politics, whereas European integration would be the overarching intertwined dynamic of the two processes. As already mentioned, the European Convention was a good example of such a domestication of European politics, taking place simultaneously at different levels. In spite of a considerable increase in studies on the Europeanisation of national politics, there is still only a small number related to the domestication of European politics (see Box 4.8).

In this volume, we have concentrated mainly on Europeanisation processes and less on domestication processes. The main reason for this is that we are interested in comparing different countries. This means that our main territorial level of analysis is, and remains, the national level. Although it is important to contextualise such national politics in the new EU political system, our main focus remains the discussion of the similarities and differences between European countries. It is also very important to differentiate between vertical top-down and horizontal Europeanisation. The vertical top-down Europeanisation is simply the process of the integration of policies defined at supranational level into national politics, policy-making or polity. Horizontal Europeanisation refers to the coordination of policies through specific soft governance methods, for example the open method of coordination, which allows best practice and benchmarking to be adopted by the member states (Radaelli, 2003: 41) (see Figure 4.6).

Top-down vertical Europeanisation of national politics

As already mentioned, this process of Europeanisation refers to the period since 1985, when member states had to implement, in a very short period of time, several policies designed at supranational level in order to implement the Single European Market (SEM) (see Table 4.3). The Single European programme comprised over 282 directives that had to be implemented between 1985 and the end of 1992. After 1992 further directives were introduced in order to fine-tune legislation in many areas. Apart from the right legal transposition into national law, national governments also had to find mechanisms to monitor the working of such directives in reality. There was considerable pressure upon national governments and institutions coming from the EU. Europeanisation as such is, therefore, a never-ending

---

Box 4.8 The Europeanisation of national politics and the domestication of European politics

The Europeanisation of national politics

A very thorough definition by Claudio Radaelli, influenced by Robert Ladrech:

> Processes of (a) construction, (b) diffusion and (c) institutionalisation of formal and informal procedures, policy paradigms, styles, 'ways of doing things', and shared beliefs and norms that are first defined and consolidated in the making of EU public policy and politics and then incorporated in the logic of domestic discourse, identities, political structures, and public policies.
>
> (Radaelli, 2003: 31)

- *Top-down Europeanisation*: The decisions taken at the supranational level are implemented at the national level, leading to a change of institution or policy-making processes (e.g., structural funds).
- *Horizontal Europeanisation*: The voluntary process of convergence of institutions or policy styles across the European Union. This is achieved through a light coordination structure at the centre, combined with a continuous review and monitoring of the process. Examples are: the European Employment Strategy (EES) (see Chapter 13); the European administrative space process through the European Public Administration Network (EUPAN) based in Maastricht (see Chapter 7); and the Bologna process in the higher education sector.

The domestication of European politics

Individual member states or alliances of member states may formulate new ideas and policy proposals that are successful at the national level at a supranational level. The European Convention leading to the constitutional treaty in 2003 internalised the public debate on the future of the European Union, taking into account constituencies at different levels of the governance system.

---

process and part of the systemic nature of European integration. Although Europeanisation processes simultaneously shape policy, politics and polity, it is important to differentiate analytically between the three, so that partial Europeanisation processes can also be understood. Moreover, it is important to add a cultural dimension and consider, in particular, how elites and populations in each of the respective countries may adjust their attitudes towards the new European Union political system. This means that Europeanisation processes are complex and can be characterised by parallel, but different, time-frames. Changes in attitudes may take a long time. A good example of this is the Labour government's difficulties when it sought to change the attitudes of the British people regarding the Economic and Monetary Union (EMU) and the adoption of the euro. The same example can also be applied to Sweden, where almost 60 per cent of the population rejected the euro in a referendum in 2004. However, the reasons for rejection were quite different. In the case of the United Kingdom it was the fear of losing sovereignty, which is strongly connected to economic and monetary issues. In Sweden, one of

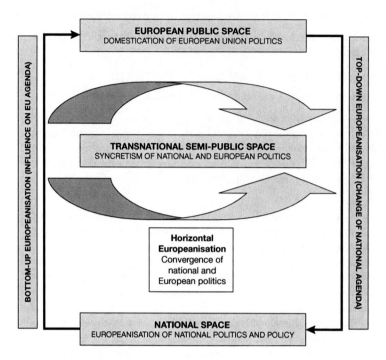

Figure 4.6 The dimensions of the Europeanisation of national politics and the domestication of European politics

the main reasons for the rejection of the euro in the referendum of 2004 was the population's fear that acceptance of the single European currency would undermine the Swedish welfare system and lifestyle.

In some countries, the population may regard the European Union as a way to overcome the negative aspects of their national political systems. This is the case in Italy, where the vast majority of the population is Europhile. The main reason is that Italians regard the European Union as an important *vincolo esterno* (external link) to overcome the vicious circle of unstable government (Dyson and Featherstone, 1996). This is the reason why Romano Prodi could advocate the raising of a special tax in order to cut the budget deficit in 1996–97, which was used to fund entry into the Economic and Monetary Union. For Italy, but also the other Southern European countries, it was a matter of prestige to be at the forefront of Economic and Monetary Union. However, the experience of Central and Eastern European countries is more mixed: there are strong Euro-sceptic groups in some countries, such as Poland, the Czech Republic and Estonia, while populations in Bulgaria and Romania have similar positive attitudes to the populations of the Southern European countries.

Since the 1980s, national political systems have changed considerably. It was Robert Ladrech who wrote one of the first studies on the Europeanisation of national politics. He studied the French political system and recognised that major adjustments had to be made to the constitution in order to be able to adopt the Treaty of European Union in 1993. His definition of Europeanisation was as follows:

Table 4.3 The dimensions of top-down Europeanisation

Layers	Institutions/actors	Description
The political system	• Central government • Parliament • Judiciary • Regional and local government • Public administration	• The impact of European integration on the political elite, the core executive, parliament, courts, subnational government and public administration • Pressures to adjust to European integration; it also includes constitutional change
Decision-making system	• Political parties • Interest groups • Organised civil society	• The role of intermediary organisations in shaping the decision-making process • This impact may have interactions with aggregated interest groups at the supranational level, which have been characterised as European organised civil society (Euro groups)
Public policy space	• Public administration • Policy networks • Private actors • Business enterprises	• The implementation of policies designed at the supranational level • It requires cooperation between government, civil society and economic actors
Political cultural space	• Political elites • Population • Interest groups • Social movements	• Political expression for and against European integration • Establishment of social movements related to the European integration process • Linkage between political parties and voters • National political culture and European integration (knowledge of European Union matters and institutions; support for the European Union; benefits of the European Union)

Source: Adapted from Magone 2004: 13

161

> Europeanisation is an incremental process reorienting the direction and shape of politics to the degree the EC political and economic dynamics become part of the organisational logic of national politics and policy-making.
>
> (Ladrech, 1994: 69–70)

Ladrech's definition was followed by more sophisticated definitions. Probably, the most sophisticated one has been presented by Christopher Knill and Dirk Lehmkuhl. They differentiate between three forms of top-down Europeanisation. The first one is labelled as positive Europeanisation, meaning that member states adopt policies based on a design developed at supranational level. The second form is 'negative' Europeanisation, which lacks a design or model and is a mere enforcement of directives. The third form is the cultural transformation of attitudes and ways of thinking in relation to the European integration process. It is a process of overcoming the poor fit between the supranational and national levels (Knill and Lehmkuhl, 2002).

The best way to understand Europeanisation, probably, is to characterise it as 'a process in which new rules of the game are constructed. Policy formation and policy change take place within these new structural conditions' (Mörth, 2003: 174). Ladrech identified, in particular, major changes in the way the French Parliament related to the European Union following the adoption of Protocol 13 (on the involvement of National Parliaments in the European Union) attached to the Treaty of the European Union (Maastricht Treaty), ratified in 1993. Indeed, the National Assembly and Senate in France were able to gain greater prominence through the interpretation of this protocol. Ladrech's findings have also been confirmed by other studies. It seems that the French Parliament was able to up-grade its role in the process of scrutiny of EU legislation and its implications for national politics as a result of the provisions in the Treaty of the European Union and Treaty of Amsterdam. Since then, the French Parliament has published excellent reports in order to inform civil society, and is an alternative source of information for the population (Szukala and Rosenberg, 2001; Sprungk, 2007; Auel, 2007).

Meanwhile, it became clear that several factors play a role in how actively parliaments are involved in the European Union decision-making process, which confirms Börzel and Risse's intervening factors, such as veto powers and/or cultural attitudes towards European integration (2003: 69). The strongest scrutiny of EU legislation can be found in the Nordic Euro-sceptic countries (for example, Denmark, Sweden and Finland) and in the United Kingdom. The German Parliament also has a strong record of EU scrutiny, but this is probably because of its strong position overall in the political system. The Austrian Parliament is also regarded as strong, while parliaments in Southern, Central and Eastern Europe are still lagging behind.

Ladrech also mentioned the impact of the structural funds, which are central to European Regional Policy, on the territorial structures of the French state. Indeed, since 1982 France has been engaged in a regionalisation process. It became a unitary regionalised state, mainly as a way of adjusting to the growing demands of globalisation. As already mentioned, Gary Marks (1993) found that the structural funds contributed to the emergence of a multilevel governance system in the European Union. Different countries were under pressure to adjust to these changes. Among them, one can mention Italy, which, since the collapse of the 'First' Republic in 1992, has been engaged in a piecemeal reform of its constitution. In 2001, Chapter 8 on the local and regional authorities of the Italian Constitution was changed in order to allow the regions to have a greater autonomy in the implementation of European public policy. According to Martin Bull and Jörg Baudner (2004), over time the structural funds had a major Europeanising impact in the Mezzogiorno. This led to a replacement of the old, domestically inspired, southern policy by a new European regional policy. The old system allowed a lack of transparency in the allocation of funds, clientelism, patronage and of course corruption. Many projects remained unfinished or were wrongly chosen. In this respect, the role of criminal organisations, such as Cosa Nostra, N'dranghetta and Camorra, in diverting public funding to pseudo-projects should not be forgotten. According to Bull and Baudner, the process of Europeanisation was not instantaneous, but took a whole decade to materialise. The authors argued that, between 1988 and 2000, the domestic reformers who based their rationale on European regional policy were able to gain the upper hand (Bull and Baudner, 2004: 1070–2). Despite these changes, there are still major asymmetrical differences in the Europeanisation processes in the north and south of the country, particularly in relation to the implementation of structural funds. Essentially, the more developed north was able to develop a more proactive policy than the southern regions could (Gualini, 2003). Similar transformations towards the EU governance system took place in most countries. For example, Sweden and Finland adjusted their territorial structures to make it more compatible with the EU multilevel governance. Although the amount of structural funds was small, there was a general thrust to make the structures more transparent and accountable, but also more flexible (Arter, 2001).

In contrast, highly federalised Germany had difficulty in adjusting the existing joint decision-making system between *Länder* and the central government to the new multilevel governance system. According to the studies of Arthur Benz, the old system of joint decision-making was geared towards creating solidarity between the German regions through generous transfers from the richer to the poorer regions, while the new EU multilevel governance system is based on competitive behaviour between the regions. This, of course, led to tension in the process of adjustment (Benz, 1998, 2000).

According to Attila Ágh, most Central and Eastern European countries also had to adjust to the EU multilevel governance system. In Poland, sixteen elected regions were created in order to achieve a more decentralised political system. The importance of the structural funds for Poland led to a strong adjustment to the structures of Germany, which also consists of 16 elected *Länder*, and this became relevant for border regions between Poland and Germany. Similarly, the Czech Republic established elected regions in 2000 in order to improve its ability to absorb structural funds. In other countries, the regionalisation process has been less clear. Throughout the 1990s, Hungary explored the best territorial structures for adjusting to EU multilevel governance, while Bulgaria and Romania decided for a de-concentrated structure, similar to the Portuguese and Greek cases (Ágh, 2003: 113–35; Jacoby, 2005: 93–101). This shows that the impact of Europeanisation on member states was asymmetric, and also led to very different responses (for more details see Chapter 10).

According to Börzel, Europeanisation can be measured according to a continuum that stretches from no change to high change. In between, she includes inertia/resistance, retrenchment/'negative change' (both are low change), absorption, accommodation/'peripheral change' (medium change) and transformation/systemic change (high change) (Börzel, 2005: 59). She also highlights that the level of transformation is dependent on mediating factors, such as the number of institutional veto points (president, judiciary, parliament, subnational actors), supporting formal institutions, or a cooperative informal culture (Börzel, 2005: 49–58). This makes the process of Europeanisation in each individual country fairly complex.

Horizontal Europeanisation or transnationalisation of politics

This form of Europeanisation is less formalised and less well framed than vertical Europeanisation. Horizontal Europeanisation can be observed in policy areas in which member states resist calls for supranationalisation, for example in areas such as social policy, employment policy, immigration policy and public administrative reform. The methods of horizontal Europeanisation include, for example, the open method of coordination (OMC), formalised as one of the European integration methods in the extraordinary European Council of Lisbon, 23–24 March 2000. (The OMC had been applied primarily to the coordination of employment policies since 1998.) The OMC is a soft form of governance, which has a minimal coordinating structure at supranational level. It sets guidelines for each member state in a particular policy area and is a medium- to long-term instrument of policy-making (Borrás and Jacobsson, 2004: 188–9).

In the case of employment policy, each country had to develop annual strategies to improve their respective labour markets. At the end of each year an employment committee attached to the Council of Ministers, consisting of representatives from the European Commission and other experts, reviews the national reports and gives recommendations on what should be changed. However, the open method of coordination had no mechanisms to enforce a change of policy. The main aim was to achieve greater employment in the most competitive knowledge-based economies of the world by 2010. The mid-term review in 2005 led to the acknowledgment that the open method of coordination had only achieved minimal improvements in the labour markets and had failed to reach the targets set out in 2000. This strategy (known as the 'Lisbon strategy') showed that horizontal Europeanisation needs time to mature and become more efficient. The mid-term review in 2005 led to a more coherent policy, but the Lisbon strategy targets were not achieved. Cultural and structural differences between member states may be an important factor in preventing success. While the Scandinavian countries and the Netherlands have the most sophisticated proactive labour market policies, the Southern European countries, as well as Belgium, France and Germany, have major difficulties in bringing about change in behaviour patterns in such policy-making (Rhodes, 2005).

Another good example of horizontal Europeanisation is the European Public Administration Network (EUPAN), which has its secretariat in the European Institute of Public Administration (EIPA) in Maastricht. Although convergence towards a European administrative space has been ongoing since the early 1990s, the thrust towards an open coordinated model started only in 1998. Since then, all twenty-eight public administrations (the EU member states and the European

Commission) are engaged in a process of convergence and adjustment in order to create a single European market in public administration. Four working groups were established, relating to priority areas of public administration: Innovative Public Services (IPSG), Human Resources Management (HRMG), e-government (eGWG) and Better Regulation (BRWG). All these priority areas are linked to the Lisbon strategy to establish the most competitive knowledge-based economy in the world (Määttä, 2004: 7; D'Orta, 2003; Schout and Bastmeier, 2003, see Chapter 7).

In the same way as for vertical Europeanisation, the effects of horizontal Europeanisation are asymmetric across Europe. While the Netherlands has a sophisticated reform programme to make public administration more citizen-friendly and enhance the participatory elements in it through the horizontalisation of public services (ICT and Government Advisory Committee, 2001: 39), most Southern, Central and Eastern European bureaucracies are lagging behind in the modernisation agenda (Sotiropoulos, 2004; Dimitrova, 2005). Additionally, this horizontal Europeanisation process is not pushed through by the European Union institutions, but by the secretariat of EUPAN, based in the semi-public European Public Administration Institute, Maastricht. This in itself clearly shows the difference between horizontal and vertical Europeanisation. The former is based on good/best practice and benchmarking and takes place over a long period of time. It is a voluntary open-ended process. The latter is more formalised and time-bound and relates to central policies of the European Union political system.

Bottom-up domestication of European politics

The 'uploading' of preferences, as referred to by Tanja Börzel and Thomas Risse, requires that national, subnational and, sometimes, transnational actors contribute to the domestication of debates about European integration. However, the best examples of domestication of European politics were probably the two conventions that led to the drafting of the Charter of Fundamental Citizens' Rights in 2002 and the constitutional treaty in 2003, respectively. The multilevel European deliberative space led to the intervention of intellectuals, think-tanks, interest groups, politicians, national parliaments and subnational parliaments in order to put forward their particular contributions. This transformed the nature of the debate. For the European Convention on the Charter of Fundamental Citizens' Rights, 70 civil society organisations submitted 900 contributions, while for the European Convention on the Constitutional Treaty 547 organisations (including think-tanks and national interest groups) sent 1,251 contributions; these figures do not include the contributions at national and subnational levels (Magone, 2006a: 179). In this sense, the whole European integration process has become more deliberative and the trend seems to be to include more and more actors in order to legitimise and democratise the outcome. In most initiatives of the European Commission, there is a lengthy consultation process that allows the public to send their views on the proposal.

Domestication of European politics can also lead to sanctioning campaigns. The best example of this was the reaction of the European Council and the Council of Ministers to the formation of a coalition government between the Austrian People's Party (Österreichische Volkspartei, ÖVP) and the new right Freedom Party

(Freiheitliche Partei Österreichs, FPÖ) in 2000. Austria was ostracised during most of the period of the Portuguese presidency, in the first half of 2000, which bowed to pressure emanating from Germany, Belgium and France. In spite of offensive Austrian diplomacy, the position of the European Council was to sustain the boycott of the country in bilateral relations. When the Austrian government contemplated holding a referendum on Austria's membership of the European Union, the European Council decided to diffuse the situation by creating the Wise Men Commission, which was to assess whether the coalition government had changed the position of democracy, human rights and protection of minorities within the country. After several months, the Commission gave a positive report about the situation in Austria, allowing the restoration of normal relations with Austria (Merlingen *et al.*, 2001; Pernthaler and Hilpold, 2000). For the first time in the history of European integration, a member state was exposed to the criticisms of the other member states. The deviation from shared European values was used as the criteria for the exclusion of another country. The Austrian case was preceded by the Slovakian one in 1997–98, still before accession, when the policies of the nationalist Vladimir Mečiar (of the Movement for a Democratic Slovakia, HZDS) against the Hungarian minority were condemned by the European Council. It led to new elections on 25–26 September 1998, in which a coalition of opposition parties won against the nationalist coalition government under Mečiar. Mečiar was removed from office and he was replaced by prime minister Mikulas Džurinda. The following year, Mečiar was also unsuccessful in his bid to become president, losing against the opposition candidate Rudolf Schuter. This change of government was regarded as an important precondition for the accession of Slovakia to the European Union.

Conclusions: the intertwinedness of the European Union multilevel governance system

The European Union has become a political system. This means that supranational and national levels are intrinsically linked. The EU multilevel governance system is a myriad of intertwined downloading and uploading processes that have become systemic over time. The formal and informal habituation of patterns of behaviour in institutions, public policy and decision-making process have led to vertical and horizontal Europeanisation of national politics. Simultaneously, political actors at national, regional, transnational and transregional levels (e.g., actors related to cross-border cooperation) try to 'upload' preferences and instigate a public debate about new public policies. This can be characterised as a bottom-up 'domestication of European politics'. As Johan P. Olsen asserts, analytically it is possible to differentiate between the two processes, but in practice it is quite complex and difficult to establish which is the more dominant process. Probably, both processes are equally important in the overall progression towards European integration. The consequence is that the two processes are interdependently linked and, probably, self-sustaining. It is important to keep in mind this dimension of comparative European politics in order to better understand today's national political systems (Olsen, 2002: 942).

A large part of decision-making is now taken in the the Council of Ministers of the European Union, where national government representatives from the EU member states decide on policies that will then have to be implemented in the respective countries. This shows that member states are still gatekeepers of most legislation coming from the European Union. This decision-making process is in the vast majority of cases consensual. Moreover, the role of national parliaments is also being redefined in the context of the evolving European integration process. All member states of the European Union stepped up their institutional structures to deal with the legislation coming from Brussels. However, as highlighted in this chapter, some parliaments are doing better than others at scrutinising EU legislation and making governments accountable. The countries doing well are the Nordic countries, Austria, Germany and the United Kingdom. The other countries are all finding it more difficult. Southern, Central and Eastern European parliaments are the weakest legislatures in terms of EU scrutiny and control of the government. The growing importance of the European Parliament in the EU decision-making process is a further factor putting pressure upon national parliaments to redefine themselves within the EU multilevel governance system.

In sum, European political systems are intrinsically linked to the European Union multilevel governance system. This creates greater complexity and also a quest for better coordination of governmental and parliamentary work at different levels. European political systems are undergoing such a transition today.

Suggested reading

Important articles and chapters

Börzel, Tanja (2005), Europeanization: How the European Union Interacts with the Member-States. In: Simon Bulmer and Christian Lequesne (eds), *The Member-States of the European Union*. Oxford: Oxford University Press, pp. 45–69.

Börzel, Tanja and Thomas Risse (2000), *When Europe Hits Home: Europeanization and Domestic Change*. European University Institute, working papers, no. 56.

Knill, Christoph and Dork Lehmkuhl (2002), The National Impact of European Union Regulatory Policy: Three Europeanization Mechanisms. *European Journal of Political Research*, 41: 255–80.

Ladrech, Robert (1994), Europeanization of Domestic Politics and Institutions: The Case of France. *Journal of Common Market Studies*, 32(1): 69–88.

Radaelli, Claudio (2003), The Europeanization of public policy. In: Kevin Featherstone and Claudio M. Radaelli (eds), *The Politics of Europeanization*. Oxford: Oxford University Press, pp. 27–56.

European Union core political system

Cini, Michele (ed.) (2007), *European Union Politics*. Oxford: Oxford University Press.

Hix, Simon (2005), *The Political System of the European Union*. Basingstoke: Palgrave.

Wallace, Helen, William Wallace and Mark A. Pollack (eds) (2005), *Policy-Making in the European Union*. Oxford: Oxford University Press.

Europeanisation of member states

Bulmer, Simon and Christian Lequesne (eds) (2005), *The Member-States of the European Union*. Oxford: Oxford University Press.

Cowles, Maria Green, James Caporaso and Thomas Risse (eds) (2001), *Transforming Europe: Europeanization and Domestic Change*. Ithaca, NY: Cornell University Press.

Featherstone, Kevin and Claudio M. Radaelli (eds) (2003), *The Politics of Europeanization*. Oxford: Oxford University Press.

Ladrech, Robert (2010), *The Europeanization of National Politics*. Basingstoke: Palgrave.

Schimmelfennig, Frank and Ulrich Sedelmeier (eds) (2005), *Europeanization of Central and Eastern Europe*. Ithaca, NY: Cornell University Press.

Schmidt, Vivien (2005), *Democracy in Europe. The EU and National Institutions*. Oxford: Oxford University Press.

National parliaments and the European Union

Holzhacker, Ronald and Erik Albaek (eds) (2007), *Democratic Governance and European Integration: Linking Societal and State Processes of Democracy*. Cheltenham: Edward Elgar.

Maurer, Andreas and Wolfgang Wessels (eds) (2001), *National Parliaments on their Ways to Europe: Losers or Latecomers?* Baden-Baden: Nomos Verlagsgesellschaft.

O'Brennan, John and Tapio Raunio (eds) (2007), *National Parliaments within the Enlarged European Union*. London: Routledge.

QUESTIONS FOR REVISION

- Define the concept of 'Europeanisation' and give examples from different European countries.
- What is the role of the Council of the European Union in the European Union political system?
- Discuss the role of national parliaments in the EU multilevel governance system.
- How much autonomy have member states in relation to the supranational institutions of the EU?
- How democratic is the European Union?

Government in multilevel Europe

- A two-headed executive: the European model
  - The head of state: moderating party politics
- The government: the centre of executive power
  - Majoritarian versus consensual patterns of government
  - The presidentialisation of the prime minister
  - Majoritarian patterns of government
  - Consensual patterns of government
  - The consolidation of government in Central and Eastern Europe: between majoritarianism and consensualism
- Conclusions: government in Europe – majoritaritarian versus consensus politics

---

SUMMARY OF CHAPTER 5

Traditionally, European politics is characterised by a two-headed executive. The head of state and the government share executive power in most European countries. However, although in most countries the role of the head of state is simply a formality, the exceptions are the semi-presidential systems in Europe, among which the French model is the most well known. In most Central and Eastern European political systems, the French model was adopted and adjusted to the needs of each country. In semi-presidential systems, the direct election of the president enhances his/her role vis-à-vis the government.

Government itself has also changed considerably in the last six decades. It is necessary to differentiate between governments with a polarising majoritarian pattern and those with a cooperating consensual one. Countries such as the UK, Greece and, increasingly, Spain and France tend to follow a polarising political dynamic, whereas countries such as Austria, the Netherlands, Switzerland and the Scandinavian countries are characterised rather by a consensual political dynamic. One of the main reasons is that, in the second group of countries, political parties are too small and so unable to achieve absolute majorities. Therefore, they have to form coalition governments and work closely with the opposition. Other European countries may have a mixture of the two patterns.

Another phenomenon is the growing presidentialisation of the office of the prime minister. The personalisation of politics has contributed to the increase in this phenomenon: for example, Silvio Berlusconi in Italy, José Maria Aznar in Spain and Tony Blair in the United Kingdom.

A two-headed executive: the European model

The head of state: moderating party politics

Apart from Switzerland and Cyprus, all the other European countries have a two-headed executive.

While the head of state (president/monarch) has merely formal functions and represents the country at international forums, the prime minister, sometimes called the president of the council of ministers, concentrates most of the executive powers of a particular country. This two-headed executive differs from the US and Latin American models, where the president is directly elected and concentrates the executive powers (Table 5.1).

The European model created the formal head of state as a moderating force of national politics. Normally, the head of state is a prestigious elderly statesmen or stateswoman who commands respect from all sectors of society. A good example in this respect was the president of Germany, Richard von Weizsäcker, between 1984 and 1994. He was perceived to be a strong moral figure by most of the population, mainly because of his critical position in relation to the political class,

Table 5.1 Political forms of democracy in Europe

	Presidential	Semi-presidential	Parliamentary	Parliamentary monarchy
Unicameral	Cyprus	Portugal Finland Bulgaria Slovakia Lithuania	Greece Latvia Estonia	Denmark Sweden Norway Luxembourg
Bicameral	US	France Austria Ireland Poland Romania Slovenia	Germany Italy Switzerland Czech Republic Malta	United Kingdom Belgium Netherlands Spain

in particular Chancellor Helmut Kohl. This outstanding president did not fit in the traditional role of a president in Germany, which was one of formal powers and low profile. Václav Havel had a similar high standing when he became president of the Czech Republic after the collapse of the authoritarian regime. His opposition to the former regime and involvement in the Charter 77 human rights movement gave him strong moral authority in the political system.

The moderating influence of the head of state goes back to the practice of the constitutional monarchies in nineteenth-century Europe, when, in some constitutions (for example, those in Portugal and Spain), the monarch would be regarded as the moderating force of the political system. Such a moderating role is more likely to be fulfilled in countries in which there is still a monarchy (for example, the Netherlands or Sweden), or a president who is elected by legislature (for example, in the Czech Republic, Hungary and Italy). In contrast, in countries where presidents are directly elected, so-called 'semi-presidential' systems, such offices can gain greater prominence and interference in national politics than is provided in the constitution. The best example of this is France, where, in spite of the fact that the president has limited powers in the constitution, in practice he/she is an important veto player in the political system. The French model of semi-presidentialism is related to France's specific national political culture, which is still shaped and framed by the French Revolution. Jack Hayward argues that, in the French case, semi-presidentialism symbolises the re-emergence of Bonapartism (Hayward, 1987: 4), however the main intention was to overcome the instability of the Fourth French Republic, which was established after 1946. In 1958, Charles de Gaulle asked constitutionalists to draft a new constitution that would ensure greater stability. As a result, the position of the president was strengthened in relation to parliament and within the executive (Knapp and Wright, 2001: 50–7). The original constitution of the Fifth Republic did not provide for the direct election of the president – this was only introduced after a revision in 1962. The first elections took place in 1965 (Elgie, 2003: 112–13). The original constitution provided for a seven-year term, which could be renewed. However, after a referendum in

2000, this term was reduced to five years, but without any limitation of terms (Knapp and Wright, 2001: 63). This is the reason why there was some speculation whether Jacques Chirac would stand for a third term between 2005 and 2007. The particular conventions of French semi-presidentialism allow the president to have strong powers in foreign policy. This is also the reason why French presidents are always present at European summits or at other international gatherings, such as the G8 or G20. The French president also has some input in domestic policy. He/she is allowed to chair and take an active part in the cabinet of ministers. However, in practice there is normally a division of labour between the two heads of the executive, with the president focusing on foreign policy and the prime minister on domestic policies and day-to-day running of the country (prime minister). Semi-presidentialism is particularly weakened when the party closest to the president has no overall absolute majority in the National Assembly, and sometimes the president may have to cooperate with an adversary party – as with Jacques Chirac and the socialist-led coalition of Lionel Jospin between 1997 and 2002. Similarly, there was a *cohabitation* between president François Mitterrand and Edouard Balladur between 1994 and 1997 (Knapp and Wright, 2001: 113–20).

Today, France still has the strongest semi-presidential model, particularly with respect to its practice. Direct election of presidents in other countries has led to semi-presidential tendencies, but in recent years scholars have been more cautious in putting those systems at the same level as the French model. Maurice Duverger was the first to coin the expression 'semi-presidentialism' (*régime semi-presidentiel*), but even his work on Western European semi-presidential systems shows that there have been major changes since 1958 (Duverger, 1970; Bahro et al., 1998). One factor to consider is that the political culture of a country may contribute to the moderation of the role of its president. This can be seen in the case of Ireland and Austria. There was an attempt by Austrian president Thomas Klestil, a former internationally recognised diplomat, to gain greater foreign powers during his term as president, but his country's conventions prevented him from doing so. Klestil was also very opposed to the highly contested coalition government between the ÖVP and the populist FPÖ in 2000, but he had to accept it after both parties signed a statement that they would endorse European integration and repudiate the Nazi regime and also that Jörg Haider would not be part of the coalition government (Welan, 2000: 26–31). In Ireland, presidents have taken the role of moral authority but have had a very low profile in national politics. They fulfil a formal role similar to those presidents in parliamentary regimes. This means that semi-presidentialism in this context is almost non-existent, owing to the fact that the Irish president only has formal powers.

In Southern Europe only Portugal has adopted the semi-presidential system. In the original constitution of 2 April 1976, the president was allocated substantial powers. The constitution itself was a product of a revolutionary process that was dominated by a military junta. The first president was General Antonio Ramalho Eanes, who clearly was sympathetic to the left and wanted to protect the achievements of the revolution. The constitution included a revolutionary council, whose main function was to oversee the democratic process and protect the revolutionary achievements. Therefore, it functioned as a constitutional court through a constitutional commission. However, after 1982 the political parties started a civilianisation process (the withdrawal of the military from political institutions that existed since the revolutionary transition of 1974–75) that led to a reduction of the powers of the president, the abolishment of the Council of the Revolution and the establishment of a constitutional court. Moreover, subsequent presidents (for example, Mário Soares (1986–95) and Anibal Cavaco Silva (president from 2006) have been civilian politicians. In Portugal, the president may become the last instance of resistance in relation to governments with strong majorities. The second term of Mário Soares (1991–96) was characterised by what was called an 'institutional guerrilla' of the president against the perceived arrogant behaviour of the absolute majority government of Anibal Cavaco Silva (Frain, 1995; Pinto and Freire, 2006).

In Finland, a semi-presidential system was introduced in 1919. During the inter-war and cold war periods it fulfilled an important function of stability. No political party was able to achieve a strong or absolute majority and therefore the parties had to form a coalition government. The closeness of the country to the former Soviet Union meant that a strong president, able to talk to the Soviet leadership, was required. The long incumbency of Urho Kekkonen (1956–82) and later Mauno Koivisto (1982–94) are symptomatic of this aspect of the Finnish political culture. Nevertheless, after 1995, a revision of the constitution led to a limitation of the term of office by any incumbent and his/her powers. These changes can be seen as part of the processes of Europeanisation that the country has been subject to since the early 1990s, especially after 1995 (see, for example, Raunio and Tiilikainen, 2003). In 2000, the four constitutional acts were integrated into one constitution, which led to the strengthening of Parliament within the parliamentarisation of the political system (Raunio and Tiilikainen, 2003: 101–2).

After 1989, many countries in Central and Eastern Europe adopted a semi-presidential system, but the standing of the president in each political system has differed considerably. As a rule of thumb, because of its stabilising moderating role, semi-presidentialism in Central and Eastern Europe has been more important than in Western Europe. The unstable period of democratic transition and consolidation allowed for a strong role for directly elected presidents. The best examples in this respect are probably Poland and Romania. In Poland, after the round table, provisional President General Wojciech Jaruzelski was replaced by the charismatic Lech Walesa, who won the elections of 1989. The small constitution of 1992 gave strong powers to the president, and with his own party in parliament, Lech Walesa attempted to further extend his powers; however, in the elections of 1995 Aleksandr Kwaniewski, the representative of the Social Democratic Alliance, became the new president. Soon after, in the constitution of 1997, the powers of the president had limitations placed on them. However, the Polish president still has a strong suspensive veto in relation to legislation, and it can only be overridden by a three-fifths majority in parliament. Normally, in the same way as the Portuguese case, the contested legislation is sent to the constitutional court for a ruling on its constitutionality (Taras, 2006: 362).

A similar process of democratic consolidation and limitation of powers took place in Romania. However, here the president may enhance their role in constitutional practice (including the dissolution of parliament if no party is able to present a viable government). Moreover, the president has powers relating to mobilisation of the armed forces. Tensions between the presidency and the government were quite frequent in the 1990s, especially under the presidency of former communist

Ion Iliescu between 1990 and 1996. Between 1996 and 2000, his successor, Emil Constantinescu, fulfilled a more traditional formal head-of-state role and kept closely to the powers assigned to him in the constitution (Gabanyi, 2002: 531–4).

In Bulgaria, Macedonia, Croatia, Slovenia and Slovakia the powers of the president are quite limited and the incumbents follow a low-profile approach to their offices. This is especially true for Croatia after the dominance of the nationalist Franjo Tudjman. He used the presidency for nation-building, leading to major controversy and to crimes against humanity in the war in Bosnia-Herzegovina. After his death, the constitution limited the powers of the president considerably; and in 2000 Croatia became a normal parliamentary democracy. In Slovenia, the directly elected president had only formal ceremonial powers. However, in 2005 considerable disagreements and conflicts began to emerge between the president and the right-centre government of Prime Minister Janez Janša. During July 2006, President Janez Drnovšek had to deal with the consequences of his office's budget being frozen by the government (one such consequence was the cancellation of his visit to Spain owing to lack of funds) (Fink-Hafner, 2007).

Similarly, the presidency in Serbia lost its importance after the collapse of the communist regime under Slobodan Milosević. Vojislav Kostunica had to deal with the Milosević legacy, particularly the constraints of the international community in relation to certain parts of the territory (for example, Kosovo). The independence of Montenegro after a successful referendum (55.6 per cent yes) and its declaration on 4 June 2006 further reduced the importance of Serbia in the Balkans. Since 2004, Boris Tadić has been a more moderate and conciliatory president than Kostunica.

What this shows is that 'semi-presidential' systems are highly dependent on the political cultures of the respective countries. This is the main reason why constitutional provisions and practices can differ so much. France, Poland, Romania and Portugal now seem to be the strongest semi-presidential systems. According to Wolfgang Merkel, it is important to create a typology of 'semi-presidential systems' according to the powers exerted by the president in each country. He differentiates between presidential–parliamentary, which is characterised by a strong president and a weak prime minister (for example, as in Russia and Ukraine), and parliamentary–presidential (found in most European countries) (Merkel, 1996: 80). I would add to Merkel's type of parliamentary–presidential the qualifications of strong, medium and weak (see Table 5.2, Box 5.1).

The presidents elected by parliament normally have fewer powers than presidents in most of the other semi-presidential systems, fulfilling more of a formal role. However, they have the very important rights to suspensive veto of legislation and the right to send such legislation to a constitutional court to rule on its constitutionality. Former President Václav Havel (1993–2003) in the Czech Republic and President Árpád Göncz (1990–2000) in Hungary have both used the suspensive veto fairly often. Whereas the suspensive veto was used in a more conciliatory form by Guntis Ulmanis (1993–99) in Latvia and Lennart Meri (1992–2001) in Estonia, particularly in relation to citizenship law (Ismayr, 2010: 24).

Although the Italian president has only formal powers, the long term of office of seven years allows him/her not only to be a strong moral authority, but also to shape national politics. The main reason for this is that post-war governments in Italy were, as a rule, very unstable. Before 1992, Italian governments lasted an

Table 5.2 Semi-presidential systems in Europe

| Presidential–parliamentary | Semi-presidential systems | | |
| | Parliamentary–presidential | | |
	Strong	Medium	Weak
Russia	France	Poland	Ireland
Ukraine		Romania	Austria
		Portugal	Iceland
		Finland	Slovenia
		Bulgaria	Slovakia
		Lithuania	Croatia
			Serbia
			Macedonia

Box 5.1 The semi-presidential government

The term 'semi-presidential government' (*régime semi-presidentiel*) was coined by the eminent French political scientist Maurice Duverger who wrote *Political Institutions and Constitutional Law* (*Institutions Politiques et Droit Constitutione*, Presses Universitaires de France, 1955/1970). It means a government that is neither clearly parliamentary nor clearly presidential. Features of a semi-presidential government are:

- direct election of the president (subsequently an alternative source of legitimacy to parliament);
- the president has considerable constitutional powers;
- the president shares power with the government;
- the government depends on parliamentary confidence, in contrast to the president who has a direct legitimacy from elections.

Duverger used this label to characterise the nature of the French political system of the Fifth Republic, which was established after 1958. It is worth noting that, long before this, Finland's political system had been semi-presidential, and that this had been the case since 1919.

Today, apart from France, semi-presidential governments can be found across Europe: Finland, Portugal, Poland, Romania, Bulgaria and Lithuania (see Bahro *et al.*, 1998).

average of only ten months, so that the president was instrumental in leading the negotiation process towards a new government (Pasquino, 1995: 162). In many cases, the president would appoint a technocratic government under a prime minister who would come from the private sector or some other Italian institution, such as the Central Bank. After 1992, the Italian governments became more stable, although in 2000 President Carlo Azeglio Ciampi had to intervene after the collapse of the centre-left coalition and appoint a technocratic government under experienced politician Giuliano D'Amato (Magone, 2003a: 75).

In Europe, there are still eight constitutional monarchies. The institutional convention for all these constitutional monarchies has led to the delegation of most governmental competences to the prime minister. In all constitutional monarchies, the monarch is a formal head of state with representative duties. In the Nordic countries, the Swedish, Danish and Norwegian monarchies have become fairly democratic. In these countries, the powers of the monarchs, and also their resources, are severely limited and are monitored by parliament. In the Netherlands, Queen Beatrix, and before her Queen Julianne, have been the formal heads of state. However, the formation of a coalition government allows the monarch to play a more active role. According to article 42, formally the king and the ministers comprise the government, but only the ministers are responsible for acts of government (article 47).

The strongest constitutional monarchy is the British one. This is largely because of the wealth and resources that Queen Elizabeth II commands. Moreover, although the royal prerogative has been delegated to the prime minister, in the UK it is still an institutional convention to consult the monarch on major issues. This practice is important, because Queen Elizabeth II is a source of political experience from which prime ministers can draw support in order to reach a decision. The relationship between Queen Elizabeth II and the various prime ministers is based very much on convention, which has itself become part of the way in which the British system operates. One important source of power for the monarchy is the House of Lords, which consists of hereditary peers and appointed life peers who form part of the modern-day nobility of the monarchy. This nobility sustains the legitimacy of the monarchy in the twenty-first century. The climax of political life in the UK is the Queen's Speech, which is read at the end of the year in the House of Lords and outlines the programme of the government of the day for the coming year. According to Dennis Kavanagh, good timing has been an essential method of survival for the British monarchy: 'The key to the monarchy's survival in Britain had been its willingness over the last three centuries to concede power in good time to head off demands for its abolition' (Kavanagh, 2001: 54).

A more modern monarchy is the Spanish one, which was reinstalled after the death of dictator Francisco Franco in 1978. King Juan Carlos became a symbol of reconciliation and unity of the new Spain. He has very formal powers, but in much the same way as the other monarchs, he has a vast political experience that is appreciated by Spain's prime ministers, including Adolfo Suarez and socialist Felipe Gonzalez. Spain remains the only monarchy that was reinstalled after a republican period (Magone, 2009a: 90–3).

In sum, the role of the head of state varies from country to country. However, in the vast majority it has purely representative functions alongside some competences in relation to the appointment of ministers or delaying legislation. Some exceptions can be found in semi-presidential systems, particularly in France, where constitutional practice and political culture allow for a stronger, more assertive role of the president.

The government: the centre of executive power

Majoritarian and consensual patterns of government

One of the best forms to categorise governments in Europe is the typology introduced by Arend Lijphart of majoritarian and consensual patterns of government. According to Lijphart, the British 'Westminster model' comes closest to the majoritarian type of government. In the UK, the prime minister holds a strong position and the government can be characterised as an 'elective dictatorship' if the prime minister is backed by a strong absolute majority, as in the heydays of Margaret Thatcher (1979–90) and Tony Blair (1997–2007). In contrast, the Dutch consociational democracy is the closest to a consensual government. Here, the prime minister is always dependent on the support of several parties. Representatives of these parties are part of a working coalition, which is based on consensus in order to keep stability in the cabinet. Lijphart defines majoritarian democracy as 'majority rule' that is responsible to a minority (Lijphart, 1984: 4–5). Such majoritarian government is elected by an electoral system that tends to create a bipolarised two-party system, such as in the UK, France, Spain or Greece. For Lijphart, such majority rule becomes less viable in plural segmented societies, such as in the Netherlands. Therefore, a different pattern of government emerges, which is characterised by consensus. Lijphart argues as follows:

> In plural societies, therefore, majority rule spells majority dictatorship and civil strife rather than democracy. What these societies need is a democratic regime that emphasises consensus instead of opposition, that includes rather than excludes, and that tries to maximise the size of the ruling majority instead of being satisfied with a bare majority: consensus democracy.
>
> (Lijphart, 1984: 21)

The importance of Lijphart's typology is that most European countries (for example, the Benelux countries, the Nordic countries, Germany and Austria) tend more towards the consensual pattern of government. However, there is also an increasing tendency towards majoritarian government, despite proportional representation systems, in France, in all Southern European countries and in many Central and Eastern European countries. Majoritarian or consensual patterns of government are not only created by electoral systems, but also by the respective political cultures. They are essentially related to the ways national political elites resolve the relationship between majority and minority, between government and opposition.

In order to achieve a better differentiation between the two patterns of government, Lijphart introduced ten elements to pinpoint the differences between them, as summarised in Table 5.3.

Table 5.3 Majoritarian versus consensus democracy

Categories	Majoritarian democracy	Consensus democracy
Executive-parties dimension		
Nature of executive power	Concentration of executive power in single party	Executive power-sharing in broad multi-party coalitions
Executive–legislative relations	Dominant executive	Balance between executive and legislative
Party system	Two-party system	Multi-party system
Electoral system	Majoritarian, disproportional electoral system	Proportional representation electoral system
System of interest intermediation	Pluralism	Neo-corporatism
Federal-unitary dimension		
Nature of territorial organisation	Unitary centralised	Federal, decentralised
Organisation of legislative power	Unicameral system	Bicameral balanced system
Constitutions	Flexible constitution, easy to amend	Rigid constitution, difficult to amend
Judicial review	Judicial review lies in parliament	Judicial review lies in constitutional court or supreme court
Central bank	Central banks that are dependent on executive	Central banks that are independent of the executive

Source: Author's own compilation based Lijphart, 1999

These ten elements are structured along two axes. One is the executive-parties dimension and the other is the territorial federal-unitary dimension. In the executive-parties dimension, five elements allow us to differentiate between the two types. While majoritarian democracies are characterised by a concentration of executive power in a single party and a strong prime minister, achieved by a majoritarian or at least a highly disproportional electoral system, consensus democracies are characterised by a power-sharing government that works consensually with the legislature and that consists of several parties without an overall majority, mainly as a result of elections based on a highly democratic proportional representation. It is important that the executive–legislative relations based on majoritarianism or consensualism are also reflected in the system of economic interest intermediation of the respective country. The UK is closest to a model of pluralism, while the Netherlands, Belgium and Austria are closer to a neo-corporatist system of interest intermediation (see Chapter 12). Similarly, the federal-unitary dimension comprises five elements. The Westminster model, at least until 1997, was characterised by a

Box 5.2 The Westminster model

The Westminster model refers to the political system of the United Kingdom. The Palace of Westminster houses the two chambers of the British parliament – the House of Commons (the lower house) and the House of Lords (the upper house). The British parliament is regarded as the mother of all modern parliaments, having a long history that reaches back to the thirteenth century. The place where parliament met was the Palace of Westminster, which was a royal residence and which later became the parliamentary building. In 1836 a major fire destroyed the Palace of Westminster and a new building was reconstructed with the famous watchtower known as Big Ben.

This long parliamentary tradition and the evolutionary development of the British political system, which is still characterised by an unwritten constitution, became an attractive model of democracy around the world. The Westminster model was exported to many Commonwealth countries including Canada and Australia, and just adjusted to meet local needs.

unicameral system (the dominance of the House of Commons) and a flexible constitution with parliamentary judicial review. However, consensus democracies are federal and decentralised, and they are characterised by a balanced bicameralism (equal power in two chambers of parliament), a rigid constitution that is difficult to amend, and judicial review allocated to a constitutional court or supreme court (see Box 5.2). Moreover, the national central bank is dependent on the executive in majoritarian democracies, but independent in consensus democracies. This typology of Lijphart is still influenced by the period before 1997, when, in the UK, the central bank was dependent on the executive. After 1997, Gordon Brown, the former chancellor and prime minister, introduced an independent statute for the central bank similar to other governments across the European Union, because of the requirements of Economic and Monetary Union. Independence of the central bank has become the rule in all European countries. In the European Union, the European Central Bank and national central banks are now independent entities that shape economic and monetary policy independently from government.

The United Kingdom is still a unitary country, but after the referenda in Scotland and Wales in autumn 1997, when devolution was introduced by New Labour, it became more regionalised and decentralised. Another feature is that most European countries, in contrast to Lijphart's typology, now have a more flexible approach to constitutional revision. This is achieved through consensual politics and cooperation between the main parties. Globalisation and European-isation are pressurising political elites in Switzerland, Belgium, the Netherlands, Romania, Bulgaria, Portugal and Finland to adjust their constitutions accordingly. As already mentioned in Chapter 1, Finland and Switzerland (in 1999 and 2000, respectively) are good examples of constitutions that had to be adjusted to take account of Europeanisation and globalisation. An important qualification for this typology is naturally the fact that most countries have both majoritarian and consensual elements in their constitutions. They may tend to one side or the other.

Pippa Norris undertook a major study to operationalise the two ideal types along two axes. Based on her results and own amendments one can categorise European democracies according to a simplified four-field table (see Table 5.4, Box 5.3). Norris clearly emphasises the impact of the electoral system as a major factor leading to consensus or majoritarian governments (Norris, 2001: 879).

Any categorisation makes it quite difficult to assess the new democracies in Central and Eastern Europe. Most of them have fragmented party systems that have only slowly been transformed into stable ones. One of the reasons for categorising most of them as majoritarian is that the cleavage between the former communists

---

Box 5.3 Majoritarian versus consensus government

Dutch-American political scientist Arend Lijphart developed a typology in order to understand government in Europe better, particularly in his own country, the Netherlands. He contrasted the British Westminster model and the Dutch model of democracy. He wrote two highly influential books – *Democracies: Patterns of Majoritarian and Consensus Government in Twenty One Countries* (Yale: Yale University Press 1984) and *Patterns of Democracy: Government Forms and Performance in Thirty-Six Countries* (Yale: Yale University Press, 1999). The main characteristics of the Westminster versus the Dutch model are summarised in Table 5.3.

Table 5.4 Majoritarian and consensus government in Europe

	Executive parties	
	Majoritarian/ majoritarian consensual	*Consensual/ consensual majoritarian*
Federal or regionalised	UK Spain Italy Poland France	Germany Austria Belgium Switzerland Czech Republic
Unitary	Ireland Malta Greece Croatia Portugal Hungary Bulgaria Romania Slovakia Slovenia	Netherlands Norway Sweden Denmark Finland Iceland

Source: Adapted and amended from Norris, 2001: 989

and the right-centre parties seems to structure most of these new democracies. In time, these countries may move towards more consensual politics.

The most stable majoritarian governments are in Western Europe. The longevity of the political systems and accumulated government traditions are an important factor in this respect. According to Jean Blondel, all countries, with the exception of Switzerland, are led by working 'cabinet governments'. The origins of such government go back to the early models set up in Britain and Sweden in the eighteenth and nineteenth centuries (Blondel, 1995: 71–2). Across Europe, there are similarities (as well as differences) in how these governments are structured and how they operate. According to Blondel, one can differentiate between three types of cabinet government: the collegial, the team, and the prime-ministerial (presidentialised).

The collegial style is where the prime minister cooperates with the ministers and formulates policy with them. This can be found in many European consensus democracies (for example, Sweden, Denmark and the Netherlands). The team style is common in the Commonwealth countries across the world, and especially in the United Kingdom, although the governments of Margaret Thatcher and Tony Blair showed strong presidentialisation traits. The prime-ministerial style has become relevant in the information age. The personalisation of politics has led to the prominence of the prime minister, who will normally have strong charismatic traits. Good examples are: in the UK, Margaret Thatcher (1979–89) and Tony Blair (1997–2007); in Spain, Felipe Gonzalez (1982–96) and José Maria Aznar (1996–2004); in Italy, Silvio Berlusconi (1994; 2001–6 and 2008–); and even in Sweden, Göran Persson (1998–2006). Normally, governments include all these styles, but can be characterised according to how strong one particular style is in relation to the others (Blondel, 1995: 276, 278).

The presidentialisation of the prime minister

One interesting aspect of European politics is that there is a tendency of both majoritarian and consensual democracies to personalise politics around the prime minister. The prime minister has to have a good relationship with the electorate. The increasing importance of electoral marketing in political campaigns has transformed the prime minister into a multifaceted politician with several skills. Additionally, the Americanisation of European politics has led to the strengthening of the importance of the political leader who is supported by political parties. This is a consequence of the growing 'cartelisation of politics' by political parties (see Chapter 10 on political parties). Normally the prime minister presides over the council of ministers, and in some countries he is called the 'president of the council of ministers', as, for example, in Spain and Italy. Indeed, political campaigns in these two countries use the word 'president' when referring to the prime minister. The charismatic Silvio Berlusconi used this analogy to the American president, in spite of the fact that Italy has a seven-year formal president who is head of state. In the United Kingdom, Tony Blair (1997–2007) used his charismatic personality to the full in order to push forward his message. Very often he was referred to in the press as 'President Blair'. Since the 1980s, similar trends could be found in Spain and in Sweden under Göran Persson, and even in consensus democracies (for example, in the Netherlands under Jan Peter Balkenende, in Belgium under

Guy Verhofstadt (1999–2008) and in Austria under Franz Vranitzky (1988–97)). One of the most successful electoral campaigners was Gerhard Schröder, who emulated the Blairite model and was able to win two elections for the Social Democratic Party (SPD) and was close to winning a third one in 2005. The role of political marketing cannot be underestimated in this respect. According to Thomas Poguntke and Paul Webb, such presidentialisation has three faces: the executive face, the party face and the electoral face:

- *executive face*: shift of intra-executive power to the benefit of the head of government;
- *party face*: shift of intra-party power to the benefit of the leader;
- *electoral face*: growing emphasis on leadership appeals in election campaigning.

The more strongly the prime minister is able to deal with these three pillars of his power, the greater the influence and power he has. According to Poguntke and Webb, prime ministers have a larger margin of autonomy towards presidentialisation in majoritarian democracies than in consensus democracies (Poguntke and Webb, 2005: 8–12) (see Box 5.4).

Majoritarian patterns of government

As already mentioned, the strongest majoritarian government is that of the United Kingdom. As a result of the simple plurality electoral system, political parties tend to receive an absolute majority in seats, in spite of a low proportional share of the votes. This naturally leads to a disproportional result, in which a government can command a strong majority. The best example is probably the strong majority of Prime Minister Tony Blair after 1997, 2001 and 2005 in the House of Commons.

Box 5.4 The presidentialisation of government

Thomas Poguntke and Paul Webb edited an important book, *The Presidentialisation of Politics: A Comparative Study of Modern Democracies* (Oxford: Oxford University Press, 2005), which described the tendency towards the centralisation of power around the prime minister. Several factors play a major role in this process, but the growing importance of the personalisation of politics around the top candidates of political parties, and ultimately the elected prime minister, is a key factor. Their definition of presidentialisation is:

[the] presidentialisation of politics can be understood as the development of

(a) increasing leadership power resources and autonomy within party and political executive respectively, and

(b) increasingly leadership-centred electoral processes.

(Poguntke and Webb, 2005: 5)

Such an absolute majority of seats strengthens the position of the prime minister, because the success in elections is linked directly to him. Charismatic leaders, such as Margaret Thatcher or Tony Blair, are nearly able to fulfil the conditions for an 'elective dictatorship'. One of the main characteristics of the British prime-ministerial government is that there is a fusion between legislative and executive powers. The government consists entirely of elected MPs and peers. According to 2004 figures, 92 MPs of the Labour parliamentary group in the House of Commons were engaged in government. In addition, there were 22 Labour peers in the House of Lords who were engaged in government. The vast majority were junior ministers who were responsible to 20 state secretaries and the prime minister, who themselves had the right to a seat in the Cabinet. The government is predominant in relation to parliament, despite occasional problems for the party in government (for example, under Prime Minister Tony Blair there were several rebellions within the parliamentary group about education and National Health Service reform bills, and under John Major in 1993 there was a rebellion against the ratification of the Maastricht Treaty).

One of the reasons why the British government still has an incomplete modernised separation of powers is that the overall political structure has evolved over centuries and is still characterised by many medieval, traditional features. One such feature was the former position of the Lord High Chancellor, responsible for the administration of the judiciary in the United Kingdom. The Lord High Chancellor had to fulfil three roles: state secretary of constitutional affairs in the Council of Ministers, the Speaker of the House of Lords, and the chief of the judiciary. Such a position was quite unheard of in the rest of Europe (Kavanagh, 2001: 344). In 2004, a major reform took place and separated the functions, although the secretary of state for justice has retained the medieval title of Lord Chancellor.

Although the prime minister is at the centre of decision-making, everything depends on how charismatic and dominant he/she is in relation to the other ministers. The cabinet principle, which binds all the ministers to decide matters collectively, is a powerful instrument that can reinforce the position of the prime minister. However, it can also undermine that position, if prominent members decide to resign. For example: Michael Heseltine resigned on 7 January 1986 because of disagreement in relation to industrial policy; Geoffrey Howe resigned on 1 November 1990 because of the rigid position of Prime Minister Margaret Thatcher against Europe; Robin Cook resigned on 17 March 2003; and Clare Short resigned on 12 May 2003 as a protest against the Iraq War (Massari, 2005: 112). The prime minister can also use a cabinet reshuffle either to renew the team or to overcome difficult crises relating to particular policy areas and ministers. Most decision-making takes place in committees attached to the prime minister's office. This means that the prime minister centralises a considerable degree of power and can reduce the time spent with the cabinet, which meets weekly on Thursdays. In her period of office, Margaret Thatcher considerably reduced the time spent in cabinet meetings. And the cabinet meetings under Tony Blair were less than an hour in duration. In comparison with the Clement Attlee government of 1945–51, which spent ninety hours per year in cabinet meetings, the Blair government spent just thirty hours per year. More recently, Prime Minister Gordon Brown is known as having a more cooperative style than Tony Blair (Massari, 2005: 122; Burch, 1988: 21).

The British prime minister also has a power of patronage. Every year he/she drafts an Honours List (scrutinised by the Queen) of people in public life who have honours conferred on them, as a result of their contribution to society. The Labour government introduced a committee to scrutinise such applications, but this led to allegations that peerages were given in return for interest-free loans to the Labour party, resulting in an investigation by the police. The 'cash for honours' scandal damaged Prime Minister Tony Blair considerably, because he was twice interviewed by the London Metropolitan police. Although such practices were common among all parties, the scandal erupted during the Labour government.

The United Kingdom comes closest to the majoritarian model as defined by Arend Lijphart. This is particularly visible in the majoritarian effects of the plurality electoral system, which has the highest levels of disproportionality when compared with other electoral systems in Europe.

Some aspects of the British tradition entered the Irish political system, however the majoritarian tendencies of the Taoiseach (chief of government) have been moderate. Even so, the Taoiseach system has been categorised as being the strongest prime-ministerial system after the British one, along with the Greek, Spanish, Portuguese and German systems (Elgie, 2000: 237). Overall, the growing importance of coalition government since 1989 has constrained the Taoiseach. According to Robert Elgie, quoting Brian Farrell, the Taoiseach tend to be either chiefs (meaning dominant) or chairmen (consensual) in their governments (Elgie, 2000: 245–6). However, it seems that a combination of the two roles and their use according to context is the best way for the Taoiseach to remain in power. Prime Minister Bertie Ahern (1997–2008) was referred to as Bertie Teflon Ahern, because of his ability to switch from one role to another according to the situation, and he was hailed for having exceptionally strong diplomatic skills as a result of the successful completion of the Intergovernmental Conference related to the Constitutional Treaty in the first half of 2004 (Giannetti, 2005: 133). The Taoiseach has an important role to play in coordinating and negotiating neo-corporatist agreements, which have become more important in Ireland in recent decades. Moreover, he/she has certain patronage rights in relation to the second chamber in the Senate, being allowed to appoint eleven members to the sixty-seat second chamber. An important constraint for the Taoiseach, probably even more powerful than the Law Lords sitting in the House of Lords in the United Kingdom, is the Supreme Court, which emulates the American model and has, in the past, led to important decisions, particularly in relation to divorce (1995), abortion (2002) and EU treaty referenda (2003). The most important decision was probably that the Taoiseach and the government should not use public funds to promote their official position. They have to use party political funding or raise private funding for this purpose. This decision, known as the McKenna decision, in 1995 was important for non-governmental campaigners (Giannetti, 2005: 146). The Taoiseach is supported by a vice-prime minister (Tanaiste) and the department of the Taoiseach, consisting of over 300 people, which includes the very important Office of the Chief Whip, the Northern Ireland Office, the Government Information Office and the Press Secretary Office (Connolly and O'Halpin, 2000: 259–61; Giannetti, 2005: 143).

In Greece and Spain prime ministers have a strong position. In Greece, the reinforced electoral system creates a bipolarised two-party system and two smaller left-wing parties. Prime ministers usually come from the two main parties – New

Democracy (Nea Dimokratia, ND) or the social democratic Panhellenic Socialist Movement (Panneliniko Sosialistiko Kinima, PASOK). They are able to rely on a strong majority in parliament (*Vouli*) which has many of the characteristics of the French National Assembly. Although cabinet meetings are held, most decision-making is taken in smaller 'mini-cabinets'(permanent committees) related to specific policy areas of the general government council (KYSIM), the foreign and defence policy council (KYSEA), the council for economic and monetary policy (ASOP) as well as the council to implement the programme of the government. This means that the cabinet principle is always undermined by these less formal settings of decision-making. During the Andreas Papandreou period (1981–89, 1993–96) and the Kostas Simitis period (1996–2004) the collegiality disappeared completely and was replaced by a presidential approach. Decision-making was done mainly by the prime minister. Kostas Karamanlis (2004–9) has reintroduced a more collegial approach, with the result that cabinets met at least once a week (Zervakis and Costeas, 2010: 834). Although the Greek prime-ministerial government is similar to the British prime-ministerial style, the prime-ministerial role in Greece is still in the making. During the Andreas Papandreou periods 1981–89 and 1993–96, clientelism, patronage and political corruption undermined the efficiency of policy-making. Europeanisation has played a major role in rationalising the Greek system, but there are still major shortcomings in the efficiency of government. The new generation of leaders, symbolised by Kostas Simitis (1996–2004) and Kostas Karamanlis (since 2004), is more strongly focused towards undertaking reforms.

Similarly, in Spain the proportional representation system reinforces the bipolarisation of the two parties. This has to do with the small size of most of the fifty-two constituencies. The system leads to a high level of disproportionality, similar to that in the French and British systems. Because of the constructive motion of censure, single-party minority governments can continue for four periods if they can count on a working majority in parliament. This means that a minority government can survive as long as the prime minister (called *El Presidente*) commands strong authority within the government. The weakest prime minister was probably Leopoldo Calvo Sotelo (February 1981 to December 1982). Since then, Prime Minister Felipe Gonzalez (1982–96) and Prime Minister José Maria Aznar (1996–2004) have commanded strong majorities, at times absolute majorities, which have reinforced their positions even more. Since 2004, José Luis Zapatero has been in charge of a minority government with parliamentary support from regionalist–nationalist parties. Like to the British system, the Spanish government is ruled by the presidential principle, the cabinet principle of collective responsibility and the ministerial principle. Although the cabinet principle of collective responsibility is important, in periods of absolute majority the presidential principle tends to gain the upper hand. There is wide autonomy for the ministries, in spite of a coordinating ministry of the presidency (*Ministerio de la presidencia*) (López Calvo, 1996: 48). Since the Al Qaeda bombings in Madrid, 11 March 2004, there has been a growing polarisation between the Spanish Socialist Workers' Party (Partido Socialista Obrero Español, PSOE) and the People's Party (Partido Popular, PP). Such a tendency towards polarisation started in the 1990s and has become more dominant in the way politics is conducted in Spain today.

As already mentioned, the French semi-presidential system leads to divided government. The prime minister is subaltern to the president, who uses his/her position in a dominant, Bonapartist way, leaving the prime minister the onerous task of coordinating all aspects of domestic and foreign policy. However, the prime minister is fairly strong in relation to parliament (Di Virgilio, 2005: 44). In the case where the prime minister is in a situation of *cohabitation* with the president, as with Edouard Balladur (1993–95) during the presidency of François Mitterrand, he/she has more autonomy. However, between 1958 and 2007 subaltern prime ministers existed for forty years out of forty-nine. This shows the weakness of the prime minister in relation to the president. There is a constant cooperation between the prime minister's office and the general secretariat of the presidency (Di Virgilio, 2005: 45) (Figure 5.1).

After 1994, the Italian government became majoritarian as a result of the new electoral system and the way pre-electoral alliances were organised. Between 1994 and 2005, the mixed system, in which 75 per cent of seats were elected by a plurality and 25 per cent by a proportional system, created a left-wing bloc called the Olive Tree coalition, led by the Party of Democratic Left, and a right-wing bloc called House of Freedoms, under the leadership of Silvio Berlusconi and his Forza Italia. This led to the emergence of a majoritarian system, in which the pro-Berlusconi camp has been successful in achieving government cohesion. In spite of differences in terms of ideology, Prime Minister Silvio Berlusconi has been reasonably successful in retaining control over the other coalition partners, the regionalist Northern League (LN) and the post-fascist National Alliance (AN). Berlusconi learned lessons from his first government in 1994, which ended at the end of the same year. In his second government, he created a more cohesive electoral alliance, which, in the end, strengthened the position of the parties of his alliance in relation to the other coalition partners. Berlusconi was the first Italian prime minister to complete the full legislature period. The new electoral system based on proportional representation will probably not change this polarisation, because pre-electoral alliances, if they win a relative majority, are entitled to receive 55 per cent of seats. This device has been important in making governments more stable. The Romano Prodi coalition government won by just a whisker in the elections of May 2006 against the Berlusconi camp, allowing Prodi to form a government. However, the cohesion of the government, which consisted of ten parties, was less than that of the former Berlusconi one, contributing to fresh instabilities. In the end, the Prodi government collapsed because of the lack of support in parliament in 2008. New elections in October 2008 led to a fresh victory for Silvio Berlusconi and his electoral coalition with the Lega Nord and National Alliance.

After the absolute majorities of Anibal Cavaco Silva between 1985 and 1995, it is probably tempting to characterise the Portuguese government as majoritarian. However, a more appropriate characterisation would be majoritarian-consensual, depending on the position of the government in relation to parliament. The proportional representation system, which favours the larger parties, the Social Democrats (PSD) and the Socialists (PS), has become more majoritarian since 1989. Smaller parties can be pivotal in creating the conditions for a coalition government. The Cavaco Silva governments were an important turning point for government stability in Portugal. Between 1976 and 1985, after democratic transition, there were nine Portuguese governments, most of which were coalition governments. None of these succeeded in completing a legislature period. Between 1976 and 1979 they lasted on average 204 days (about seven months) and between 1979 and 1985

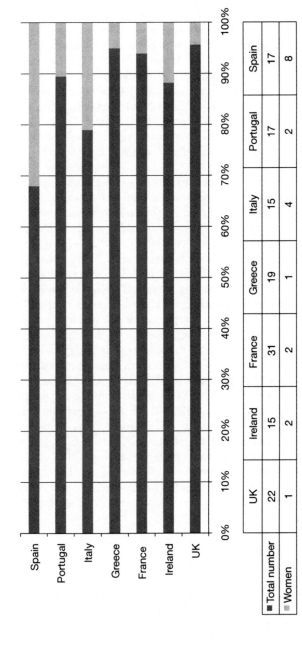

	UK	Ireland	France	Greece	Italy	Portugal	Spain
Total number	22	15	31	19	15	17	17
Women	1	2	2	1	4	2	8

Figure 5.1 Cabinet sizes in majoritarian government countries, 2005

Source: Van Biezen and Katz, 2005: 1023–4

16 months (Magone, 1997: 46). Cavaco Silva's charismatic style allowed a consolidation of government in Portugal, and this benchmark was then followed by other leaders. However, they were less charismatic and dominant than Cavaco Silva. In the same way as some other European countries, the prime minister's office has become more important and has been expanded, giving the prime minister a strong position, which, in the case of an absolute majority, can dominate parliament as well. The only veto player remains the president, who has a suspensive veto and can send legislative bills to the constitutional court. According to Marina Costa Lobo, over a period of time, the prime minister is able to gain substantial autonomy inside the respective political parties, in relation to parliament, and within the cabinet. He has become a central figure in the coordination of policy-making. The profiles of successive prime ministers such as Antonio Guterres, Manuel Durão Barroso and José Socrates, show that they are less charismatic than Cavaco Silva, but that, nonetheless, they have strong coordinating and organisational skills (Lobo, 2005: 215–38).

The Hungarian core political system has taken many devices from the German model. However, in contrast to the German system it has majoritarian effects. The prime minister's position in relation to the cabinet and parliament is stronger. Between 1990 and 2007 there were five prime ministers, which indicates that it is a reasonably stable system, certainly when compared with Poland (Müller-Rommel and Ilonski, 2001: 93–4). Since the Orbán government, the power of the prime minister's office has increased substantially. Prime Minister Ferenc Gyurcsány, of the Socialist Party, was clearly able to stay in power, even though he lied to the population about the disastrous economic situation before the elections of 2006. In 2009, Prime Minister Gyurcsány was replaced by one of his fellow ministers, Gordon Banaj, who remained in office until the end of the legislature period in 2010. This contributes to political stability in Hungary. The Hungarian government orientates itself considerably towards the German and Austrian chancellor model of government, indicating that government stability is an important factor in Hungarian politics. This is ensured by the constructive motion of censure copied from German Basic Law (Schiemann, 2004: 130). This also means that, over time, the Hungarian government has gained more resources and power in order to implement its policies. At the centre of this 'chancellorisation' is the prime minister's office, which was substantially reinforced in 1998 (Schiemann, 2004: 131, 137–9). The polarisation of government is between the coalition of the Hungarian Socialist Party (MSZP) and the Free Democrats (SzDSZ) on the one hand and the bourgeois bloc under the leadership of the Citizen's Alliance (Fidesz) and the Democratic Forum (MDF) on the other.

Consensual patterns of government

The traditional consensus democracies can be found in central Western Europe – consisting of Belgium, the Netherlands, Luxembourg, Switzerland, Austria and Germany – and the Nordic countries. The main characteristic of consensual government is coalition government alongside strong cooperation between the main parties in most areas of politics. In these countries, such coalition governments are necessary because the party systems are so fragmented that no party is able to achieve an absolute majority. The political culture established since the beginning of the twentieth century has adjusted to this fact and accommodates diversity through compromise. One of the factors that allows diversity to be expressed in elections is the proportional representation system. The Netherlands is the country with the most favourable conditions for representation, because MPs are elected in one constituency, which matches the Dutch territory and the threshold is 0.67 per cent. In some countries, for example Belgium and the Netherlands, a coalition government has become a way of life. After the electoral results, from which no party is able to win, there is a formalised process to select a new government. This ritual of coalition formation entails the use of an *informateur* (appointed by the queen in the case of the Netherlands and by the king in Belgium). The main task of the *informateur* is to find out what the different parties seek to achieve within the coalition. The process may take quite a long time. This is followed by a second phase, when a *formateur* is appointed. The *formateur* is in charge of putting the new government together and writing down an extensive coalition agreement in which all the rules of the game are set out. The whole process of *informateur* and *formateur* together may last between three and four months, depending on the difficulty of the negotiations. The four main questions that a *formateur* has to deal with are:

1   Which parties will form the new cabinet?
2   What will be the content of the new government's programme?
3   How will ministerial portfolios be distributed among governing parties? And finally
4   Who will be nominated as ministers?

(adapted from De Winter et al., 2000: 309)

In Belgium, coalition government formation is fairly complicated, because of the federalisation of the country. The doubling of political parties along francophone and Flemish lines has contributed to a change of the majorities. The decline of the Christian Democrats led to the rise of the Flemish Liberals, under Guy Verhofstadt. Federalisation has led to a considerable devolution of policies, including foreign policy, and the national government has now only a *primus inter pares* position in relation to the other subnational units, with its main function being that of coordination. This means that the coalition government requires a high level of consultation and coordination in different cabinet committees. One important protecting factor in relation to parliament is the constructive motion of censure, which makes it quite difficult for the opposition to topple the government (Fiers and Krouwel, 2005: 130). Another important aspect of Belgian politics is that it is dominated by parties. Since 1945, this 'party-ocracy' has developed a patronage system, which is still relevant across different parts of the political system. However, European integration, federalisation and new social movements asking for greater transparency are undermining its viability and financial sustainability in view of the poor financial record of the Belgian state (De Winter *et al.*, 2000: 342; De Winter *et al.*, 1996).

In the Netherlands, because of the need to accommodate the interests of the different coalition partners and factions inside the party, the position of the prime minister is formally one of *primus inter pares*. However, as in Belgium, the position

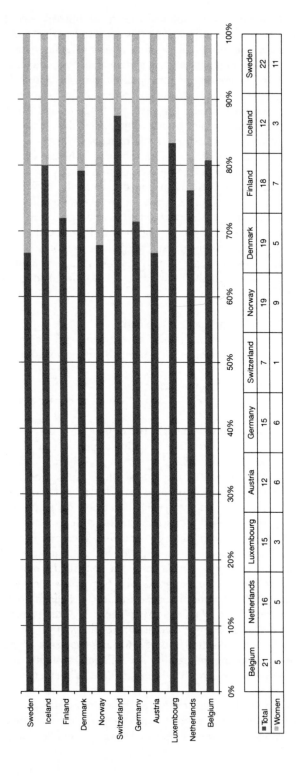

	Belgium	Netherlands	Luxembourg	Austria	Germany	Switzerland	Norway	Denmark	Finland	Iceland	Sweden
Total	21	16	15	12	15	7	19	19	18	12	22
Women	5	5	3	6	6	1	9	5	7	3	11

Figure 5.2 Cabinet sizes in consensus government countries, 2005

Source: Van Biezen and Katz, 2005: 1023–4

of the prime minister has gained a greater reputation because it is central to the cohesion of the cabinet. The importance of coordination in order to have a successful government has become crucial. There is also an increasing longevity of government. which is helping to strengthen the executive. As in Belgium, the prime minister's office has gained more resources over time. In both countries, the prime ministers are required to be actively involved in foreign relations, particularly the Belgian prime minister, because Brussels is host to so many international organisations (Fiers and Krouwel, 2005: 135–6). In the Netherlands, Prime Minister Wim Kok and Prime Minister Jan Peter Balkenende have taken a dynamic role in foreign affairs (Figure 5.2).

Informateurs and *formateurs* are used also in the Nordic countries, particularly in Finland and Denmark, while in Norway, Sweden, Germany and Austria coalition bargaining is more free-style.

Last, but not least, Luxembourg also belongs to this pattern of government. Since 1945, all governments in Luxembourg have been coalition governments and, in the same way as in Belgium, a highly sophisticated model of coalition governance has been created, which requires the coalition partners to be extremely loyal to the government. This has created a stable government in the country (Dumont and De Winter, 2000: 424–5).

Although, since 1945, the Benelux countries have almost always had coalition governments, other countries have also had periods of single-minority government. An updated version of coalition governments in Europe would largely confirm the findings of Wolfgang C. Müller and Kaare Strøm, that between 1945 and 2008, Germany, the Netherlands and Luxembourg were the countries with the longest periods of coalition governments, while Belgium, Finland, France, Italy, Austria and Denmark closely followed (Müller and Strøm, 2000: 2).

It is important to note that, over time, coalitions became more stable in all these countries. Until the 1960s, the collapse of coalitions before the end of their legislatures was quite common, however, since the 1970s, most countries have been able to achieve a more stable coalition governance. The role of extensive coalition agreements stipulating the rules of the game has been important in achieving this, but the practice of creating smaller core government cabinets has proved to be the best way to deal with conflictive issues.

In Germany, the chancellor's office plays a major role in controlling the way government runs. Several interdepartmental cabinets work together to solve most of the problems of the government. According to Thomas Saalfeld, it was common practice to reject cabinet agenda items if they were not previously agreed between the ministers (Saalfeld, 2000: 60–3). The constitutional position of the chancellor is fairly strong, leading to a position of strength in the cabinet. Moreover, the chancellor will usually also be head of the strongest party, and this strengthens the position even more. In spite of coalition governments, there are presidentialising tendencies in chancellorships that allow very stable governments to be created. However, because of the practice of consultation with interest groups and other important social and political actors, German political culture does not lead to majoritarian rule. The federal system, through the changing Bundesrat composition, is an important suspensive veto player, which contributes to a more consensual style of leadership despite of the presidentialising tendencies of the political system

(Poguntke, 2005: 65–7). Helmut Kohl (1982–98) and Gerhard Schröder (1998–2005) represent these presidentialising tendencies of the German government, but Chancellor Angela Merkel (from 2005) shows that for a grand coalition between the CDU/CSU and the SPD there is a need for a consensual approach and strong managerial and coordinating abilities. In all three cases, the complex checks and balances of the German political system act as a moderating influence with regard to any movement towards full presidentialisation and a majoritarian style of politics.

Similarly, in Austria, the chancellor democracy creates stability and most decision-making is taken outside the formal cabinet structure, which leads to an increasing lack of transparency of decision-making (Pallaver, 2005: 26; Müller, 2006b: 104–5; Müller, 2000: 104–5). In coalition governments, which have been more frequent since the long absolute majority period under Chancellor Bruno Kreisky (up to 1983), a coalition committee was an important factor in coordinating and deciding policy. Despite the existence of presidentialisation tendencies resulting from the mediatisation of politics, the Austrian chancellor's democracy is embedded in a political culture emphasising consensualism (Pallaver, 2005: 33–9). After 1983, the decline in the share of the two main political parties was a major factor leading to greater competition. In particular, the rise of new parties, such as the Greens and the transformed Freedom Party under Jörg Haider, led to greater polarisation between left and right. European integration led to a decline of the social partnership (*Sozialpartnerschaft*) of the main economic interest groups (Pelinka and Rosenberger, 2003: 64–9, 192–8). It is difficult to predict whether the split of the Freedom Party and the subsequent collapse of its vote will lead to a reduction in the polarisation between left and right. Chancellor Wolfgang Schüssel of the OVP gained a very good reputation during his term between 2000 and 2006. However, the difficulties in building a grand coalition between the SPÖ and the ÖVP following the elections of 2006 may be a sign of a re-emergence of competition and a decline in consensual politics. That said, the legislative elections of October 2008 led again to a grand coalition between the two main parties. The pragmatic approach of new Social Democratic Party leader Werner Faymann has been an important factor in restoring a consensual approach to politics. The difficult global financial crisis has been a major constraint for disagreements between the two parties.

The most stable government system is probably the Swedish one, which has a strong dominant party in the political system: the Social Democrats. Similar to other political systems, there was an increase in the presidentialisation of the prime minister during 1996 and 2006 when Göran Persson was able to rule with a large majority. His strong electoral performance led to his holding a good position in relation to both the party and parliament, which are normally major constraints for a prime minister. In spite of this, the whole political culture in Sweden remains consensual. This presidentialisation has also led to a considerable increase of resources for the prime minister since the 1970s, especially over the last fifteen years (Aylott, 2005: 179–84). The consultation of interest groups in the over-300 royal committees before policies are decided is an important feature of the system. There are lots of meetings in the main government building, which leads to the characterisation of Sweden being labelled as the 'democracy of Harpsund', after the name of the building. In this sense, the social partners are still very important, although less so than they were in the

1970s (Poli, 2005: 299–305). Coalition governments have been rare in Swedish politics and asymmetrically practised among the right-centre parties. In spite of the dominance of the Social Democrats in the political system, there has been a strong preoccupation with achieving consensually balanced cabinets, taking into account gender, age and socioeconomic interests. Since membership of the EU in 1995, it has also been important to have critical Euro-sceptic voices in the cabinet (Poli, 2005: 290).

In contrast, Norway, Denmark and Finland are more dependent on coalition governments, hence undermining the position of the prime minister.

In the case of Finland, the semi-presidential system was weakened by the revised constitution, adopted in 2000, which had the purpose of increasing the parliamentarisation of the political system. Consensualism is an important feature of the Finnish political system and consultation with civil society groups and the main economic groups is an important aspect of national politics. Similar to Belgium and the Netherlands, the council of ministers is fairly egalitarian. However, until the constitution reform, Finland had a strong semi-presidential system in which the president was the strongest actor and the government was confined to the implementation of the president's policies. Following the constitutional reform of 2000, the president's strong position was weakened and that of the government was strengthened. In spite of this, the president and the government still share power. Many of the important policies are decided in smaller, formalised committees. There are three important committees that make important policy decisions: the economic policy committee (since 1977), the financial committee (since 1917) and the foreign policy committee (since 1923). This is complemented by an informal 'evening school' (*iltakoulu*) at the prime minister's residence on the evening before the meeting of the Council of Ministers. At this evening school, government ministers and officials discuss policy and make informal decisions, which are then decided formally in the Council of Ministers (the state council) on Thursday mornings. The evening school goes back to the period 1937–39, when it was created to improve the relationship between agrarians and social democrats. It lost some of its importance in the 1990s and, more recently, such meetings have become less regular (Auffermann, 2009: 232–3; Nousiainen, 1988: 221–2). Overall, ministers have a high level of autonomy in relation to their policy area. One day later, on Fridays, the president takes part in the Council of Ministers to decide on issues that are within his competence or shared with the government.

In Denmark, there is ministerial autonomy and responsibility, and the position of the prime minister is one of a coordinator who seeks compromise and flexibility, avoiding confrontation (Pedersen and Knudsen, 2005: 160). There are six cabinet committees for specific policy areas, including economic policy and EU affairs. The role of the prime minister in monitoring the ministers has increased over time, and he/she is responsible for the good performance of ministers, being obliged to intervene if necessary. A court of impeachment was established in 1910, with power to force a prime minister to resign. The impact of Europeanisation and internationalisation has increased the responsibilities of the prime minister in foreign policy. Poul Nyrup Rasmussen (1993–2001) and Anders Føgh Rasmussen (2001–9) both increased their involvement in international affairs. Anders Føgh Rasmussen resigned from office to become the new NATO Secretary-General.

Since the 1960s, there has also been a substantial increase in the resources of the prime minister's office, which clearly led to a stronger centralisation of power in his/her hands (Pedersen and Knudsen, 2005: 163–6). Consensualism through the consultation of interest groups is similar to that in other Nordic countries.

The position of the prime minister in the Norwegian political system can be considered weak. Until the late 1980s, prime ministers tended to resign before the end of the legislation, usually because of problems with coalition partners or other ministers (Eriksen, 1988: 193). The prime minister is not hierarchically superior to the ministers, he/she only has the right of information about what is happening in other ministries. The overall pattern is one of collegiality. Although a coalition government is typically formed along the left–right spectrum, consensualism prevails in the way policy-making is undertaken. However, owing to the fragmentation of the party system, governments may be able to survive, even without a majority in parliament. The lack of an alternative majority among the opposition parties may allow for what has been labelled as 'negative parliamentarianism' (coined by Bergman, 1993; quoted from Narud and Strøm, 2000: 166–7).

In Iceland, ministerial autonomy is also one of the features of government. Individual ministers are required to take charge of several ministries, making the Icelandic government one of the smallest in Europe (Eythórsson and Jahn, 2009: 202–3).

The consolidation of government in Central and Eastern Europe: between majoritarianism and consensualism

The Portuguese case is helpful in understanding the processes towards government stability in Central and Eastern Europe. After the transition to democracy between 1974 and 1976, Portugal was characterised by weak governments, most of them coalition governments, which were not able to complete the legislature period. In the decade between 1976 and 1987, Portugal had ten governments, yet between 1987 and 1999 it had only three governments. The lesson to be learned is that *time* is needed to achieve a consolidation of political institutions, including government. Most governments were quite unstable in Central and Eastern Europe, and it is probable that, because of the instability of the party systems, Central and Eastern European governments have more difficulties with governmental consolidation than Southern European ones. Although we have categorised them as having majoritarian tendencies, one has to recognise that their political systems are still consolidating and the rules of engagement for governments are still in the making. In many ways, any categorisation is a simplification.

Today, the Polish party system is still far from being consolidated. The emergence of a right-wing majority, which included the extremist right-wing Euro-sceptic Samoobrona (Self-defense) of Andrzej Lepper, under the leadership of Lech Kaczynsky, leader of the Law and Justice Party between 2005 and 2007, shows how large is the inter-bloc volatility between left and right. After the legislative elections of 2007, Donald Tusk's Civic Platform, a liberal democratic party, led again to a change of party system configuration. In spite of this problem, since 1997 there has been increasing stability of government in Poland. In the early years, divided government led to conflicts between the president and the prime minister. Moreover, the lack of experience of coalition governance contributed to the collapse of governments up to 1997 (Taras, 2006: 364–5). According to Jean Blondel and Ferdinand Müller-Rommel, between 1991 and 1997 there were six prime ministers and seven governments, most of them coalition governments. Moreover, there was a large turnover of personnel. In an eight-year period, there were 107 ministers who had an average incumbency of 1.48 years (Blondel and Müller-Rommel, 2001: 58). There was also a tendency towards a majoritarian two-alliance system, induced by the proportional electoral system introduced in 1993. After 1997, the majoritarian system led to greater longevity of government. Between 1997 and 2007 there were four prime ministers and four governments. The cabinet has normally between seventeen and twenty-three ministers, and cabinet meetings are prepared by the secretariat of the cabinet. The chancellery can be regarded as a prime minister's office to which the economic, social and defence affairs committees are attached (Blondel and Müller-Rommel, 2001: 58–9). During the premiership of Jaroslaw Kaczynsky he was able to count on the support of his brother Lech Kaczynsky, who was president until his tragic death in a plane crash in 2010.

In contrast, Hungary and the Czech Republic were able to achieve an early consolidation of government. In Hungary, the electoral system produced a left and a right alliance that contributed to majoritarian politics. The most important exponent in this regard is probably Viktor Orbán (1998–2002), who strengthened the government by emulating the German chancellor's office (see above).

In the Czech Republic, the Václav Klaus government of the Civic Forum (ODS) was instrumental in undertaking major reforms towards the liberalisation of the political economy. The Klaus government allowed a smooth transition after the 'Velvet Divorce'; however, the economic scandals that began to emerge in 1998 led to a change of government to the Social Democrats (ČSSD). The scandals also led to the creation of a more moderate party system, with the ČSSD minority government of Miloš Zeman supported by the ODS through an agreement with the opposition that divided these two parties. In spite of the difficulties in building coalitions, Czech governments have developed important rules of engagement that allow for strong stable governments. The prime minister has a strong position in the political system. One problem that still remains in the Czech system is that two parties, the former communists (KSČM) and the radical republicans (SPR–RSČ) are still not able to take part in the political system (Vodička, 2005: 249–51; Figure 5.3).

In Slovakia, the dominance of the Movement for a Democratic Slovakia (HZDŠ) under the nationalist Vladimir Mečiar created a polarised system. The HZDŠ was supported by the nationalist SNŠ. However, the attitudes of Mečiar against the Hungarian minority and other nationalist policies led to an increasing concern in the European Union in 1997–98, which led to the end of the Mečiar government and its replacement by the moderate coalition government of Mikulas Džurinda. Džurinda formed a four-party coalition, which included the Party of the Democratic Left (SDL) and the Hungarian coalition party. The lack of clear majorities and the polarisation between nationalists and the left coalition allowed for some majoritarianism. In 2006, the populist Social Democratic Party-Direction (SMER) formed a coalition with the nationalist parties, the Slovak National Party

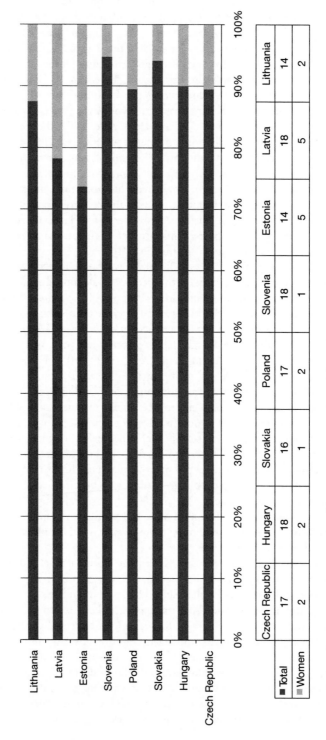

	Czech Republic	Hungary	Slovakia	Poland	Slovenia	Estonia	Latvia	Lithuania
Total	17	18	16	17	18	14	18	14
Women	2	2	1	2	1	5	5	2

Figure 5.3 Cabinet sizes in Eastern Central European countries and the Baltic countries, 2005

Source: Van Biezen and Katz, 2005: 1023–4.

(SNŠ) and the Movement for a Democratic Slovakia (HSDŽ) under Prime Minister Robert Fico. This was regarded as a negative step, moving away from democracy (*The Economist*, 12 August 2006: 33). However, the Slovak government under Prime Minister Fico has already achieved a great success by steering the country towards the adoption of the euro. One of the main reasons for this success is that all three parties have common ground in relation to economic policies (*The Economist*, 26 August 2008).

In Eastern Europe, the consolidated party systems now allow for more stable governments. In Romania, after a very unstable decade in the 1990s with high levels of turnover, governments have been more stable. The Social Democratic Party in Romania, which emerged out of the former Communist Party, formed a minority government under Adrian Nastaše between 2000 and 2004, creating conditions for stability. After 2004, a right-centre pre-electoral coalition called Democratic Alliance for Justice and Truth, which consisted of the National Liberal Party, the Democratic Party, the Humanist Party and the party representing the Hungarian minority (UDMR), won the elections, and the coalition government under Prime Minister Călin Popescu-Tăriceanu (2004–8) was able to survive the full legislative period. In Bulgaria, the coalition for Bulgaria dominated by the Social Democratic Party won the elections of 2005 and created a grand coalition with the National Movement Simeon II. The new Social Democratic prime minister, Sergej Stanishev, was able to count on the support of President Georgi Parwanov (2002–) from the same party. In these two cases, the accession to the European Union on 1 January 2007 was an important factor leading to these changes. In both cases, the semi-presidential tendency was weakened and the position of the prime minister strengthened.

The Baltic states are still characterised by a high level of government in-stability, although the longevity of governments has improved since 2000. Both in Estonia and Latvia, because no party has been able to achieve an absolute majority, coalition governments have been the rule. Problems and tensions between the coalition partners are often the main reason for the collapse of governments in the two countries. In case of Latvia, most parties in the coalition are right of centre and are defined against the huge Russian minority. On the left, there are several parties that represent the Russian minority, but they have so far been ostracised from the political system. Although Lithuania has a strong economic record with 7.5 per cent growth per year, corruption scandals related to the main parties, in particular the new populist pro-Russian Labour Party, led to the collapse of the 2004 coalition government under Algirdas Brazauskas. However, the Lithuanian government can be regarded as the most stable of all three countries.

The Balkan countries also have governments that are still consolidating. Many of them are characterised by multi-ethnic communities that are still dealing with the scars of the Balkan wars. The processes of normalisation and democratisation are advancing slowly, and the European integration process may contribute to further stabilisation of the region. Thus far, the Bosnia-Herzegovina experiment has been important in transforming the region; however, divisions still prevail and undermine a proper transition to a consociational society. In this respect, Macedonia has been more successful in changing patterns of behaviour and streng-thening the position of the Albanian minority in government.

Conclusions: government in Europe – majoritarian versus consensus politics

Government in Europe expresses itself differently in each European country. According to the typology of Arend Lijphart, it can be categorised as majoritarian and consensual government types. Majoritarian government is characterised by polarisation between two main parties, which are regularly able to achieve absolute majorities and form a single-party government, while consensual government is characterised by cooperation between political parties, because none of them are able to achieve an absolute majority and therefore have to form coalition governments. In spite of similarities, there are differences within majoritarian and consensual government countries. Classic examples of Lijphart's typology are the United Kingdom as a majoritarian example and the Netherlands as an example of consensualism. In the past four decades, there has been considerable change in all these countries, so that both majoritarian and consensual governments have introduced elements of the other. In Central and Eastern Europe, it is still too early to make an assessment about which countries are adopting a more majoritarian or consensual pattern of government.

Suggested reading

Crucial book

Lijphart, Arend (1999), *Patterns of Democracy: Government Forms and Performance in Thirty-Six Countries*. New Haven, CT: Yale University Press.

General textbooks

Blondel, Jean (1995), *Comparative Government: An Introduction*. London: Prentice Hall.

Blondel, Jean and Maurizio Cotta (eds) (2001), *The Nature of Party Government*. Basingstoke: Palgrave.

Gallagher, Michael, Michael Laver and Peter Mair (2007), *Representative Government in Modern Europe: Institutions, Politics and Governments*. Boston, MA: McGraw-Hill, chapters 3, 5 and 12.

Western Europe

Blondel, Jean and Ferdinand Müller-Rommel (eds) (1997), *Cabinets in Western Europe*. 2nd edition. Basingstoke: Palgrave.

Central and Eastern Europe

Blondel, Jean and Ferdinand Müller-Rommel (eds) (2001), *Cabinets in Eastern Europe*. Basingstoke: Palgrave.

Blondel, Jean, Ferdinand Müller-Rommel and Darina Malova (eds) (2007), *Governing New European Democracies*. Basingstoke: Palgrave.

Divided government/semi-presidential governments

Elgie, Robert (ed.) (2001), *Divided Government in Comparative Perspective*. Oxford: Oxford University Press.

Coalition governments

Müller, Wolfgang and Kaare Strøm (eds) (2001, 2003), *Coalition Governments in Western Europe*. Oxford: Oxford University Press.

Presidentialisation of government

Poguntke, Thomas and Paul Webb (eds) (2005), *The Presidentialization of Politics: A Comparative Study of Modern Democracies*. Oxford: Oxford University Press.

Delegation and accountability

Müller, Wolfgang, Kaare Strøm and Torbjörn Bergman (eds) (2003), *Delegation and Accountability in Parliamentary Democracies*. Oxford: Oxford University Press. (Rational choice approach, but very useful in terms of data richness.)

QUESTIONS FOR REVISION

- Compare the main features of majoritarian and consensus governments. Use examples of at least two different countries.
- What are the main differences between government in the United Kingdom and in Germany?
- What is understood under a 'semi-presidential' political system and how widespread is it in Europe? Discuss, using examples of at least two different countries.
- Is 'presidentialisation' of government in Europe an old or a new phenomenon? Discuss, using two different countries as examples.
- Explain the main steps in the formation of coalition government in the Netherlands and/or Belgium.

Chapter 6

The diversity of parliamentarianism in multilevel Europe

- The main functions of parliament in postmodern European
  political systems: patterns of parliamentarianism in Europe
  - Strong reactive policy-influencing legislatures: the Nordic
    countries and the Netherlands
  - Medium reactive policy-influencing legislatures: UK,
    Germany, Austria, Belgium, Ireland and Italy
  - Weak reactive policy-influencing legislatures
- New democratic parliaments in Central and Eastern Europe
  - Central and Eastern European parliaments: Hungary, the
    Czech Republic, Slovakia, Poland and Slovenia
  - The Baltic parliaments: Lithuania, Estonia and Latvia
  - Eastern European parliaments: Bulgaria and Romania
  - The parliaments in the Balkans: Croatia, Serbia, Bosnia-
    Herzegovina, Macedonia, Montenegro and Albania
- Conclusions: parliament as a moderating institution

SUMMARY OF CHAPTER 6

National parliaments are the most important democratic institution of a polity. However, each European country gives a different importance to the role of parliamentarianism in politics and society.

This chapter uses Philip Norton's typology of policy-making legislatures (USA) and policy-influencing legislatures (Europe). However, among the policy-influencing legislatures, differentiation between weak, medium and strong parliaments is needed. Weak legislatures can be found mainly in Southern, Central and Eastern Europe, whereas strong ones are located in the Nordic countries and the Netherlands. Most other legislatures, including those of the United Kingdom and Germany, are considered to be medium reactive policy-influencing ones.

The chapter also addresses the consolidation and institutionalisation of legislatures in Central and Eastern Europe. Finally, the parliaments in the Balkans are discussed at the end of the chapter.

The main functions of parliament in postmodern European political systems: patterns of parliamentarianism in Europe

Symbolically, one can characterise parliament as the centre of democracy of the modern European political system. In many countries, for example the United Kingdom and France, the government emerged as a specialised committee of parliament in the nineteenth and early twentieth centuries, becoming slowly independent from the assembly (Figure 6.1, Box 6.1).

The British case still shows this strong relationship between the government, consisting of elected MPs and members of the House of Lords, and parliament. The British system was unique, because of the strong fusion between the three powers, until the reforms introduced by the Blair government in 2004. The core of the British system is based on indivisible parliamentary sovereignty, which is also a major difference from other countries. This makes it difficult for many British citizens to accept a sharing of sovereignty with the European Union, or even with the emerging subnational parliaments in Scotland, Wales and Northern Ireland. The symbolic importance of national parliaments has been challenged by the growing dominance of the work of governments and public administrations in Europe. Moreover, globalisation, internationalisation and Europeanisation have played a major role in transposing many international legal acts into national legislation. Apart from the European Union, there are also the intergovernmental organisations, such as the Council of Europe, the Organisation for Economic Cooperation and Development and the United Nations. All the countries in Europe are under pressure to implement these international legal acts by making them national law. The international monitoring of such implementation may lead to naming and shaming or pariah status if not undertaken. The European Court of Human Rights (ECHR) in Strasbourg and the European Court of Justice (ECJ) in Luxembourg have become courts of the last instance, if all possibilities at national level have been exhausted by defendants.

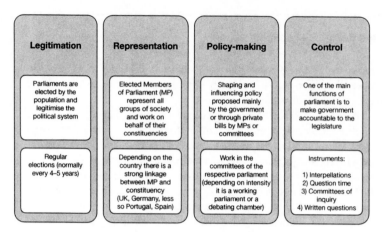

Figure 6.1 The functions of democratic parliaments

Box 6.1 The origins of European parliamentarianism

The origins of modern European parliaments go back to more oligarchical assemblies in the Middle Ages, the main function of which was to approve funding for enterprises of the monarch. Such assemblies can be traced back to the thirteenth century in England, leading up to the Magna Carta in 1215, to the early fourteenth century in France, and to the twelfth century in Spain at the regional level.

According to Samuel E. Finer, parliamentarianism as we know it today owes a great deal to the developments that took place in England in the seventeenth century, where parliament was able to push the monarchy away from its absolutist form of government and towards limited government. Although, parliamentarianism and assemblies existed in other countries during the seventeenth and eighteenth centuries (e.g., États Généraux (General Estates) in France, Cortes in Spain) it is only in England that it became part of the way of life of government and politics. In England it was an oligarchical parliamentarianism, which was steadily democratised in the nineteenth century. For Finer, parliamentarianism is a major distinctive feature in the development of European politics.[1]

1 Samuel E. Finer (1999), *The History of Government. Vol.III: Empires, Monarchies and the Modern State* (Oxford: Oxford University Press), pp. 1335–6, 1372–4.

The best characterisation for categorising parliaments is probably that developed by Philip Norton, who was inspired by M. Mezey's typology of legislatures (Mezey, 1979) (see Box 6.2). Norton developed two categories for legislatures: policy-making and policy-influencing legislatures. The former is appropriate for the US bicameral Congress because of its independence from the White House and because of the human and material resources that it commands. In contrast, the policy-influencing legislatures are all *reactive* legislatures, not active ones. All European legislatures can be characterised as policy-influencing and therefore

---

Box 6.2 Michael L. Mezey's typology of legislatures

Political scientist Michael L. Mezey developed a typology for the analysis and classification of legislatures in his book *Comparative Legislatures* (Durham, NC: Duke University Press, 1979). There are three clusters of functions: policy-making, system-maintenance and representation activities. They can be subdivided into two further sub-functions.

- **policy-making functions**: law-making (initiation and deliberation); and control (legislative oversight)
- **system-maintenance activity functions**: recruitment and socialisation of political elite; and conflict management
- **representation activity functions**: articulation (with interest groups); and intermediation (representing the constituency).

---

reactive. However, European legislatures differ in the strength with which they can influence the proposed legislatures (Norton, 1998a: 3).

Several internal and external factors help us to determine to which category a legislature belongs. Among the external factors Norton speaks of are the political culture, the constitutional constraints and the position of parliament in the political process, while among the internal factors he closely follows Nelson Polsby's institutionalisation thesis (Polsby, 1968) that emphasises the level of specialisation, the agenda control, the rules and organisation, and the resources (Norton, 1998a: 8–13; Table 6.1, Figure 6.2, Box 6.3, 6.4).

If we follow Norton's typology for policy-influencing legislatures, then we have to acknowledge that most European legislatures are weak reactive ones. The most specialised and institutionalised are in the northern countries – the Netherlands, Austria, the UK, Germany and Italy. All the countries of Southern, Central and Eastern Europe are weak reactive because of their low level of institutionalisation. Most of these countries are still taking part in a process moving towards qualitative democratisation. This process is characterised by fragmented or unstable party systems, a high level of rotation of MPs in parliament, weak committee work and organisational consolidation. Although these new democratic legislatures can learn from the institutional and behavioural experiences of the more advanced democracies in Europe, a culture of parliamentarianism takes time to set in.

Table 6.1 A typology of parliaments in Europe

Policy-influencing legislatures	Countries
Strong reactive	Sweden, Finland, Netherlands
Medium-term reactive	UK, Germany, Austria, Denmark, Norway, Italy
Weak reactive	Switzerland, Belgium, Luxembourg, France, Ireland, Portugal, Spain, Greece, Hungary, Poland, Latvia, Lithuania, Estonia, Bulgaria, Romania, Slovenia, Croatia, Macedonia, Serbia, Montenegro, Albania

Source: Author's own categorisation based on Norton (1998a)

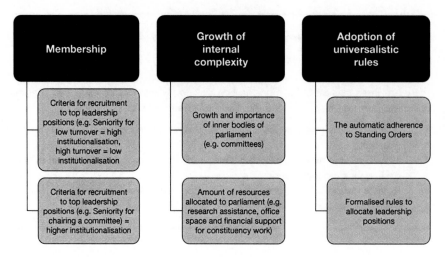

Figure 6.2 Institutionalisation indicators of legislatures, according to Nelson W. Polsby, 1968

Box 6.3 Philip Norton's typology of European legislatures

In 1998, Philip Norton edited a comparative book entitled *Parliaments and Governments in Western Europe* (London: Frank Cass). He presented there a typology of policy-making and policy-influencing legislatures. While the US legislature is characterised as policy-making because it commands so many resources and was devised as a check and balance power to the presidency, all European legislatures are characterised as reactive policy-influencing. In some cases, they are very weak, in others fairly strong.

See also Philip Norton, *Parliament in British Politics* (Basingstoke: Palgrave, 2005), Chapter 1.

Moreover, because of the low salaries and the value of the MPs' position in the political system, the professionalisation of parliamentarians may take a long time.

In a study commissioned by the Swiss Parliament, Heidi Z'Graggen and Wolf Linder identified major differences in professionalisation between European legislatures (see Table 6.2). However, none of the European legislatures has the level of professionalisation of the US Congress.

Strong reactive policy-influencing legislatures: the Nordic countries and the Netherlands

The Swedish Parliament (Rijksdag) consists of 349 MPs elected for four years by a proportional representation electoral system.

> ## Box 6.4 Nelson W. Polsby's institutionalisation process of legislatures
>
> One of the most quoted articles on parliaments is from US political scientist Nelson W. Polsby under the title 'The Institutionalization of the US House of Representatives', which was published in the prestigious *American Political Science Review* in 1968 (vol. 62, issue 1, pp. 144–68). His main focus is on how an organisation, in his case a legislature, is able to gain autonomy in the overall systemic context (political system). Such autonomy is established through a long-term internal institutionalisation process. Polsby identifies three different ways of analysing such institutionalisation:
>
> - lower turnover of membership means higher institutionalisation;
> - growth of internal organisational complexity means higher institutionalisation (e.g. differentiation of committees);
> - adoption of universalistic rules (e.g., following the Standing Orders, clear rules of selection to leadership positions).
>
> In Europe, the Nordic countries, the UK, Germany, Benelux, France and Italy are more institutionalised legislatures, while the Southern (Portugal, Spain and Greece), Central and Eastern European ones are less institutionalised, mainly because of late or interrupted development towards democracy.

Table 6.2 Professionalisation index based on the income of MPs, the costs of parliament and workload

	Professionalisation	Countries
High	At least two variables in this category	• United States of America
Between middle and high	At least one variable in this category	• UK (workload) • Italy (workload) • Canada (income)
Middle	At least two variables in this category	• Netherlands • Germany • France • Finland (workload, income) • Denmark (workload, income) • Australia (costs of parliament, income)
Between low and middle	At least one variable in this category	• New Zealand (workload) • Luxembourg (income) • Norway (income) • Belgium (income) • Austria (income)
Low	All three variables in this category	• Sweden • Portugal • Switzerland • Spain

Source: Simplified from Z'Graggen and Linder, 2004: 18

Since the constitutional reform of 1975, Sweden has moved towards a full parliamentary system. The role of the king has been substantially reduced, while that of the president of the Rijksdag has been strengthened. It is the president who appoints the prime minister, not the king. Moreover, the new government has to be approved by parliament. The king is still important as a formal head, but parliament has become the centre of political life in Sweden. The Instrument of Government, the institutional part of the Swedish constitution, states that the 'Riksdag is the foremost representative of the people. The Riksdag enacts the laws, determines state taxes and decides how state funds shall be employed. The Riksdag shall examine the government and administration of the Realm' (Chapter 1, article 4).

According to Bergman and Larue this was an adjustment of the constitution to the practice in the political system (Bergman and Larue, 2004: 232). In 1971, the second chamber of parliament was abolished and the Rijksdag became unicameral. In terms of legislation, the government proposes laws, which are checked *ex ante* on their constitutionality by the Council of State (Lagrådet); however, parliament has the right to ignore the advice. Moreover, *post facto*, if the law is against the constitution, any sector of public administration can refuse to apply the law. This enhances democracy and accountability (Bergman and Larue, 2004: 233). The committee system within the Riksdag is well institutionalised. Committees match the number of governmental ministries and play an important role of scrutiny and control. Parliament also has the right to audit the government, if necessary through committees of enquiry. Parliament has a well-resourced audit bureau (*Riksdagens Revisorer*), which is, however, not as strong as the Governmental Audit Agency (Riksrevisionsverket) (Bergman and Larue, 2004: 242).

The Danish unicameral Folketing consists of 179 MPs elected for four years by a proportional representation electoral system. It is a working parliament that concentrates most of its time in the twenty-four standing committees. Over time, the Danish MPs have been able to get better resources in order to carry out their work. Indeed, office space and research assistants are allocated to each individual MP. Although over 90 per cent of legislation approved was initiated by government, the whole approach has been one of cooperation and consensus. There are very few occasions when the government has not won a vote. While between 1982 and 1993 the government lost, on average, in 6.9 per cent of a total 2,147 votes, between 1993 and 2000 this decreased to almost zero, which is similar to the period between 1971 and 1982 (Nannestad, 2009: 84).

Between 1988 and 2005, the Folketing approved on average about 210 laws per legislature period. Although these were mainly a result of government initiatives, they were nonetheless also negotiated with the opposition in committees (Nannestad, 2009: 71). This means that consensus on legislative acts is achieved at committee level. In terms of parliamentary control, parliament can express its censure to an individual minister and press charges against him in a special court (Rigsretten). Moreover, in a similar way to other Nordic countries, it also has an office controlling budget spending (Rigsrevision) that consists of six revisers appointed by parliament (Nannestad, 2009: 73–4).

The Finnish unicameral Eduskunda consists of 200 MPs elected by proportional representation for a four-year period. In Finland, the main objective of the constitution of 2000 was to achieve a parlamentarisation of the political system.

As already mentioned, the strong position of the president in the political system during the cold war was weakened in favour of a parliamentary system. Rather like the Swedish parliament, the Finnish parliament has a sophisticated committee system that matches the governmental departments. Tapio Raunio and Teja Tiilikainen characterise it as a *working* parliament in contrast to a *debating* parliament, as most of the work takes place in the committees. The number of committees may vary according to the number of government departments, but there are certain committees that are constitutionally enshrined. The Grand Committee (Suuri valiokunta) comprises twenty-five members and is probably the most important parliamentary committee, as it deals with EU legislation (it has similar powers to the Swedish Committee of European Affairs). The Committee of Foreign Affairs and the Finance Committee, two very important departments within the government, are further committees recognised by the constitution. Normally committees have at least eleven members. The fragmentation of the party system contributed to the institutionalisation of a consensual style of politics in parliament, because no party is able alone to achieve a working majority (Raunio and Tiilikainen, 2003: 76–7).

The Norwegian Storting can be considered as one of the oldest parliamentary assemblies of Europe. It was established by the constitution of 1814, and was fully democratised after 1884. In principle, it is a two-chamber parliament, consisting of an upper house called Lagting, to which one-quarter of the 169 MPs belong, and Odelsting, which the vast majority of the MPs are part of. In reality, the Storting acts as one chamber – only 20 per cent of business is dealt with through the two-chamber system, while 80 per cent is dealt with by the whole chamber (Gross and Rothholz, 2009: 155). Two of the main reasons for establishing a two-chamber system was to create a proper impeachment procedure and a thorough legislative process scrutinised by both houses (Narud, 2003: 301). The Storting is elected for a four-year period and there is no possibility of having early elections; this diverges completely from the practice in other European countries. In this sense, the Norwegian Storting is not a debating parliament, but rather a working parliament, like the other Nordic ones. Central to the whole parliament are the standing committees, which match the departments of government, although a major reform in 1993 has made the system more flexible by distributing and coordinating the work between the committees more evenly (Narud, 2003: 301). Although Norway can be considered a consensus democracy, it seems that the number of conflicts over legislation has been increasing since 1973. In spite of that, most legislation is agreed consensually and by very disciplined parliamentary groups (Gross and Rothholz, 2009: 159).

The Icelandic Parliament (Althingi) is considered to be the oldest parliament of the world. Today's Althingi follows the Nordic model by investing a lot in committee work. It consists of sixty-three MPs elected for four years by a proportional representation system. There is a consensual approach to the legislative process. Parliamentary groups have a strong position in relation to the main political party (Eythórsson and Jahn, 2009: 199).

In all Nordic countries, MPs are appointed to undertake an audit of the budget and its components (so called *rijksrevision*) and also supervise the Ombudsman, who deals with administrative complaints of the population.

The place of the bicameral Dutch parliament in the political system is very important. It consists of a lower house, called the Second Chamber (Tweede Kamer), which consists of 150 MPs elected by a generous proportional representation system for four years, and an upper house, the First Chamber or Senate (Eerste Kamer), which is elected by the members of the twelve provincial assemblies after they themselves have been elected by the population.

The nature of the proportional representation electoral system, which creates a fragmented party system, compels the main parliamentary groups to work together consensually and with the government. Instead of an adversary style of politics, the Dutch parliament is an important arena where the amendments of the opposition parties to proposed government legislation are normally included. The Dutch States-General is a strong parliament, in spite of being dominated by government legislation. The strong committee system and the existing resources strengthen its position in relation to the government. Interestingly, in contrast to the British system, there is limited dualism between government and parliament, which is evident in the fact that members of the government cannot be members of parliament. According to Rudy Andeweg and Galen Irwin, the Dutch parliament has elements of both presidential and parliamentary systems. It clearly has a high level of autonomy, but the nature of coalition government in the Netherlands dilutes the presidential adversary tendencies between government and parliament (Andeweg and Irwin, 2002: 122). The government and the coalition parties in parliament are the main actors in charge of the decision-making process.

The relationship between the two chambers is important. The upper chamber, known as the First Chamber as well as, unofficially, the 'Senate', consists of the seventy-five elected members from the twelve provincial legislatures after subnational provincial elections have been conducted. In the past, elections for the provincial legislatures were staggered, however today they take place on the same day, leading then to the election of the members of the First Chamber in each individual assembly. The First Chamber has an important right of absolute veto that has been used sparingly. Although there have been proposals to reduce this absolute veto to a suspensive one, the First Chamber has been able to resist. The queen also has the right of veto, but has avoided using it and has allowed the First Chamber to fulfil this task (Andeweg and Irwin, 2002: 123).

The Dutch Tweede Kamer (lower house or Second Chamber) dominates the legislative process. It has twenty committees, which are organised to match the governmental departments. It can also use inquiry committees (eight between 1945 and 2001, the last one being on the conduct of Dutch soldiers in the Srbrenica massacre in Bosnia-Herzegovina). Furthermore, the individual MPs are considerably constrained by their respective parties. Greater autonomy is granted to policy specialists, but overall the Dutch MPs are not linked to a particular constituency. However, although the territorial linkage is weak, the functional representation of interest groups plays an important part in MPs' activities (Thomassen and Andeweg, 2004: 60–3).

In sum, although these six strongest national parliaments are considerably constrained by the activity of each government, they are nonetheless central to the political system.

Medium reactive policy-influencing legislatures: UK, Germany, Austria, Belgium, Ireland and Italy

The early development of parliamentarianism in the United Kingdom was an important factor in developing well-established procedures and practices, which led to a high level of institutionalisation. The bicameral parliament is presently in transition owing to the constitutional reform introduced by the Tony Blair government in 1997. One factor that is challenging parliamentary sovereignty in Westminster is the emergence of subnational parliamentary assemblies in Scotland, Wales and Northern Ireland. In particular, the Scottish Parliament has been gaining greater competences since its establishment in 1997, creating questions about the right of Scottish MPs to sit in the House of Commons and decide about English matters (the 'Westlothian question'). In reality, the lack of regional assemblies in England has created this unevenness of representation as well as creating some tensions between London and Edinburgh. The second factor is the constitutional reform needed to make the House of Lords a more representative chamber by making it a hybrid chamber with hereditary, life and *elected* peers. However, to date, further reform of the House of Lords has been put on hold because of the lack of consensus between the parties. Presently, there are 750 members: 630 appointed life peers, 92 hereditary peers (inclusive of the Law Lords as part of the highest Appeal Court) and 26 bishops. However, the different parties cannot agree on a final formula to reform the House of Lords. In this sense, the reform initiated in 1997 has been stagnating and remains only half completed. Moreover, in spite of the introduction of a committee to appoint life peers, based on merit and contribution to public life, the 'Cash for Honours' scandal severely damaged the government and the image of the House of Lords. All political parties, especially the party in government, were accused of using the appointment of peerages to obtain party political donations. This led to a major discussion about the reform of the present party political financing system from private donors to a more transparent public financing model. In the end, the police had to give up their investigations, because there was not sufficient proof to prosecute particular persons involved in the scandal (*The Economist*, 1 February 2007, 26 June 2007).

Although the right of suspensive veto of the House of Lords has been eroding since the beginning of the twentieth century, today it still plays an important role in deliberating on important bills of the government. In this sense, it remains a significant chamber, where party political differences can be overcome for the common good. Indeed, members of the House of Lords have a less adversarial approach in the work of the committees than the House of Commons (information provided by Philip Norton, who is a member of the House of Lords).

The centre of British parliamentarianism is the directly elected House of Commons, which consists of 646 members. The House of Commons is dominated by the government agenda, which is presented in the Queen's speech at the beginning of the one-year legislative period. Apart from very important bills, MPs usually vote completely along party lines; according to Richard Rose, MPs vote along party lines for nine out of ten bills (Rose, 2006: 102) (see Table 6.3).

The House of Commons has a very well-established committee system as a result of its long evolutionary tradition. The most important committees are the select committees, organised to match the government departments. The chairing of such

Table 6.3 The legislative output of the British Parliament, 2001–7

	2001–5			Just 2005–6 and 2006–7 legislative period		
	Total	Total receiving royal assent (absolute numbers and percentage)	Total amended in House of Lords	Total	Total receiving royal assent (absolute numbers and percentage)	Total amended in House of Lords
Bills brought from House of Commons	116	110 (94.8%)	55 (47.4%)	63	61 (38.43%)	32 (50.8%)
Government bills	90	85 (94.4%)	53 (58.9%)	56	55 (98.2%)	31 (55.4%)
Private bills	26	25 (96.2%)	2 (7.7%)	7	6 (85.7%)	1 (14.3%)
Bills introduced in House of Lords	95	42 (44.2%)	51 (53.6%)	67	28 (41.8%)	29 (43.3%)
Government bills	43	40 (93%)	34 (79%)	27	1 (3.7%)	24 (88.9%)
Private members' bills	52	2 (3.8%)	18 (34.6%)	40	27 (67.5%)	5 (12.5%)
Total	211	142 (73.2%)	106 (54.6%)	130	89 (68.5%)	61 (46.9%)

Source: House of Lords (2001–9), Public Bills Sessional Statistics, available online at: www.publications.parliament.uk/pa/ld/billstat.htm (accessed 25 January 2009)

committees is assigned to the most experienced MPs and can be a very good position to hold in terms of the career of a MP. In contrast, the standing committees, which preceded the select committees, were not well-resourced, tended to be characterised by an adversarial style (similar to the plenary sessions), and were non-specialised. The select committees, established in 1979, are clearly a considerable improvement on the standing committees, because they really challenge the government by taking evidence and, as Philip Norton asserts, 'are empowered to "send for persons, papers and records"'. According to Norton, most of the committee time is spent taking evidence from witnesses (Norton, 1998b: 32). Central to British parliamentarianism are the prime minister's questions, which before Tony Blair came to power, were scheduled for Tuesdays and Thursdays for fifteen minutes each. After Blair became prime minister, this was changed to Wednesdays, early afternoon for thirty minutes. Prime minister's question time is an important aspect of British parliamentarianism, during which the leader of the opposition is able to challenge the prime minister on major policy decisions. The style is quite adversarial. This is important, because all members of the government are also members of parliament. However, since 1945, prime ministers have been spending less and less time in parliament. As prime minister, Tony Blair's record of participation in voting sessions was one of the worst of modern prime ministers (Dorey, 2004: 111).

The bicameral German Parliament has often been characterised as a working parliament (Arbeitsparlament). A central role is assigned to the standing committees in the lower house, the Bundestag, which consist of between fifteen and forty members each according to the strength of the political parties in the legislative assembly. Most of the work is undertaken in these committees and is usually conducted consensually between government and opposition. This means that the high rate of approved legislation proposed by the government is the result of compromises and the inclusion of amendments from the opposition parties. In this sense, parliamentarianism in Germany is less adversarial, and is dominated by a consensual style of cooperation between the parties (see Table 6.4).

During the 1980s and 1990s the Greens were exceptional in being more adversarial than the established parties, but the overall legislative process continued to be framed by consensual politics. One factor that makes the German Bundestag so effective is the level of resources that it has at its disposal. According to Thomas Saalfeld, quoting Werner J. Patzelt, the number of research assistants per MP increased by a factor of 8 from 0.7 to 6.05 between 1969 and 1991. Originally most of the staff were placed in the Bundestag, but since the 1970s most of them have been placed in the constituency. Saalfeld gives a ratio of 3:2 in favour of the constituency (Saalfeld, 1998: 53). This, of course, strengthens the position of parliament in relation to the government. In spite of this strength, the constitutional framework has created a system of checks and balances in which the Bundestag is embedded. One of these is the upper house of Parliament, the Bundesrat, which consists of sixty-nine representatives, appointed by the regional governments in the Länder, following their elections. The representatives are bound by the instructions of their respective regional governments. The votes of the respective regional government cannot be divided. The majority in the Bundesrat is always changing as a result of the staggered elections in the sixteen Länder. The number of votes in the Bundesrat is related to the population in each Land.

Table 6.4 The legislative output of the German Bundestag, 1994–2005

Legislature/ Chancellor	13th Legislature 1994–98 Helmut Kohl			14th Legislature 1998–2002 Gerhard Schröder			15th Legislature 2002–5 Gerhard Schröder		
	Submitted	Approved	Percentage of submitted	Submitted	Approved	Percentage of submitted	Submitted	Approved	Percentage of submitted
Government bills	449	403	89.7	450	394	87.5	362	400	90.5
Bills from *Länder*	235			224			187		
Private bills	329	102	31	328	108	32.29	211	85	40.3
Other		25			34			16	
Total bills	1013	566	55.8	1002	559	55.8	760	400	52.6

Source: Database of the German Bundestag, available online at: www.bundestag.de (accessed on 25 January 2009)

For most important consent laws (Zustimmungsgesetze) the Bundesrat has absolute veto. This sometimes leads to conflict between government and Bundesrat. In order to overcome differences a Joint Mediation Committee (Vermittlungsausschuss) of the two houses can be appointed. Originally it was quite a small committee, but, with unification, there are currently thirty-two members. Therefore, before being discussed in the Joint Mediation Committee, there is a small round of negotiations. Until 1972, 100 per cent of all such vetos were overcome in the Joint Mediation Committee and between 1972 and 1990 over 90 per cent of such conflicts were overcome, however between 1990 and 1998 this figure was reduced to just 66 per cent. During the legislatures of 1998 and 2002 and 2002 and 2005, the rate of success increased to 86 and 88 per cent respectively (GESTA, 2010). Moreover, the Bundesrat has suspensive veto over simple laws, which can only be overcome by the Bundestag with an absolute majority of MPs (Rudzio, 2006: 234–5, 271–82).

A second factor that constrains the powers of the Bundestag is the fact that Germany is a federal state. Most of the competences are devolved to the *Länder*, so that the Bundestag has only limited oversight over implementation of legislation. The main task of the Bundestag is to make sure that the framework laws at federal level are well drafted in order to create equality over the territory. In this sense, detailed negotiation of legislation is an important factor in the committees. This 'cooperative federalism' (*Politikverflechtung*) is strengthened by the watchful eye of the Bundesrat.

Last, but not least, the strong position of the chancellor in the political system compels the German Parliament to cooperate and negotiate with the government in order to achieve a broader majority for the bill. The experience of the Weimar Republic, where seventeen cabinets each lasted on average 287 days (less than a year) and which for 58 per cent of this period had no majority, contrasts heavily with the stable majority-seeking system of the present German system. The constructive motion of censure is an important instrument in preventing an early downfall of a government. This means that the opposition has to present an alternative candidate for the position of chancellor and eventually an alternative programme before it can submit a constructive motion of censure. This is an understandably difficult task, because such attempts may fail and considerably damage the main leader of the opposition (Rudzio, 2006: 216–17).

The German Bundestag also has many instruments to oversee the work of the government. Among the most important instruments are the forms of interpellation (for example, the *Grosse Anfragen* ('Big Question')) and, since 1965, the *Aktuelle Stunden*, which comprises short one-hour debates on current issues. The use of this latter instrument has increased considerably and it is widely used as a weapon of control by the opposition parties (Saalfeld, 1998: 65).

There are strong similarities between the German and Austrian Parliaments, as both have a chancellor democracy and are federal states. However, the German Parliament is probably better resourced than the Austrian one. In a study by the Austrian Parliament in 2000, it was established that the Austrian Parliament receives just 0.12 per cent of the budget and in 2005 this declined to 0.10 per cent (Schefbeck, 2006: 150). This means that, in terms of financial resources, it is at the lowest level among Western European parliaments. This also leads to joint administration of both the lower house, Nationalrat (National Council), and the upper house, Bundesrat (Federal Council). In spite of this fact, the Nationalrat, has been able to gain more human and financial resources since 1992. In a similar way to Germany, most of the work is done in the standing committees (*ständige Auschüsse*) and there is a culture of consensualism allowing the opposition to make amendments to the bill. The vast majority of the legislation is proposed by the government. About 60–70 per cent of bills are from the government, while only 20–30 per cent are from the opposition (Schefbeck, 2006: 152). The upper house, the Bundesrat, has a suspensive veto only. In the case of Austria, the Bundesrat consists of appointed representatives of the regional parliaments, the *Landtage*, and not the regional governments as in Germany. However, both the annual rotation of the presidency among the Bundesländer and the changing composition of the assembly resulting from the staggered elections bear strong similarities to the German system. The use of written questions (*schriftliche Anfragen*) is the most common instrument used by the opposition parties to control the government. This is complemented by oral question time, which is highly regulated and formalised. Moreover, there has also been a growing quantity of urgent questions through *aktuelle Stunden* (topical question time) and *dringlichen Anfragen* (urgent questions) (Schefbeck, 2006: 158–60).

The lack of absolute majorities by one party since 1979 has contributed to a strong connection between government and parliament. The need to keep a broad absolute majority through a coalition of parties leads to a culture of compromise and consensus.

Until the collapse of the First Republic in Italy, which resulted from the exposure of the web of systemic corruption created by the Christian Democracy Party (Democrazia Cristiana, DC) over a forty-year period, the balanced bicameral Italian parliament was central to the political system. One of the main reasons was the instability of government. The lack of absolute majorities by a single party strengthened the positions, as individuals, of MPs of any party. Maurizio Cotta called it the 'centrality of parliament', because of this dependency of government on the majority in parliament (Cotta, 1994). The collapse of the large part of the 'political class' and the respective government parties – the Christian Democracy Party, the Socialist Party (Partito Socialista Italiano, PSI) and other smaller parties – after the Tangentopoli affair in 1992 led to the establishment of the Second Republic based on a new electoral system, which reinforced the majoritarian tendencies (75 per cent of seats elected by a plurality system, 25 per cent by a proportional representation list system), and a new party system. Since 1994, Italians have experienced the reconstruction of parliamentarianism, moving towards the Westminster model largely successfully. The bipolarisation of the political system was pushed very much by Silvio Berlusconi through the foundation of his 'firm-party' Forza Italia. However, the stabilisation of the pre-electoral coalitions came about only after the victory of the House of Freedoms (Casa delle Libertá) under Silvio Berlusconi in 2001. The collapse of the former political elite led to a major reshuffle of the MPs, resulting in the vast majority of MPs having no real experience. In 1994, 70 per cent of members were elected for the first time, with only a small minority having had experience in the 'First' Republic (Verzichelli, 1995: 118).

However, by 2001, 70–80 per cent of MPs had had previous experience in parliament, showing a low level of rotation and and high degree of professionalisation. Additionally, the number of senior members of the Chamber of Deputies had increased to 30 per cent. Moreover, the number of MPs renewed in the same committees reached 67 per cent in 2001 (Verzichelli, 2004: 143–5). This means that, in a very short period of time, parliament regained its position in the political system.

Since the Tangentopoli scandal of 1992, there has been a rationalisation of the work done in committees, particularly related to the clientelistic use of 'small laws' (*leggine*). There has also been a shift of final decision-making from the committees to the plenary in order to avoid such proliferation of laws. The scrutiny of government decrees and legislation has become more important than the approval of micro-sectional legislation (Della Sala, 1998: 87–8).

Moreover, the role of parliament as a supervisory and controlling institution of the executive has become more important in the Second Republic. The majoritarian style of politics is certainly a factor that has led to a more active role of the opposition parties. There is also a general concern that successive Italian governments have tended to use government decrees to bring through legislation, and Luigi Gianniti and Nicola Lupo have criticised this chaotic approach to legislation. The alternative suggested is the 'British model' in which, through a similar device to the Queen's Speech, the government sets out the priorities of legislation and allows parliament to organise itself accordingly. A more formalised and rationalised approach to the role of government in parliament is regarded as a solution to overcome the poor quality and inflationary nature of Italian legislation (Gianniti and Lupo, 2004: 237–44).

Weak reactive policy-influencing legislatures

In contrast to strong and medium policy-influencing legislatures, weak legislatures have greater difficulty in making government accountable to parliament. Apart from the limited availability of resources, the overall structure of parliament is only partly fit for purpose.

The French unbalanced bicameral parliament, consisting of the National Assembly (Assemblée Nationale) and the Senate (Sénat), was considerably weakened after the introduction of the constitution of the Fifth Republic in 1958. It was one of the main objectives of Charles de Gaulle to weaken the position of parliament in relation to the executive. This meant that the scrutiny of legislation was dominated by the executive (see Table 6.5).

Table 6.5 The legislative output of the French Parliament in the Twelfth Legislature, 2002–7

	Submitted	Adopted	Percentage of approved
Government bills	811	411	30.26 (with bills in transition)
Government bills in transition	547		50.7 (without bills in transition)
Government bills in total	1,358		
New private bills	1,586	60	1.05 (with bills in transition)
Private bills in transition	4,091		3.8 (without bills in transition)
Private bills in total	5,677		

Source: Annual reports of activities of the Assemblée Nationale, available online at www.assemblée-nationale.fr (accessed on 25 January 2009)

One major problem is the lack of a strong committee system. There are only eight standing committees, which are normally too large to be effective. Such committees are overcrowded, with over eighty MPs each (12th legislature period 2007 onwards) – almost small parliaments (Assemblée Nationale, 2002–7). The annual legislative period is also quite restricted (170 days, article 28), creating problems in dealing with the ever-growing legislative work (Elgie, 2003: 164–5). A major factor that weakens parliamentarianism is that senators and MPs are allowed to accumulate mandates. Most senators are elected out of the local constituencies and therefore are important local councillors or even mayors. It means that both houses of parliament have high levels of absenteeism.

However, according to Eric Kerrouche, individual French MPs are still able play a strong role in shaping the legislative process. Both in terms of private bills and amendments MPs are active, particularly among the right-centre parties. It seems that amendments are a way of integrating most of the concerns of the opposition and the majority parties. According to Kerrouche, MPs have a better strategic chance to submit amendments at committee level than at floor level (Kerrouche, 2006: 357). Moreover, there has been a shift towards more active and conflictive behaviour since 1981. The processes of socialisation have been important in enhancing the role of parliament, in spite of the dominance of the executive (Kerrouche, 2006: 362).

The Irish unbalanced bicameral Oireach, consisting of the lower house (Daíl) and the Senate (Seanad), was structured along the lines of the Westminster model, although, as Michael Gallagher asserts, it has both features of this model and of consensus democracy. The Irish Parliament has to be considered as weak. In 1983, it tried to create more effective standing committees, emulating the British ones after 1979, but, despite several attempts, the committee system has been inadequate in making the executive accountable to parliament (Gallagher, 2010b: 217). One of the consequences is a politicisation of the other control instruments, in particular question time that takes place over one hour three times a week (Gallagher, 2010a: 219). The Senate is also weak, because the government of the day is very keen to have a majority through the eleven appointees of the government.

The federalisation of Belgium, after approval of the constitution of 1993, led to major devolution of competences to the subnational parliaments. A major reform of national parliament was undertaken, in which the Senate (Senat) was transformed into a chamber representing the interests of the subnational units. The main forum of policy-making is now the lower house, the Chamber of Deputies (Chambre de Deputés). Among the reforms was the strengthening of the position of the government in relation to parliament by introducing the constructive motion of censure. This may indeed work both ways, because it makes the opposition better able to express its discontent with government policy without calling for a resignation. The number of MPs in the two houses was substantially reduced. Moreover, MPs are not allowed to be part of the government, thus ensuring a separation of powers (de Winter, 1998: 115–18). The Belgian Parliament has been provided with increased human and material resources since the 1980s, including research assistance and office space for individual MPs (de Winter, 1998: 105–6). According to Paul Magnette, there has been a considerable quantitative use of instruments of control by the government, such as interpellations, written questions and oral questions. However, it is difficult to assess whether this has had any impact on government behaviour (Magnette, 2004: 99–103).

The Swiss Parliament is a symmetrical bicameral parliament. The lower house, the National Council (Nationalrat, Conseil Nationale, Consiglio Nazionale), consists of 200 MPs elected by proportional representation, while the upper house, the Council of States (Ständerat, Conseil d'Etats, Consiglio di Stati), consists of forty-six MPs (twelve from each of the twenty cantons and six from the half cantons) elected for four years by a simple majority system. Parliament is the centre of the Swiss political system. It elects the seven members of the government, called Federal Council (Bundesrat, Conseil Federal, Consiglio Federale). The consensual nature of decision-making is an important feature of the whole political system.

The Swiss case is probably the most difficult to categorise. Its status as a militia parliament disguises to some extent how much MPs work in the two houses. MPs are not paid a salary for their work and only receive reimbursement for expenses. This means that MPs have to have a normal job and do their parliamentary work as an additional voluntary part-time activity. There have been calls for a reform in the direction of professionalisation, but this has been so far resisted by the vast majority. This lack of professionalisation is reinforced by a low level of human and financial resources supporting the MPs, which means that MPs have no office space and do not get much support from parliament. In spite of this, they work hard in committees and in the plenary sessions. However, the growing complexity of the policy process is creating problems for MPs in keeping up with new developments. According to a study commissioned by the Swiss Parliament, only Spain is less professionalised based on income, parliamentary costs and workload (see Table 6.2).

All three Southern European parliaments in Portugal, Spain and Greece are quite weak. The increasing importance of strong minority or absolute majority governments has undermined the position of parliament even more. The Portuguese Assembly of the Republic (Assembleia da Republica), the Spanish Cortes and the Greek Vouli are regarded as parliaments in new democracies and, as such, still engaged in a process of institutionalisation and professionalisation. One characteristic of all three parliaments is the dominance of the executive in the legislative process. The role of committees, which have high levels of rotation in all three countries, can lead to some amendments from the opposition, but overall their role is quite weak. One of the major problems is that all three parliaments have limited human and material resources. These parliaments tend to be debating parliaments, rather than working parliaments.

Probably, the weakest of the three is the Greek Vouli, consisting of 300 MPs, which has large committees (inspired by the French model) and is dominated by government legislation. Normally, the respective permanent committees have only five to eight days to discuss a bill and prepare a non-binding report. Most of the work is done in the plenary session, which also works over the summer with a smaller parliament of 100 MPs. Between 90 and 95 per cent of legislation is initiated by the government and, because of the majoritarian nature of the political system, there is only minimal involvement of the opposition in the legislative process. Indeed, the low quality of legislation of the Greek parliament, resulting from the low level of scrutiny by MPs, is a major problem for the country. One growing problem is the fact that the government often reverts to passing laws by decree, which is only intended to be used in exceptional circumstances, bypassing the scrutiny of parliament. After the adoption of the revised constitution in 2001, the incompatibility of the position of MP with other activities was enshrined in the constitution. As a trade-off, MPs were allocated increased resources in terms of living expenses benefits, increase of salary, office space and research assistants. Each MP has, on average, five assistants (three civil servants, one of whom will be an academic, a personal assistant and a security officer) (Zervakis and Auernheimer, 2009: 826, 837). This has also meant the end of what has been called 'part-time parliamentarianism'. However, it will take some time to change a culture that has existed since 1952 (Zervakis, 2002: 694–5). In a similar way to the United Kingdom, the government is selected from the elected MPs. Governments in Greece are large (48–50 members), with ministers and junior ministers, meaning that all MPs belonging to the dominant party have a good chance of being part of the cabinet. This strengthens the political patronage opportunities for the government (Foundethakis, 2003: 97–9).

The Spanish Parliament is characterised by an unbalanced bicameral system consisting of the lower house, the Congress of Deputies (Congreso de Deputados), and the upper house, the Senate (Senado). The former is the main policy-making forum, while the Senate can delay legislation, but not veto it. Today the Senate is stilll awaiting reform – something that Elisa Roller has called 'an impossible mission', because of the diversity of opinions on how to achieve it. The main aim is to make it more compatible with the existing state of autonomies consisting of seventeen regional governments, but the main parties and regionalist parties cannot agree on a final model (Roller, 2002). The Spanish Parliament tends to be more active and dynamic when a party does not achieve an absolute majority and needs support from some of the parliamentary parties. This was the case in 1993–96 in the final phase of the socialist government under Felipe Gonzalez, in 1996–2000 during the first term of José Maria Aznar, and in 2004–8 during the Zapatero government (Capo Giol, 2003). However, the government is protected by the constructive motion of censure, which gives a high level of stability to the political system (Magone, 2009a: 94).

The unicameral Portuguese Assembly of the Republic consists of 230 MPs and has become a more efficient legislature over time. In spite of a low level of human and financial resources, Portuguese parliamentarianism has improved its profession-alisation and institutionalisation. The decade during which Cavaco Silva dominated Portuguese politics was crucial. Although the absolute majority government used its position to bring through a reform programme, the high level of political and economic stability allowed restructuring and, as Cristina Leston-Bandeira writes, the 'maturing of parliamentarianism in Portugal' (Leston-Bandeira, 2004) One of the reasons for this is that some MPs and parliamentary staff have become more professionalised and are able to build long-term careers within parliament. Although there are reasons for optimism, the Portuguese Parliament continues to be weaker than other West European parliaments, nonetheless the institutional structuring process has created stronger committees, which are able to scrutinise the government and play a role in shaping legislation. Additionally, the use of hearings that invite members of civil society, interest groups and government members to take part has become a more frequent feature. However, there are still major problems in the use of control instruments such as questions to the government and committees of inquiry (Leston-Bandeira and Freire, 2003: 77–8).

The Maltese and Cypriot legislatures should be categorised as weak. The unicameral Maltese House of Representatives closely follows the British model.

Although the sixty-five MPs are elected by the single transferable vote, only two parties are represented in parliament: the conservative Nationalist Party and the leftist Labour Party. The Maltese Parliament is dominated by the government because, in the same way as in the Swiss Parliament, most MPs only work part time (Bestler and Waschkuhn, 2009: 875). They meet three times a week in the evening. There is a strong parliamentary group discipline in the two parties, so that normally legislation is adopted in a second reading, instead of the prescribed three readings (Waschkuhn and Bestler, 2009: 879–80).

Cyprus has two legislatures, one in the Greek Republic of Cyprus and the other in the Northern Turkish Republic of Cyprus. Internationally, only the Greek Republic of Cyprus is recognised; however, in recent years the European Union and the United Nations have tried to resolve the dispute between the two republics, which has lasted since 1974. The Greek Cypriot House of Representatives (Vouli ton Antiprosopon) consists of eighty members, of which fifty-six are Greek Cypriot representatives and twenty-four Turkish Cypriot representatives. Nevertheless, the Turkish representatives have boycotted the assembly since 1963/64. Until 1985, the Vouli was insignificant in the presidential system of Cyprus, however since then it has stepped up its engagement (Zervakis, 2002: 860). In contrast, the Northern Turkish Assembly of the Republic (Cumhuriyet Meclisi) consists of fifty Turkish Cypriot MPs elected for a five-year period. Although they are elected democratically, the electoral system is defined in favour of the ruling National Unity Party (UBP). In many ways, the Assembly of the Republic is largely a rubber-stamp assembly for policies advocated by the UBP (Zervakis, 2002: 872–3).

New democratic parliaments in Central and Eastern Europe

The new democratic parliaments in Central and Eastern Europe are characterised by different historical legacies and transitions to democracy. David Olson and Philip Norton differentiate between legislatures that followed their national traditions and even practices during the communist period and those that decided to break with the past and search for models from Western Europe. The more established legislatures decided for continuity, while those that had to establish new legislatures every time a new regime was established usually chose to create new parliaments (Olson and Norton, 1996: 4–5). It could be said that there was a stronger continuity of parliamentary practices in the Central European democracies (Hungary, the Czech Republic, Slovakia, Poland and Slovenia) than in Eastern Europe (Romania and Bulgaria) and the Balkans. The Baltic states could revert to periods of inter-war democracy, which allowed the re-establishment of some democratic continuity. Among the three countries, it was Latvia that decided to link the continuity of the new Saeima to that of the inter-war period.

In spite of historical legacies, all these new parliaments were operating during a period of political and economic instability. The process of professionalisation and institutionalisation is still continuing. In some cases, as in Eastern Europe, Moldova and the Balkans, the level of institutionalisation and professionalisation is still low: the result of both internal factors, such as a low level of human and financial resources, and external factors, such as the nature of the political parties. One of the characteristics of political parties in Central and Eastern Europe is their lack of grass roots in society. Most of these parties are 'cartel parties' meaning that they are dependent on state subsidies. The low level of electoral participation further reinforces this crisis of representation in Central and Eastern Europe (Ágh, 2006; see Chapter 6).

Central and Eastern European parliaments: Hungary, the Czech Republic, Slovakia, Poland and Slovenia

Probably the most researched parliament in Central and Eastern Europe is Hungary, which, since its inception after 1989, has been monitored by a research team led by Professor Attila Ágh from Corvinus University, Budapest. This research has led to four excellent volumes on the Hungarian Parliament covering the first legislature periods between 1990 and 1998. The Hungarian National Assembly (Országgyülés) consists of 386 MPs: 176 (45 per cent) are elected by a French-style two-ballot majority system, while the rest are elected by a proportional representation electoral system. From the very start, the National Assembly had the ambition of becoming a parliament that would represent a new democratic political culture. Therefore, it was characterised as a working parliament (*Arbeitsparlament*) in the first two legislature periods between 1990 and 1998. In this context, the German Parliament was a powerful model for the new Hungarian political elite. One characteristic of the Hungarian Parliament was that committee work was central. Moreover, each week would start with two days reserved for plenary sessions in which the opposition could challenge the government. The rest of the week would be used for committee and parliamentary group work. This was changed through parliamentary reform during the incumbency of the conservative prime minister, Viktor Orbán, from the Federation of Young Democrats (Fidesz) (1998–2002). He changed the parliamentary schedule to a three-week cycle, thereby reducing the power of the opposition in parliament: one week for parliamentary committees, one week for plenary sessions, and one week for constituency work. This led to major conflicts with the left-wing social democratic opposition (Körösényi, 2002: 317).

Table 6.6 Government, private and committee bills in the Hungarian Parliament, 1990–2006

Bills by	1990–94		1994–98		1998–2002		2002–6	
	Init.	Pass.	Init.	Pass.	Init.	Pass.	Init.	Pass.
Government	54.3	80.9	62.3	87	51.5	85.9	53.7	82
MPs	38.6	13	35.6	10.8	44.6	9.6	43.9	15.7
Committee	7.1	6.1	2.1	2.2	4	4.5	2.4	2.3
Total	788	430	755	499	858	464	968	973

Note: Init. = bill proposal, Pass. = approved bills.
Source: Author's own calculations based on data provided by Hungarian Parliament in July 2007

After 2002, parliament returned to the old weekly system (written information provided by Hungarian Parliament, July 2007). Over time there was a considerable increase of standing committees from 10 (1990) to 19 (1995) and then 25 (2002–6). In view of efficiency and making savings, after 2006 this was reduced to 18 standing committees. In the 2002–6 legislature period, only 6 MPs sat on 3 committees, 141 in 2 committees and 197 in 1 committee. Apart from the standing committees, there are also ad hoc committees that deal with specific aspects and committees of inquiry that can be established by the opposition or the government in order to investigate certain issues (Hungarian Parliament website, 2007). About 55–60 per cent of legislation is initiated by the government and 80–90 per cent of laws passed are initiated by the government. This is reinforced by a six-month legislative programme of the government, which has priority over other legislation. According to Gabriella Ilonski, the Hungarian Parliament was assessed as a working parliament, but during its third term it declined considerably in output. The government was able to dominate parliament and impose a strict legislative programme. Moreover, instruments of scrutiny and parliamentary control were not used to compensate for the loss of power (Ilonski, 2007: 53–4; Table 6.6; see also Hungarian Parliament website).

Basically, the first two parliaments were characterised by a high level of turnover. According to Gabriella Ilonski, there has been a decline in the numbers of new incumbents from the first to the third legislature (1998–2002). In the third legislature new MPs still represented 47.9 per cent of parliament (Ilonski, 2001: 223; Kukorelli, 2001: 35). However, the fourth legislature (2002–6) had only a 31.3 per cent turnover (Ilonski, 2007: 50). This has undermined the early professionalisation and institutionalisation of parliament. Moreover, the number of people with an academic education increased considerably (91.7 per cent), while the number of employees and working-class representatives was reduced to zero, and the number of women declined from 21 per cent in the communist legislature of 1985 to 7.3 per cent in 1990 (Ilonski, 2001: 220–1). Since the 2006 legislative elections, this number has risen to a modest 10.36 per cent (IPU, 2010).

Overall, the Hungarian Parliament has lost considerable power and therefore Gabriella Ilonski compares it to the same processes that happened in Southern Europe. Indeed, the Parliamentary groups are quite selective in keeping the rules of the standing orders. Party political interests may lead to exceptions, such as the number required for the formation of a political parliamentary group, which is fifteen, but has been lowered to accommodate junior coalition partners, which were not able to achieve the required number of MPs. Ilonski calls this 'formal institutionalisation' meaning that the rules are there, but political parties may choose to circumvent them (Ilonski, 2007: 56–7).

The Slovakian Parliament was designed during a period of 'revolutionary democratism' (Malová and Sivaková, 1996b: 344). Indeed, the first decade was characterised by weak governments and a weak party discipline, both of which helped parliament to establish itself. The constitution provides for parliament to be reasonably independent from government. The National Council (Narodna rada) consists of 150 MPs, who are directly elected by a proportional representation system, and has staggered thresholds for parties and coalitions of parties depending on size. Although Slovakia has a directly elected president, the constitutional framework really emphasised the centrality of parliament in the political system.

According to Darina Malová and Danica Sivacová, it has vast powers over government, including the dismissal of ministers subject to presidential approval. Moreover, government has to seek parliament's approval to deploy troops abroad (Malová and Sivacová, 1996a: 108). This became evident during the Vladimir Mečiar government of autumn 1993. Several ministers resigned, were dismissed by government or were voted down by parliament (Malová and Sivaková, 1996b: 343).

The bicameral Czech Parliament emerged after the 'Velvet Divorce'. It consists of a lower chamber called the Chamber of Deputies (Poslanecká Sněmovna), with 200 MPs elected by proportional representation, and has staggered electoral thresholds for parties and coalitions of parties depending on size. The upper chamber, the Senate, consists of eighty-one Senators elected for six years by a plurality electoral system, normally involving two rounds. Czech bicameralism is asymmetrical, meaning that the lower chamber is the dominant one, while the Senate is simply a chamber to reflect on proposed legislation. The adoption and/or change of constitutional laws need a majority of three-fifths in both houses. After two years, one-third of senators have to stand for elections. The Senate was only established in 1998, four years after the Velvet Divorce. Initially, the lower house considered that there was no need for a second chamber. Although there was some tradition of bicameralism in the inter-war period, and after 1968 in the communist period, the experiences were not very positive. Therefore, the Senate had difficulty in finding a place in the new political system (Kysela, n.d.). The lower house has the right to scrutinise and control the government. However, the Senate has the right to start impeachment procedures against the president and to evaluate his appointees to the constitutional court.

In the last two decades, the Czech Parliament has been able to evolve towards a Western model of parliamentarianism. The role of coalition government in Czech politics is crucial and negotiated bargains of coalition partners with the opposition take place in the Chamber of Deputies. Moreover, government ministers are allowed to be members of parliament simultaneously, something that encourages greater cooperation between executive and legislative. However, minority governments have considerable difficulty in imposing themselves – governments need a majority in parliament to bring through some of the legislation. The relationship

Table 6.7 The legislative output of the Czech Parliament, 1992–2004

Bills by	1992–96		1996–98		1998–2002		2002–4	
	Init.	Pass.	Init.	Pass.	Init.	Pass.	Init.	Pass.
Government (%)	58	75	22	76	70	73	63	83
MPs (%)	42	25	47	23	36	25	31	15
Senate (%)			1	1	2	2	2	1
Regions (%)					1	1	4	2
Absolute numbers of bills	436	260	221	116	785	465	438	252

Note: Init. = bill proposal, Pass. = approved bills.
Source: Simplified from Linek and Mansfeldová, 2007: 33

between the Chamber of Deputies and Senate has become settled over time. While in the early years, until 2002, the Senate was fairly confrontational towards the minority government of the Social Democratic Party (ČSSD), it then became more cooperative. In the early period it tended to seek major changes and amendments to bills that, finally, failed to achieve a majority in the Chamber of Deputies; however, it changed its pattern of behaviour by concentrating on minor changes that were more easily accepted by the Chamber of Deputies (Linek and Mansfeldová, 2007: 20–1, 34) (see Table 6.7).

In a similar way to other countries, the legislative process has been dominated by the government (see Table 6.7). Between 75 and 85 per cent approved legislation was initiated by government. The period between 1998 and 2002 led to a considerable number of laws being approved, largely because of the Czech government's need to absorb the EU *acquis communautaire* into national law. A growing institutionalisation of the Czech Parliament has taken place in the last eighteen years that can be measured by the increased number of plenary sessions, and increased complexity of its committee system (including the creation of subcommittees in order to discuss bills in more detail). In 2006, there were fourteen committees, which did not mirror the government departments, but allowed ministers to be full members because of their dual membership. Over time, the Czech Parliament has introduced the requirement for three readings in order to ensure that legislation would be properly scrutinised before being approved.

Such institutionalisation can be seen in the decreasing turnover in both chambers. At the end of 2006, new MPs with no previous experience comprised 41 per cent (Linek and Mansfeldová, 2007: 21).

The Polish Parliament is also an asymmetrical bicameral system, based on a lower house (Sejm), with 460 MPs elected by proportional representation for four years, and an upper house (Senate), with 100 MPs elected in forty pluri-nominal constituencies by single majority voting. The Sejm is the central chamber of the political system. The Senate is a revising chamber, although, during and shortly after transition, it tried to take a more important role. Such ambitions settled down over time and today, the Sejm dominates the parliamentary system and is the main chamber to which the governments are accountable. After adoption of the constitution of 1997, the powers of the president in relation to the Sejm declined. The Sejm now needs only three-fifths of the votes in order to override the presidential suspensive veto, as opposed to the two-thirds of votes required before adoption. Moreover, the president cannot use the constitutional court *before* using the veto: now he/she has to approve a bill, veto it, or send it to the constitutional court, which ruling will be binding (Sanford, 2001: 119–20).

The Polish Parliament is considered to be a working parliament, focusing most of its work on the committees. Since 1989 the number of committees has grown gradually from 23 in the transition tenth Sejm (1989–1991) to 28 since the third Sejm (2001–5). The committees match the government departments and, apart from their legislative workload, they play a major role in scrutinising the work of the government. The use of subcommittees is widespread and designed to draft pending legislative bills with more care. According to George Sanford, there were 1,217 subcommittees in the tenth Sejm, 855 in the first Sejm, 516 in the second Sejm and 3,028 in the third Sejm. Sanford compares their powers and role to the Third and Fourth French Republics or their equivalent in the United States. Indeed,

Table 6.8 The legislative bills of Sejm, 1989–2005

Bills by	10th Sejm (1989–1991) Init.	Pass.	1st Sejm 1991–93 Init.	Pass.	2nd Sejm 1993–97 Init.	Pass.	3rd Sejm 1997–2001 Init.	Pass.	4th Sejm 2001–5 Init.	Pass.	5th Sejm 2005–7 Init.	Pass.
Legislative proposals passed by Sejm (absolute numbers)	441	248	335	94	826	473	1152	753	1264	891	708	384
Approved bills (%)	56.2		28		57.3		65.4		70.5		54.2	
Change proposals of Senate (absolute numbers)	84		47		207		372		495		175	
% of all legislative proposals	19		14		25		32.3		39.2		24.7	
% of accepted proposed changes of Senate by Sejm	79.8		78.7		93.7		92.4		96.8		90.9	
% of total legislative proposals of Sejm rejected by Senate	0.6		2		1.3		No data		0.47		0.56	
% of legislative proposals rejected by Senate and accepted by Sejm	50		42.8		36.4		No data		16.6		25	
Legislative proposals of Senate in absolute numbers	27		9		19		27		26		19	
% of accepted legislative proposals of Senate by Sejm	55.6		44.4		26.3		55.6		61.5		15.8	

Source: Author's own calculations based on Sanford, 2001: 117, and Nalewajko and Wesolowski, 2007: 67–8; Ziemer and Matthes, 2010: 232. Statistics of Sejm posted on website at: www.sejm.gov.pl/archiwum (accessed 26 April 2010). Percentages are own calculations. Init.: Submitted legislative bills; Pass.: Passed legislative bills

committee chairmanship may be an important step towards a ministerial position (Sanford, 2001: 120–1; website of Sejm, 2007). However, the reality seems to tell a different story. According to Ewa Nalewajko and Wlodzimierz Wesolowski the quality of legislation has been poor, despite three readings and a considerable amount of work in the committees (Table 6.8).

One of the main reasons for this can be related to the high turnover of MPs without experience and lack of training in the legislative process. This is reinforced by the fact that first-time MPs are required to chair committees, and yet are extremely faithful to their parties, thus creating a tense adversarial culture (Nalewajko and Wesolowski, 2007: 80). Moreover, parliamentary party groups are not stable and party discipline is not strong, so MPs may defect or, more likely, create rival parties. In the fourth term, at the beginning of 2001, eight parliamentary groups and one group of non-affiliated MPs were created; by the end of the legislature, however, there were fourteen parliamentary groups and one of non-affiliated members, which had increased from seven to thirty-two members (Nalewajko and Wesolowski, 2007: 75). In this sense, the Senate was able to play an important role in scrutinising legislative bills and looking for erroneous wording and logic. It thus became an important reflective chamber for dealing with the growing adversarial culture in the Sejm (Nalewajko and Wesolowski, 2007: 80). As Table 6.8 shows, until 1997 MPs and committees were able to achieve a high level of approved legislation. Government legislation dominated, although it was counteracted by a strong input from the Sejm. This pattern changed considerably in the third and fourth Sejm, after 1997, in which government legislation dominated completely – the main reason being the huge amount of EU legislation that had to be transposed into national law.

This fragmentation has been continuous throughout the past five legislatures. Among the reasons are personal animosities between leaders and/or differences in policy. In some ways, the Polish Parliament shows similarities to certain features of Southern European parliamentarianism, which clearly was and still is dominated by personalisation of politics.

The Slovenian Parliament is also a bicameral parliament, although the second chamber is elected by different interest groups. At the centre is the lower house, the National Assembly (Državni Zbor), which consists of ninety MPs, eighty-eight of whom are directly elected by proportional representation. Two MPs are non-elected representatives of the Italian and Hungarian minorities. The upper house, the State Council (Državni Svet), consists of representatives of interest groups that are normally closely linked to the political parties. It consists of forty members – twenty-two representatives of local interests, six representatives of non-commercial activities, four representatives of employers, four representatives of employees and four representatives of farmers, crafts and trades and independent professionals. Although the design of the second chamber was influenced by the Senate of the Bavarian state (as it was until 1999), at national level within Europe only Ireland has a similar system. The Slovenian second chamber draws from the legacy of the socialist period, in which there was three-chamber parliamentarianism, and the inter-war period. The second chamber has predominantly a consultative corrective role, but it can also initiate legislation and has a right to a suspensive veto (Lukšič, 2002: 614–15).

In terms of performance, the Slovenian National Assembly has developed a functioning committee system and has an impressive legislative output for its size.

However, as in other Central and Eastern European countries, government is the dominant initiator of legislation and most of its laws are passed. In the second term (1996–2000) and third term (2000–4), 82.4 and 91.51 per cent , respectively, of total legislation passed was initiated by government (Zajc, 2007: 94). Once again the need for the transposition of EU law should be emphasised here. However, as Zajc points out, the quality of legislation has been poor at times, particularly when the government has used fast-track procedures (almost half of legislation declared urgent) to bring through many legislative bills, which were not of a high standard (Zajc, 2007: 93). Furthermore, the high level of turnover – about 50 per cent in the third term (2000–4) – prevents the professionalisation of parliament. This is reinforced by a high level of politicisation of control instruments, undermining a proper serious scrutiny (Zajc, 2007: 90, 93–4).

The Baltic parliaments: Lithuania, Estonia and Latvia

The three Baltic unicameral parliaments have also achieved stabilisation and institutionalisation; however, their different political systems have led to different dynamics in each case. According to Vello Pettai and Ulle Madise, the Estonian Riigikogu, consisting of 101 MPs, is the strongest parliament largely because of the autonomy of its MPs and the centrality of the assembly in the political system, while the Latvian Saeima, consisting of 100 MPs, is the weakest because of the dominance of the executive in the political system. This dominance exists mainly because the executive is able to pass emergency laws or important regulations through a fast-track procedure. Between these two lies the Lithuanian Seimas, consisting of 141 MPs, which is embedded in a weak semi-presidential system. The president does not interfere in domestic policies and concentrates his/her activities on foreign policy (Pettai and Madise, 2006: 291). The greater autonomy of Estonian and Lithuanian MPs is partly because of the different electoral systems. Latvia elects its MPs through a proportional representation system. However, although the Estonians also have a proportional representation system, the Estonian system allows for preference voting, leading to 'personal mandates' and 'district mandates', through which MPs can become entrepreneurial politicians in order to get re-elected. And Lithuanian MPs are elected by a mixed proportional representation and simple majority system, so that basically at least half of them have a strong mandate from their local constituencies (Pettai and Madise, 2006: 296). In spite of thresholds, all three parliaments have had to deal with the fragmentation of parliamentary groups; this was worse in Latvia and Estonia, and, in particular, the Latvian Parliament has had to deal with very weak unstable governments.

The differences between the three parliaments are also evident in the rights that MPs and committees have in each parliament. Individual MPs are fairly strong (in terms of the their power and influence in shaping legislation) in Estonia, but less so in Latvia and Lithuania. The differences are also demonstrated in the success of passed legislation. In all three countries there has been an increasing share of success of legislation passed by the government. However, Latvia has the highest share, in spite of having the weakest governments. In the seventh Saeimas (1998–2002), 77.2 per cent of legislation passed was that of the Latvian government, compared to the ninth Riigikogu (1999–2003) in Estonia and the seventh

Saeima(1998–2002) in Lithuania with 70.6 per cent and 54.5 per cent respectively. In contrast, in the same period, private members' bills by single MPs and committees account for only 22.6 per cent in Latvia, but for 29.4 per cent in Estonia if we include the parliamentary group, and 30.1 per cent in Lithuania (where only MPs have a right to initiate legislation). Of course, EU legislation has been rushed through in the cases of Latvia and Lithuania, but in the case of Estonia it seems there has been greater deliberation in parliament, particularly because of its three readings (Pettai and Madise, 2006: 305–6).

Committee work is important, yet human and financial resources are modest. In Latvia, in the ninth Saeima (which started in 2006), there are seventeen committees and several subcommittees; in Estonia, in the tenth Riigikogu (2004–8), there were eleven committees; and in Lithuania, there are fifteen committees (websites of Estonian, Latvian and Lithuanians Parliaments, 2007).

With growing rationalisation, all three parliaments are likely to move towards similar patterns shown in other European countries. There is a strong affinity with the Baltic states and the Nordic countries, so that the long-term perspective may offer the possibility of learning from the latter.

Eastern European parliaments: Bulgaria and Romania

Both Bulgaria and Romania are characterised by weaker parliamentarianism than Central European and Baltic legislatures. Apart from the fact that a historical legacy of genuine democratic parliamentarianism has been almost non-existent, both countries had difficult transitions to democracy. The inter-war period was characterised by periods of democracy and authoritarianism. Afterwards, in both cases, the communist period clearly further undermined a culture of democratic parliamentarianism. Although Bulgaria is generally at ease in relations with the former Soviet Union and today's Russia, Romania is not. Bulgaria defines itself positively as a Balkan country, while Romania wants to be part of Central Europe (Wagner, 2006: 3–4). In both cases, the executive dominates parliament far more than in the other Central and Eastern European parliaments.

The Bulgarian unicameral National Assembly (Narodno Sabranie) consists of 240 MPs, who are elected for four years by proportional representation. The Bulgarian Parliament is embedded in a semi-presidential system that has been rationalised over time, particularly since the constitutional reform of 2005. Indeed, it has a limited right of veto that can be overridden by parliament with a simple majority. During the 1990s, conflict between the presidency and parliament dominated political life to the extent that it became known as the 'war of institutions'. The polarisation between the Bulgarian Socialist Party and the conservative anti-communist Union of Democratic Forces was a major factor fuelling this conflict (Karasimeonov, 1996: 46–7). In the 1990s, parliament was quite unstable, and it is only since 1997 that parliament has begun to be able to complete the four-year legislature period. There was considerable use of the motion of censure in order to topple coalition governments; however, only the Dimitrov government of 1992 resigned after a failed motion of confidence (Riedel, 2002: 569). This was reinforced by control of the standing committees by the government, which allocated only a few to the opposition. Moreover, ministers are allowed to chair parliamentary committees; this happened in the 39th National Assembly (2001–5) in which Mehmet Dikme, minister for agriculture and forestry, and Solomon Pasi, foreign minister, from the coalition government under Simeon Saksecoburga, chaired the respective parliamentary committees (Riedel, 2002: 570).

Over time, the government has gained control over the legislative process. This became crucial after 2000, when EU legislation had to be transposed into national law within a very short period of time, which undermined the position of parliament in relation to the government. In general terms, parliament does not have the human and financial resources to undertake a critical review of EU legislation (Stoykova, 2007: 264–8).

The Romanian Parliament is characterised by a symmetrical bicameralism. The lower chamber, Chamber of Deputies (Camera Deputatilor) consists of 334 MPs, who are elected for four years by a mixed member system (but before 2008, this was by a proportional representation system). The upper chamber (Senatul) consists of 137 senators, elected directly for four years. The communist legacy is still present in many aspects of the standing order. Parliament is a hybrid between the legacy of the inter-war period and the communist regime (Crowther and Roper, 1996: 149). Like Bulgaria, parliamentarianism is embedded in a 'rationalised parliamentarianism' following the constitutional reform of 2000. The president can veto bills, but this veto can be overridden by parliament with a simple majority. Moreover, the president has the option to send a bill to the constitutional court in order to be examined on its constitutionality. As in Bulgaria, there is a tendency for successive governments to rush through legislation using emergency procedures; and this has been highlighted as putting parliamentarianism in danger by the legislative council, which oversees and examines the content of legislation. According to Ute Gabanyi, in 1999 the government was able to approve more regulations (339) than actual legislative bills (210) (Gabanyi, 2002: 542). However the quality remains low. Similarly to Bulgaria, the European integration process has further reinforced this trend towards an overwhelming dominance by the government.

The parliaments in the Balkans: Croatia, Serbia, Bosnia-Herzegovina, Macedonia, Montenegro and Albania

Parliaments in the western Balkans were and are embedded in political systems that are still dominated by high levels of political corruption, patrimonial networks between criminal organisations and political parties, and ideological polarisation between the different political parties. Croatia had to deal with the Franjo Tudjman legacy, which was characterised by a belligerent style against its neighbours and authoritarianism. Today, the Croatian Parliament (Hrvatski Sabor) is still fragmented and divided in terms of parliamentary groups. The fluid situation of party membership is a major feature that it shares with other Balkan countries. After the death of President Franjo Tudjman in March 2000, the constitution was revised from a semi-presidential to a pure parliamentary system. Moreover, it changed from a bicameral to a unicameral parliament by abolishing the upper house, the Chamber of Counties. The Croatian Parliament consists of 153 directly elected members (for four years by proportional representation). Five members are elected by ethnic minorities in Croatia. Moderate leaders, such as president Stipe

Mesić, who was elected for a second term on 16 January 2005, and a revamped Croatian Democratic Party (HDZ) have contributed to a democratisation of politics in Croatia, which is supposed to join the European Union in the near future. In spite of improvements, the selective cooperation with the International Criminal Tribunal of Former Yugoslavia (ICTY), which is biased towards indicted Serbs and less forthcoming in relation to Croats, is still a major problem (Bideleux and Jeffries, 2007b: 226–9).

Similar nationalist tendencies can also be found in Serbia. The Serbian National Assembly (Narodna skupština) consists of 250 members (directly elected for four years by proportional representation). In March 2004, the Serbian Parliament approved a financial package to support Serbians indicted by the ICTY, which included support and payment of travel costs to the ICTY in The Hague for family members (Bideleux and Jeffries, 2007b: 313). Moreover, in October 2006 the Narodna skupština unanimously voted to keep Kosovo as part of Serbia, defying the international negotiations relating to the potential independence of this region. Furthermore, Montenegrin independence was not accepted by all political parties, both the ultranationalist Serbian Radical Party (SRS) and the Serbian Socialist Party (SPS) kept away from the official ceremony in the Narodna skupština on 5 June 2006 (Bideleux and Jeffries, 2007b: 320). Since 2005, the international community has been more supportive of moderate political parties and leaders in Serbia. In June 2007 negotiations in relation to the Stability and Association Agreement were relaunched. This may help to reduce the power of the SPS and SRS. Legislative elections in May 2008 gave a strong relative majority to the pro-European party; however, both SPS and SRS are strong enough to prevent an absolute majority (*The Economist*, 15 May 2008, 18 September 2008).

In spite of major political and financial investment by the international community, Bosnia-Herzegovina still has a long way to go. Until June 2007, Bosnia-Herzegovina was an international protectorate under the United Nations. A High Commissioner was responsible for assisting with institution-building and economic reconstruction. A moderate parliamentarianism is crucial to heal the wounds of the war between 1991 and 1995. The ethnic divisions between Bosniak-Muslims, Serbs and Croats are still salient and difficult to heal and the political-institutional design tried to use the Swiss model to accommodate the different ethnic groups. The Bosnian Parliament (Parlamentarna skupština) is bicameral and MPs are elected from the three ethnic groups within the Serbian Republic (Republika Srpska) and the merged Bosnian and Croatian Federation. Each constituency also has its own parliament. The House of Representatives (Predstavnički dom/ Zastupnički dom) consists of forty-two members elected according to the ethnic groups (twenty-eight from the Bosnian-Croatian Federation and fourteen from the Serbian Republic). The speaker of the house rotates every eight months in order to accommodate the three ethnic groups. The upper house, the House of Nations (Dom Naroda), consists of fifteen appointed members, ten of them from the Bosnian-Croatian Federation and five from the Serbian Republic. The inter-ethnic party for Bosnia and Herzegovina got only eight seats in the lower house. The international community also wants the individual entities to devolve more powers to the central government. Parliamentarianism has so far been dominated by what the High Commission wants, the best example of this being the law on presidential succession, approved after long negotiations by parliament in 2000. However, the

High Commission rejected the law because of the potential for conflict between the three ethnic groups. In other cases, it would usually issue decrees in order to fill the gaps left by bills that did not achieve approval in parliament. This further undermines the confidence of MPs in Bosnia-Herzegovina (Hayden, 2005: 248–9). The role of the High Commission is reinforced by the constitutional court that includes three foreign judges and overrides any laws that may harm the balance between the three ethnic groups (Hayden, 2005: 249).

Macedonian and Montenegrin parliamentarianism show similar features to the other Balkan countries already mentioned. The Macedonian Parliament (Sobranie) is unicameral and consists of 120 MPs, who are directly elected for a four-year period. The overall performance of parliament has been poor. The standing committees are used for party political imposition of certain laws by the government. Moreover, party discipline is low, leading to regular defections or creation of new parties. The relationship between Macedonians and the Albanian minority is tense, creating major problems for the cohesion of the country (Willemsen, 2002: 742–4,749–50). The peace between the ethnic groups is kept by European Union troops.

Montenegro became independent after the referendum in May 2006. A Montenegrin Parliament existed within the Yugoslav Federation and later on in Serbia and Montenegro. It will take some time for the new Montenegrin Parliament to adjust to the new challenges posed by a sovereign country.

The Albanian unicameral Assembly (Kuvend) consists of 140 members, elected by a mixed system in which 100 are elected by a simple majority system in uni-nominal constituencies and 40 nationally by proportional representation. The legacy of the communist period still plays a major role in the behaviour of politicians and political parties. Parliamentarianism is normally sidelined by the continuous polarised fight between the Albanian Socialist Party and the Albanian Democratic Party. Until 1998, it was quite difficult to undertake any reforms. However, the Stability and Association Agreement has become an important instrument for investing in institution-building. However, parliamentarianism shows many features that can be found in other Balkan parliaments, such as party defections, the creation of new parties, the dominance of government in the legislative process, and ideological polarisation between the main political parties (Schmidt-Neke, 2002: 774–7, 779–82).

Conclusions: parliament as a moderating institution

European parliamentarianism is not characterised by adversarial politics (as in the United States). Parliament in Europe is closer to government and tends to act as a force of moderation in terms of legislation. However, in periods of absolute majority or in some countries with majoritarian patterns of politics, governments may impose legislation on the opposition. This can create a dynamics of its own at the elections that follow. Again, unlike the US, parliamentarianism in Europe is not a policy-making legislature, but policy-influencing. It means that the government initiates legislation and the parliamentary groups inside parliament will usually review, amend or change it. In Europe we can differentiate between weak, medium and strong reactive policy-influencing legislatures. Weak legislatures can be found in France, Southern Europe and Central and Eastern Europe, and strong legislatures can be found in the Nordic countries and the Netherlands. All the others, including the United Kingdom and Germany, are in between these two groups.

In the Balkans and Central and Eastern Europe legislatures are still consolidating and institutionalising. Their parliaments are crucial for the further democratisation of these countries.

Suggested reading

Arter, David (ed.) (2007), *Comparing and Classifying Legislatures*. London: Frank Cass. (Also electronically available as special issue of *Journal of Legislative Studies*, 12 (3/4).)

Helms, Ludger (ed.) (2008), Parliamentary Opposition in New and Old Democracies. London: Frank Cass, special issue, *Journal of Legislative Studies*, 14(1/2).

International Parliamentary Union (IPU), excellent website with database on all parliaments under www.ipu.org accessed 22 August 2009.

Norton, Philip (ed.) (1998), *Parliaments and Governments in Western Europe*. London: Frank Cass.

Norton, Philip and David M. Olson (eds) (2007), Post-Communist and Post-Soviet Legislatures. London: Frank Cass, special issue, *Journal of Legislative Studies*, 13(1).

Olson, David M. and Philip Norton (eds) (1996), The New Parliaments of Central and Eastern Europe. London: Frank Cass. (Also electronically available as special issue, *Journal of Legislative Studies*, 2(1).)

Journal of Legislative Studies is an important electronic journal, excellent for research studies on European parliaments.

See also *West European Politics* and *East European Politics and Societies*

QUESTIONS FOR REVISION

- What are the main functions of legislatures in contemporary European politics? Discuss, using examples from at least two countries.
- What are the main features of executive–legislative relations in Germany and France?
- How consolidated are Central and Eastern European parliaments?
- Compare Nordic and Southern European legislatures. Discuss, using at least one country from each region.
- Compare the influence of parliamentary opposition on policy-making in the Netherlands and the United Kingdom.

Chapter 7

Towards the European public administrative space?
The Europeanisation of national governance

- The introduction of public management principles
- National patterns of public administration
  - The British Isles model: UK and Ireland
  - The French model
  - The Drei-Sat/Germanic model: Germany, Austria and Switzerland
  - The Benelux model: Belgium, the Netherlands and Luxembourg
  - The Nordic model: Sweden, Denmark, Norway, Finland and Iceland
  - The Southern European model: Italy, Spain, Portugal and Greece
  - The Central and Eastern European models
- Towards a European administrative space: rhetoric and reality
- Conclusions: towards a European administrative space

SUMMARY OF CHAPTER 7

In the last four decades (1970–2010), national public administrations have been subject to major transformation. The rigid Weberian public administrations of the 1950s and 1960s, which were both hierarchical and bureaucratic, have been replaced by more flexible, market-oriented public administrations. The new philosophy of public administration is called 'new public management'. Its aim is to make public administration more efficient. One of the main reasons for this change came from the growing welfare states, which were creating major financial problems in the 1970s. 'New public management' instruments were introduced, such as the principles of 'value for money', establishing a 'customer-oriented' relationship between civil servant and citizen, and using a 'result-oriented budget'. One particular feature was the subcontracting of social welfare services to the private sector. Public–private partnerships were set up in most European countries in order to improve efficiency in the delivery of services and simultaneously reduce costs. The expansion of 'new public management' led to a transformation of government into governance. The growing necessity to steer all these public–private networks has become a central task of postmodern governance.

In this chapter, we show how different countries adjusted to these transformations, with particular focus on how bureaucracies had to change and adopt these principles.

Finally, the process of administrative convergence between the EU27 and the European Union is fully discussed.

The introduction of public management principles

In most European countries there has been a substantial transformation of the state. The original Weberian state, based on a neutral civil service, had become less and less viable by the end of the twentieth century (see Box 7.1).

The huge welfare states in most advanced countries were absorbing funds and creating stagnation in the national economies. The problem became evident during the 1970s, with the two oil shocks of 1973 (resulting from the war of the Arab states against Israel and the 1979 Iranian revolution), when all advanced democracies had to deal with oil shortages. This meant that, by the mid 1970s, the growth of state and public administration had reached its limits.

Since then there has been a new transition, similar to that of the nineteenth and early twentieth centuries, identified by Karl Polanyi (1944). This great transformation of the late twentieth century affects all aspects of life, but particularly the relationship between state and civil society.

The main international organisation facilitating this transformation of public administration and public policy among developed economies is the Organisation for Economic Cooperation and Development (OECD), which was originally the Organisation of European Economic Cooperation (OEEC) – founded under American auspices in 1948 in order to coordinate US Marshall aid to countries in Western

Box 7.1 Max Weber and modern state bureaucracy

The German sociologist Max Weber (1864–1920) is one of the founding fathers of modern political sociology. His main work was a very thorough volume entitled *Economy and Society* (*Wirtschaft und Gesellschaft*) published posthumously in 1922. Weber used a historical–sociological method to understand the emergence of modernity in the West in general, and the modern democratic state in particular. He differentiated between the pre-modern (feudalism, patrimonial, absolutist monarchy), in which arbitrary rule dominated, and the modern state based on the rule of law and a specialised civil service implementing it. This 'rational–legal state' was based on six bureaucratic principles:

1   There is the **principle of fixed and official jurisdictional areas**, which is generally ordered by rules, that is, by laws or administrative regulations.

2   The **principles of office hierarchy and of levels of graded authority** mean a firmly ordered system of super- and subordination in which there is a supervision of the lower offices by the higher ones.

3   The **management of the modern office is based upon written documents** ('the files'), which are preserved in their original or draft form. There is, therefore, a staff of subaltern officials and scribes of all sorts.

4   **Office management**, at least all specialised office management, which is anyway distinctly modern, usually presupposes thorough and expert training. This increasingly holds for modern executives and employees of private enterprises, in the same manner as it holds for state officials.

5   **When the office is fully developed, official activity demands the full working capacity of the official, irrespective of the fact that his obligatory time in the bureau may be firmly delimited.** In the normal case, this is only the product of a long development, in the public as well as in the private office. Formerly, in all cases, the normal state of affairs was reversed: official business was discharged as a secondary activity.

6   The **management of the office follows general rules, which are more or less stable, more or less exhaustive, and which can be learned.** Knowledge of these rules represents a special technical learning, which the officials possess. It involves jurisprudence, or administrative or business management.
(Max Weber quoted from Gerth and Mills, 1946: 196–8)

Today we take all these principles of public administration for granted, but during Weber's time at the turn of the nineteenth to the twentieth centuries, most public administrations in Europe were engaged in moving towards a rational–legal state. He analysed and described something that was happening between 1850 and 1945 in most European countries.

Europe. Originally, the OEEC had the overall aim of European economic integration, but this was resisted by most European countries. So, by 1960, the OEEC had become an intergovernmental international organisation based in Paris. From the 1970s, the OECD developed benchmarking and best practice of public administration based on the principles of new public management. At the forefront is a transition from a Weberian model of civil service and public administration to the new public management model (Peters, 2003). The whole process had already started in the 1970s, as a result of the increasing crisis caused by the growth of the welfare states and the stagnation of most OECD economies (Scharpf, 1999). According to Sabino Cassese, such reforms were started in the late 1970s in Germany (1978) and the United Kingdom (1979), followed by France (1989), Spain (1992) and then various other countries (Cassese, 2003: 131; Pollitt and Bouckaert, 2004).

One could characterise this transformation as one from government to governance, meaning that the separation between the public and private sector is not clear any more. This also means that the state has introduced more and more administrative devices taken from the private sector, such as evaluation, competition and flexibility, in order to make their organisational structures more efficient.

Although government and governance share similarities, both refer to purposive behaviour, goal-oriented activities and to systems of rule. However, while government undertakes activities that are backed by 'formal authority and by police powers that ensure the implementation of duly implemented policies', governance comprises activities that are backed 'by shared goals that may or may not derive from legal and formally prescribed responsibilities and that do not necessarily rely on police powers to overcome defiance and attain compliance'. Briefly, government is quite formalised, while governance includes both formal and informal elements (Rosenau, 2000: 4).

According to Cassese, seven main elements of this new rationale can be identified:

1   'Agencification': the establishment of special independent bodies to either regulate or perform duties once performed by the state. In the United Kingdom, good examples are agencies such as Ofcom (for control of the communication sector) and the Strategic Rail Authority (for the railway system).

2   'Process re-engineering': the revision of procedures inside the public administration in order to reduce the administrative burden on citizens.

3   'Value for money': the reduction of costs by introducing commercial principles and increasing the productivity of services.

4   'Result-oriented budget': enhanced accountability of public accounts accompanied by measurement of performance of expenditure.

5   'Public–private partnerships': the contracting out of public services to the private and voluntary sectors and/or seeking financial support for certain services, such as education or transport.

6   'Marketisation': opening up public services to private competition.

7   'Customer orientation': the identification of quality indicators and productivity standards, and the measurement of user satisfaction.

(The above list is the author's summary from Cassese, 2003: 131–2.)

This growing marketisation of public administration raises questions about its neutrality and the possibilities for interest groups to control policy-making processes of the state as a result of the state's dependency on their expertise. Today the state is losing its monopoly in the delivery of public services. It has to compete in the market, based on principles of 'value for money'. It becomes *primus inter pares* (first among equals) and works through public–private partnerships (PPP) with private economic actors and civil society actors in the delivery of public services and other state-related activities (Jessop, 2002: 243) (see Box 7.2). This means that governance seeks to overcome the rigidity and strong separation that existed between the public and private sectors until at least the 1970s. In this sense, governance in a particular policy field can be interpreted as greater than the sum of interactions between the governmental institutions, the private sector actors and the civil society actors.

The concept of 'governance' began to be part of the language of political scientists in the 1990s, but the transition began after 1979/80, when Margaret Thatcher came to power and started to introduce radical reforms in order to restore the competitiveness of the British economy. Reform of the state was an important element in this strategy. Rod Rhodes called this the 'hollowing out' of the state (Rhodes, 1997), meaning that Prime Minister Margaret Thatcher ensured that the state/public administration would minimise any attempt to use public resources to bail out declining industries or to provide specific clientele with additional funds. Moreover, the Conservative government made sure that the taxpayer would get the best value for money for services, at least in theory. In this sense, the contracting out of public social services that were inefficiently run by public agencies contributed to the move from government to governance. The establishment of public–private partnerships and networks that comprised public and private providers was a major factor in establishing governance as a mode of regulation.

According to Rod Rhodes, governance can be defined as 'self-organising inter-organisational networks' (Figure 7.1). Thus, the interaction between public, private and voluntary-sector actors and institutions leads to a sustainable system. Hence, during the 1980s and 1990s many public services delivered by the state were gradually taken over by networks of organisations comprising the public, private and voluntary sectors. Such networks work interdependently and are reciprocal (Rhodes, 1996: 660). Moreover, governance has now become a non-hierarchical third mode of organisation that clearly differs from hierarchies (government) and markets (economy) (Rhodes, 2003: 66).

Most members of the European Union are engaged in this *OECD-isation* or transformation process from government to governance, which is also the basis for transnational Europeanisation and integration of public administrations. EU member states are all implementing public administrative reform in order to create more competitive state structures for the Single European Market. Essentially, most public administrations are now engaged in a long transition of structural and cultural overhaul.

National patterns of public administration

In comparative terms, there are big differences in the performance of the public sector, which also affect confidence in public administration. In a sophisticated

---

Box 7.2 New public management and governance

The crisis of the 1970s also represents the climax of the expanding welfare state based on Weberian principles of a neutral civil service and a strict separation between public and private sectors. Many countries had large public economic sectors (for example, Austria and Italy) and they were used as strategic motors for the economy. However, in the 1970s the competition coming from non-European countries, particularly in Asia, led to a major crisis of the economy. Governments tried to use Keynesian policies to curb the economy, but without much success. In the United Kingdom, the 'winter of discontent' in 1978–9 almost led to the collapse of the British economy.

These experiences led to the introduction of public management reform. The 'new public management' (NPM) introduced market principles into the rationale of the rigid Weberian state. Separation between the public and private sectors was replaced by cooperation and learning between the two. However, such a process of learning was asymmetrically favourable to the private sector. 'Thatcherism' (1979–90) in Britain and 'Reaganomics' (1981–92) in the USA set the pace of movement towards radical reform (see Chapter 2).

NPM became the new philosophy of public administration across the world. The Organisation for Economic Cooperation and Development (OECD, founded in 1960) disseminated NPM across all advanced economies of the world. NPM is now an integral part of the reforms of all European Union member states, particularly through the European Public Administration Network (EUPAN) based in Maastricht (see below, pp. 273–6).

As a consequence of the growing integration of market mechanisms into public administration and the public sector, a third form of regulation, called governance, emerged parallel to hierarchies (Weberian government) and markets. Governance is more than simply the merging of elements of the two. It is a more flexible form of regulation that leads to the creation of networks between government institutions and actors and those from the private economic sector and civil society. Governance is broader than government, more flexible, but uses fewer public enforcement mechanisms, and relies much more on voluntary benchmarking and good practice agreements. It allows for steering and regulation to be informed by such 'private governance' soft mechanisms. Although the emergence of governance wanted to improve the efficiency, transparency and democratic accountability of public administration and the public sector, the growth in complexity and differentiation may actually have led to the opposite effect. Quasi-governmental organisations, such as Ofgem (Office for gas and electricity markets, in the United Kingdom) or the huge German BnetzA (Federal Network Agency – Bundesnetzagentur – responsible for gas, electricity, telecommunications, post and railways) have the difficult task of overseeing the running of privatised utilities.

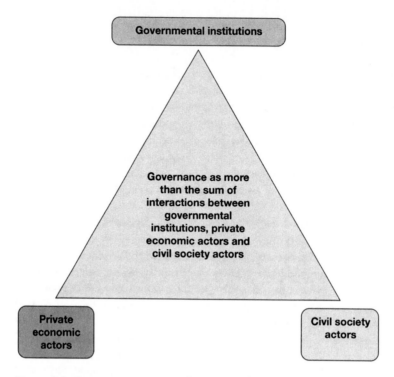

Figure 7.1 Governance as a complex system of interactions

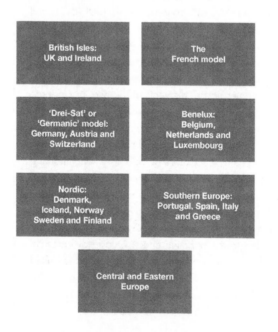

Figure 7.2 Types of public administration in Europe

Table 7.1 The ranking of performance in the public sector

	Country	Group
1	Finland	Northern European Group
2	Denmark	
3	Luxembourg	West European Group
4	Sweden	Northern European Group
5	Austria	West European Group
6	Netherlands	
7	Ireland	
8	Belgium	
9	Czech Republic	Central Eastern European Group
10	Canada	Anglo-Saxon Group
11	Australia	
12	France	West European Group
13	Spain	Southern European Group
14	Germany	West European Group
15	Slovakia	Central European Group
16	United Kingdom	Anglo-Saxon Group
17	United States	
18	Hungary	Central European Group
19	Italy	Southern European Group
20	Greece	
21	Portugal	
22	Poland	Central European Group

Source: Simplified from Kuhry and Pommer, 2004: 288; see also Kuhry and Pommer, 2007

study by Bob Kuhry and Evert Pommer, OECD countries were ranked according to performance of the public sector. They included several variables, such as stability and growth of the economy, distribution of welfare, financial allocation to public services, and quality of public administration and came up with six clusters of countries: Northern Europe, Western Europe, Southern Europe, Central Europe, Anglo-Saxon countries and France. In their ranking, Northern European countries had the best scores in terms of performance, while Southern and Central and Eastern European countries were at the bottom (Kuhry and Pommer, 2004: 279–85; see also Kuhry and Pommer, 2007) (see Table 7.1).

Similarly, Edward Page developed a typology of six national administrative patterns that are related to geographic location and also have common features: the British Isles model, the French model, the 'Germanic' model, the Nordic model, the Southern European model, and the Central and Eastern European model (Page,

Table 7.2 Components of bureaucratic character, according to Edward Page

Categories	Description
Pervasiveness	Range of competences under its influence
Cohesion	Universalisation or particularisation of civil servants elites
Political control	Institutionalised patterns of political control over civil servants. Three forms: 1 Top officials appointed by politicians (politicisation) 2 Norm of neutrality (insistence on neutral behaviour of civil servants) 3 Supervisory administrative body
Caste	Higher civil servants often come from privileged social classes and build a class for themselves in public administration and the public at large
Permeability	Relationship of bureaucracy with interest groups: 1 Low level (UK, France) 2 Structured cooperative high level (Scandinavia) 3 Unstructured high level (Southern Europe, Central and Eastern Europe)

Source: Adapted from Page, 1995: 259–74

1995: 278–80). This differentiation between the six types helps to simplify the highly complex and varied reality of Europe. Page's typology is based on a combination of several characteristics, as presented in Table 7.2.

Influenced by the Edward Page typology on public administrative patterns, we can use a geographically defined typology of models of public administration. Naturally, any typology simplifies the reality of each of these public administrations quite a lot. In what follows, we consider all six patterns identified by Page and add to them the Benelux pattern, which is certainly a hybrid system between the Germanic, Scandinavian and French models, depending on the country.

The British Isles model: UK and Ireland

In spite of the new agenda of administrative reform, the British civil service remained reasonably stable over time. One of the main characteristics of the British civil service is that it is fairly neutral: governments can come and go, but, in general, terms there is a strong separation between politics and public administration. Historically, modern British public administration was established during the second half of the nineteenth century. The Northcote-Trevelyan report of 1854 set the guidelines for the restructuring of public administration. According to John Kingdom, the Indian civil service (in British India) was taken as the model to overcome the nepotistic, fragmented and patronage-ridden British civil service until then. It took decades to establish a modern and neutral civil service. Recruitment was based on merit and competition and the different departments were merged

Table 7.3 A typology of national patterns of public administration, according to Ed Page

	Pervasiveness	Cohesion	Institutionalised political control	Caste	Permeability
British Isles pattern	High level of pervasiveness owing to unitary nature of political systems	'Village community', high level of cohesion	Least politicised higher civil service	'Oxbridge' recruitment still relevant	Controlled low permeability through pluralistic inclusion of interest groups in consultative committees
Nordic pattern	High level of pervasiveness, moderated by growing decentralisation	Careers pursued within ministries, particularised	Non-politicised civil service	Wide variety of degrees, professionalisation of civil service	High permeability through institutionalised consultation process, cooperative approach
'Germanic' pattern	Highly limited pervasiveness owing to federalism	Ressortpartikularismus, particularised civil service (departmental and/or ministry)	Politicisation of higher civil servants 'Politische Beamte', good to have political skills	Staatsexamen, law degree	High permeability owing to cross-party cooperation in the federal system and the attached interest groups
French pattern	High level of pervasiveness, in spite of regionalisation of 1980s	Grands corps high level of cohesion within these groups, however fragmented in relation to the whole	Neutrality perceived as part of higher civil service.	École Nationale d'Administration (Enaistes) or École Polytechnique	Low permeability, weak interest groups, strong bureaucracy
Southern European pattern	High level of pervasiveness in Portugal and Greece; declining pervasiness in regionalised Italy and Spain	Fragmented, divided higher civil service	Legalistic neutral perception, however political patronage as an important tool of recruitment	Law degrees, highly legalistic civil servant culture	Weak interest groups and weak bureaucracy, tendencies towards 'clientelism' and patronage
Central and Eastern European pattern	High level of pervasiveness, still legacy of former communist regimes	Problems of developing a new civil service	Tendency towards emulating Western counterparts depending on geographical position	No overall pattern, additional qualifications outside the country relevant	Weak interest groups and weak bureaucracy, pluralistic systems of interest intermediation still in the making

Source: Adapted from Page, 1995, partly own interpretation

into a unified home service. Since then, the new model has not undergone major changes. The civil service grew considerably over the decades until it reached its peak in 1976 with 751,000 civil servants (Kingdom, 2000: 21). This also represented the climax of the post-war expansion of the social democratic welfare state, which entered a crisis in the mid 1970s.

Britain, like many other European countries, was no longer able to afford further expansion of the welfare state. In 1979, Prime Minister Margaret Thatcher came to power and began to implement neo-liberal policies in order to reduce the size of the state. The philosophies of 'the limited state' and of 'new public management' became important in order to 'reinvent government'. Thatcherism introduced private sector principles into several aspects of public administration, including the National Health Service. Margaret Thatcher particularly wanted two things from the civil service in terms of reform. First, she wanted to achieve greater efficiency by substantially reducing the civil service, and, second, she intended to dismantle its 'privileges'. Efficiency was achieved by a considerable reduction in the number of civil servants (from 732,000 in 1979 to 593,000 in 1988). The vast majority of cuts took place among industrial employees who worked for the government across the country. In spite of a major civil service strike in 1981, the Thatcher government introduced standardisation and unification of pay scales, at least for the senior civil service, changed pensions rights because of the costs and, in 1981, abolished the civil service department, which represented the civil servants within the government and was a powerful lobby group (Fry, 1989: 101–6).

The Thatcher government pioneered in 'hollowing out' the state, particularly through several waves of privatisation of public sector enterprises, such as British Airways, British Railways, British Telecom and British Gas. It opened up the market to allow competition between providers in the main public utilities sectors. The privatisation waves were paralleled by the creation of watchdog agencies, such as Oftel (later merged with Ofcom) for the telecommunications sector and Ofgas (later merged with the electricity sector to form Ofgem) for the gas market sector (Dunleavy and Rhodes, 1989: 134–42). The introduction of private sector managerial principles in the National Health Service and a squeeze on the finances of local authorities, through cutting back on block grants, were further elements of the strategy to slim down the state (Dunleavy and Rhodes, 1989: 119–26).

One particular phenomenon was the emergence of single-issue quasi-governmental organisations (known as Quangos, for example Manpower Services) and quasi-elected local government organisations (known as Quellgos, for example the Police Authorities or the London Regional Transport Board (established in 1984; replaced in 2000 by Transport for London under the supervision of the Mayor), which was created to deal with the coordination of transport in Greater London and to implement and oversee specific concrete tasks (Dunleavy and Rhodes, 1989: 130–3). The Ibbs report, under the title 'Improving Management in Government: The Next Steps', published by the Efficiency Unit in 1988, was crucial. It led to a separation of the core policy-making departments from agencies dedicated exclusively to operational policy implementation. This process was implemented throughout the 1990s and continued by the Labour government (Dargie and Locke, 1999: 180–1). The Thatcherite re-invention of government also gained momentum across Europe, being particularly successful in the Scandinavian countries.

The Thatcherite period of reform was followed by more moderate changes during the John Major, Tony Blair and Gordon Brown governments.

Since 1997, the devolution process has also considerably changed the civil service. The Scottish, Welsh and Northern Irish civil services gained greater independence from Whitehall and Westminster as a result of the different programmes of the regional governments. However, this seriously undermined the powers of a unitary bureaucratic structure – something that became evident in Scotland, where, after a full decade of the devolution process, many policies differed considerably from those in England, particularly in education and health.

One particular area in which the Blair and later the Gordon Brown governments invested was e-government. This innovative approach is also one of the most controversial aspects of the new public management agenda. It means that public administration uses electronic means to join services together and to integrate the information flows within public administration. The Government Secure Intranet (GSI) has been at the forefront of British public administrative reform. Since Thatcher's administrative reform programme, called 'The Next Steps', which was clearly influenced by the new public management philosophy, the United Kingdom has been at the forefront of pushing the boundaries of e-government. Both the 1996 Green Paper *Government Direct: A Prospectus for the Electronic Delivery of Government Services* and the 1999 White Paper *Modernising Government* show enthusiasm for using the new technologies to slim down public administration. In 2005, the Labour government introduced a strategy paper that included the offering of public services through the digital television platform. This also included a proposal for growth of the new economy based on new technologies. The BBC is engaged in expanding digital television until 2012, when the analogue signal will be switched off. At the time of writing, it is too early to assess whether the rapid changes introduced by e-government will, in the end, make public administration more efficient. Independent evaluations are still to be commissioned and presented. There is always the problem of the digital divide. According to a study by BT it is estimated that 23 million (35.9 per cent) out of a population of 64 million will be digitally excluded in 2025 in the UK; something that will particularly affect the elderly (British Telecom, 2004: 3).

The original British model recruited most of its civil service from Oxford and Cambridge, but, with time, the recruitment pool was widened to other institutions. In spite of this, the civil service continues to be quite a privileged group, a large part still having an 'Oxbridge' background. There is a general preoccupation with preserving what are regarded as the core values of the British civil service, such as 'honesty, personal disinterestedness, a respect for intelligence, an enormous capacity for hard and often rapid work, and loyalty to colleagues'. However, the British civil service also has the reputation of being conservative and elitist (Dargie and Locke, 1999: 194). The recent trends towards managerialism and the opening up to the private sector have, not surprisingly, contributed to some insecurity in this traditional understanding of the civil service (Dargie and Locke, 1999: 195; Figures 7.2 and 7.3).

The Republic of Ireland inherited the British model of public administration. In this sense, colonialism played a major role in shaping the way government is run in Dublin. However, Ireland has also integrated major features from other European models. This became even more important when Ireland joined the

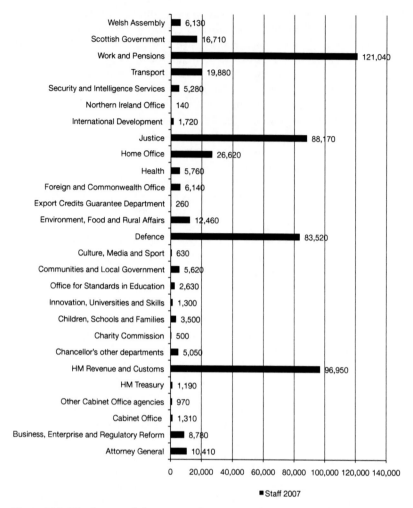

Figure 7.3 Distribution of the core civil service in the UK, according to departments, 30 September 2007

Source: Office for National Statistics, Civil Service Statistics, available online at www.statistics. gov.uk (accessed 7 August 2008)

European Community in 1973. In the 1980s, the country faced a difficult period of recession and new austerity policies had to be introduced to transform the situation. In 1987, a major decision was taken to restructure the state and public administration. The inclusion of the social partners in the process of restructuring led to the adoption of neo-corporatist structures in the Republic of Ireland. Such restructuring has been continuous throughout the 1990s and has not yet been completed. The central policy was the 'Strategic Management Initiative' in 1995, which led to the report, 'Delivering Better Government' in 1996. The main objective was to make the Irish state and public administration more competitive in an age of accelerating globalisation (Collins and O'Shea, 2000: 105–8; Figure 7.5).

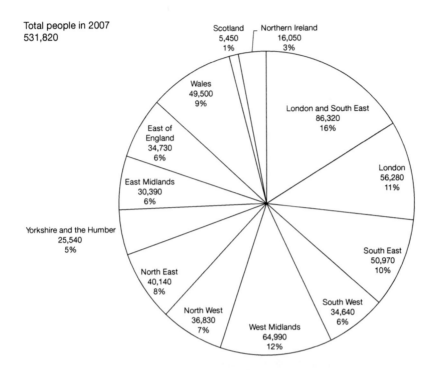

Figure 7.4 The civil service in the UK, according to regions, 2007

Source: Office for National Statistics, Civil Service Statistics, available online at www.statistics. gov.uk (accessed 7 August 2008)

In 2004, a further report focused on 'Regulating Better', which was to be based on six principles: transparency, consistency, necessity, accountability, proportionality and effectiveness (Department of the Taoseach, 2004). The reform of public administration fits with the overall worldwide trend to introduce new public management instruments and to open up to the private sector. The successful implementation of the structural funds also helped to show the importance of the Irish model. The 'Celtic tiger' is very keen to create a competitive public administration in order to sustain the economic growth that it enjoyed, at least until the financial crisis of 2008–9. According to a study commissioned by the government, Ireland had 213 agencies, of which 204 were regulatory agencies. This shows the level of agencification reached in a small country (Better Regulation, 2007: 7).

The French model

At the centre of the French model is the higher civil service, characterised by Pierre Bourdieu as the new 'Noblesse d'État' ('State Nobility') – an allusion to the 'Noblesse de Robe' of the *Ancien Régime*, meaning that the civil service represents a very privileged administrative elite recruited from the prestigious National School of Administration (École Nationale d'Administration, ENA) and the École Poly-technique. This administrative elite organises itself according to professions in the

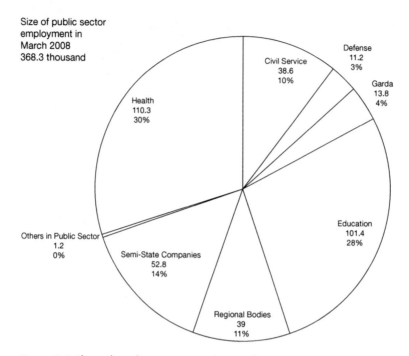

Size of public sector
employment in
March 2008
368.3 thousand

Defense
11.2
3%

Civil Service
38.6
10%

Garda
13.8
4%

Health
110.3
30%

Education
101.4
28%

Others in Public Sector
1.2
0%

Semi-State Companies
52.8
14%

Regional Bodies
39
11%

Figure 7.5 The Irish civil service, according to departments, March 2008

Source: Central Statistics Office, Public Sector Employment and Earnings, 31 July 2008; available online at: www.cso.ie/releasepublications/documents/earnings/current/pearnpearn.pdf (accessed 11 August 2008)

grands corps that can be traced historically to the late phases of the *Ancien Régime* in the nineteenth century (Bourdieu, 1989). Although today there has been an increase in the *grands corps* in order to accommodate new professions, the oldest are the technical Mines, Bridges and Highways Corps (whose members were recruited from the École Polytechnique), the administrative Council of State, the Finance Inspectorate, and the Council of State (whose members were recruited from the ENA). The French model is also characterised by the fact that *énarques*, graduates from the ENA, can move freely from the administrative field to the political or private economic fields. This, of course, makes the whole administrative system fairly non-transparent. What is more, these *grands corps* are not juridically enshrined in any document even though they are central to the organisation of the higher civil service. The *grands corps* have a strong *esprit de corps*, based on the values and the long historical legacy of their origins (Kessler, n.d.; Owen, 2000: 56–9). However, according to Andrew Knapp and Vincent Wright, this elitist dominance of the *énarques* and *grands corps* has been declining in the past decades. Many of the *énarques* are attracted by more lucrative jobs in the private sector, as well as by more strategic positions within French administration, especially positions that are shaping the relationship of France with the European Union (Knapp and Wright, 2001: 291–2; Table 7.4).

Moreover, at the local level, *les grands élus* (elected notables, such as mayors or regional presidents) exert considerable power in preventing a change of the political and administrative system. *Les grands élus* are usually mayors of major cities

Table 7.4 The number of civil servants and public employees in France, 2005

	Total	State civil service	Territorial civil service	Hospital civil service
France	4.8 million	2.3 million	1.1 million	800,000

Source: Luxembourg Presidency, 2005c: 21–3

or presidents of the twenty-two administrative regions of France (created in 1982 by President François Mitterrand). Both mayors and regional presidents are politicians and heads of their respective administrative services. They have considerable access to public resources, which they use in order to stay in power. There have been several attempts to reform the system, but, instead of change, the old system was able to absorb the changes and preserve the status quo of a non-transparent system (Thoenig, 2005: 701–5). Between 1985 and 1997, there were five attempts to reform the administrative system and the state. Among those attempts, the most successful was the one instigated by socialist Prime Minister Michel Rocard, under the second term of President François Mitterrand, between 1988 and 1991. Rocard had to include the powerful civil service trade unions in the consultation process, otherwise he would have faced defeat. Some aspects of the new public management were introduced in this reform. A more radical approach by conservative Prime Minister Alain Juppé between 1995 and 1997, under President Jacques Chirac, led to major protests by the civil service trade unions confederations (Bezes, 2001; Cole and Jones, 2005). Further attempts to introduce change by socialist Prime Minister Lionel Jospin (1997–2002) and conservative Prime Minister Jean-Pierre Raffarin (2002–5) were met with resistance (Thoenig, 2005: 705). In spite of a high level of decentralisation to the regional and local levels, the powerful notables at local level have recentralised at their level and use the *cumul de mandat* ('accumulated public offices') to control the political system. The *cumul de mandat* allows mayors to be members of the national Parliament or Senate as well (see Chapter 6). The most evident case is probably that of Jacques Chirac, who was able to be both mayor of Paris and prime minister between 1986 and 1988. Prime Minister Lionel Jospin tried to reform the system by reducing the *cumul des mandats* to two, however the power of the notables continues to be strong.

The Drei-Sat/Germanic model: Germany, Austria and Switzerland

As already mentioned in Chapter 1, Drei-Sat refers to Germany, Austria and Switzerland; all three countries have developed common television channels called SAT1 and 3SAT and they exchange programmes. 'Drei-Sat' is an artificial expression used to show the commonalities between the three countries. Although Switzerland has a large French population, most of its people are German-speaking and share a common culture with Austria and Germany. One particular characteristic unites the three countries: they all have federal systems and therefore highly decentralised administrative systems (see Table 7.5).

The German administrative system has achieved a high level of decentralisation since the 1950s. According to figures by Hans-Ulrich Derlien *et al.* there has been a considerable decrease of central government – from 40 per cent in 1950 to 13 per cent in 2003. Over this period, the civil service has been federalised among the sixteen *Länder*. The federal structure of Germany gives a lot of power to the regions as well as autonomy for the implementation of any framework laws decided at federal level (see Chapters 5, 6 and 9). Most civil servants have a law degree (over 60 per cent in 1999), although since the 1960s there has also been recruitment of economists (14.3 per cent in 1999) and social scientists (2.1 per cent in 1999) (Derlien, 2003: 405).

According to Derlien, there has been an increasing politicisation of the civil service since 1983. Apart from the fact that there is a growing number of civil servants with a declared political affiliation (72 per cent in 1970 compared to 40.4 per cent in 1995) (Derlien, 2003: 409), higher civil servants have developed political and social skills in order to serve politicians better. The longevity of the Helmut Kohl governments (1982–98) led to a strong attachment of the higher civil service to Kohl's government. This, of course, had serious implications when the new coalition government between the SPD and the Greens came to power in 1998. Derlien characterised it as the 'political bloodshed' of the higher civil servants who were connected to the previous government: they were replaced by civil servants who supported the new political parties. According to Derlien's figures, 52.2 per cent of all higher civil servants at state secretary and ministerial director level were replaced by the new coalition government. Traditionally, civil servants who have been removed have to retire temporarily or simply move to other positions (Derlien, 2003: 410). 'Political' civil servants who have the necessary political and social skills can be very useful in helping politicians fulfil or present political programmes (Derlien, 2003). Unification led to a transfer of some of the 22,000 core public servants attached to the main ministries from Bonn to Berlin. However, many of them still remain in Bonn (see Figure 7.5).

Although Austria is a federal system, it is more centralised than Germany and Switzerland. One speaks of an 'executive federalism', meaning that the nine Bundesländer normally just implement policies decided at the central level. This relates to the importance of Vienna in the political system. The capital of the then Austro-Hungarian Empire was a huge city (*Wasserkopf Wien*). However, after

Table 7.5 The number of civil servants in public administration in Germany, Austria and Switzerland

	Total	Federal level	Länder/canton level	Local level
Germany (2005)	4,550,000*	481,400	2,076,900	1,337,800
Austria (2005)	389,187	133,287	180,500	70,400
Switzerland (2001)	468,312	36,000	201,374	140,494

* Germany: includes indirect administration 652,400

Source: Luxembourg Presidency, 2005: 4–5, 24–26; Christophe, Trippolini and Traimond, 2006: 7; BMI, 2007: 7–8; Bundeskanzleramt (n.d.)

the break-up of the Austro-Hungarian Empire it became the capital of the small German-speaking part of the former Empire (known as Deutsch-Österreich (German Austria)) after 1918. It was, however, a disproportionately large capital city for such a small population and territory. Since 1945, there has a been a strong trend towards a decentralisation and modernisation of the public administration. According to Gerhard Hammerschmidt and Renate Meyer, in 2002, out of the 490,000 civil servants, 39.8 per cent worked for the central government, 29.6 per cent for the Bundesländer, 14.6 per cent for the city of Vienna, and 16.4 per cent for local government (Hammerschmid and Meyer, 2005: 715). According to the latest figures, the Austrian administration at federal level reduced its personnel between 1997 and 2006 from 115,575 to 88,218, which corresponds to a decrease of 24.7 per cent (*Kurier*, 30 July 2007: 2).

State and administrative reform have always been on the agenda. The integration into the European Union and globalisation were major pressures to modernise and adjust the public administration accordingly. The decline of neo-corporatism represented by social partnership (*Sozialpartnerschaft*) opened up new opportunities to overhaul the administrative system.

New public management aspects had already emerged in 1988. A programme called 'Administrative management'(*Verwaltungsmanagement*) was introduced in 1988, aimed at increasing the productivity of public administration by 20 per cent. Six years later, the final report presented quite sober conclusions. Resistance among the higher-ranking officials made it very difficult to steer Austrian public administration towards a more horizontal structure (Neisser, 1997). Despite

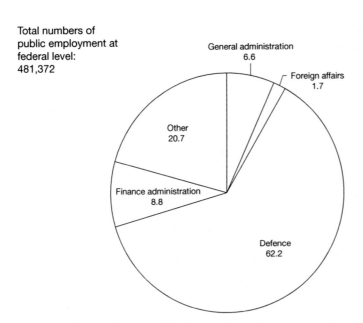

Total numbers of public employment at federal level: 481,372

General administration 6.6

Foreign affairs 1.7

Other 20.7

Finance administration 8.8

Defence 62.2

Figure 7.6 The distribution of public employment at the core federal level in Germany, 30 June 2005

Source: BMI, 2007: 22

this, the impact of Europeanisation and globalisation reinforced the pressures upon the political system to make public administration more efficient and competitive. Here the path-dependency is very relevant. European Union membership reduced the power of neo-corporatist interests, which were semi-institutionalised through social partnership. The thrusts towards liberalisation and privatisation reduced the power of the social partners and allowed for a pluralistic economic structure (Pelinka and Rosenberger, 2003: 198). Calls for a restoration of confidence in the political system after decades of a system of patronage and clientelism created by the two main parties and the social partners led to a debate about the quality of democracy (Campbell *et al.*, 2002). Public administration had to respond to these demands for a less hierarchical structure between the citizenship and the civil service.

Such reforms were undertaken during the SPÖ–ÖVP coalition government between 1995 and 1999, which wanted to reduce the number of civil servants and make employment more flexible. The reduction of tenure appointments, known under the label of 'Pragmatisierung', was an important change.

The highly controversial coalition government between the ÖVP and the FPÖ after 2000 became a turning point against the over-dominant position of the two main parties in the political system and major reforms were introduced in order to achieve a more competitive state structure. Most of the reform programme addressed the reduction of personnel, resulting in the simplification and reduction of bureaucratisation, and the modernisation of practices (Hammerschmidt and Meyer 2005: 727).

The use of IT for e-government and e-democracy is a major issue in Austrian public administration reform. The discussion is about the ways to strengthen the position of the citizens vis-à-vis public administration (Wisse, 2006: 66–9).

The Swiss system is the most decentralised administrative system of the three countries. The federal system of Switzerland emerged in 1848 after a civil war between Catholic and Protestant cantons. The resultant political system gave a high level of autonomy to the cantons. Since then, the twenty cantons and six 'half cantons' have resisted against too much centralisation by the federal government (Linder, 2005: 139–40). However, the pressures from globalisation and Europeanisation have led to the accumulation of some more competences at federal level. Originally, until the 1960s, Switzerland had a light welfare state, but by 2010 social security has become the major expenditure of the country. The welfare state is shared between the federal and the cantonal levels. The transport system is managed at the federal level. And last, but not least, defence has always been a competence at federal level. The autonomy of the cantons also allowed for a continuing diversity of taxation systems and a resistance to uniformisation or even federalisation. It means that, still, the cantons have not been able to agree on a common taxation system. Until 1990, civil servants were employed with temporary contracts of four years, both at federal as well as cantonal levels, with only the canton Vaud and Geneva issuing permanent contracts. This was then abolished and replaced by a more modern statute for civil servants in 2000 that came into force in 2002 (UN, 2006: 12). According to 2001 figures, 468,312 persons worked in the public sector, out of which 35 per cent were at federal level (although only 7 per cent, about 36,000, were civil servants), 43 per cent at cantonal level and 30 per cent at local level (Koller *et al.*, 2006: 7).

At cantonal level, there is a higher level of centralisation in the Romandie (francophone Switzerland) than in the German-speaking part of the country (Linder, 2005: 165). Since 1993, there also exists a conference of the cantonal governments, which tries to better coordinate their position in relation to central government. This is an attempt to avoid the doubling-up of efforts and the overburdening of the administrations of the smaller cantons (Linder, 2005: 194).

In sum, one can say that all three countries pursue policies of consensus in central-periphery relations; this is the only way to make the three systems work. The *Politikverflechtung* ('policy intertwinedness') in the three countries requires a positive form of cooperative federalism. The role of subsidiarity and appropriateness of level for certain policies is an important consideration for allocating competences.

The Benelux model: Belgium, the Netherlands and Luxembourg

The Benelux economic union between Belgium, the Netherlands and Luxembourg is the main reason to group these three countries together. All three countries are consensus democracies and their histories are intrinsically linked. They show similar features to the Drei-Sat countries and all of them can be subsumed under the geographical label of 'West Central Europe', coined by Gerhard Lehmbruch (1996) (see Table 7.6).

Belgian public administration, which was established after 1830, was influenced by French public administration and was quite centralised. This centralisation was to dominate the country until the end of the 1950s. One of the main reasons for the dominance of the francophone majority in Belgium was that it was also wealthier than the northern, Flemish, part of the population. However, after 1945 the Flemish population increased in size considerably, until it became the majority. Moreover, Flanders was able to invert the economic situation to its advantage, with the result that today Flanders is the wealthiest part of the country, while Wallonia has to deal with the aftermath of de-industrialisation and the decline of the coal industry. This new situation has had major implications for public administration. A peaceful movement towards federalisation of the country has taken place since the 1960s, culminating in the approval of the new federal constitution in 1993, which led to the establishment of three regions (Flanders, Wallonia and Brussels) and three linguistic communities (Flemish, Francophone and German). The region of Flanders and the Flemish community merged their structures

Table 7.6 The size of public employment in the Benelux countries, 2005

	Total	Central/ federal level	Region/ province	Local	Other services
Belgium	934,290	268,229	363,218	285,843	
Netherlands	806,004	607,871	11,647	161,733	24,753
Luxembourg	14,212	5,018			8,994

Source: Luxembourg Presidency, 2005: 6–8, 38–41, 62–3; Arends, 2008: 25

into one, making it better prepared to defend their interests. The federalisation process was accompanied by decentralisation of public administration with a small central government administrative structure that is in charge of coordinating policy-making across the country.

Belgian public administration always emphasised the strict separation between the neutral civil servant and the politician. Until the federalisation process and the reform of the civil service in 1993, Belgian public administration was organised according to the Camu statute, a royal decree issued in 1937 and changed and updated several times thereafter. The nature of the consensus model of democracy based on coalition government and 'partyocracy' led to a substantial encroachment of party politics on public administration. Party patronage also affected public service. Moreover, the rationale of the neutral civil service led to problems with regard to loyal support of party politics because of high levels of patronage. This meant that politicians would usually hire short-term cabinet staff that they could trust. Even if civil servants had the correct party label, they would still be less well trusted than the cabinet staff. This point is important because higher civil servants were therefore marginalised from their essential role as a link between public administration and the political world (Dierickx, 2003: 328–30). After 1993, the decentralisation process led to the introduction of major reforms in order to achieve the modernisation of public administration. The most important reforms were undertaken in Flanders, which is strongly influenced by the Anglo-Saxon and Dutch model of public administration. Major changes were also undertaken at central government level. One important reform was related to the status of cabinet staff and higher civil service in the different ministries. This was necessary to overcome the role of party patronage in public administration. In the Francophone public administration, which is influenced by the French model, modernisation has been much slower, one of the reasons seems to be the fact that the dominance of the Socialist Party reinforces the principle of maintaining the status quo in order to protect working places (Dierickx, 2003: 336–41). The result, thus far, has been an asymmetrical reform of public administration, with Flanders being a leader and Wallonia a laggard. The administrative reform at federal level, which started in 2000, was important. It was a comprehensive plan to introduce the new public management rationale in public administration, although its implementation led to mixed results, with the Francophone administrations still implementing piecemeal reforms. Flanders is regarded as an early moderniser in relation to the other parts of Belgium, largely because it implemented a comprehensive package of reforms from the outset thus gaining an advantage over the other public administrations (Brans *et al.*, 2006: 990–1). In 2000, there were only 29.7 per cent of civil servants at federal level, and only 6.8 per cent in the ministries. Most competences, including education and health, were devolved to the regions. Only the courts, the army and the federal police remained at the central level (Brans *et al.*, 2006: 979).

The Dutch decentralised state was created by Johan Thorbecke after 1848, and it clearly allowed for some autonomy at local and regional level (Nomden, 2000; Neelen *et al.*, 2003). Therefore, Dutch public administration was always characterised by a decentralised system of public employment, in which government departments had their own personnel policy. Departmentalisation and compartmentalisation of the civil service and public administration were the main characteristics of the Dutch civil service until the 1990s. This general development has to be qualified by the fact that, by the 1980s, there were efforts by the coalition government between the Christian democrats and liberals to reduce the size of the civil service (Thoonen and van der Meer, 2005: 842).

This meant that civil servants tended to remain in the same department for their whole working life and therefore mobility between departments was low. New public management contributed to major reforms of the Dutch public service, the most important one probably being the creation of a senior civil service in 1995, with the purpose of making it more mobile and more able to move from one department to another based on 'competency management' skills – skills that could be applied in any department. This was an important step towards making the public administrative system more mobile. However, the small number of members belonging to the higher civil service meant that the degree of change achieved was also small. Therefore, reform was widened to other groups so that a greater impact could be achieved (Thoonen and van der Meer, 2005: 847–9). In contrast to Belgium and Germany, politicisation of the civil service has been moderate, the tradition of depoliticisation of policy-making issues being a major characteristic in Dutch politics (Andeweg and Irwin, 2002: 153). The fact that there is a widespread use of specialised regulatory and administrative agencies, which thus allows the civil service to remain small, is important. The Independent Administrative Bodies (Zelfstandige Bestuursorgane, ZBOs) are an important factor in keeping policy-making depoliticised and this clearly follows the new public management model of agencification (Andeweg and Irwin, 2002: 153).

The present doctrine of public administration in the Netherlands emphasises the need to give greater autonomy to administrative units, so that they are flexible enough to respond to the emerging information society. The autonomisation of public administrative units has to be followed by a growing horizontalisation of hierarchical organisations. There is a strong emphasis on using the new information technologies to push this kind of development forward, although there is a general scepticism that vertical collective accountability and transparency can be maintained. However, the model of a 'individualised transparency', an increased transparency for the benefit of the individual, is being implemented. This entails the growing management and control of personal data by the citizen in relation to government and other private organisations (Ministry of Interior and Kingdom Relations, 2006: 39). This model ought to become a central principle of constitutional democracy. This approach is also highlighted in the new vision of government that wants to restore the confidence of the population in government (Ministry of Interior and Kingdom Relations, 2006). Indeed, the declining confidence of the populations in their governments in advanced democracies was studied thoroughly by the Dutch public administration, with the conclusion that most advanced democracies are suffering from a widening gap between citizens and government (Wisse, 2006: 109–10). The Dutch case shows that, among small states within the European Union, the debate is informed by its historical legacy. The Dutch debate is about enhancing and facilitating citizenship in a context of the information society and it clearly identifies several processes that are changing society (Ministry of Interior and Kingdom Relations, 2006: 11–12). In this sense, government is no longer something separated from private life. Indeed, government becomes a facilitator for democratic processes, particularly for the interactions between citizens, but also for the interactions between citizens and other civil associations (Ministry of Interior and Kingdom Relations 2006: 32).

The Luxembourg public administration is quite small, comprising only 14,212 civil servants. However, only 5,018 (35.3 per cent) are employed by the general administration, with the rest working in education (46.9 per cent), the police (12.7 per cent), the judiciary (3.1 per cent), and the religious sector (1.9 per cent) (United Nations, 2006c: 7). Similarly to other more advanced democracies the Benelux countries are engaged in improving the relationship between public administration and citizens. At the centre is the expansion of e-government and the new public management agenda (MFPRA, 2007: 40–76).

The Nordic model: Sweden, Denmark, Norway, Finland and Iceland

The Nordic model comprises Sweden, Denmark, Norway, Finland and Iceland and is based on the inclusion of all relevant interest groups. This cooperative administrative approach has been intrinsically linked to the very generous welfare states built in all five Nordic countries since the inter-war period. A dualism between core small ministries that concentrate on decision-making and large administrative agencies responsible for implementation policies is a strong feature of Nordic public administration and decentralisation of public services to the local level has been an important characteristic of the Nordic model. All this has been changing, because of the introduction of new public management reforms, such as marketisation, autonomisation and privatisation. However, such administrative change has been undertaken at a slow pace, moderately and within the framework of lengthy consultation with relevant stakeholders.

Swedish public administration has a strong tradition of separating out the decision-making processes into the small departments of ministries. It is based on using inclusive advisory committees and large administrative agencies that implement the policies. Since the 1980s, there has been a major effort to further delineate the tasks between these two parts of public administration. The position of the politician as a decision-maker was strengthened in relation to the civil servant. This dualism of Swedish public administration has a long historical legacy and remains a key feature of its workings. The over-dominance of the Social Democratic Party until the mid 1970s contributed to the expansion of the public sector, which consumed on average about 60 per cent of the gross domestic product (GDP) and employed about 30 per cent of the working population. This contrasted strongly with the average in OECD countries of 40 per cent and 20 per cent respectively (Ehn et al., 2003: 431). It had already become evident in the 1970s that reform was needed. However, the timid attempts at reform did not do much to change the situation. It was only in the 1990s, because of both the loss of competitiveness of the Swedish economy (16 per cent of GDP budget deficit in 1993 (Ehn et al., 2003: 430)) and the prospect of joining the European Union, that major reforms were undertaken that also included the new governance agenda.

The higher civil service is very committed to the party in power. This would usually mean that members of the top level of the civil service would be removed from the centre of power and moved to another department within the civil service when the party in power changed. However, because of the strong position of the social democrats in the political system, changes at the top level have been only moderate (Yates, 2000: 155). Apart from the politicisation of the civil service and the increase in the number of civil servants belonging to particular parties (100 per cent at the top level of under-secretaries) (Ehn *et al.*, 2003: 443–4), there is also a low level of interdepartmental mobility, which in turn can lead to isolationism and lack of contact with other realities beyond the departmental one (Pierre and Ehn, 1999: 257). About two-thirds of civil servants have studied either in Uppsala or Stockholm and come from the Stockholm area. Moreover, they typically have socially an upper-middle-class background. At one time there was a predominance of lawyers, but this has now been largely balanced by civil servants with social sciences and economic sciences degrees (Ehn *et al.*, 2003: 437; Table 7.7).

A central feature of the decision-making process is the inclusion of 'laymen boards' (*lekmannastyrelser*), which consist of representatives from interest groups relevant to a particular policy area, and which have decision-making powers. Although administrative agencies tended to resist these boards, because of their lack of administrative professionalism, this has nonetheless been regarded as an important democratising element of the political system (Pierre and Ehn, 1999: 256).

The European integration process has led to a considerable flexibilisation of territorial governance, with the regional level gaining in importance. The twenty-four country administrations have become important tiers of policy coordination in view of the growing impact of the European Union; and the partnership principle has become a central instrument in making the regions more competitive in view of globalisation. However, it is still difficult to assess whether these transformations at subnational level will in the end lead to a reduction in the influence of national government (Hudson, 2005: 319–22). Although the subnational level has a considerable amount of freedom of action, there is a strong fiscal control by the centre in order to avoid a spiralling of expenditure (Yates, 2000: 161–3; Figure 7.7).

The Danish structure of public administration shows similarities to the Swedish model; however, it has to be remembered that it is a much smaller country. One characteristic of Danish public administration is the level of de-concentration of its civil servants, of whom 80 per cent are placed at local level (*amtskommuner*) and only about 20 per cent are in the central government. In the same way as in Sweden, decision-making processes are taken within smaller ministries and then implemented by larger agencies. This model was prevalent until the late 1970s, however in the 1980s and 1990s it was restructured and made more compatible with a globalising economy. Many agencies received a considerable amount of autonomy, and others were integrated into the ministries. New public management became important after 1982, when a right-centre coalition government had to

Table 7.7 The size of public employment in Nordic Europe, 2004

	Total	Central	Regional	Local
Sweden	1,330,000	230,000	250,000	850,000
Denmark	743,700	185,000	141,700	398,000
Finland	544,000	128,000	416,000*	

* Both regional and local levels.

Source: Luxembourg Presidency, 2005c: 14–15, 21–3, 60–1

Core civil service in 2006:
205,221
(Full time equivalent)

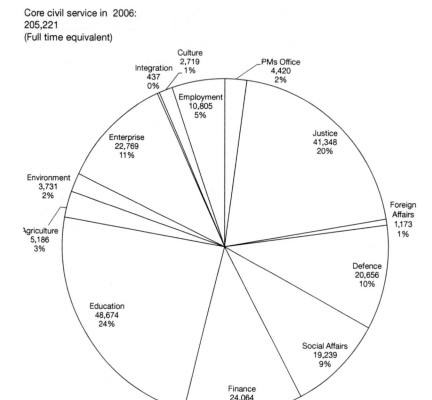

Figure 7.7 The core civil service in Sweden in full-time equivalents, 2006
Source: Regeringskansliet, 2007b: 36

deal with an economic crisis and a large, inefficient public sector. The changes made led to a transformation of public administration that took into account marketisation and privatisation principles (Jensen and Knudsen, 1999: 231). This transformation formed part of the overall transformation of the state, which was taking place in order for Denmark to remain competitive in the globalised economy. Many aspects of the private sector were introduced in public administrative reform (Campbell and Pedersen, 2007). Nonetheless, new public management tools and policies have been implemented more moderately in Denmark than in Sweden. In several welfare areas there was a reluctance to follow the route of marketisation and privatisation completely, one of the main concerns being that inequalities would emerge if too much contracting out and privatisation were to take place (Green-Pedersen, 2002).

In contrast to civil servants in Sweden, Germany and Belgium, in Denmark both civil servants in general and top civil servants in particular do not belong to a political party and are neutral in the Weberian sense. They resemble the British model of the civil service. Political appointees are the exception to the rule. About 95 per cent of top civil servants have an academic degree and they are rather conservative in their behaviour (Jensen and Knudsen, 1999: 239). Similarly to Sweden, the Danish civil service was formerly dominated by lawyers, but it is slowly being balanced by civil servants with social science and economics degrees (Jensen and Knudsen, 1999: 242–3).

In Norway, Danish dominance for four centuries and Swedish rule in the nineteenth century shaped the way Norwegian public administration is organised. Until the 1970s, Norway had a very centralised administrative system that, because of the increase in complexity of modern society, had to gradually give greater autonomy to the large administrative agencies, basing it on the technical expertise of such agencies. Major reforms based on new public management began to take place in the 1990s. However, in the same way as Sweden and Denmark, they were largely integrated into the previous pattern of administration, and the inclusion of interest groups in a myriad of committees remained a central feature of Norwegian public administration. According to Tom Christensen: 'it is one of the most encompassing national consultative and bargaining communities of the world, covering nearly 3,000 national interest groups today' (Christensen, 2005: 727). Some interest groups have resisted the introduction of new public management, and others have negotiated compromises with civil servants. Most of the reform goals were directed towards decentralisation and autonomisation of agencies. The growing use of regulatory agencies has also become a feature of this reform. According to Christensen, since the early 1990s, sixty units have changed their 'organisational status and became formally more autonomous' (Christensen, 2005: 728). The consequence was a loss of political control by government ministers and an increase of power for the executives of such autonomous units. The Storting gained powers of control over this vast autonomous sector and the Office of the Auditor General was upgraded and reinforced to this effect (Christensen, 2005: 731; Figure 7.8).

Although Finland was dominated by Russia during the nineteenth century, it was the Swedish model of public administration that was emulated. This was possible because of the high level of autonomy and self-rule granted by the Russian czars, Alexander I and Alexander II, during this period. The traditional dualism that characterised most Nordic public administration can also be found in the Finnish case (Auffermann, 2009: 240). Although reform of the Finnish administrative system started in 1987, it was the collapse in 1991 of the Soviet Union – until then Finland's main trading partner – that accelerated the reform of public administration. As in other Nordic countries, the reform also concentrated on granting greater autonomy and freedom to the administrative agencies. This was paralleled by a process of decoupling the large public sector from the main public administration, transforming them into state-owned enterprises subject to commercial and market principles, with the result that public administration could be slimmed down considerably and the core government ministries could remain largely untouched. In a similar way to Sweden, Finland also started a major reform of territorial governance by granting more powers of economic coordination to the regional tier. European integration has led to a considerable adjustment to the principles of the multilevel governance model of the European Union (e.g. partnership and subsidiarity). As in Sweden, the partnership principle became important. Finland has a strong tradition of local government autonomy, with about 75 per cent of civil service being located at local level. Implementation of new public

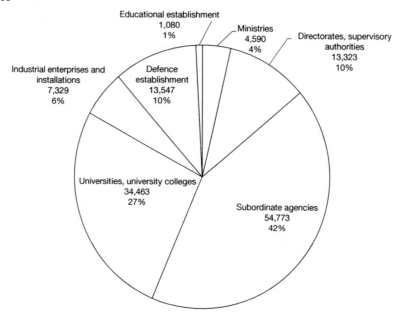

Core civil service in 2006:
129,105

Figure 7.8 The core civil service in Norway, 2006

Source: Norwegian Ministry of Government Administration and Reform, 2007: 2

management has been moderate and has taken place after lengthy consultation with interest groups. As a result, the essential pattern of public administration did not change, despite the inclusion of innovative dynamic elements from marketisation and privatisation (Pollitt and Bouckaert, 2004: 241–2).

The politicisation of the three highest levels of civil service is a feature that Finland shares with Sweden. However, the Finnish system is constrained by the dominance of coalition governments, so that such politicisation is undertaken following a 'quota system' (Pollit and Bouckaert, 2004: 241).

Iceland's public administration also follows the Nordic model, especially in terms of the high degree of decentralisation to the local level. The core government consists of fourteen ministries (run by only nine ministers). It is a small public administration, which has adjusted to the needs of the country. Membership of the European Economic Area (EEA) has been regarded as a challenge for the modernisation of Iceland's public administration. However, the process of negotiation towards accession to the EU should be unproblematic, so that, in the near future, Iceland will be able to follow and implement new public management reform through institutional learning and transfer from the EU.

In sum, the Nordic model has been subject to change so that the state could become more competitive and innovative in a globalised world. However, the core features of the Nordic model, such as inclusive consultation of all relevant interest groups and preservation of equality through a generous welfare state, continue to be dominant. There is concern that 'Nordic or Scandinavian exceptionalism' may be threatened by the growing pressures of Europeanisation and globalisation (Strandberg, 2006). In spite of these concerns, however, it is quite remarkable how this group of countries has been able to adjust to major international changes thus far. The role of public administration cannot be emphasised enough in this context.

The Southern European model: Italy, Spain, Portugal and Greece

In contrast to the clear Nordic model, Southern European democracies had difficulties in creating efficient public administrations. The Southern European public administrations considered here include: Italy, Portugal, Spain and Greece. Nevertheless, all four countries followed similar trajectories for their public administrations from the second half of the nineteenth century up to the Second World War. Clientelism, patronage and political corruption were major features of all four public administrations, and authoritarianism in all four countries used this to legitimise its rule. According to Dimitris Sotiropoulos (2006: 200–3), one can recognise seven features of Southern European public administrations:

- *Political clientelism at the top*: Party organisations engineer political clientelism in public administration among top civil servants, known as 'bureaucratic clientelism' (Lyrintzis, 1984).
- *Political clientelism 'from below'*: Political parties in power use clientelism and patronage among supporters to ease social pressure on government. Political parties facilitate selective recruitment without objective criteria into the public sector and bureaucracy.
- *Uneven staffing of the public sector*: In some parts of public administration there is over-staffing, in others under-staffing.
- *Legal rigidity and excessive legalism*: There is an overproduction of laws and decrees and their selective and fragmented application. According to R. Spence, in the early 1990s Italy enacted between 100,000 and 150,000 pieces of legislation, while the figures for Germany and France over the same period were 6,000 and 7,000, respectively. As in Italy, Southern European political systems are over-legislated and under-regulated, however, because of a 'lack of financial resources' and 'administrative expertise', the legislation is not implemented (Spence, 2000: 126–7).
- *Lack of an institutionalised administrative elite*: This applies more to the Greek and Italian cases, in which a higher civil service has been difficult to establish. In Spain (through the *cuerpos*) and Portugal there is an established higher civil service.
- *Perceived administrative inefficiency*: Public administration in Southern Europe is notorious for being slow and documents are issued in a legalistic language that the ordinary citizen has difficulty in understanding. The quality of public services is also very uneven across all four countries.
- *Widespread political corruption in the lower ranks of public administration*: Political corruption still exists in all four countries, although it does not reach the same levels as in Central and Eastern Europe. Most recently, there were

cases of political corruption at municipal level in Spain. Cases of corruption were also found in the customs service in Portugal with respect to the increasing importance of global criminal organisations (Morgado and Vegar, 2003). In the corruption perception index issued annually by Transparency International, corruption in Italy and Greece is clearly perceived to be greater than in Portugal and Spain.

An eighth feature should probably be added to Sotiropoulos's list, which is still is important in some countries:

- *Excessive over-centralisation of public administration*: Although Spain has now become one of the most decentralised political systems in Europe, and Italy is pushing forward major reforms for the decentralisation of financial resources and competences from the centre to the regions (in view of adapting to Europeanisation and globalisation), Portugal and Greece continue to be highly centralised. Indeed, they are among the most centralised states in Europe. In fact, the ratio between central and local public administration for Portugal is the inverse of that for Denmark. Almost 80 per cent of public administration is that of central government, which is concentrated in the two main cities of Lisbon and Oporto, and 20 per cent is at local level. A similar situation exists in Greece, with the concentration of public administration in Athens and Thessaloniki.

These general traits of Southern European public administration do not take into account developments in the individual countries, so the following pages give more detailed comments on each country. It is probably useful to discuss Italy separately from the other three countries, which only became stable democracies in the mid 1970s, whereas Italy became a democracy soon after the Second World War.

In spite of six decades of Italian democracy under a Republican government, thus far public administration in Italy has remained non-transparent, fragmented and inefficient. The collapse of the First Republic as a result of the Tangentopoli scandal in 1992 showed that public administration was used, and abused, by the political parties to create clienteles and establish patronage networks, resulting in over four decades of systemic political corruption (Rhodes, 1997).

Among many of the corrupt practices was the circumventing of the formalised system of entrance into the civil service based on competition. The reality showed that between 1970 and 1990 about 350,000 entered without exams in contrast with 250,000 with exams. This was a method generally used by political parties to absorb unemployment at local level (Spence, 2000: 135). This high level of political interference was related to the systemic corruption that prevailed until 1992.

Another recruitment practice in public administration has been labelled 'southernisation of the public administration': essentially it means that a disproportionately higher number of southern Italians are recruited into public administration than northern Italians. According to Sabino Cassese, in 1995, 73 per cent of civil servants and 93 per cent of director-generals came from the centre and south of Italy, contrasting strongly with the population distribution of 55 per cent in the north and 45 per cent in the centre and south (Cassese, 1999: 56; Table 7.8).

Table 7.8 The size of public employment in Southern Europe, 2004

Country	Total	Central	Regional	Local
Italy (2002)	3,377,918	2,080,564	605,392*	
Spain (2004)	2,364,866	542,233	1,162,057	567,874
Portugal (2005)	716,418	560,823	33,804	116,076
Greece	518,562	440,591	77,971*	
Malta	47,285	30,069		
Cyprus	62,407	58,433		3,974

* Both regional and local levels.
Source: Luxembourg Presidency, 2005c: 9–11, 27–38, 34–5, 48–50, 42–3, 60–1

The top level of civil service consists of about 400 director-generals distributed among the twenty-plus ministries. These director-generals are career officials holding permanent jobs and cannot be removed by the incoming governments. This is reinforced by the fact that there is a very low level of mobility among this top level of civil service. Last, but not least, the high level of instability of government since 1948 strengthens the position of the director-generals in relation to the politicians. Ninety-five per cent of director-generals hold an academic degree, the vast majority being in law, with only a minority having engineering degrees. There is also a very low proportion of women as director-generals, which did not exceed 5 per cent in the 1990s. Because of the career-dependent trajectory of the civil service, there is also only a low level of mobility to positions outside the civil service, or even within the civil service (Cassese, 1999: 57–9). Cassese characterises Italy as 'an administration without a centre', because of the lack of an *esprit de corps*, in strong contrast with, for example, the French case. However, it is difficult to develop this *esprit de corps* because of the lack of common training and common culture. The vast majority of civil servants come from the southern parts of Italy, where unemployment is highest, and they seek job security, are very legalistic in their approach to public administration, and reject competition. This is also the reason for the lack of mobility and lack of influence in the policy-making process. There is considerable resistance to change at the lower levels of civil service (Cassese, 1999: 63).

Major reform to public administration became imperative in order to restore confidence in the political system. Initially, such reforms were undertaken by the technocratic governments led by Giuliano Amato and Carlo Azeglio Ciampi between 1992 and 1994. These two technocratic governments used the vacuum left by the political parties of the First Republic to make these changes. This not only affected the core public administration, but also the relationship between centre and periphery. There was a general effort to make public administration more compatible with the latest developments in new public management and the European Union multilevel governance system. The aims of the reforms were to make public services more accessible to the citizen/consumer, to simplify the machinery of state by increasing its efficiency, to reduce the costs of public administration (a central aspect of new public management), to reduce political interference with and corrupt practices in public administrative services, and, last but not least, to make public administration more compatible with the pressures coming from Europeanisation (Spence, 2000: 133).

Reforms continued throughout the 1990s and the new millennium, with the purpose of transforming Italy's political system into a more transparent and democratic one. At the centre of these reforms was the introduction of a more flexible territorial governance system, which was more compatible with the pressures stemming from European public policy. Apart from the direct election of the mayor in Italy's larger cities in 1993, the Bassanini laws of 1997 and 1998 gave greater autonomy to local authorities. Additionally, a small constitutional reform (Constitutional Law 3/2001) led to an upgrading of the competences and autonomy of the regions in relation to the central state. The centre-right coalition government of Silvio Berlusconi between 2001 and 2006 sought to go one step further and move to federalism. Although this step would not change the 2001 reform very much, it was an important concession to the coalition partner, Lega Nord (Cotta and Verzichelli, 2007: 186–95). In the end, the proposed constitutional change to federalism was rejected by the population in a referendum on 25–26 June 2006. At the core of the 'devolution' of competences of the regions was the complete transfer of health, education, and law and order (Lanzilotta, 2007: 7).

Furthermore, downsizing the huge public sector that had grown during the post-war period was an important aspect of the reform, so that the state could not be used by political parties to distribute spoils to their respective electoral clienteles (Della Sala, 1997). Several of these huge state holdings, for example the Institute for Industrial Reconstruction (IRI), the National Electrical Energy Corporation (ENEL) and the National Hydrocarbon Corporation, were privatised or decoupled from the main public administration. It was estimated that over and above the large enterprises, the state owned 50,000 to 60,000 organisations in the fields of social welfare, education, sport and cultural activities (Spence, 2000: 137).

Reforms also affected the core public administration. Although the vertical hierarchical model is still strong in the organisation of ministries, in the last fifteen years there has been a growing introduction of innovative, less vertical elements of a departmental model, which delegates more to the responsible units of the department. Today, only 8 per cent of the civil service is employed by central government. There have been also attempts to modernise the top civil service, by introducing a stronger performance-related element to pay structures, encouraging mobility, and changing its social and gender make-up. Moreover, 'agencification', intended to regulate most industries in Italy, became important after 1999 (Cotta and Verzichelli, 2007: 217–30). And, furthermore, Italy, like all other European Union countries, is engaged in an e-government strategy in order to improve the access of public services to citizens.

Among the three democracies that emerged out of authoritarian rule in the 1970s, Spain may be regarded as the most successful in terms of public administration reform. The constitution of 1978, stipulating that Spain was a 'state of autonomies', was the catalyst for the decentralisation process that has been taking place since then. The 'state of autonomies' provided a structure of opportunities to change a legacy of centralisation that goes back to the early nineteenth century.

As in most other Southern European countries, Spain kept most of its civil servants from the previous authoritarian regime. This meant that the whole process towards reform of public administration had to take place over a longer period of time. A key to this transformation was the dynamics created by the 'state of autonomies', which allowed for a steady decentralisation of civil service and public administration. Today, two-thirds of public administration is placed at subnational level and one-third is at central level.

One important feature of the Spanish higher civil service has been the role of the *cuerpos*, which emerged in the nineteenth century in response to the hiring and firing of civil servants by patronage (*cesantes*). The *cuerpos* emulated the French *grands corps* and consisted of specialists in certain professions, whose entrance was strictly regulated by exam, and who had their 'corporatist' organisation to represent their interests. They were able to provide leadership in the Spanish civil service because of their expertise, Moreover, they had common values and a common academic trajectory. In 1911, the statute of Prime Minister Antonio Maura created a permanent civil service based on the *cuerpos*. In the 1960s, Franco's regime tried to complement this specialised *cuerpos* with a top civil service with more general skills. However, this did not diminish the power of the *cuerpos*. During the UCD and PSOE governments of the 1970s and 1980s, there was considerable resistance by the *cuerpos* to any changes to their statute. Prime Minister Felipe Gonzalez wanted to modernise the civil service by allowing outsiders to compete for civil service positions and also by abolishing the practice of reserving certain posts for the civil service. His attempt was rejected by the constitutional court, for reasons based on Article 103 of the constitution, which stipulates that a permanent civil service based on merit should be maintained. The socialist government was able to reform part of the structure of the civil service, but the *cuerpos* continue to be an important force within the civil service (Molina Alvarez de Cienfuegos, 1999: 35–8). The most famous representative of the *cuerpos* is probably the former prime minister, José Maria Aznar, who was an inspector of taxes and therefore integrated in the appropriate *cuerpo*. The politicisation of the higher civil service has been one of the characteristics of Spanish public administration (Molina Alvarez de Cienfuegos, 1999: 50–1). This became evident during the Aznar governments (1996–2004), when a large number of civil servants at both the top and the provincial levels were replaced by loyal supporters of the party in power (*El Pais*, 6 April 1997: 16). Most of the top civil servants come from the core regions of Spain – Castille-León and Madrid; and the vast majority hold degrees in law (almost one-half of them) or economics (one-fifth), or technical diplomas (also one-fifth). A small number hold degrees in humanities and the social sciences. And most originate socially from wealthy families of the upper middle classes (Molina Alvarez de Cienfuegos, 1999: 43–4).

The modernisation of the Spanish public administration is markedly linked to the decentralisation of competences to the subnational level and democratisation. New public management, marketisation and privatisation were introduced into the public administration in the 1990s and in the new millennium. This was started under the socialist governments, but more radically implemented during the two Aznar governments. Basically, the decentralisation process meant that most public services could be managed by the different regional administrations and that both financial as well as human resources were delegated to regional level. Further attempts to reform the core central administration have been partly successful. Steps towards a simplification of administrative processes and the introduction of citizens' charters in most public services have been important (Ramió, 2001: 554–9).

The Portuguese public administration can be considered to be fairly fragmented and divided. Throughout the 1970s until the mid 1980s, governmental and economic instability prevented a proper reform of public administration in the context of democracy. The modernisation of public administration started after 1985, during the ten years of government under Prime Minister Anibal Cavaco Silva. New public management was used to transform the closed-minded public administration that existed under the authoritarian regime that existed before the transition to democracy (1974–76) into an open-minded citizen-friendly one within a democratic political system (Corte-Real, 2000; Magone, 2004: 110–14).

This administrative reform was continued by the subsequent governments. Two of the most important aspects of the reform of public administration were the downsizing of the public sector, which had grown considerably during the revolutionary transition process, and the reduction in the size of the civil service, which had been used for patronage purposes or to solve unemployment problems by successive governments. According to a census in 1999, the number of civil servants had risen to about 700,000, however the vast majority had poor qualifications. One problem was the lack of job mobility within the civil service and the concentration of about 75–80 per cent of it within the large cities in Lisbon and Oporto. Only about 20 per cent were working at the local level or in the autonomous regions of Azores and Madeira (Magone, 2004: 115). This has been a major problem for government. There has been a resistance on the part of many civil servants to move to the eighteen districts and be part of these deconcentrated services. However, in 2002 Portugal exceeded the budget deficit criterion relating to Economic and Monetary Union and since then successive governments have been under considerable pressure to reduce public expenditure (Magone, 2006b). Therefore, the José Manuel Barroso (2002–4), Pedro Santana Lopes (2004–5) and José Socrates (2005–) governments have prioritised the reform and modernisation of public administration.

The Barroso government was crucial in defining the priorities of such administrative reform. One particular aim was to de-bureaucratise public administration, hence reducing the services as well as the use of human resources. Such approach was pursued by the Barroso and Santana Lopes governments with the aim of bringing the budget deficit below 3 per cent of GDP. However, despite extraordinary efforts to reduce services in public administration, the budget deficit has always remained close to 3 per cent of GDP. Trade union confederations have also been vociferous against any reforms without consultation (consulation having been the norm in Portuguese politics). Reforms also include the transition to e-government, marketisation and 'agencification' (Carapeto and Fonseca, 2005: 29–35). The new government of Prime Minister José Socrates was able to count on an absolute majority achieved in the legislative elections of February 2005 but, as previous governments, it had to tackle the problems of an inefficient public administration. On 30 March 2006, a restructuring of all ministries was approved. The Programme for the Restructuring of the Central State Administration (Programa de Reestruturação da Administração Central do Estado, PRACE) proposes a reduction of 518 existing structures and bodies to 331 (Programa de Restruturação, 2006: 17). Although it is planned to close 246 units, 60 new ones will be created. This programme is affecting all ministries and has the aim of pushing Portuguese public administration towards a model of governance based on the new public management tools advocated by the OECD. Outsourcing, contracting out, public–private partnership are all part of the language used in this attempt to reform public administration (Programa de Reestruturação, 2006: 4, 6–8, 14). It is also proposed that this attempt at reform will be accompanied by measures to simplify administrative and legislative procedures, the Simplex programme, which envisages the implementation of 333 measures in different areas. Overall, this also will certainly be reinforced by the policies of e-government.

Hence, although later than other countries, Portugal's transition to governance is beginning to take place. One basic problem that public administration will encounter, however, is that a weak state is compounded by a weak economic infrastructure. In this sense, the opportunities to create public–private partnerships with the private sector economy are probably very limited (Sá et al., 2001). This can be seen particularly in the area of social services, in which the independent third sector is actually financially dependent on state subsidies and contracts – without which it would simply collapse (Hespanha et al., 2000). The permanent crisis of the health sector, which is always on the verge of bankruptcy, shows that the overall political system and its leadership are characterised by high levels of inertia (Oliveira et al., 2005).

Greek public administration is probably the one that has had the greatest difficulties in introducing a modernisation programme. It is a top-heavy, politicised and highly fragmented public administration. During transition to democracy, Prime Minister Kostas Karamanlis introduced some reforms in public administration that, in reality, led to clientelistic practices (Sotiropoulos, 2006: 204–5). Such practices were also dominant during the PASOK governments between 1981 and 1989, under Prime Minister Andreas Papandreou. In 1982, the higher civil service was abolished with the intention of achieving a more egalitarian public administration. However, the vacuum this action left led to an increase in the politicisation of the civil service, largely because it was filled with political appointees (Sotiropoulos, 1999: 15). The over-dominance of the socialists also led to a strengthening of the position of the sectorial socialist trade union PASKDY in public administration. Although efforts were made to achieve a professionalisation of the civil service and create an objective entrance system based on examinations, the politics of clientelism seemed to prevail (Sotiropoulos, 2006: 216–17; see also Sotiropoulos, 2006). After 1981, European integration later led to the introduction of thirteen non-elected administrative regions, imposed on Greece by the European Community in 1986 in order to achieve the better implementation of the structural funds – known as the Integrated Mediterranean Programmes, to which Greece was tentitled (Paraskevopoulos, 2005: 450).

In 1990, after an interlude of coalition governments, New Democracy (ND), under Kostas Mitsoutakis, came to power and introduced major reforms, which were partly modernising, partly traditional. One important change was the reinstatement of the director-generals in the higher civil service. The new public management rationale also began to be introduced in the Greek administrative services. Although the Mitsoutakis government only lasted until 1993, it reversed many of the reforms and measures undertaken by the previous PASOK government. This was paralleled by the strengthening of ND's sectorial trade union DAKDY (Sotiropoulos, 2006: 217).The dynamics between the two political parties led to a cancelling out of policies introduced by the previous government, and this, understandably, further undermined morale and efficiency within the Greek civil service (Spanou, 1996). A serious, comprehensive modernisation programme was undertaken only after 1996, under the leadership of socialist Prime Minister Kostas Simitis. Between 1996 and 2004, he particularly tackled economic and social issues in order to make the Greek economy more competitive (Featherstone, 2005: 226–8). The privatisation programme of the Simitis government, which included the National Telecommunications Corporation (OTE) and other public enterprises, was a very important step. There was also general pressure from Europeanisation to dismantle state monopolies and allow more competition in the market. The privatisation policy, which was both unilateralist and centralised, was achieved without any consultation with the unions (Pagoulatos, 2005: 374–5; Dimitrakopoulos, 2001). Simitis also encountered major resistance to the reform of the pension system from within his own party, and it took a long time to achieve some changes in this area (Featherstone *et al.*, 2001).

In 1999, the socialist government introduced a new Civil Service Code in a bid to restructure public administration, making it more efficient. However, politicisation, lack of interdepartmental mobility, and a reluctance to adopt the new modernising programmes based on new public management continue to be obstacles to achieving greater efficiency in the decision-making process and the delivery of public services. Clientelism and patronage also continue to be a major problem in public administration (Sotiropoulos, 1999: 28–9).

In sum, Southern European public administrations are still characterised by many of the features mentioned by Sotiropoulos. However, the European integration process is a major catalyst for modernisation and Europeanisation. This means that the external dimensions of reform should be taken into consideration in this group of countries and the European Union should be regarded as an important *vincolo esterno* (external link) (Dyson and Featherstone, 1996) that helps the countries to overcome the negative features of their public administrations. A similar assessment can be given to the final group of countries, that of Central and Eastern Europe.

The Central and Eastern European model

In contrast to these more advanced democracies in the European Union, the new democracies in Central and Eastern European countries have similar problems of adjustment to those of the Southern European countries. The fall of the Berlin Wall allowed for a democratisation of these countries, which, until 1989, were dominated by communist regimes. Since 1991, the EC/EU has been engaged in a dialogue with these new democracies. The establishment of the Copenhagen criteria in the Danish presidency of 1993 allowed a more organised, structured process towards integration to take place. The new member states had to fulfil political, economic and administrative criteria. It is the administrative criteria that are relevant for our discussion of public administrative reform in Central and Eastern Europe. According to Antoanetta Dimitrova, period between 1989 (the start of democratic transition) and 2004 (the accession to EU membership) should be divided into two. The first period can be characterised as the necessary process of democratic transition, which lasted until 1997, and the second period can be labelled as Europeanisation based on conditionality. In fact, administrative conditionality became an essential tool of the EU to push through reforms in central administration, including encouragement to regionalise and decentralise structures.

The main rationale for this administrative restructuring was to increase the capacity of the new Central and Eastern European countries to absorb the *acquis communautaire* of over 80,000 pages of European legal directives and regulations (Dimitrova, 2005: 75–9). This structured way of dealing with Central and Eastern European enlargement deviates considerably from the experience in the Southern European enlargement of the mid 1980s. Indeed, the demands made on the new Southern European democracies were much lower than those made on the Central and Eastern European countries, partly because the number of candidate countries was much larger, and also because, since 1985, the *acquis communautaire* had grown exponentially.

The blueprint for Central and Eastern European reform was the SIGMA-PUMA programme developed by the OECD and commissioned by the European Union. The Support for Improvement and Governance and Management in Central and Eastern European Countries (SIGMA) established the 'baselines' for a modern reformed public administration. Initially, these baselines introduced a Weberian model of public administration, before moving towards the more mixed system of the new public management rationale (Dimitrova, 2005: 81). In the annual progress reports of the European Union, reform of public administration in general and the civil service in particular were flagged up as central to any future membership. In spite of this conditionality, different countries reacted in different ways and still today some countries are more advanced in implementing public administrative reforms than others. However, all of them are engaged in a transition from a centralised public administration based on egalitarian principles to one that has adjusted to a market-oriented environment, deconcentration and decentralisation. In the case of the new member states from Central and Eastern Europe, it means a considerable transformation of the modus operandi. This is confirmed in John A. Scherpereel's excellent study on civil servants in Czech and Slovak ministries in Central and Eastern European public administrations, which shows clearly how the civil service and public administrations cope with this transition in cultural and paradigmatic terms. Over the last two decades, civil servants in the Czech Republic and Slovakia in particular, but also in all other Central and Eastern

Table 7.9 The number of public employees including civil servants in Central and Eastern Europe, 2004

	Total	Central	Regional	Local
Hungary	550,000	110,000		
Czech Republic		101,071	5,342*	
Slovakia	473,237	41,618		
Poland	356,874	162,244	194,665*	
Slovenia (2003)	144,049	140,549		3,500

*Regional and local governments.

Source: Luxembourg Presidency, 2005c: 12–13, 38–41, 44–7, 51–3, 54–6

European countries, have been and are still in a state of transition from the state socialist administrative space, which was more closed-minded and less international-ised, to the new European administrative space, which is open-minded and dynamic (Scherpereel, 2004; Goetz, 2001: 1033–4). This transition has been and is being pushed and monitored by the European Union.

Europeanisation and modernisation are two interlinked processes that are still taking place. The public administrations needed to 'catch up' with Western-inspired ideas of government. Klaus Goetz quite rightly emphasises similarities to Southern Europe and Latin America. The 'Latinisation' of the public administrations of the Central and Eastern European countries is related to the fact that these different regions are trying to transform their public administrations within a cultural context of past legacies. The present public administrative cultures, in the same way as in Southern Europe and Latin America, are mixed. However, Europeanisation is making these public administrative cultures and structures more compatible with the EU multilevel governance system (Goetz, 2001: 1037).

A major problem for Central and Eastern European public administrations is political corruption. One of the reasons for this is the low salaries of civil servants and public employees across the region. However, it seems that the level of political corruption is higher in the western and eastern Balkans than in central Eastern Europe. A major study on political corruption shows that too much reform and replacement of legislation has led to confusion and a resistance to change (Miller *et al.*, 2001: 312–15). There is also a general expectation, or rather perception, in many of the countries that small gifts/bribes to public employees are necessary in order to receive better treatment. Again, there are major differences between the Czech Republic and Bulgaria. In the Czech Republic there is a larger gap in behaviour between the public and the respective public employee (e.g. hospital doctors or benefits officials) than in Bulgaria (Miller *et al.*, 2001: 207–9). Alexandru Grigorescu's study (2006) demonstrates that international organisations (in particular the European Union) actually play a major role in keeping political corruption as a salient issue in the press of the Central and Eastern European countries. This acts as pressure upon the political elite to put certain procedures in place in order to make public administration more predictable. It is difficult to assess whether these measures will finally lead to a decline of political corruption (Grigorescu, 2006: 548–9).

The fight against political corruption is essential to restore the confidence of the populations in the respective political systems. Across Central and Eastern European countries trust in political institutions is particularly low (Grigorescu, 2006: 519–20). A lack of transparency in government policy improves the opportunities for populist movements to achieve greater success in the political arena. Indeed, nationalist and xenophobic populism have been increasing across all the Central and Eastern European countries, especially Slovakia, Poland, Bulgaria and Romania. Although all public administrations are struggling with political corruption, Bulgaria and Romania are certainly the two countries perceived to be most corrupt. Apart from the fact that civil servants have low salaries, it is estimated that one-third of the population in each country lives below the poverty line. Since 2000, the two member states have introduced several institutions designed to combat political corruption, as well as drawing up plans to tackle and prevent it. In October 2001, Romania announced their National Plan against Corruption and the National

Programme for Corruption Prevention. In 2002, this was followed by the creation of a National State Prosecutor for the Fight against Corruption (NAPO) and an Anticorruption Agency (PNA) that, among other successes, led to the resignation of three politicians. In October 2005, a directorate-general for the fight against corruption was created in the Ministry of the Interior and Public Admnistration, in order to tackle such crimes in the public sector. Similarly, since 2001 Bulgaria has had an anti-corruption strategy, which was complemented by several training programmes in governmental units and other public sector agencies in order to raise awareness of corruption and corrupt behaviour. There is also a stronger screening process of civil servants (Leiße, 2006: 10). In 2006, Bulgaria and Romania remained at the bottom in the ranking of the annual Corruption Perception Index (CPI) of the non-governmental organisation, Transparency International, along with other Balkan countries – Poland, Turkey and Russia (see Figure 7.9).

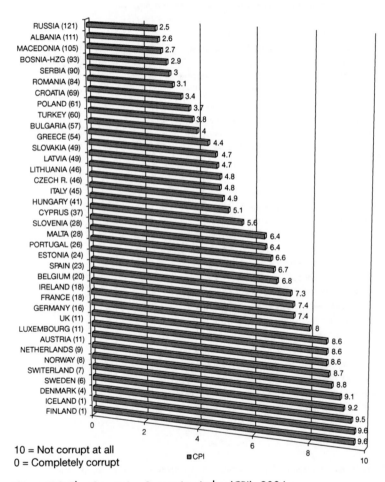

Figure 7.9 The Corruption Perception Index (CPI), 2006

Source: Transparency International, available online at: www.transparency.org/policy_research/surveys_indices/cpi/2007 (accessed 21 June 2010)

After decades of war, public administration reform has become an important issue in the reconstruction of the Balkan countries. Such reform is important, because all of these countries have high levels of political corruption. Croatia, although it does not want to be counted as a Balkan country, has made the most progress in this field. Even so, it has a long way to go before it can overcome the legacy of the Tudjman period, which was based on patrimonialism and authoritarianism. Similar problems can be found in the other Balkan countries (see Figure 7.9).

However, in terms of evaluation of public administration, Romania and Bulgaria differ completely. Romania has a positive evaluation of public administration that comes closer to the almost-European countries of Nordic Europe or even higher, while Bulgaria has the lower evaluation, followed by Portugal and Croatia. This means that there is no clear East–West divide in terms of positive

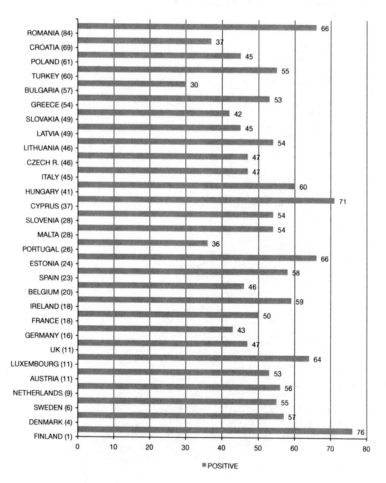

Figure 7.10 The positive evaluation of public administration performance, 2006

Note: Numbers in parentheses following country names denote the position of that country in the CPI (see Figure 7.9)

Source: Eurobarometer 67, 2007: Question 28,10.

evaluation of public administration. The highest positive evaluation can be found in Finland (see Figure 7.10).

Not surprisingly, political corruption is also widespread in other Central and Eastern European countries. In 2007, several cases of political corruption were found among the police and the political elite in Latvia. Sometimes small-scale corruption can be seen as part of the tradition of a country and the case of Latvian president Valdis Zatlers highlights this clash between the transitional culture of the past and the present priorities. Zatlers was a well-known surgeon in Latvia and he used to receive envelopes with money after offering his services to patients. Such unsolicited gifts are a tradition inherited from the former Soviet Union and as such have remained part of daily life in post-Soviet Latvia. However, these envelopes were linked to inappropriate payments from patients and classified as small-scale corruption. President Valdis Zatlers confessed that he had received such payments and that he did not declare them to the tax office. This highlights the point that certain practices of a previous culture may need to be eradicated in a new democratic era, where public employees are expected to offer their services impartially and without any incentive from patients or administrative clients (*Baltic Times*, 6 June 2007) (Table 7.10).

This is not the place to review all Central and Eastern European public administrations. However, some examples may suffice to highlight the problems that all of them are facing. Hungary is regarded as the front-runner of public administration reform; however, after four civil administrative reforms undertaken by different governments, it continues to have major problems of politicisation in the higher civil service (Meyer-Sahling, 2005: 693–4).

In 1992, even before the period of administrative conditionality, Hungary started to introduce major reforms in line with European Union requirements (Dimitrova, 2005: 83–4; Ágh, 2003: 115–19). There was also an attempt to introduce seven decentralised regions in Hungary, but the process has been far from smooth because of the lack of tradition for such tiers (Goetz, 2005: 273). However, the growing distrust between left and right parties after the consensual transition to democracy led to a more politicised approach to the reform of public administration. The level of personnel turnover after a new government taking control began to be a major characteristic of Hungarian politics in the mid 1990s. Viktor Orbán's centre-right government contributed to the polarisation of left and right. In spite of four reforms of public administration (in 1992, 1996, 2001 and 2002), political parties retained political discretion to circumvent the rules concerning the civil service (Meyer-Sahling, 2005: 705). This was reinforced by

Table 7.10 The size of public employment in the Baltic states, 2004–5

	Total	Central	Regional	Local
Latvia (2005)	37,498	29,852		
Estonia (2004)	28,540	19,386		4,870
Lithuania (2005)	27,000			

Source: Luxembourg Presidency, 2005c: 16–18, 36–9

an economic policy that focused on overspending. In 1995, there was an attempt to implement a stabilisation package, but when the signs of the crisis were gone, any commitment to further austerity was abandoned. Such polarised distrust between the parties contributed simultaneously to growing disappointment and low trust by the population (Györffy, 2006: 253–4).

All other countries in Central and Eastern Europe delayed their reforms until the second half of the 1990s and the new millennium. The Czech Republic resisted the implementation of any kind of civil service reform for a long time. Indeed, it was very keen to move towards a market-based system of hire-and-fire. Nevertheless, before joining the European Union, legislation was adopted on civil service reform (Dimitrova, 2005: 87). Although it was only approved in 2002, two years before accession, and implementation only started in 2007 – and is still ongoing. The results have so far been very mixed and resistance to change is a major problem (Meyer-Sahling, 2005: 701; Kotchegura, 2008: 144–8; Cardona and Dannequin, 2010: 3–4, 5; Table 7.11).

According to a study by Miro Hacek on the Slovenian Civil Service, in 2004 about 75 per cent of the higher civil servants were recruited from families in which the father had already some managerial experience. Although this group could come from all possible classes, it came mainly from classes where the father could be categorised as lower non-manual (28 per cent), skilled manual (30 per cent), and semi-skilled and unskilled (11 per cent). In contrast, the combined higher categories of high and low management and professionals represented only 27 per cent of the administrative elite. Because the new democratic public administration is only twenty years old, it may still contain a legacy from communism, in which belonging to the working class and egalitarian values were important (Hacek, 2006: 166–7). Another interesting finding is that, in the Slovenian case, neither politicians nor civil servants are able to have dominance over each other. The complexity of the policy-making process makes these two groups interdependent, because of the complementary skills that they have. Hacek demonstrates that the nature of the process weakens and moderates the politicisation of the civil service (Hacek, 2006: 181–3).

Although legal frameworks have been implemented in recent years, the whole relationship between government and higher civil servants is still very fluid in Central and Eastern Europe. It is still difficult to make a final assessment (Goetz and Wollmann, 2001: 882).

In sum, this short comparative overview of the different trajectories of European countries and public administrative reform shows that there is no single approach towards a European administrative space. All these countries have been influenced by processes induced by the OECD, which is slowly becoming part of an pan-European *acquis administratif*.

Table 7.11 The size of public employment in Bulgaria and Romania, 2004

	Total	Civil servants
Bulgaria	84,799	25,338
Romania	110,000	

Source: Luxembourg Presidency, 2005c: 67–71

Towards a European administrative space: rhetoric and reality

The transformation of government to governance has also to be contextualised in the European integration process. The construction of the Single European Market and the implementation of its policies needs national and European public administrations that are compatible with each other. Such a process of convergence of public administration has been taking place since the mid 1990s and has been referred to as a process towards the 'European administrative space' (see Box 7.3).

A reform of the European Commission has been taking place since the beginning of the new millennium and this has been supplemented by similar processes of public administrative reforms in the member states. This has led to the establishment of the European Network of Public Administration (EUPAN) among the twenty-eight public administrations. There is a growing open coordination taking place among the different public administrations in order to create a Single European Market in this sector. Exchanges of civil servants between different public administrations, including the European Commission, take place regularly. One of the main problems of the concept of a 'European administrative space', though, is that it lacks an agreed definition (Olsen, 2003; Burnham and Maor, 1995; Everson, 1998).

In a stricter sense, one might speak of the relationships between the administrative Euro-elites of the EU member states (Magone, 2004: 174). Indeed, this would

---

Box 7.3 The European administrative space

One of the main aims of the Lisbon Strategy of the European Union, which was formulated in 2000, was to achieve the most competitive knowledge-based economy of the world in 2010. For this purpose, all aspects that might lead to a more competitive Single European Market (SEM) need to be readjusted towards this ultimate aim. Although the ultimate goal of the Lisbon Strategy will not be achieved by 2010, the overall thrust has already given a new dynamic to the European integration process.

One aspect that needs to be readjusted in line with the Lisbon Strategy's ultimate goal is public administration reform. Based on the principles of new public management, the twenty-seven national public administrations of the member states and the European Commission are engaged in convergence processes in order to achieve better compatibility between them. This process started in 1998 and has become more sophisticated and structured over time. The whole process is coordinated by the European Institute of Public Administration in Maastricht.

The twenty-eight public administrations (twenty-seven national plus the European Commission) established the European Union Public Administration Network (EUPAN). Soft governance methods, such as the open method of coordination, benchmarking and good practice, are being used to sustain this voluntary process of horizontal Europeanisation (see Chapter 4). The Organisation for Economic Cooperation and Development is an important partner in this respect.

include all civil servants involved in the national coordination of European policy-making. It would mean that the members of the permanent representations in Brussels, the directorate-general responsible for European affairs, the European policy units in the individual ministries and the European civil servants in the European Commission, European Council and European Parliament would be the main actors within this European administrative space. According to Maurizio Bach, in the mid 1990s an estimated 30,000–40,000 people were involved in the European administrative space (Bach, 1995: 54–5). The recent enlargement may have increased this figure to at least 50,000 people. Over time, the stable patterns of relationships have been contributing to the emergence of a common transnational culture with common European values and shared experiences. Indeed, all these actors are part of a transnational administrative culture and are, therefore, less rigid in terms of national preferences. They empathise with the positions of fellow civil servants from other countries and are geared towards the development of a compromise in the working groups of the Council. Such administrative Euro-elites would also include the different national representatives in the comitology of the European Commission (Kassim *et al.*, 2000, 2001; Zwaan, 1995; Beyers and Dierickx, 1998; Lewis, 1998) (see Chapter 4).

Moreover, the European Institute for Public Administration (EIPA) is an important socialisation institution for training national civil servants into a European rationale. EIPA is at the core of the European administrative space. In a wider sense, the European administrative space means that a slow process of integration and socialisation of all parts of national administrations into common frameworks is taking place. This is a long process, but it is already happening. The best examples are the regular six-monthly meetings of national director-generals of the departments of administrative reform. Starting in the 1970s, by May 2008 fifty such meetings had taken place (Irish Presidency, 2004; Dutch Presidency, 2004; Luxembourg Presidency, 2005a; Slovenian Presidency, 2008). This is paralleled by meetings of the national ministers of administrative reform of the member states, introduced in 1988 (with twelve such meetings up to 2005) (Italian Presidency, 2003; Luxembourg Presidency, 2005b). In spite of this long period of cooperation, it was only during the Austrian presidency of the second half of 1998 that the ministers responsible for the reform of public administration, in their meeting of 12 November 1998 in Vienna, agreed to move to the 'European administrative space', which would in turn gradually lead to a common framework assessment in relation to the quality of delivery of administrative services.

Since 1998, an informal network of director-generals responsible for public administrations in the EU member states was established, coordinated by the European Institute of Public Administration in Maastricht. The European Public Administration Network (EUPAN) is pushing forward the agenda of public administrative reform in order to create a European administrative space. The overall aim is to create a more competitive European public administration that will support the Lisbon strategy of making the European Union the most competitive and dynamic knowledge-based economy. It is intended that this will be achieved through sustainable and economic growth, so that more and better jobs can be created and social, economic and environmental cohesion preserved – a very ambitious task that reflects this optimistic 'Euro-jargon'. The reality is always a little more modest. The cooperation mechanisms were only set up after the

Portuguese presidency in the first semester of 2000. Four main working groups were set up, later reduced to three, with the purpose of drawing up ideas for mid-term programmes (see Box 7.3).

A first mid-term programme was drawn for 2004–5; this was followed up by continuing programmes in 2006–7, 2007–8 and 2008–9. The language of EUPAN is based on new public management and the approach is citizen-oriented (although informed by the priorities of the information society). Coordination between the different sectors of public administrative reform was regarded as an important priority for the mid-term programme of 2006–7 (Luxembourg Presidency, 2006).

Since 1998, one of the more concrete results of this intensified cooperation was the creation of the Common Assessment Framework (CAF) in order to enhance efficiency and quality in the delivery of services in the public sector. The CAF was developed during the Austrian (second half of 1998), German (first half of 1999) and Finnish (second half of 1999) presidencies. It was finished and polished during the Finnish and Portuguese presidencies. The CAF is a lighter version of the European Framework for Quality Management (EFQM). The European Institute for Public Administration (EIPA) and the German Academy for Administrative Sciences in Speyer undertook the academic work leading up to the CAF. One of the advantages of the CAF is its simplicity and ease of implementation. EUPAN agreed to establish a CAF resource centre in EIPA that would lead to research projects and the collection of data relating to the implementation of CAF in the individual member states. Meanwhile, there were two surveys on the implementation of the CAF in the member states in 2003 during the Italian presidency and most recently in the first half of 2005 during the Luxembourg presidency (EIPA, 2003, 2005). The results showed an increase in the use of the CAF. Apart from the Netherlands, which developed its own Instituut Nationaal voor Kwaliteit (National Institute of Quality, INK), all other countries had some experience with the CAF. In both the 2003 and 2005 surveys, the main reason for using it was related to the wish to improve the organisation, particularly by identifying weak and strong points (Staes and Thijs, 2005a: 37–8; 2005b: 44). The CAF model of assessment is already creating an asymmetrical level of implementation among countries. Some countries are adopting it and recommending it strongly, others are using the CAF in parallel with other quality enhancing tools, and yet others are still learning to deal with the new instrument. In this sense, after five years of implementation of the CAF, it is possible to recognise an asymmetrical interdependent structuring of a European administrative space.

Looking at other areas such as e-government, we would probably find similar asymmetrical interdependence structures. The dominance of the Scandinavian countries, the UK and Germany in this area and the lagging behind of Southern European countries shows similar asymmetries.

In the case of the new member states from Central and Eastern Europe, this means a considerable transformation of the modus operandi. According to John A. Scherpereel's study of civil servants in Czech and Slovak ministries, Central and Eastern European public administrations are still in a transition from the state socialist administrative space, which was more closed-minded and less international-ised than the new European administrative space (Scherpereel, 2004). This kind of transition was also experienced by Portuguese public administration until the late 1990s, as Joaquim Aguiar showed in his work (Aguiar, 1985; 1986). In general, post-communist public administrations have many similarities to post-authoritarian ones, being a mixed culture of old authoritarian/communist values and new democratic ones. However, with the passing of time a democratic public administration will emerge.

The dissemination of best practice is important for any public administration, with regular quality conferences designed to promote it, currently held every second year. The first one was held during the Portuguese presidency in 2000. Additionally, examples of best practice are collected by the EUPAN network and posted on the EIPA website.

The different national trajectories of public administration will show different impacts of these initiatives in different countries. However, despite this, the EUPAN network is certainly creating the conditions for a blurring of boundaries between different national public administrations, creating an all-encompassing European network. The long-term aim has to be a public administration network in order to improve efficiency of implementation of legislation across the European Union. Last, but not least, programmes designed to enhance the mobility of civil servants across the European Union help to transform the national compartmentalised spaces into a large transnational one. This means that the core area of the European administrative space will be able to expand to the more nationally defined periphery of national public administrations. This is key in sustaining the ongoing reforms of European governance micro-institutionally. Furthermore, the present EUPAN network is creating – parallel to macro-institutional change – the vocabulary and structure for the dynamic integrative transformation of the twenty-eight public administrations into a public administration network (Olsen, 2002b: 594–7).

The reform of the European Commission after 2000 initiated by the European Commissioner is a sign of encouragement that there is a synchrony of institutional transformation at different levels of the emerging European Union political system (Christiansen and Grey, 2004: 23–4). Nonetheless, in spite of these remarkable changes, there is a still a long way to go. It is expected that the European Commission will have to become more politicised and increasingly characterised by a functioning communication policy, otherwise the problem of leadership will continue to be a major problem for the EU (Christiansen, 1997; Schmidt, 2002: 246–50). This also means that policy-makers will need to focus on prioritising their policies sensibly in order to avoid an overburdening of the EU's agenda (Schout and Bastmeijer, 2003: 13). As Carlo D'Orta points out, the main reason for the emergence of a European administrative space is the acceleration of globalisation and the need to create a more competitive public administration. Such an attempt can be achieved through a shared regime of public administrative governance, in which experiences and tools are shared and used across the European Union (D'Orta, 2003).

Conclusions: towards a European administrative space?

The European integration process is contributing to a convergence of public administrative practices. In the European Union, the twenty-eight public administrations (the national ones and the European Commission) are engaged in major public administrative reform. At the centre of the reform is the creation of a single European market in the administrative sector. In spite of the convergence, there are still major differences in national public administration patterns. In this chapter, we have identified seven patterns that are also almost identical with their geographical location: the British, French, Drei-Sat/Germanic, Benelux, Scandinavian, Southern European and Central and Eastern European patterns. The historical legacy of each one influences the way new public management tools, instruments and philosophy are being incorporated in public administrative reform, with the result that, in spite of a common purpose, European diversity will remain a major feature of public administration.

Suggested reading

Introductory essay

Page, Edward C. (1995), Administering Europe. In: Jack Hayward and Edward C. Page (eds), *Governing the New Europe*. Cambridge: Polity Press, pp. 257–85.

General books on public administration in Europe

Chandler, J. A. (eds) (2000), *Comparative Public Administration*. London: Routledge.

Hayward, Jack and Anand Menon (eds) (2003), *Governing Europe*. Oxford: Oxford University Press (Part II on Public Administration).

Pollitt, Christopher and Geert Bouckaert (2004), *Public Management Reform: A Comparative Analysis*. 2nd edition. Oxford: Oxford University Press (important text about new public management reform).

Bureaucratic elites in Europe

Page, Ed and Vincent Wright (eds) (1999), *Bureaucratic Elites in Western European States*. Oxford: Oxford University Press (excellent edited volume on the administrative elites in several European countries).

Public sector performance

Kuhry, Bob (ed.), *Public Sector Performance.An International Comparison of Education Health Care, Law and Order and Public Administration*. The Hague: Social and Cultural Planning, pp. 271–92, website www.scp.nl (accessed 13 August 2008).

Kuhry, Bob and Evert Pommer (2007), *Public Sector Performance. An International Comparison*. Mimeographed document, published as Publication 2007/1 in Social Cultural Planning, website www.scp.nl, this version is on www.irspm2007.org/Fullpaper/PT_Metrics_Kuhry%20Pommer.pdf (accessed 13 August 2008).

Europeanisation of national administrations

Kassim, Hussein (2003), Meeting the Demands of EU Membership: The Europeanization of National Administrative Systems. In: Kevin Featherstone and Claudio Radaelli (eds), *The Politics of Europeanization*. Oxford: Oxford University Press, pp. 83–111.

Kassim, Hussein, Guy Peters and Vincent Wright (eds) (2000), *The National Co-ordination of EU Policy. The Domestic Level*. Oxford: Oxford University Press.

Kassim, Hussein, Anand Menon, Guy Peters and Vincent Wright (eds) (2001), *The National Co-ordination of EU Policy: The European Level*. Oxford: Oxford University Press.

On European Public Administration Network: please see database on website www.eupan.eu accessed 22 August 2009.

QUESTIONS FOR REVISION

- What are common features of public administrations in Europe? Discuss using examples from at least two countries.
- What is understood under 'new public management' and what impact does it have on national public administrations?
- Compare the main features of British and German administrative styles.
- How efficient are public administrations in Southern, Central and Eastern Europe? Discuss, using examples of at least one country for each region.
- Discuss the impact of European integration on national public administrations.

Judicial power in multilevel Europe

SUMMARY OF CHAPTER 8

The independence of the judiciary is one of the most important aspects of European politics. However, governments always tend to gain influence over judiciary power through legislation or other means. The relationship between the government and the judiciary is therefore crucial. There is also a major tension between the constitutional text and the reality of judiciary power.

This chapter deals with the different patterns of judiciary power, taking account of the different systems adopted by different countries. There are at least five law systems that have similarities, even though they have evolved from different traditions: the common law countries (the UK, Ireland and Malta), the Napoleonic Code countries (France, Belgium, Luxembourg and Latin Southern Europe), the Germanic law countries (Germany, Austria, Switzerland, in part, and Greece), the Nordic law countries (Scandinavia and Iceland), and the law systems of Central and Eastern Europe (which are highly influenced by Germanic law).

In this chapter, a special section is dedicated to constitutional courts as the means of achieving constitutional review in Europe. The German Federal Constitutional Court became the model for all the other countries in Europe, particularly in Southern, Central and Eastern Europe (e.g. Spain, Portugal, Hungary, Poland and Albania).

As with many other institutions, the power of the judiciary is being challenged by the European dimension. EU law supersedes national law and this has led to major conflicts at the national level.

Introduction

The separation of powers, as advocated by the French philosopher and political scientist Montesquieu in his *L'Esprit des Lois* (*Spirit of Laws*) in 1748 has remained a central doctrine of European politics. We have shown in Chapter 6 that across Europe the legislative branch is weak in relation to the executive one. European legislatures are considerably weaker than the American legislature, which also has considerably greater financial and human resources as well as greater power to challenge the executive. Although there are differences in the impact of European national legislatures on their particular executives, all of them should be characterised as reactive. The outcome is a more cooperative approach between executive and legislature (Box 8.1).

Although executives are able to dominate legislative politics, the independence of the judiciary has always been an important issue in European politics. Political pressure on the judiciary is usually regarded as negative by a country's citizens. The politicisation of the judiciary can lead to corruption of judicial activity and, in the end, erode the legitimacy of the political system. The Italian case shows how important it is to have an independent judiciary. The 'Mani Pulite' ('Clean Hands') investigation of judge Antonio di Pietro and his team uncovered a web of systemic

---

Box 8.1 The judiciary and the rule of law

Throughout the eighteenth and nineteenth centuries, the bourgeoisie in Europe fought against the absolutist state in order to achieve a modern state based on the rule of law. The absolutist state was characterised by some judicial order, for example as in France; however, the monarch held absolute power and could decide arbitrarily about any subject. The 'Glorious Revolution' in England in 1688–89 and the French Revolution of 1789 led to the emergence of the rule of law based on a written constitution.

The idea of the rule of law was first mentioned by English philosopher James Harrington in his book *The Commonwealth of Oceana* (1656, p. 37) in which he proposed an ideal republic during Oliver Cromwell's Republican intermezzo (1650–58). He called it the 'empire of laws' and equalled it to 'government'.

There are, of course, different traditions of the rule of law. In England, the rule of law is based on individual freedom and is about citizens' rights in relation to the state. On the continent, rule of law means mainly *Rechtsstaat* (the legal state), meaning that public administrations are confined by the legal framework, thus preventing arbitrariness of decision-making. In France in particular, the significance of the rule of law means administrative law (*droit administratif*) in relation to public administration. In this context, the Weberian 'rational state' is an essential part of the independence of the judiciary as we understand it today. The judiciary is probably the most important check and balance to government.

Although some convergence has occurred between these three interpretations of the rule of law, the diversity of traditions still persists. The dogmatic approach of Napoleonic law based on codes is quite different to the more flexible common law traditions. Germanic and Nordic countries show a mix of the two approaches.

---

corruption, called Tangentopoli ('Kickback City'), which had been going on for over forty years and was sustained by the main governing parties, particularly Christian Democracy (Democrazia Cristiana, DC) and the Italian Socialist Party (Partito Socialista Italiano, PSI). This led to the collapse of the entire political class as well as the two main parties. A new political system, called the Second Republic, with a new party system emerged after 1994 (Guzzini, 1994; Della Porta and Vannuci, 1999, Rhodes, 1997).

This chapter tries to assess the importance of judicial power in Europe. It begins by looking at several dimensions of the judicial power in Europe; and afterwards the role of the constitutional courts, which grew in importance in Europe after the Second World War, is discussed. This is followed by a section on the European dimension of judicial politics and the supremacy of European law over national law. Finally, the last part of the chapter is dedicated to the creation of the European Union's area of freedom, security and justice, in which national prosecutors and police forces are moving towards greater integration in order to deal with organised crime and the management of the Single European Market.

Patterns of judicial power in Europe

One of the characteristics of European politics is that there are different legal traditions shaping judicial power across Europe. One can identify at least five such legal traditions.

In the British Isles, the common law tradition led to the development of law based on precedent. Case law is central to the common law tradition both in the UK and Ireland, although each country has its own traditions (see Figure 8.1).

In Western Europe, including Benelux, France, Portugal, Spain, Italy and Switzerland, the main tradition is Napoleonic, being based on the systematic integration of the different legal codes during the dominance of Napoleon over Europe between 1804 and 1811. This influence of the extremely structured Napoleonic tradition created a fairly rigid criminal and civil legal code.

The Germanic legal tradition comprises Germany, Austria and Switzerland. It is mainly influenced by Roman law, which was rediscovered at the end of the Middle Ages.

The fourth tradition can be found in Scandinavia and evolved from Scandinavian legal traditions, incorporating many elements from other systems.

Figure 8.1 Legal traditions in Europe

The full development of legal systems with a modern judiciary goes back to the nineteenth century. One particularly important aspect is the inner-Scandinavian institutional transfer, which led to the creation of similar judiciaries across the regions (Bell, 2006: 234).

The fifth legal tradition can be found among Central and Eastern European countries. One unifying element is that all these Central and Eastern European countries were dominated by the socialist law tradition until 1989. Since then, these countries have been rediscovering their previous legal traditions and integrating new elements from the long-standing democracies of Western Europe, with the Germanic model in particular having a strong impact. This became clear by the establishment of constitutional courts with the power of constitutional review in most of these countries. However, as Rafal Manko argues for the Polish case, which can certainly be taken as a good example for the other countries, there are still many continuities and elements from the fifty years of the socialist legal system in the present new democratic legal order (Manko, 2007: 89–103).

The common law countries: the UK and Ireland

The independence of the judiciary is one of the most important features of European democratic societies. The constitutional guarantees of such independence are the basis for the non-arbitrary just rule of law. In spite of this generally accepted principle, there are still major differences between the different countries within Europe. In the common law tradition, the judiciary is very keen to defend its independence from political pressure. One major problem for the British judiciary was that, until 2005, the Lord High Chancellor was the chair of the judiciary, but was also in charge of ensuring that the courts were working properly and that the independence of the judges was protected. However, he was also the Speaker of the House of Lords and sat in the cabinet. The position of Lord High Chancellor clearly contradicted the principle of the separation of powers. A major reform by the Tony Blair government, introduced in 2004 and adopted in 2005, limited the role of the Lord High Chancellor, by transferring some powers to other incumbents. The role of the presiding officer of the House of Lords was taken over by the Lord Speaker and the administration of the judiciary became the competence of the Lord Chief Justice. The position of the Lord High Chancellor was merged with the position of State Secretary of Justice, the first incumbent being Jack Straw. The modernisation of the judiciary in the United Kingdom also required the introduction of more transparent procedures for judicial appointments. Since the reform, there is now a Judicial Appointments Committee and the Lord Chief Justice is appointed by this committee. According to John Bell, until the 1970s the judicial community was quite small and most appointments were made informally, partly according to merit, but also partly through patronage and clientelism. However, from the 1970s, the judiciary became a more complex, diversified system that needed reform, meaning that more transparent procedures of appointment had to be developed in order to make the judicial class more accountable. The recent reforms are the culmination of this evolutionary transformation of the British judiciary (Bell, 2006: 312).

The 2005 reform also led to the unification of the administration of the court system under one agency, Her Majesty's Court Service (HMCS), which is in charge of the governance of the complex UK judicial system. This is an important stepping stone towards the modernisation of the court system. In 2007, the operational costs of the judiciary were over £1.3 billion (€1.6 billion; US $2.4 billion). The HMCS manages the magistrates' courts, the Crown Court, the county courts, the Supreme Court and the Court of Appeal (HMCS, 2006, 2008).

In contrast to other European countries, the jury system is central to the British system, allowing the population to be involved to some degree in the management of justice. The number of judges has increased over the years. In 2007, there were thirty-seven Lord Justices in the Appeal Courts, 108 High Court judges, 639 circuit judges (District) in England and Wales, and 29,816 lay justices of the peace (50 per cent men and 49 per cent women). The use of lay justices means that laymen and laywomen can be involved in the judiciary (Ministry of Justice, 2007: 156–7). They are appointed for a limited period and are particularly important in specialised courts, where a professional judge normally moderates the proceedings. Between 2001 and 2004 there was a decline in justices of the peace, but since 2005 their number has recovered (Ministry of Justice, 2007: 160).

Although the Republic of Ireland is a common law country, its judiciary is more accountable than that of the United Kingdom. The Republican-written constitution ensures a considerable independence for Irish judges, who are appointed by a governmental committee. Once appointed, the Irish judges can only be removed from office if they misbehave or show incapacity. Such removal can only be achieved by a majority in both houses of parliament (Oireachtas) – the Dail and the Seanad. Ordinary Irish judges interact with the political system because they can shape the constitution through the interpretation of its text. Any Irish judge has judicial review powers when interpreting the constitutional articles. This brings the Irish judicial system closer to the American model. In the same way as the United States, the Irish system also has a Supreme Court with similar powers of judicial review (Gallagher, 2010: 84–95). In 2005, there were 131 judicial positions that took on a case load of 770,000. The overall courts services system was administered by the courts services with 1,003 employees and a budget of €900 million (Courts Service, 2005: 33).

The Netherlands: a hybrid system

Although located on the continent of Europe, the Netherlands has a legal system closer to that of the United Kingdom. The constitution upholds the principle of parliamentary sovereignty and therefore forbids any review by the judiciary. This is denied by article 120 of the constitution. This also means that there is no constitutional court in the Netherlands (Andeweg and Irwin, 2002: 152). There is a Supreme Court (Hoge Raad), five appeal courts, nineteen district courts and sixty-one first instance courts. The Council of State (Raade van der Staat) not only advises the government on legal matters, but is also the highest appeal court for administrative issues. Although the Netherlands has a civil and criminal code that has supremacy, it also allows case law to shape the legal system. The recent reform of 2002 led to a better definition of the accountability of judges, while at the same time there has been a reinforcement of the autonomy and the independence of the judiciary. The self-management of courts is a major feature of the Dutch judiciary. In 2002, the Council of the Judiciary was established, with operational tasks such as the allocation of the budget and human resources for the courts. At its core is a bureau of 120 persons. In 2004, the management of the Dutch court system cost €690 million. There are 2,108 judges (45 per cent are women) and 5,050 people working in the Dutch judicial system (Ministerie van Justitie, 2008).

The Napoleonic Code countries: France, Italy, Spain, Portugal, Belgium and Luxembourg

In contrast to the common law countries, law is codified in all the other European countries. In France, the Napoleonic Code (with updates) is still central to the legal system. The civil and criminal courts are interpreted rigidly and there is less room for judges in the Napoleonic legal tradition to be creative in the interpretation of the law. According to Alec Stone Sweet, such canonisation of the law has become the pattern for dealing with constitutional law; indeed there is also a *code constitutionel*, which is studied almost dogmatically by law students (Stone Sweet, 2000: 138). In spite of the number of constitutions that have existed in France since the French Revolution, the different legal codes have remained central to the French judiciary. There is a territorially organised court system for criminal and civil matters. At the top there are the courts of appeal and, as last instance, the Court of Cassation, which becomes involved when all legal means have been exhausted. The French judiciary consists of thirty-five appeal courts at regional and national levels, 181 high courts *(tribunaux de grand instance)*, 473 district courts *(tribunaux de instance)*, 271 labour courts *(conseils de prud'hommes)*, 191 commercial courts *(tribunaux de commerce)* and 151 children's courts *(tribunaux pour enfants)* (Direction de l'Administration Générale et de l'Équipement, 2007: 3).

In 2008, 72,993 people were working in the justice department, 8,140 of whom were judges. A further 22,215 employees worked in the judicial system. The overall budget for the justice department was €6.5 billion; however, this also included the administration of the prison service (Ministére de Justice, 2008). Judges normally follow a career pattern that starts with a specialised course in the National School of the Judiciary (École Nationale de Magistrature, ENM), from which a successful graduation will lead to a judiciary career. The administrative body of the courts system and the judiciary is the Higher Council of the Judiciary (Conseil Superieur de la Magistrature, CSM), which was established in 1958. It emulates the Italian Consiglio Superiore della Magistratura (CSM), which has the same name and was founded in 1948/1956 after the Italian constitution was adopted.

Similar bodies were also established in Spain through the Consejo General del Poder Judicial (CGPJ) in 1978 and in Portugal through the Conselho Superior da Magistratura (CSM) in 1976. In France and Portugal the Council consists of politicians and judges in equal share, however in Italy and Spain it consists of judges only. In France as well as the other countries in this group these administrative agencies are responsible for the good governance of the judiciary in terms of the good functioning of the courts, resource allocation, and the appointment, promotion and conduct of disciplinary processes of judges. In the three Southern European countries in this category, political influence or pressure upon the judiciary has been low (Magalhães *et al.*, 2006: 156). In spite of this strong independence of the judiciary, the collapse of the Italian First Republic in 1992 precipitated by the investigations of the judiciary under Antonio di Pietro, led not so much to a 'politicisation of the judiciary' but to a 'judicialisation of politics', at least until 1995. The judges merely filled the vacuum left by the politicians, and some of them, such as Antonio di Pietro, became politicians themselves. The new political class gained control over the political field and over the judiciary after 1995 (Nelken, 1996).

According to Yves Meny and Andrew Knapp, a similar, more moderate, judicialisation of politics took place in France during the political corruption scandals of the 1980s (Meny and Knapp, 1998: 326–7; Knapp and Wright, 2001: 398–9). In all the countries in this group there are also ideological currents within the judiciary. In France, there are trade unions of judges on both the left (for example, the Syndicat de la Magistrature (Judiciary Trade Union)), and the right (for example, the Union Syndacale des Magistrats (Trade Union of Magistrates) and the Association Professionelle de Magistrats (Professional Association of Magistrates)) (Knapp and Wright, 2001: 408). This leads to some politicisation of the judiciary, because these ideological currents are normally sympathetic to the political parties on the left or right respectively. In Italy, there is a National Association of Magistrates (Associazione Nazionale de Magistratura, ANM) in which different ideologies compete for dominance. On the left, one can find *Magistratura democratica* (Democratic Magistrature) and on the right *Magistratura indipendente* (Independent Magistrates). Both left and right groups have clear ideas about the Higher Judiciary Council and their politics have considerable influence over the decision-making process within this body (Cotta and Verzichelli, 2007: 242).

Similarly, the Spanish General Council of the Judicial Power (CGPJ) is sharply divided between judges sympathetic to the conservative People's Party and those sympathetic to the Socialist Party (Magone, 2009a: 125). In a similar way, in Portugal the presidency and vice-presidency are highly contested between the Trade Union Association of Portuguese Judges (Associação Sindical de Juizes Portugueses, ASJP) and the more left-wing grass-roots Movement for Justice and Democracy (Association of Judges) (Movimento para a Justiça e Democracia – Associação de Juizes, MJD–AJ) (*Diário de Noticias*, 4 September 2006).

The dual French court system of criminal/civil and administrative courts was emulated in all three Southern European countries in this group. Italy also has a Court of Cassation (Corte de Cassazione). In Spain, this court is called the Supreme Court (Tribunal Supremo) and it had already been mentioned in the constitution of Cadiz in 1812, but was only established in 1834. In Portugal, there is the Supreme Court of Justice (Tribunal Supremo da Justiça, STJ), which has existed since 1833. In the quasi-federal organisation of Spain, there are seventeen High Judiciary Courts (Tribunal Superior de la Justicia) that fulfil cassation work before being sent to the Supreme Court in Madrid.

One the whole, Italian, Spanish and Portuguese courts are not very efficient, largely because, particularly in the cases of Portugal and Spain, the judiciary is under-resourced. In Spain there has been an effort to take on more judges and improve the human and material resources of the court system. This has been supported by the main parties PSOE and PP since they signed a pact of justice in

2002. In 2007, there were 4,543 judges sitting in court – about 10 judges per 100,000 inhabitants. This figure contrasts heavily with the equivalent figures for France (8,140) and Italy (9,056 judges in 2006) (General Council of the Judiciary, 2007).

In 2006, Portugal, a much smaller country, had 1,780 judges – about 17 judges per 100,000 inhabitants. However, this figure reduces considerably if we exclude the judges in the higher, constitutional and special courts. In the courts of first instance the ratio is about 12 judges per 100,000 inhabitants (information provided by Portuguese Ministry of Justice, October 2008).

In terms of organisation, both Portugal and Spain are still reforming the judiciary, moving towards the creation of more efficient territorial structures. While in Spain there are too many scattered courts at local level, in Portugal there is a lack of economies of scale. Both countries are engaged in changing their out-dated geography of the judiciary (Bell, 2006: 174; information provided by Portuguese Ministry of Justice, October 2008).

The geographical proximity of Belgium and Luxembourg to France has also led to the establishment of similar judicial systems. The overall structures match the French model in many ways. Both countries have a cassation court (Cour de Cassation), an appeals court and, depending on the territorial organisation, the local and regional courts. In case of Belgium there are the 187 justices of the peace (*justices de paix*) at the lowest level to deal with minor issues and the thirty-four police courts (Tribunaux de Police) for minor offences. Above them are the twenty-seven courts of first instance (Courts de Premiére Instance), the two labour courts (Tribunaux de Travail) and two commercial courts. At the top are the appeal courts, the labour court, the assizes court, and, as already mentioned, the cassation court. In 2007, there were 2,446 judges and the overall budget was €846.8 million (Service Publique Federal Justice, SPF, 2008a: 10). In the same way as in the Southern European countries, there is also a constitutional court adjudicating in constitutional matters (Service Publique Federal Justice, SPF, 2008b: 23–32). In spite of federalisation, there is still a nationally organised judicial system in Belgium (Service Publique Federal Justice, SPF, 2008b: 8). A federal public service for the judiciary, which has existed since 1830, was reformed in 2002 in order to adjust to the new system.

The Germanic or Drei-Sat model: Germany, Austria and Switzerland

Typologies can tend to simplify the complex historical legacy of different countries. In spite of many similarities between Germany, Austria and Switzerland, their historical backgrounds are quite different. There has been a borrowing of institutions from each other, so that the similarities have been achieved over a long period of time.

The German legal and judiciary system was established in the nineteenth century. The Prussian judiciary was the core model, which was then emulated by or transferred to the other German states. The bureaucratic–legal model achieved its completion at the end of the nineteenth century and many features of the model remained important until today. The 1949 Grundgesetz (Basic Law) clearly streng-thened the judiciary as a reaction to the traumatic experience of the national socialist period. Apart from the fact that the catalogue of rights became central to the constitution, particularly the protection of human dignity, a constitutional court, which is separate from the ordinary judiciary system, was established to adjudicate on all constitutional issues. The fact that judges can only be removed by a two-thirds majority in both houses of parliament, the Bundestag and Bundesrat, is also important. Judges are probably the most important civil servants of the country in terms of pay and status. On one hand, this strong position of the judges allows for a strong autonomy and independence, but, on the other hand, it may cause problems of inertia under the bureaucratic–legal organisation of the courts. John Bell outlines the trade-off as follows:

> The ideal of the bureaucratic judge has both positive and negative elements. Positively, he is willing to commit himself to operating the system in which he works. It is this aspect of the ideal that was stressed by Weber at the beginning of the twentieth century. The bureaucratic, rational and impartial decision-maker applied the rules in a predictable and even-handed way. In a democratic society, this involves a commitment to the separation of powers and the priority of the democratically elected legislature. Negatively, the idea contains values of impersonality and a lack of critical judgement with respect to the orders that are given. This latter aspect was supported by ideas of legal positivism and *Begriffsjurisprudenz*. The bureaucratic idea was reflected in the traditions of judicial appointment and judicial life. It was a public service position and many of the rules applying to Beamten [civil servants] applied to judges, unless specific provision was made. The impersonality of the collegial decision (broken only in the Bundesverfassungsgericht [Federal Constitutional Court]) emphasised the role of the institution, not the person, in coming to decisions, and the individual could escape blame. The idea of the *Rechtsstaat* as the rule of law and not men seemed to reinforce this.
>
> (Bell, 2006: 144–5)

The reputation of the judiciary suffered a lot during and after the collapse of national socialist rule. In the same way as in Italy, the Allies decided not to prosecute any judges that worked during the nationalist period. This meant that many middle- and lower-ranking judges were brought over from the previous totalitarian regime without charge. By now, most of these older judges have retired and younger generations have replaced them. There was also some solidarity of judges, which allowed for this continuity (Conradt, 2001: 210–11).

The German judicial system is federalised, meaning that there are sixteen different regional judiciaries as well as the federal level. Although most of these regional legal systems need to be compatible with federal law, there may be differ-ences in handling minor offences in the different parts of the country. In 2008, there were 667 local courts (Amtsgerichte), 116 regional courts (Landesgerichte) and 24 higher regional courts (Oberlandesgerichte). Besides these, there were 67 administrative courts, 18 tax courts (Finanzgerichte), 139 labour courts (Arbeitsgerichte) and 83 social courts (Sozialgerichte). At federal level, the different federal high courts were placed in different German cities (Bundesamt für Justiz, 2008). This reinforces federal solidarity and also enhances loyalty between the *Länder* (Bundestreue). The constitutional court (Bundesverfassungsgericht) is based in Karlsruhe, the federal court (Bungesgericht) is in Karlsruhe and Leipzig (criminal section), the federal administrative court (Bundesverwaltungsgericht) is in Leipzig, the federal tax court (Bundesfinanzgericht) is based in Munich, the federal labour court (Bundesarbeitsgericht) in Erfurt, and the federal social court (Bundessozialgericht) in Kassel.

In 2006, there were 20,138 judges, of which 33 per cent were women. The vast majority worked in the regional judicial system (98 per cent), whereas only very few judges worked in the federal court system (2 per cent). Moreover, 74 per cent worked in the ordinary criminal and civil court system, while the rest were distributed among the other specialised courts (Bundesamt für Justiz, 2006).

Institutionally, German unification in 1989 particularly affected the judiciary in the eastern *Länder*. The tradition of the German Democratic Republic (GDR) was to have a partisan judiciary that would adhere to the ideology of the Socialist Unity Party (Sozialistische Einheitspartei, SED). In this sense, many judges were party members and supportive of the regime. After 1989, the whole East German judiciary had to be restructured. According to Hellmut Wollmann, this process took place between 1990 and 1995. About 62 per cent of the 1,625 GDR judges applied to be taken on within the new system, however only 650 (40 per cent) were successful. The implementation of the complex new judiciary system consisting of the ordinary and specialised courts led to an increase in the number of positions to 3,331. However, these new positions were filled with West German judges, who were either reallocated or were newly recruited. This meant that the proportion of East German judges declined even further, to 18 per cent by 1992 (Wollmann, 1996: 103–4).

The Austrian system is similar to the German one. There is a stronger centralising tendency because of the nature of Austrian executive federalism. However, in terms of structure there are many similarities. As in Germany, there are 141 district courts (Amtsgerichte) at local level, 20 regional courts of justice (Landesgerichte) and 4 regional courts of appeal (Oberlandesgerichte). At the head of the whole system is the Supreme Court. There are about 1,700 judges working in the Austrian judicial system (Bundesministerium für Justiz, 2007: 10–11, 22).

In both Germany and Austria there is the judicial position of *Rechtspfleger* – full-time court workers, who have particular competences and deal with very specialised issues, such as bankruptcy proceedings, and maintain the land and trade register. They have to undertake specialised training in higher education institutions (Bundesministerium für Justiz, 2007: 31).

The Austrian judiciary system is extremely relevant for European judicial politics, particularly in relation to constitutional review. Indeed, the first constitutional court was established in 1920 in Austria and was designed by the legal scholar Hans Kelsen (see section on constitutional courts, pp. 294–8).

Although Switzerland has many similarities to Germany and Austria, the highly decentralised federal system gives a strong position to the twenty-six cantons. A kind of 'soft federalisation' of the legal system took place in 1898. Until 1874, the federal dimension was almost non-existent and parliament was both a legislature and the last instance of the judiciary. A civil code was only established in 1912 (Kälin, 2002: 189). Today, each canton still has its civil and criminal process, and in spite of attempts to standardise to a national one, such efforts have only been partially successful. Since 2000, there has been a greater interest among the cantons in harmonising their criminal law process, largely because of the increase in economic and organised criminality. Less successful has been the attempt to harmonise the civil law process (Kälin, 2002: 191).

The federal Supreme Court is at the top of the hierarchy. It consists of thirty judges and is divided into five sections. It adjudicates not only in civil and criminal law, but also in administrative law (Kälin, 2002: 188). Although the Supreme Court cannot adjudicate on constitutional matters, because of article 190 in the constitution, the constitutional reality has been quite different from those of other countries, particularly because of the complex system of competences that exists in Switzerland. The Supreme Court balances the rights of the federal government and the cantons, and has so far been fairly well balanced in its decisions (Kälin, 2002: 198). At canton level, there are district courts and canton courts. The vast majority of cantons have no regional higher court – some just have a regional cassation court in civil or criminal law (or both) (Kälin, 2002: 198). Another peculiarity of the system is that the judicial system of the Francophone part of Switzerland has been influenced by the French model. The cantons of Geneva, Waadt and Neuenburg use, for example, justices of peace (*justices de paix*) at the lowest level of the judiciary system and labour courts. In contrast, German-speaking Switzerland (for example, Zürich, Bern, St Gallen and Aargau more closely follow the German model, particularly in the use of commercial courts (Kälin, 2002: 190).

The Nordic model: Sweden, Denmark, Norway, Finland and Iceland

The geographical proximity of these five countries led to the institutional transfer and convergence of judicial models during the last 200 years. According to John Bell, the Swedish system evolved out of its own legal tradition. Such a process has been evolutionary and has been taking place since 1809. One salient characteristic of the Swedish and Nordic systems in general is the entrenched culture of consensus and compromise of government that also affects the judiciary (Bell, 2006: 234).

The Swedish court system consists of, on the one hand, civil and criminal courts and, on the other hand, administrative courts. The civil and criminal courts are organised in fifty-three district courts (Tingsrätt), six regional courts of appeal (Hövrätt) and the Supreme Court (Högsta Domstol). The administrative courts have twenty-three county administrative courts (Lansrätt), four courts of appeal (Kammarrätt) and a supreme administrative court (Regeringsrätt). The court system is managed by a National Courts Agency (Domstolsverket), founded in 1975 in order to ensure the independence of government. It employs over 5,500 staff and has an annual expenditure of €670 million (£804 million, US $938 million). Since 2008, the National Courts Agency has advisory board under a director-general. It consists of nine members, most of them from the judiciary system, but also two members from the Rijksdag (Domstolsverket, 2008). This National Courts Agency has some input in the appointment of judges, which is carried out by the Appointments Proposal Board for the Swedish Judiciary. At district and county level, lay judges, appointed by the municipal councils, are also used by the judiciary (Regeringskansliet, 2007b: 10–13).

There are also several special courts, such as the labour court for workplace disputes, the market court for competition policy issues and the Swedish Migration Board and the higher migration court for immigration issues (Regeringskansliet, 2007b: 13).

The Swedish judicial system uses precedent law, but now this is mainly done by the higher courts. A Europeanisation process is taking place, largely as a result of the integration of Sweden into the EU. The inclusion of the European Human Rights Convention of the European Court of Human Rights based in Strasbourg, which allowed for the convergence of law towards other European countries, was crucial for the Europeanisation of the Swedish legal system (Bell, 2006: 243–4). Judges also participate in government-organised committees of reform. One factor that led to a democratisation of the judiciary was the longevity in government of the Social Democratic Party (1933–76). They used their power to make the judiciary more accountable, transparent and closer to the population. One such reform was the abolition of special clothing for officers and judges in courts (Bell, 2006: 255).

In the same way as the Swedish system, the Danish judicial and legal system has its roots in its own evolutionary development towards democracy. A key date is 1849, when a democratic Danish constitution enshrined the separation of powers.

According to John Bell, Swedish judges are particularly impressed by the management of the court system in Denmark, which is undertaken by the Danish Court Agency (Domstolsstyrelsen) and is run by judges solely. This was introduced in 1999 after a unanimous vote in the Folketing, making the agency independent from the Ministry of Justice (Bell, 2006: 243). The reform also allowed for the independent appointment of judges through a Judicial Appointments Council. Apart from this difference, the Danish judiciary system is very similar to the Swedish system and has adjusted to the needs of the country. In 2006, the Folketing decided to undertake a major reform to improve the efficiency and management of the courts. Since 2007, the judiciary system comprises the Supreme Court, two high courts and twenty-four district courts. Moreover, at national level there are the specialised Copenhagen maritime and commercial court and land registration court. The Supreme Court is the final instance of appeal for the civil and criminal courts and for the maritime and commercial courts. Like many other European countries, the new court system is the result of reforms that started to come into force in 2007. Among these reforms, there was a considerable reduction in the number of district courts – from eighty-two to twenty-four – as well as the improvement of the efficiency and length of trials and the management of the court system. Moreover, the reforms were designed to make the rules of procedure more flexible, and included the introduction of courts consisting of a judge and experts. The reforms strengthened the position of district courts, which have greater managerial and budgetary autonomy within the system. District Courts also function as appeals courts. Only fundamental issues can be referred to the Supreme Court, if permission is granted by the Appeal Permission Board (Domstolsstyrelsen, 2008).

The Norwegian judiciary system shows the same features as the Swedish and Danish systems. In the same way, there is a Supreme Court (Hoyessteretts) as the final instance of appeal. There are six regional appeals courts (Lagmannsrettene) and fifteen district courts (Tingretts). It has a special supervisory committee for judges that deals with disciplinary and promotion issues. As in Sweden and Denmark, there is an agency for the administration of courts (Domstol administrasjonen) (Domstol, 2008).

In both Finland and Iceland, the judiciary systems have similar structures as Sweden, Denmark and Finland. The judiciary systems of Finland and Iceland are also based on their own individual legal traditions as well as institutional transfer between the different Scandinavian countries. The Europeanisation of the legal and judiciary system has become important through the European network of the councils of the judiciary.

The Central and Eastern European countries: continuities and discontinuities

After decades of a socialist judiciary system, most Central and Eastern European countries had to restructure their judiciary systems. The rule of law based on liberal principles became a central aspect of the restructuring of the judiciary in these countries. The transformation of the judiciary has been difficult, partly because of the need for new personnel trained in liberal democratic legal systems (after decades of socialist legal systems) and partly because of the difficulty of rewriting complete civil and criminal codes. Some aspects of the period of socialist law had to be taken over by the new regimes. It is more appropriate here to give a general overview of these countries, rather than to discuss each one in detail.

The most pragmatic country was probably Hungary, which simply revised the socialist constitution and adjusted to the new liberal order. The historical legacy of the nineteenth century and the inter-war period allowed some continuity with previous regimes to be achieved. The present Hungarian model is strongly influenced by German and Austrian law. The Austro-Hungarian monarchy, even after the Ausgleich of 1867, has remained an important reference of the Hungarian legal system. The unification process of the courts began in 1872 and continued until the end of the nineteenth century (Hoensch, 1989: 49). This Austro-Hungarian codification of law remained in place until the end of the Second World War, to be replaced at that point by the new socialist civil and criminal codes. In spite of its transition to democracy in 1989, Hungary simply adjusted these socialist codes to meet the demands of the European Convention on Human Rights. There have been no major revisions of the codes since 1990, although there were some further adjustments in 1997. These adjustments led to a complete separation of the Ministry of Justice from the court system. The National Council of Justice, which is in charge of running the judiciary, was also created in 1997. It is completely independent of the government and is directly accountable to parliament. The Hungarian judicial system consists of four tiers: the 111 local courts, the 20 county courts, 5 regional appeals courts and the Supreme Court. Such a model, in one form or another, was largely implemented in all the new democracies of Central and Eastern Europe. In 2004, there were 2,757 judges (27 judges per 100,000 inhabitants) and 7,557 support staff worked in the judiciary. The number of incoming cases was about 1.19 million and the overall budget €276.6 million (Montgomery, 2006: 422–3; Magyar Köztarsasag Bírosagai, 2008).

For most Central and Eastern European countries, the independence of the judiciary was an important principle during the constitutional settlement (which was quite a difficult process in Poland). A new constitution was only adopted in 1997 and the independence of the judiciary became a very important aspect of it. The structure of the judiciary in Poland largely follows the Hungarian model, though with three tiers. One important court is the Tribunal of State to which the acts of office holders are accountable in terms of their constitutionality should incumbents become involved in criminal activities or abuse their power (Taras, 2006: 365–6). There are also administrative and military courts. In a similar way to Hungary, a council of the judiciary, which is independent from government, is responsible for the running of the courts. As already mentioned, the Polish legal system has many continuities from the old socialist system. According to Rafal Manko, the Polish civil code of 1964, which was in force in the socialist period and which had adopted many aspects from the civil code of the inter-war period, in spite of adjustments, is still used in civil law courts (Manko, 2007: 90). According to Manko, there are also many aspects of civil proceedings, as used during the socialist period, which were taken over with only slight adjustments (Manko, 2007: 92). This shows that legal traditions grow and are not necessarily confined to a particular regime; there is some continuity and some discontinuity in this process.

The Czech judiciary system shows that institution-building was a difficult and long process. The best example of this was the late establishment of the Supreme Administrative Court in 2003, ten years after the 'Velvet Divorce'. Currently, in 2010, the court system has eighty-six district courts, eight regional courts, two high courts and the Supreme Court. According to Karel Vodička, the Czech judiciary system is quite slow and inefficient and has lost many good judges to the private sector because of the low pay (Vodička, 2005: 228–30). The nationalist tendencies of the Mečiar government until 1998 in Slovakia led to a substantial catalogue of rights that should be protected by the courts, particularly the newly founded constitutional court, with the protection of minorities as a central principle (Malová, 2001: 370–3). The communist legacy led other countries to develop similar constitutional safeguards, supported by an independent judiciary.

This became relevant in the Baltic states when they declared independence from the Soviet Union. The judiciary became a central institution with the purpose of restoring a sense of justice. The restructuring of the judiciary was particularly difficult, because of the lack of expertise of the incumbents. In all three Baltic republics there was a shortage of qualified personnel to serve in the restructured judiciary system. The overall restructuring also created major problems of continuity, so that instability in the courts was common throughout the 1990s. In Latvia, international organisations, such as the Soros Foundation, the American Bar Association and the United Nations Development Programme, played a major role in supporting the efforts of the judges to get adequate training in a liberal democratic context. A judicial training centre was established in 1995 in order to give training to judges and their support personnel. In legal and judicial terms, several international conventions were transposed to national law, sometimes creating harmonisation problems (Sprudzs, 2001: 157–8). Similar processes took place in the other Baltic states, all of them creating a three-tier judiciary system consisting of district, regional and Supreme courts. Both Latvia and Lithuania decided to establish constitutional courts as a further safeguard to protect the constitutionality of laws and procedures. Estonia did not establish a constitutional court, but the Supreme Court has a Constitutional Review Chamber dealing with the constitutionality of laws and procedures (Pettai, 2001: 129–30).

In contrast to the Central European and Baltic countries, the western and eastern Balkans are still lagging behind in terms of creating a functioning judiciary system. In the cases of Bulgaria and Romania, corruption has been a major obstacle in the quest to create an independent impartial judiciary. Low wages and low morale have undermined any reform attempts to make the two countries more compatible with the norms of the European Union and the Council of Europe. Despite joining the EU on 1 January 2007, the problems relating to corruption and the slow process of judiciary reform have been highlighted by several reports of the European Commission since then. In July 2008, a further report highlighted the continuing problems of judiciary reform in both countries. In early January 2008, this led to the freezing of structural funds for Bulgaria, because of the high level of irregularity in the financial accounting (Miller *et al.*, 2001; Leiße, 2006: 10; European Commission, 27 June 2008; IP 07/948 of 27 June 2008; IP 08/1195 of 23 July 2008).

The restructuring of the judiciary is of central importance in the countries of the western Balkans, the successor states of the former Yugoslavia. The ethnic wars between the countries has led to the dominance of nationalism, which has prevented the establishment of a democratic judiciary. The European Union has been at the forefront in building new judiciary institutions. The International Criminal Tribunal for the Former Yugoslavia (ICTY) has only partially helped to bring justice to the millions of victims of the senseless wars of the 1990s. The ideological and ethnic divisions still shape politics in some of these countries, particularly in Serbia and Bosnia-Herzegovina. It will be some time before there is a genuine move towards democratic judiciary structures in most of these countries, including Croatia.

The judicialisation of politics and the politicisation of the judiciary: a constitutional review, European-style

One of the innovations of European constitutions following the Second World War was the introduction of constitutional courts that would adjudicate on the constitutionality of laws and, sometimes, procedures. One of the reasons for the wish to strengthen constitutional law in European democracies was the negative experience recently undergone with authoritarian and totalitarian regimes. The theoretical foundations were laid down by the Austrian legal scholar, Hans Kelsen (1881–1973), who was central to the drafting of the Austrian constitution of 1920. In 1929, he developed the idea of a constitutional court, which would be separate from ordinary law, in order to adjudicate the constitutionality of laws. Kelsen's overall idea was based on a self-contained legal architecture, in which all legal norms of a particular polity could be referred back to a single fundamental document, the constitution. The constitutional court would be intended to act as a negative legislator, reviewing the laws accepted by parliament in order that they should be compatible with the constitution. One of his strongest opponents was the highly controversial German scholar, Carl Schmitt (1888–1985), who regarded the Kelsenian model of a constitutional court as a 'super legislature' and, as such,

Country	Foundation	Number of judges	Term (years)	Renewable	Citizen's complaints
Albania	1992	9	9	No	Yes
Andorra	1993	4	8	No	No
Austria	1920–9	14	Lifetime	–	Yes
Belgium	1980/2007	12	Lifetime	–	Yes
Bosnia-Herzegovina	1995	9	9*	No	Yes
Bulgaria	1991	12	9	No	No
Croatia	1963/1990	13	8	No	Yes
Czech Republic	1992	15	10	Yes	Yes
Latvia	1949	16	12	No	Yes
Lithuania	1993	9	8	No	
Montenegro	1963/1992	4	Lifetime	–	Yes
France	1958	9	9	No	No
Germany	1949	16	12	No	Yes
Hungary	1990	11	9	Yes (once)	Yes
Italy	1948/1956	15	9	No	No
Poland	1985–6/1992	15	9	No	Yes
Portugal	1982	13	9	No	Yes
Romania	1992	9	9	No	No
Serbia	1963/1990	10	15	No	No
Slovakia	1992	13	12	No	Yes
Slovenia	1992	9	9	No	Yes
Spain	1978	12	9	Conditional	Yes

* 3 from European Court of Human Rights/Council of Europe

Figure 8.2 Constitutional courts in Europe

one to be rejected (Stone Sweet, 2000: 34–47). In the second half of the nineteenth century, the Austro-Hungarian monarchy already had an imperial court (Reichsgericht), that was established through the constitution of 1867. Citizens were able to file complaints against the state relating to the violation of political rights. There was a state court (Staatsgerichtshof) that dealt with trials against MPs or ministers. After the collapse of the Austro-Hungarian monarchy, Austria adopted the new constitution of 1920, which established a constitutional court as we know it today. The Austrian constitutional court became a model for other countries, particularly Germany (Verfassungsgerichtshof, 2008).

Following the end of the Second World War, several countries had to adopt new constitutions as a result of the ending of the authoritarian and totalitarian period and also decided to introduce constitutional safeguards in order to prevent such undermining of democratic rule from happening again. Apart from Austria (Verfassungsgerichtshof), other countries, such as Germany (Bundesverfassungsgericht) and Italy (Tribunale constituzionale), included constitutional courts in their constitutions. Later, the constitution of the French Fifth Republic of 1958 introduced a constitutional council (Conseil constitutionel), which was designed to strengthen the government in relation to parliament. The model of constitutional review became important in the new democracies of Southern Europe, such as Portugal (Tribunal constitucional) in 1982 and Spain (Tribunal constitucional) in 1978, and later in those of Central and Eastern Europe, such as Hungary, Poland, the Czech Republic, Slovakia, Lithuania, Latvia, Romania, Bulgaria and Slovenia. This meant that the constitutional courts became a highly respected means for the solution of legislative and competence disputes in most European countries.

The German federal constitutional court has been regarded as a model for many Southern and Central and Eastern European countries. It allows constraints to be put on politicians and also on certain controversial legislative programmes. The decriminalisation of abortion has been a key issue in many European countries. The constitutional courts needed to find a legal–ethical answer that would satisfy both the pro-life and pro-choice parties. This became crucial in West Germany in 1975, in unified Germany in 1992, and in Catholic Spain in 1985. The constitutional courts did not endorse abortion, but allowed it under certain extreme circumstances. In Germany, politicians frequently try to anticipate rulings by the constitutional court and act accordingly, and this was the case with regard to the law on abortion. Governments generally tend to take over the precise guidelines set by the constitutional court (Landfried, 1992: 54–5). Constitutional courts are particularly important to the process of democratic consolidation in new democracies. In the case of Spain, the constitutional court adjudicated and shaped the emerging state of autonomies, and also decided on disputes over competences between central and regional governments. The important work of the constitutional court in Spain took place between 1979 and 1989, after which such disputes became less relevant. The constitutional court may also be used by the opposition to block government legislation. Again in the case of Spain, the People's Party tried to block the new Catalan Statute as being too far reaching and contravening the principles of the constitution in many respects: the main criticism was that it gave Catalonia a privileged bilateral relationship with the national Spanish government. Therefore, there was general opposition on the part of the other autonomous communities in relation to the Catalan Statute. Although the reformed Catalan Statute was negotiated in 2006 and approved by national parliament, the constitutional court came to a decision on its constitutionality four years later, in June 2010. The decision was a compromise, declaring some aspects as unconstitutional, however not the statute itself. Meanwhile, the political parties supporting and opposing the Catalan Statute exerted pressure upon particular judges, according to where their sympathies lay. This has contributed to a deterioration in the reputation of the constitutional court in Spain.

Until 1971, the French constitutional council was a dormant institution. That year represented a turning point, because the constitutional court judged the preamble of the 1958 constitution, which took over from the constitution of 1946, as part of constitutional law. This meant that several other legal documents had to be included in the constitution; for example, the 1789 Declaration of Rights of Man, the Fundamental Principles Recognised by the Laws of the Republic, and additional rights mentioned in the 1946 preamble, such as:

> equality of sexes; the right to work, to join a union, to strike and to obtain social security; and the responsibility of the state to guarantee a secular school system and to nationalise all industries that have taken on the character of a monopoly or public service.
>
> (Stone, 1992: 33–4)

Since then, the constitutional council has almost come to resemble a third chamber of the legislature, because of the weak nature of parliamentarianism in France (see Chapter 6). In the 1980s, the increased activity of the Council of State led to changes in the law of nationalisation proposed by the socialist government in 1982. It increased the level of compensation payments, which were originally presented by the government in its bill (Stone, 1992: 36).

In spite of the fact that the Italian constitutional court was enshrined in the 1948 Italian constitution, it was only established in 1956. Between 1948 and 1956, the regional high court in Sicily had many competences of the Italian constitutional court, which was founded later. The constitutional court was quite cautious initially, but then aggressively began to annul many legislative acts of the fascist period. Moreover, the constitutional court was instrumental in changing the legal relationship between the Catholic Church and the Italian state. Last, but not least, the constitutional court, in a similar way to the Spanish case, adjudicates on disputes between the central and regional governments. According to Maria Elisabetta de Franciscis and Rosella Zannini the constitutional court lost credibility at the end of the First Republic as a result of a string of bad rulings (Franciscis and Zannini, 1992: 71–8).

According to Alec Stone Sweet, we can differentiate between the more restrictive Italian constitutional court and the French constitutional council, which both write very short declaratory opinions and rulings, and the longer opinions and rulings of the German and Spanish constitutional courts (Stone Sweet, 2000: 145). There is also better direct access to the constitutional court for German and Spanish citizens than for Italian and French citizens. In Germany, there is the instrument of the *Verfassungsbeschwerde* (constitutional complaint), which citizens can call on if they feel that rights are being violated. In Spain the same procedure is called *amparo*. In both cases, the constitutional court considers such complaints and whether they should proceed to be discussed.

Also, according to Alec Stone Sweet, constitutional courts increased their repertoire of instruments over time. In many respects, they have almost become a legislating body when asked about the constitutionality of certain laws. This became especially relevant in the legislation on abortion in Germany and Spain. The constitutional courts also developed the instrument of corrective revision. According to Stone Sweet, corrective revision is

> the re-elaboration of a censured text in conformity with constitutional jurisprudence in order to secure promulgation. Corrective revision processes occur after full or partial annulments. They are highly structured by case law, to the extent that the judges have already made their legislative choices explicit, and that oppositions work to monitor the majority's compliance with the ruling.
>
> (Stone Sweet, 2000: 83)

The constitutional courts are also engaged in the protection of rights enshrined in the constitution or incompatible with the European Convention of Human Rights. The importance of rights of citizens before the interest of state institutions has been particularly important in Germany, Italy and Spain, but also in the Central and Eastern European countries. All these countries have undergone periods of authoritarian–totalitarian rule, so this provision is a safeguard against the return of such regimes (Stone Sweet, 2000: 95).

This means that today European politics must take into account a triad of relationships between government, parliament and the constitutional court (in those countries where the constitutional court exists). However, as mentioned before, other countries, for example Switzerland, the UK and the Netherlands, are finding ways of allowing constitutional review to take place, even if forbidden by the constitution.

In sum, constitutional review through constitutional courts or similar institutions has become an integral part of European politics since the Second World War. Most European countries, apart from the Republic of Ireland, have avoided following the American model of judicial review, adopting rather the Kelsenian model of separate constitutional review. This again is a distinctive feature of what European politics constitutes.

The European dimension: the growing impact on national legislation

The European Court of Justice in Luxembourg

Alec Stone Sweet characterises the European Court of Justice (ECJ), one of the institutions of the European Union, as a European constitutional court. The supremacy of the EU over national law further confrms this enhanced position of the European Court of Justice. According to Stone Sweet, such a constitutionalisation process was undertaken through the interaction between private litigants, national judges and the European Court of Justice. It was developed over two phases. The first phase was between 1962 and 1979, during which the European Court of Justice was able to secure the supremacy of the EU over national law and the doctrine of direct effect of European legislation, which delcared that the Treaty of Rome established individual rights that courts had to protect. Therefore not only governments but also individuals could appeal to the European Court of Justice. The second phase took place in the 1980s, when the doctrine of indirect effect of European legislation was also secured, which states that national courts have to interpret domestic law according to European law. It also allowed for the liability of the state, if a directive is not properly implemented or not implemented at all (Stone Sweet, 2000: 162–3).

The European Court of Justice, the Court of First Instance and the judicial courts are all part of this judiciary branch of the European Union, which interacts with other European institutions, institutions of the member states, enterprises and citizens. The European Court of Justice normally solves disputes between these actors by issuing binding rulings that contribute to the further development of European law. In many ways, European law can be regarded as a hybrid between continental law and common law systems. Since the Nice Treaty, which entered into force in 2003, the European Court of Justice has gained additional powers in the third pillar on justice and home affairs, which was upgraded in response to the common problems of member states relating to crime and immigration and the requirement to protect the Single European Market. Prior to this, most of the work of the ECJ was confined to adjudication on rights and disputes related to the emerging Single European Market.

The European Court of Justice is the most important supranational institution in the world. It is clear that it sets precedents that are studied by other courts. The workload of the European Court of Justice increased considerably over the years, especially since 1985. Therefore, the ECJ developed the Court of First Instance to look at cases before they reached the main chamber. However, even this reform was not enough to deal with the workload, so, following the Nice Treaty, the Court of First Instance became a separate institution, which functions as an antechamber of the European Court of Justice, although it consists of the same judges. Furthermore, the European Union Civil Service Tribunal was established in 2005 with specialised courts designed to support the Court of the First Instance in dealing with its workload. Former judges of the ECJ form part of this expanded court system at supranational level (Kapsis, 2007: 189–90). The ECJ is involved in the infringement proceedings of member states, which may be started by the European Commission. Such infringement proceedings can be found particularly in key policies (e.g., environmental policies) or the transposition into national law of directives concerning the Single European Market. Moreover, the ECJ gives preliminary rulings on particular cases submitted by the national courts. In this sense, the ECJ is used as a court above the national judiciary systems, reinforcing the supremacy of law.

This means that national courts in general and constitutional courts in particular have become 'Europeanised', i.e., that they have, even if reluctantly, accepted the supremacy of European law. The courts of the Central and Eastern European countries, both before and after joining the European Union, were under pressure to accept the supremacy of European law. This was difficult for these new institutions, because these countries had barely gained their sovereignty and were already under pressure to change their legislation according to European law precedents. Many of these constitutional courts developed strategies to avoid confrontation with the ECJ by accepting supremacy, but at the same time stating principles concerning the importance of national law. The Czech constitutional court was probably one of the most Euro-friendly constitutional courts, accepting that European law is part of the inheritance of Czech national law, and hence stating that there was no problem in accepting the supremacy of European law (Piqani, 2007: 16–17). In contrast, the Polish constitutional tribunal was very reluctant to accept the supremacy of European law and developed complex legal arguments to make the case for the supremacy of national law, while accepting the importance of European law for the specific issue of a European arrest warrant in 2004. The Polish constitutional tribunal tried therefore to establish a balanced ruling, in which national law would still be the most relevant, creating a hybrid system comprising both national and European law (Piqani, 2007: 10–15; Sadurski, 2008: 18–24). The highly respected Hungarian constitutional court, considered to be the most powerful constitutional court in the world because of its importance in shaping the new Hungarian democratic political system, was quite cautious and adopted a strategy of conflict avoidance. This was particularly important for the question of implementing certain European regulations on the surplus stock of agricultural products. The Hungarian constitutional court decided to deal with this as a domestic issue, and thus avoided including of the ECJ in this matter (Piqani, 2007: 9–10; Sadurski, 2008: 9–11).

In this sense, the ECJ has become an important agent in the constitutionalisation process of the European Union. A process of legal integration is taking place, in which European and national laws are becoming integrated and therefore transforming a dominant dualist conception of the legal architecture into a monist one. Slowly, the member states have had to reluctantly accept this growing integration of their national law systems with the European law system (Stone Sweet, 2000: 193).

The European Court of Human Rights in Strasbourg

The European Court of Human Rights (ECHR) was founded in 1959 under the auspices of the Council of Europe. Its main task is to adjudicate on violations of the European Convention of Human Rights and Fundamental Freedoms (ECHRFF), adopted by the Council of Europe in 1950 and entered into force in 1953. Since then, thirteen further protocols have been added to the ECHRFF. Both the Convention and the thirteen protocols are based on the United Nations Universal Declaration of Human Rights of 1948. Since 1959, the ECHRFF has been a reference point for all European countries, allowing the convergence and harmonisation of human rights across Europe, especially within the European Union. Reluctantly, the United Kingdom also had to integrate the European Convention of Human Rights and Fundamental Freedoms into their constitutional order in 1998, requiring that many incompatibilities with the European Convention had to be removed within the UK. The ECHRFF also allows citizens to appeal to the European Court of Human Rights when all national appeal courts have been exhausted. From 1959 until the late 1970s, the ECHR was not very well known and not very active, but this has changed in the past three decades (Storey, 1995: 141–2). ECHR rulings have been on particularly difficult issues, such as the right to a dignified death through euthanasia, those relating to artificial insemination, and those relating to the suspension of freedom arising from the new security threats from terrorism.

The European Audit Court and European Anti-Fraud Office (OLAF)

The European Audit Court is one of the controlling bodies of the European Union. It has built a network with its counterparts and similar institutions within the member states. It is a very important institution because of its power to look into the accounting practices of the European Union institutions and the member states. In 2006, 32.5 per cent of the EU budget was spent on structural funds, which member states have to implement. A further 51.6 per cent was spent on agricultural subsidies. And the proper spending of these funds is controlled by the European Audit Court. Cases of corruption, deviation of funds or misappropriation of funds can be prosecuted by the European Union. In early 2008, structural funds to Bulgaria worth €500 million were frozen, because there had been cases of corruption and the misappropriation of funds. One important body that contributes to the investigation of such cases is the Office of Fight against Fraud (Office Européen de Lutte Contre Fraude, OLAF), which has about sixty-five national police and judicial bodies cooperating with it. Examples of the cases handled are: forged time-sheets; fraud in several EC-funded projects in Spain; the rehabilitation of a power station in Serbia; the illicit trade of non-quota milk and milk products between two member states; European social fund fraud; and regional development fund fraud (European Anti-Fraud Office, 2008). Although there was a unit against fraud in the EU before 1999, the negative report of the Wise Men Commission, in which systemic cases of cronyism, nepotism and clientelism were found, led to a reform of the body and its upgrading to the embryo of a European-wide prosecution service with a staff of 300 people. OLAF coordinates European-wide investigations with similar institutions at national level.

The fight against corruption has become a global effort, and it is one where the European Union seeks to be at the forefront (Nelken, 2003: 222). One major problem so far has been the difficulty of finding common ground concerning what constitutes corruption. Different national traditions have lower or higher thresholds in relation to specific aspects of corruption, clientelism and patronage. OLAF plays a major role in harmonising such practices and creating a level playing field in the emerging Single European Market. So far, a major problem for the European Union has been the high level of corruption in Central and Eastern Europe, particularly in Bulgaria, Romania, Lithuania and Latvia (Holmes, 2003: 205). It will take at least a decade to reduce corruption and fraudulent activities substantially in Central and Eastern Europe.

The creation of a European area of freedom, security and justice

All this is linked to the growing importance of a European space for home and justice affairs, in which European and national institutions have created special bodies (e.g., Europol and Eurojust) to better fight against organised crime and to coordinate immigration and asylum policies. The process of harmonisation and the integration of anti-criminal, immigration and asylum policies had already started in 1975. The Trevi group was a loose network of member states who worked together in four main areas: immigration policy, asylum policy, police cooperation and judicial cooperation (Uçarer, 2007: 206). Until 1985, the whole process of cooperation was fairly dormant. However, in 1985, several member states decided to go one step further and abolish the internal borders between them. The Schengen Agreement was signed in 1985 and originally comprised France, West Germany and the Benelux countries. Today the 'Schengen Area' also comprises most of the Central and Eastern European countries. This means that it is possible to travel from Lisbon (Portugal) to Talinn (Estonia) without being stopped at any of the borders of the member states that lie between these two cities. Bulgaria and Romania are still outside the Schengen Area, because they have not yet met the criteria. The UK and Ireland take part in some policies, such as police and judicial cooperation, but have not given up their border controls.

In the Maastricht Treaty of 1993, a third pillar on justice and home affairs, allowing closer cooperation in this area among the member states, was included (den Boer and Wallace, 2000: 494–504). This was reinforced by the Amsterdam and Nice Treaties. The role of the European Commission was upgraded, so that it now has the right of co-initiative in justice and home affairs. The European Commission has its own general-directorate in the European Commission dealing with these issues. A turning point for increased cooperation was the Tampere Council, during the Finnish presidency in 1999, in which the implementation of the area of freedom, security and justice enshrined in the Amsterdam Treaty was discussed and led to several important decisions. Throughout the first decade of the new millennium, different policies (e.g., immigration and asylum policies) and judicial instruments (e.g., the European arrest warrant) were harmonised and institutional mechanisms were found to achieve stronger cooperation. The 9/11 terrorist attacks against the New York twin towers and the Pentagon in 2001 were a major factor in accelerating the process (Lavenex and Wallace, 2005: 463–6) (Box 8.2).

Since 1993, several institutions and cooperation networks have been established that have contributed to a better integration of European and national agencies. The Schengen Information System (SIS) can be named as one of the many devices that exist to track down nationals from countries that are not members of the EU when they enter the European Union or European Economic Area. In terms of judicial cooperation, Eurojust should be mentioned. It was established in 2002 and was designed to coordinate cross-national judicial issues. It is supported by the European Judicial Network, a pool of identified experts on cross-national matters in the member states, which was established in 1998. Further structures are being established, such as the Network of Experts on Joint Investigation Teams. With regard to the security forces, the EU established a police force called Europol in 1992, based in The Hague. It clearly has an important coordinating task helping national police forces to track down criminals or facilitating cross-national work. Although, after its foundation in 1992, the remit was restricted to the fight against drugs trafficking, the Treaties of Amsterdam and Nice allowed a considerable extension to the areas of activity, which now comprise illicit drug trafficking, illicit immigration networks, terrorism, forgery of money (counterfeiting of the euro) and other means of payment, trafficking human beings including child pornography, and money laundering (Europol, 2010). Furthermore a European Police College was established in 2005, which allows the integration of national training programmes

---

Box 8.2 The European space of freedom, justice and security

The establishment of the Single European Market (SEM) and the Schengen area has led to a growing cooperation between national judiciaries and the state prosecutors of the European Union. This process of cooperation is geared towards the creation of a European space of freedom, justice and security. Freedom refers to the rights of European citizens enshrined in the Charter of Fundamental Rights. Justice means a growing convergence of practices, such as the court processes or standardisation of evidence management. Security comprises fight against organised criminality and terrorism within the European Union and internationally. Although cooperation has been happening since the 1970s, the third pillar 'Home and Justice Affairs' of the Treaty of the European Union adopted in 1993 and amended by the Treaty of Amsterdam in 1999 and the Treaty of Nice in 2003 contributed to a reinforcement of this cooperation. In the 1999 Helsinki European Council during the Finnish presidency an action programme was adopted that was implemented until 2005. A further action programme was adopted in the The Hague European Council during the Dutch presidency in 2005. One of the major problems has been the reluctance of some member states to devolve powers to such shared networks. In this context several institutions emerged out of this cooperation:

EUROJUST: Founded in 2002 as the first judicial cooperation network of the world.

EUROPOL: Founded in 1992 as a coordinating institution of the EU national police, which has gained more powers over time. It fights against money laundering, terrorism, child pornography, organised crime, illegal trafficking of people and trafficking of drugs.

---

into a European framework. Several programmes were also established to achieve greater cooperation in the administrative and operational sectors as well as other sectors (Lavenex and Wallace, 2005: 476). Since the beginning of the millennium, there has been a general trend to combine the justice and home affairs policy and the common foreign and security policy, because the external dimension of judicial and police matters is extremely important for the success of EU domestic policies (Uçarer, 2007: 313; Lavenex and Wallace, 2005: 476–7).

In sum, the Europeanisation of judicial and security policies shows that today European politics has to take into account the interactions between national governments and both supranational and international levels. The success of such cooperation should allow the creation of greater political, economic and social stability at national level.

Conclusions: the Europeanisation of judicial power

In this chapter, we have argued that judicial power has gained greater prominence since 1945. The creation of a constitutional review through constitutional courts has become an important aspect of this increased judicial power, which has evolved in the different European political systems. In spite of the difficulties of institution-building, an independent judiciary has become of crucial importance for countries in Southern Europe and Central and Eastern Europe. In some countries, such as Italy and France, the judiciary increased its level of activity during periods of crisis in both countries in the 1980s and 1990s.

The European integration process has put the judiciaries under considerable pressure. The supremacy of EU law restricts the jurisdiction of national law, but is leading to an increasing integration between European and national laws. The growing importance of the Single European Market is also increasing cooperation and institution-building between the member states and the EU. In this sense, national politics is intrinsically linked to supranational politics. The dynamics of the interactions between national and supranational levels no longer allow analysis of European political systems to be separated from each other. As the Scandinavian and Southern European cases show, there is a mutual learning and institutional transfer taking place, which is leading to convergence of judicial systems. As such, we can speak of a substantial Europeanisation of national judicial systems.

Suggested reading

Bell, John (2006), *Judiciaries within Europe: A Comparative Review*. Cambridge: Cambridge University Press.

Kapsis, Ilias (2007), The Courts of the European Union. In: Michelle Cini (ed.), *European Union Politics*. Oxford: Oxford University Press, pp. 188–201.

Stone Sweet, Alec (2000), *Governing with Judges: Constitutional Politics in Europe*. Oxford: Oxford University Press.

—— (2004), *The Judicial Construction of Europe*. Oxford: Oxford University Press

Volcansek, Mary L. (ed.) (1992), Judicial Politics and Policy-Making in Western Europe. London: Frank Cass, special issue of *West European Politics*, 15(3), July.

Wilhelmsson, Thomas, Elina Paunio and Annika Pohjolainen (eds) (2007), *Private Law and the Many Cultures of Europe*. Amsterdam: Kluwer Law.

QUESTIONS FOR REVISION

- What are the main judicial traditions in Europe? Discuss, using examples from countries from each region.
- Compare the executive–judiciary relations in Italy and Germany.
- Assess what kind of problems judiciaries have in the new democracies of Central and Eastern Europe.
- Explain the role of constitutional courts in Europe. Discuss, using examples from at least two countries.
- Is European integration eroding national judicial traditions? Discuss, using examples from at least two countries.

Regional and local government in multilevel Europe

SUMMARY OF CHAPTER 9

There are different patterns of territorial organisation in Europe. According to a slightly changed typology by John Loughlin (2000), there are five patterns of territorial organisation in Europe: federal states (Germany, Austria, Switzerland, Belgium), a confederal state (Bosnia-Herzegovina), regionalised unitary states (Italy, Spain, France, the UK, Poland, the Czech Republic), decentralised unitary states (the Netherlands, Denmark, Sweden, Finland and Norway) and centralised unitary states (Portugal, Greece, Luxembourg, Baltic states, Hungary, Bulgaria and Romania and most of the Balkan countries).

The importance of decentralisation in Europe fits in with the principles of governance (see Chapter 7, pp. 233–6), which has allowed a multilevel governance system to emerge in the European Union. The European dimension is relevant to the increasing significance of the regions in national, supranational and international politics.

The European integration process has led to the emergence of a myriad of regional actors who are using the multilevel structure of opportunities of the EU governance system to enhance their political status and/or gain greater influence at supranational level. Moreover, a new phenomenon of 'paradiplomacy', the parallel foreign policy of subnational actors to that of national governments has led to new interregional partnerships and cross-border cooperation.

Decentralisation in Europe

As we mentioned in Chapter 3, Stein Rokkan identified the silent revolution taking place in the 1970s and early 1980s, which was related to the growing self-confidence and self-consciousness of many European regions. Indeed, in the past three decades, the centralised nation-state has had to move towards a more decentralised structure as a result of the growing pressure coming from the subnational level, seeking greater autonomy, as well as in response to the challenge of globalisation, which requires a more flexible structure (Christiansen and Jørgensen, 2000). In this regard, the region was identified as probably being a more flexible geographic unit than the nation-state to respond directly to global challenges. Michael Keating characterised this revival of the region as 'new regionalism' (Keating, 1998). The European integration process further contributed to a transformation of centre-periphery relations in each country. The present political geography of Europe has become quite diverse, with some countries being fully-fledged federal states (e.g., Austria, Belgium, Germany and Switzerland), others being centralised, despite consequent high costs in terms of inefficiency (e.g., Portugal and Greece), and many others developing their own new centre-periphery relations between these two extremes. Probably, the two best examples in this regard are Spain and the United Kingdom. Both countries were very centralised in the 1970s, but moved towards more regionalised, decentralised structures after

1978 and 1997 respectively. Many countries remained unitary but decentralised and have de-concentrated their administrative structures (e.g., Sweden, Denmark, Norway, Finland and the Netherlands). All these countries developed new governance structures that allowed a more flexible and dynamic relationship between centre and periphery. In particular, Sweden and Finland restructured their governance after joining the European Union in 1995, as did Italy after Tangentopoli in 1992. Pressures from the Northern League under Umberto Bossi led to a piecemeal restructuring of the constitution, moving towards fully-fledged federalism. However, in spite of major efforts on the part of the Berlusconi government, a referendum on federalism held on 25 June 2006 was rejected by almost two-thirds of the population (*International Herald Tribune*, 25 June 2006).

The re-emergence of regional consciousness in many parts of Europe has been an important factor. After 1978 Spain became a regionalised unitary state, which, after more than three decades of authoritarianism, allowed regions to regain their autonomy and their own institutions. Catalonia, the Basque Country and Galicia are regarded as historical nations within Spain. There is discussion about declaring Spain a pluri-national country, in which Spain and the other historical nations within it have equal standing. However, this has led also to opposition from the other regions, who do not want to accept asymmetrical federalism or similar arrangements.

In the United Kingdom, the devolution process introduced by the Labour government under Prime Minister Tony Blair led to the re-establishment of the Scottish Parliament and Welsh Assembly, which in turn had spillover effects upon regional and national politics and policies. Moreover, after years of negotiations and setbacks, in 2007, before Prime Minister Tony Blair left office, the Northern Ireland Assembly was finally able to elect a power-sharing government, which included the loyalist Democratic Unionist Party (DUP) and the Irish nationalist Sinn Fein. During the transition to democracy in Czechoslovakia after 1989, the Velvet Divorce of 1993 allowed a peaceful separation of the Czech and Slovak Republics, which was more a demand of the latter than the former. The Velvet Divorce is also regarded as a model for the xenophobic Vlaams Belang (Flemish Interest, VB), which should be implemented in Belgium in order to achieve a separation of Flanders and Wallonia. As mentioned earlier, in Italy Lega Nord, under leader Umberto Bossi, advocated independence of the northern regions with the new name of 'Padania'. In 2001, when Lega Nord became part of the Berlusconi government, Umberto Bossi as minister for state reform developed a more moderate proposal of federalism that was nonetheless rejected by the above-mentioned referendum in June 2006.

The most traumatic experience in Europe was probably the breakdown of the former Yugoslavia, which led to the Balkan wars of the first half of the 1990s. There are now seven new states: Slovenia, Croatia, Serbia, Macedonia, Montenegro, Bosnia-Herzegovina and Kosovo. These wars have led to inter-ethnic violence and crimes against humanity, which are now being dealt with by the International Criminal Tribunal for the former Yugoslavia (ICTY). Yugoslavia is a negative reminder of how virulent nationalism can be on the European continent.

In this chapter, patterns of territorial administration in Europe are looked at initially. This is followed by a section on the European dimension of subnational government. And, last but not least, some conclusions are drawn at the end of the chapter.

Table 9.1 National territorial organisation in Europe

	Country	Regional units	Municipalities/ communes
Federal states	Germany	16 Länder	12,900
	Austria	9 Bundesländer	2,357 (2005)
	Switzerland	20 cantons 6 Half cantons	2,715
	Belgium	3 regions 3 cultural communities 10 provinces (5 in Flanders and 5 in Wallonia)	589 308 (Flanders) 262 (Wallonia)
Confederal states	Bosnia-Herzegovina	Confederation of two parts – Bosnian–Croatian Federation 10 cantons – Republika Srpska Just communes, no in-between tier	Bosnian–Croatian Federation 79 Republika Srpska 61+2 cities
Regionalised unitary states	Spain	17 autonomous communities	About 8,109
	United Kingdom	4 regions Scotland Wales Northern Ireland England (9 non-elected subregions)	England and Wales 410 Scotland 32 Northern Ireland 26
	Italy	15 regions 5 special regions	104 provinces 8102 communes
	France	22 regions 4 regions overseas 102 departements (4 outside France)	36,781
	Poland	16 województwo 315 counties 65 cities with county status	2,500
	Czech Republic	14 regions and city of Prague	6,249
	Hungary	7 non-elected regions 19 elected counties	3,152 communes
Unitary, but decentralised states	Netherlands	12 provinces	467
	Ireland	8 non-elected coordinating regions 2 regional assemblies	5 city councils, 29 county councils, 75 town councils and 5 borough councils
	Sweden	2 directly elected and 18 non-elected counties	290

Table 9.1 Continued

	Country	Regional units	Municipalities/communes
	Norway	19 counties	443
	Denmark	5 regions 14 counties	98 municipalities
	Finland	19 counties/regional councils	444
Unitary centralised states	Albania	12 regions	309 communes and 65 municipalities
	Bulgaria	Six planning macro-regions 28 districts (*oblasti*)	264 municipalities 3,850 mayoralties and local districts
	Croatia	20 counties	121 towns and 421 municipalities
	Estonia	15 county governments	227
	Greece	13 non-elected coordinating regions 54 directly elected prefectural self-government	1,034 (900 urban municipalities and 134 rural communes)
	Iceland	23 regional districts	79 Town and rural districts
	Latvia	26 districts	430 rural municipalities 36 amalgamated municipalities
	Lithuania	10 counties	60
	Luxembourg		116
	Macedonia		84 and city of Skopje
	Portugal	5 non-elected coordinating regions Provisional non-elected 18 districts in continental Portugal 2 autonomous regions (Madeira and Azores)	308 municipalities (subdivided in 4,261 municipalities)
	Romania	8 non-elected development regions 42 counties and Bucharest	103 municipalities 265 towns 2,864 communes
	Serbia	29 districts Two autonomous regions Vojvodina Kosovo (controversial)	190
	Slovakia	8 kraj 79 districts	About 2,891
	Slovenia	58 decentralised state administrative units	193 municipalities

Source: Committee of the Regions (February 2008) and government websites

Patterns of territorial administration in Europe

One of the simplest and easiest ways to differentiate patterns of territorial administration was devised by John Loughlin. In a seminal article, Loughlin differentiated between four categories of territorial organisation: federal states, regionalised but unitary states, unitary but decentralised states, and unitary centralised states (Loughlin, 1998; 2000). We have added here a tentative fifth category of a confederal state, because Bosnia-Herzegovina is still far from achieving a reconciliation between the Serbs and the Bosniak-Muslims and Croats (Tables 9.1 and 9.2, Figure 9.1).

Federal states: Germany, Austria, Switzerland and Belgium

The most decentralised countries are in the western central part of Europe: Germany, Austria, Switzerland and Belgium. Germany is by far the largest federalised country in Europe. It was divided into sixteen *Länder* after reunification

Figure 9.1 The territorial organisation of European countries

Table 9.2 General government expenditure in the European Union and European Economic Area members, 2006

		General government	Central government	Regional government	Local government
EU average	EU27	46.8	25.6	4.3	11.4
	Euro-area	47.8	21.8	6	10.2
Federal states	Belgium	49	27.7	14.1	7
	Germany	54.8	20.6	13.3	8.1
	Austria	48.9	29.2	9.2	7.9
Unitary regionalised states	Spain	38.5	14.8	14.6	6.2
	Italy	50.1	28.4	0	15.6
	France	53.4	22.3	0	11.1
	United Kingdom	44.6	41.1	0	12.9
	Poland	47.7	31.3	0	11
	Czech Republic	42.5	30.7	0	11.7
	Hungary	52.5	36.7	0	12.8
	Slovakia	37.3	21.5	0	6.6
Unitary decentralised states	Netherlands	46.7	26.9	0	15.6
	Sweden	55.6	30.6	0	25
	Finland	48.6	24.8	0	19.5
	Denmark	51.4	31.7	0	33
	Iceland	41.4	30	0	12.7
	Norway	40.8	32.7	0	12.8
Unitary centralised states	Luxembourg	40.4	29.1	0	5.1
	Ireland	34.1	27.6	0	7.1
	Slovenia	46.3	29.3	0	9
	Greece	46.1	33.3	0	3.3
	Cyprus	43.9	38.9	0	2
	Malta	43.1	43	0	0.6
	Portugal	46.2	30.9	0	5.9
	Bulgaria	36.6	25.2	0	6.2
	Romania	32	17.5	0	8.1
	Estonia	33.2	25.4	0	8.2
	Latvia	37	22.7	0	10
	Lithuania	33.6	20.7	0	8.6

Source: Eurostat database, http://epp.eurostat.ec.europa.eu/portal/page?_pageid=1073,46870091 &_dad=portal&_schema=PORTAL&p_product_code=TEC00023 (accessed 1 February 2009)

in 1989–90. There are twelve *Länder* in the west, and four new *Länder* in the east. The overall pattern of distribution of budget and personnel is one of cooperative federalism based on consensual agreement and negotiation. The *Länder* are an important stepping stone for national politics, and this is also true vice versa. There is a *Politikverflechtung* (joint policy-making) that allows diversity to be set alongside agreed frameworks that set the guidelines and limits for the respective policies.

The conference of first ministers (*Konferenz der Regierungschefs*) is important for achieving coordination and harmonisation of policy-making between the *Länder* and the federal government. There are also several intergovernmental meetings between the ministers of the *Länder* governments, which allow more specialised discussions between the representatives of the *Länder* and the federal government (*Ressortministerkonferenzen*) to take place. Moreover, a complex network of committees between the federal government and the *Länder* has been established over the last sixty years, making the decision-making process less transparent and accountable (Figure 9.2).

The *Länder* have exclusive competences in education, culture, policing, media and local government, but have to share a bulk of other competences with the federal government. According to Wolfgang Rudzio, most of the interesting domestic policy areas are shared between the *Länder* and the federal government

Figure 9.2 The *Länder* in Germany

(Rudzio, 2006: 316). One of the main reasons is that there are general principles underlying the governance of the Federal Republic of Germany. First of all, there is the general principle of creating a level playing field across the country in terms of life chances and quality of life. Second, in spite of diversity, the economic and legal conditions are intended to be largely the same in all parts of the country. This sets boundaries for policy-makers at the regional level. Despite this small number of exclusive competences, the *Länder* are central to implementation of federal policies, so that Germany is characterised by an executive federalism (*Verwaltungsföderalismus*). According to Rudzio there is no dualist structure between federal level and *Länder*, as is common in the United States and Canada, but rather an integrated one in which there is cooperation (Rudzio, 2006: 319).

The *Länder* have their own governments and parliaments, which are elected every four years. This has become an important factor for the dynamics of domestic politics. Positive or negative results at regional elections may create problems for a party that is represented in the federal government in Berlin. *Länder* also have a suspensive veto power in the upper chamber of the national parliament, the Bundesrat (Federal Council), and a final veto in a limited number of areas.

Austria has a similar territorial structure to Germany with nine *Bundesländer*. The only major difference is that it is more centralised in terms of competences and there is more emphasis on executive federalism. This has to do with the Austrian historical legacy, in which Vienna was the centre of administration and the political system was highly centralised. From 1945, the historical legacy shaped the way the country has been organised up to the present day. However, Austria is one of the most decentralised countries of the European Union in financial terms (Pelinka and Rosenberger, 2003: 223–32). In a similar way to Germany, there are regular elections to a regional parliament (*Landtag*) every four years. Also, since the 1960s, an informal conference of first ministers (*Konferenz der Landeshauptleute*) regularly takes place. Last, but not least, the regional parliaments send representatives to the Bundesrat (Federal Council), the upper chamber of the national parliament. However, in comparison to the German system, the Austrian Bundesrat is fairly weak (see Chapter 6) (Figure 9.3).

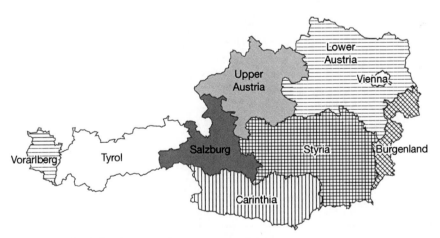

Figure 9.3 The federal territorial organisation of Austria

2005	Territory in sq km	Population in thousands
Aargau	1,404	574.3
Appenzell Ausserroden	243	53.2
Appenzell Innerroden	173	15.4
Basel – country side	517	267
Basel – city	37	185.1
Bern	5,961	959.1
Fribourg	1,671	257.6
Ginebra	282	433.8
Glaris	685	38.1
Glaubuenden	7,105	187.8
Jura	837	69.2
Luzern	1,493	359.1
Neuchatel	803	168.4
Nidwalden	276	40.1
obwalden	491	33.6
Schaffhausen	299	73.8
Schwyz	909	138.8
Solothurn	791	248.3
St. Gallen	2,076	462.1
Turgau	991	235.9
Ticino	2,813	324.6
Uri	1,077	35
Valais	5,225	294.6
Vaud	3,212	661.9
Zug	239	107.7
Zurich	1,729	1.283

Linguistic groups
German: Aargau, Appenzell, Basel, Bern, Glarus, Graubuenden, Luzern, Unterwalden, Schaffhausen, Schwyz, Solothurn, St. Gallen, Thurgau, Uri, Zug, Zurich. *Share of population*: 63.67%
Francophone: Fribourg, Ginebra, Neuchatel, Valais, Vaud. *Share of population*: 20.4%
Italian: Ticino, Jura. *Share of population*: 6.5%
Raetoroman: Graubuenden. *Share of population*: 0.5%

Share of foreign population: 20.4%

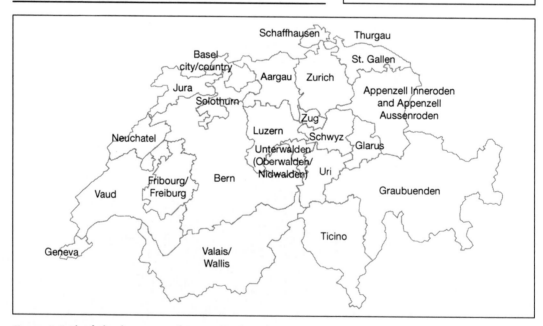

Figure 9.4 The federal structure of Switzerland
Source: Fischer Taschenbuch Verlag (2008: 414–22)

Switzerland is the most decentralised of the three countries, although the central government has gained in importance since 1945. There are twenty cantons and six half cantons, each with their own parliament and government (see Figure 9.4). Because of the high level of decentralisation, intergovernmental structures are of great importance in order to achieve the harmonisation and coordination of policies. This fragmentation and high level of autonomy creates major administrative problems and some policy areas, such as taxation, are still far from harmonised. The consequence is the establishment of a very expensive administrative structure because most cantons are small.

One important principle of Swiss federalism is subsidiarity, which prevents the central government from being too powerful. A more formalised horizontal conference of cantonal governments (Konferenz der Kantonalregierungen, KdK) was only established in 1993. However, according to Nicole Bolleyer, a whole institutionalised network of horizontal conferences and committees has been in existence since the end of the nineteenth century. According to Bolleyer, Switzerland has about 500 horizontal inter-cantonal conferences. Moreover, the sixteen conferences of directors (Direktorenkonferenzen, DK), responsible for different policy areas, are central to intergovernmental relations. Although the DK was originally a conference to shape federal policy on the European Union, it has become the main coordinating structure of the intergovernmental network. One particular characteristic of Switzerland is that there are only coalition governments at both cantonal and federal level. This leads to consensualism and a model of cooperative federalism (Bolleyer, 2006: 400–1). While in Germany about two-thirds of policies originate from concurrent shared legislation, in Switzerland this is roughly only 17.4 per cent. This shows the high level of autonomy of Swiss cantons in comparison with other federal systems (Bolleyer, 2006: 387).

In spite of the consensualism in cantonal governments and parliaments, it would be a fallacy to assume that all cantonal systems are the same. In an excellent study by Adrian Vatter, it was found that among the different cantonal political systems there were also different forms of consensus democracy (Vatter, 2002). This shows how difficult it is to understand all the complexities of the Swiss political system and its subnational government. Another characteristic is the strong position of the cantonal representatives in the Council of States (Ständerat), the upper chamber of the national parliament. It has equal status to the lower chamber, the National Council (Nationalrat), and shapes policy in the interests of the represented cantons (see Chapter 6).

Belgium is the youngest federal state in Europe. It was established after the ratification of the new constitution in 1993. This was the culmination of a process of decentralisation that had been taking place since the 1960s. At the centre was an ongoing latent conflict between the Francophone region of Wallonia and the Flemish-speaking region of Flanders. Although there is a third German linguistic group, in the south-west of Belgium, it has remained outside the major conflict between the two regions. Before the Second World War, when Wallonia dominated the unitary state, the Flemish-speaking population felt disadvantaged in Belgium. After the Second World War, Flanders gradually became the richest part of Belgium and began to demand greater autonomy. Moreover, the population ratio between the two parts of Belgium inverted. Although before the Second World War, the majority of the population was living in Wallonia, in the 1960s there was a larger share of the population in Flanders. Since the 1960s, there has been a process of decentralisation and also some separation of the two populations. Piecemeal reforms were undertaken, so that greater autonomy could be granted to the three regions. However, this period was also characterised by many conflicts (Leton and Miroir, 1999). The new federal structure comprises six subnational units: three regions and three cultural communities. The three regions are Flanders, Wallonia and Brussels and the cultural communities the Flemish, Francophone and German communities. The Flemish region and community have merged and built one government. Overall, judging by the results of opinion polls, the population seems to be happy with autonomy, however the nationalist xenophobic party VB (mentioned above) is seeking to achieve more and is demanding independence. This has created tensions in Belgium. The share of personnel and expenditure has shifted in favour of the regions. There is still no fiscal federalism, and subnational governments are dependent on federal government grants, which total about three-quarters of their budgets (Swenden and Jans, 2006: 885) (see Figure 9.5).

The whole process of federalisation is still being developed. According to Wilfried Swenden and Maarten Theo Jans, there is a deliberation committee to sort out the differences between the federal and subnational levels in Belgium, but, so far, it has not been very successful at dealing with the issues. This means that many intergovernmental agreements are reached outside this framework. As this involves a smaller number of partners, it has resulted in greater success. As well as the deliberation committee, sixteen intergovernmental conferences, involving the different areas of cooperation, complete this intergovernmental network (Swenden and Jans, 2006: 887–8). One characteristic of Belgian politics is that there is no

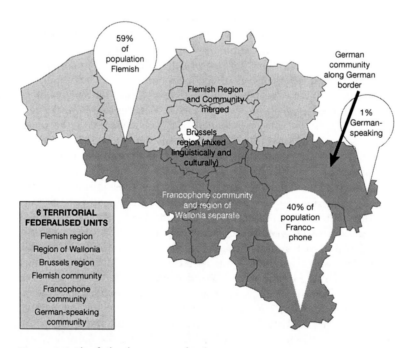

Figure 9.5 The federal structure of Belgium

national party system. There are now two party systems, one in Wallonia and the other in Flanders, and, depending on the national strength of each party in each of the two regions, they then negotiate a coalition government at national level. Such attempts have become more difficult because of the tension between the two communities, especially after the general elections of 10 June 2007. A coalition government under Prime Minister Yves Leterme collapsed on 15 July 2008, because his coalition partners could not agree on the future of devolution to both Wallonia and Flanders. Since then, it has been difficult to form stable coalition governments in Belgium.

A confederal state: Bosnia-Herzegovina

Although the international community used the Swiss model to devise the political system, the bitter divisions between the Serbs on the one hand and the Bosnian-Muslims and Croats on the other hand still prevent a normal relationship between the two parts of the country (*El Pais*, 6 October 2008: 7). The independence of Kosovo in February 2008 reignited the desire of the Serbian Republic (Republika Srpska) to become an independent identity. The bitter war fought between the different ethnic groups before the Dayton Agreement of 1995 left many scars, which are still conditioning the behaviour of political actors. One major difficulty with the Bosnian-Herzegovina confederal status is that it was imposed by the inter-national community. The United Nations is in charge of rebuilding the fragile institutions of this independent country. This means that many decisions, including the flag itself, were imposed by the high representative of the United Nations for Bosnia-Herzegovina. The high representative acts as an external governor, who can intervene in the political process and take action against those that violate the Dayton Agreement. This creates greater resentment against the international community. The top-down approach of creating a political structure that would bring all relevant groups on board has led to a complete exclusion of the population, thus creating an artificial identity, similar to the former Yugoslavia, with the same dangers of compartmentalisation and division that existed before (Hayden, 2005; Oschlies, 2003: 712–13).

The overall structure allows an equal distribution of representation for all ethnic groups in parliament and the executive. The head of the collective presidency rotates every eight months, so that each ethnic group is represented equally. The country consists of two large entities: the Federation of Bosnia and Herzegovina, which comprises both the Bosnian-Muslims and the Bosnian-Croats; and the Republika Srpska, populated by the Bosnian-Serbs. The overall territorial share is 51 to 49 per cent respectively. Each entity has its own political structure, consisting of a president, a vice-president and a prime minister. American influence has led to the establishment of a bicameral parliament, consisting of a directly elected house of representatives, with forty-two-MPs, and a nominated house of peoples, with fifteen MPs. The overall structure is, of necessity, fairly complex, so that the different ethnic communities can be accommodated.

There is a danger that these arrangements have consolidated rather than overcome the ethnic divisions and segregation that existed between the different communities. Moreover, issues related to government inefficiency, slow development of a market economy and political corruption have prevented greater progress in bringing the ethnic communities closer together (Bideleux and Jeffries, 2007b: 399–404). According to a study by Zdravko Zlopaka, local government is poor in terms of efficiency in both parts of the Federation, and the population is dissatisfied with the provision of public services (Zlopaka, 2008: 180). The two parts have different local government structures: in the Bosnian-Croatian Federation there are ten cantons, which are treated as federal units and which are different in size and level of competences, and seventy-nine municipalities; the Republika Srpska is far more centralised with only one local government tier, sixty-one municipalities and two cities (Zlopaka, 2008: 182–8). In both parts of the country, centralisation is dominant. The only major difference is that in the Bosnian-Croatian Federation centralisation takes place at cantonal level, while in the Republika Srpska it comes from the central government (Zlopaka, 2008: 199). Apart from budgetary constraints, which are still highly centralised, there are also other factors that lead to inefficiencies of local government. First, the municipalities are far too small to create economies of scale, so services become expensive. Second, lack of skilled and well-educated leadership is a major disadvantage in creating strategic plans at local level. Third, there is a lack of cooperation between the different municipalities, which reinforces the problem of creating economies of scale for public services (Zlopaka, 2008: 200–1).

Regionalised unitary states: Spain, Italy, France, the UK, Poland, the Czech Republic, Hungary and Slovakia

The regionalised unitary states can be divided into two broad categories: those that allow autonomy because of the strong regional consciousness of some parts of the country (such as Spain, the UK and, to some extent, Italy) and those that are engaged in administrative decentralisation and de-concentration (such as France, Italy, Poland, the Czech Republic, Hungary and Slovakia). The former want to accommodate centre-periphery tensions, while the latter want to modernise the state through the introduction of more flexible. decentralised structures.

Among the first group, Spain is probably the most interesting case. In the constitution of 1978, Spain was defined as a 'state of autonomies'. This was a compromise between the Francoist right, which wanted to preserve the unitary nature of Spain, and the left-wing democratic opposition, which was keen to move towards a federal structure and, if not, at least to restore the autonomy of the historical regions of Catalonia, the Basque Country and Galicia, all of which had their own languages. However, between 1979 and 1982, the granting of autonomy to the historical regions led to a movement towards the creation of autonomous communities in other parts of the country. At the end of 1982, there were seventeen autonomous communities, some with a comprehensive level of autonomy, which included policing and education, and others with lower levels of autonomy. Four regions were able to achieve a considerable level of autonomy according to article 151: Andalucia, the Basque Country, Galicia and Catalonia. The others had autonomy conceded through article 143, which allowed for a limited autonomy. However, all autonomous communities were granted directly elected regional parliaments and their own executives (Figure 9.6).

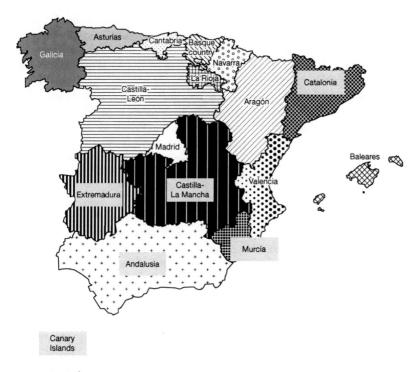

Figure 9.6 The autonomous communities in Spain

Such an asymmetrical construction of the state of autonomies was reviewed in the 1990s by the two main parties, the People's Party (Partido Popular, PP) and the Socialist Party (Partido Socialista Obrero Español, PSOE) (Magone, 2008: 194). In 1992 and 1994, they signed agreements to upgrade the competences of the autonomous communities with limited autonomy. This process of levelling the competences of all the autonomous communities towards a more symmetrical model was reinforced during the government of Prime Minister José Maria Aznar between 1996 and 2004. During this period, the highly successful National Health Service was decentralised, thus creating seventeen regional systems (Magone, 2009a: 198–9). Since 2004, the Zapatero government pushed for further decentralisation and allowed for a review of the statutes of the autonomous regions. The most controversial was the Catalan Statute, which led to major opposition by the PP under Mariano Rajoy. The Catalan Statute was sent to the constitutional court in order to check its constitutionality. One particular issue of contention was the use of the word 'nation' for Catalonia in the statute. The more radical conservative factions inside the PP regarded this as an assault on the unity of Spain. However, the different historical communities in Spain do regard themselves as nations and would like to change the Spanish constitution to enshrine the pluri-national identity of the country. The country could follow the British model, which allows for a full acknowledgment of the different nationalities – Scottish, Welsh, Irish and English – within the state. Apart from the Catalan Statute, several other autonomous communities undertook review processes. The one with fewest problems was

Valencia. In contrast, in Andalucia there were some disagreements about the word 'nationality'. In spite of these differences, all the autonomous communities were eventually able to get their statute reviews approved by the Cortes. The approval of the Catalan Statute is still waiting for the decision of the constitutional court, which is split between supporters and opponents. In many ways, the debate in the constitutional court has become quite politicised because of the polarisation between the two main parties, the Socialist Party and the People's Party. Although the Catalan Statute was approved and confirmed in a referendum in Catalonia in 2006, as of May 2010 the constitutional court had not yet reached a decision.

The relationship between the Spanish government and the Basque government has been even more difficult. Since 2001, former Basque President Juan José Ibarretxe has proposed various plans for the independence of the Basque Country from Spain. The plan initially proposed was rejected by both main political parties as being against the Spanish constitution. Known as the 'Ibarretxe plan', it proposed a path that could be taken towards independence. Such a step would require a positive result in a referendum put to the Basque people. As an intermediate solution, before independence, the Ibarretxe plan proposed an association of the Basque Country with Spain, before it became independent. Although endorsed by the Basque Parliament, it was rejected by the Cortes in February 2005. In September 2007, regional President Ibarretxe presented a similar revised plan to Prime Minister José Luis Zapatero, who rejected it vehemently. Moreover, an appeal to the constitutional court by the Basque government resulted in Ibarretxe's plan being declared unconstitutional. The rigid position of Ibarretxe has created tensions inside his own party, the Basque Nationalist Party (Partido Nacionalista Vasco), because more moderate forces can see the successful improvement brought by statutes for other autonomous communities including Catalonia, while the process in the Basque Country is stagnating (El Pais, 27 September 2008: 11). After the 1 March 2009 Basque elections, in spite of winning the elections, it was not possible to form a government owing to the lack of an absolute majority. The PSOE (Spanish Socialist Workers' Party) as the second largest party and supported by the People's Party was able to form a single-party government under the socialist leader Patxi Lopez. This is important, because it represents a turning point in Basque politics. For the first time, a non-nationalist party is governing the Basque Country without the Basque Nationalist Party (El Pais, 3 March 2009: 9–11).

One major issue in the Basque Country, which is putting moderate nationalist parties under pressure, is the Basque separatist organisation Basque Country and Freedom (Euskadi ta Askatasuna, ETA). The ETA has been active since 1959 and demands independence from Spain. Between 1959 and 2009, 855 people died as a result of their terrorist attacks, two-thirds in the Basque Country and the rest in other autonomous communities (Guardia Civil, 2010). Since 2003 both the PP and PSOE governments have reinforced their fight against the organisation. The new law of political parties, ratified in 2002, forbids any association of political parties with terrorist organisations. This allowed the Spanish government, after a judicial process, to forbid the existence of parties connected to ETA. Apart from Herri Batasuna (People's Union, HB), other proxy parties such as the Communist Party of the Basque Countries (Partido Comunista de las Tierras Vascas, PCTV) and the Nationalist Basque Association (Associación Nacionalista Vasca, ANV), which took part in the Basque elections of September 2005 and the local elections of May 2007 respectively, were investigated and their leaders questioned, if not imprisoned. ETA and its youth organisation Jarrai have terrorised the Basque Country through street violence (*kale borroka*) and the 'revolutionary tax' on entrepreneurs working in the Basque Country. However, reinforced joint action by Spanish and French police has substantially reduced the operational capabilities of ETA. Similar joint actions have also increased between the Spanish and Portuguese police (Magone, 2009a: 246–51).

Spanish intergovernmental relationships have increased over time. At the centre are the top-down sectorial conferences (*conferencias sectoriales*) between the central government ministries and their counterparts in the regions. Initially, in 1981 there were four such meetings, by 2005 this had increased to seventy-nine in one year. In 2005, there were fifty-five sectorial areas in which meetings were taking place. Moreover, a special committee dealing with European Union affairs was established in 1988 to allow consultation with the autonomous communities. The Committee of European Community Affairs (Comisión de Asuntos Relacionados con la Comunidad Europea, CARCE) plays a major role in selecting the two representatives of the autonomous communities for the Spanish Permanent Representation in Brussels (Magone, 2009a: 201–3).

Furthermore, the Zapatero government introduced the conference of presidents, which has decision-making powers on issues related to the autonomous communities. It is comprised of the Spanish prime minister, known as *El Presidente* in Spain, and the presidents of the seventeen autonomous communities. The first conference took place in October 2004, and a further two were organised in 2005 and 2006 (Magone, 2008: 204).

The Spanish model of a state of autonomies is unique and quite original. It developed a dynamics of its own, largely unintended by the founding fathers of the new democratic constitution in Spain.

When the New Labour government under the leadership of Tony Blair came to power in 1997, devolution of powers to Scotland, Wales and Northern Ireland were top priorities. In November 1997, two referenda in Scotland and Wales led to the approval of the establishment of a Parliament in Scotland and an Assembly in Wales. Such a bold move by the first Blair government was perceived by many (especially in the Conservative Party) as the dismantling of the United Kingdom; however, for the Labour government, it was part of a major modernisation of the constitution of the United Kingdom, which also entailed transformations in the House of Lords (see Chapter 6), in the Judiciary (see Chapter 8) and other parts of the political system. After more than a decade of devolution, it can be assessed as being very successful for all three regions of Wales, Scotland and Northern Ireland. The Scottish Parliament and Executive have been able to develop their own policies in education and health, which are now quite distinctive from those of England. This variable geometry led to new questions about the equity of opportunities across the territory. While the Welsh Assembly, the Scottish Parliament after 1997 and the Northern Ireland Assembly after 2007 profited considerably from the new territorial arrangements, the advantages became less clear for England, the largest part of the United Kingdom. Attempts by former Deputy Prime Minister John Prescott to implement English regions across the territory through referenda failed after rejection in the referendum for the north-east region by an overwhelming majority of 78 per cent against 22 per cent on 4 November 2004 (BBC, 5 November 2004).

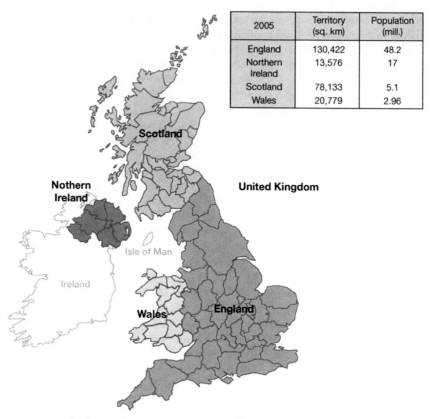

2005	Territory (sq. km)	Population (mill.)
England	130,422	48.2
Northern Ireland	13,576	17
Scotland	78,133	5.1
Wales	20,779	2.96

Figure 9.7 The regionalised structure of the United Kingdom after 1997

The most difficult process was probably that for Northern Ireland, which required strong negotiating skills by the British government. Prime Minister Tony Blair followed in the footsteps of John Major trying to achieve reconciliation between the nationalist Sinn Fein on the one hand and the loyalist Ulster Democratic Party (UDP) and Ulster Unionist Party (UUP) on the other. US Senator George J. Mitchell was appointed to mediate in the negotiation process, but this took a decade to become reality. Finally, a power-sharing agreement between Sinn Fein and the UDP was reached that allowed the restoration of devolution to take place. Between 1998 and 2007, there were many interruptions in this process, which led to the suspension of the Northern Ireland Assembly (BBC, 26 March 2007).

In the May 2007 Scottish elections, the Scottish National Party was able to gain a relative majority and form a minority government with some support in the Scottish Parliament. The party received 32.2 per cent of the vote and forty-seven seats, while New Labour got one seat less. The Conservatives with seventeen and the Liberal Democrats with sixteen remained in third and fourth place respectively (BBC, 6 May 2007). The new First Minister Alex Salmond formed the first Scottish Nationalist government, with the long-term aim of achieving the independence of the country. This may be difficult to achieve because the majority in Scotland want to keep the union with the rest of the United Kingdom.

In the Welsh elections of May 2007, Plaid Cymru, the Nationalist Party of Wales, was able to improve its results and gain three seats from Labour. While New Labour got twenty-six seats, Plaid Cymru achieved seventeen, followed by the Conservatives with twelve and the Liberal Democrats with six (BBC, 7 May 2007).

Among the second group of countries of regionalised unitary states, Italy has to be regarded as a hybrid because of the recent regional mobilisation of the northern regions by the Northern League.

The regionalisation of Italy was enshrined in the constitution of 1948, although elected regions were only established in 1970. This delayed the process of decentralisation and de-concentration inherited from fascism. In total, twenty regions were established, of which fifteen were ordinary regions and five special regions. The special regions were established where linguistic or ethnic minorities were considered, such as Vale d'Aosta (French-speaking minority), Trentino-Adige (German-speaking minority) and Friuli-Venezia Giulia (Croat and Slovene minorities) or for those with island status such as Sicily and Sardinia. Most devolution in competences and budgetary terms took place in the 1970s. Until the collapse of the First Republic in 1992, the regional governments had very limited powers and constrained budgetary means. The regions were regarded as extended arms of the Italian government. This meant that Italian regions had almost no autonomy (Hine, 1993: 269). The political structure comprises a regional assembly elected every five years and a regional executive (*giunta regionale*) that implements the policies.

In spite of this, some regions have done better than others. According to a seminal study by Robert Putnam with Bob Leonardi and Laura Nanetti undertaken in the late 1980s, the northern regions were doing considerably better than the southern regions. Historical legacy factors combined with government efficiency were presented as reasons for the gap between north and south. The tradition of civic culture of the northern city-states and the good coordinating performance of regional government allowed the establishment of social capital over time. Social capital is based on the virtuous interaction of business enterprises, civil society and governmental institutions in order to create wealth for the community. According to Putnam, this can be found in the northern regions as a result of their historical legacy and government efficiency. In contrast, the southern regions, with a historical legacy of feudalism and foreign occupation, did not develop civic culture leading to social capital. Regional government inefficiency and difficulties in overcoming the structures that prevent a virtuous cycle of social capital emerging are the main reasons for the continuing stagnation of the southern regions (Putnam, 1994: 152–62). The findings of Putnam and his team help to explain the major gap between north and south in terms of gross domestic product per capita. In this context, the Mafia, N'Dranghetta and Camorra have been able to dominate politics and society and keep the status quo intact. However, one has to be cautious with these generalisations. Although there was an asymmetrical dominance of civil society associations in the north of Italy until the 1980s, at the end of that decade the spread of civil society was more balanced territorially. The Anti-Mafia movement was a subnational democratic movement in Sicily that consisted mostly of women's groups. According to Allison Jamieson, the Anti-Mafia movement contributed to a strengthening of civil society in the south. In 1992, there were 6,400 civil society associations in the south of Italy, similar to the levels existing in

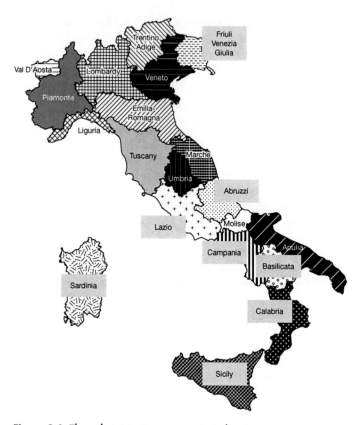

Figure 9.8 The administrative regions in Italy

northern Italy (Jamieson, 1998: 152–3; see also an overall assessment by Paoli, 2007) (Figure 9.8).

After several failed attempts to revise the constitution in the Second Republic after 1992, the political elites agreed on a piecemeal approach. One of the most important aspects of the revision was Chapter V of the constitution, which deals with subnational government. The reforms began in 1995 with the introduction of new electoral laws for the local and regional levels. In 1997, the Bassannini laws allowed autonomy and decentralised decision-making processes for the over 8,000 communes and towns in Italy to take place (Gilbert, 1999; Cotta and Verzichelli, 2007: 189). In 1999, the direct election of the mayor in each major urban centre was introduced, allowing a bipolarised competitive process between ideologically different coalition alliances to take place. The dual role of the mayor as the political head of large municipalities and also as the head of local administration was reinforced by providing more competences as well as increased human and financial resources. Finally, in 2001, a major revision of the constitution was undertaken, which increased the powers of the regions and created the conditions in Italy to take advantage of a more flexible multilevel governance system. The regions were granted more competences and autonomy within the context of multilevel governance (Baldini and Vassalo, 2001: 127–32).

In 1995 and 1999, the electoral system for regional governments and assemblies was changed to a reinforced PR system, which gives a bonus of 20 per cent to the winning coalition. This creates greater stability in regional government. The personalisation of politics at regional level is intentional in order to regenerate democratic politics. According to Maurizio Cotta and Luca Verzichelli, this 'Americanisation of regional politics' resulted in many regional presidents being called 'governor', an allusion to the same term used for the leaders of the individual states in the US (Cotta and Verzichelli, 2007: 188–9).

Finally, in 2006, the Silvio Berlusconi government proposed the introduction of a new territorial organisation for Italy, similar to that of Spain. The new federal territorial structure was submitted to a referendum in June 2006, but two-thirds of voters rejected the proposal. The proposal was mainly designed by Umberto Bossi, the former minister of state reform and leader of the Northern League. The overall aim was not only to accommodate the demands of the Northern League, but also to create more flexible and malleable structures, able to respond quickly to national, European and global challenges.

According to Martin Bull and Gianfranco Pasquino, the myriad of institutional reforms introduced since 1993 has actually put the whole political system under stress, because the different political parties are not able to agree consensually on the way forward. The consequence is that each party in power will try to impose its own design, creating major tensions among the political elite. The Italian constitution has become a political battleground between the main left-wing and right-wing coalitions and there has so far been no compromise about the overall design (Bull and Pasquino, 2007: 671–2).

In spite of Italian unification, a strong regional consciousness characterises the country, which is still relevant today. However, regional political parties are almost non-existent in Italy, apart from the Northern League that emerged as a collection of smaller leagues in the 1980s. In electoral terms, it gained in importance shortly before the collapse of the First Republic in 1992. The political discourse of the Northern League was directed against the waste of resources by the government in Rome and was clearly against the southern part of the country. One particular criticism was that the government in Rome was dominated by southerners. The 'southernisation' of the central administration has been regarded as an impediment for the development of the country (see Chapter 7, p. 260). Moreover, the Northern League was also quite xenophobic, in particular with regard to the Muslim population. The Lombardy has become the centre of demands for greater regional autonomy and federalism in Italy. In the mid 1990s, Umberto Bossi, the leader of the Northern League, demanded independence for 'Padania', the name his party gave to the northern part of Italy. Such demands were moderated considerably in the late 1990s and at the beginning of the new millennium.

French administrative regionalisation started in the 1960s as a consequence of the new regional planning philosophy, the Constituencies of Regional Action and Commissions of Regional Economic Development (Circonscriptions d'Action Régionale et des Commissions de Developpement Économique Régional, CODER) in 1964 and the Public Regional Bodies (Établissements Public Regionaux) in 1972 (Balme, 1998a: 182).

Directly elected regions were only established in 1982. Before that regions did exist, but consisted of appointed members coming from the *départements*.

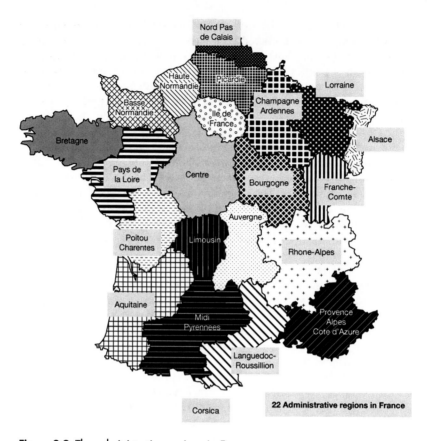

Nord Pas de Calais

Haute Normandie

Picardie

Lorraine

Basse Normandie

Champagne Ardennes

Île de France

Alsace

Bretagne

Pays de la Loire

Centre

Bourgogne

Franche-Comte

Auvergne

Poitou Charentes

Limousin

Rhone-Alpes

Aquitaine

Midi Pyrennees

Provence Alpes Cote d'Azure

Languedoc-Roussillion

Corsica

22 Administrative regions in France

Figure 9.9 The administrative regions in France

The highly centralistic tradition of the Napoleonic state began to be quite inefficient in a period of growing Europeanisation and globalisation. In spite of the centralistic tendencies of the French state, the territorial structure was and remains highly fragmented. There are over 36,000 local authorities and they remain important in the political system. The representatives of the twenty-six regions (twenty-two in continental France plus four islands) are elected for six years and have important competences of policy-making (Figure 9.9).

France has a regional assembly that elects a regional executive. It clearly plays a coordinating role in other territorial subnational structures such as the *départements* and the municipalities. Most of the legislation for the directly elected regions was adopted between 1982 and 1992. De-concentration of public services from Paris to the regions took place in the 1980s and 1990s, so that the new structures were able to offer better arrangements for the citizens. French regions have become important engines of economic development, which are better adjusted to the globalisation and Europeanisation process. However, the budgetary allocation is not extensive and most of the competences are quite specialised. Central to all of them is economic development. Richard Balme characterises regionalisation as follows:

The reform of decentralisation leads much less to the constitution of a regional government endowed with autonomous public policies, than a regionalisation of public policy, *that is to say, the establishment of a regional space of interdependence and collective action among participants taking part in public policy processes.*

(Balme, 1998a: 182; emphasis in original)

According to Andrew Knapp and Vincent Wright, the decentralisation process of the 1980s and 1990s contributed to three important improvements: subsidiarity, rationalisation and democratisation. After decades of centralistic decision-making, regionalisation allowed these to be taken at a more appropriate level, thus reinforcing better services for citizens. This also allowed the rationalisation of services caught between centralisation and fragmentation. The new tier allowed these services and territorial organisation to be more efficient. Last, but not least, all this contributed to a democratisation of the policy and decision-making process, allowing for more access points for citizens (Knapp and Wright, 2001: 365–9).

In spite of the historical legacy of centralism, weak regional consciousness still exists in Brittany and, more so, in Corsica, where several separatist groups tried to gain independence through political violence. However, the separatist movement is ideologically divided, allowing the French state to continue to control the territory (Molas, 2001).

European integration and the enlargement process was a major factor shaping the development of the new territorial organisation in the Central and Eastern European countries. After decades of a centralised communist regime, decentralisation was an important issue in all these countries. However, until the end of the 1990s, the political parties had difficulty in coming to agreement about how regionalisation should be implemented.

Regionalisation also took place in Poland, the Czech Republic and Hungary, although the extent has been much more limited in these countries than in West European ones. Polish regionalisation goes back to the communist period, in which the subnational government was subordinated to the centre. Throughout the 1990s there was a restructuring of the Polish territorial organisation. Up to 1998, there was a major effort to set up a democratic local government system. In 1998, the forty small regions (*województwo*) were replaced by sixteen directly elected large ones. The intermediate structure of counties (*powiat*) that existed until 1974, was restored in 1998, resulting in 315 counties and 65 cities of county status. Moreover, there are 2,500 municipalities (*gmina*) (Swianiewicz, 2006: 11). It is probably too early to make an assessment, but the Polish model of regionalisation bears similarities to the French model. It has limited budgetary means and limited competences, but it is essential for the coordination of regional policy-making (Swianiewicz, 2006: 14).

A similar process of redesigning of the territorial structure of the country took place in the Czech Republic. Throughout the 1990s, the new structures of local government were implemented, although it was only in 1999 that an agreement was reached on regionalisation. In the end, the political parties agreed on the creation of thirteen regions (*kraj*) and the independent region of the city of Prague. The first regional elections for the new regions took place in 2000, and for the city of Prague in 2002 (Illner and Vajdova, 2006: 11–18). One of the reasons for the delay was the resistance of the Civic Forum (ODS) of Vaclac Klaus to the implementation of regionalisation, which was enshrined in the constitution of 1992. However, the European Commission clearly pressed the Czech government to implement some kind of regional structure in order to better absorb the structural funds for which the country would be eligible when it joined the EU (Baun and Marek, 2006: 412–13). The overall rationale of the regions is to develop a regional policy that is compatible with the national strategies. It has competences that are shared with the national government. Among these competences are spatial planning and regional development, education, culture, transport and communication, health care, social welfare, environment and the protection of public order (Illner and Vajdova, 2006: 30–1). However, the Czech regions are highly dependent on government grants in order to fulfil their function and autonomy in terms of funding is quite limited. In spite of this, after two electoral cycles, regionalisation has gained an important place in Czech politics (Baun and Marek, 2006: 418–19).

Similarly, throughout the 1990s, there was discussion about the merits of decentralisation and regionalisation between the left-wing and right-wing parties in Hungary. In 1990, a first structure was established that allowed some auton-omy of the regions, though still under strong central government supervision. Commissioners of the Republic were placed in the intermediate county regions in order to control the policy-making process. Directly elected county regions were established in 1994. In total nineteen county regions (*megye*) were established, with on average about 537,000 inhabitants in each region. The commissioners of the Republic (1990–94) were replaced by non-political technical county public adminis-tration officers, controlled by the minister of the interior in Budapest. The regions were established primarily to facilitate the coordination and implementation of EU structural funds, however the financial devolution process in respect of these regions has been slow and cumbersome. Above them, seven non-elected adminis-trative regions, with a regional development council consisting of central govern-ment representatives and local representatives, steer regional development policies. In spite of this, the new tier strengthened the position of the regions and allowed the establishment of a new arena of politics. In contrast to the Czech Republic and Poland, where the upper house of parliament, the Senate, functions as a territorial chamber adjusted to the new regions, Hungary has refrained from creating any such representation at national level (Rószás, 2004: 80–7; Brusis, 2002: 536). In Slovakia, there are eight directly elected regions (*kraj*), but regions are not represented at national level.

Unitary decentralised states: the Netherlands, Denmark, Sweden, Finland and Norway

Among the unitary decentralised states one has to include the Netherlands and the Nordic countries. All of them are unitary states, but the administration is extremely decentralised. All these advanced democracies have also moved towards new forms of governance that allow for a stronger cooperation between the public and private sector as well as allowing civil society to shape the policy-making process.

The Netherlands consists of twelve directly elected provinces; the elected representatives then elect the members of the Senate. The provinces have a tiny budget of about 10 per cent of all public expenditure; most of the public expenditure is made by the central government through its de-concentrated services and the municipalities. The provinces are not very conspicuous in the political system and merely fulfil a coordinating role at the provincial level. The provinces are very much a product of Dutch history, and, in terms of territorial organisation, not well adjusted to the new realities. Therefore, the debate has shifted to the consideration of creating smaller regions between the provincial and municipal levels (Thoonen, 1998: 143–4). Over the past forty years, the Netherlands has tried to develop a new, more efficient regional structure, but the attempts have always ended in failure. In the 1990s, the main idea was to create 'city-provinces' (*stadsprovincies*). The model was the Rotterdam city-region which, if successful, was to be expanded to other parts of the country, particularly Amsterdam and The Hague. In total, there was a general plan to establish twenty-five such regions. An important factor in this process was the consultation of the population, so that decision-making would not be top-down, but supported by bottom-up social movements. Suffice to say that the Rotterdam city-province was rejected and therefore the regionalisation project did not go any further (Schaap, 2003). This has complicated the situation, because the Dutch meso-level was already overcrowded with 'functional regions'. These functional regions have different demarcations, which do not match the provincial territorial boundaries. A streamlining and simplification of governance structures is something the Dutch government is trying to undertake, but with limited success (Thoonen, 1998: 142–3). Despite these failures, the territorial governance system of the Netherlands has become fairly complex with civil society actors and the private economic sector playing an important role in shaping the policy process (Schaap, 2003: 166–7; Arendsen, 2003: 21).

The discussion in Denmark has been less complicated. A major reform of subnational government took place in the 1970s, which led to the amalgamation of the 24 counties and over 1,200 municipalities. The outcome was a more efficient territorial organisation consisting of 14 counties and 275 municipalities. In terms of public expenditure, subnational government represents 60 per cent of the gross domestic product (this is similar to Finland and Sweden). The welfare state is a central aspect of the decentralised Danish system. The welfare provision in respect of the allocation of funding is a further characteristic of the Danish subnational system (Mouritzen, 2004: 7–11). The municipalities form the most important tier because they are responsible for most of the welfare services, such as education, social policy and health. The counties are responsible for larger tasks, such as the governance of hospitals, major roads and special services (Mouritzen, 2004: 12–13). Both the National Association of Local Authorities and the National Association of County Councils are extremely strong interest groups, which are able to shape national policy (Mouritzen, 2004: 15–16). Only the municipalities are directly elected, not the counties.

In Sweden and Finland, a similar decentralisation of public services and public expenditure has taken place in the past forty years. There are also counties in these two countries. Both countries became members of the European Union in 1995, and there has been major pressure to adjust the territorial structures to the EU multilevel governance system. Since the mid 1990s both countries have been engaged in making their subnational structures more flexible in relation to the context of the EU multilevel governance system.

Since 2000, Sweden has been engaged in a restructuring of the territorial governance system. The basic system of 21 counties (*landsstincommuner*) and 290 municipalities (*kommuner*) has become more complex as a result of the recent reforms introduced by central government. The counties are non-elected structures, apart from two larger councils Västra Götland (a merger of three counties with the city of Göteborg) and Scania (a merger of two former counties in the province of Scania). In much the same way as in Denmark, the process of rationalisation of local government took place between 1950 and 1970. Until 1955, the Swedish local government was fragmented into 2,500 municipalities – a very large number in comparison to the 290 today (Bäck, 2007: 7–8). The recent thrust towards further reform has to do with the wish to increase the competitiveness of the regions in the global arena. The two new larger counties were first set up on an experimental basis, in order to see how they worked. Now, they have become permanent structures in the new territorial governance of Sweden. The counties have so far been responsible mainly for health care. According to Henry Bäck, 88 per cent of total expenses of the county are in health, and all the other public policies, such as education and infrastructure, are devolved to the local authorities. In particular the administration of the hospitals is central to the tasks of the counties (Bäck, 2007: 18). However, the overall thrust for more flexible structures has led to the emergence of new structures, such as the association of municipalities, which can be created in order to improve coordination and efficiency of some specific tasks common to all actors. There are now bodies of regional cooperation (*regional samwerksorgan*) between the counties and the municipalities, which have coordinating functions for the overall county (Bäck, 2007: 25).

As is happening in many other countries, according to Christine Hudson there has been a major shift from government to a governance system, in which stakeholders in regional policy are included in the whole process of decision-making. This was not very difficult for Sweden, because of the political culture of consultation with relevant stakeholders that was already in existence. However, other aspects relating to new public management (for example public–private partnerships, the establishment of less rigid structures, and the activation of the regional stakeholders for regional policy) were introduced through the present reforms. In spite of these changes, Hudson argues that central government remained a stakeholder at regional level through its presence in its county administrative boards (*lansstyrelsen*), which are extended arms of public administration. This means that, in spite of transformation of the territorial governance structure, central government oversees the policy-making processes at subnational level (Hudson, 2005: 314, 320).

Finland and Norway have similar models of territorial organisation, and have also been engaged in transforming into more flexible structures in order to adjust to growing Europeanisation and globalisation processes (Arter, 2001).The provision of welfare is central to local government in these Nordic governments. Overall, all of them spend about 18–20 per cent of the GDP in local government. Finland's subnational government consists of 19 counties and 444 municipalities; however, at intermediate, there are also 20 regional districts for hospitals and 17 regional districts for the care of the disabled. There are also over 200 joint municipal authorities for regional policy coordination in particular areas. Additionally, Finland has granted self-government to the Åland Islands (with their own local government act) (Sandberg, 2005: 9–15).

In Finland, in contrast to Denmark and Sweden, there was strong protest against the amalgamation of municipalities between 1965 and 1980, so that the number of municipalities in Finland remained fairly high (it was only reduced by 100) (Sandberg, 2005: 18).

In Norway, a major debate is taking place about the usefulness of the nineteen county councils (*fylkeskommuner*), which have had their importance reduced over the past thirty years, particularly since 2002 when competences for hospitals and the health sector were taken away from these subnational bodies and reallocated to the central government. This was a bid by the government to develop an integrated National Health Service similar to that in Britain. It meant that the county councils lost substantial funding and as well as their standing within the whole framework. In 1985, the county councils represented 12.3 per cent of expenditure, but this declined to 4.1 per cent in 2003. Compensatory competences for the county councils, such as environmental protection, did not lead to a resurgence of this level of government (Baldersheim and Fimreite, 2005: 769–70). According to Harald Baldersheim and Anne Lise Fimreite the debate about the future of the regional tier has been between abolitionists and revivalists. The former want to create a similar system that existed in the United Kingdom before devolution was implemented in 1997, which would comprise only the central and local government levels, while the revivalists advocated an amalgamation of these towards larger regions, called *landsdelen*. The revivalists advocated the establishment of five provincial assemblies (Northern Norway, Mid-Norway, Western Norway, Southern Norway and Eastern Norway) with more powers and competences than the existing county councils (Baldersheim and Fimreite, 2005: 765, 770).

At the local level, an amalgamation process of municipalities has taken place. Since the 1950s and 1960s, the number of municipalities has declined from 774 to 443 today. And there is further pressure at national level to reduce the present number by 100 (Rose, 2006: 21–2; Baldersheim and Fimreite, 2005: 768).

Unitary centralised states: Southern Europe, Central and Eastern Europe and the Baltics

About fifteen countries in Europe can be considered to be unitary centralised states. In many cases, this has to do with the sheer size of the country, which really does not warrant any sophisticated form of decentralisation.

In Southern Europe, the decentralising efforts of Spain and Italy are in clear contrast to the highly centralised countries of Greece and Portugal.

Democratisation after 1974 did not change the highly centralised Greek administrative structure, which has concentrated most of its administration in the two cities of Athens and Thessaloniki. In Greece, centralisation is a legacy of the history of unification of the country. Today, this historical legacy still shapes the way the country portrays itself. There is a general concern that too much decentralisation will compromise the unity of the country (Hlepas, 2005: 9–11).

Greek territorial governance comprises two directly elected levels of local government – the 50 prefectural self-governments *(nomarhiakes Autodiekesis)* at prefectural level *(nomos)* and, below these, the 1,003 municipalities (900 urban municipalities (*demoi*) and 133 rural communes (*koinotites*)). The elected prefectural level was introduced in 1994 as a further reform of the highly centralised Greek political system. In order to better absorb and coordinate the structural funds to which Greece is entitled, 13 administrative regions (*perifiaie*) were established, which are merely extended decentralised administrative structures of central government. These non-elected structures are chaired by a secretary general of the regions appointed by the central government (Hlepas, 2005: 7). According to Hlepas, disappointment about prefectural self-government set in when it was found that it functioned merely as an extended arm of central government. Clientelism, patronage and inefficiency have also contributed to a negative perception of this level and there has been a continuing discussion about how to 'repair' the reform (Hlepas, 2005: 17). At local level there has been a major thrust to reduce the number of municipalities. While in 1996 there were 5,825 municipalities, of which 88.6 per cent had fewer than 1,000 inhabitants, this changed dramatically after 1999 through the Capodistria plan, which was implemented between 1997 and 2001 and achieved a reduction of municipalities of 80 per cent through amalgamation. In 1999, there were 1,033 municipalities, still a large number, but considerably less than before the plan (Hlepas, 2005: 26–8). Such transformations have been part of the Europeanisation processes geared to make local government more professional and rationalised (Ioakimidis, 2001: 84–6).

Similar problems of centralisation can be found in Portugal. Although there are two autonomous regions in the islands of Madeira and Azores, continental Portugal continues to be highly centralised. For the moment, continental Portugal consists of two elected levels: the national level and the local level. Including Madeira and Azores, there are 308 municipalities (*municipios*) consisting of 4,252 parishes (Nunes da Silva, 2004: 8), with regular elections to the municipalities. In spite of being enshrined in the Portuguese constitution, no elected administrative regions have been established until now, although this continues to dominate the debate. On 8 November 1998, there was a referendum on regionalisation in continental Portugal, in which two-thirds of voters were against the proposed regionalisation of Portugal in 8 regions; although the referendum was not binding because it failed to achieve more than the required 50 per cent turnout (Magone, 2000: 505–7; 2004: 33–4). The present intermediate structure includes the 18 districts (*distritos*), which are non-elected and are supervised by a general governor (*governador-geral*) appointed by the central government. The de-concentrated public services have different territorial demarcations, so that currently the Portuguese government is engaged in a state modernisation programme in which such confusing overlapping of structures is to be simplified (Nunes da Silva, 2004: 13). There are 5 commissions of regional development (Comissões de Desenvolvimento Regional, CDRs), which are de-concentrated non-elected structures and play an important role in coordinating regional policy. In the past three-and-a-half decades local governments were allocated more powers, but this was not accompanied by corresponding funding. Only about 10 per cent of public expenditure is spent at local level. The amount of own revenues out of taxes and fees has been on the increase, however it has not been enough to overcome the high dependency on government block grants (Nunes da Silva, 2002: 204–6; 2004: 23–8).

The Irish local system is strongly influenced by the British legacy, although after independence it developed its own structures. The transition from British rule to independence led to a high level of confusion, corruption and inefficiency, so that, from early on, local government was controlled by central government. Professional managers were appointed to deal with the operational policy-making process and the management of the specific local council. They are appointed by an independent Local Appointments Committee and are a distinctive feature in comparison to other European government systems (Quinlivan, 2006: 25–7; Chubb, 1992: 274–8).

Although there were several reforms to make local government more efficient, a final structure was not achieved. In 2002, the country was divided between 29 counties and 5 cities, resulting in a total of 5 city councils, 29 county councils, 75 town councils and 5 borough councils (Quinlivan, 2006: 17–18). Until 1991, centralisation was fairly common in central-local government relations. This improved slightly following the Local Government Act of 1991 and also after the recommendations of the Devolution Commission of 1995, which gave more powers to local government (Quinlivan, 2006: 23–4). As already mentioned, several reforms were undertaken after the 1970s, however they showed only limited success. In the 1990s, new public management reforms became crucial to making local government more accountable through the use of principles such as value for money or quality control of public services. The Local Government Acts of 2001 and 2003 tried to redress many of the problems of Irish local government, such as duplication of structures, lack of accountability and decentralisation (Quinlivan, 2006: 41–56).

Countries such as Luxembourg, Latvia, Estonia, Lithuania and Slovenia do not need high levels of decentralisation, because both populations and territories are quite small. In the Baltic states and Slovenia there was, of course, debate about creating some kind of decentralised regional structures to absorb the structural funds better. All three Baltic republics as well as Romania and Bulgaria chose to implement non-elected administrative regional structures that are, in essence, extended de-concentrated bodies representing the central government at regional level. In Lithuania, ten de-concentrated county governments were established in order to coordinate regional development. They are, in effect, extended structures of central government. Below this structure are the elected 60 municipalities, which today are still inefficient in implementing policy as well as being characterised by high levels of mismanagement and corruption. In Latvia, 26 districts (*rajons*) and 530 municipalities (*pasvaldiba*) were established. And in Estonia, 15 county governments and 227 municipalities were established. So, for both countries, adjustment to EU multilevel governance, particularly with a view to the absorption of incoming structural funds, was undertaken. Estonia also established regional associations of municipalities in order to better coordinate certain policy areas and has been engaged in a process of amalgamation of municipalities since 2006 (Ministry of the Interior of Estonia, 2008: 2–4). In Estonia, in terms of budget, most of the expenditure goes on education (44 per cent) and most of the receipts come from 11.8 per cent of the total collected income tax (which represents 42 per cent of the local authorities budget). Earmarked grants from the state budget represent only 18 per cent, and 22 per cent of investments are included (Ministry of the Interior of Estonia, 2008: 17).

Similar problems of adjustment to the EU multilevel governance system could be found in Bulgaria and Romania. In Bulgaria, the main subnational directly elected tier consists of the 264 municipalities (*obshtini*). Above this are 28 districts (*oblasti*), which are merely extended de-concentrated structures of central government. They are in charge of implementing and coordinating regional policy. Moreover, 6 planning macro-regions (*rayone za planirane*) at NUTS2 were established in order to implement the structural funds better. In spite of this restructuring of the Bulgarian local government system, not enough funding from central government was allocated in order for local communities to fulfil their tasks, and their own revenues remain quite limited (Nikolova, 2007: 239–42). Moreover, the new regional structures were not able to overcome the continuing culture of corruption without the support of better accountability and transparency structures, leading to the suspension of a transfer of 0.5 billion euros in structural funds in early 2008. The Romanian subnational government consists of 42 counties (*judete*) and Bucharest, 265 towns (*orase*) and 2,686 communes. These are directly elected non-hierarchical tiers. Moreover, in the counties there are also prefects (similar to the French model) to oversee the county and local government. In a similar way to Bulgaria, 8 NUTS2 level administrative regions were created to coordinate regional development. In spite of major changes since the early 1990s, subnational government is still highly fragmented, preventing the establishment of economies of scale, particularly at village level. Increased competences and tasks over the years were not accompanied by the respective funding (Nikolov, 2006: 14–16).

In spite of major reforms, Slovenia is still constructing its new local government system. Presently it has 210 municipalities, but has failed so far to create an intermediate subnational structure between central and local government. There is a discussion to introduce 14 regions of different sizes that will be responsible for the coordination of regional development (Ploštajner, 2008: 39–43). As is the case for all the other Central and Eastern European countries, funding for the increasing number of local government tasks has been insufficient. In 2002, it accounted for only about 12 per cent of public expenditure and 5.17 per cent of GDP (Ploštajner, 2008: 63).

Although these Central and Eastern European countries have already made some considerable progress towards more efficient subnational government structures, such democratisation of local government has been more difficult in the western Balkans. In the case of Croatia and Macedonia, two candidate countries for accession to the EU, the European integration process has been important in pushing for a more decentralised territorial organisation. However, there are still major problems in the definition of the strategy for regional development, which is essential for the absorption of structural funds when Croatia joins the European Union. After several laws on territorial organisation since 1992, presently Croatia has 20 counties, the city of Zagreb, 121 towns and 421 municipalities (Kopajtich- Škrlec, 2008: 84). A major programme of decentralisation was only approved in 2004 and ran until 2007. One of its main tasks was to overcome the continuing fragmentation and consequently weakening of subnational government (Kopajtich- Škrlec, 2008: 82). The county councils have a coordinating function in relation to regional development. The share in public expenditure is 14.7 per cent and therefore still insufficient for local government to fulfil all their competences (Kopajtich- Škrlec, 2008: 105).

In Macedonia, territorial organisation has been carried out at least twice. Most recently in 2005, it established 84 municipalities and the city of Skopje (Angelov, 2008: 132–3). Apart from this territorial instability, central government devolved only 0.5 per cent of GDP in the early period following independence between 1990 and 1996. Since then, own revenues of municipalities have been on the increase. Between 2002 and 2007, there has been a considerable transfer of human resources to the local level (Angelov, 2008: 135–6, 148). In May 2007, a law on equitable regional development was passed that allowed two planning and development regions to be created. They do not belong to the local government structure, but are extended de-concentrated arms of the government in order to achieve more equitable development over the territory (Angelov, 2008: 139). This has to be seen as part of the process of adjustment to the European multilevel governance system and to the forthcoming structural funds, after joining the European Union.

In Albania, a major restructuring of subnational government took place in 2000. The two-tier subnational structure replaced the thirty-six historic districts by twelve regions. Below the regions are 309 communes and sixty-five municipalities. A national strategy plan was established in 2000, but has not so far been fully implemented. Some regions have already begun to implement their strategies; however, so far this has been a centralised top-down process dominated by central government (Dhimitri et al., 2007: 13–16).

In sum, the Balkans is probably still a region where decentralisation of subnational government is lagging considerably behind in relation to other parts of Europe. Several international organisations, including the European Union, are advising these countries in their quest to democratise their subnational government. It is too early to make an assessment of the success of these efforts.

The European dimension of subnational government

The European integration process has led to a growing cooperation between the regional and local authorities. There are several aspects related to a Europeanisation of subnational government. The emergence of the multilevel governance system of the European Union opened new access points to regions and local authorities beyond the main gatekeeper, the European Union. According to Gary Marks and his team, in the 1980s and 1990s regions were able to gain influence at the supranational level through a 'multiple crack' policy (Marks et al., 1996: 45). The doubling of the structural funds in the 1988 reform, and then a further doubling after the Edinburgh summit in 1992, created new funding possibilities for the region. Indeed, the region was regarded as the appropriate level to develop a regional strategy (Marks, 1993). In the 1980s, the European Commission worked closely with the regions in order to push forward the structural funds and other policies. According to Ingeborg Tömmel, the European Commission formed a strategic alliance with the regions in order to push forward its agenda (Tömmel, 1998: 53–4). Since the 1980s, regional and local authorities have been establishing representative offices in Brussels in order to gain access to information and to lobby for more funding or specific legislation. According to Lorenza Badiello, by 2002 there were 244 regional offices in Brussels (Badiello, 2004: 328). Some offices, such as Catalonia and Baden Württemberg, which had more resources, were able to develop fairly extensive networks in Brussels, while the poorer representations had to restrict themselves to gathering the information and sending it to the appropriate bodies in the particular region (Marks et al., 2002).

This fairly disorganised and unstructured access of the regions to different parts of the European administration was formalised through the establishment of the Committee of the Regions and Local Authorities (CoR) in 1993, after the Maastricht Treaty was approved (Box 9.1). Originally, many regional decision-makers, such as the president of the Catalan regional government, Jordi Pujol, or the Mayor of Barcelona, Pascual Maragall, overestimated the role of the Committee of Regions, which was assigned only deliberative and consultative powers. In spite of this, the CoR became an important institutionalised structure, allowing the regions to shape important legislation that affected their constituencies. After fifteen years of existence, the CoR has become an important deliberative body in questions relating to regional policy (Ramón, 2004).

One of the consequences of structural funding is that it has led to the establishment of a new governance structure across Europe. The Central and Eastern European countries in the pre-accession phase had to deal with issues relating to regionalisation and regional planning as well as the best way to adjust to supranational policies. Another aspect was the growing importance of cross-border

---

Box 9.1 The Committee of the Regions and Local Authorities

The Treaty of European Union (1993) created a new advisory body called the Committee of Regional and Local Authorities, also shortened to the Committee of the Regions. In 1993, there was great hope among regional policy-makers that they would be able to take part in EU decision-making. Soon, however, it became clear that the new committee was only an advisory body, with its main task being to comment on legislative proposals that might affect regional governance.

One peculiarity of the Committee of the Regions is that the members do not sit according to countries, but according to the party group to which they belong. There is no single system of appointment for these regional and local representatives, as each country has its own system. In some centralised countries, the representatives are appointed by the government of the day.

The committee consists of 344 members.

Member states	Number of members of CoR
France, Germany Italy and the United Kingdom	24
Poland and Spain	21
Romania	15
Austria, Belgium, Bulgaria, the Czech Republic, Greece, Hungary, the Netherlands, Portugal and Sweden	12
Denmark, Finland, Ireland, Lithuania and Slovakia	9
Estonia, Latvia and Slovenia	7
Cyprus and Luxembourg	6
Malta	5

cooperation through the INTERREG programme of the European Union. Meanwhile the INTERREG programme includes three different sub-programmes for (a) cross-border, (b) transnational, and (c) interregional cooperation. After two decades as a parallel programme to the structural funds, it has now become an integral part of objective three for regional cooperation for the period 2007–13 (see Chapter 13). Another important aspect of INTERREG is that it also finances projects along the border with non-EU member states countries such as Russia, Ukraine and Morocco. In some parts of Europe, cross-border cooperation preceded the INTERREG programme and has advanced to more permanent structures. This is the case in the Saar-Lorraine-Luxembourg (Saar-Lor-Lux) Great Region between Germany, Luxembourg, France and Belgium, which created an economic and social committee and other structures to make cross-border cooperation more sustainable. This region consists of the German Rheinland-Pfalz, Luxembourg, French Lorraine, the Belgian Francophone Wallonia, the Belgian French-speaking and German-speaking communities and comprises 65,400 square kilometres and 11.4 million people (Grande Région, 2010). It already has structures of interregional and socioeconomic cooperation that contribute to further integration of this territory. Another more institutionalised cross-border cooperation is the EUREGIO Maas-Rhine, which was founded in 1974, and originally funded by the Dutch and German governments. It comprises the regions of Limburg, Liége, Wallonie and the German-speaking community in Belgium, the province of Limburg in the Netherlands and the Regio Aachen in Germany (EUREGIO MaasRhine, 2008).

In other parts of Europe, cross-border, interregional and transnational cooperation are less institutionalised. In the Baltic, several networks were created to achieve greater cooperation between the countries, but the funding has so far been quite low for the territory.

Particularly interesting are cross-border INTERREG projects along difficult parts of Europe, such as the German-Polish border or the Portuguese-Spanish border. INTERREG projects mean that these different countries can be brought closer together through the development of common projects. Moreover, the investment of the European Union has led to spillover effects, for example the establishment of a network of interregional trade union councils (ITUCs) across the European Union. These trade union councils were formed to protect the rights of cross-border workers. Examples of successful ITUCs can be found along the Portuguese-Spanish or the Italian-French borders. In both cases, they were able to strengthen the position of cross-border workers in these regions. In the case of Portugal, the North Portugal-Galicia ITUC achieved the establishment of a branch of the European Service of Employment, which was to be funded by the European Union. This brought economic and civil society interest groups of the region together in order to improve the economic situation. A similar process can be stated for the Piemonte, Rhone Alps and Val D'Aosta ITUC on the Italian-French border. Such thickening of cross-border cooperation strengthens the position of the regions (Magone, 2001b; Ciampani and Clari, 2005).

Another innovative project is the Arco Latino along the northern Mediter-ranean coast. It was founded in 2001 and consists of 71 members from Italy (41), France (12) and Spain (18). Overall it comprises 8,004 municipalities and 45.5 million people. It seeks to overcome regional imbalances in the Mediterranean and push forward the position of the south within the European Spatial Development

Strategy, which was adopted by the Council of Ministers of the European Union in 2001 (Arco Latino, 2008).

The overall rationale of INTERREG is to make the neglected border regions more dynamic, to soften the borders of the European Union and to increase the level of cooperation between the different regions and local authorities in Europe. Such processes contribute to the establishment of the Single European Market by softening the internal borders and replacing them with harder external ones. This restructuring of the territory has political implications as well, because it allows for an increasing number of powers to be transferred from central government not only to the subnational and cross-border level, but also to the supranational one (Bartolini, 2005: 177–241; Christiansen and Jørgensen, 2000).

European regions are also able to shape decision-making processes in the Council of Europe through the Congress of Regional and Local Authorities, whose main task is to create a level playing field in subnational democracies and disseminate best practice and the new benchmarks (Caciagli, 2006: 86–8).

Another important aspect of the growing cooperation of regions is the level of associationism among European regions. Probably the most important interest group of regional governments is the Assembly of European Regions (AER). The AER was founded in 1985 and comprises 270 regions from 33 countries. It is seeking to increase the influence of the regions in the European institutions. Another important association is the Conference of Peripheral and Maritime Regions (CPMR), which was founded in 1973 and represents the interests of disadvantaged regions. It comprises over 159 regions from 29 countries and it has established 6 geographically defined commissions to push forward the interests of its members. A third major interest group is the Association of European Border Regions (AEBR), which was founded in 1971 and comprises 90 of 115 working cross-border regions. Its focus is to lobby for the interests of the border regions. Also important is the Council of European Municipalities and Regions (CEMR), which was founded in 1951 and consists of 50 national associations from 37 countries. The CEMR concentrates its work on promoting self-government at local and regional level and works closely with the European institutions (Caciagli, 2006: 83–6; Balme, 1998b: 76, 86–7; AER, 2008; CPMR, 2008; AEBR, 2008; CEMR, 2008).

The most interesting aspect of the increased role of the regions is probably the level of parallel diplomacy of the regional to central governments, particularly among the more aware regions. This 'paradiplomacy' has contributed to a new approach to International Relations, which is based on global governance issues. Until the 1970s, nation-states were the main actors in the system of international relations, however in the past four decades other actors, such as non-governmental organisations (NGOs), advocacy alliances (comprising interest groups from different countries), and regional and local authorities, have become involved in global politics (Magone, 2007c). Paradiplomacy has so far been a specific aspect of Europe. Some regions have advanced and sophisticated paradiplomatic structures, for example Catalonia, Baden-Württemberg, Scotland, Flanders and Wallonia (Hocking, 2004). In a comparative study of eighty-one regions from Germany, Belgium, the United Kingdom and Austria, Joachim Blatter and his team found that the Belgian and German regions have the strongest foreign policies; this is also supported by the constitutional framework of the countries. One weakness of the study was probably the non-inclusion of Spain (Blatter et al., 2008; on

Belgium see also: Bursens, 2002; Gozi, 2004). The most famous cooperation between the regions is the Four Motors of Europe comprising Baden-Württemberg, Lombardy, Catalonia and Rhone-Alps. It was founded on 9 September 1988 as a flexible response to the emerging Single European Market in 1993. Apart from the cultural and economic cooperation between them, they organise joint missions to international fairs, such as Shanghai in 2006 and India in February 2007 (Harvie, 1994: 60–3; Four Motors, 2008).

In sum, there is major territorial restructuring taking place across Europe. The growing importance of shared experiences through best practice and benchmarking are allowing a convergence of standards and structures of local government to take place. The emergence of a complex multilevel governance system with overlapping boundaries, depending on the particular regional cooperation issue, allows the restructuring of the territory. Regional actors are taking advantage of the new opportunities for cooperation that have emerged, partly as a result of Europeanisation, but also as a result of the globalisation processes, in which the nation-state is no longer the only actor in the system of global governance.

Conclusions: towards a Europe of the regions

This chapter assesses the growing importance of subnational government in European politics. Decentralisation of most territorial organisations began to be widespread in the 1980s and 1990s. Such transformations were encouraged by several factors, including the European integration process. This chapter, following John Loughlin, differentiates national territorial organisations in five main categories: federal states, confederal states, regionalised unitary states, unitary decentralised states and unitary centralised states. In spite of differences between the countries, there is a commitment to further decentralisation. National territorial organisations are adjusting to the EU multilevel governance system by creating more flexible structures, which enable regions or similar structures to play a more relevant role in regional development policy. In parallel with this decentralisation and flexibilisation of regional and local government structures across Europe, subnational actors have also developed their own international policies through cross-border cooperation within an integrated Europe; however, some regions, such as Wallonia, Flanders and Baden-Württemberg, have more ambitious, worldwide international policies, mainly in the economic and cultural fields.

Suggested reading

Introductory articles

Brusis, Martin (2005), Between EU Requirements, Competitive Politics and National Traditions: Re-creating Regions in the Accession Countries of Central and Eastern Europe, *Governance: An International Journal of Public Administration and Institutions*, 15(4), October: 531–59.

Goldsmith, Mike (2003), Variable Geometry, Multilevel Governance: European Integration and Subnational Government in the New Millennium. In: Kevin Featherstone and Claudio Radaelli (eds), *The Politics of Europeanization*. Oxford: Oxford University Press, pp. 112–33.

Keating, Michael (2008), Thirty Years of Territorial Politics, *West European Politics*, 31(1): 60–81.

Loughlin, John (2000), Regional Autonomy and State Paradigm Shifts in Western Europe, *Regional and Federal Studies*, 10(2): 10–34.

—— (2009), The 'Hybrid' State: Reconfiguring Territorial Governance in Western Europe, *Perspectives on European Politics and Society*, 10(1): 51–68.

Introductory books

Jeffery, Charlie (ed.) (1997), *The Regional Dimension in the European Union. Towards a Third Level in Europe*. London: Frank Cass.

Keating, Michael (1998, 2000), *The New Regionalism in Western Europe*. Cheltenham: Edward Elgar.

Keating, Michael (ed.) (2005), *Regions and Regionalism*. Cheltenham: Edward Elgar.

Keating, Michael and John Loughlin (eds) (1996), *The Political Economy of Regionalism*. London: Frank Cass.

Loughlin, John (ed.) (2004), *Subnational Democracy in the European Union*. Oxford: Oxford University Press.

Electronic journal: *Federal and Regional Studies*

Publius: The Journal of Federalism

QUESTIONS FOR REVISION

- What are the main forms of territorial organisation in Europe? Discuss, using examples for each form.
- Compare the advantages and disadvantages of devolution in the United Kingdom and Spain.
- Discuss the challenges to the federalisation of Belgium since 1993.
- How efficient are federal countries? Discuss, using examples from at least two countries.
- Are we moving towards a Europe of the regions? Discuss, using examples from at least two countries.

Political parties in Europe

- The Americanisation of European parties and party systems
- The transformation of political parties: from cadre to cartel parties
- The decline of party membership
- The importance of public funding for political parties
- The main party families
  - The liberal party family
  - The Christian democrats and conservatives
  - The social democratic party family
  - The communist party family and other left-wing parties
  - Extreme right-wing and new right parties
  - New populism and Euro-scepticism
  - The green party family
  - The regionalist party family
- Conclusions: the Americanisation of European politics

SUMMARY OF CHAPTER 10

Political parties are the most important intermediary groups between civil society and the state. Their role is central to politics and policy-making in Europe. This chapter deals with the main transformation of political parties since the 1970s. One particular feature has been the 'Americanisation' and 'marketisation' of political parties in electoral markets.

Some important characteristics of political parties in the postmodern world are:

- the decline of the mass party and its transformation into a cartel party;
- as a consequence, the decline of party membership; and
- the decline of dependency on public funding.

After discussing thoroughly these three aspects, the chapter gives an account of the most important party families that can be found in most countries across Europe. The main families are:

- liberals
- Christian democrats and conservatives
- social democrats
- communists and other left-wing parties
- greens
- the extreme right and new right
- new populism and Euro-scepticism
- the regionalist party family.

The Americanisation of European parties and party systems

European party systems are undergoing considerable change owing to the changing social structures in most European countries. The encapsulation of the electorates that existed until the 1950s, which allowed for the establishment of strong linkages between political parties and particular social classes or groups in society, have been replaced by a more socially volatile society, in which class is still relevant, but no longer the main determining factor in elections. Chapter 3 discussed thoroughly the role of political parties in structuring national politics and the impact of socioeconomic change since 1945. Stein Rokkan's pioneering work contributed to a better understanding of the patterns of European politics. When Stein Rokkan died in 1979, parties and party systems were changing very fast. As already mentioned, some countries such as Denmark and the Netherlands experienced a considerable fragmentation of the party system in the 1970s. In 1967, Seymour Martin Lipset and Stein Rokkan presented their freezing hypothesis of the party system since the 1930s. This stated that most West European party systems were reproducing the same kind of electoral results that the same parties had been producing since the 1930s. They came to the conclusion that the encapsulation of the electorate up to the 1930s led afterwards to the formation of stable social cleavages that translated into political ones. This became known as the 'freezing hypothesis', meaning that no major changes of party systems took place after the 1920s (see Chapter 3).

However, soon after they published their seminal chapter, party system change was happening in many West European countries (Lipset and Rokkan, 1967: 50; see also Bartolini and Mair, 1990; Kitschelt, 1997: 134–5). Today, all party systems are more volatile, and traditional political parties, such as the social democrats, Christian democrats, liberals and communists cannot rely any more on returning the same results, election after election. The cultural and social group cohesion has eroded over time. Traditional party systems based on mass parties such those in Austria, Belgium, the Netherlands and the Scandinavian countries have experienced major transformations, and fragmentation of the electorate has forced parties to use new technologies to appeal to the voters. Today 'mediatisation of politics' through a vast range of instruments, including continuing opinion polling, focus groups and targeted media campaigns, has become an integral part of electoral politics. Parties appeal to a fragmented electorate with different interests and requirements and they therefore need to use new approaches. The strategies of parties have to take into account which kind of electorate they want to address. The larger parties have to address a very diverse electorate and are beginning to resemble assembly line 'supermarket parties' more and more, while the smaller parties, sometimes known as 'boutique parties', specialise and target particular groups on the left or right (Kitschelt, 1997: 149).

Parties compete today in electoral markets. Political marketing has become essential for political parties. This also means that, similar to the United States, European political parties are becoming less ideological and more pragmatic. This can be observed in the growing tendency of the main parties on the left and right to move towards the centre. Because of this growing pragmatism and de-ideologisation, political parties require other means to make themselves heard. Among them is the growing importance of personalisation in politics. Charismatic leaders have become an important factor in postmodern politics. There are now lots of examples, confirming this trend – formidable politicians such as Margaret Thatcher, Tony Blair, Gerhard Schröder, José Maria Aznar, Silvio Berlusconi, and, most recently, Nicolas Sarkozy, were able to take advantage of this new structure of opportunities by using the media. Political management, particularly in electoral campaigns, has become fairly common across Europe. According to Pippa Norris, there has been a transformation from pre-modern to postmodern electoral campaigns (Norris, 1997: 3) (Table 10.1).

Table 10.1 shows how electoral campaigns have become more expensive, more permanent and more media-oriented. The mediatisation of politics has become a major aspect of current European politics. Such practice has always been common in the United States, so that there is a general trend among political scientists to call it 'Americanisation of electoral politics'. However, such processes of diffusion from the United States to other parts of the world, particularly Europe, may have different effects and impacts in different countries. According to Alexander Geisler and Ulrich Sarcinelli, one can interpret 'Americanisation' in three ways. First, it can be interpreted as 'diffusion', which is a selective integration of

Table 10.1 The transformation of electoral campaigns

	Pre-modern	Modern	Postmodern
Campaign organisation	Local and decentralised	Nationally coordinated	Nationally coordinated, but decentralised operations
Preparations	Short-term and ad hoc electoral campaigns	Long campaign	Permanent campaign
Central coordination	Party leaders	Central headquarters, coordinating body, more specialist consultants and party officials	More outside consultants, pollsters, and specialist campaign departments
Feedback	Local canvassing	Opinion polls	Opinion polls, focus groups, internet websites
Media	National and local press; local handbills, posters and pamphlets, radio leadership speeches	Television broadcasting through major territorial channels	Television narrowcasting through fragmented channels, targeted mail, targeted ads
Campaign events	Local public meetings, limited whistle-stop leadership tours	Media management, daily press conferences, TV publicity, photo-operations	Extension of media management to 'routine' politics, leadership speeches, policy launches, etc.
Costs	Low budget and local costs	Higher costs for producing television ads	Higher costs for consultants, research and television ads

Source: Norris, 1997: 3. From *Politics and the Press: The News Media and Their Influences*, edited by Pippa Norris. Copyright © 1997 by Lynne Rienner Publishers, Inc. Used with permission by the publisher

US patterns that are regarded as the models and objectives of modernisation. Second, one may regard this as a process of 'global standardisation', which would be conceptualised as an interactive exchange of new forms of electoral politics between the USA and Europe. Finally, it can be seen as modernisation leading up to universal convergence processes in media democracies. In this last interpretation, the USA would be the pioneer of such social modernisation (Geisler and Sarcinelli, 2002: 51).

In this chapter, Americanisation is understood primarily in the latter sense. It means that there has been a convergence of electoral politics of European countries to the US model. Hans Georg Soeffner and Dirk Tanzler summarised the most important features of this Americanisation in electoral campaigns as follows:

1 *Personalisation*: concentration on the candidate, neglect of campaign issues.

2 *Electoral campaign as 'horse race'*: competition as in sport events.

3 *Use of negative campaigning*: in order to destabilise the opponent or even destroy his/her credibility.

4 *Professionalisation of electoral campaigns*: electoral campaign experts, sometimes independent from the party, run the campaign.

5 *Marketing approach of political adverstisements*: use of well-known and successful means of the marketing industry to promote a candidate.

6 *Events and issues management*: choreographed and controlled organisation of events and presentation of issues.

(Soeffner and Tanzler, 2002: 130)

Political marketing has become an important aspect of contemporary European politics. The erosion of socioeconomic cleavages, and encapsulated political cleavages through subcultures with their own institutions and social rituals, led to the individualisation of most European societies. The citizen has become an individualised political consumer and as such looks at the products of political parties, their policies and politics. They are now political consumers in all fields of public life, particularly when using public services or using their purchasing power to change policies, nationally or abroad (Micheletti *et al.*, 2006; Føllesdal, 2006). Therefore, political parties are now acting in electoral markets and need to either apply product- or market-oriented marketing strategies. While political parties, mostly smaller parties, that use product-oriented marketing strategies are quite specialised in a specific issue and target particular groups in society, those that apply market-oriented marketing strategies are always concerned with adjusting to the changing expectations of the political consumer (Lees-Marshment, 2004: 9–11; Newman, 1999).

Owing to its close relationship to the United States, political marketing and political management strategies gained central importance for political parties in the United Kingdom. In particular, the Labour Party has been at the forefront with its success in political marketing. Political marketing strategies became important in the electoral campaign that brought New Labour, under the leadership of Tony Blair, back to power. Before long, the Conservative Party had to adjust to the new reality, but only after the election of David Cameron as leader in 2007 have their prospects at elections improved. Smaller parties such as the Scottish National Party or the Scottish Socialist Party tend to use product-oriented marketing strategies and focus on particular constituencies. However, the ambitions of the Scottish National Party have contributed to the use of marketing strategies in order to transform it into a catch-all party in the context of Scottish politics (Lees-Marshment, 2004: 16–42).

Similarly, the campaign of the Social Democratic Party of Germany (Sozialdemokratische Partei Deutschlands, SPD) under the leadership of Gerhard Schröder in 1998 set a new trend that was later emulated by other parties. Similar to the British case, the longevity in power of the coalition government between the Christian Democrats (Christlich-Demokratische Union/Christlich-Soziale Union, CDU/CSU) and the Liberals (Freie Demokratische Partei – FDP) led to a strong wish for change. An electoral campaign conducted by professional political managers who were independent of the party hierarchy with their own 'war room',

cus groups and new technologies, contributed to the victory of the
t Helmut Kohl's CDU/CSU in 1998. Gerhard Schröder's electoral
llowed for a personalisation of the electoral campaign (Soeffler and
002: 95–106; Altendorfer, 2000: 71–2).

France, the new Union of the People's Majority (Union de Majorité du
UMP) used its party conference on 14 January 2007 to launch the electoral
ntial campaign of Nicolas Sarkozy. He was elected with 98 per cent of the
vou...1 a highly orchestrated party conference. The personalisation of the electoral
campaign clearly had strong resemblance to presidential elections in the United
States (*The Guardian*, 15 January 2008). The Spanish prime minister, José Luis
Zapatero, also began his electoral campaign, which was managed by a marketing
firm, one-and-a-half years before the general elections. There was a constant
dialogue between the Spanish leadership and the marketing firm. This shows the
'permanent campaign' approach that has to be carried out in order to achieve a
successful outcome at elections (Campmany, 2005). The most successful leader has
probably been the Italian prime minister, Silvio Berlusconi, who created a political
party, Forza Italia (FI), from scratch in January 1994. Within three months Forza
Italia had won the general election. Berlusconi, a media tycoon, was able to use his
media network and the marketing techniques of his business empire to launch his
party. Forza Italia is chanted in the stadiums to support the national sports teams
and means 'Go on Italy'. In this sense, the highly populist–opportunist approach
allowed the successful expansion of the party. Meanwhile the party, after fourteen
years of success, merged with the post-fascist National Alliance (Alleanza Nazionale,
AN) to become the Party of Freedom (Partito delle Libertá, PdL). In 2010, Silvio
Berlusconi was already chairing his third government since 1994 (McCarthy, 1996;
Fix, 1999; Donovan, 2008). This success had consequences for the other parties,
epecially the former Communist Party, which transformed itself into a social
democratic party and, just before the 2008 October elections, formed the Democratic
Party with other centre and left-wing parties (Partito Democratico, PD) (Lazar, 2008).

The transformation of political parties: from cadre to cartel parties

Both the present party systems and the political parties are quite different from
those of the past. The main typology for Europe is the transformation of the cadre
party into the mass party and later into the catch-all party. Finally, today we are
experiencing the transformation of the catch-all party into a cartel party.

Political parties as we know them today emerged after the French Revolution
in 1789. The French Revolution was crucial in creating the main dimension of
party competition, the left–right cleavage (see Chapter 2). During the nineteenth
century, the cadre party was the dominant form of intermediary structure between
the state and civil society. The cadre party consisted of notables who were elected
through a census electoral system and had therefore to deal with a very small
electorate. Most politicians were not making their living from politics; on the
contrary it was their wealth that allowed them to engage in politics. One main
characteristic of this kind of electoral politics is that the socioeconomic basis of
the cadre parties was not achieved through membership or support for a political

party, but through patronage networks at the local level. It was very much a pre-modern way to organise politics, because no party structures existed in the nineteenth century. There was also no central office for the party. The main locus of the party was the parliamentary group consisting of wealthy notables with regional or local power. In some countries, particularly in Southern Europe and Central and Eastern Europe, there was a tendency to manipulate elections through governmental electoral machines – this allowed certain parties or people to remain in power for long periods of time. For example, such government electoral machines could be found in Hungary during the premiership of Kalmán Tisza between 1875 and 1890, leading to the expression 'Hungarian elections' (meaning that they were rigged) (Hoensch, 1989: 52). There was a similar case in Italy, which was dominated by the Liberal Party (divided into left-wing and right-wing factions). The Liberal Party remained in power as a result of systemic manipulation, called *transformismo* (transforming clientelistically socioeconomic interests into political votes), and later as a result of *giolittismo* (a co-option method used by Prime Minister Giuseppe Giolitti at the beginning of the twentieth century (Duggan, 1994: 161–88). There was also a similar case in Spain during the period of restoration (1874–1923), when the interior ministry would simply pigeonhole (*encasillado*) the right candidates, so that the governmental electoral machinery could manage their election or re-election (Kern, 1974: 33–9). The model followed by all of these countries was the British two-party system consisting of the Conservative and Liberal Parties, which was spearheading democratisation across Europe. The extension of suffrage throughout the nineteenth and twentieth centuries allowed later on for the emergence of the Labour Party, which in the 1920s and 1930s slowly replaced the Liberal Party as the second largest party. The evolutionary development of the British party system based on a growing electorate became an attractive model across Europe. However, some national cultures in Southern, Central and Eastern Europe, using clientelism, patronage and corruption, prevented such a system from flourishing.

The transition from the nineteenth to the twentieth century led to the emergence of the mass party. The extension of suffrage now required larger bureaucratic structures to encapsulate and mobilise the electorate. In this regard, Robert Michels' study on political parties, which focused on an empirical analysis of the German Social Democratic Party, still remains an important source for understanding the making of party elites and the development of party organisations from the pre-modern to the modern world (Michels, 1999). Such mass parties emerged particularly in the more industrialised countries in continental Europe. In Germany, Austria, Belgium, the Netherlands, Italy and the Scandinavian countries, mass parties emerged both on the right and the left. The traditional mass parties were the social democratic and the Christian democratic parties; both drew their support from two large social groups, the growing working class and the mass of faithful followers of the Catholic Church who felt their privileges under threat, owing to the expansion of the modern state in areas such as education and welfare provision respectively. While the social democratic parties could rely on a working class subculture with their own social and economic institutions, Christian democratic parties relied mainly on the structures of the Catholic Church to establish a mobilising network of followers. A very good example is the Italian People's Party (Partito Popolare Italiano, PPI) founded in 1919 that overnight was able to challenge electorally the Italian Socialist Party (Partito Socialista Italiano, PSI). However, after 1922 the leader of the party, Don Luigi Sturzo, had to leave the country, because Benito Mussolini, after his march on Rome on 31 October 1922, started to persecute all other political parties until they were completely eliminated from the political system (Webster, 1968).

Another mass party was the Catholic State Party (Roomisch-Katholieke Staatspartij, RKSP) in the Netherlands, which was quite successful in blocking the advance of the social democrats among the Catholic working class in the 1930s.

After 1921, the foundation of the Third Communist International, steered by Moscow, led to the emergence of communist parties across Europe that were originally splinter groups of the social democrats. Communist parties were able to rely on the growing working class. The emergence of such parties became particularly apparent in France, Germany, Italy, Belgium, Spain and Finland.

In the mid 1960s, the mass party was replaced by the catch-all party. On one hand, this was a response to the 'end of ideology' (Bell, 1962) and the emergence of an affluent society in most West European democracies. On the other hand, it resulted from the effort of these mass parties to broaden their socio-economic bases and strive for absolute majority governments. The catch-all party is inter-classistic and seeks to be a party for everybody. According to Otto Kirchheimer, these *Volksparteien* (people's parties) (or catch-all parties) are fairly pragmatic and vote-seeking. They have already begun to develop strategies for staying in power or obtaining the best possible electoral results within the electoral market. Although the core of these *Volksparteien* are the core subcultures of the social democrats, Christian democrats or conservatives, they want to add new constituencies to their supporters' social mobility through the socially oriented welfare states of these industrialised democracies (Kirchheimer, 1965). According to Peter Mair, Kirchheimer's catch-all party entails seven features:

1 Drastic reduction of ideology.
2 Oligarchisation of top leadership groups.
3 Declining role for party member.
4 Less subculturally oriented towards class or denominational group, but more inter-classistic approach.
5 Seeking support of wide variety of interest groups.
6 Party is less in touch with electorate.
7 Top-down approach and competition in an electoral market.

(Mair, 1997: 37–8)

Among the best examples of catch-all parties are the German SPD and the CDU/CSU, which both moved towards the centre in the late 1950s and hoped thus to increase their share of the vote. Similarly, the erosion of the Catholic and Protestant subcultures in the Netherlands during the 1960s and 1970s led to the merger of the Catholic People's Party, formed after the war as a follow-up of the RKSP, with the Protestant Christian-Historical Union (CHU) and the Anti-Revolutionary Party (ARP). The new party was founded in 1980 and was called the Christian Democratic Appeal (Christen-Democratisch Appél, CDA). Since then, the CDA has been quite successful in forming governments with other parties, showing a high level of pragmatism and flexibility.

According to Richard S. Katz and Peter Mair there has been a further change from the catch-all to the cartel party. The growing importance of mediatisation and the decline of membership of the political parties since the early 1980s, has led to the emergence of the cartel party. The cartel party is an office-seeking party and is interested in keeping close to the structures of power, because this is crucial for organisational survival. The cartel party relies on public funding and additional private funding, uses new media and technologies and has a light organisational structure. This means that it has considerably reduced the number of functionaries working for the party. It is clearly a party that has adjusted to the emerging electoral markets and the electorate as political consumers (Katz and Mair, 1995: 17–21).

Owing to the marketisation of electoral politics, most parties are becoming cartel parties. The decline of membership across Europe has been a major factor leading up to this situation. Parties cannot rely anymore on membership fees, and electoral campaigns are so expensive that apart from public funding, they have to engage in fund-raising. Katz and Mair, therefore, differentiate between the party in office, the party on the ground and the party in central office. According to them, the party on the ground was quite important during the phase of the mass party until the late 1950s, but has lost importance nowadays. The party in the central office was quite important during the catch-all phase, but has more difficulties in imposing itself today. It is now the party in office that dominates decision-making processes within the party. Although all three party faces are important, in the end office-seeking has become central to the aims of the party. Owing to the interdependence of all three party faces and the structures of the parties for success at the next elections, present parties are creating 'stratarchies', meaning that there is lots of autonomy for each party face (Katz and Mair, 1995: 21) (see Table 10.2).

Although most West European democracies experienced all these models of parties in the past 150 years, such a process cannot be extrapolated to the rest of the continent. Southern Europe and Central and Eastern Europe are defined as 'new democracies' and as such they never experienced such a transformation of political parties. In these new democracies, political parties became cartel parties from the outset, being highly dependent on the media and public funding. According to Ingrid van Biezen these parties had no time to encapsulate an electorate. The competitive pressure led to the use of the media to address potential voters. She asserts as follows:

> Parties in new democracies lack the stable constituencies with relatively durable political identities that enable them, like their Western European counterparts, to encapsulate the electorate and to narrow down the electoral market. While, as Sartori (1968, 2005) has emphasised, the mass party played a crucial role in the structural consolidation of West European party systems, parties in new democracies lack the organisational capacities ultimately to stabilise the party system.
>
> (van Biezen, 2003: 36)

This is confirmed by Paul G. Lewis who emphasises that the Lipset–Rokkan freezing hypothesis does not apply to the new democracies, because 'Central and

Table 10.2 The transformation of parties

	Pre-modern	Modern		Postmodern
	Nineteenth century	1880–1960	1945–	1970–
Type of party	Cadre party	Mass party	Catch-all party	Cartel party
Social–political inclusion	Restricted suffrage	Mass suffrage	Mass suffrage	Mass suffrage
Principal source of party's resources	Personal contacts	Members' fees and contributions	Contributions from a wide variety of sources	State subventions
Relations between party elite and membership	Small and elitist	Bottom-up, elite accountable to members	Top-down; elites dominate membership	Stratarchy, mutual autonomy
Membership	Small and elitist	Large homogeneous subcultural membership	Large heterogeneous inter-classistic membership	Declining or small membership
Party channels of communication	Inter-personal networks	Party provides its own channels of communication	Party competes for access to non-party channels of communication	Party gains privileged access to state regulated channels of communication
Position of party between civil society and state	Unclear boundary between state and politically relevant civil society	Party belongs to civil society, particularly as representative of particular subculture	Parties as competing brokers between state and civil society	Party becomes part of state
Representative style	Trustee	Delegate	Entrepreneur	Agent of the state

Source: Simplified from Katz and Mair, 1995: 18

Eastern Europe is (an) unstructured political field and conditions for party system formation are open rather than tightly constraining' (Lewis, 2003: 143).

Although some countries such as Hungary and the Czech Republic were able to develop stable party systems, many other countries are still consolidating. The pragmatic nature of the parties and their only interest being to maximise the number of votes became a crucial characteristic. Klaus von Beyme calls it 'Americanisation', because the approach towards the electoral market is similar to that of political parties in the USA. Parties in new democracies are more or less electoral machines (von Beyme, 1996: 140).

According to Attila Ägh there has been what he calls 'overpartycisation' in Central and Eastern Europe. Many parties emerged in the early 1990s, but few survived over time owing to lack of linkages to civil society and resources. Slowly, the surviving parties had to build strong party organisations with a disciplined membership. However, these parties, sometimes supported by international democracy assistance institutions such as the German foundations attached to the political parties, remained just cartel parties (Ägh, 1998a: 88; 1998b: 204). Similarly, processes of consolidation of parties took place one-and-a-half decades earlier in Portugal, Spain and Greece. In Spain, 579 parties registered before the Constituent Assembly elections of 1977, but only a few were able to achieve representation. Some of them were called taxi parties, because they had no membership and all possible members fitted in a car (Montero, 1998: 76–8). After the elections of 1982, the Union of Democratic Centre (UCD), which was the pivotal party of the political system, collapsed and disappeared because it was not well-connected to the grass roots and consisted of a coalition of parties that were not able to achieve a common platform (Hopkin, 1999).

In this sense, it is a good idea to differentiate between continuous, discontinuous and new democracies when discussing the development of political parties. The continuous democracies experienced all these party models since the nineteenth century and the process has not been interrupted. The discontinuous democracies had a major interruption during the authoritarian/totalitarian age of the 1920s and 1930s, but experienced more or less all party models. Last, but not least, the new democracies had quite long interruptions of around forty years, which led to complete disruption of such party development. These new democracies experienced very corrupt cadre parties in the nineteenth century, but did not, with the exception of Spain, experience the development of mass parties. Such typology of countries is summarised in Table 10.3.

Owing to weak party organisation, political parties in Southern Europe and Central and Eastern Europe had to spend considerable amounts of money on the media in order to reach their potential voters. In their very interesting study on consolidation in Central and Eastern Europe, Jon Elster, Claus Offe und Jürgen Preusse assert that it was easier for political parties in Central and Eastern Europe to play the electoral game than to dedicate more resources to building a party organisation. Television played a major role in attracting supporters. Therefore, without a local, regional or national grass-roots organisation, parties became even more dependent on the media to mobilise voters (Elster et al., 1998: 134–5).

Although some of the political parties, such as the Christian Democratic and Agrarian Parties, could refer to their past legacy in the inter-war period (1918–39), they were not in any advantageous position in relation to the new parties. On the contrary, after such a long period of interruption, the 'historical parties' could no longer rely on a particular constituency. They hd the same starting conditions as all the other parties (Olson, 1998: 434).

In this regard, the Southern European democracies of Portugal, Spain and Greece were able to show more continuity to the pre-authoritarian period. All three countries had communist and social democratic parties in exile fighting against the authoritarian regime. The communist parties in Portugal and Spain were quite well organised and therefore with an advantage in relation to all other parties. However, international assistance of sister parties led to the establishment of social demo-

Table 10.3 Party development in different parts of Europe

	Continuous democracies	Discontinuous democracies	New democracies
Description of typology	No interruption of democratic regime (apart from German Nazi Occupation of many European countries (1939–45))	Interruption of democratic regime (authoritarian, totalitarian period 1920, 1930, but democratic after 1945)	Over four decades of interruption of democratic regime and phases of democracy characterised by manipulation and corruption. Genuine democracies after 1974 as representatives of the third wave of democratisation
Countries	• United Kingdom • France* • Belgium* • Netherlands* • Luxembourg* • Switzerland • Norway* • Sweden • Finland • Denmark*	• Germany • Italy • Austria	• Greece • Spain • Portugal • Hungary • Czech Republic • Slovakia • Poland • Slovenia • Bulgaria • Romania • Moldavia • Croatia • Serbia • Bosnia-Herzegovina • Montenegro • Macedonia • Kosovo • Albania
Colonies that acquired independence	• Iceland (from Denmark), Malta and Cyprus (from the UK)		

* Countries under German occupation during the Second World War (1939–45).
Source: Author

cratic and right-centre parties in all these countries. The Portuguese Soci (Partido Socialista) and the Spanish Workers' Socialist Party (Partido Obrero Español, PSOE) were supported financially and logistically by th Friedrich Ebert foundation, the Swedish Social Democratic Work (Socialdemokratiska Arbetareparti, SAP) and the Austrian Social Democ (Sozialdemokratische Partei Österreichs, SPÖ) (Eisfeld, 1984; Mateus, 1996).

Another major difference is that in general the Southern European party systems consolidated quite fast and have remained stable until today. In Greece, Portugal and Spain we see a growing polarisation between the two main parties on the left and right. In Portugal and Greece three smaller parties are represented, but they are always in danger of losing further votes from election to election. In Spain, the two main parties, PSOE and PP, dominate the national arena, and the third national party United Left (Izquierda Unida, IU) is losing votes to them from election to election. Overall now, after the 2008 general elections, the two main parties together have over 83 per cent of the vote, while the IU's share has declined to 3.8 per cent and it had to form a parliamentary group with other smaller regional parties (*El Pais*, 28 April 2008: 16). Approximately 13 per cent of the vote is divided among the other regionalist parties. In Portugal, the two main parties together have 73.77 per cent of votes in 2005, while in Greece after the 2007 legislative elections this figure reached 79.93 per cent (see Magone, 1998; 2003a).

The decline of party membership

The transformation from the mass party to the catch-all and cartel parties led to the decline of mass membership. Parties such as the Italian Christian Democracy (Democrazia Cristiana, DC) and Italian Communist Party (Partito Comunista Italiano, PCI) saw their membership decline, even before the Tangentopoli affair in 1992. The same has been happening to the Austrian, Belgian, Dutch and Scandinavian mass parties since the 1980s. According to Ronald Inglehart and Christian Welzel, there has been a departure from the traditional institutions of modern society, such as political parties, trade unions and church organisations, to more postmodern, flexible organisational types such as non-governmental organisations (NGOs) (Inglehart and Welzel, 2005: 262). Citizens as political consumers are much better informed and critical when looking at institutions, and particularly political parties. This cognitive (knowledge-based) mobilisation has contributed to the development of electoral market behaviour of citizens and political parties. The traditional parties relied on the fees of its members, but today public funding for political parties and the impact of the media have made having large memberships obsolete. The erosion of traditional subcultures based on class or religious denomination has contributed considerably to the end of the traditional mass party. The excellent work of Peter Mair and Ingrid van Biezen in collecting data for the end of the 1990s raises awareness that such an exercise has been neglected by political scientists, so that figures remain only estimates. Moreover, political parties give inflated or wrong numbers of party membership. Such problems can be found in all countries, but particularly in Southern, Central and Eastern Europe, which means that any membership figures have to be read with a degree of caution (Mair and van Biezen, 2001: 6–7).

e importance of public funding for political parties

Today, only three countries in Europe still have no system of public funding for political parties: the United Kingdom, the Netherlands and Switzerland. All other countries have introduced generous public funding systems that include not only annual grants to the parties represented in parliament according to their share of the vote at the last elections, but also coverage of national, regional, local and European elections. In spite of this, many parties are dependent on private donors in order to fund the expensive use of the media in politics in the 'permanent campaign' during and between elections.

In the UK, the 'cash for honours' scandal during 2006 and 2007 engulfed the New Labour government under former Prime Minister Tony Blair. In spite of being in power, the New Labour Party was in debt, and, allegedly, one strategy used to overcome this debt was to raise cash for the party through secret loans from benevolent lenders in exchange for promised honours (peerages, etc.) at a later stage. This broke the UK law of 1925 that stipulated that honours (peerages) could not be sold. The former prime minister, Tony Blair, was interviewed twice by the police to ascertain whether he was aware of these transactions. Labour's chief fund-raiser, Lord Levy, was arrested twice, and after sixteen months' investigation no one was prosecuted, although the leading police investigator was unhappy about the abrupt end to the investigations. According to the BBC, 136 people were interviewed and a lengthy report (6,300 pages) was submitted by Scotland Yard to the Crown Prosecution Service (BBC, 20 July 2007).

In Italy, the First Republic collapsed because Christian Democracy, the Italian Socialist Party and other smaller parties were involved in illicit private funding. The widespread pattern of behaviour led to the imprisonment of an entire political class, and the emergence of a new party system. It was a web of systemic corruption affecting all aspects of public life. In spite of this negative experience, there is still small-scale corruption in Italy (Della Porta and Vanucci, 1999; Della Porta, 2001a).

In new democracies, one of the major problems is the lack of accountability and transparency of public and private funding. In Portugal and Spain the respective controlling institutions always get incomplete information in the annual, very delayed reports of the political parties. This, of course, gives opportunities for political parties to continue practices that perpetuate a situation of intransparency (Magone, 2004: 58; Sousa, 2001).

Throughout the 1980s and 1990s, several scandals related to illicit party financing, such as the Elf affair, in which Chancellor Helmut Kohl was allegedly involved (Miguet, 2004: 2), or the many corruption scandals linked to the socialist government led by former Prime Minister Felipe Gonzalez (Magone, 2009b: 115–18).

In Europe, there are many public funding models. However, Arnault Miguet was able to categorise them along three main groups. The first model finances almost every aspect in which political parties are involved. This system is widespread in Portugal, Spain, France, Italy and Central and Eastern European countries. The second model of public financing is less generous, just funding about 50 per cent of the activities of the political parties. Belgium, Austria, Switzerland, Germany and Greece belong to this category. The last model of public financing is the almost complete absence of such a system. In this category, one can find the UK and the Netherlands (see Table 10.4).

The main party families

In spite of the differences between them, most European countries have political parties with similar ideologies and common origins. The origins of the political parties are related to the junctures of European politics (see Chapters 1 and 2). In the mid 1980s, Klaus von Beyme wrote an excellent study on political parties in Western Europe and he identified several party families (von Beyme, 1984). There has been change since then, so it is necessary to update such classification. Any typology simplifies the reality considerably, but we may differentiate between at least eight party families:

- liberals
- Christian democrats and conservatives
- social democrats,
- communists and extreme-left-wing parties,
- neo-fascist parties
- greens
- regionalists, and
- new populism (the Euro-sceptics, the new right and the new left).

Many of these parties, particularly those of the new right, may combine elements of Euro-scepticism with topics of the extreme right. Therefore will discuss these new parties under the label of 'new populism parties' at the end of this section.

Table 10.4 Three models of public funding of political parties

	Generous public financing system	Mixed system (about 50% state funding)	Almost no public funding
Countries	Portugal	Belgium	UK
	Italy	Ireland	Netherlands
	Spain	Austria	Switzerland
	France	Germany	
	Hungary	Greece	
	Poland	Sweden	
	Czech Republic	Norway	
	Slovakia	Denmark	
	Bulgaria	Finland	
	Romania		
	Latvia		
	Lithuania		
	Estonia		

Source: Table based on Miguet, 2004: 8; with author's own amendments

The liberal party family

The liberals can be considered as the oldest party family. They emerged in the nineteenth century as part of the democratisation movement. They responded to arbitrary absolutist monarchies and became important in the 1848 democratic revolution. The word 'liberal' is Spanish and was used to characterise the liberals in 1807 when the Cadiz constitution was adopted (von Beyme, 1985: 45). Liberals were instrumental in democratising education and in many countries such as the Netherlands, Belgium and Germany were very keen to reduce the power of the Catholic Church. Liberals can be found in the UK, Scandinavia, Germany, Italy, Austria, Switzerland, Hungary, Poland and other Central and Eastern European countries. The ideology of liberalism emphasises freedom and individualism. Since 1947, the Mount Pellerin Society founded by Friedrich von Hayek, promoted the ideas of liberalism, which include the demand for a limited state and the protection of the individual from state interference. After 1945, most liberal parties had to adjust to the expansion of the welfare state and include the social dimension in their programmes. However, the crisis of the 1970s led to the return of neo-liberal ideas. Particularly, the British conservatives under Margaret Thatcher and US president Ronald Reagan took on the new liberal ideas. Most liberal parties are quite small, but in Belgium, the Netherlands and the Scandinavian countries they play a major role, because of the fragmented nature of the political system (De Winter and Marcet i Morera, 2000: 13–16) (see Figure 10.1).

In Germany, the Free Democratic Party (Freie Demokratische Partei, FDP) was re-founded on 11–12 December 1948 under the leadership of Theodor Heuss. According to their own self-understanding, their history goes back to 1807, when some liberal policies were introduced in Prussia, particularly the abolition of certain forms of slavery common in the agricultural sector, university reform and economic reforms (FDP, 2007: 2). The party was engaged in the building up of the social market economy along with other major political parties (Müller-Rommel, 2000: 98–101). From the very beginning it was a party of the establishment. It took part in a coalition government with the SPD between 1970 and 1982 and with the CDU/CSU between 1982 and 1998. Probably, one of the most influential liberal politicians was Hans-Georg Genscher who acted as foreign minister during the Kohl governments of the 1980s and was instrumental in establishing good relations with Eastern Germany, the *Ostpolitik*. (Müller-Rommel, 2000: 91–8). The present leader, Guido Westerwelle, had difficulties in establishing himself in the party and national politics owing to early poor electoral results; however, with the passing of time he was able to gain a good reputation as a principled person among the population and his fellow politicians from other parties.

After a difficult period between 1998 and 2005, the party was able to recover both at federal and regional level. In the 2005 elections it achieved 9.5 per cent and became again the third largest party. After the general elections of 2009, the FDP became a junior partner to the coalition with the CDU/CSU under Chancellor Angela Merkel.

In Switzerland, the Free Democratic Party of Switzerland (Freisinnig-Demokratische Partei der Schweiz, FDP/Parti radical-démocratique suisse, PRD) is an important party of the Swiss political system. It has one seat in the federal government. The party supports the social dimension of the economy, but is for

LIBERAL PARTIES IN EUROPEAN UNION

- Established traditional Liberal Parties
- Newcomers
- No Liberal presence

Figure 10.1 The liberal parties in Europe

a limited citizen-friendly state and reduction of tax. Like most other parties, it also advocates more freedom for the citizen.

In the Netherlands, the People's Party for Freedom and Democracy (Volkspartij voor Vrijheid en Democratie, VVD) was founded on 25 January 1948 and remains one of the most important parties in the fragmented Dutch party system. It includes the traditional demands of liberal ideology, such as freedom, social justice, limited engagement of the state and reduction of tax and welfare state. It took part in some of the grand coalitions of the late 1940s and 1950s. After 1959, it became a crucial coalition partner of the two main parties, the CDA and the PvdA. The party played a major role in opening up the Dutch economy in the 1980s through participation in a coalition with the CDA. It also took part in a coalition with the PvdA, the 'purple coalition' between 1994 and 1998, in which issues such as euthanasia, gay marriages and economic liberalisation were adopted. This was the first time that the Christian democrats were not part of a coalition, and therefore it was regarded as an historical event. In 1998, the VVD received 25 per cent of the vote and became the second largest party (Koole, 2000: 128–31). Since then the electoral support for the party has been declining. In the 2007 elections, the VVD got 14.7 per cent and twenty-two seats. In 1966, the Democrats 66, a smaller party with representation in parliament, split from the VVD, because they were unhappy with the establishment (Koole, 2000: 132–3). They wanted a reform of the political system.

The federalisation process in Belgium led to the emergence of two separate liberal parties in Wallonia and Flanders. The Flemish Liberals and Democrats (Vlaamse Liberalen en Democraten, VLD) are quite a strong party in the fragmented two-party systems of Belgium. It became an important party for overcoming the growing tensions between Flanders and Wallonia. The Wallonian Reform Movement (Movement Reformateur, MR) is smaller, but still achieves over 11 per cent of the vote. Between 1999 and 2007, the main leader of the VLD, Guy Verhofstadt, became the prime minister of a coalition government, because the Christian democrats failed to win the elections for the first time. One of the reasons for the decline of the Christian democrats was the political scandals that erupted during the 1990s, including the paedophilia and arms scandals. Owing to the difficulties of the Christian democratic prime minister, Yves Leterme, to put together a new government, Verhofstadt remained in power until mid 2008. Meanwhile, the Leterme government collapsed in December 2008, and thereafter several attempts to form a lasting coalition government failed throughout 2009 and 2010.

In the United Kingdom, the liberal democrats are the successors of a long tradition of liberalism in the country, which goes back to the eighteenth and nineteenth centuries. Throughout the nineteenth century the Liberal Party was one of the major parties. It began to decline at the end of the nineteenth century and during the inter-war period, when it was replaced by the Labour Party as second largest party, and remained then a smaller party. They were re-founded in 1988 as a merger of the Liberal and Social Democratic Parties, not to be mixed up with the Labour party. In the 1990s, the party was able to improve its electoral performance owing to the leadership of Paddy Ashdown and later Charles Kennedy (Thomas, 2000). Charles Kennedy was forced to resign in 2006 and was followed by leaders Menzies Campbell and Nick Clegg. The party is very sympathetic towards the European Union, advocating a written constitution, investment in public services through progressive taxation and an international policy based on international law. After 2003, the Liberal Democrats were the main party to oppose the Iraq War. After the general election of May 2010, the Liberal Democrats became a junior partner of a coalition government with the Conservative Party.

In the Nordic countries the liberals were traditionally one of the five parties. All these parties are supporters of the European integration process and advocate social liberalism. This means that they support some intervention of the state in order to achieve social justice, but remain loyal to their principles of liberalism, including a reduction of the state in economy and society. However, since the 1970s some of them have lost electoral support. Particularly, the Norwegian Liberals (Venstre) had to deal with a substantial decline in the 1990s. The People's Party Liberals (Folkeparti-liberalema) has been an important partner of conservative (moderate) led governments in Sweden. Its electoral support has been volatile since the mid 1980s. It declined considerably up to 1998, but in the 2002 and 2006 elections its electoral support increased markedly. Last but not least, one must also mention the Danish Liberals (Venstre) – a central party on the right that remains a pivotal party of the party system. It has been part of coalition governments since 1945. The present prime minister, Anders Føgh Rasmussen, has been incumbent since 2001 leading a right-centre coalition, and is from the Liberal Party. Many of the agrarian parties of the nineteenth century, moved to the centre and became part of the liberal family. The Centre Party (Senterpartiet, SP) in Sweden is a good example in this respect.

In Central and Eastern Europe there are also several liberal parties. Among the most important is the National Simeon II Movement for Stability and Progress, founded by former King Simeon Borisov Sakskoburggotski. It achieved over 42 per cent of the vote and 120 seats in the Bulgarian general elections of 2001. The minority government implemented liberalisation policies between 2001 and 2005, which created more social inequality in society. Therefore, after the 2005 general elections, its support declined considerably and the Bulgarian Socialist Party was able to return to power.

In Hungary, the Alliance of Free Democrats (Szabad Demokraták Szövetsége – a Magyar Liberális Párt-SzDSz, MLP) is central to the polarisation politics between left and right. It was a partner of the Hungarian Socialists and was part of the coalition, but left the coalition in May 2008 as a result of the behaviour of the senior partner, the Hungarian Socialist Party. Electoral support for the party has declined considerably since its foundation in November 1988. In Romania, the National Liberal Party (Partidul National Liberal, PNL) was re-founded in 1991 and became the most important right-centre party in Romania. However, in 2007 a splinter group founded the Democratic Liberal Party (Partidul Liberal Democrat, PDL), which merged with the Democratic Party (Partidul Democrat, PD) in December of the same year. It has been able to stay in power since 2004 and contribute to the liberalisation of the Romanian economy and society.

The Estonian Reform Party (Eesti Reformakond) and the Estonian Centre Party are the two main parties in a highly fragmented party system. The small Latvian First Party–Latvian Way (Latvijas Pirmā Partija–Latvijas Ceļš, LPP–LC) took part in several coalitions, but was also embroiled in corruption scandals.

The Christian democrats and conservatives

The Christian democrats have their origins in the Reformation of the sixteenth century. The growing importance of the state and the reduced influence of the Catholic Church in the nineteenth century finally led to the emergence of Christian democratic parties. Christian democratic parties were linked to the Catholic Church and were supported by the Church hierarchy. In Germany, the German Centre Party (Deutsches Zentrumspartei-Zentrum) was founded in 1870 and was the oldest party in Germany. It became an important party up until First World War, attracting between one-fourth or one-fifth of votes in elections in Wilhelmine Germany. In the Weimar Republic, though, the Zentrumspartei declined to about 10–11 per cent and ended up with quite a negative reputation for allowing Adolf Hitler to come to power. A particular challenge for the party were Bismarck's policies to reduce the power of the Catholic Church. This *Kulturkampf* (cultural fight) between state and Church was not confined only to Germany, but to other countries as well, particularly the Netherlands. The rise of social democratic parties and their support from the growing working class also led to stronger engagement of these Christian democratic parties among the working class. Therefore, German Chancellor Otto von Bismarck changed the policies of antagonism towards the Zentrum, forming an alliance against social democracy, which led to the introduction of social legislation in order to achieve more social protection for the working class. Strong parties could be found in Italy, Austria, Switzerland, Belgium, Germany and the Netherlands. In all these countries, social cleavages were translated into political cleavages, particularly in Austria, the Netherlands, Belgium and Switzerland. Pope Leo XIII was instrumental in providing the ideological framework for such social engagement through the 1891 *Rerum Novarum* encyclical and later through the 1901 *Crucis de communi* encyclical. The latter introduced the concept of Christian democracy (Democratia Christiana, DC).

In terms of ideology, Christian democracy is not easy to define. David Hanley characterises Christian democracy as 'an elusive and shifting phenomenon', but still easier to study and define than the conservative sister parties (Hanley, 1996: 2). In spite of the transformation of traditional Christian democratic parties to catch-all parties (*Volksparteien*), there are some characteristics that make them distinctive from other party families. First, the view of an individual as a person, who is directed towards solidaristic communities, summarised under the label of 'personalism', is an important feature. The dignity of the person is an important aspect of Christian democracy. Moreover, the Christian religious dimension plays a major role in shaping the ideology of personalism. The emphasis on the social dimension of capitalism is, therefore, important. Social capitalism or social market economy are integral parts of the ideology, especially so until the early 1980s. Since then, there has been a liberal shift towards reducing the welfare state, however inconsequently implemented (Keesbergen, 1996: 35–42). A more pragmatic issue-oriented approach has been adopted since the 1960s, relating to controversial issues such as abortion, same-sex marriages and state subsidies to private faith-based schools.

After the Second World War, many of the inter-war parties were replaced by successor parties. The most important of all of them was probably the German CDU/CSU, which united both Catholics and Protestants under the banner of Christian democracy. The successor parties across Europe slowly evolved to catch-all parties, largely because religious cleavages were eroding from decade to decade. The CDU/CSU had already become a *Volkspartei* in the 1950s and 1960s and the Christian democrats dominated the new Federal Republic of Germany until 1970. Politicians such as Konrad Adenauer and Ludwig Erhard of the CDU/CSU were supporters of a social market economy (*Soziale Marktwirtschaft*). Some parts of the party would emphasise the social protection aspects of the market economy, others more the liberal aspects. The CDU/CSU was reasonably successful until the late 1960s, however generation change led to anti-establishment social movements that contributed to a shift of the electorate to the left. The CDU/CSU only came back to power in 1982 under Chancellor Helmut Kohl. He remained in office until 1998 and became the 'Chancellor of Reunification' as a result of his involvement with the German integration process during 1989 and 1990. However, in spite of several half-hearted reforms of the labour market and the economy, he lost the election of 1998. Moreover, a major scandal related to illicit party financing related to payments by the French Elf Firm, which Kohl refused to disclose to a parliamentary committee of the Bundestag, contributed to the damage done to his reputation. He was replaced by Wolfgang Schäuble and, later, by Angela Merkel. Angela Merkel. Merkel been instrumental in streamlining the party and delivering the necessary reforms in order to make the party competitive again. In 2005, she became Chancellor of a coalition government with the SPD.

Similar processes from mass to catch-all party could be seen in Italy, France, the Netherlands, Belgium and Luxembourg (see Figure 10.2). In this context, the Italian Christian Democracy (Democrazia Christiana, DC), founded in 1945, became an important party against the growing electoral success of the Italian Communist Party (Partito Comunista Italiano, PCI), which was considered a danger. DC consisted of many factions that were formed around important national and regional politicians, such as Aldo Moro and Giuliano Andreotti, and factionalism remained an important characteristic of the party until its collapse after the Tangentopoli affair of 1992. DC was a strong party, but had difficulties in reaching an absolute majority, so it formed coalitions with smaller parties such as the Italian Republican Party (Partito Republicano Italiano, PRI), Italian Liberal Party (Partito Liberale Italiano, PLI), the Social Democratic Italian Party (Partito Socialdemocratico Italiano, PSDI) and the Italian Socialist Party (Partito Socialista Italiano, PSI) to prevent the PCI coming to power. The main reason was that there was fear

Figure 10.2 The Christian democratic parties in Europe

that the PCI was just an agent of communist Russia and sought to take over power in Italy. In this sense, the cold war shaped politics in Italy (Leonardi and Wertman, 1989). The DC was not only based on Christian social teachings, but was extremely anti-communist. Therefore, through a web of systemic corruption involving illicit party financing, DC remained in power between 1948 and 1992. In the 1980s the electoral support for DC declined below the 30 per cent threshold and it had to cooperate with larger parties such as the PSI. In this climate of electoral decline and a high level of dissatisfaction in Italian society, a new generation of judges was able to uncover the huge network of systemic corruption, leading to the collapse of the party in 1993 (Guzzini, 1994). As a result of internal factionalism, the successor parties aligned themselves either on the right supporting Berlusconi's right-centre coalition or on the left associating themselves with the Party of Democratic Left. The most prominent party that emerged after 1994, was the Christian Democratic Centre (Centro Cristiano Democratico, CDC), which suffered a further split with the emergence of the United Christian Democrats (Cristiani Democratici Uniti, CDU) in 1995. These right-wing parties were always close to the Berlusconi right-centre coalition. In spite of its weak electoral support, personalities tended to create new splits, leading to quite a fragmented group. On the left, the Italian People's Party (Partito Populare Italiano) under Romano Prodi was more fortunate in its association with the left-wing coalition dominated by the DS. In 1996, the left-wing coalition Olive Tree (Ulivo) won the general elections. Romano Prodi became prime minister for the next two years. However, after Prodi's nomination as the new president of the European Commission by the Council of Ministers of the European Union in 1998, the PPI combined with other groups to form a new party called La Margherita, which was part of the left-wing coalition. On the left, these Christian democrats became part of the new Democratic Party (Partito Democratico) (Furlong, 1995; Bull and Newell, 2005: 52–9).

In Austria, the Austrian People's Party (Österreichisches Volkspartei, ÖVP) became an important rival to the social democrats. It was the successor party to the Christian socials of the inter-war period, who were discredited after the establishment of an authoritarian corporatist dictatorship between 1934 and 1938. Although there was some continuity, the new party wanted to start anew and followed a conciliatory policy in relation their main rivals, the social democrats. After the animosities of the two opposite camps (*Lager*) during the inter-war period and the annexation of the country by national socialist Germany (1938–45), both parties decided to work together and rebuild the country. They created the informal institutions of neo-corporatism, the social partnership (*Sozialpartnerschaft*) between the employees' and employers' organisations. This gave considerable stability to the country until the 1980s.

Until 1966, the ÖVP was in a grand coalition with the SPÖ, however between 1966 and 1970, it governed alone. After 1970 the predominance of the SPÖ prevented the party from coming to power until 1986. It then formed a grand coalition with the SPÖ between 1986 and 1999 and later on a coalition with the new right Freedom Party (FPÖ) as a junior partner between 1999 and 2006 (Müller, 2006). The coalition with the FPÖ was quite controversial and led to considerable protests from sister parties across Europe after 2000. After the report of the Wise Men (12 September 2000, commissioned by the European Commission), the European Union was assured that, despite of the participation of the FPÖ, no major negative changes to democracy of the country were undertaken (Kopeinig and Kotanko, 2000). The gamble of party leader Wolfgang Schüssel paid off. The infighting within the FPÖ led to the emergence of a new splinter group led by charismatic Carinthian Regional Government President Jörg Haider, under the label of Union for the Future of Austria (Bündnis für die Zukunft Österreichs, BZÖ) (Luther, 2006). After the general elections of 2006, the ÖVP formed a coalition with the SPÖ as a junior partner. However, disagreements within the coalition led to early elections in October 2008, in which both main parties lost votes and the two small new right parties were able to considerably increase their vote. The ÖVP lost over 8.7 percentage points and achieved only 25.6 per cent, less than the two new right parties FPÖ and BZÖ together (*Wiener Zeitung*, 2008).

As already mentioned, in the Netherlands, the denominational religious parties had to deal with the erosion of their constituencies during the 1960s and 1970s. In the end, they had to merge into the Christian Democratic Appeal (CDA) in 1980 and became a fairly pragmatic party that, after 1982, formed a coalition with the Liberals (VVD) until 1992 (Lucardie and ten Napel, 1994: 66–7). After a period in opposition until 1998, the CDA came back to power. Prime Minister Jan Peter Balkenende was able to follow a steady course of reform of the Dutch Polder system. In spite of a challenge by the Pim Fortuyn List in 2002, Balkenende was able to adopt some of the policies of this new right party and, owing to infighting inside the Pim Fortuyn List, to win the early elections of 2003 and the legislative elections of 2007. However, well into the 1960s, these denominational parties dominated coalition politics in the Netherlands.

In Belgium, the Christian democrats, through the Flemish Christian-Democratic People's Party (Christen-Democratisch Volkspartij, CVP) and the Christian Social Party (Parti Social Christien, PSC), were able to dominate between 1945 and 1997, although always in coalition with other parties. The federalisation of the country has led to a division of party systems; now two independent party systems in Wallonia and Flanders have led to almost identical parties in the two regions. The only major difference is that the renamed Christian Democratic and Flemish Party (Christian-Democratisch en Vlaams, CD&V) now emphasises its Flemish identity, while the renamed Christian Socials as Democratic Humanist Centre Party (Centre Démocratie Humaniste, CDH) emphasises a cross-denominational identity, reaching out to the immigrant communities. The CD&V is becoming more strongly integrated in the logics of the Flemish party system, which is moving towards nationalism. The Flemish Christian democrats are still the strongest party in Belgium, in spite of a short period of hegemony by the liberals between 1997 and 2007. The CDH suffered considerably from the erosion of religion in Wallonia, and had to broaden its appeal to new social groups (Delwit, 2003: 101–4, 123–32).

In Scandinavia, as well as the core traditional Christian democratic parties, there are also the small parties to consider. There has been a recent revival of these small parties, as a result of the fast-expanding secularisation of society. They represent small communities in Norway, Sweden, Finland and Denmark. The Christian People's Party (Kristellig Folkeparti, KFP) in Norway, the Finnish Christian Party (Suomen Kristilinen Liitto, SKL) in Finland, the Christian Democrats (Kristendemokraterna, KD) in Sweden and the Christian Democrats (Kristendemokraterne, KD) in Denmark were able to take off in the late 1980s and since then have become important junior partners in right-centre coalitions (Karvonen, 1996: 122–3).

Small Christian democratic parties can also be found in Central and Eastern Europe. Normally, they are referred to as 'historical parties', because some of them existed during the inter-war period. This is the case of the Hungarian Christian Democratic People's Party which is very small and, in 2006, had to join forces with the Fidesz-Hungarian Civic Forum to achieve representation. In the Czech Republic, in the 2006 legislative elections, the Christian Democratic Union–Czech People's Party (Křesťansko-demokratická unie–Československá strana lidová, KDU–CSL) received 7.3 per cent of votes and thirteen seats. It is an important coalition partner for the right-centre government under the Civic Democratic Party. In Slovakia, two Christian democratic parties compete with each other. The Slovak Democratic and Christian Union–Democratic Party (Slovenská demokratická a kresťanská únia – Demokratická strana, SDKU–DS) was founded in 1998 and is popular in Slovakia. In the elections of 2006, it achieved 18.35 per cent and thirty-one seats and, in 2010, it was the second largest party. The Christian Democratic Movement (Kresťanskodemokratické hnutie, KDH) was founded in the early 1990s, but remains small. It got 8.5 per cent of the vote and fifteen seats in 2010. In Romania, there is a Christian Democratic National Peasants' Party (Partidul Naţional Ţărănesc–Creştin Democrat, PNŢ–CD), however it has no representation in parliament. There are no Christian democratic parties in Bulgaria. In the Baltic countries, the only Christian democrat party was in Lithuania: the Christian Democratic Party (Lietuvos krikščionys demokratai, LKD) which can refer to its legacy from the inter-war period. However, after a promising start the party began to decline soon after 1996, so that by the 2004 election it did not get any representation. However, in 2008 it merged with the Homeland Union, a conservative party, and became the largest party in Lithuania.

The Spanish People's Party (Partido Popular, PP) certainly has some Christian democratic roots, but its late development and the continuity of some of its members with the former authoritarian regime makes it difficult to count as part of the traditional family. The PP has changed considerably since its foundation in 1977. It has been able to overcome the negative connotations about the party's connection with the previous authoritarian regime and transform itself into a *Volkspartei* in Spain. The religious dimension is underplayed and the party has developed a more liberal outlook in economic terms. Former Prime Minister José Maria Aznar was instrumental in transforming the party into a more pragmatic catch-all formation. He was also quite successful in broadening the appeal of the International Christian Democratic Union by pushing it towards a more centrist position. Although abortion is a major issue for the Christian democrats in Spain, the party decided to underplay it and moderate its position in many areas. However, there are strong connections to the Church and some personalities of the PP are connected to the Opus Dei, an elitist organisation associated to the Church hierarchy. One particular issue is the role of private faith schools associated with the Catholic Church, which are generously funded by the state. This has become increasingly contested, because of the very fast secularisation process of Spanish society (Magone, 2009a: 150–7).

The conservative parties are very close to the Christian democratic parties. In both cases the parties are ideologically right-centre parties. In general, the conservative parties are considered to be very pragmatic, and, in contrast to the

Christian democrats, strongly nationally oriented. They are strong in the United Kingdom and in the Scandinavian countries.

The Conservative Party in the United Kingdom was founded in 1832 and has evolved into a modern, pragmatic political formation. Ideologically it has always changed and adjusted since its foundation. It is basically a party that is very keen to protect British values, at the same time taking into account the balance between conservatism and change. Until the 1970s there was the notion that, owing to its catch-all appeal, it was a one-nation party overcoming the main cleavage between left and right. However, after the general election of 1979, the Conservatives under Prime Minister Margaret Thatcher shifted their ideological foundations towards a stronger emphasis on British nationalism and economically on neo-liberalism. The latter contributed to a major transformation of British society. Prime Minister Margaret Thatcher had inherited an economy that was losing competitiveness, because social and wage costs were spiralling out of control and innovation in enterprises was stagnating. The climax of demands by trade unions was the 'Winter of Discontent' during the winter 1978–79. Between 1979 and 1990, Margaret Thatcher was able to open up the British economy and increase its competitiveness. She took on the trade unions, reducing their power and making them more accountable to their members, amd she limited spending on social and public services. The consequence was that the National Health Service suffered from lack of investment up to 1997.

Another radical policy was the privatisation of public utilities such as water, electricity and transport. In 1989, a major recession set in, and one of Margaret Thatcher's policies suffered a setback – that of house ownership. The recession led to a considerable number of houses being repossessed. Additionally, Thatcher was opposed to the Maastricht Treaty, particularly Economic and Monetary Union, and finally opposition inside the party led to her resignation and replacement by John Major. In spite of all expectations that Labour would win the elections in 1992, John Major was able to hold on to power until 1997. However, the economy was suffering considerably under these last years of Conservative government. After the victory of New Labour led by Tony Blair in 1997, the Conservative Party had difficulties in adjusting to the new political reality. Between 1997 and 2007 the party had five leaders, each of them resigning after or before elections. There has been an attempt at rebranding the party, but until 2007 this met with limited success. On 15 August 2007, David Cameron became the new Tory leader and initiated a process of change in the Conservatives. After the resignation of Tony Blair as prime minister, his rival Gordon Brown had difficulties in dealing with the new young leader (BBC, 15 August 2007). The major problem for the Conservatives has been that, in legislative elections, they have almost no representation in Scotland and in the larger metropolitan areas (see Figure 10.3). In spite of this, after the May 2010 general election, the Conservatives formed a coalition government with the Liberal Democrats and returned to power.

Conservative parties exist also in the Scandinavian countries. In Norway, the Right (Høyre) wants reduction of state intervention in the economy. Its share of the vote is between 14 and 22 per cent. The Moderates (Moderata samlingspartiet) is the second largest party in Sweden, and after 2005 formed the government in coalition with other, smaller, right-centre parties. Historically, the Moderate Party goes back to its predecessor, the General Electoral League, founded in 1904.

Figure 10.3 The conservative parties in Europe

The Norwegian Høyre is similar to the British Conservative Party. It advocates liberal policies related to less intervention of the state and more freedom for the individual. In Finland, the National Coalition Party (Kansallinen Kokoomus, Kok), founded in 1918, is the largest party. It also advocates liberal policies, especially limited intervention of the state in private life and the economy. All three parties are strongly pro-European. In Denmark, the Conservative People's Party (Konservative Folkepartiet, KFP) has a similar ideological make-up to the other conservative parties.

In Greece, New Democracy (Nea Dimokratia, ND) founded in 1974 is presently one of the strongest parties in the country. Its policies are quite liberal and nationally oriented. However, the party is also able to attract the religious vote, which is important in Greece because of the strong role of the Greek Orthodox Church.

In Central and Eastern Europe there is the Civic Democratic Party (Občanská demokratická strana, ODS), founded by Vaclav Klaus, a strong supporter of Thatcherism – the party also tends towards Euro-scepticism. ODS took a key role in shaping the Czech Party system. In Hungary, Fidesz – Hungarian Citizens

Federation (Fidesz – Magyar Polgári Szövetség) follows right-wing conservative positions and has become a fierce opponent of the Hungarian Socialist Party.

The Citizens for the European Development of Bulgaria (Grajdani za evropeisko razvitie na Bulgarija, GERB) is a new right-centre party, founded in 2006, under the leadership of the Mayor of Sofia Boyko Borisov. It achieved second place in the 2007 European elections and won the July 2009 general elections. It formed a minority government supported by other right and centre parties in parliament.

The social democratic party family

Social democracy can be considered as the third major party family. It was a response to the industrial revolution and the very bad conditions that the working class were subjected to in the nineteenth and twentieth centuries. The First (1864–76) and the Second (1889–1919) Internationals were important here. Although social democracy started as a radical movement seeking to achieve a classless society, after the death of Karl Marx its members became increasingly interested in achieving results through the democratic institutions. This moderation of social democracy led to success in elections during this period of expanding suffrage. Strong parties emerged in Italy, Austria, Germany, Switzerland, Belgium, the Netherlands, France and Sweden (Sassoon, 1997: 4–26). However, social democracy became more established after the Second World War, particularly in countries with strong working class subcultures. According to Stefano Bartolini, we can differentiate between the types of left movements according to organisational and electoral mobilisation. The four types were founded and/or dependent on:

1 union lefts, which are organisationally and electorally over-mobilised;
2 encapsulated lefts with strong subcultures, which are both organisationally and electorally over-mobilised;
3 under-mobilised lefts with strong constituencies, which are both organisationally and electorally under-mobilised; and
4 ideological lefts with weak organisations, which are extremely over-mobilised (Table 10.5).

Britain and Ireland represent examples of union lefts; Sweden, Austria, Denmark and Norway are examples of encapsulated lefts; Belgium, Germany, Switzerland and the Netherlands are examples of under-mobilised lefts; and Italy, Finland and France are examples of ideological lefts (Bartolini, 2000: 305). These characteristics have remained part of the identity of social democratic parties until today. However, since the late 1950s, social democratic parties such as Christian democratic and conservative parties have adopted strategies taking into account the complexity of emerging electoral markets.

The erosion of modern industrial society and the decline of the working class forced social democratic parties to broaden their appeal. Traditional working-class parties such as the Austrian, Swedish and Dutch social democrats evolved to become catch-all parties in the 1950s and 1960s. Many parties had to struggle with factionalism within their party arising from disagreements over the direction the party should take. The transformation of European social democracy took place

Table 10.5 Types of left movements by organisational and electoral mobilisation, according to Stefano Bartolini

Organisationally over-mobilised	Union lefts Britain Ireland	Encapsulated lefts Sweden Austria Denmark Norway
Organisationally under-mobilised	Under-mobilised lefts Belgium Germany Switzerland Netherlands	Ideologically over-mobilised Italy Finland France
	Electorally under-mobilised	**Electorally over-mobilised**

Source: Simplified from Bartolini, 2000: 305

between the 1970s and the mid 1990s. This transformation particularly saw a change from the traditional mass party to catch-all or cartel parties. Most of this change took place in the 1980s and 1990s. Some parties were quite quick to recognise the need to change strategies, but others had difficulties in adjusting to the national electoral markets. Herbert Kitschelt identified three groups of parties related to the adjustment to new challenges and the demands of the electoral market: the electoral victors, the electoral stabilisers and the electoral losers. The electoral victors were the French, Italian and Spanish socialist parties. However, it should be noted that the Italian Socialist Party (Partito Socialista Italiano, PSI) collapsed after the Tangentopoli affair. The electoral stabilisers consisted of Belgium, the Netherlands and Sweden. All three social democratic parties adjusted to the new reality, some changes to internal organisation being undertaken to address the new challenges. The third group, the electoral losers, consisted of Austria, Germany and Britain which were not able to adjust to the new times (Kitschelt, 1995b: 232–52). However, an Americanisation of social democracy set in during the second half of the 1990s. The influence of the more pragmatic policies of the Democratic Party and the Clinton administration led to major transformations in the British Labour Party and the German SPD. The Third Way between traditional social democracy and neo-liberalism became a new framework for change among social democratic parties (Giddens, 1998; Lipset, 2001; Marlière, 1999) (Figure 10.4).

At the forefront of this change from traditional ideological social democratic parties to modern inter-classistic pragmatic centrist politics was and is the New Labour Party. The Labour Party was founded in 1900 as a political pressure group of the trade unions. In comparison to the social democratic parties of the continent, Marxism was not part of its ideology. Between 1900 and 1979 it became a strong subculture within British society. In the 1960s and 1970s, the more radical left-wing factions inside the party were dominant. This led to a major crisis in the 1970s, the climax of which was the 'Winter of Discontent' in 1978 and 1979. The Winter of Discontent and the mismanagement of the crisis by the Labour government of Prime Minister James Callaghan, led to the electoral victory of Margaret

Figure 10.4 The social democratic parties in Europe

Thatcher in 1979, which kept the Labour Party out of power for seventeen years. It took a long time for Labour to become a more pragmatic party. Such transformation took place after 1979 and lasted until Tony Blair came to power in May 1997. Tony Blair's New Labour Party no longer appealed to voters with an ideological programme or common subcultural values, but with pragmatic policies designed to improve the living conditions of the population. This 'Third Way' between neo-liberalism and social democracy followed a catch-all strategy in order to replace the Conservative Party, which governed Britain from 1979 to 1997. New Labour under the leadership of Tony Blair and Gordon Brown used techniques of marketing to position the Labour Party in a favourable position in relation to the Conservatives (Lees-Marshment, 2004: 20–3, see above). In 1997, a New Labour government under Tony Blair came to power, committed to quite an ambitious agenda. After thirteen years in power, it must be conceded that such reforms have achieved mixed results. There has been more pragmatism in the decision-making, implementation and delivery of policies, but owing to its new nature, the New Labour Party conducted a permanent campaign that was exposed regularly by the media. The role of 'spin doctors' and political advisers shaped the work of the government and also of the party. The support of the British government for the US-led Iraq War in 2003 caused a general discontent within the party. Many dedicated party activists left the party. Owing to reliance on the new marketing techniques and the permanent electoral campaign, the party needed considerable cash to finance all these electoral operations. The 'Cash for Honours' scandal during 2006 and 2007 was an important tipping point in the popularity of Prime Minister Tony Blair within the party. He resigned shortly after completing ten years in office. He was replaced by the Chancellor of the Exchequer Gordon Brown. However, the party has so far not recovered from this growing popular dissatisfaction. In May 2010, the New Labour government lost the election to the Conservative Party.

The Irish Labour party, founded in 1912, became the third largest party of the Irish party system and took part in elections after the creation of the Republic of Ireland. As such it took part in several coalitions as a junior partner with one of the two main parties. Although the Irish Labour Party is quite conservative and reformist, it also has strong pragmatic credentials and is able to adjust quickly to new situations (Holmes, 1999: 130). In the 2002 and 2007 general elections the party got 10.1 per cent and twenty seats.

Among the traditional social democratic parties, the Austrian social democratic party (Sozialdemokratische Partei Österreichs) should be mentioned. The party was founded in 1889. The leadership of the party was involved in major discussions about strategy and ideology at the turn of the nineteenth to the twentieth century. One particular ideological current of Austrian social democracy became known as *Austromarxismus* of which the main representative was Otto Bauer. *Austromarxismus* advocated that social democratic parties should first get an absolute majority through parliamentary elections before introducing revolutionary change. Such an approach was relevant during the First Austrian Republic between 1918 and 1934, but became less so after 1945 when the party was re-founded. The difficult international position of Austria between 1945 and 1955 led to the participation of the social democrats in the grand coalition, which continued until 1966. However, between 1970 and 1994 the party was able to remain in power. Between 1983 and 1986, the party formed a coalition with the FPÖ, and subsequently it formed a coalition government with the ÖVP until 1999. Between 1970 and 1983, the SPÖ clearly transformed Austrian society through its redistributive policies. Party leader and Chancellor Bruno Kreisky was charismatic and influenced by the Scandinavian welfare state model. Most policies were geared towards the creation of a stable economy with strong welfare policies. After 1986 Chancellor Franz Vranitzky was able to introduce major reforms in the economy and prepare Austria's integration into the European Union, but in 1997 he resigned from office and was replaced by Viktor Klima. In 1999 the SPÖ lost considerably in electoral support. The SPÖ had difficulties in adjusting to the new realities and the electoral vote declined between 1970 and 2008 from 48.5 per cent to 29.5 per cent. After the resignation of Franz Vranitzky the SPÖ was unable to find a new charismatic leader that would change its fortunes. A new party programme was adopted in the party conference of 1998, which allowed the party to adjust to new contemporary issues, such as the environment, and to acknowledge the role of the market with regard to the well-being of society (Učakar, 2006: 334–5). Moreover, the SPÖ had not developed proper strategies to deal with the new mediatised electoral markets (Učakar, 2006: 335–40). In terms of membership, it declined from the 721,262 in 1979 to 301,251 in 2005 (Učakar, 2006: 332). On 8 August 2008, the SPÖ nominated Werner Faymann, the minister of transport of the government of Alfred Gusenbauer as party leader for the election of October 2008. It seems that his dynamic personality has contributed to a better image for the party, particularly in a period of financial crisis. He became chancellor of the grand coalition of the SPÖ and the ÖVP.

The Swedish Social Democrats Party (Socialdemokraterna) has been the most successful in this party family. They have been able to govern for almost seventy years with only short interruptions. All the other right-centre and liberal parties have to join together to create a balance of power on the right in Sweden. Swedish social democracy has become a model for many other similar parties, because of the positive record in terms of the welfare state and the dynamic economy based on research and development. This 'Swedish model' was designed by Gösta Rehn and Rudolf Meidner, two economists of the main trade union confederation LO (Aylott, 1999: 191). Ideologically, the party programme uses the concept of 'democratic socialism': 'Social Democracy aims to build a society based on the ideals of democracy and on the equal value of everyone. Free and equal people in a solidaristic society are the goal of democratic socialism' (Socialdemokraterna, 2001: 1). The party was founded in 1889 in Stockholm. Like its Austrian sister party, the Swedish social democrats have close historical relations with the trade unions. Trade union affiliation would automatically lead to membership of the party. Such overlapping membership was only abolished in 1987 leading to a decline of membership from 1.23 million in 1983 to 260,000 in 1997 (Aylott, 1999: 197). In 2010 there were 100,000 party members. Between 1994 and 2007 Göran Persson led a social democratic government, but in the 2007 elections it did not have a strong enough majority to be able to form a minority government.

Since 1998, the party has not been able to pass the threshold of 40 per cent, and in 2006 received only 35 per cent of the vote – the lowest share since 1920. However, it remains the largest party of the Swedish party system.

Other Scandinavian social democratic parties in Norway, Denmark and Finland have had to deal with continuing decline in electoral support. All these parties have to agree coalitions with other left-wing parties to form government.

Although the history of the SPD goes back to 1848, it was the Eisenach unification conference in 1875 between supporters of Ferdinand Lassalle, the Lassalleans and the social democrats, that led to the establishment of the Social Democratic Workers Party (Sozialdemokratische Arbeiterpartei, SDAP). The popularity of the party grew in the late nineteenth century, in spite of the fact that Chancellor Otto von Bismarck introduced the 'Sozialistengesetze' (Law to forbid the activities of the social democrats) in 1878, which prevented the free activity of the SDAP. This changed only after 1890, when Chancellor Bismarck was forced to resign by the new German emperor, William II. From then on, the social democrats grew steadily with the increase of suffrage. In the Weimar Republic it became the most important party on the left, however it had to deal with the growing enmity of the communists and national socialists in the 1930s.

After the Second World War the re-founded SPD became even more moderate and moved slowly towards the format of an inter-classistic party.

The Bad Godesberg party conference of the SPD in 1958 led to a break with the traditional subcultural working class-based approach to electoral politics.

The SPD became a catch-all party like the CDU/CSU. It was not until 1966 that the SPD was able to take government responsibility in a grand coalition with the CDU/CSU, but that was just for three years. Afterwards, the SPD was able to form a coalition government with the liberals between 1970 and 1982. However, this was a difficult period because of the two oil crises and the economic recession. Between 1982 and 1998, the SPD was out of power. The turning point was in the election of 1998, when Gerhard Schröder came to power. Gerhard Schröder had been the regional president of the *Länd* of Niedersachsen (1990–98). Schröder used his charisma and new marketing techniques imported from the United States to conduct the campaign against Helmut Kohl. The SPD was influenced by the British New Labour 'Third Way' model and emulated it using the concept der 'Neue Mitte' (New Centre) which was characterised by the ideological change towards more liberal policies. During Schröder's first and second term in office several social and economic reforms were undertaken such as that of the labour market (Hartz-Reform) which aimed at making public employment services more efficient and increasing the number of people in work. Moreover, the reform of the pension system through the introduction of incentives to have additional private pension schemes (known as *Riester Rente*) was a further measure of the Schröder red–green government. In spite of the reforms, unemployment remained high during his period, reaching an historic 5 million in 2005.

On 31 October 2005, the SPD had 523,966 members (Sozialdemokratische Partei Deutschlands, 2008), quite a considerable decline from the climax figure of 998,471 members in 1975 (De Deken, 1999: 85). After a negative period under the leadership of Kurt Beck between 2006 and 2008, a new party leader was chosen, former Foreign Minister Walter Steinmeier of the coalition government of Chancellor Angela Merkel. One of the new challenges of the SPD is to deal with the new left-wing political formation Die Linke (The Left) which is a merger of the former communists of the German Democratic Republic, a splinter group of the SPD and other smaller left-wing groups. The success of Die Linke is among the poorer parts of the population who are suffering under the reforms (particularly the Hartz-Reform) introduced by the governments of Chancellor Gerhard Schröder and continued by Chancellor Angela Merkel. This led to splits within the SPD parliamentary group in the *Länd* of Hessen, resulting in the failure to elect social democratic candidate Andrea Ypsilanti as regional president because of four rebels in the SPD who rejected any cooperation with Die Linke. Ypsilanti was dependent on the parliamentary support of Die Linke to become regional president (*Der Spiegel*, 7 March 2008).

The Social Democratic Party of Switzerland, founded in 1888, also has to deal with a fragmented party system. In the past two decades it has become one of the strongest parties in Switzerland, although the right-wing Swiss People's Party (SVP) was able to become the strongest party in the elections of 2003 and 2007. The Swiss Social Democratic Party had to deal with the major socioeconomic changes since the 1960s and adjust its position. Traditionally, the party was a supporter of state intervention and improvement in the living conditions of the poorer parts of the Swiss population. However, since the mid 1980s, it has made a shift towards the centre, being less adversarial towards the market and developing a more pragmatic approach to policy. It also advocated coalitions with the greens at local and cantonal level, which has led to a strengthening of its position in the overall multilevel party system (Ladler, 2005: 230–1).

The Dutch Party of Labour (Partij van der Arbeid, PvdA) was founded in 1946, but its historical development goes back to the Social Democratic Workers' Party (Sociaal Democratische Arbeiderpartij, SDAP). The SDAP was fairly successful in the inter-war period. In comparison to other sister parties, the SDAP evolved towards a catch-all party that also appealed to the middle classes before the Second World War (van Kersbergen, 1999: 156). The newly founded PvdA followed similar strategies. In a highly fragmented society, it worked with other political parties, including the Christian democratic parties until 1958. However, in the late sixties it adopted a polarisation strategy in order to reduce the power of the Christian democrats. Major ideological transformation took place during the 1990s. One can also speak of a bourgeoisification of the working class, meaning that the welfare state led to considerable improvement of living conditions and social mobility of its constituency, the working class. Some of the working class became part of the middle classes. In terms of party organisation, the membership declined sharply from 142,853 members in 1960 to 64,573 in 1995 (van Kersbergen, 1999: 159). In 2004, the membership was around 60,000.

In Belgium, the Belgian Workers' Party (Parti Ouvrier Belge – POB) was founded in 1885 and can be counted as part of the traditional mass party. A Flemish and a Wallonian section worked together in the party. This was continued after federalisation in 1993, which led to the separated general elections in the two parts of the country. The stronghold of the socialist party was Wallonia, which was highly industrialised in the 1950s and 1960s. Since then economic power has shifted to Flanders and Wallonia, which have had to deal with many financial problems and a declining industrial sector. In 2001, the Flemish party merged with the social liberal party and created the Socialist Party – Different (Socialistische Partij – Anders, SP.A). In the 2003 elections it was able to improve considerably in electoral terms and take part in the government of Verhofstadt II. However, in 2007 it lost considerable electoral support and seats.

The Socialist Party (Parti Socialiste – PS) in Wallonia is also declining and has considerable difficulties in overcoming past legacies. The entrenchment of the Socialist Party in the society and economy of Wallonia has led to the disclosure of several corruption scandals that have clearly undermined the position of the party.

The French Socialist Party (Parti Socialiste, PS) was re-founded in 1971. Historically, it goes back to the French Section of the Workers' International (Section Française de l'Internationale Ouvriére, SFIO). However, the SFIO had been declining electorally since 1945, so its re-foundation was a way of modernising the party and its message. In the 1970s, the PS was quite traditional, advocating a common programme with the communists. In the Fifth Republic, the communists were a traditional ally of the Socialist Party because of the dynamics of the electoral system. In 1981, François Mitterrand became the first socialist president to be elected by the population in the Fifth Republic. The Socialist Party also won also the general elections and tried to implement left-wing policies in order to curb the economy. In 1983, PS acknowledged that the French economy had to become more competitive. Laurent Fabius introduced a major privatisation programme and rolled back the state from the economy. The overall policies of the French government became more liberal and the PS moved towards the centre (Merkel, 1993; Sassoon, 1997: 534–71). After two years out of power, the PS formed a new government under Prime Minister Michel Rocard, and tried to solve the existing economic problems. However, in 1991 Rocard was forced to resign from his position because of the deteriorating economic situation. In 1997, Lionel Jospin was able to win a majority and form a socialist government with the Green Party and the communists. He also became the main representative of the opposition against the Third Way. Jospin emphasised more policies of social cohesion, inclusion and social regulation. He was instrumental in putting employment policies on the agenda of the European Union. This was included in one of the chapters of the Treaty of Amsterdam. However, he created a major crisis inside the Socialist Party when he ran for president against Jacques Chirac in the presidential elections of 2002. He came only third after Jean Marie Le Pen, the leader of the extreme right-wing Front National, in the first round and was not able to make it to the run-off – this bitter disappointment led to his resignation. His successor, François Hollande, initiated a process of modernisation and adjustment to new realities. Hollande's wife, Sególene Royal, became the new candidate for the presidential election in 2007 against Nicolas Sarkozy and lost, although she succeeded in reaching the second round without difficulty. The Socialist Party also lost the general elections in the same year against the UMP. In the primaries of November 2008, Martine Aubry, the mayor of Lille, won against Sególene Royal by 100 votes and became the new secretary general (PS, 2009).

In Italy, before and after the Fall of the Berlin Wall, the Italian Communist Party (Partito Comunista Italiano – PCI) faced decline of electoral support. The negative image of the Soviet Union contributed to an erosion of the subculture that was established after 1921. The PCI was the strongest left-wing party after 1945 but, owing to the cold war, was excluded from power. However, it was an important party at both the regional and the local levels. In 1976 the party had almost the same share of the votes as Christian democracy. This was a result of leader Enrico Berlinguer's strategy of moving towards the centre and working with Christian democracy through an 'historical compromise' (compromesso storico). However, the kidnapping of Christian Democratic Prime Minister Aldo Moro by the terrorist organisation Red Brigades led to the failure of this policy. From 1979 to 1992, the share of the party declined from 36 per cent to 16 per cent. After several party conferences in 1991 the party renamed itself the Party of Democratic Left (Partito Democratico della Sinistra, PDS) and, later, it joined the Socialist International. A splinter group, called the Party of Communist Refoundation (Partido della Refondazione Comunista, PRC), under the leadership of Fausto Bertinotti, continued the communist tradition; however, it remained close in terms of alliances to the PDS. In 1998, it merged with all smaller parties and changed its name to Democrats of the Left (Democratici della Sinistra). The PDS/DS became the strongest party on the left and formed alliances with small Christian democratic and liberal parties against the right-centre alliances led by Silvio Berlusconi. In spite of electoral success in 1996 in the Olive Tree (Ulivo) coalition and in 2006 in the Union (Unione), the electoral coalitions in which the DS was involved tended to fragment while in power, so the reputation of the left suffered considerably. In order to avoid such fragmentation in the future, several parties decided to form the Democratic Party (Partito Democratico, PD), on 14 October 2007. However, this new party has had difficulties in creating a common position, because of the diversity of the parties involved in it. Apart from the DS, there are other Christian democratic parties. There has so far been no decision as to which European party the democratic party should be attached to (Lazar, 2008).

In Spain, Portugal and Greece, strong social democratic parties emerged after 1974. In Spain, the Socialist Party could refer to a historical background that went back to 1879. The party was quite successful during the Second Republic, but became the main victim of persecution during the authoritarian regime of General Francisco Franco. In the 1970s, Felipe Gonzalez and Alfonso Guerra had tried to set up a new organisation, but encountered many difficulties. However, after the death of General Franco, the Spanish Socialist Workers' Party (Partido Socialista Obrero Español, PSOE) was able to build a new organisation, in spite of the advantages that the communists had. Under the charismatic leadership of young Felipe Gonzalez, the party modernised, by taking out all references to radical language. The new modern party moved towards the centre and was able to win an absolute majority in the historical elections of 1982. Under the leadership of Felipe Gonzalez, the PSOE remained in power until 1996. During this period, Gonzalez introduced major changes in Spanish society and the economy. Similar to the French socialists, he also used neo-liberal policies to open up the Spanish economy. This was necessary after decades of authoritarianism that had practised a very regulated form of capitalism. However, after 1989 the socialist government was embroiled in several corruption scandals leading to a decline of support in the 1993 and 1996 elections. Between 1996 and 2004, the PSOE was in opposition. It was quite difficult to find an alternative to Gonzalez, who decided to withdraw from public life. After a difficult period between 1996 and 2000, the PSOE chose José Luis Zapatero as its new leader at the 35th party congress. He was able to modernise the party and adjust to the new changes and topics. After winning the 2004 general elections he became prime minister and introduced major reforms in education, legalised same-sex marriages, and changed the financing system between the government and the Church. In the 2008 general elections, the PSOE was able to extend slightly the relative majority of 2004 (Magone, 2009a: 157–64).

The Portuguese Socialist Party (Partido Socialista, PS) can be traced back to its roots when it was founded in 1875, but it never became a mass movement. It remained until the 1930s a party of cadres. One of the major reasons was the lack of an industrial proletariat. Portuguese industrialisation started quite late, mainly after 1945, when several socialist organisations tried to coordinate their efforts against the authoritarian regime. However, only in the late 1960s did a new, re-founded Socialist Party emerge. In 1973, the PS was re-founded in Bad Münster-eiffel under the auspices of the Friedrich Ebert Foundation and the German SPD. The PS became a pivotal party during the revolutionary process of 1974–75, forming alliances with other democratic right-centre parties to prevent a take-over by the communists or extreme left-wing parties. A central figure of the party was Mario Soares, who led three short governments in the constitutional period (1975–78; 1978; 1983–85). A climax for the Socialist party was the election of party leader Mario Soares to president of the Republic between 1986 and 1996. He was followed by Jorge Sampaio who remained president until 2006. After Mario Soares became president, the party had a very difficult period, owing to its severe financial problems and the lack of a charismatic leader to face Prime Minister Anibal Cavaco Silva. The fortunes of the party began to change when Antonio Guterres, considered a technocrat within the party, took over the leadership and moved the party towards the centre. The PS became a 'Third Way' party, but the economic reality of the country was that it was still lagging behind. Between 1995 and 2001, it was able to hold on to power, and, after a short period of right-wing coalition government, it returned to power in 2005 under the leadership of José Socrates (Magone, 2004; 2007). For the first time, the PS got an absolute majority. This allowed a major restructuring agenda of Portuguese institutions, particularly public administration, education, health and social policy.

In Greece, Andreas Papandreou founded the Panhellenic Socialist Movement (Panellinio Socialistiko Kinia, PASOK) on 3 September 1973. Originally, the party was verbally radical and had a strategy oriented towards the third world. It also viewed the Socialist International negatively, because of its integration in the capitalist system. The radicalism of PASOK appealed to the Greeks in a period in which anti-Americanism was quite strong after the fall of the authoritarian dictatorship of the colonels. PASOK came third in the 1975 elections, but was able to improve considerably to second place in the 1977 elections. Finally, in 1981, PASOK came to power under the motto of '*alagi*' (change). Between 1981 and 1989, Papandreou introduced radical policies that were expensive and undermined the economy. In spite of joining the European Union quite early, in 1981, the PASOK government was not able to benefit from this. The charismatic personality of Andreas Papandreou was sometimes a major hindrance to the development of the party and the country. The 'charismatic organisation' (Panebianco, 1988) was extremely dependent on its leader. After a period of catharsis and a right-centre government under Kostas Mitsotakis, Papandreou returned to power in 1993 until 1996 – when he died and power had to be transferred to Kostas Simitis.

Prime Minister Kostas Simitis was pragmatic in his approach to government. He was able to change the mood of the country and begin major reforms, particularly in view of joining Economic and Monetary Union. Simitis had to deal with considerable resistance within the party and the trade unions. In spite of this, he remained in power until 2004, after which Andreas Papandreou's son, Giorgios, took over the party. However, he was not regarded as very charismatic and in both the 2004 and the 2007 elections, his party was defeated by Kostas Karamanlis' New Democracy (Nea Dimokratia, ND).

The social democratic party family changed considerably when several former communist parties in Central and Eastern Europe embraced social democracy overnight. The Hungarian Socialist Party (Magyar Szocialista Párt, MSzP) is one of these reformed communist parties. It was founded on 9 November 1989 and continues to be one of the two main parties in Hungary. It retained many of the assets of the previous Communist Party, and members of the Communist Party also continued to play a role. The Bulgarian Social Democratic Party (Bulgarska Socialist-isheka Partija, BSP), founded in 1990, and the Romanian Social Democratic Party (Partidul Social Democrat), founded in 2001, after several mergers with smaller parties, are also strong parties on the left of the respective party systems. The Lithuanian Social Democratic Party (Lietuvos socialdemocratu partija, LSP) founded in 2001, having undergone many mergers since 1993, and, in Poland, the Democratic Left Alliance (Sojusz Lewicy Demokratycznej, SLD), founded in 1999, and also after several mergers, are examples of these transformed communist parties, which are now quite pragmatic and less ideological. All of them renounced Marxism and communism, although factions of members of the former Communist Party still exist.

The main exceptions are in the Czech Republic and Slovakia. The Czech Social Democratic Party (Česká strana sociálně demokratická, ČSSD) can trace its history back to 1874. It was originally part of the Social Democratic Party in the Austro-Hungarian monarchy, and was able to re-establish itself during and after the transition to democracy. The ČSSD is the strongest party on the left, achieving about one-third of votes in general elections. It is a pragmatic party (Vodička, 2005: 158). In Slovakia, the Social-Democracy-Direction is actually a populist party and, because of its coalition with nationalist parties since 2006, is not accepted by the Socialist International.

In sum, social democratic parties evolved from highly ideological to pragmatic parties. This transformation was particularly fast in Southern Europe and Central and Eastern European countries. The Americanisation of the left is a major factor in this respect.

The communist party family and other left-wing parties

After the Bolshevik Revolution of 1917 in Russia, particularly after the foundation of the Third Communist International (COMINTERN) in 1920, the more radical factions of the social democratic parties split to form communist parties in most countries. They became an important rival party to social democracy. In some cases, communist parties tried to destroy social democratic parties, for example during the Spanish Civil War in Spain and the Weimar Republic in Germany.

The Stalinist experience, the persecution and murder of Leon Trotzky in Mexico in 1941 and the emergence of communist regimes in China and Albania were reasons for some left-wing intellectuals to create new smaller political parties which opposed the official communist parties. These parties emerged particularly in France and Southern European countries in the 1960s and 1970s, and some of them have survived until the twenty-first century (see Figure 10.5).

Two decades after the Fall of the Berlin Wall, there are few electorally significant parties in Europe. In Western Europe, we can find important communist parties in Portugal, Spain, France, Italy, Greece, Germany and Finland. In Central and Eastern Europe, it is important to highlight the Communist Party of Bohemia and Moravia (Komunistická strana Čech a Moravy – KSČM) in the Czech Republic. The latter still has a large membership and is able to achieve between 12 and 20 per cent of the vote. The party did not give up on a Marxist ideology and continues to be a strong anti-systemic subculture in the Czech Republic, which is quite critical of market-oriented policies. However, the party members are getting older, having been members of the party for over forty years, and it has difficulty in attracting young members and voters (Vodička, 2005: 164–9). In 2006, the Ministry of the Interior decided to ban the communist youth branch of the KSČM, because of the inclusion of sentences in the programme that called for the overthrow of the democratic regime, and the refusal to withdraw these from the programme. This was upheld by a court. However, the same court cancelled the ban in 2010.

In Portugal, the Portuguese Communist Party (Partido Comunista Portugues, PCP) founded in 1921, was very active during the revolutionary process. It had a close relationship with the military who took over after 25 April 1974. Other political parties were concerned about the influence of the Communist Party in the context

Figure 10.5 The communist and new left parties in Europe

of the cold war. Afer the revolutionary process, the PCP was quite isolated because of its behaviour during the first years of democratic transition. It remains ostracised from the centre of power, although it was able to build a reputation at the local level. The party has an ageing membership, which is probably slightly below 100,000 members. For a long time it was dominated by *éminence grise* Alvaro Cunhal, even after his retirement. In 2005, new leader Jerónimo de Sousa was able to start a renewal of the party. In general elections the Communist Party may achieve on average between 6 and 7 per cent of the vote.

Since 1999, the party has had to deal with competition from the small Block of the Left (Bloco da Esquerda, BE) that consists of different groups related to other communist and postmodern new age currents. It consists of young leaders who seem to appeal to a younger population in the urban centres of Lisbon and Oporto.

In Spain, the Communist Party is part of the coalition of United Left (Izquierda Unida, IU), which was founded in 1986, but has been losing votes since 1996. It is the third largest party in national elections in terms of share of the vote, but not in terms of seats. There has been tension within the IU, particularly between the Communist Party and the central leadership of the coalition. The party is in dire straits financially, because of its electoral losses. In the 2008 general elections the party achieved 3.8 per cent and two seats. Subsequently, it had to form a parliamentary group with other regionalist parties. It has approximately 50,000 members (Ramiro Fernandez, 2003).

A similar trend of decline can be found in the French Communist Party, which was in the 1950s and 1960s one of the strongest representatives of this party family. The French Communist Party (Parti Communiste Français, PCF) was founded in 1921 and attracted many French intellectuals. It was able to build a subculture that lasted until the early 1980s. De-industrialisation and liberalisation have contributed to a decline of the working class, subsequently the Communist Party had difficulties in keeping high levels of mobilisation. It became an important partner for the Socialist Party from the 1970s, particularly after agreeing on a common programme (*programme commun*). Communists took part in several socialist-led governments.

In the 1970s, the party tried to move towards a more moderate position by adopting a new course called Eurocommunism. It formed a block of new communist parties with the Spanish and Italian communist parties. These new Eurocommunist parties were not trusted by other parties because of their sudden transformations. However, the growing integration of communist parties in the electoral processes of Western democracies led also to moderation of its ideology. In Italy, the historical compromise and in Spain the consensual approach of the communists during the transition process are examples of this change of heart. The party began to decline considerably after 1986, because its members did not agree with the policies of the socialist-led government and withdrew their ministers. While in the early 1980s, they were able to achieve about 20 per cent of the vote, in the late 1990s this was only about 9–10 per cent. In the new millenium, the party achieved slightly above 4 per cent in the 2002 and 2007 elections. Some modernisation has been initiated since 2002, but with limited success.

France is also known for other communist currents on the left of the PCF. Among these are the Trotzkyite Party of Workers (Parti des Travailleurs, PT), the Communist Revolutionary League (League Communiste Revolutionaire, LCR) and Workers' Struggle (Lutte Ouvriere, LO), all of them with electoral support below those of the Communist Party. However, they may become important in presidential elections, because each of these parties also tends to present a candidate, leading to a fragmentation of the left-wing vote. This was one of the reasons for the failure of Lionel Jospin to make it to the run-off in the presidential elections 2002 – there were about ten different candidates on the left competing with each other.

After the PCI changed its name to PDS in Italy, a splinter party called the Party of Communist Refoundation (Partito di Rifondazione Comunista, PRC) was founded. The PRC has strong linkages to the trade unions and the anti-globalisation movement. It typically achieved about 6 per cent in general elections. It was allied to the left-wing coalition of Unione in 2006 and, more recently, to the Democratic Party in 2008. There is also an even smaller party called Party of Italian Communists (Partito dei Comunisti Italiani, PCI) that split from the PRC in 1998. Since 2006, there has been talk of reunification of the two parties.

In Greece, two communist parties have been successful in getting some representation in parliament, in spite of the electoral system that favours larger parties and penalises smaller ones. The Communist Party of Greece (Kommounistiko

Komma Elladas, KKE) was founded in 1918 and has a strong tradition in Greece. It is a party that has a good reputation in the left, because it played a major part in the anti-fascist movement during the occupation of Greece between 1941 and 1945. It was also ostracised from the political system during the right-wing democracy of the 1950s and 1960s. In 1968 there was a split in the party. One group formed the Communist Party of the Interior, with tendencies towards Eurocommunism and moderation, and the other group, the hardliners, were called the Communist Party of the Exterior (KKE-es). The strongest party was the KKE-es with its popular leader, Aleka Papariga. It has continued to enjoy a strong reputation as a resistance party and is strongly engaged in anti-globalisation movements. It achieved 8.25 per cent and twenty-two seats in the 2007 legislative elections. The more moderate Communist Party of the Interior formed a coalition with other parties, forming the United Left (Synaspismos) and, since 2004, the Coalition of the Radical Left, with a considerable number of left-wing, environmental and new-age parties. In 2007 they got 5.04 per cent and fourteen seats – a considerable improvement on the 2004 results.

In Germany, there has been a revival in the left-wing subculture. This was possible after a merger between a splinter group of the SPD under the leadership of former SPD leader Oskar Lafontaine and other smaller formations with the successor formation of the East Communists of the Party of Democratic Socialism (Partei des Demokratischen Sozialismus, PDS). The new party is called the Left (Die Linke). It was founded in 2007 and has changed German politics considerably. Neither the SPD nor the CDU/CSU wish to work with the PDS at federal government level. However, the party has gained considerable support in East and West Germany at both the regional and the national levels. There was the possibility that the SPD in the *Land* of Hessen would elect Andrea Ypsilanti as regional president against incumbent Roland Koch with the votes of Die Linke. However, in the voting session at the Hessen regional parliament, Ypsilanti failed to get the votes of the whole SPD, and some rebels decided not to vote for her. Die Linke is successful largely because it is able to attract protest voters and also many people who live in difficult conditions, particularly after the Labour market reforms made during the government of former Chancellor Gerhard Schröder (especially pensioners and the working classes). The party is fairly strong in the eastern *Länder*, such as Sachsen, Thüringen and Berlin and its success in the regional elections of Saarland, where it achieved 21 per cent of the vote and became the third largest party after the CDU and the SPD, was surprising. One of the reasons is that the former president of the region Oskar Lafontaine is one of the leaders of the party.

Several smaller left-wing parties were able to improve their electoral positions in the past decade. Most of them are in Northern Europe. One such party is the Dutch Socialist Party (Socialistische Partij, SP), founded in 1972, which has its origins in Marxism–Leninism and Maoism, but which has moderated its ideology towards democratic socialism. The party has an extensive organisation and in the 2006 elections got 16.6 per cent and twenty-five seats. It became the third largest party after the CDA and PvdA. The Danish Socialist People's Party (Socialistisk Folkeparti, SFP), founded in 1959 and with a more radical ideology than the Social Democratic Party, got 13 per cent and twenty-three seats and has become the fourth largest party in Denmark. The Socialist Left Party (Socialistisk Venstreparti, SV) in Norway has become the fourth largest party and is part of the coalition under the social democratic leadership. The party is very keen to preserve or extend the welfare state and puts its emphasis on equality in most areas of society. Other similar smaller parties are the Swedish Left Party (Vänsterparti) and the Finnish Left Alliance (Vasemmistoliitto). Both were former Communist Parties that adjusted their party strategy to a changed society. The Finnish Left Alliance is a merger of several left-wing parties, including a feminist party.

Extreme right-wing and new right parties

The legacy of authoritarianism and totalitarianism in Italy, Germany and many other countries led to the establishment of an extreme right-wing party family that led to the emergence of neo-fascist parties after the Second World War. These parties have a nationalist ideology, are against the European Union and are xenophobic. Apart from that, they are partly anti-systemic, and want to establish an authoritarian regime. In Germany, the National Democratic Party of Germany (National Demokratisches Partei Deutschlands, NPD), in the UK, the British National Party (BNP) and in France Jean Marie Le Pen's National Front (Front National, FN) are all representatives of this party family. All these parties are small parties and many of them have retained an extreme right-wing ideology. In Germany, the NPD was founded in 1964 and regards itself as a successor party to the National Socialist Party. The party had some success in the 1960s at regional level, but since then has remained a small party. However, the reunification has led to a rise of support in the eastern *Länder* of Vorpommern-Mecklenburg and Sachsen. The party works closely with the German People's Union (Deutsche Volksunion, DVU) that was founded in 1971. The ideology of both parties is xenophobic, nationalist and authoritarian. Both parties are regarded as extreme right-wing and are being monitored by the Verfassungsschutz (protection of the constitution) authorities. Several attempts to ban the NPD through the constitutional court have failed. In the 2005 general elections, the NPD got just over 1 per cent and no seats. A slightly more moderate party are the Republikaner founded in 1983, although the ideology and demands are quite similar. They were able to play a role at regional level, particularly in Bavaria and then in Berlin in the late 1980s. Since then the party has almost disappeared, achieving only minimal electoral support, below 1 per cent.

In Britain, the British National Party, founded in 1982, pursues a nationalist, xenophobic policy. Central issues for the party are also law and order and opposition to immigration, with a strong undercurrent against the Muslim population. They have been able to achieve some representation at local level, particularly in city districts dominated by the Muslim population. However, they have not been able to achieve representation at a national level. Nevertheless, in the last European parliament elections of 2009 the BNP got over 940,000 votes, 6.2 per cent and two seats nationally. However, the turnout was poor at 34.4 per cent – in the normal first-past-the-post system, it is more difficult to achieve representation in legislative elections when there is a higher turnout.

In France, Jean Marie Le Pen's National Front (Front Nationat, FN) was founded in 1972. It shares a xenophobic, nationalist and anti-immigration ideology with the extreme right in other countries. Leader Jean Marie Le Pen is a charismatic figure and was able to achieve second place in the 2002 presidential elections with over 17 per cent of the vote. Apart from that, the party was unable to achieve representation in parliament due to the majoritarian electoral system that requires parties on the left and the right to form a coalition in order to overcome the high thresholds for the second round. However, no party on the left or right wanted to work with the FN. Regionally, the FN is strong in the south, Corsica and the suburbs of major cities. In Belgium, a sister party with the same name (Front National) can be found in Wallonia. It got less than 2 per cent of the vote in the 2007 elections. However, the situation is quite different in Flanders, where the popularity of Flemish Interest (Vlaams Belang, VB), which is represented at local level, is growing. VB is the third largest party in Belgium and the second largest in Flanders and has been winning votes and seats in both the national and regional parliaments since the early 1980s, although, so far, it has only gained power at local municipal level because other parties have boycotted it. VB seeks the independence of Flanders from Belgium, and proposes a peaceful Velvet Divorce, like that between the Czech Republic and Slovakia. Its ideology includes strong xenophobic tendencies, particularly against the Muslim population. The other parties have refused to cooperate with VB, because of its extreme views (see Figure 10.6).

Figure 10.6 The extreme right-wing, new right and new populist parties in Europe

New populism and Euro-scepticism

Since the 1980s, a transformation of extreme right-wing parties into something more moderate (but which, nonetheless, operate with similar arguments against further immigration and integration into the EU and are xenophobic) has become evident. This was paralleled by the emergence of new parties or reinvigorated old parties on the right that use single issues such as European integration or immigration. This has been labelled as 'new right' or 'new populist'. However, new populist parties can also be found on the left, so that new right is probably a more suitable label.

New populist parties have a less well-defined ideology. In some cases, there is no clear distinction between extreme right and new right. In some parties, extreme right splinter groups may still be present, in spite of the fact that the leadership tries to move away from this legacy (they can be on the left or right, although the vast majority of them are on the right). The parties tend to emphasise a world that is being lost, because of European integration or globalisation, and they propose nationalist policies to deal with the new realities, appealing directly to the people through charismatic leaders (for example, Jörg Haider and Pim Fortuyn). This period of transformation from the industrial to the post-industrial society creates zones of insecurity, particularly for those who are not able to cope with rapid social and economic change. Therefore, Cas Mudde characterises contemporary Europe as being in a 'populist Zeitgeist' that he defines as follows:

> I define populism as *an ideology that considers society to be ultimately separated into two homogeneous and antagonistic groups, 'the pure people' versus 'the corrupt elite', and which argues that politics should be an expression of the* volonté générale *(general will) of the people*. Populism, so defined, has two opposites: elitism and pluralism. Elitism is populism's mirror-image: it shares its Manichean worldview, but wants politics to be an expression of the views of the moral elite, instead of the amoral people. Pluralism, on the other hand, rejects the homogeneity of both populism and elitism, seeing society as a heterogenous collection of groups and individuals with often fundamentally different views and wishes.
>
> (italics in original; Mudde, 2004: 543–4)

According to Paul Taggart, there are five characteristics of new populist parties that should be taken into account.

1 *New populist parties are hostile to representative politics*: they seek a direct relationship with the people in the political system. They are characterised by anti-elitism and pluralism.
2 *Identification with an idealised 'heartland'*: this is an imagined community that is under threat from contemporary processes such as European integration (losing national sovereignty and national identity) or globalisation.
3 *Lack of core values*: there is no clear ideology. They may change ideological suppositions in order to increase their electoral support or take part in government.
4 *Reaction to a period of extreme crisis*: the present transformation from industrial to post-industrial society creates zones of insecurity that include unemployment, change of welfare to workfare state or waves of immigration.

5   *Use of short-term appeal using new politics and charismatic leaders*: a charismatic leader can be a very easy way to catapult a new populist party into
the mainstream discussion. Pim Fortuyn in the Netherlands, Jörg Haider in
Austria until 2008 or Christoph Blocher in Switzerland are good examples
(adapted from Taggart, 2004: 273–6; see also Taggart, 2000: 91–114).

Last, but not least, the Euro-sceptic parties had already emerged in the 1970s,
particularly in the Nordic countries and later on in the UK. The Treaty of the
European Union, which was signed in Maastricht and came into force in 1993, led
to a considerable rise of these parties in electoral terms. Some parties were adamant
in rejecting the European Union, while others were against the move towards the
Economic Monetary Union and eventually Political Union. Particular concerns of the
Euro-sceptics are the lack of democratic accountability at European level and the loss
of sovereignty of the individual country. According to Taggart, there are different
Euro-sceptic parties, some being more moderate than others. The strongest parties
can be found in Scandinavia and Central and Eastern Europe, particularly the Czech
Republic and Poland. However, Euro-scepticism has almost no expression in South-
ern Europe. Taggart differentiates the different Euro-sceptic movements as follows:

1   Complete opposition to the EU, because parties oppose its ideal.
2   Not opposed to the EU in principle, but are not convinced that this is the
best way to achieve inclusion, owing to the diversity of countries. These
parties emphasise the rights of states and want to prevent the EU becoming
a gateway for immigration.
3   Not opposed to the EU in principle, but are convinced that the present model
is too exclusive. The majority of left-wing Euro-sceptic parties fear that the
EU will lead to more inequalities in a global perspective (adapted from
Taggart, 1998: 365–6).

In Austria, the Austrian Freedom Party (Freiheitliche Partei Österreichs,
FPÖ) and the 2005 splinter party the Union for the Future of Austria (Bündnis
für die Zukunft Österreichs, BZÖ) are representatives of the new right, new
populism and Euro-scepticism. Both parties have right-wing policies based on
control of immigration, exhibit xenophobic tendencies and focus on law and order
issues. The FPÖ was originally a liberal party founded in 1956. However, the party
also offered a political home for many sympathisers and supporters of national
socialism. In 1986, the party was hijacked by Jörg Haider and became a new
populist party on the right, leading to a considerable increase in support for the
party. The liberal ideology was replaced by a more nationalist and anti-immigration
approach. It led to substantial gains in legislative elections. The climax came after
the 1999 elections, when the party got more votes than the ÖVP. This led to a
coalition government that caused some protests in Belgium and France. In spite of
this success, political infighting inside the party led to its split. Jörg Haider then
created the BZÖ in 2005. However, in spite of the split, both parties were able to
achieve considerable electoral success in the October 2008 legislative elections.
The death of Jörg Haider in a car accident on 11 October 2008 may contribute
to a reunification of both parties (*The Economist*, 16 October 2008).

The Swiss People's Party (Schweizerische Volkspartei, SVP) led by Christoph Blocher has become the largest party in Switzerland, in spite of its main leader being ostracised by the main parties. The SVP has roots among the rural parts of Switzerland that focus their resistance against the federal government in protecting the traditions of the country, particularly the militia democracy. However, these core attitudes are mixed with growing xenophobic and Euro-sceptic language. This was the main reason for the exclusion of Christoph Blocher from the federal government. In spite of the dominance of Blocher in the SVP, the party also has moderate politicians who are interested in preserving the consensual style of Swiss politics (McGann and Kitschelt, 2005).

The Danish People's Party (Dansk Folke Parti, DF), founded in 1995, is normally referred to as the successor of the Progress Party that emerged in the 1970s. The leader of the party is Pia Kjærsgaard. This is a new right party that advocates limitation of immigration and is Euro-sceptic. Since its inception it has been able to achieve 12–14 per cent of the vote and supported the government of Anders Fogh Rasmussen, which led a coalition government between 2001 and 2009 (Rydgren, 2004).

In 1946, Giorgio Almirante founded the Italian Social Movement (Movimento Sociale Italiano, MSI), which succeeded the Fascist Party of the inter-war period. The best electoral results were achieved in the 1970s, during a period of considerable instability in Italian politics. After 1993, new leader Gianfranco Fini decided to modernise the party by overcoming its association with fascism. He established a more moderate, new right party called the National Alliance (Alleanza Nazionale, AN), which moved towards the centre. AN became an important coalition partner of Forza Italia and Lega Nord on the right between 1994 and 2008. The party was keen to preserve the Italian identity, control immigration and prevent a federalisation of Italy (Ruzza and Schmidtke, 1996). Afterwards it merged with Forza Italia to form the People of Freedom (Popolo della Libertá, PdL) (*El Pais*, 30 March 2009: 8).

In the Netherlands, the former Pim Fortuyn List was reasonably successful in 2002, achieving more than 17 per cent of the vote. Pim Fortuyn was a sociology professor from Erasmus Rotterdam University. He was well liked by the population, because he tended to speak out on issues that were not necessarily politically correct, but struck a chord with the public. His controversial opinions on the relationship of Islam to homosexuality, or the lack of integration of the Muslim population in the Netherlands, were seen as provocative. Shortly before the elections, after a radio talk, he was shot by an environmentalist. This led to a sympathy vote at the 2002 elections. The party became part of the Balkenende II government, but after continued infighting within the party, early elections were called in 2003, and the party saw its electoral support disappear overnight. The party was dissolved in 2007 (van Holsteyn *et al.*, 2003; Bélanger and Aarts, 2006).

In Central and Eastern Europe several parties emerged that can be considered xenophobic and populist. In Slovakia, the People's Party – Movement for Democratic Slovakia (Ľudová strana – Hnutie za demokratické Slovensko, LS–HZDS) of Vladimír Mečiar used nationalist xenophobic language against minorities in Slovakia, particularly the Hungarians. In the 1990s it was one the strongest parties. The populist nationalist language was condemned by the European Union in 1998, leading to a change of government. The party is presently (in 2010) part of a coalition of populist parties such as Social-Democracy-Direction and the Slovak National Party. In Romania, the Great Romanian Party (Partidul Romania Mare, PRM) was founded in 1991 and is a neo-fascist party with xenophobic tendencies. The party has been able to achieve about one tenth of the votes in general elections. The main target group are the Hungarians living in Transylvania close to the Hungarian border, but also other minorities. In Bulgaria, the party National Union Attack (Natsionalen Săyuz Ataka) achieved 8.1 per cent and twenty-one seats in the 2005 elections. It is a xenophobic, populist party against the Turkish minority and it is also nationalist and therefore against NATO and the EU. In Poland, the Self-Defence of the Republic of Poland Party (Samoobrona Rzeczpospolitei Polskiei, SRB) of Andrej Lepper has so far been a Euro-sceptic populist party. It was part of the right-centre government of Jaroslaw Kaczynsky and lost considerably in the elections of 2007.

The green party family

The crisis of the exponential model of growth in most industrialised West European democracies and growing dissatisfaction of the younger generation with the established parties led to the emergence of green parties across Europe in the early 1980s. They formed a new party family that is quite established nowadays. The findings of the Club of Rome in its report (organised by Dennis Meadows, called *The Limits of Growth*), in which the scarcity of major raw materials, especially oil was predicted, contributed to the emergence of the model of sustainable development. This was reinforced by a UN conference in Stockholm in 1972. A milestone was the report of former Norwegian prime minister Harlem Grø Brundtland to the United Nations in 1987, in which sustainable growth and sustainable development are recommended for the way economic policy is undertaken. Another factor was the slow emergence of new set of cultural values in industrialised countries that also included concern over the deterioration of the environment. These post-materialist values were identified by Ronald Inglehart as the 'silent revolution' (see Chapters 3 and 13) (Inglehart, 1977; Inglehart and Welzel, 2005; Inglehart, 2008).

Among the most important green parties are those in Germany, Austria, Scandinavia, the Netherlands and Belgium. Most of these parties attract post-materialist voters, who want a change towards new clean and green technologies in all aspects of life, protection of the environment and more decisive steps towards an economic strategy of sustainable growth.

Green parties can be found mainly in the northern parts of Europe such as Germany, the Netherlands, Belgium and the Nordic countries. In Central and Eastern Europe one can find strong green parties in Estonia and the Czech Republic (see Figure 10.7).

Among the most prominent green parties are the German Greens (Bündnis '90/Grüne). During the 1970s, a vast movement against nuclear plants, proliferation of nuclear weapons and a strong peace movement in Germany had already started. Many of these groups decided to form the Green Party in 1980. Its ideology was related to the growing problems of a complex democracy and the deteriorating environment. The greens were then supporters of direct democracy and the social

Figure 10.7 The green parties in Europe

state. However, the green movement was quite divided between fundamentalists (*fundis*) and realists (*realos*). The *fundis* wanted to keep an anti-establishment, anti-party position, reinforcing the principles of direct democracy, particularly through prevention of professionalisation of politicians. The *realos* wanted to adopt a more moderate position and build a party that was able to take part in government and shape policy-making. In the end, the *realos* were able to win the debate in the Green Party, although some splinter groups left the party. For a long time, the greens were excluded from federal government, but were able to build some reputation as a coalition partner at regional level. During the reunification process, the greens made the mistake of being against it, and the party almost lost representation at the 1990 elections, failing to overcome the 5 per cent threshold. The greens fusioned with Federation '90 (Bündnis '90), which consisted mainly of the greens of East Germany. After 1990, the party was able to regain its previous electoral support. Between 1998 and 2005, the greens were part of the coalition government under Gerhard Schröder, finally achieving full integration into the political system. The Green Party is today regarded as an important party in Germany. It is supported mainly by a younger generation (Conradt, 2001: 126–9; Rudzio, 2006: 133–5).

In the Netherlands, the Green Left (Groenlinks), founded in 1990, is a small party achieving between 4 and 7 per cent of the vote. The party was a merger of several left-wing parties and combines both a left-wing critical ideology and green policies.

In Belgium, the federalisation process split the green movement into a Wallonian and a Flemish party. Both parties are small. The party Flemish Green! (Groen!) was founded in 1979 and can be considered one of the oldest members of this party family. It remained quite small, advocating similar issues to the German Greens, particularly ecological policies, participatory democracy and peace. It is very tolerant of alternative lifestyles. The Wallonian greens, Ecolo (Écologistes confédérés pour l'organisation de luttes originales, ECOLO), founded in 1980, also remained small (Delwit, 1999; Rihoux,1999). Both parties took part in the Verhoftstadt I government between 1999 and 2003. However, lack of experience and mismanagement of policy issues led to the collapse of the vote in the 2003 election. Nevertheless, the two parties were able to improve their position considerably in the 2007 general election. Groen! lost representation in 2003, but was able to return to parliament in 2007.

In the Nordic countries, there are also many small green parties. The most important are the Swedish Greens (Miljöpartiet de Gröna) founded in 1980. They receive about 4–6 per cent of the vote and are on the left of the party system. The Danish Greens (Enhedslisten–De Rød–Grønne–El), founded in 1983, are a Eurosceptic, anti-capitalist party. The Greens in Norway (Miljøpartiet Dei Grøne) were founded in 1988 as a merger of several lists.

In 2006 a Green Party was founded in Estonia: the Estonian Greens (Erakond Eestimaa Rohelised) got 7.1 per cent and six seats in the 2007 elections. And last, but not least, the Czech Green Party (Strana zelenych, SZ) was founded in 1990. Although the party has been characterised by bitter infighting, it was able to achieve parliamentary representation in the 2006 elections, receiving 6.1 per cent of the vote and six seats.

The regionalist party family

Stein Rokkan had already recognised in the 1970s that regionalism as a political movement was becoming more important. Since then, many European countries have formed strong regionalist parties that have been able to shape politics at national level (Rokkan and Urwin, 1983: 118) (see also Chapter 9; and Figure 10.8).

Transition to democracy in Spain led to the rise of the 'state of autonomies' (*estado de autonomias*) that allowed for the emergence of seventeen regional party systems.

Parties such as the right-centre Catalan Convergence and Union (Convergencia i Unió, CiU), the Basque Nationalist Party (Partido Nacionalista Vasco, PNV) and the Nationalist Galician Block (Bloque Nacionalista Gallego, BNG) have been able to achieve high levels of autonomy for their autonomous communities. The CiU consists of two parties that are right-centre with a mixed pragmatic Christian democratic and liberal ideology. It is the strongest party in Catalonia and wants to achieve more autonomy for the region. In 2005, leader Artur Mas renegotiated the Catalan Statute, the regional constitution, with the PSOE

Figure 10.8 The regionalist and ethnic minorities parties in Europe

government, which is still awaiting the decision of the constitutional court on its constitutionality. Although it is a small regionalist party in national terms, it may play a role in national politics if one of the main national parties is not able to achieve an absolute majority. Between 1979 and 1983, the autonomous community was dominated by CiU. Between 1979 and 2003, charismatic regional president Jordi Pujol played a major role in shaping the ideology of political Catalanism. For example, he would never speak in Spanish but only in Catalan (Magone, 2009a: 167–70; Etherinton and Fernandez, 2006).

The PNV is one of the oldest parties in Spain, originally founded in 1894. It is a moderate Basque regionalist party that seeks independence from Spain. However, it is quite divided between factions that want a referendum and adopt similar strategies to the Parti Quebecois in Canada, and those that want to achieve it through the parliamentary institutions. In 2001, Juan José Ibarretxe of PNV became regional president and tried to push the idea of 'association' with Spain, before full independence and the conduct of a referendum. This was rejected by the main parties in Madrid in 2005. Ibarretxe tried to revive his plan in 2007, but with growing opposition from the party. This rigid position of the regional president has delayed any reform of the statute. It really shows the difference between a pragmatic inclusionist model of nationalism as in Catalonia and a more rigid exclusionist one represented by the Basque Country. Owing to Basque terrorism through the terrorist organisation Basque Country and Freedom (Euskadi ta Askatasuna, ETA) and its radical positions, PNV is always under pressure to reconcile moderation with the radical aim of independence (Magone, 2009a: 170–1; Letamendia, 2006).

The Galician National Block (Bloco Nacionalista Galego, BNG) was founded in 1982 as a merger of several nationalist and left-wing small parties. Between 1982 and 2005, the charismatic Xosé Manuel Beiras was able to transform the party into the second largest party in Galicia. In spite of this success, infighting about strategy led to his replacement by Anxo Quintana. Between 2005 and 2009, BNG was a junior coalition partner of the regional government in Galicia (Keating, 2006). However, in the 1 March regional elections both the socialists and the Block were voted out of office (*El Pais*, 3 March 2009: 14).

In the United Kingdom, there are nationalist parties in the stateless nations of Scotland, Wales and Northern Ireland. The devolution process introduced by Tony Blair's government in 1997 led to the establishment of new regionalist party systems. In Scotland, the Scottish Nationalist party (SNP) was founded in 1934 and pursues independence for Scotland. The party has become the largest party in Scotland after the Scottish elections of 2007. It formed a minority government under First Minister Alex Salmond. The devolution process has led to different policies in Scotland and England, creating inequalities of access to university places and health care. In spite of its demand for independence, the SNP has been quite moderate in its policies and is very keen to achieve independence through peaceful democratic means.

The Party of Wales (Plaid Cymru, PC) was formed in 1925 and wants more autonomy for the region. It is a left-wing party and has improved its electoral support in the past decade. It is the second largest party after Labour achieving 25.5 per cent and fifteen seats (Jones, 2007b: 325–36).

In Northern Ireland there are several regionalist parties. They are divided into nationalist parties that want to join the Republic of Ireland such as Sinn Fein and the Social Democratic and Labour Party (SDLP), and loyalists to the British Crown such as the Democratic Unionist Party (DUP) and the Ulster Unionist Party (UUP). After very difficult negotiations between 1997 and 2007, a power-sharing agreement between the main political parties was achieved. Probably, the most Irish of the four political parties is Sinn Fein ('We, Ourselves'), which allegedly had links to the terrorist organisation Irish Republican Army (IRA). Many leaders of Sinn Fein were allegedly involved in the IRA. Certainly links between the two organisations exist, although denied by Sinn Fein. Sinn Fein is quite a traditional party founded in 1905 that played a major role in the Irish independence struggle. The party is also active in the Republic of Ireland. It campaigned against the Lisbon Treaty in the Irish referendum of 2008. The SDLP was founded in 1970 and is a moderate nationalist party. It was always committed to a peaceful settlement of the Northern Ireland problem. The movement of Sinn Fein to the centre has led to a decline in support for the SDLP. However, it remains an important party in Northern Irish politics because of its pragmatic and compromising attitude.

Among the unionists, the more radical is the DUP which was for many years under the leadership of Reverend Ian Paisley. More compromising, but always under pressure from the DUP, is the UUP, which was central to the peace process, particularly owing to the hard work of leader David Trimble. Together with John Hume, the former leader of the SDLP, he got the Nobel Prize for Peace in 1998. The vote of the UUP collapsed in 2005, while the DUP profited from its radical uncompromising position, which became a better position for negotiations with Sinn Fein, leading, as already mentioned, to the decommissioning of weapons and subsequently a power-sharing agreement (Tongue, 2007).

In Italy, the Northern League (Lega Nord per l'indipendenza della Padania, LN) was founded in 1991 as a merger of several small regional leagues, of which the Lombardian League (Lega Lombarda) was the strongest. It is a separatist party with populist and xenophobic tendencies led by Umberto Bossi. Throughout the 1980s the different leagues were only partly successful in gaining representation. However, the collapse of the Italian First Republic allowed the Northern League to expand in the north of Italy. Dissatisfaction with the government in Rome was a major factor for the success of the Northern League. LN refers always to the territory of 'Padania' which is defined as being all the regions north of the Po Valley. In the mid 1990s, Umberto Bossi tried to achieve the independence of Padania, however since 1998 there has been a shift towards greater autonomy and federalism. The party joined the Berlusconi coalitions of 1994, 2001 and 2008. During 2001 Umberto Bossi was minister for state reform and was instrumental in proposing a federal system for Italy. However, the referendum in the summer of 2006 led to rejection by the population. A negative aspect of the ideology of the LN is the anti-immigration discourse, particularly against African and Muslim immigrants. In the 2008 legislative elections, the LN won nationally 4.58 per cent and twenty-six seats (Diamanti, 1996; Donovan, 2008).

In Belgium, the separatist Flemish Interest (Vlaams Belang, VB), founded in 1979, has received increasing electoral support. The party advocates the independence of Flanders from Belgium through a 'Velvet Divorce' similar to that between the Czech Republic and Slovakia. The party is fairly xenophobic, particularly against the Muslim population and, like many other extreme right-wing/new right parties, it opposes Turkey joining the European Union. The predecessor Vlaamse Blok was found guilty of discriminatory language against foreigners by the Belgian Supreme Court in 2004, and therefore it changed the name to Vlaamse Belang. The other Belgian parties created a political *cordon sanitaire* around it, because of its xenophobic and law and order policies, with the result that VB is able to gain representation at the local level, but, despite its electoral strength, is prevented from joining the Flemish and the federal governments (Erk, 2005).

In Finland, the Swedish People's Party (Svenska Folkparti, SFP) was founded in 1906 and represents the Swedish minority, which is heavily concentrated in the south-western part of the country. The party is fairly socially heterogeneous and regularly takes part in coalition governments.

In the German *Land* of Schleswig-Holstein there is a small party representing the Danish and Frisian minorities: the South Schleswig Voter Federation (Südschleswigscher Wählerverband, SSW) was founded in 1948 and plays a major role in regional coalition politics. For example, following the 2005 regional elections its members decided to support the social democratic–green coalition government, though without taking part in it. This led to major protests from the CDU, which characterised this as an abuse of their status as a representative of the minorities. The party gets just 3–4 per cent of votes and is exempt from the 5 per cent threshold. Their policies are close to those of liberal parties in the Nordic countries that advocate social liberalism, meaning a strong welfare state and a flexible labour market (known as flexicurity).

Similar arrangements were made in Central and Eastern Europe for many parties representing minorities. This is the case of Hungarian minorities in Slovakia (Party of Hungarian Coalition – Strana maďarskej koalície – Magyar Koalíció Pártja) and in Romania (Hungarian Democratic Union of Romania – Uniunea Democratică Maghiară din România). The former achieves about 11–12 per cent of the vote, while the latter gets 6–7 per cent. In Romania, there are also representatives of other smaller minorities. In Bulgaria, the large Turkish minority is represented through the Movement for Rights and Freedoms (Dviženie za Prava i Svobodi, DPS) which achieved 12.9 per cent and thirty-four seats in the 2005 legislative elections.

Conclusions: the Americanisation of European politics

Throughout this chapter we discussed the importance of political parties in European politics. In spite of all the differences between party systems, all countries were or are being framed by traditional party families. The European parliament has become a centre of dissemination and learning processes between political parties.

Electoral market behaviour has become inherent to political parties in multi-level party systems. The growing importance of political marketing has led to moderation and even almost complete disappearance of ideological discourses and its replacement with personalisation and pragmatic electoral campaigns.

The traditional party families still have an important role to play in shaping electoral politics. Due partly to historical legacy, partly to ideological inclinations of the voters, they allow for a structuring of the party system. Although the larger parties, mainly social democrats and Christian democrats, tend to move to the centre and become similar in terms of ideology, it is still possible to recognise the divisions between left and right regarding, for example, how much the state should intervene in economy and society, the relationship between the state and the Church, the role of religion in public education, and how to decide moral issues (for example abortion and gay marriage).

Suggested reading

Important chapters and articles

Katz, Richard S. and Peter Mair (1995), Changing Models of Party Organization and Party Democracy, *Party Politics*, 1(1): 5–28.

—— and —— (2002), The Ascendancy of the Party in Public Office: Party Organizational Change in Twentieth-Century Democracies. In: Richard Gunther, José Ramón Montero and Juan J. Linz (eds), *Political Parties: Old Concepts and New Challenges*. Oxford: Oxford University Press, pp. 113–35.

Kitschelt, Herbert (1997), European Party System: Continuity and Change. In: Martin Rhodes, Paul Heywood and Vincent Wright (eds), *Developments in West European Politics*. Basingstoke: Macmillan, pp. 131–50.

Lipset, Seymour Martin (2001), The Americanization of the European Left, *Journal of Democracy*, 12(2): 74–87.

Mair, Peter (1993), Myths of Electoral Change and the Survival of Traditional Parties. The 1992 Stein Rokkan Lecture, *European Journal for Political Research*, 24: 121–33.

Mair, Peter and Ingrid van Biezen (2001), Party Membership in Twenty Democracies (1980–2000), *Party Politics*, 7(1): 5–21.

Olson, David M. (1998), Party Formation and Party System Consolidation in the New Democracies of Central Europe, *Political Studies*, 46(3): 432–64.

Important books

General on political parties

Gunther, Richard, José Ramón Montero and Juan J. Linz (eds) (2002), *Political Parties: Old Concepts and New Challenges*. Oxford: Oxford University Press.

Central and Eastern Europe

van Biezen, Ingrid (2003), *Political Parties in New Democracies*. Basingstoke: Palgrave. (*Party Politics*, electronic journal.)

Lewis, Paul G. (2003), *Political Parties in Post-Communist Eastern Europe*. London: Routledge.

Mair, Peter (1997), *Party System Change. Approaches and Interpretations*. Oxford: Oxford University Press.

Mair, Peter, Wolfgang C. Müller and Fritz Plasser (eds) (2004), *Political Parties and Electoral Change. Party Responses to Electoral Markets*. London: Sage.

Panebianco, Angelo (1988), *Political Parties: Organization and Power*. Cambridge: Cambridge University Press.

Pennings, Paul and Jan-Erik Lane (eds) (1998), *Comparing Party System Change*. London: Routledge.

Sartori, Giovanni (2005), *Parties and Party Systems: A Framework for Analysis*. Colchester: ECPR Press. (First published in 1976 by Cambridge University Press.)

On Western Europe

Broughton, David and Mark Donovan (eds) (1999), *Changing Party Systems in Western Europe*. London: Pinter.

On social democracy

Kitschelt, Herbert (1995), *The Transformation of European Social Democracy*. Cambridge: Cambridge University Press.

Ladrech, Robert and Philippe Marlière (eds) (1999), *Social Democratic Parties in the European Union: History, Organization, Policies*. Basingstoke: Palgrave.

Christian democracy and conservative parties

David Hanley (ed.) (1996), *Christian Democracy in Europe: A Comparative Perspective*. London: Continuum.

Communist parties

Bull, Martin J. and Paul Heywood (eds) (1994), *West European Communist Parties after the Revolutions of 1989*. London: Macmillan.

On populism

Taggart, Paul (2000), *Populism*. Buckingham: Open University Press.

QUESTIONS FOR REVISION

- What is understood under the 'cartel party'? Discuss, using examples from at least two countries.
- Compare the ideologies of the main political party families.
- Why is membership of political parties declining? Discuss, using examples from at least two different countries.
- Compare political parties in 'old' and 'new' democracies. Discuss, using examples from at least two countries.
- How would you explain the emergence of 'new populist' parties in Europe?

Chapter 11

Elections and party systems

- The impact of electoral systems on party systems
- Party systems in Europe
  - The Nordic model
  - The British model: majoritarian democracy at work
  - The French model
  - The Drei-Sat model: Germany, Austria and Switzerland
  - Party systems and the single transferable vote: Ireland and Malta
  - The Benelux countries
  - The Southern European countries
  - The Central European countries: Hungary, the Czech Republic, Slovakia and Poland
  - The Baltic countries
  - The south-eastern model: Bulgaria and Romania
  - Party system consolidation in the Balkans
- Multilevel electoral arenas
- Conclusions: the intertwinedness of electoral and party systems

SUMMARY OF CHAPTER 11

In this chapter, we discuss the intertwinedness of electoral and party systems. The electoral system chosen by the political elites will lead to a certain party system. Electoral engineering can create more consensual or polarised party systems. There is also the possibility that electoral systems may not work, which could lead to the collapse of a political system, such as, for example, during the Weimar Republic and the Spanish Second Republic.

There are at least three important aspects in the design of electoral systems:

- the type of electoral system: for example, proportional representation, plurality system or mixed system among others;
- the electoral threshold that parties need to achieve to get representation in parliament (for example, Germany: 5 per cent; Sweden: 4 per cent; Austria: Grundmandat/first elected seat);
- the magnitude of the constituency: at one extreme are large constituencies (for example, the whole country of the Netherlands is the constituency) and, at the other, small constituencies (for example, Spain has fifty-two mainly small constituencies).

In Western Europe, party systems are shaped by political traditions and political cleavages have evolved over time. Marketisation and Americanisation have limited the role of the socio-political cleavages, nevertheless today new parties still have difficulties in challenging established ones.

In Southern Europe and Central and Eastern Europe party systems have had to be built anew during democratic transition and are less connected to previous socio-political traditions because of the long authoritarian/totalitarian periods. Many party systems in Central and Eastern Europe (e.g. Poland, Bulgaria and Latvia) are still awaiting consolidation.

Today, electoral systems are multilevel, including local, regional, national and European elections. Party systems are therefore multilevel as well, and electoral strategies have to take into account the sequence of the elections.

The impact of electoral systems on party systems

Before we turn to an analysis of the party systems in Europe, it is important to review the main aspects of the relationship between party and electoral systems. The selection of an electoral system during the constitutional settlement is probably one of the most important tasks of a political elite. It has to take into account whether it wants political stability or whether to emphasise representation of all political forces. For example, during the Spanish constitutional settlement, the political elite opted for political stability by creating small constituencies with a threshold of 3 per cent, while preserving some proportionality through the adoption of the D'Hondt electoral system. Furthermore, political parties dominate the electoral process and, because the lists are closed, there is no preferential voting. MPs represent the whole country, not the constituency in which they were elected. The result is an electoral system that favours the larger parties and discriminates against the smaller parties. However, it is a system that allows strong regionalist parties to achieve representation at national level (Magone, 2009b: 133–41). For example, in 1949 the Federal Republic of Germany opted for political stability, although it tried to balance this with a high level of proportional representation, meaning that half the seats are elected by a plurality system (first-past-the-post) and half by proportional representation. There is a 5 per cent threshold, so that fragmentation of the party system is avoided. In each election, the citizen has two votes, one for the constituency seats, and one for the proportional representation section. In this sense, the Germans may act strategically by splitting the vote among two parties in order to achieve a coalition government on the right or on the left. The German system also shows that, after adopting the basic aspects of the electoral system, it can take some time before an electoral system becomes permanent and fine-tuning will often be necessary. For example, it took until 1956 to finally fine-tune the German electoral system to ensure it is valid at both national and *Länder* level (Scarrow, 2003: 62). In both Spain and Germany, the national political elites wanted to adopt an electoral system that would produce stable party systems in order to prevent the instability and uncertainty of the Second Republic and the ensuing Spanish Civil War, in the case of Spain, and those of the Weimar Republic and the ensuing national socialist dictatorship in the case of Germany. Other devices were also developed to strengthen party government and prevent insecurity zones when choosing the prime minister or chancellor.

A mixed system is used in Hungary. In the same way as in Spain, the electoral system was a complex compromise achieved in round-table negotiations in 1989 during the democratic transition. Political stability was an important point of deliberation in these negotiations (Benoit, 2003: 478). The Hungarian electoral system differs slightly from the German one in that 45.5 per cent of the 386 MPs are elected in single-member constituencies, 38 per cent in multi-member constituencies and 16.5 per cent from national lists. The third level can be compared to the compensatory seats of the German system, which are redistributed according to proportional representation in order to compensate for any inequalities in the distribution of seats at the lower levels. Another difference from the German system is that Hungary uses a version of the two-ballot electoral method for the single constituency seats. The threshold to participate in the second round is 15 per cent (Benoit, 2003: 478). The Hungarian model emulated the German system, and was able to create one of the most stable party systems in Central and Eastern Europe.

In Lithuania, the electoral system is similar to the Hungarian system, using the two-ballot system for single constituencies, but it does not allocate compensatory seats. This means that the two systems are independent from each other, so it is known as a parallel system.

More radical approaches were used by France and Italy. In 1958, President Charles de Gaulle introduced a new constitution that was designed to overcome the unstable situation of the Fourth Republic (1946–58). One of the crucial changes in the new constitution was the introduction of a new majoritarian two-ballot system that aimed at making governments more stable. Moreover, the new constitution weakened the powers of parliament considerably, so that power was transferred to the executive. Furthermore, in 1962 the direct election of the president for a seven-year period with the possibility of re-election was introduced, however in 2000 the time span was changed to five years with the possibility of re-election. The outcome of the new electoral system for legislative elections was that political parties were forced to form electoral coalitions in order to survive the first round and take part in the second. Each coalition supports the candidate with the best chance of election at constituency level, regardless of which party he or she belongs to. A candidate is elected if they win the election with at least 25 per cent of the vote in the first ballot and only candidates who pass the 12.5 per cent threshold are allowed to take part in the second round (however, if there is only one candidate who achieves this threshold, the runner-up can also take part). In contemporary French politics, this leads to coalitions on the right and on the left. The Union of People's Majority (UMP) will often form coalitions with smaller right-centre parties, such as the Union of French Democracy (UDF), and the socialists will often do so with the communists and greens.

The changes to the political system have indeed led to more stability in the French political system; however, this was at the cost of proportional representation of all the different groups. The French electoral system is one of the most disproportional of Europe (Knapp and Wright, 2001: 252–5).

After the implosion of the Tangentopoli corruption scandal in 1992, the new Italian political elite tried to reform the political system in general and the electoral system in particular. Until 1992, Italy used a system that largely favoured proportional representation, with multiple preferential choices. This led to a highly fragmented party system and considerable governmental instability (forty-eight governments between 1948 and 1992). The new electoral system, designed to create greater political stability (Katz, 2003) and applied for the first time in 1994, was a mixed system, with 75 per cent elected at the single-constituency level and 25 per cent through a national proportional list. This meant that parties were forced to create electoral alliances in order to be able to compete. One consequence was the establishment, on the one hand, of a right-centre coalition consisting basically of Silvio Berlusconi's Forza Italia, Umberto Bossi's Lega Nord and Gianfranco Fini's National Alliance, and, on the other hand, of a left-centre coalition consisting of the Party of the Democrats of the Left and some other smaller parties. The new electoral party system bipolarised the party system along the left–right ideological axis.

The left-centre coalition had more difficulty in competing in the new electoral system than the right-centre. In 2001, Silvio Berlusconi's House of Freedoms alliance was able to win an absolute majority and create the first government that was able to govern through the five-year period of the legislature.

However, in December 2005, the Berlusconi government changed the electoral system back to proportional representation. The only difference was that the alliance with most of the votes would get an automatic absolute majority in the Chamber of Deputies. This new electoral system was designed to achieve greater political stability by awarding the strongest party an automatic absolute majority of 55 per cent in the lower Chamber of Deputies. In the 2006 elections, the left-centre won the elections and Romano Prodi became the prime minister. However, the coalition government began to fragment, and some MPs left their parties to form new ones. At one stage, the coalition government could not rely on a majority

Table 11.1 Electoral systems for national elections, lower chamber

Electoral systems		Countries
Majoritarian systems	Plurality, simple majority, first-past-the-post-system (FPTP)	UK
	Two-ballot system	France
Parallel systems		Lithuania
Mixed systems	Simple majority/ PR Sainte-Laguë	Germany
	Two-ballot system/ Hagenbach-Bischoff	Hungary
Proportional representation	Simple majority/ PR Hare-Niemeyer/ Hagenbach-Bischoff	Greece, Austria (first level) Slovakia
	D'Hondt	Portugal Spain Belgium Netherlands, Luxembourg Bulgaria (until 2009) Czech Republic Poland Romania (until 2008) Austria (second level) Switzerland Estonia (second level modified D'Hondt) Italy Slovenia Croatia Serbia Montenegro Macedonia
	Modified Saint-Laguë	Denmark Sweden, Norway Iceland Latvia Estonia (first level) Bosnia-Herzegovina
	STV	Ireland Malta

Source: Parline, Database of International Parliamentary Union, www.ipu.org (accessed 4 June 2010)

Figure 11.1 Electoral systems for national general elections, lower chamber

in the Senate, therefore early elections were called in 2008. In October 2008, Silvio Berlusconi's Party of Freedoms won the legislative and was able to profit from the new electoral system (see Table 11.1. and Figure 11.1).

The British electoral system has probably been the most stable of all European systems. The simple plurality system (also popularly called first-past-the-post system, FPTP) is constituency based and declares the candidate that gets the most votes to be the winner. This means that one can get elected with a simple majority of one vote over all other candidates. In this sense, it is important to have the resources of large political parties to achieve a majority of seats across the country. The party machinery allows for organised politics, otherwise it would be very fragmented. Party discipline through the team of whips becomes an important issue, so that such parties do not fragment in order to represent only the interests of the constituencies. This also means that some parties may achieve a respectable proportional share of the vote, but still have no seats in parliament. The constituency-based election is the most important one, and therefore proportional representation electoral results are not relevant. This system creates stability, but the price is distorted representation, with only two-and-a-half parties represented at national level: Labour, Conservative and the Liberal Democrat.

The fairest electoral systems in terms of proportional representation are probably those found in the Netherlands and the Nordic countries, all of which use some form of proportional representation and also have quite fragmented party systems. In the Dutch Parliament there are regularly ten or more parties, and the same is true for Denmark, Norway and Finland. In the Netherlands, there is only one national constituency, although candidates are allocated to eighteen sub-constituencies. Parties need only to overcome the low threshold of 0.67 per cent to get representation in the lower chamber, the Tweede Kamer. In Sweden the 4 per cent threshold prevents party system fragmentation and its party system, in which the social democrats dominate is more stable. Proportional representation systems for the lower chamber are also dominant in Southern Europe, in Bulgaria (until 2009), Romania, Poland, the Czech Republic, Slovakia and Slovenia. Many Central and Eastern European countries have experimented with electoral systems, but political instability has forced many of them to include electoral thresholds in order to prevent fragmentation of the party system. Today, all Central and Eastern European countries have some kind of electoral thresholds (mostly about 5 per cent) for single parties and staggered higher thresholds for coalitions.

In terms of proportional representation electoral systems, it is important to differentiate between different methods: the d'Hondt system, the Saint-Lague, the Hare system and single transferable vote. The difference is that the d'Hondt and Saint-Lague systems use a division quotient, whereas the Hare system is calculated based on a subtraction quotient.

- *D'Hondt system*: This system was developed by the Belgian mathematician Victor D'Hondt at the end of the nineteenth century. It was adopted in 1899 in Belgium and in 1906 in Finland. The D'Hondt system divides the quotient by 1, 2, 3 until it has allocated all the seats. The steep division is favourable to larger parties. This system is used in Portugal, Spain, Belgium, the Netherlands, Luxembourg, the Czech Republic and Bulgaria.
- *Saint-Lague system*: This system was developed by the French mathematician André Saint-Lague and is based on the largest average, so that the quotient is divided by 1, 2, 3, 4 and so on. It is more moderate and helps smaller parties.
- *Modified Saint-Lague system*: This system lies between the d'Hondt and the pure Saint-Lague system. It uses a quotient of 1, 4, 3, 5. It is used in most Nordic countries with the exception of Finland that uses the d'Hondt system. It is also used in Latvia and Bosnia-Herzegovina.
- *Hagenbach-Bischoff'sche system*: This also uses a quotient that is based on the total number of votes received by the parties divided by the number of seats plus one. Afterwards the votes of each party are divided by the quotient to see how many seats can be allocated. Remaining seats are allocated based on who gets the highest quotient when divided by the already allocated seats plus one. This electoral method is used in Greece, but also at first level in Austria. It is a system that favours larger parties, something which is evident in Greece.

- *Single transferable system (STV or Hare-Clark system)*: This uses a subtraction quotient based on division of total sum of votes by number of seats. STV also includes the opportunity to rank candidates according to preference, so there is a lengthy electoral process before the results can be announced. Indeed, it may take several days until one knows the exact results. It is used in Ireland, as well as in Northern Ireland and in Malta.

The variety of electoral systems in Europe has allowed for the creation of different party systems and also for different styles of politics, contributing to the establishment of majoritarian or consensus democracies (see Chapter 5).

According to Douglas Rae, all electoral systems favour the larger parties, the only question that remains is about the extent of such disadvantage. Electoral engineering plays a major role in shaping such relationships between larger and smaller parties (Rae, 1967), and once the electoral system has been agreed on, it is difficult to change the rules of the game. However, some parties have tried to do this. For example, in 1986 the French government, controversially, changed the electoral system to proportional representation, only to have the two-ballot system reinstated in time for the following elections. In Greece, Andreas Papandreou changed the electoral system before the 1989 general elections, in order to gain an advantage for his party PASOK against his main opponent New Democracy (ND). The result was a hung parliament, which led to a coalition government between ND and the communist parties against PASOK (Pridham and Verney, 1991). Therefore, it is important that the electoral system that is agreed on should be supported by all the political parties, otherwise democracy and the stability of the political system may suffer.

As already mentioned, there are at least three devices that can shape the electoral system towards more stability with a reduced number of parties or more proportional representation with a large number of parties.

First, the creation of an electoral threshold contributes to a reduction of small parties being represented in parliament. Many countries use a threshold at national level to reduce party fragmentation, for example Germany (5 per cent), the Czech Republic (5 per cent) or Sweden (4 per cent). On the other hand, Spain uses a threshold of 3 per cent at the constituency level, while some countries, such as France (12.5 per cent) and Hungary (15 per cent), use thresholds for candidates in single-constituency elections to advance to the second round.

Second, some countries use the direct mandate (*Grundmandat*), which means that a party is able to achieve a seat in a constituency and is therefore eligible to take part in the second round of allocation of seats. This is the case in Austria. Germany has a similar system for parties that do not achieve the 5 per cent threshold but are able to get seats in their electoral strongholds. The Party of Democratic Socialism (PDS) was able to profit from this rule in the 2002 legislative elections, because they achieved direct mandates in Berlin. However, the PDS was not allowed to form a parliamentary group (*Fraktion*) in the Bundestag, but just a group (*Gruppe*) with fewer rights in the internal workings of parliament.

Third, inclusion or exclusion of parties can be achieved through the size of the constituency. A very large multi-member constituency with a low threshold is favourable to small parties, whereas a small multi-member constituency contributes to the exclusion of small parties. General elections in the Netherlands are conducted in a very large constituency that actually comprises the whole country, meaning that the threshold is very low at 0.67 per cent. The result is a high level of representation of small parties. In contrast, Spain is divided into fifty-two constituencies, most of which are quite small. This is reinforced by a threshold of 3 per cent, which means that only the larger parties, PSOE and PP, are able to achieve representation; smaller parties such as IU only have a limited chance of getting MPs elected. However, parties strong in a particular region, such as the regionalist parties in Spain, have a better chance of getting MPs elected than smaller parties that put forward candidates nationally.

All this shows that electoral systems produce different levels of disproportionality. Even if countries have the same electoral system, the particular characteristics of the individual system may lead to different levels of disproportionality. In this context, the UK and France have probably the most disproportionate systems because they use plurality/majoritarian systems (see Table 11.2). In spite of the use or partial use respectively of proportional representation of the Polish and Lithuanian electoral systems, both can match the levels of disproportionality of

Table 11.2 Categorisation of some electoral systems, according to disproportionality (simplified)

Level of disportionality	Majoritarian/ plurality	Mixed	Proportional representation
High level	UK France		Lithuania Poland Greece Spain
Middle level			Norway Iceland Czech Republic Portugal
Low level		Germany Hungary	Ireland Belgium Luxembourg Finland Malta Austria Slovakia Sweden Slovenia Bulgaria Latvia Switzerland Denmark Netherlands

Sources: Adapted and simplified from Farrell, 2000: 157–9

the UK and France. Although high levels of disproportionality can also be found in the Greek and Spanish electoral systems, which considerably favour the larger parties and are disadvantageous for the smaller parties, these electoral systems still have lower levels of disproportionality than the UK and France.

In sum, the design of electoral systems matters. Sometimes, political systems may be characterised by high levels of political instability because of an ill-designed electoral system. In this sense, there is a close relationship between electoral and party systems (Table 11.3).

Table 11.3 Electoral cycles and levels in Europe

Electoral levels	Countries
National and local level elections	Norway Iceland Croatia Serbia Macedonia Montenegro
National, local and European elections	Portugal Ireland Greece Netherlands Luxembourg Sweden Finland Denmark Lithuania Latvia Estonia Bulgaria Romania Slovenia
National, local and regional	Switzerland Bosnia-Herzegovina
National, local, regional and European elections	Germany Austria Spain Belgium UK France Italy Poland Slovakia Czech Republic

Source: Author

Before we turn to a description and analysis of national party systems, it is important to just make a note on turnout in general elections. As Figure 11.2 shows, turnout is quite diverse among European countries. On average, turnout is quite high in the Nordic countries, the Netherlands, Belgium, Luxembourg, Italy, Malta and Cyprus. In contrast, it is quite low in Central and Eastern European countries. The pattern is that in the first founding elections most populations in the Central and Eastern European countries tend to go to the polls achieving a high turnout, however, disappointment and disenchantment with the political elites can lead to a steep decline in turnout in subsequent elections. There were, therefore, major differences between elections in Central and Eastern European countries in the 1990s and after 2000. In the 1990s, there were still figures above 70 per cent in many countries, but after 2000 turnout declined to below that figure. Germany, Austria, Greece, Portugal, Spain, France, the United Kingdom and Ireland fall in between the Nordic and Central and Eastern European countries. Turnout is important, because, if low, it can open a range of opportunities for more radical parties.

Figure 11.2 Turnout at general elections in European countries on average, between 2000 and 2009 in percentage

Party systems in Europe

The Nordic model

Scandinavian parties were characterised by considerable stability until the 1960s. A freezing of party systems occurred during the inter-war period, and in the post-1945 period, five parties regularly gained electoral representation in the different parliaments: the social democrats, the conservatives, the liberals and the centre party. In all the party systems in Scandinavia, the Social Democrats were the strongest party and were able to implement strong welfare policies in coalition with other parties. In the 1970s and 1980s, a high level of electoral volatility led to the emergence of new political parties (for example, the greens and the Christian democrats), including Euro-sceptic parties (for example, the Progress Party in Norway and the Danish People's Party in Denmark). This fragmentation of the electoral vote also led to considerable volatility between the main parties (Table 11.4).

Traditionally, Nordic electorates have a high turnout. In Sweden, Denmark and Iceland turnout in the past two decades has been over 80 per cent, while in Norway the turnout has been above 70 per cent. In fact, over the same period, turnout has declined in Finland considerably, where it is now at 65 per cent. However, in the 1970s Sweden, Iceland and Denmark had turnout figures of over or around 90 per cent. Finland and Norway had a turnout of over 80 per cent. In spite of this decline, Nordic electorates have the highest turnout in Europe.

One particular aspect of party system change has been the declining electoral support for social democratic parties across the regions. Some of the parties achieved over 40 per cent of the vote in the 1950s and 1960s, but this has declined considerably since the 1970s.

This is the case in Finland, where three main parties dominate: the social democrats, the conservatives and the centre party. in the past decade the centre party has been successful in dominating the political system. Other parties able to establish themselves in the past three decades are the Christian democrats and the greens, both of which play an important role in coalition-building – the main form of government in Finland because of the lack of clear majorities. In contrast, the liberals declined considerably and now (in 2010) have no representation. Since 1999, a new right party called True Finns, which is Euro-sceptic and uses anti-immigration language, has been increasing its vote (Figure 11.3).

In Sweden, the Social Democratic Party has declined considerably since the 1970s. However, it is still the largest party, and is the only party that achieves more than 30 per cent of the vote. The Social Democrats governed the country for most of the post-1945 period. The right-centre opposition is fragmented into different parties, of which the moderates are the strongest. A considerable decline in social democracy and the popularity of the Social Democrats in the elections of 2006 led to the establishment of a right-centre coalition government, led by Fredrik Reinfeldt from the Moderate Party. Other parties that formed the coalition are the Christian Democrats, the Centre Party and the Liberals. This bipolarisation between left and right has become more marked since the 1970s. The threshold of 4 per

Table 11.4 Old and new political parties in the Nordic countries, before and after 1970

| Party systems until 1970s | Party system after 1970 | | | | | | |
	Social Democrats	Conservatives	Centre	Liberals	Communists/ Radical Left	Greens	Christian-Democrats	Eurosceptic/ xenophobic parties
Sweden	Sveriges socialdemokratiska arbetareparti (SAP)	Moderata samlingspartiet (M)	Centerpartiet (C)	Folkpartiet liberalerna	Vänster partiet	Miljöpartiet de Gröna	Krist demokraterna	
Finland	Suomen Sosialidemokraattinen Puolue (SDP)	Kansallinen Kokoomus, KOK	Suomen Keskusta, KESK	Svenska folkpartiet (SFP)	Vasemmis Toliitto (VAS)	Vihreät, Vihr	Kristillis demokraatit,	Perussuomalaiset
Denmark	Socialdemokraterne	Det Konservative Folkeparti		Venstre Danmarks Liberale Venstre	Socialistisk Folkeparti	Enhedslisten	Kristen demokraterne	Dansk Folke parti
Norway	Det norske Arbeiderparti	Høyre	Senterpartiet	Venstre	Sosialistisk Venstreparti	Miljøpartiet De Grønne	Kristelig Folkeparti	Fremskritts partiet)
Iceland	Samfylkingin (Socialdemocratic Alliance)	Sjálfstæðis flokkurinn (Independence Party)	Ramsóknar flokkurinn (Progressive Party)	Frjálslyndi flokkurinn (Liberal Party)		Vinstrihrey fingin – grænt framboð		

Source: Author

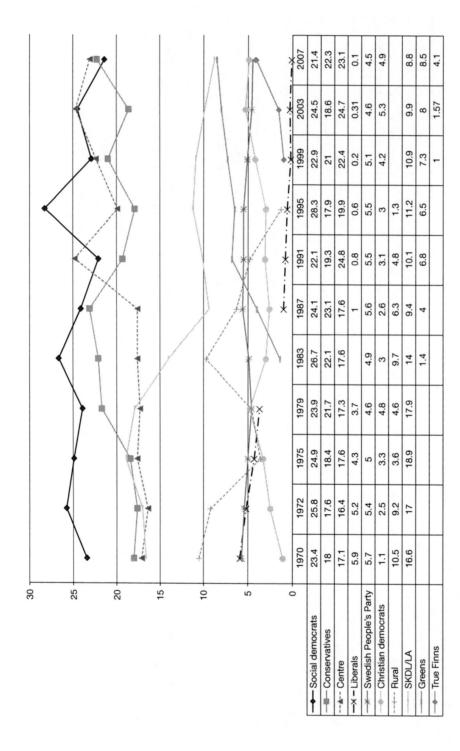

	1970	1972	1975	1979	1983	1987	1991	1995	1999	2003	2007
Social democrats	23.4	25.8	24.9	23.9	26.7	24.1	22.1	28.3	22.9	24.5	21.4
Conservatives	18	17.6	18.4	21.7	22.1	23.1	19.3	17.9	21	18.6	22.3
Centre	17.1	16.4	17.6	17.3	17.6	17.6	24.8	19.9	22.4	24.7	23.1
Liberals	5.9	5.2	4.3	3.7		1	0.8	0.6	0.2	0.31	0.1
Swedish People's Party	5.7	5.4	5	4.6	4.9	5.6	5.5	5.5	5.1	4.6	4.5
Christian democrats	1.1	2.5	3.3	4.8	3	2.6	3.1	3	4.2	5.3	4.9
Rural	10.5	9.2	3.6	4.6	9.7	6.3	4.8	1.3			
SKDL/LA	16.6	17	18.9	17.9	14	9.4	10.1	11.2	10.9	9.9	8.8
Greens					1.4	4	6.8	6.5	7.3	8	8.5
True Finns							1	1.57	1	1.57	4.1

Figure 11.3 General elections in Finland, 1970–2007

Source: Ministry of the Interior, Finland, available online at: www.vaalit.fi (accessed 4 June 2010) (Auffermann, 2009: 231)

cent is a major hurdle for small parties, with only the Greens and the Left Alliance (a follow-up organisation of the former Communist Party, with a more pragmatic, less ideological approach to social issues) able to get representation. The orthodox Communist Party no longer achieves representation. Both the Greens and the Left Alliance are potential coalition partners for the Social Democrats, although the Social Democrats usuallyprefer a minority government than to form a coalition with other parties (Figure 11.4).

Since the elections of 1973, the Danish electoral system has been considerably fragmented, which has also led to polarisation between left and right. The Social Democrats declined considerably electorally, whereas right-centre parties have been able to improve their electoral position in the past decade. The Liberals have become a pivotal party in gathering together the right-centre parties. Between 2001 and 2009, former party leader Anders Føgh Rasmussen has led a right-centre coalition government with the parliamentary support of the Euro-sceptics and anti-immigration Danish People's Party, which has been growing steadily since 1998 to its current 13.9 per cent of the vote. The right-centre coalition consists of the Conservative People's Party, the Liberals and the Centre Party (Figure 11.5).

In Norway, the Labour Party has declined considerably, as have the conservatives. In the 1970s, the Euro-sceptic and anti-immigration Progress Party was able to establish itself as part of the party system. The Conservatives usually join with with the Liberals, Christian Democrats and Centre Party to form a government coalition. In 2001, Conservative leader Kjell Magne Bondevik formed a coalition government with the Liberals, Christian Democrats and Centre Party, which was dependent on the parliamentary support of the Progress Party. However, in the 2005 elections a coalition of the Labour Party with the Socialist People's Party and Red–Green Alliance led to a change of government. This means that individual parties are not able to achieve absolute majorities and have to build coalitions on the right or left accordingly. Furthermore, a moderate polarisation between left and right is taking place in Norway (Figure 11.6).

In Iceland, the Independence Party and Social Democrats are the dominant parties of the political system. There has been greater cooperation between the Conservatives, the Social Democrats and the Progressive Party and, despite the differences, consensual politics among parties of different ideological positions has also been common since independence. Among the new parties, one has to emphasise the Green Party that emerged only after 1999. However, the global financial crisis hit Iceland quite hard and led to the resignation of the government under the leadership of Prime Minister Geir Haarde after massive protests by the population. The April 2009 legislative elections led to considerable losses for the conservative Independence Party which had run the country since independence, and this, in turn, led to substantial gains for the Social Democratic Alliance and the Left Green movement. Both formed the first left-wing coalition government in the history of Iceland under the first female premiership of Johanna Sigurdardottir (Figure 11.7).

In sum, all the Nordic countries have been affected by party system changes since the 1970s, with the traditional five party system of Social Democrats, Conservatives, Liberals, Centre Party and Communists being challenged by new parties, such as the Greens or the Progress Party, in the 1970s. Today, the Danish,

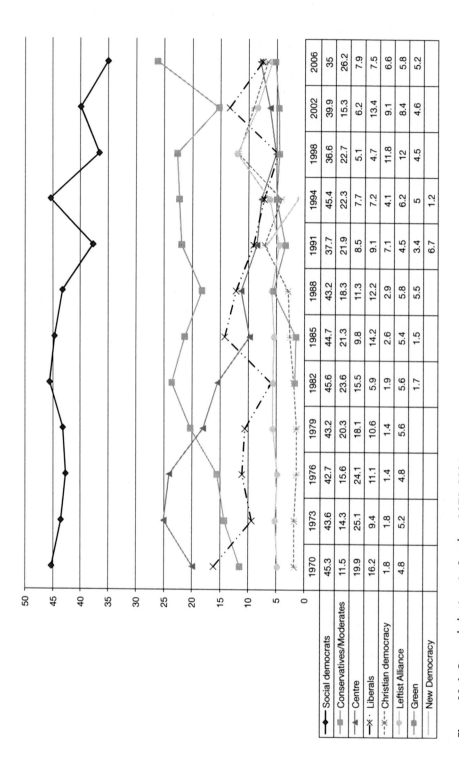

	1970	1973	1976	1979	1982	1985	1988	1991	1994	1998	2002	2006
Social democrats	45.3	43.6	42.7	43.2	45.6	44.7	43.2	37.7	45.4	36.6	39.9	35
Conservatives/Moderates	11.5	14.3	15.6	20.3	23.6	21.3	18.3	21.9	22.3	22.7	15.3	26.2
Centre	19.9	25.1	24.1	18.1	15.5	9.8	11.3	8.5	7.7	5.1	6.2	7.9
Liberals	16.2	9.4	11.1	10.6	5.9	14.2	12.2	9.1	7.2	4.7	13.4	7.5
Christian democracy	1.8	1.8	1.4	1.4	1.9	2.6	2.9	7.1	4.1	11.8	9.1	6.6
Leftist Alliance	4.8	5.2	4.8	5.6	5.6	5.4	5.8	4.5	6.2	12	8.4	5.8
Green					1.7	1.5	5.5	3.4	5	4.5	4.6	5.2
New Democracy								6.7	1.2			

Figure 11.4 General elections in Sweden, 1970–2006

Source: Statistics Sweden database, available online at: www.scb.se/Pages/ProductTables_____12287.aspx (accessed 4 June 2010)

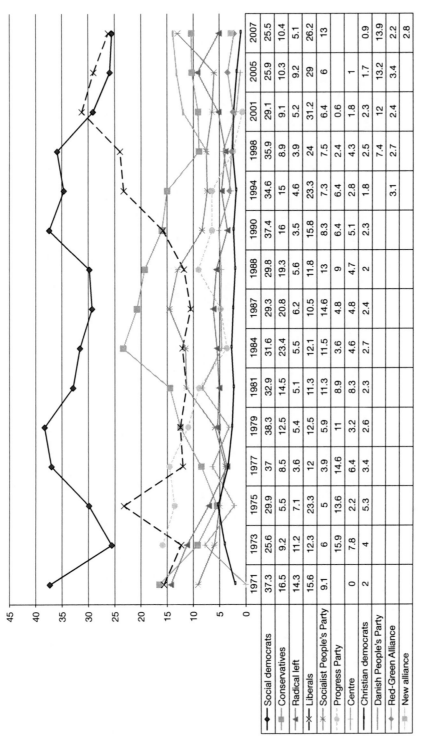

	1971	1973	1975	1977	1979	1981	1984	1987	1988	1990	1994	1998	2001	2005	2007
Social democrats	37.3	25.6	29.9	37	38.3	32.9	31.6	29.3	29.8	37.4	34.6	35.9	29.1	25.9	25.5
Conservatives	16.5	9.2	5.5	8.5	12.5	14.5	23.4	20.8	19.3	16	15	8.9	9.1	10.3	10.4
Radical left	14.3	11.2	7.1	3.6	5.4	5.1	5.5	6.2	5.6	3.5	4.6	3.9	5.2	9.2	5.1
Liberals	15.6	12.3	23.3	12	12.5	11.3	12.1	10.5	11.8	15.8	23.3	24	31.2	29	26.2
Socialist People's Party	9.1	6	5	3.9	5.9	11.3	11.5	14.6	13	8.3	7.3	7.5	6.4	6	13
Progress Party		15.9	13.6	14.6	11	8.9	3.6	4.8	9	6.4	6.4	2.4	0.6		
Centre	0	7.8	2.2	6.4	3.2	8.3	4.6	4.8	4.7	5.1	2.8	4.3	1.8	1	0.9
Christian democrats	2	4	5.3	3.4	2.6	2.3	2.7	2.4	2	2.3	1.8	2.5	2.3	1.7	
Danish People's Party												7.4	12	13.2	13.9
Red-Green Alliance											3.1	2.7	2.4	3.4	2.2
New alliance															2.8

Figure 11.5 General elections in Denmark, 1971–2007

Source: Nannestad, 2009: 88

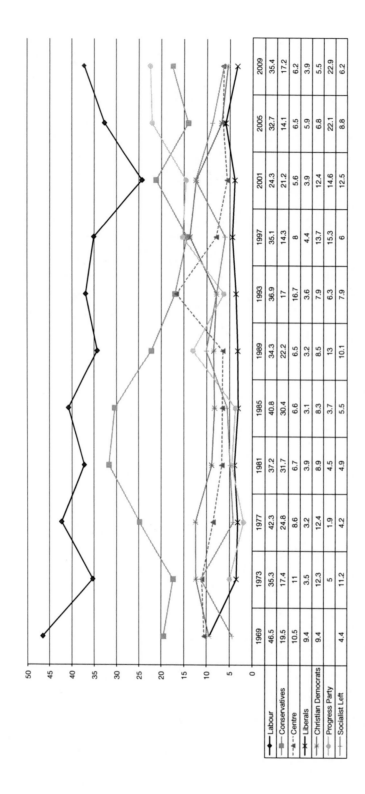

	1969	1973	1977	1981	1985	1989	1993	1997	2001	2005	2009
Labour	46.5	35.3	42.3	37.2	40.8	34.3	36.9	35.1	24.3	32.7	35.4
Conservatives	19.5	17.4	24.8	31.7	30.4	22.2	17	14.3	21.2	14.1	17.2
Centre	10.5	11	8.6	6.7	6.6	6.5	16.7	8	5.6	6.5	6.2
Liberals	9.4	3.5	3.2	3.9	3.1	3.2	3.6	4.4	3.9	5.9	3.9
Christian Democrats	9.4	12.3	12.4	8.9	8.3	8.5	7.9	13.7	12.4	6.8	5.5
Progress Party		5	1.9	4.5	3.7	13	6.3	15.3	14.6	22.1	22.9
Socialist Left	4.4	11.2	4.2	4.9	5.5	10.1	7.9	6	12.5	8.8	6.2

Figure 11.6 General elections in Norway, 1969–2009

Source: Gross and Rothholz, 2009: 173; Ministry for Communes and Regional Department for 2009 result posted at www.scb.se/Pages/ProductTables_____12287.aspx (accessed 4 June 2010)

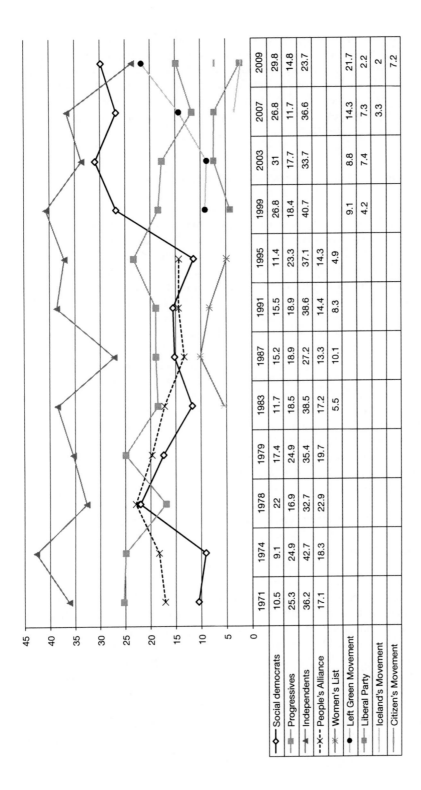

	1971	1974	1978	1979	1983	1987	1991	1995	1999	2003	2007	2009
Social democrats	10.5	9.1	22	17.4	11.7	15.2	15.5	11.4	26.8	31	26.8	29.8
Progressives	25.3	24.9	16.9	24.9	18.5	18.9	18.9	23.3	18.4	17.7	11.7	14.8
Independents	36.2	42.7	32.7	35.4	38.5	27.2	38.6	37.1	40.7	33.7	36.6	23.7
People's Alliance	17.1	18.3	22.9	19.7	17.2	13.3	14.4	14.3				
Women's List					5.5	10.1	8.3	4.9				
Left Green Movement									9.1	8.8	14.3	21.7
Liberal Party									4.2	7.4	7.3	2.2
Iceland's Movement											3.3	2
Citizen's Movement												7.2

Figure 11.7 General elections in Iceland, 1971–2009

Source: Eythorsson, 2009: 206; Elections and Parties database, available online at: www.parties-and-elections.de/iceland.html (accessed 4 June 2010)

Finnish and Norwegian party systems are considerably fragmented, with no party being able to achieve an absolute majority or even a strong majority. In Sweden and Iceland, the fragmentation has so far been contained because of the high electoral threshold. Moreover, in Sweden the Social Democratic Party continues to be the strongest party by far. However, the potential decline of its electoral share in other European countries raises the question whether it can hold this position in the next decade.

The British model: majoritarian democracy at work

The simple majority electoral system tends to lead to a bipolarisation of the party system. The British model is also the classic majoritarian democracy in Arend Lijphart's typology (see Chapter 6). Two main parties dominate the party and political system, with the main axis of competition being the left–right ideological spectrum: the Labour Party is on the left and the Conservative Party on the right. However, since the early 1990s, the Liberal Democrats, who are on the left of the Labour Party in many respects, have re-emerged. There has been considerable change in the party system in the UK since the 1960s, with the decline in the class-based vote for the Labour Party contributing to the emergence of an electoral market with spiralling campaign costs. Today, in 2010, British parties compete in an electoral market that has similar properties to that of the United States. The vast majority of the 646 constituencies are regarded as safe seats for the main parties, however a small, though increasing, proportion of these seats are leading to real contests between the parties and may change hands from election to election. Moreover, smaller parties, such as the Liberal Democrats, the regionalist Scottish Nationalist Party (SNP) and Plaid Cymru, are also able to create embarrassment for the main parties when they succeed in taking safe seats from them. It all depends on the changing popularity of a particular party at a given time.

The majoritarian nature of the British electoral system creates major distortions in terms of the distribution of seats (Table 11.5). This considerably helps the two main parties, which have greater resources, allowing them to field candidates in all constituencies. A candidate has to make a monetary deposit in order to participate in the elections at constituency level and this can be a burden for smaller parties. The distortion in the distribution became very clear in the general elections of May 2005, in which the Labour Party with 35.2 per cent share of the vote got 55.1 per cent of seats, while the Conservative Party with 32.2 per cent share of the vote got 30 per cent of seats. The big loser from election to election has been the Liberal Democratic Party, which got about 23 per cent of the vote, but only 9–10 per cent of seats. The Conservative Party is also disadvantaged, because, since 1997, it has essentially become an English party, having low national representation both in Scotland and Wales. The Labour Party has become the main national party, because of its strong support in the large urban centres, along with Scotland and Wales. However, both parties have considerable competition from the Liberal Democrats, who have been successful in gaining some of the less safe seats from either the Labour Party or the Conservatives. The 2005 elections also showed that the centre-periphery cleavage has become important for electoral politics in the

Table 11.5 The electoral system in general elections in the United Kingdom

	UK	England	Scotland	Wales	Northern Ireland
Number of constituencies	646 (2009: 650)	529 (2009: 533)	59	40	18
Electoral system	Simple plurality system (first-past-the-post)				
Political parties	Labour Conservative Liberal Democrat		Scottish National (SNP)	Plaid Cymru	Ulster Unionists (UUP) Democratic Unionists (DUP) Sinn Fein (SF) Social Democratic and Labour Party (SDLP)

Source: Author

UK. Regionalist parties can be important competitors at the national level, particularly in Scotland. However, the regionalist cleavage seems to work better for Labour and the Liberal Democrats, which are both strong in Wales and Scotland, traditional working-class strongholds. In contrast, England has become a battlefield for all three parties. One of the main objectives of New Labour after 1997 was to move towards the centre in order to gain votes from the highly volatile middle classes, often labelled 'Middle England'. This is a constituency of voters who are middle class, moderate in ideological terms, and very concerned about issues such as the National Health Service, the quality of education in both school and university sectors, social policies, immigration, and law and order. Both political parties are now competing for these centrist voters and hence trying to avoid extremist views in order not to alienate them (Figure 11.8).

In comparison to the Nordic countries, the turnout of the electorate in the UK has been decreasing since the 1970s, reaching an all-time low of 59.6 per cent in the 2005 election. In particular, young people are showing less interest in politics, which is in itself becoming a major problem for the legitimacy of the political system. Another interesting aspect is that the threshold for achieving an absolute majority has been decreasing in the past decade, particularly since 1997. Owing to the weakness of the Conservatives in Wales and Scotland, the contest has been dominated by the Labour Party, which has been more successful in winning at constituency level despite a similar electoral share of the vote (see Table 11.6). In the May 2010 general election, no party could win an absolute majority; the Conservatives won the election and formed a coalition with the Liberal Democrats.

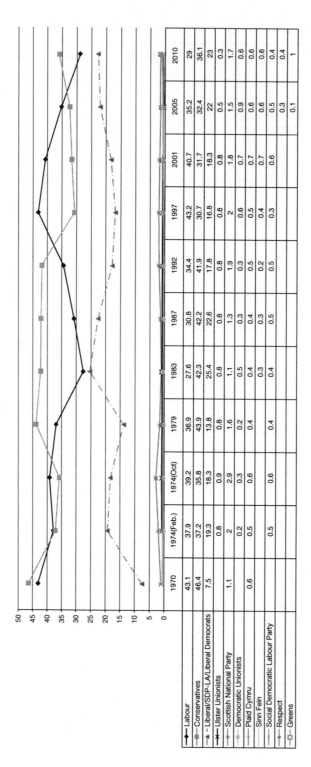

Figure 11.8 Electoral results of general elections in the United Kingdom, 1970–2010

	1970	1974(Feb.)	1974(Oct)	1979	1983	1987	1992	1997	2001	2005	2010
Labour	43.1	37.9	39.2	36.9	27.6	30.8	34.4	43.2	40.7	35.2	29
Conservatives	46.4	37.2	35.8	43.9	42.3	42.2	41.9	30.7	31.7	32.4	36.1
Liberal/SDP-LA/Liberal Democrats	7.5	19.3	18.3	13.8	25.4	22.6	17.8	16.8	18.3	22	23
Ulster Unionists	0.8	0.8	0.9	0.8	0.8	0.8	0.8	0.8	0.8	0.5	0.3
Scottish National Party	1.1	2	2.9	1.6	1.1	1.3	1.9	2	1.8	1.5	1.7
Democratic Unionists		0.2	0.3	0.2	0.5	0.3	0.3	0.6	0.7	0.9	0.6
Plaid Cymru	0.6	0.5	0.6	0.4	0.4	0.4	0.5	0.5	0.7	0.6	0.6
Sinn Fein					0.3	0.3	0.2	0.4	0.7	0.6	0.6
Social Democratic Labour Party		0.5	0.6	0.4	0.4	0.5	0.3	0.3	0.6	0.5	0.4
Respect										0.3	0.4
Greens										0.1	1

Source: Electoral Commission database, available online at: www.electoralcommission.org.uk/publications-and-research/election-reports (accessed 4 June 2010); http://news.bbc.co.uk/2/shared/election2010/liveevent/ (accessed 4 June 2010); Political Parties and Elections in Europe database available online at www.parties-and-elections.de (accessed 4 June 2010)

Table 11.6 The distribution of seats according to UK region after the 2005 general election (difference with respect to the 2001 general election shown in parentheses)

	England	Scotland	Wales	Northern Ireland	United Kingdom
Labour Party	286 (–37)	41 (–5)	29 (–5)		356 (–47)
Conservative Party	194 (+29)	1 (+1)	3 (+3)		198 (+33)
Liberal Democratic Party	47 (+7)	11 (+2)	4 (+2)		62 (+11)
Scottish National Party		6 (+2)			6 (+2)
Plaid Cymru			3 (–1)		3 (–1)
Democratic Unionists				9 (+4)	9 (+4)
Ulster Unionists				1 (–5)	1 (–5)
Sinn Fein				5 (+1)	5 (+1)
Social Democratic and Labour Party				3 (0)	3 (0)
Others	2 (+1)		1 (+1)		3 (+2)
Totals	529	59	40	18	646

Source: BBC Online, www.bbc.co.uk, 8 September 2005

The French model

After 1958, the party system of the Fifth Republic was a response to the highly fragmented parliament of the previous regime. The new political system had as its priorities stability and the ability to govern. The weakening of the parliamentary institution was paralleled by a strengthening of the presidency of the Republic and the government. Therefore, the French party system is also strongly connected to the directly-elected incumbent president. The new Fifth Republic led to the major change of the electoral system from proportional representation at *département* level to the two-ballot majoritarian system, with a threshold of 12.5 per cent for candidates to reach the second round. Although the electorate continues to be highly fragmented, the majoritarian electoral system forces parties to form coalitions on the right or left in order to increase their overall chances in terms of seats. The main cleavage goes back to the French Revolution, which divided France into a right-wing camp with stronger confessional roots in the Catholic Church, and a left-wing camp, which is secularised and adheres to a staunch republicanism (Table 11.7).

One major problem of the French party system is that there are not many parties, especially those on the right, which have been changing their labels over the past three decades. The main right-wing party is the Union for a People's

Table 11.7 The French electoral system

System	Constituencies	Election threshold for candidate in first round	Threshold for candidates who qualify for second round
Two-ballot electoral system	577	At least 25% of the vote	12.5% of vote in first round

Source: Author

Movement (Union pour un Mouvement Populaire, UMP), which not only includes the Gaullists, but also other right-wing groups, such as the Christian democrats and the liberals. The second largest party of the right, the Union for French Democracy (Union de la Democratie Française, UDF) lost many of its supporters to the UMP before the 2002 presidential elections. It re-founded itself as the Democratic Movement (Mouvement Democrate, MoDem) in December 2007. These right-wing parties are reasonably pragmatic. On the left, there is the Socialist Party (PS), the Communist Party (PCF), the greens and several smaller, splinter, radical left-wing parties. The Communist Party has lost a considerable number of its supporters and hence its share of the vote, and it really only survives when it is in coalition with the PS. The greens are somewhat divided, however they remain a force to be reckoned with, particularly as a junior coalition partner, as happened, for example, during the Lionel Jospin government between 1997 and 2002.

Although the extreme right-wing National Front has been able to achieve a considerable share of the vote in elections since the 1980s, its isolation from the other parties because of its ideology and policies leaves them with no seat. Only in 1986, when the socialists changed the electoral system to proportional representation did they achieve considerable success. However, this was changed in the subsequent elections of 1988 back to the two-ballot system. The National Front may become less attractive for the electorate in the long term, because Jean Marie Le Pen is due to retire, and his daughter, Marine, is not charismatic enough to achieve the same level of electoral success, therefore infighting over the succession to Le Pen is expected in the next few years. One reason for the decline of the National Front is the fact that President Nicolás Sarkozy took on many of the issues of the National Front such as immigration and law and order and introduced them into mainstream politics (*El Pais*,15 December 2008, p. 6).

One major change to the '*quadrille bipolaire*' (bipolarised four-party system) is that the smaller partners on the right and the left have lost support in the past two decades. The decline of the Communist Party has been fairly dramatic, with its support halving from one decade to the next. This decline will create greater bipolarisation between the PS and the UMP as well as greater fragmentation on the periphery of these two centrist parties (Figure 11.9).

In sum, the French party system has gained considerably in stability, however this has in turn led to bipolarisation between left and right and the decline of smaller parties (Table 11.8).

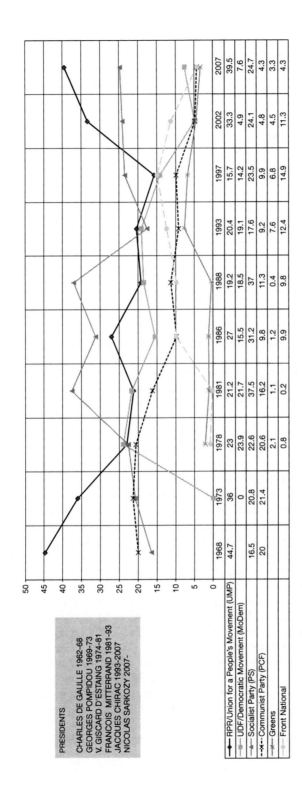

Figure 11.9 General elections in France, 1968–2007

Source: Ministry of the Interior database, available online at: www.interieur.gouv.fr/sections/a_votre_service/elections/resultats (accessed 4 June 2010); Wright and Knapp, 2001: 168–9

	1968	1973	1978	1981	1986	1988	1993	1997	2002	2007
RPR/Union for a People's Movement (UMP)	44.7	36	23	21.2	27	19.2	20.4	15.7	33.3	39.5
UDF/Democratic Movement (MoDem)		0	23.9	21.7	15.5	18.5	19.1	14.2	4.9	7.6
Socialist Party (PS)	16.5	20.8	22.6	37.5	31.2	37	17.6	23.5	24.1	24.7
Communist Party (PCF)	20	21.4	20.6	16.2	9.8	11.3	9.2	9.9	4.8	4.3
Greens			2.1	1.1	1.2	0.4	7.6	6.8	4.5	3.3
Front National			0.8	0.2	9.9	9.8	12.4	14.9	11.3	4.3

Table 11.8 The distribution of seats in the first and second rounds in the French general elections, 2007

	First round	Second round	Total
Union for a People's Movement (UMP)	98	215	313
Democratic Movement (MoDem)	3	0	3
Socialist Party (PS)	1	185	186
Communist Party (PCF)		15	15
Greens	0	4	4
New Centre	8	14	22
Radical Party of the Left (RDG)	0	7	7
Movement for France (MPF)	0	1	1
Others		26	26
	110	441	551

Source: Interior Ministry, through website www.interieur.gouv.fr (accessed 6 December 2008)

The Drei-Sat model: Germany, Austria and Switzerland

Although Germany, Austria and Switzerland have distinctive political cultures, they share many commonalities. In spite of different electoral systems, all of them want to achieve the highest level of proportional representation in their respective assemblies.

One of the main characteristics of these three party systems is that they all have similar parties that belong to the traditional party families, and in all three countries, the traditional cleavages have had their expression in party politics (see Tables 11.9 and 11.10).

In Germany, there has been a five-party system at least since 2005, if not earlier. The main representative of the confessional cleavage is the CDU/CSU. The CSU (Christian Socials) is the largest party in Bavaria, an extremely Catholic *Land*, and until 2008 it was able to achieve between 50 and 60 per cent of the vote in the region. However, in the recent Bavarian elections of October 2008 it declined considerably to below 43.2 per cent and this was regarded as a major failure by the party elites (*The Economist*, 2 October 2008). The Christian Democrats (CDU) are the strongest nationwide right-centre party and, as already mentioned, the traditional catch-all party (*Volkspartei*, according to Otto Kirchheimer, 1965). On the left, the main party is the Social Democratic Party (SPD), re-founded after 1945, but with a long tradition going back to the nineteenth century. Neither the CDU/CSU nor the SPD have been able to get an absolute majority, and therefore these two main parties have had to form coalitions with the smaller parties. Among the smaller parties, the liberal Free Democratic Party (FDP) is the most established. It already has a long history of coalitions with the CDU/CSU in the 1950s, 1960s, 1980s and 1990s and with the SPD in the 1970s. Although, until the 1990s, there was a tendency to reject any coalition with the Greens, because of their leftist tendencies and radicalism, this changed at the end of the 1990s. The SPD formed

Table 11.9 Electoral systems in Germany, Austria and Switzerland

	Electoral system	Constituencies/seats	Size of constituencies	Threshold
Germany	Mixed system 50% elected in pluri-nominal constituencies 50% through proportional representation system (Saint Lague method)	299 constituencies (but 598 seats) Proportional representation Use of Hare-Niemeyer at *Länd* level (16 constituencies) Compensatory seats (*Überhangsmandate*) in order to reduce disproportionality of distribution of seats	Uni-nominal Depending on population	5% or direct seat (*Grundmandat*)
Austria	Proportional representation system (two levels: constituency and national) First level: Hare electoral method Second level: D'Hondt	9 multi-member seats (*Bundesländer*) Subdivided into 46 regional constituencies	Pluri-nominal (7 to 36 seats according to population)	1 direct seat (*Grundmandat*) 4%
Switzerland	Proportional representation with preferential voting, also including candidates from other parties (panachage) Uni-nominal constituencies elected by simple plurality system	26 constituencies (cantons)	Uni-nominal and pluri-nominal (1 to 35)	No threshold

Source: Adapted from Parline Database of International Parliamentary Union, www.ipu.org (accessed 4 June 2010)

Table 11.10 Political parties in Germany, Austria and Switzerland

	Social Democrats	Christian Democrats	Liberals	Other parties	Parties after 1970
Germany	Sozialdemokratische Partei Deutschlands (SPD)	Christlich-Demokratische Union (CDU) Christlich-Soziale Union (CSU)	Freie Demokratische Partei Deutschlands (FDP)		Grüne/Bündnis '90 Die Linke
Austria	Sozialdemokratische Partei Österreichs (SPÖ)	Österreichische Volkspartei (ÖVP)	Freiheitliche Partei Österreichs (FPÖ) (new right after 1986)	Kommunistische Partei Österreichs (KPÖ)	Grünen-Alternativen Bündnis für die Zukunft Österreichs (BZÖ) (new right party)
Switzerland	Sozialdemokratische Partei der Schweiz (SP)/Parti Socialdemocrate de la Suisse (PS)	Christlich-Demokratische Volkspartei (CVP)/ Parti Democrate Christien (PDC)	Freisinning Demokratishce Partei (FDP)/ Parti Radicale Democratique (PRD)	Schweizerische Volkspartei (SVP)/ Union Democratique du Centre (UDC) (Swiss People's Party)	Grüne

Source: Author

a coalition with the Green Party in 1998, integrating this once new social movement into mainstream politics. The cooperation between SPD and the Green Party is now well established at regional and national level, leading to ticket splitting of voters for the two parties. This means that social democrats and greens tend to vote for one party at the uni-nominal constituency level (mainly for the Social Democrats or for the candidate that has the better chance of being elected) and for another party (usually the Green Party) in the proportional representation list system. In recent years the CDU/CSU (black party colour) has been considering a 'Jamaica flag' option (so named because of the colours of the party), forming a coalition with the Greens and the FDP (yellow) (Alex Jakubowski, 2005) (Figure 11.10).

Since the Fall of the Berlin Wall, there has been a new political party shaping German politics. The former East German Socialist Unity Party of Germany (Sozialistisches Einheitspartei Deutschlands, SED) created a new party called the Party of Democratic Socialism (Partei des Demokratischen Sozialismus, PDS), which became fairly strong in the East German *Länder*, in particular in East Berlin. In 2005, the PDS joined a new, smaller party in the western part of the country, and formed the Left Party (Die Linke) in 2007. This party was able to comfortably pass the threshold of 5 per cent in the 2005 general elections, and has been fairly successful in providing a platform for protest voters, particularly against the liberalisation policies of the government (Table 11.11).

Electoral support for the two main parties has been declining and is currently (in 2010) at almost the same level, with the result that the smaller parties have gained a very important position in the political and party systems. The main cleavage is between the rich conservative south (with the wealthy *Länder* of Bavaria and Baden-Württemberg) and the poorer, left-wing northern and eastern regions. One particular aspect of the German party system is that there is some polarisation between left and right, however the approach to politics follows a similar pattern

Table 11.11 The distribution of seats after the general elections in Germany, 2005

	Uni-nominal constituencies		Proportional representation regional lists		Compensatory seats	
	Share of vote	Seats	Share of vote	Seats	Seats	Total seats
SPD	38.4	145	34.2	68	9	222
CDU	32.6	106	27.8	68	6	180
CSU	8.2	44	7.4	1	1	46
Greens	5.4	1	8.1	50	0	51
FDP	4.7		9.8	61	0	61
Left Party	8	3	8.7	51	0	54
Other	2.7		3.9			
	100	299	100	299	16	614

Source: Bundeswahlleiter, 2006 and election website, www.election.de (accessed 18 December 2008)

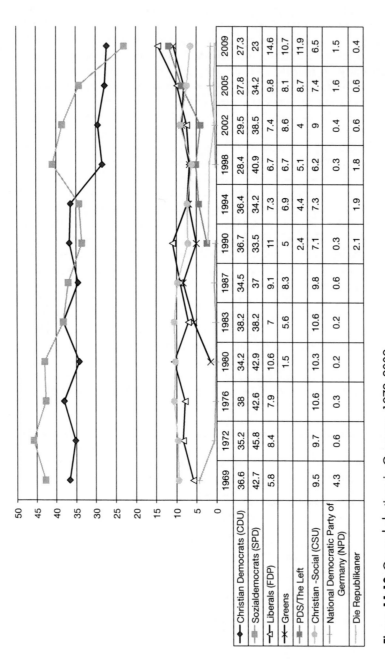

	1969	1972	1976	1980	1983	1987	1990	1994	1998	2002	2005	2009
Christian Democrats (CDU)	36.6	35.2	38	34.2	38.2	34.5	36.7	36.4	28.4	29.5	27.8	27.3
Sozialdemocrats (SPD)	42.7	45.8	42.6	42.9	38.2	37	33.5	34.2	40.9	38.5	34.2	23
Liberals (FDP)	5.8	8.4	7.9	10.6	7	9.1	11	7.3	6.7	7.4	9.8	14.6
Greens				1.5	5.6	8.3	5	6.9	6.7	8.6	8.1	10.7
PDS/The Left							2.4	4.4	5.1	4	8.7	11.9
Christian -Social (CSU)	9.5	9.7	10.6	10.3	10.6	9.8	7.1	7.3	6.2	9	7.4	6.5
National Democratic Party of Germany (NPD)	4.3	0.6	0.3	0.2	0.2	0.6	0.3		0.3	0.4	1.6	1.5
Die Republikaner							2.1	1.9	1.8	0.6	0.6	0.4

Figure 11.10 General elections in Germany, 1972–2009

Source: Bundeswahlleiter electoral database, available online at: www.bundeswahlleiter.de/de/bundestagswahlen/fruehere_
bundestagswahlen/ (accessed 4 June 2010)

to the traditional consensus democracies (for example, the Netherlands, Austria and Switzerland). This fact also brings the German party system closer to those of Austria and Switzerland. The mixed system that includes compensatory seats after the elections creates quite an even distribution between the parties represented in the Bundestag, so that it is difficult to achieve absolute majorities.

The Austrian party system was characterised by a four-party system until 1956. The two main parties were and still are the Social Democrats (SPÖ) and the People's Party (ÖVP). The original party system was complemented by two small parties, the Communist Party (KPÖ) on the left and the Liberals (FPÖ) originally known as the Association of Independents (Verband der Unabhängigen, VdU until 1953) on the right. However, in the 1960s the Communists lost representation in parliament, so that it became a three-party system until 1983. Until 1966, Austria was ruled by a grand coalition, so that polarisation between the two main parties was moderate. The main aim was to achieve the independence of the country, which came about after the signing of the state treaty with the Allied Forces in 1955. However, in the 1960s the main political parties transformed themselves into catch-all parties. After a short absolute majority government of the ÖVP between 1966 and 1970, the SPÖ became the strongest party between 1970 and 1999. This hegemonic position of the Social Democrats led to a continuous participation of government during this period. Between 1971 and 1983, they were able to achieve absolute majorities and extend the welfare state considerably. The architect of such improvement of the living conditions of the population was Chancellor Bruno Kreisky, who was quite charismatic. However, after failing to achieve an absolute majority in 1983, Bruno Kreisky decided to resign. The SPÖ formed a coalition with the FPÖ. Nevertheless, the growing divisions and infighting inside the FPÖ led to the rise of new leader Jörg Haider who was known as having xenophobic and nationalist tendencies. After he became the new leader, the SPÖ ended the coalition with the FPÖ. From 1986 to 1999, both the SPÖ and the ÖVP were under pressure from the now populist-nationalist FPÖ under the leadership of Jörg Haider. They formed a coalition under social democratic Chancellor Franz Vranitzky and after 1997 under Viktor Klima. However, in the elections of 1999, the FPÖ was able to match the electoral result of the ÖVP. A growing polarisation along the left-right axis between the two main parties led ÖVP leader Wolfgang Schüssel to form a coalition with the FPÖ. The international community, particularly the European Union, condemned the formation of such a coalition. Even Federal President Thomas Klestil was quite sceptical and opposed to such a coalition. However, after negotiations the two parties formed a coalition government that lasted until 2006.

This meant that the SPÖ had to go into opposition. The emerging new party system now consisted of three political parties with almost the same share of the vote. While the SPÖ and the ÖVP were able to keep the cohesion and party discipline, the FPÖ began to fall apart owing to permanent infighting. Former party leader Jörg Haider decided to step down from the leadership position, in order to facilitate the coalition government between the two parties. The consequence was a permanent fight for leadership positions. Owing to this infighting the ÖVP was able to improve considerably in the 2002 elections, while share of the FPÖ vote plummeted from 26.9 to 10 per cent. Moreover, in April 2005, followers of Jörg Haider decided to leave the FPÖ and create a new party called the Alliance for the Future of Austria (Bündnis für die Zukunft Österreichs, BZÖ). Originally, only a few members of the

FPÖ, mainly those in Carinthia, the stronghold of Haider, joined the BZÖ. Only after the 2006 elections did the membership of the BZÖ improve. In the 2006 elections, both FPÖ and BZÖ parties had a combined vote of 15.1 per cent; this increased to 27.5 per cent in 2008. This means that if the two parties reunite, they may be able to challenge the two main parties again. The tragic death of Jörg Haider in a car accident on 11 October 2008 may contribute to a decrease of votes, particularly for the BZÖ. New leaders have emerged such as H.C. Strache in the FPÖ who also successfully uses a populist language and follows many of the anti-immigration and law and order policies of former leader Jörg Haider. This threatening situation of a strong new right block based on a populist message contributed to the return of the grand coalition between the two main parties after the elections of 2006 and 2008. The decline of support for the two main parties, and increase in vote for the new right populist parties is creating considerable insecurity in the Austrian party system. In this triadic constellation of the party system, the greens have so far remained outside of governmental politics (Figure 11.11).

The Swiss party system has been characterised by the dominance of a group of traditional parties, none of which was able to achieve an absolute majority. The fragmented party system created a consensus-oriented political system that has at its core the Executive Federal Council (Bundesrat). The Federal Council consists of seven members, two from each of the three main parties and one from the fourth largest party. This 'magic formula' was introduced in 1958 and has since then characterised the allocation of government seats between the political parties. Each member is elected by the joint Houses of Parliament, and, until 1987, the system worked quite well, leading to stability of the party system. The main political parties were able to achieve approximately the same level of support, so there was no major change in the allocation of seats to the Federal Council.

Until the mid 1990s, the main political parties were the Social Democrats (SPS/PSS), the Radical Democrats (FDP/PRD) and the Christian Democrats (CVP/PDC), each of them being among the parties that received most of the votes. However, after the mid 1990s, while the Social Democrats steadily gained votes, the Christian Democrats either stagnated or lost votes, with the resut that the main contest was then between the Social Democrats and the Radical Democrats. Until 1995, the fourth largest party was the Swiss People's Party, which was traditionally a party of the farmers, artisans and citizens, who resisted the centralisation tendencies of the federal government and wanted to protect the traditional institutions and values of Switzerland. In 1971, this traditional subculture of Switzerland, particularly in the German-speaking part of the country, re-branded itself as the Swiss People's Party. In 1991, Christoph Blocher from the canton Zurich became the new leader and updated the discourse of the party by introducing a new right populist language against increased taxation, immigration and membership of the European Union. The rejection of membership of the European Economic Area (EEA) in December 1992 was a key victory for the party. Since then, the popularity of the Swiss People's Party has been increasing from election to election.

Since 1999, there has been some discussion about changing the magic formula, because the SVP overtook all the parties in 2003 and 2007. The main reason for the rise of the SVP is that it has considerable financial resources and uses new political marketing techniques that communicate a clear message. According to Clive Church, the technique is simply called KISS ('Keep it Simple Stupid').

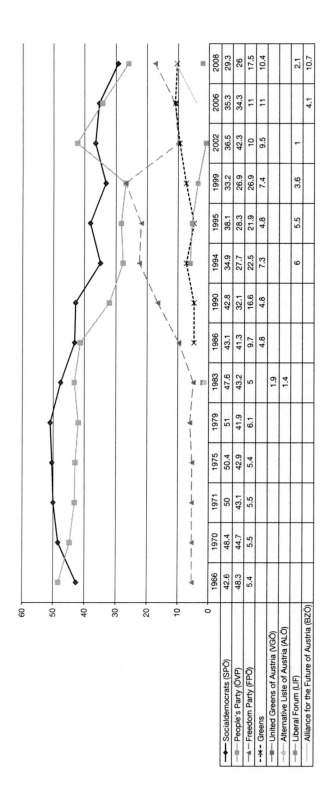

	1966	1970	1971	1975	1979	1983	1986	1990	1994	1995	1999	2002	2006	2008
Socialdemocrats (SPÖ)	42.6	48.4	50	50.4	51	47.6	43.1	42.8	34.9	38.1	33.2	36.5	35.3	29.3
People's Party (ÖVP)	48.3	44.7	43.1	42.9	41.9	43.2	41.3	32.1	27.7	28.3	26.9	42.3	34.3	26
Freedom Party (FPÖ)	5.4	5.5	5.5	5.4	6.1	5	9.7	16.6	22.5	21.9	26.9	10	11	17.5
Greens							4.8	4.8	7.3	4.8	7.4	9.5	11	10.4
United Greens of Austria (VGÖ)						1.9								
Alternative Liste of Austria (ALÖ)						1.4								
Liberal Forum (LIF)									6	5.5	3.6	1		2.1
Alliance for the Future of Austria (BZÖ)													4.1	10.7

Figure 11.11 General elections in Austria, 1966–2008

Source: Ministry of Interior, Austria, electoral database, available online at: www.bmi.gv.at/cms/BMI_wahlen/nationalrat/NRW_History.aspx (accessed 4 June 2010)

It seems that the SVP outspent the other political parties, with an overall spend of about 20 million Swiss francs in comparison with an average of 1 million by each of the other parties (Church, 2008: 611). According to Church, the party particularly targets those who could be considered the losers in the globalisation process – the rural population, the elderly, small businesses and employees (Church, 2008: 618). Although most of the traditional cleavages, such as religion and class, have been eroded, there is a growing cleavage between the populations of the main urban centres and those of the rural areas and small towns. This would also explain the continuing rise of the greens, whose share of the vote has been increasing (from 0.6 in 1979 to 9.6 per cent in 2007). It is a sign that the post-materialist vote has increased considerably in the past two decades. The Swiss party system is extremely fragmented and the proportional representation system allows parties with small percentages to achieve representation. Many parties have only regionalist support at canton level. However, due to the proportional representation system, they are able to get MPs elected to the National Council, the lower house of Parliament. Additionally, many small regional parties form electoral coalitions, so that they stand a better chance at national level.

In spite of the success of Christoph Blocher's SVP, the traditional parties have formed an alliance against Christoph Blocher, because of his xenophobic populist politics, creating an impasse in the Federal Council. Blocher was not able to get enough votes in parliament in order to be part of the Federal Council, so that other members of his party were elected. The ostracism of Blocher led to the expulsion of any member of the SVP who agreed to be part of the government. This created considerable tension in Swiss politics. Following the 2007 election, two members of the SVP were elected by Parliament to be part of the government: Eveline Widmer-Schlumpf and Samuel Schmid accepted the election and became members of the Federal Council. However, they were expelled from the SVP soon afterwards. They decided to form a new party called the Citizens Democratic Party (Bürgerlich-Demokratische Party, BDP), which is moderate and recruits most of its members from the canton Bern, which is less radical and populist (Church, 2008: 620–2; *The Economist Intelligence Unit*, 17 September 2008; Figure 11.12). A vacancy after Samuel Schmid was forced to resign from the Citizens Democratic Party because of a political scandal, led to the election of Ueli Maurer, a long-standing member of the SVP and more moderate than Christoph Blocher. Maurer is more willing to compromise on immigration policy, promising to adjust his position to that of the government, particularly in relation to the extension of the free movement of people to the new members of the European Union, Bulgaria and Romania, which is strongly opposed by the hard core of the SVP (*Focus online*, 10 December 2008).

Party systems and the single transferable vote: Ireland and Malta

Ireland and Malta are the only European countries that use the oldest electoral system in the world (see Table 11.12): the single-transferable vote (STV), which is a proportional representation system that allows voters to rank candidates according to their preferences. All preferences are counted, so that it takes a long

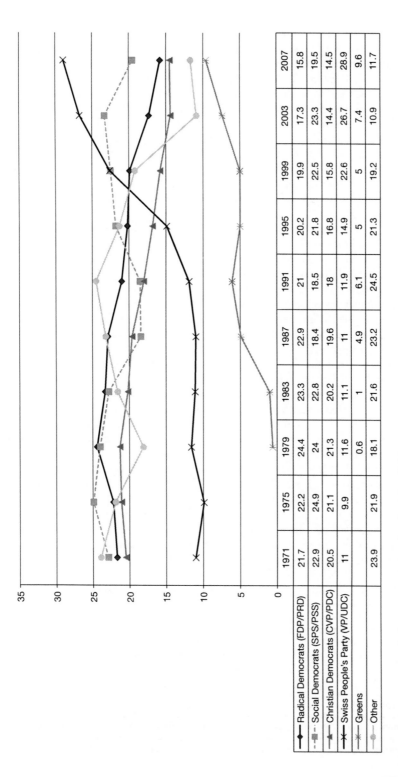

	1971	1975	1979	1983	1987	1991	1995	1999	2003	2007
Radical Democrats (FDP/PRD)	21.7	22.2	24.4	23.3	22.9	21	20.2	19.9	17.3	15.8
Social Democrats (SPS/PSS)	22.9	24.9	24	22.8	18.4	18.5	21.8	22.5	23.3	19.5
Christian Democrats (CVP/PDC)	20.5	21.1	21.3	20.2	19.6	18	16.8	15.8	14.4	14.5
Swiss People's Party (VP/UDC)	11	9.9	11.6	11.1	11	11.9	14.9	22.6	26.7	28.9
Greens			0.6	1	4.9	6.1	5	5	7.4	9.6
Other	23.9	21.9	18.1	21.6	23.2	24.5	21.3	19.2	10.9	11.7

Figure 11.12 General elections in Switzerland, 1971–2007
Source: Federal Chancellery of Switzerland, electoral database, available online at: www.bk.admin.ch/themen/pore/nrw/index.html (accessed 4 June 2010); Lindner, 2005: 91

time to get an accurate result. In a similar way to the United Kingdom, MPs are strongly involved with their particular rural or urban constituency. The dangers of clientelism and patronage are always a present reality in this system of party politics (Farrell, 1999: 31–2). The Irish system is also different in that the class or confessional cleavage is less salient. In a country where the Catholic Church is a very important institution, despite secularisation, this means that none of the parties is elected based on confession. After independence in 1921, the four industrialised counties remained in Northern Ireland, however the Republic of Ireland was quite rural. Industrialisation and a working-class-based vote only began to play a role in the 1950s and 1960s; however, it was less salient in Northern Ireland than in the Nordic countries or in the UK (see Chapter 3).

The main cleavage is a historical one, which goes back to the emergence of the Irish Free State out of the British Empire, and the Treaty that was signed with the British government. The main party struggling for independence, Sinn Fein ('Ourselves'), split into two. One party supported the Treaty and became known as Fine Gael ('family group of the Gaels' [Irish]), while the opponents to the Treaty formed Fianna Fail ('the warriors of destiny'). After 1932, Fianna Fail became the predominant party. Fine Gael had a weaker social base and had to form coalitions with other smaller parties, particularly the Labour Party, in order to come to power (Farrell, 1999: 30–1). Similarly to the UK, the Irish party system is traditionally regarded as a two-and-a-half party system, with, in 2010, one predominant party, Fianna Fail (Farrell, 1999: 32).

However, since the late 1980s there has been a considerable party system change that has led to the emergence of new parties, all of which emerged as breakaway factions of the main parties. One important new party is the Progressive Democrats, which emerged out of a breakaway faction of Fianna Fail in 1987. Previously, in the 1960s and 1970s, Sinn Fein split and one of the new parties became the Workers' Party; then, in 1992, seven MPs of the Workers' Party formed the Left Democrats. Furthermore, the green parties emerged in the late 1980s. The consequence of all this is that the Irish party system has become fairly volatile in the past few decades (Farrell, 1999: 40–4), with a change of government at almost every election since the 1970s. Irish political parties are extremely pragmatic, and the main parties will adopt centrist positions in order to catch the highest number of voters. The MPs themselves, as charismatic human resources, are very important for the electoral competition, as Irish politics is more personal and direct than in other European countries (Figure 11.13).

Table 11.12 The use of single transferable voting in Ireland and Malta

Country	Number of seats	Number and size of constituencies
Ireland	166	43 constituencies • 12 with 5 seats • 13 with 4 seats • 18 with 3 seats
Malta	65	13 constituencies with 5 seats to be elected

Source: Author's own calculations, based on Database of Elections, Ireland, available online at: http://electionsireland.org/results/general/30dail.cfm#results (accessed 4 June 2010); database on Malta Elections, available online at: www.maltadata.com (accessed 4 June 2010)

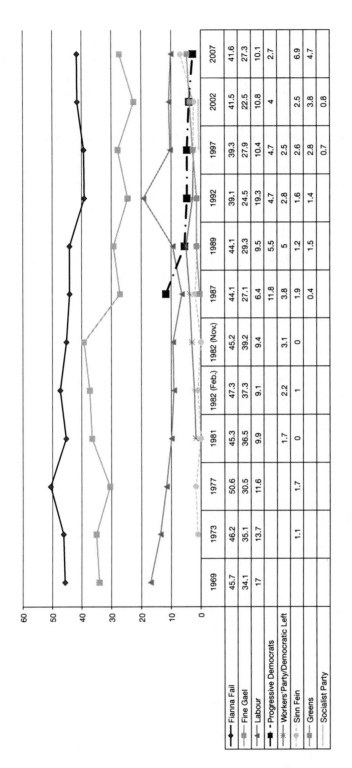

	1969	1973	1977	1981	1982 (Feb.)	1982 (Nov.)	1987	1989	1992	1997	2002	2007
Fianna Fáil	45.7	46.2	50.6	45.3	47.3	45.2	44.1	44.1	39.1	39.3	41.5	41.6
Fine Gael	34.1	35.1	30.5	36.5	37.3	39.2	27.1	29.3	24.5	27.9	22.5	27.3
Labour	17	13.7	11.6	9.9	9.1	9.4	6.4	9.5	19.3	10.4	10.8	10.1
Progressive Democrats							11.8	5.5	4.7	4.7	4	2.7
Workers'Party/Democratic Left				1.7	2.2	3.1	3.8	5	2.8	2.5		
Sinn Féin		1.1	1.7	0	1	0	1.9	1.2	1.6	2.6	2.5	6.9
Greens							0.4	1.5	1.4	2.8	3.8	4.7
Socialist Party										0.7	0.8	

Figure 11.13 Irish general elections, 1969–2007

Source: Author's compilation based on Database on Irish General Elections, available online at: http://electionsireland.org/results/general/general.cfm (accessed 4 June 2010)

Although the Maltese party system is more polarised than in Ireland, the constituency-based networks of clientelism and patronage play an important role in the political system. The Labour Party and the conservative Nationalist Party are the two main parties, regularly alternating in power. Since 2005, there have been thirteen districts with five seats each (a total of sixty-five seats). Because of the complexity of the voting system, some parties were able to get more seats than the actual electoral share. This led to the introduction of a rule in 1982, that the party that gets most first preference votes will form the government. Another feature of the Maltese party system is that the personal relationship of candidates to their constituencies leads to highly partisan campaigns at local level. This also translates into high turnout of more than 90 per cent of registered voters. In spite of the complexity of the voting system, the number of spoiled ballot papers is quite low and has been reducing over time (Hirczy de Miño and Lane, 1999; Farrell *et al.*, 1996; Figure 11.14).

In sum, the use of the single transferable vote in Ireland and Malta has produced two quite different party systems. The Irish party system is fragmented, while the Maltese system is characterised by a polarisation of the two main parties.

The Benelux countries

In Belgium, the Netherlands and Luxembourg proportional representation is the electoral system used. Owing to the fragmentation of the party system, political parties have to work together. All three are considered consensus democracies, and Arend Lijphart highlighted that the Netherlands was the country used for his typology of consensus and majoritarian democracies (see Chapter 5).

The most complex case of the three is probably Belgium. The federalisation of Belgium after 1993 led to the establishment of two independent party systems in Wallonia and Flanders, but in spite of these two separate electoral areas with their own dynamics, the political parties are almost the same in the two parts of Belgium. The electoral results in the two electoral arenas are also counted together in terms of the national vote, which means that political parties of the same ideological family are formally separate and independent entities. Nonetheless, their ideological affinity and common history leads to cooperation at national level. The complexity of the Belgian party system started in the 1980s, when the parties divided into two and created their dynamics in the two parts of the country. Moreover, after the 1999 elections, many Belgian parties decided to change their labels in order to appeal to particular electorates. The two regional electoral markets produced an extremely fragmented party system.

The main parties in Wallonia are the Wallonian Liberals and the Social Democrats. Traditionally, the Social Democrats were the strongest party in Wallonia and the Christian Democrats in Flanders. However, in the past fifteen years the Liberals in both Wallonia and Flanders have been able to challenge the main parties. In 1999 and 2003, the Flemish Liberals overtook the Christian Democrats. This was regarded as a historical turning point, because of the dominance of Christian democracy in the political system since the nineteenth century. One of the main reasons for this shift was that the length of time the Christian Democrats had been in power, even in coalition with other parties, had led to several political scandals

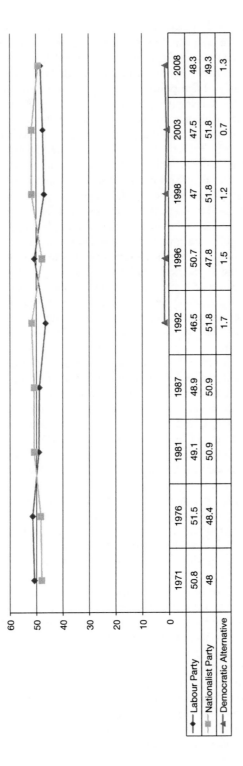

	1971	1976	1981	1987	1992	1996	1998	2003	2008
Labour Party	50.8	51.5	49.1	48.9	46.5	50.7	47	47.5	48.3
Nationalist Party	48	48.4	50.9	50.9	51.8	47.8	51.8	51.8	49.3
Democratic Alternative					1.7	1.5	1.2	0.7	1.3

Figure 11.14 Maltese general elections, 2001–8

Source: Author's compilation based on Database on Maltese Elections, available online at: www.maltadata.com (accessed 4 June 2010)

(including the uncovering of a paedophile network and an illicit arms scandal), which seriously tarnished the reputation of the Christian Democrats. The Liberals became a viable alternative, partly as a result of the electoral and then governmental performance of leader Guy Verhofstadt. While the re-founded CD&V recovered in 2007 and became the largest party of the political system, its sister party in Wallonia was troubled by a major crisis of identity. It renamed itself the Democratic Humanist Centre (Centre Democrate Humaniste, CDH) so that it would appeal to other ethnic communities. In spite of this re-branding, the electoral vote has been stagnating or decreasing since 1995. Similarly, the Social Democrats have been losing votes since the 1980s, mainly because of the lack of renewal both within the party and within Wallonia, where they are considerably entrenched in the political structures. Both the party and political systems are being challenged by the rise of Flemish Interest (Vlaamse Belang, VB), which was called Flemish Block until 2004, but was then banned by the Supreme Court because of the xenophobic language used in the programme of its youth organisation (Erk, 2005). The VB has become the third largest party in the country and has been increasing its vote from election to election. The party is quite strong at local council level and it can govern without the other parties, but it is excluded from government in national and regional politics by the main political parties because of its xenophobic and populist programme. While class and religion have declined as major cleavages in Belgian politics, the linguistic/cultural divide between northern Flanders and southern Wallonia has become central for the country. This cleavage is particularly salient in Flanders, which is strongly in favour of independence from Belgium (De Winter *et al.*, 2005). Such tension has now become an inherent problem in coalition-building, as Prime Minister Leterme experienced after the elections of 2007, when it took almost a whole year to find a compromise between the main coalition parties. In December 2008, the coalition government collapsed again, leading to the appointment of a new prime minister, Christian Democrat Hermann Van Rompuy (*SpiegelOnline*, 22 December 2008; *DeutscheWelle*, 30 December 2008). The two liberal parties have become pivotal in the Belgian political system, because they are able to achieve consensus and moderation among the other parties (Figure 11.15).

The Dutch party system changed considerably in the 1970s, with the decline of the Christian democratic parties. In particular the Catholic People's Party contributed to a realignment in the party system. After 1977, Catholic and Protestant parties merged into the Christian Democratic Appeal and were reasonably successful in restoring an influential position. The liberal People's Party for Freedom and Democracy (VVD) also had to deal with the splinter reform liberals D'66 from 1967. Moreover, other parties emerged in the 1970s and 1980s, particularly the greens. As a result of the very friendly electoral system, parties are able to achieve representation easily. A political party only needs 0.67 per cent of the vote to get a seat. This means that the Dutch Parliament is highly fragmented, with over ten parties in it. The 1980s and early 1990s were dominated by the Christian Democrats and the Liberals, which contributed to a reform of the ailing economic system. And between 1994 and 2002 the Social Democrats and Liberals, in a coalition sometimes known as the 'purple coalition', shared government (Ten Napel, 1999). However, CDA leader Jan-Peter Balkenende was able to achieve a relative majority in the 2002, 2003 and 2006 elections. None of the major parties have been able to achieve more than 30 per cent of the vote, so it is important for

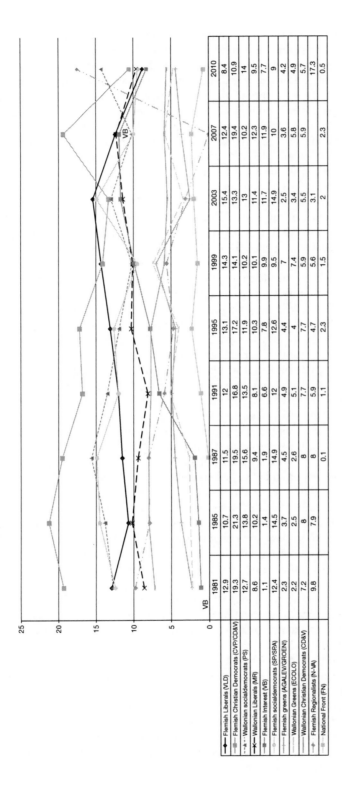

	1981	1985	1987	1991	1995	1999	2003	2007	2010
Flemish Liberals (VLD)	12.9	10.7	11.5	12	13.1	14.3	15.4	12.4	8.4
Flemish Christian Democrats (CVP/CD&V)	19.3	21.3	19.5	16.8	17.2	14.1	13.3	19.4	10.9
Wallonian socialdemocrats (PS)	12.7	13.8	15.6	13.5	11.9	10.2	13	10.2	14
Wallonian Liberals (MR)	8.6	10.2	9.4	8.1	10.3	10.1	11.4	12.3	9.5
Flemish Interest (VB)	1.1	1.4	1.9	6.6	7.8	9.9	11.7	11.9	7.7
Flemish socialdemocrats (SP/SPA)	12.4	14.5	14.9	12	12.6	9.5	14.9	10	9
Flemish greens (AGALEV/GROEN!)	2.3	3.7	4.5	4.9	4.4	7	2.5	3.6	4.2
Wallonian Greens (ECOLO)	2.2	2.5	2.6	5.1	4	7.4	3.4	5.8	4.9
Flemish Christian Democrats (CD&V)	7.2	8	8	7.7	7.7	5.9	5.5	5.9	5.7
Flemish Regionalists (N-VA)	9.8	7.9		5.9	4.7	5.6	3.1		17.3
National Front (FN)			0.1	1.1	2.3	1.5	2	2.3	0.5

Figure 11.15 Belgian general elections, 1981–2010

Source: Deschouwer, 2009: 128

them to keep all options open for coalition-building after the elections. Traditional Dutch politics were shaken up by the appearance of a charismatic new politician called Pim Fortuyn in 2002. Fortuyn was a Professor of Sociology at Rotterdam Erasmus University and used very direct language in order to address issues that were relevant for at least part of the Dutch population, including immigration, policies of integration and other law and order issues. Although he had a populist right-wing discourse in certain areas, it was fairly liberal in others. Shortly before the elections of 2002, Pim Fortuyn was killed by Volkert van der Graaf, an animal protection activist (who, allegedly, opposed Pim Fortuyn's policies against the Muslim population). The death of Fortuyn led to a considerable share of the vote for his PFL – his list got 17 per cent of the vote and it was interpreted by most commentators as a sympathy vote for him. The PFL became part of the first coalition government of Jan Peter Balkenende, but their participation did not last long, because of the continual infighting of the leaders of the PFL over policy and personal issues (van Praag, 2003: 16–18). After early elections in 2003, the PFL declined to 5.7 per cent and, later, in the elections of 2006 it further declined to 0.2 per cent. The party had to dissolve at end of the year. In the 2006 elections, a new populist anti-immigration party called Party of Freedom, under the leadership of charismatic Geert Wilders, emerged. It won 5.4 per cent of the vote and nine seats. All this shows that the immigration and integration discussion is far from over in the Netherlands. It also means that the CDA is under pressure to follow harder policies on immigration. In terms of immigration, the Netherlands has moved from being one of the most tolerant countries in the world to being one of the most strict within a twenty year period (Joppke, 2007: 5–9). Furthermore, the radical left-wing Socialist Party (SP) achieved a remarkable improvement from 6.3 per cent in 2003 to 16.6 per cent in 2006. One of the main reasons for the rise of the Socialist Party was that the population was extremely dissatisfied with the implementation of quite an austere reform plan on the part of the government that particularly affected the weaker parts of Dutch society. Overall, Dutch parties have become fairly pragmatic and have adjusted to the electoral market. The consensual nature of politics allows for coalition-building based on the results.

All this confirms that the electorate has become quite volatile in the past three decades, with the 'heartlands' of the Christian Democrats, Social Democrats and Liberals (based on class and religion cleavages) being eroded and replaced by a battlefield in which parties have to compete for all the votes. This is a process that has been taking place since the 1970s. It means that the CDA is trying to broaden its base to include those who follow other religions, basing its appeal on moral values, while the Liberals are concentrating on the liberalisation of markets, and the Dutch Labour Party is focusing on state intervention in the economy and the protection of the welfare state (Pellikaan et al., 2003: 38) (Figure 11.16; Table 11.13).

In contrast to Belgium and the Netherlands, the party system in Luxembourg has been less fragmented and more stable. The Christian Democrats (CSV) dominate the political system, the other two main parties being the Social Democrats (LSAP) and the Liberals (DP). Although all these main political parties have been losing votes to smaller parties from election to election, it has been a slower process for the CSV. Other smaller parties play an important role in coalition-building. The Greens emerged in the 1984 elections and were able to double their share from

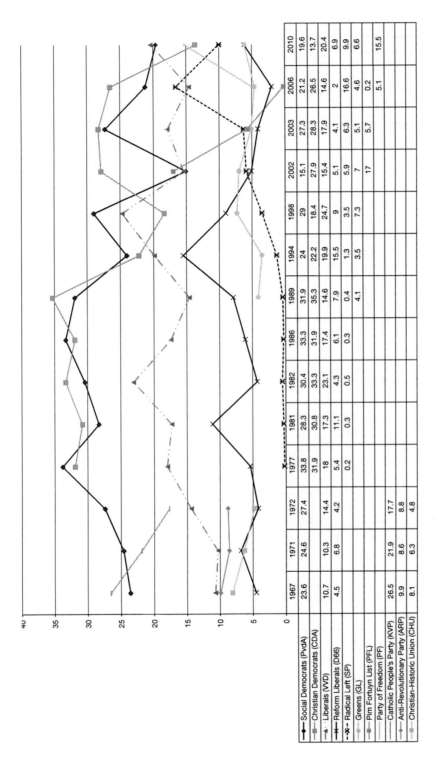

	1967	1971	1972	1977	1981	1982	1986	1989	1994	1998	2002	2003	2006	2010
Social Democrats (PvdA)	23.6	24.6	27.4	33.8	28.3	30.4	33.3	31.9	24	29	15.1	27.3	21.2	19.6
Christian Democrats (CDA)				31.9	30.8	33.3	31.9	35.3	22.2	18.4	27.9	28.3	26.5	13.7
Liberals (VVD)	10.7	10.3	14.4	18	17.3	23.1	17.4	14.6	19.9	24.7	15.4	17.9	14.6	20.4
Reform Liberals (D66)	4.5	6.8	4.2	5.4	11.1	4.3	6.1	7.9	15.5	9	5.1	4.1	2	6.9
Radical Left (SP)				0.2	0.3	0.5	0.3	0.4	1.3	3.5	5.9	6.3	16.6	9.9
Greens (GL)								4.1	3.5	7.3	7	5.1	4.6	6.6
Pim Fortuyn List (PFL)											17	5.7	0.2	
Party of Freedom (PF)													5.1	15.5
Catholic People's Party (KVP)	26.5	21.9	17.7											
Anti-Revolutionary Party (ARP)	9.9	8.6	8.8											
Christian-Historic Union (CHU)	8.1	6.3	4.8											

Figure 11.16 General elections in the Netherlands, 1967–2010

Source: Andeweg and Irwin, 2002: 98; see also online: www.nlverkiezingen.com/index_en.html (accessed 4 June 2010)

Table 11.13 Electoral systems in Belgium, the Netherlands and Luxembourg

	Electoral system	Constituencies/ seats	Threshold
Belgium	Proportional representation D'Hondt system	Eleven constituencies	5%
Netherlands	Proportional system D'Hondt system Closed list system	One national constituency, subdivided into 19 electoral districts Electing 150 seats	No threshold (0.67%)
Luxembourg	Proportional representation Hagenbach-Bischoff calculation of electoral quota, distribution of seats through D'Hondt system Panachage: preferential voting for candidates of different lists or just for one list	Four pluri-nominal constituencies electing 60 seats	No threshold

Source: Own compilation based on Parline database online of International Parliamentary Union, www.ipu.org (accessed on 22 December 2008)

5.2 to 11.6 in 2004. The other two smaller parties are the former party of pensioners, which, since 1989, has tried to broaden its support by calling itself Alternative Democratic Reform Party (ADR) and a left-wing coalition called Left (Lénk), in which the Communist Party is taking part. In the 2004 general elections the CSV was able to gain about 35 per cent in all constituencies and end up with 40 per cent of the 60 seats (Dumont and Poirier, 2005: 1110–11). The LSAP was able to win about 1 per cent and became the new junior partner for the coalition government under the leadership of Jean-Claude Juncker. In spite of being the richest country in Europe, Luxembourg is facing some economic problems as well as some policy issues, particularly in relation to education. The poor performance of the education sector in the OECD PISA studies became a major issue in the 2004 campaign (Dumont and Poirier, 2005: 1107).

Turnout in all three countries has been particularly high. Compulsory voting in Belgium and in the Netherlands between 1917 and 1970 were important in keeping the numbers above the 80 per cent threshold (Figure 11.17).

The Southern European countries

Party systems in Southern Europe have become more bipolarised since the 1980s, and this has led to the establishment of two main parties/electoral coalitions with equal electoral strength as well as two or more smaller parties. Although party

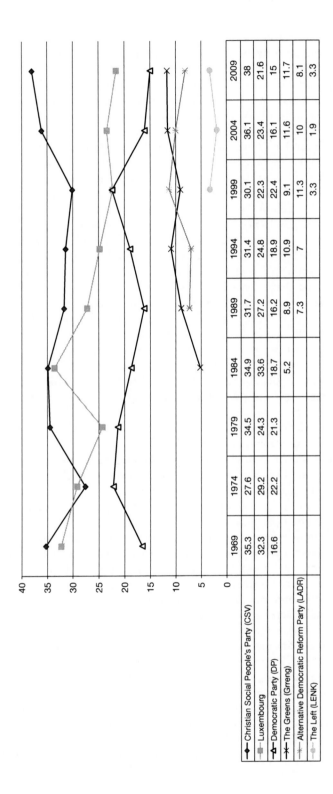

	1969	1974	1979	1984	1989	1994	1999	2004	2009
Christian Social People's Party (CSV)	35.3	27.6	34.5	34.9	31.7	31.4	30.1	36.1	38
Luxembourg	32.3	29.2	24.3	33.6	27.2	24.8	22.3	23.4	21.6
Democratic Party (DP)	16.6	22.2	21.3	18.7	16.2	18.9	22.4	16.1	15
The Greens (Grreng)				5.2	8.9	10.9	9.1	11.6	11.7
Alternative Democratic Reform Party (LADR)					7.3	7	11.3	10	8.1
The Left (LENK)							3.3	1.9	3.3

Figure 11.17 General elections in Luxembourg, 1969–2009

Source: Official electoral website on Luxembourg elections, available online at: www.elections.public.lu/fr/elections-legislatives/1994/index.html (accessed 4 June 2010); Parties and Elections in Europe, available online at: www.elections-and-parties.de (accessed 4 June 2010)

systems in Southern Europe have many common features, there are still major differences, for example, between Italy and the democracies of Portugal, Spain and Greece that emerged after 1974–75.

The party system of the Italian First Republic (1948–92) was framed by an almost pure proportional representation system, which meant that the party system was quite fragmented. Just two parties were able to achieve a share of more than 30 per cent: Christian Democracy (DC) and the Communist Party (PCI). The cold war was an important factor in conditioning the development of the Italian party system. From the very beginning, the communists were excluded from power, so that over four decades Christian Democracy dominated the party and political system (Leonardi and Wertman, 1989), co-opting other smaller parties such as the Liberal Party, the Republican Party, the Social Democratic Party and the Socialist Party into coalition governments. However, a major bribery scandal affecting Christian Democracy as well as the other parties led to the collapse of the party system of the First Republic in 1992. Since the early 1990s, there have been attempts to reform the party system. There was a reduction of preferential voting from four to one at constituency level (Daniels, 1999: 70–81).

The collapse of the old party system and the imprisonment of a large part of the political elite, led to the creation of a new electoral system that intro-duced 75 per cent election of MPs by a simple plurality system in uni-nominal constituencies and 25 per cent by proportional representation with a 5 per cent threshold. This was accompanied by the emergence of the Second Republic, which still used the old constitution, but led to the emergence of a new party system with new political parties. In December 2005, the electoral system was changed back to a proportional representation system, but with the slight difference that the winning electoral coalition would automatically get 55 per cent of seats in the lower house, the Chamber of Deputies (Bardi, 2007: 712).

The consequence of these changes is that the old, fragmented party system has been slowly replaced by a bipolarised two-party system, in which smaller parties either join the left-wing or the right-wing party alliance. The realignment and polarisation has also led to a de-ideologisation of the party programmes and a growing personalisation (Bardi, 2007: 728–9).

Among the most innovative parties is the former Forza Italia, characterised as a 'firm party' (*partito azienda*) or a 'media-mediated personality party', because it was founded and established by the firms of tycoon Silvio Berlusconi using marketing techniques usually used in business (Seisselberg, 1996: 717). Forza Italia was founded in 1994 and, since then, has been shaping the way the party system has evolved. Berlusconi created a coalition with the transformed post-fascist party, National Alliance (AN), led by the charismatic Gianfranco Fini, and the separatist–autonomist Northern League (LN) under the leadership of Umberto Bossi. Since the first elections in 1994, this coalition was able to win three further elections and can be regarded as being more stable than the left-wing coalition. A key label used in the electoral coalition is 'freedom'; this branding remained quite stable since 1994. Other smaller parties, such as the right-centre Christian Democrats, also joined the coalition and, in 2007, the electoral coalition became a political party called People of Freedom (Popolo della Libertà) comprising FI, AN and several smaller parties. However, the Northern League did not join (Donovan, 2008).

The other electoral coalition still has major difficulties in achieving the same level of cohesion and stability as the 'freedom' electoral coalition. In 1994, the left-centre coalition was in disarray and had difficulties adjusting to the new, predominantly majoritarian, electoral system. However, in 1996 the former communists, now Social Democrats, known as the 'Democrats of the Left', left-centre Christian Democrats and Liberals (Margherita), and the Greens (Girasole) formed the Olive Tree (Ulivo) coalition. However, Prime Minister Romano Prodi was nominated president of the European Commission in 1998, following which the coalition fragmented, so that by 2000 a technocratic government had to be appointed by the president of the Republic, Carlo Azeglio Ciampi, to complete the legislature period. The left-centre coalition tended to change labels in the elections that followed. After five years of a right-centre coalition government, the left-centre coalition again came to power in 2006 under Prime Minister Romano Prodi; however, two years of growing dissent between the political parties, and sometimes between the political personalities within the coalition, led to early elections in October 2008. In 2006, the Democrats of the Left and Margherita became the Olive Tree coalition.

In September 2007, it was decided the electoral coalition would be transformed into a political party, to be called the Democratic Party (Partito Democratico, PD) (Lazar, 2008) (Table 11.14).

The process outlined above could be described as a growing consolidation of a bipolarised party system. One positive effect, particularly as a result of the longevity of the coalitions under the leadership of Berlusconi, is that more stability was achieved at governmental level, although such consolidation was still not achieved in the left-centre coalitions. In spite of this, there is a progressive integration of all major parties, reducing the opportunities for smaller parties that depend on particular personalities (for example, Italy of Values led by former judge Antonio di Pietro) to dominate the political scene. It is interesting that Silvio Berlusconi, his party Forza Italy and his coalition-building skills have all been extremely innovative and a major source of party system-building in Italy since

Table 11.14 The main Italian political parties, 2008

Party of People of Freedom (Partito del Popolo della Libertá) right-centre	Democratic Party (Partito Democratico) left-centre	Other parties
• Forza Italia (FI) • Alleanza Nazionale (AN) • Unione Cristiana Democratica (UDC) • Partito Socialista Nuovo (PSN) • Other smaller parties	• Democratici della Sinistra (DS) • Margherita (Christian Democrats and Liberals) • Other smaller parties	• Lega Nord (LN) • Partito della Riconstruzione Comunista (PRC) • Federazioni di Verdi • Italia dei Valori (Antonio di Pietro)

Source: Author

the fall of the First Republic. Overall, it seems that volatility between parties of the same ideological block on the left or the right was still high in the 1996 and 2001 elections, but declined considerably in the 2006 elections. Although this intra-block volatility is quite high, volatility between blocks is negligible. This shows that the two-party system is becoming more consolidated (Bardi, 2007: 720) (Figure 11.18; Table 11.15).

Table 11.15 Electoral systems in Italy, 1948–2008

	Electoral system	Constituencies/seats	Thresholds
1948–93	Proportional representation D'Hondt Preferential voting up to 4 in constituencies with more than 16 seats until 1987 (reformed in 1991 from 4 to 1) Elected for 5 years	31 pluri-nominal constituencies, 630 seats 1 uni-nominal constituency for Val D'Aosta	No threshold
1994–2005	Mixed system 75% uni-nominal constituencies elected by simple plurality, 25% pluri-nominal constituencies elected by proportional representation (first nationally, then at constituency level) using Hare quota system	26 pluri-nominal constituencies returning 155 MPs, 474 single-member constituencies Val D'Aosta as separated uni-nominal constituency	4% threshold
2005–	Proportional representation with a bonus of majority of seats (55%, 340 seats) for winning electoral coalition	27 pluri-nominal constituencies for 629 seats, 1 uni-nominal constituency for Val D'Aosta	• 10% for electoral coalitions • 2% for political parties outside electoral coalitions of total valid votes • 4% for political parties inside electoral coalitions nationwide • 20% for language minority groups within the constituency

Source: Parline datatase online of Interparliamentary Union posted on website www.ipu.org accessed 17 January 2009

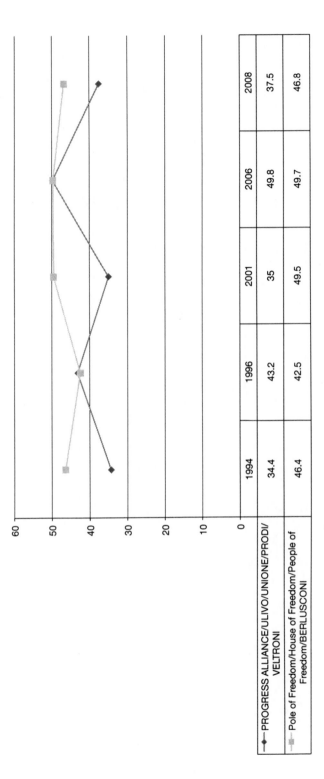

	1994	1996	2001	2006	2008
PROGRESS ALLIANCE/ULIVO/UNIONE/PRODI/ VELTRONI	34.4	43.2	35	49.8	37.5
Pole of Freedom/House of Freedom/People of Freedom/BERLUSCONI	46.4	42.5	49.5	49.7	46.8

Figure 11.18 Elections in Italy according to the two main electoral coalitions/parties, 1994–2008

Source: Author's compilation, available online at: http://parties-and-elections.de (accessed 4 June 2010)

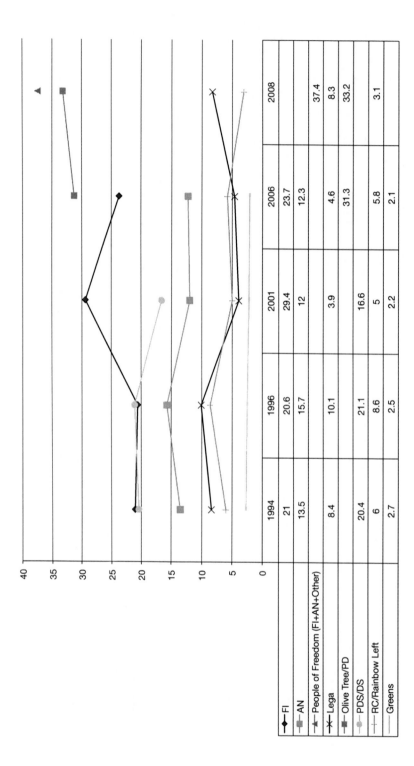

	1994	1996	2001	2006	2008
FI	21	20.6	29.4	23.7	
AN	13.5	15.7	12	12.3	
People of Freedom (FI+AN+Other)					37.4
Lega	8.4	10.1	3.9	4.6	8.3
Olive Tree/PD					33.2
PDS/DS	20.4	21.1	16.6	31.3	
RC/Rainbow Left	6	8.6	5	5.8	3.1
Greens	2.7	2.5	2.2	2.1	

Figure 11.19 General elections in Italy according to the main parties, 1994–2008

Source: Author's compilation, available online at: http://parties-and-elections.de (accessed 4 June 2010)

One of the big successes of democratisation in Portugal, Spain and Greece is that all three party systems are fairly well consolidated. Between 1974 and 2008, there was, generally, continuity of the political parties and also of the electoral share of the vote (Tables 11.16 and 11.17). The big exception was Spain in 1982, when the governmental party, the right-centre Union of Democratic Centre (Unión del Centro Democratico, UCD), collapsed and contributed to the emergence of the Socialist Party (PSOE) as the dominant party. As already mentioned, Southern European and Central and Eastern European political parties have only partially had a similar development to the more established democracies in the north and west of Europe. From the very beginning, new political groups were cartel parties that were and are highly dependent on public funding.

Table 11.16 Electoral systems in Southern Europe

	Electoral system	Constituencies/seats	Threshold
Portugal	Proportional representation based on D'Hondt system Closed lists	22 pluri-nominal constituencies electing 230 seats	No threshold
Spain	Proportional representation based on D'Hondt system Closed lists	50 pluri-nominal constituencies electing 348 seats 2 uni-nominal constituencies of Melilla and Ceuta electing each one seat	3% threshold in pluri-nominal constituencies
Greece	Reinforced proportional representation Bischoff-Hagenbach system	56 pluri-nominal and uni-nominal constituencies electing 300 seats Three levels: • constituency with preferential voting • 13 electoral districts for remaining seats • single national constituency for remaining seats 12 'state deputies' nominated by most successful parties are elected by proportional representation in a national single constituency	3% threshold, above it respective party receives at least 6 seats

Source: Parline archive, Interparliamentary Union, www.ipu.org (accessed 21 December 2008)

Table 11.17 The main parties in Southern Europe

	Social Democrats	Christian Democrats/ Conservatives	Communists	Radical Left	Other parties
Portugal	Partido Socialista (PS)	Partido Socialdemocrata (PSD) Centro Democratico Social-Partido Popular (CDS–PP)	Partido Comunista Portugues (PCP)	Bloco da Esquerda	
Spain	Partido Socialista Obrero Español (PSOE)	Partido Popular (PP)	Izquierda Unida (IU)		Convergencia i Unió (CiU) Partido Nacionalista Vasco (PNV) Bloque Nacionalista Galego (BNG) Coalición Canaria (CC)
Greece	Panhellenio Sosialistisko Kinima (PASOK)	Nea Dimokratia (ND)	Kommunistiko Komma Ellada (KKE)	Synaspismos tis Rizospastikis Aristeras (SYRIZA)	

Source: Author

In Portugal, the party system has remained almost the same since the founding elections of 1975. It is a five-party system with two dominant parties, the socialists and the social democrats, with an almost equal share of the vote. While the socialists belong to the Socialist International and are left-centre, the social democrats were originally a liberal party, but later joined the European People's Party and are right-centre. Three small parties, the conservative Democratic Social Centre–People's Party (CDS–PP), the Communists in coalition with the Greens (PCP–PEV) and the left–new age Block of the Left (BE) can be important for coalition government or parliamentary support for the two main parties. Both the CDS–PP and the Communists are disappearing at local level, although they continue to be present at national level. The Block of the Left is a new party that emerged in 1999 and is supported by the younger generations. It combines new left issues related to new social movements and anti-globalisation with postmodern environmental themes. It has been a major competitor with the Communist Party, which is still quite orthodox in comparison with its counterparts across Europe. It overtook the vote of the Communist Party in the 2009 European elections, although both are in the same parliamentary group of the European Left Group – Nordic Green Left.

A major political earthquake was caused by the Democratic Renewal Party of former president Antonio Ramalho Eanes, which got 17 per cent of the vote in the 1985 elections; however, in the following early elections of 1987, the party lost two-thirds of the vote and by 1991 it had disappeared from the scene. The main winner of the collapse of the vote was the PSD under the leadership of Anibal Cavaco Silva. Between 1985 and 1995, he was able to achieve two absolute majorities that contributed to the stabilisation of the party and political systems. One of the characteristics of the Portuguese party system that bears similarities to the others in Southern Europe is the high level of volatility at the centre owing to the emergence of the new middle classes, which can be characterised as the winners of the European integration process. At the margins, we see the smaller parties competing for the groups left behind by the prosperity induced European integration. Joaquim Aguiar therefore characterises the Portuguese party system as having a hidden fluidity in an ultra-stable party system (Aguiar,1985; see also Jalali, 2007). The CDS–PP was a Christian democratic party, but became Euro-sceptic during and after the adoption of the Treaty of the European Union in 1993. However, leader Paulo Portas has so far been quite pragmatic. In a coalition government with the PSD between 2002 and 2004 Euro-scepticism was almost absent from the demands of the CDS–PP. In the 2005 elections, the Socialist party achieved an absolute majority for the first time, something that they came close to in 1995 and 2001. This means that both main parties, socialists and social democrats, were able to get absolute majorities and contribute to the consolidation of the party system. There is a high level of electoral inter-block volatility between these two main parties (Magone, 2006b) (Figure 11.20).

The Spanish party system can also be regarded as reasonably stable. Until 1982, the Union of Democratic Centre, led by Prime Minister Adolfo Suarez, was the dominant group with about 35 per cent of the vote. It was a pivotal party in the negotiations of the constitutional settlement. One major problem was that it consisted of several social democratic, Christian democratic and liberal parties that were not able to merge into a single party. After the constitution was approved in a referendum in December 1978, the party began to fall apart. The decline was particularly visible after the resignation of Adolfo Suarez in January 1981.

In the elections of 1982, the UCD vote collapsed completely and most voters went to the socialists (PSOE) or the Francoist People's Alliance (AP), which was to become the second largest party (Gunther and Hopkin, 2002).

Owing to the historical legacy of the People's Alliance under former Francoist minister Manuel Fraga Iribarne, the party remained a weak second not reaching more than 25–26 per cent of the vote during the 1980s, known as the 'ceiling of Fraga' (*techo de Fraga*) (Hopkin, 1999: 22). In contrast, the PSOE became the strongest party, achieving a renewed absolute majority in 1986 and failing to achieve a third majority by a narrow margin in 1989. It was able to implement a progressive agenda of reforms, including liberalisation of the economy and the labour market, expansion of the welfare state and democratisation of the education

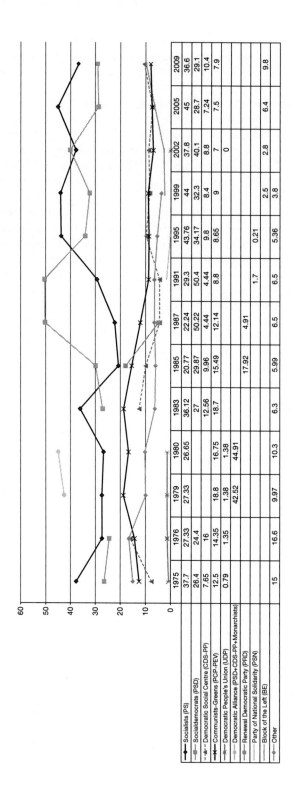

	1975	1976	1979	1980	1983	1985	1987	1991	1995	1999	2002	2005	2009
Socialists (PS)	37.7	27.33	27.33	26.65	36.12	20.77	22.24	29.3	43.76	44	37.8	45	36.6
Socialdemocrats (PSD)	26.4	24.4			27	29.87	50.22	50.4	34.17	32.3	40.1	28.7	29.1
Democratic Social Centre (CDS-PP)	7.65	16			12.56	9.96	4.44	4.44	9.8	8.4	8.8	7.24	10.4
Communists-Greens (PCP-PEV)	12.5	14.35	18.8	16.75	18.7	15.49	12.14	8.8	8.65	9	7	7.5	7.9
Democratic People's Union (UDP)	0.79	1.35	1.38	1.38									
Democratic Alliance (PSD+CDS-PP+Monarchists)			42.52	44.91									
Renewal Democratic Party (PRD)						17.92	4.91						
Party of National Solidarity (PSN)								1.7	0.21				
Block of the Left (BE)										2.5	2.8	6.4	9.8
Other	15	16.6	9.97	10.3	6.3	5.99	6.5	6.5	5.36	3.8			

Figure 11.20 General elections in Portugal, 1975–2009
Source: Author's compilation based on database posted on Portuguese National Electoral Commission website, available online at: www.cne.pt
(accessed 4 June 2010)

sector. The PSOE was able to rule between 1982 and 1996. Owing to the weakness of the AP, the Spanish party system evolved towards a predominantly one-party system in the sense of Giovanni Sartori (Hopkin, 1999: 221). This longevity of power led to the establishment of clientelistic networks and political corruption, which James Petras called patrimonial socialism. The inability of the AP, also known as the Democratic Coalition (CD) in the 1986 general elections, to challenge the PSOE contributed to this situation. Because many political scandals began to erupt in the early 1990s, the AP decided to rejuvenate its leadership and re-found the party. Between 1989 and 1996, new leader José Maria Aznar transformed the party into the People's Party (PP) and modernised the whole approach to electoral politics. The growing deterioration of the image of the PSOE resulting from the political scandals contributed to the rise of the PP in terms of electoral share. In 1993, the PP broke the 'ceiling of Fraga' by achieving 34.8 per cent, and in 1996 it won the elections by one percentage point. The 1993 and 1996 elections represented a major party system change, because the Spanish party system was no longer an imperfect two-party system, but had moved to a bipolarised one. Other parties almost disappeared from the landscape. Jonathan Hopkin calls the present party system 'adulterated', meaning that in spite of a considerable number of small regionalist parties, the tendency is towards majoritarianism and a bipolar two-party system (Hopkin, 2005: 10–14). The best example is the development of the third largest national political group, the United Left.

In 1986, the Communist Party formed a coalition with other parties called United Left (IU), which achieved a respectable 9–10 per cent until 1996. Since then, the electorate of IU has been shifting to the PSOE. In the new millennium, the share has declined to below 6 per cent, resulting in the loss of parliamentary group status. The party was forced to join a parliamentary group with the regionalist Catalan Republican Left (ERC) and its sister party, Initiative for Catalonia – Greens (IC-V). Such parliamentary group status was important, because it had an impact on public funding. Since 1996, the IU has had to make major cuts in personnel and expenditure, because of its dependence on public funding. Apart from the United Left, there are no other national parties, with most of the other parties being regionalist parties coming from the autonomous communities, which achieve representation because they are strong in their regional constituencies. One of the reasons for the lack of representation of other parties at national level is the size of the fifty-two constituencies (fifty in Spain plus Melilla and Ceuta), which are quite small with a threshold of 3 per cent. This means that smaller parties have the best chances of winning in the larger pluri-nominal constituencies of the larger cities, and are disadvantaged in most constituencies in the rural areas.

Thus, apart from the left–right cleavage between PSOE and PP, there is also a major cleavage between the national and regional vote. Among the most prominent regionalist–nationalist parties are Convergence and Union (Convergencia i Unio, CiU) in Catalonia, the Basque Nationalist Party (Partido Nacionalista Vasco, PNV) and the Galician Nationalist Block (Bloco Nacionalista Galego, BNG).

This means that the main parties PSOE and PP, who avoid working with the IU because of its communist legacy, are sometimes dependent on the support of the regionalist parties. The PSOE under Prime Minister Felipe Gonzalez had to rely on the support of the Catalan CiU during the legislature period 1993 and

1996. However, at end of 1995 CiU withdrew its support and PSOE had to call for early elections. The same situation happened during the first Aznar government between 1996 and 2000. Prime Minister Aznar had to make major concessions to the regionalist parties in order to get parliamentary support for his policies. After the elections of 2004 and 2008 Prime Minister Zapatero had to rely on support from the regionalist parties, in spite of strong majorities (Magone, 2009a: 99–101) (Figure 11.21)

In Greece, the reinforced proportional representation electoral system is conducive to a polarised two-party system. The electoral system favours larger parties against the smaller ones. The Socialists (PASOK) and New Democracy have been the main parties of the party system, but some smaller parties are also represented in the Greek *Vouli* (parliament). Ideological differences between the two main parties have declined considerably, so that both are competing for the voters in the centre, mainly consisting of the new middle classes (Nicolacopoulos, 2005). Among the smaller parties is the orthodox Greek Communist Party (KKE) that represents a strong subculture in Greek politics. The ostracism of the Communists during the right-wing democracy of the 1950s and 1960s and the anti-dictatorship resistance made them attractive to a large part of the more radical youth. Leader Aleka Papariga has played a major role in cultivating this subcultural importance of the party in Greek politics. A coalition of several postmodern and left-wing parties is the Coalition of the Radical Left (Synaspismos), which has also been successful in achieving some representation in parliament. Apart from these four parties, there were some splinter parties from the major parties led by strong personalities that achieved representation at a particular election, but disappeared after a while.

Therefore, the Socialists and New Democracy have no other political adversary. There is a tendency in Greece to use the party machinery to create networks of clientelism and patronage. Christos Lyrintzis has called this 'bureaucratic clientelism', which extends to civil society organisations associated to each of the political parties. The heydays of such bureaucratic clientelism were in the 1980s during the absolute majority governments of PASOK under the leadership of Andreas Papandreou (Lyrintzis, 1984; 2005). Europeanisation has contributed to a hollowing out of the state and a decline of such practices, although they are still present. Another characteristic of Greek politics is the dominance of certain political families over several generations. This is the case of the Papandreou and Karamanlis families, which have dominated Greek politics since the 1950s (see Figure 11.22).

While the Southern European party systems achieved a considerable level of party system consolidation, in spite of a high level of volatility at the centre, those of Central and Eastern Europe are still in the middle of such a process. There is also no clear regional pattern, although there is a stronger consolidation of party system in Hungary, the Czech Republic and Slovenia. On the way to consolidation are Slovakia, Bulgaria and Romania. However, the vast majority are characterised by high levels of volatility, and the constant emergence and disappearance of new political parties create major problems in finding the emergence of a consolidated party system.

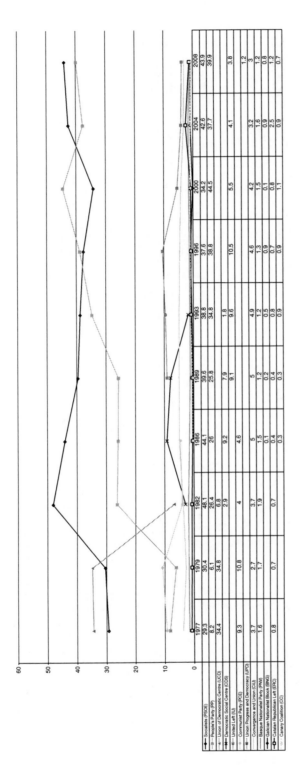

	1977	1979	1982	1986	1989	1993	1996	2000	2004	2008
Socialists (PSOE)	29.3	30.4	48.1	44.1	39.6	38.8	37.6	34.2	42.6	43.9
People's Party (PP)	8.2	6.1	26.4	26	25.8	34.8	38.8	44.5	37.7	39.9
Union of Democratic Centre (UCD)	34.4	34.8	6.8							
Democratic Social Centre (CDS)			2.9	9.2	7.9	1.8				
United Left (IU)				4.6	9.1	9.6	10.5	5.5	4.1	3.8
Communist Party (PCE)	9.3	10.8	4							
Union Progress and Democracy (UPD)										1.2
Convergence and Union (CiU)	3.7	2.7	3.7	5	5	4.9	4.6	4.2	3.2	3
Basque Nationalist Party (PNV)	1.6	1.7	1.9	1.5	1.2	1.2	1.3	1.5	1.6	1.2
Galician Nationalist Block (BNG)				0.1	0.2	0.5	0.9	0.1	0.9	0.8
Catalan Republican Left (ERC)	0.8	0.7	0.7	0.4	0.4	0.8	0.7	0.8	2.5	1.2
Canary Coalition (CC)				0.3	0.3	0.9	0.9	1.1	0.9	0.7

Figure 11.21 General elections in Spain, 1977–2008

Source: Author's compilation based on electoral database of Spanish Ministry of Interior, available online at: www.elecciones.mir.es/MIR/jsp/resultados/index.htm (accessed 4 June 2010)

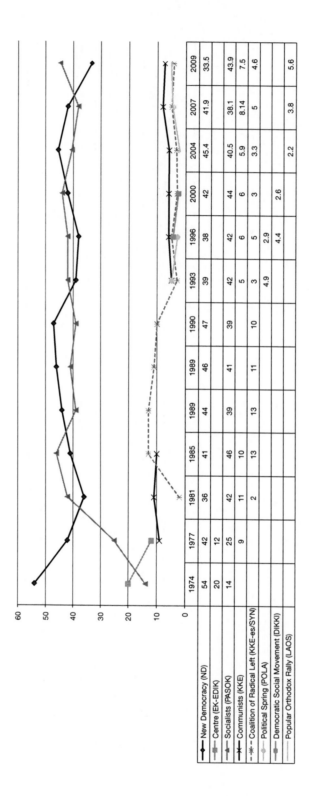

	1974	1977	1981	1985	1989	1989	1990	1993	1996	2000	2004	2007	2009
New Democracy (ND)	54	42	36	41	44	46	47	39	38	42	45.4	41.9	33.5
Centre (EK-EDIK)	20	12											
Socialists (PASOK)	14	25	42	46	39	41	39	42	42	44	40.5	38.1	43.9
Communists (KKE)	14	9	11	10	13	11	10	5	6	6	5.9	8.14	7.5
Coalition of Radical Left (KKE-es/SYN)			2	13	13	11		3	5	3	3.3	5	4.6
Political Spring (POLA)								4.9	2.9				
Democratic Social Movement (DIKKI)									4.4	2.6			
Popular Orthodox Rally (LAOS)											2.2	3.8	5.6

Figure 11.22 General elections in Greece, 1974–2009

Source: Zervakis and Auernheimer, 2009: 842

The Central European countries: Hungary, the Czech Republic, Slovakia and Poland

Hungary and the Czech Republic were the two countries where party systems consolidated at a very early stage. In the case of Hungary, the early transition led to an advantageous position for the incumbent Communist Party, which transformed itself into a social democratic party. This strategy of the 'reform communists' was practised in most other countries of Central and Eastern Europe (see Tables 11.18 and 11.19).

The Hungarian party system has evolved towards a majoritarian democracy, resulting from the polarisation between the Social Democrats (former Reform Communists, MSZP) and the Hungarian Civic Union (Fidesz). These are the two main parties that have their respective junior partners for eventual coalition building. The Social Democrats tend to join with the Liberals (SDSZ) while Fidesz with the Hungarian Democratic Forum and the Christian Democrats (KDNP). There is a general tendency towards a bipolarised two-party system (Körösényi et al., 2010: 387–98). Such strategy was pursued particularly by Viktor Orbán, leader of the Fidesz, during his government between 1998 and 2002. It led to a concentration of the vote among the two main parties. In spite of the financial crisis, the left–right polarisation between the Civic Union and the Social Democrats continued to dominate Hungarian politics (Figure 11.23).

The Czech party system also became consolidated soon after the transition to democracy. The former communists remained fairly orthodox, so that a re-founded social democratic party emerged to occupy the left-centre position. Although the ČSSD was re-founded in 1992, its long historical legacy goes back to Austria–Hungary in the nineteenth century. On the right, there is the conservative Euro-sceptic Democratic Civic Party, which was first established as an umbrella party for all conservative and liberal opposition forces. Prime Minister Vaclav Klaus, who became president of the Republic after 2003, is the best known politician of the ODS. He is a strong supporter of the market economy and was inspired by Margaret Thatcher and Ronald Reagan. The ODS is quite pragmatic, as shown by the way it was able to negotiate a coalition agreement, following the 2006 elections, with the Greens (who achieved representation for the first time after a long period of internal infighting) and the Christian Democrats (KDL–ČSL). The only anti-systemic party remains the Communist Party, which is fairly orthodox and is supported mainly by the groups left behind in the transition process to democracy and the market economy. The Communist Party still has considerable support, but may become less and less important because of its rigid ideological tendencies, and also because its members are ageing. The Christian Democrats could also regain their historical legacy from the inter-war period and play an important role in coalition-building, particularly on the right.

Overall, the Czech party system is well consolidated, partly because of the quality of its leaders, and partly because of the historical legacy of democracy inherited from the inter-war period. Pragmatism has dominated the relationship between the political parties, despite their ideological differences. However, issues of clientelism, political corruption and power cartelisation supported by the ČSSD and the ODS have undermined the quality of democracy (Vodička, 2005: 151–3) (Figure 11.24).

Table 11.18 Electoral systems in east Central Europe

	Electoral system	Constituencies/seats	Thresholds
Hungary	Mixed system Two-ballot majoritarian system (absolute majority for first round) And proportional representation Two votes (each for majoritarian and proportional representation part)	176 (45.6%) elected by two-ballot majoritarian system, only candidates with more than 15% of vote can move to second ballot, 25% is enough for winning seat in second ballot Less than 50% turnout at constituency level leads to repetition of ballot Two levels of allocation of proportional representation seats: 146 seats in 20 pluri-nominal constituencies 64 seats allocated at single national constituency	5% threshold
Czech Republic	Proportional representation using D'Hondt system Up to two preferential votes at constituency level	14 multi-member constituencies electing 200 MPs	5% for political parties 10% for coalitions of two parties 15% of coalitions of three parties 20% for coalitions of four parties
Slovakia	Proportional representation Closed party lists using Hagenbach-Bischoff method	1 national constituency electing 150 MPs	5% for political parties 10% for coalitions
Poland	Proportional representation Closed lists Modified Saint-Lagüe	41 multi-member constituencies (depending on population) electing between 7 and 19 seats each Overall 460 seats	5% for political parties 8% for coalitions
Slovenia	Proportional representation Preferential voting D'Hondt	8 electoral units, divided in 11 single-member constituencies electing 88 seats, 2 seats reserved for Hungarian and Italian minorities	4% threshold

Source: Interparliamentary Union, Parline Database, www.ipu.org (accessed 22 December 2008)

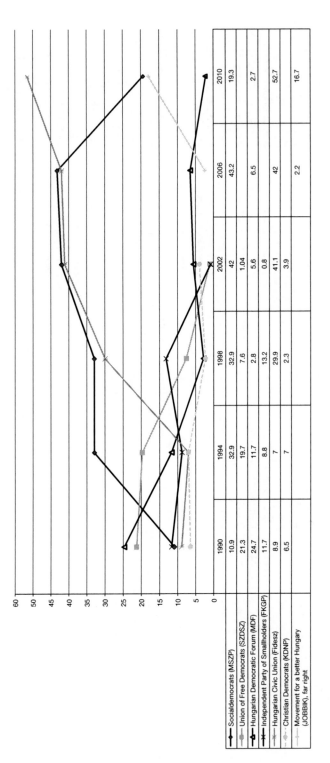

	1990	1994	1998	2002	2006	2010
Socialdemocrats (MSZP)	10.9	32.9	32.9	42	43.2	19.3
Union of Free Democrats (SZDSZ)	21.3	19.7	7.6	1.04	6.5	2.7
Hungarian Democratic Forum (MDF)	24.7	11.7	2.8	5.6		
Independent Party of Smallholders (FKGP)	11.7	8.8	13.2	0.8		
Hungarian Civic Union (Fidesz)	8.9	7	29.9	41.1	42	52.7
Christian Democrats (KDNP)	6.5	7	2.3	3.9		
Movement for a better Hungary (JOBBIK), far right					2.2	16.7

Figure 11.23 General elections in Hungary, 1990–2010

Source: Körösényi *et al.*, 2010: 386; see also online at: www.parties-and-elections.de (accessed 4 June 2010)

Table 11.19 Political parties in east Central Europe, 2008

Country	Social democrats	Conservatives	Liberal	Christian democrats	Other
Hungary	Magyar Szocialista Párt (MSZP) Hungarian Socialist Party	Fidesz – Magyar Polgári Szövetség (FIDESZ) Fidesz – Hungarian Civic Union/Magyar Demokrata Fórum (MDF) Hungarian Democratic Forum	Szabad Demokraták Szövetsége (SZDSZ) Union of Free Democrats	Kereszténydemokrata Néppárt (KDNP) Christian Democratic People's Party	Jobbik, Movement for a Better Hungary (extreme right)
Czech Republic	Česká Strana Sociálne Demokratická (ČSSD) Czech Social Democratic Party	Občanská Demokratická Strana (ODS) Civic Democratic Party		Kresťanská a Demokratická Unie (KDU–CSL) Christian and Democratic Union (2002: KDU–CSL + US–DEU)	Komunistická Strana Čech a Moravy (KSČM) Communist Party of Bohemia and Moravia Strana Zelených (SZ) Green Party
Slovakia	Smer – Sociálna Demokracia (SMER–SD) Direction – Social Democracy		Aliancia Nového Občana (ANO) Alliance of the New Citizen	Slovenská Demokratická a Kresťanská Únia (SDKU–DS) Slovak Democratic and Christian Union Krestanskodemokratické Hnutie (KDH) Christian Democratic Movement	Magyar Koalició Pártja (MKP) Hungarian Coalition Party (Minority) Slovenská Národná Strana (SNS) Slovak National Party (Nationalist) L'udová Strana – Hnuti za Demokratické Slovensko (LS–HZDS) People's Party – Movement for a Democratic Slovakia (Nationalist)

Table 11.19 Continued

Country	Social democrats	Conservatives	Liberal	Christian democrats	Other
					Komunistická Strana Slovenska (KSS) Communist Party of Slovakia (Communist)
Poland	Sojusz Lewicy Demokratycznej (SLD) Democratic Left Alliance Socjaldemokracja Polska (SDPL) Social Democracy of Poland	Prawo i Sprawiedliwosc (PiS) Law and Justice	Partija Demokratyczna (PD) Democratic Party	Platforma Obywatelska (PO) Civic Platform Polskie Stronnictwo Ludowe (PSL) Polish People's Party	Samoobrona Rzeczpospolitej Polskiej (SRP) Self-Defense of the Republic of Poland (right-wing populism) Liga Polskich Rodzin (LPR) League of Polish Families (Christian right, populist)
Slovenia	Socialni Demokrati (SD) Social Democrats	Slovenska Demokratska Stranka (SDS) Slovenian Democratic Party	ZARES (Z) For Real Liberalna Demokracija Slovenije (LDS) Liberal Democracy of Slovenia	Slovenska Ljudska Stranka (SLS) Slovenian People's Party Nova Slovenija – Krščanska Ljudska Stranka (NSI) New Slovenia – Christian People's Party	Demokratična Stranka Upokojencev Slovenije (DeSUS) Democratic Pensioners' Party of Slovenia Slovenska Nacionalna Stranka (SNS) Slovenian National Party (Nationalist) Stranka Mladih Slovenije (SMS) Youth Party of Slovenia (Greens)

Source: Author's own compilation

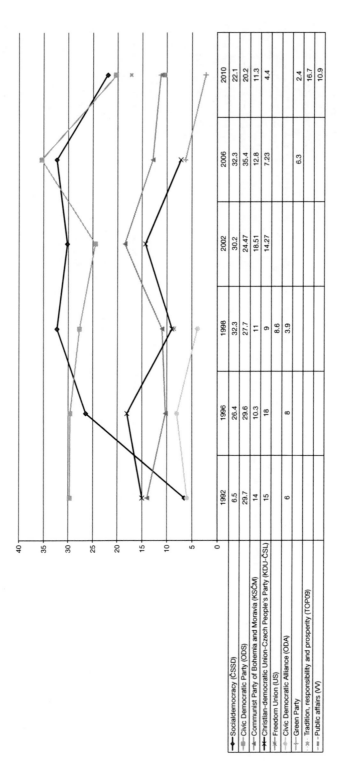

	1992	1996	1998	2002	2006	2010
Socialdemocracy (ČSSD)	6.5	26.4	32.3	30.2	32.3	22.1
Civic Democratic Party (ODS)	29.7	29.6	27.7	24.47	35.4	20.2
Communist Party of Bohemia and Moravia (KSČM)	14	10.3	11	18.51	12.8	11.3
Christian-democratic Union-Czech People's Party (KDU-ČSL)	15	18	9	14.27	7.23	4.4
Freedom Union (US)			8.6			
Civic Democratic Alliance (ODA)	6	8	3.9			
Green Party					6.3	2.4
Tradition, responsibility and prosperity (TOP09)						16.7
Public affairs (VV)						10.9

Figure 11.24 General elections in the Czech Republic, 1992–2006

Source: Author's graph based on Lewis, 2003: 62; see also online at: www.parties-and-elections.de (accessed 4 June 2010)

In contrast, the Slovak party system is fairly volatile. Populist parties dominate in the party system, although it is difficult to assess whether they are able to survive over the long term. Populism becomes less appealing when such parties come to power and have to face the reality of daily politics. From the start, the Movement for Democratic Slovakia (HZDS) under the leadership of Vladimír Mečiar dominated the political system. However, the fragmented party system was a major constraint for radical policies. Mečiar became known for his xenophobic language and policy tendencies against the large Hungarian minority. He was able to count on the support of the Slovak Nationalist Party (SNS), but both together were unable to achieve an absolute majority (Szomolányi and Mesesnikov, 1997: 135–42).

Slovakia was under pressure from the European Union to change these policies, so that in 1998 a coalition government of five parties, which were opposed to Mečiar, was formed. The Slovak Democratic Coalition, which included the Christian Democratic parties, the Hungarian minority party, the Liberals (DS), the Social Democrats (SDSS later SDL) and the Greens, was able to replace Mečiar's coalition government. The Christian democrat, Mikulas Džurinda, became the main leader and remained in power from 1998 to 2006. The main aim of Džurinda's government was to achieve accession to the European Union (Haughton and Malová, 2007).

The volatility of the party system led to the decline of the Social Democratic Alliance (SDL) and its replacement by the new populist party Direction – Social Democracy. In contrast to the Czech Republic, the SDL originated from the former Communist Party and moved towards social democracy. Leader Robert Fico was the best-known personality in the previous SDL, but he decided to leave and create his own party, called Direction – Third Way. Therefore the new party won the 2006 general elections. However, Fico's subsequent coalition government with Mečiar's HZDS and the xenophobic SNS, which led to the suspension of the SMER from the Party of European Socialists, has been controversial. Although in political terms the present coalition has partners with irreconcilable positions, all three political parties agree on economic issues. Both SNS and HZDS have a strong affinity to socialist economic principles, particularly anti-market tendencies and the expansion of the welfare state. According to a study on the general elections in 2006 by Vladimir Pčolinsky and Antónia Štensová, there were at least three main cleavages symbolised by political parties in Slovakia. The left–right cleavage was symbolised by the social democrats and the Christian democrats, who also had the most economic resources to spend on the campaign, and it was personalised through the leaders of the respective parties, Robert Fico and Mikulas Džurinda. SMER was against the necessary reforms in the economy and welfare state, whereas the incumbent SDKU wanted to continue on the path of reform. In terms of opinion polls, Robert Fico was the clear winner of this cleavage. The second major cleavage was between the nationalists (SNS) and the Hungarian minority (SMK). The SNS led a very aggressive campaign against the Hungarian minority and this was responded to in the campaign by the SMK. The third cleavage was less salient, and was played out between the HZDS and the smaller Christian Democratic Movement (KDH). While the HZDS emphasised social protection and health care issues, the KDH stressed the role of the family, ethical, and law and order issues. The main loser of the 2006 elections was the HZDS, which took a moderate position, in order to preserve good opportunities in terms of coalition-building after the elections (Pčolinsky and Štensová, 2007: 106–9).

Although there has been a consolidation of the party system, populism can still create instability and uncertainty. The volatile nature of the electorate may lead to the sudden decline of some parties and the emergence of new ones. The xenophobic tendencies of some parties, such as the SNS and the HZDS against the Hungarian minority, continue to be problematic (Figure 11.25).

In comparison to Hungary, the Czech Republic and Slovakia, Poland is probably a less consolidated party system. Originally, Solidarity and its parties formed the main opposition to the Reform Communists (SLD); however, over time other conservative and liberal parties emerged on the scene and old parties declined. This became particularly evident in the 2005 elections, which saw the share of the vote of the SLD slump to 11.5 per cent. Instead, conservative nationalist parties emerged and founded a coalition government led by the Law and Justice Party (PiS). The other partners were the Self-Defence of the Polish Republic (Samoobrona, SRP), which was Euro-sceptic and populist, and the anti-semitic conservative League of Polish Families (PSL) (Jasiewicz and Jasiewicz-Betkiewicz, 2006).

After the 2005 general elections, Jaroslaw Kaczysnky became prime minister, while his brother had been elected president of the Republic some months before. PiS emerged out of the Solidarity Electoral Action (AWS, later AWPS) founded in 1997 and consisting of thirty parties, but collapsed in the 2001 elections. The PiS emerged out of the AWS as a result of the popularity of Lech Kaczinsky, who was justice minister of the minority government formed by the AWS (Jasiewicz and Jasiewicz-Betkiewicz, 2006: 1242–5).

The League of Polish Families (PSL) is a far-right party with strong Catholic ties, emphasising social conservative values. Moreover, the party can be nationalist and anti-semitic according to the circumstances. Owing to its uncompromising positions it has been able to gain a substantial share of the vote. Similarly, Samobroona under leader Andrej Lepper is also populist and appeals directly to the losers of the transition to democracy and the European integration process. However, in the 2007 elections support for the party eroded completely.

The liberal Civic Platform (PO) under leader Donald Tusk, which has strong American ties, also emerged after 2001 as a moderate follow-up party of the AWPS. After the social democrats (2001–5) and the conservatives (2005–7), the liberals have become the largest party. This shows the high level of volatility that exists in the Polish party system. At present we can speak of a four-party system in Poland: on the right-centre we can find PiS, on the left-centre PO, on the left SDL and in the centre the agrarian Polish People's Party (PSL). One important positive aspect is that the number of parties represented in parliament has decreased considerably, allowing for more stable coalitions, for example the Civic Platform formed a coalition with the moderate PSL (*The Economist*, 25 October 2007).

One major problem of Polish elections has been the low turnout. In 2001, the turnout was 46.3 per cent, in 2005 40.5 per cent and in 2007 53.9 per cent. This leads to a distortion of results, owing to the stronger mobilisation either of the left or the right. One of the reasons why PiS and other right-wing parties performed so well in 2005 was probably related to the extremely low turnout (McManus-Czubinska *et al.*, 2004) (Figure 11.26).

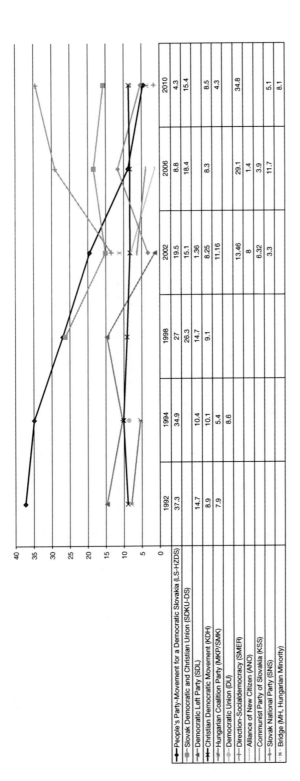

Figure 11.25 General elections in Slovakia, 1992–2010

Source: Author's graph based on Lewis, 2003: 63; see also online at: www.parties-and-elections.de (accessed 4 June 2010)

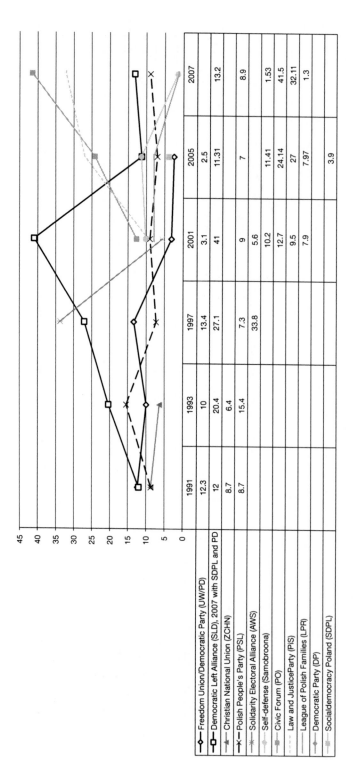

	1991	1993	1997	2001	2005	2007
Freedom Union/Democratic Party (UW/PD)	12.3	10	13.4	3.1	2.5	
Democratic Left Alliance (SLD), 2007 with SDPL and PD	12	20.4	27.1	41	11.31	13.2
Christian National Union (ZChN)	8.7	6.4				
Polish People's Party (PSL)	8.7	15.4	7.3	9	7	8.9
Solidarity Electoral Alliance (AWS)			33.8			
Self-defense (Samobroona)				5.6	11.41	1.53
Civic Forum (PO)				10.2	24.14	41.5
Law and JusticeParty (PiS)				12.7	27	32.11
League of Polish Families (LPR)				9.5	7.97	1.3
Democratic Party (DP)				7.9		
Socialdemocracy Poland (SDPL)					3.9	

Figure 11.26 General elections in Poland, 1991–2007

Source: Lewis, 2003: 62; see also online at: www.parties-and-elections.de (accessed 4 June 2010)

Geographically Slovenia can be placed as part of the western Balkans, but politically it has been part of the Central European pattern of politics. The former Slovenian communists were instrumental in paving the way towards democracy in the country. The party system has been dominated by the Social Democrats (SD), the Democrats (SDS) and the Liberal Democrats (LDS). The dominant party was the LDS, which was able to form governments with other parties between 1992 and 2004 almost without interruption. However, in 2004 the conservative Democratic Party (SDS) won the elections and formed a government with other right-centre parties including the Christian People's Party (NSi), the Slovenian People's Party (SLS) and the Pensioners' Party (DeSUS). The main reason for decline of the vote for the liberal democrats was basically the consequences of longevity in power, particularly the eruption of several corruption scandals. Moreover, the LDS moved towards the left, and this vacuum was filled by the right-centre SDS (Fink-Hafner, 2005: 1183–4). Furthermore, the SD moved towards the centre. Soon after the elections, the LDS split into two. A new party called ZARES-Nova Politika emerged that challenged the liberal democrats. In the 2008 elections, Janez Janša was not able to repeat the victory of the previous elections. A further major shift took place, owing to the rise of the social democrats from the third to the strongest political party in the country. Prime minister Borut Pahor formed a coalition government with the LDS that lost considerably at the 2008 elections to the new party ZARES-Nova Politika (Figure 11.27).

> After the collapse of the vote of the LDS, the Slovenian party system remains quite volatile. Nevertheless, one can see a cleavage emerging between the leftcentre social democrats and the rightcentre Democratic party. Both are able to co-opt junior partners which are respectively on the left and right. The only anti-systemic populist party is the National Party of Slovenia which have a small share of the vote. The overall ideology cannot be pinpointed to the right or left, because it mixes right-wing xenophobic populism with left-wing socially oriented policies. It shares similarities to its Slovak counterpart, and represents a major current across most countries of Central and Eastern Europe.
>
> (Kopeček, 2007: 288–90)

The Baltic countries

While the east Central European countries were able to preserve some kind of sovereignty during the Soviet period, this was not the case of the three Baltic states, Lithuania, Latvia and Estonia, that were occupied by Germany during the Second World War and in 1942 annexed by the Soviet Union. They became integral Republics of the Soviet Union. The newly found independence after 1991 led to the establishment of political parties, although the strong russification of the population during the Soviet period led to considerable tensions with the Soviet Union and today with Russia. The exclusion of the Russian minority who did not learn either Estonian or Latvian led to considerable social tensions in these countries. Such tensions continue to determine the political situation in both countries. A more tolerant approach was chosen by Lithuania but, in spite of that, tensions with Russia have

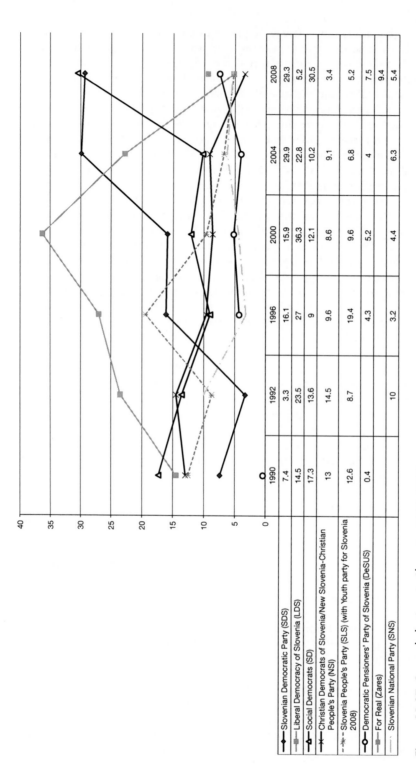

	1990	1992	1996	2000	2004	2008
Slovenian Democratic Party (SDS)	7.4	3.3	16.1	15.9	29.9	29.3
Liberal Democracy of Slovenia (LDS)	14.5	23.5	27	36.3	22.8	5.2
Social Democrats (SD)	17.3	13.6	9	12.1	10.2	30.5
Christian Democrats of Slovenia/New Slovenia-Christian People's Party (NSI)	13	14.5	9.6	8.6	9.1	3.4
Slovenia People's Party (SLS) (with Youth party for Slovenia 2008)	12.6	8.7	19.4	9.6	6.8	5.2
Democratic Pensioners' Party of Slovenia (DeSUS)	0.4		4.3	5.2	4	7.5
For Real (Zares)						9.4
Slovenian National Party (SNS)		10	3.2	4.4	6.3	5.4

Figure 11.27 General elections in Slovenia, 1990–2008

Source: Lewis, 2003: 63; see also online: www.parties-and-elections.de (accessed 4 June 2010); http://volitve.gov.si/dz2008/en/index.html (accessed 4 June 2010)

continued to shape the bilateral relationship, particularly in relation to energy policy. In both countries the party systems tend to be right-centre, with most left-wing parties being dominated by the large Russian ethnic groups.

One characteristic of all three party systems is that they are fairly volatile and the political parties are reasonably small. This is especially true for Estonia and Latvia. Lithuania managed to create greater stability, although in recent years new populist parties have undermined this early consolidation (see Tables 11.20 and 11.21).

The Latvian party system is probably the least consolidated of all three countries. Most political parties are quite nationalist or populist in nature, and personalisation of politics is important in Latvian politics. There is a general cleavage between left and right, which coincides with ethnic divisions between the large Russian minority and the Latvian population. Most Latvian parties support a tough language policy towards the Russians who do not speak the language. Although Latvian Way (LC–LPP) was the dominant party up until 2002, corruption scandals and disenchantment with its policies led to its decline. This is a liberal party, but also conservative on many issues. Since 2002, the People's Party has been able to become the dominant party with roughly 20 per cent of votes. In the

Table 11.20 Electoral systems in the Baltic countries

Country	Electoral system	Constituencies/seats	Threshold
Latvia (100 seats)	Proportional representation Preferential vote Modified Saint-Lagüe	5 multi-member constituencies (14 to 29 seats)	5%
Estonia (101 seats)	Proportional representation Preferential vote Simple electoral quotient at constituency level D'Hondt at national level	Constituency level: 12 multi-member constituencies (6–13 seats according to population) National level: 26 compensatory seats	5%
Lithuania (141 seats)	Parallel system Two-ballot majoritarian system and proportional representation	70 single-member constituencies with 2 rounds, if none of candidates achieve at least one-fifth of the vote when there is less than 40% of turnout If there is more than 40%, 50% of votes is required, otherwise a second ballot is conducted 70 seats are allocated by proportional representation system in a single national constituency	5%

Source: Interparliamentary Union, Parline database online www.ipu.org (accessed 23 December 2008)

Table 11.21 Political parties in the Baltic states, 2008

	Social democrats	Conservatives	Liberals	Agrarian/Green	Other
Latvia	Latvijas Sociāldemokrātiskā Strādnieku Partija (LSDSP) Latvian Social Democratic Workers' Party	Tautas Partija (TP) People's Party Jaunais Laiks (JL) New Era	Centriska Partija – Latvijas Zemnieku Savienība (LZS) Centre Party – Latvian Peasants Union Latvijas Pirmā Partija – Latvijas Ceļš (LPP/LC) Latvia's First Party – Latvia's Way	Latvijas Zaļā Partija (LZP) Latvian Green Party	Tēvzemei un Brīvībai/LNNK (TB/LNNK) Fatherland and Freedom (National conservative) Saskaņas Centrs (SC) Harmony Centre Russian minority) Par Cilvēka Tiesībām Vienotā Latvijā (PCTVL) For Human Rights in United Latvia
Estonia	Sotsiaaldemokraatlik Erakond (SDE) Social Democratic Party	Isamaa ja Res Publica Liit (IRL) Pro Patria and Res Publica	Eesti Reformierakond (RE) Estonian Reform Party Eesti Keskerakond (K) Estonian Centre Party	Eestimaa Rohelised (ER) Estonian Greens Eestimaa Rahvaliit (ERL) Estonian People's Union	
Lithuania	Lietuvos Socialdemokratu Partija (LSDP) Lithuanian Social Democratic Party	Tevynes Sąjunga – Lietuvos Krikscionys Demokratai (TS–LKD) Homeland Union – Lithuanian Christian Democrats (2004: TS)	Lietuvos Respublikos Liberalu Sajūdis (LRLS) Lithuanian Republic Liberal Movement Liberalų ir Centro Sąjunga (LiCS) Liberal and Centre Union Naujoji Sąjunga – Socialliberalai (NS) New Union – Social Liberals	Lietuvos Valstiečių Liaudininku Sąjunga (LVLS) Lithuanian Peasant Popular Union (2004: VNDS) (Agrarian)	Tautos Prisikelimo Partija (TPP) National Revival Party (National Conservative) Tvarka ir Teisingumas (TT) Order and Justice (2004: LDP) (National Conservative) Darbo Partija (DP) (radical left) Labour Party Akcja Wyborcza Polaków na Liwie (AWPL) Electoral Action of Poles in Lithuania (Polish minority)

Source: Author

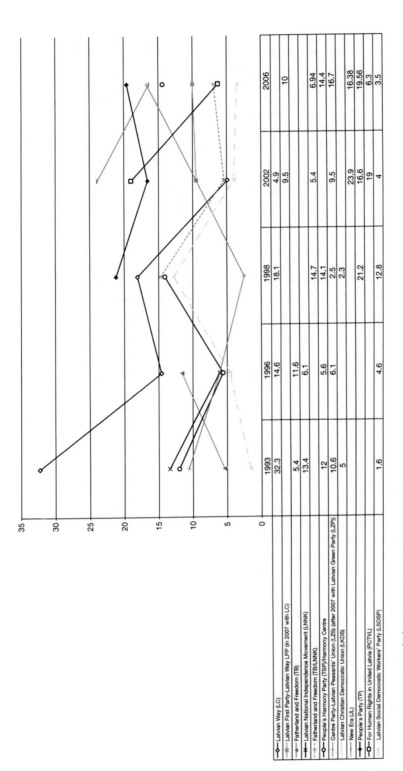

	1993	1996	1998	2002	2006
Latvian Way (LC)	32.3	14.6	18.1	4.9	
Latvian First Party-Latvian Way LPP (in 2007 with LC)				9.5	10
Fatherland and Freedom (TB)	5.4	11.6			
Latvian National Independence Movement (LNNK)	13.4	6.1			
Fatherland and Freedom (TB/LNNK)			14.7	5.4	6.94
People's Harmony Party (TSP)/Harmony Centre	12	5.6	14.1		14.4
Centre Party-Latvian Peasants' Union (LZS) (after 2007 with Latvian Green Party (LZP))	10.6	6.1	2.5	9.5	16.7
Latvian Christian Democratic Union (LKDS)	5		2.3		
New Era (JL)				23.9	16.38
People's Party (TP)			21.2	16.6	19.56
For Human Rights in United Latvia (PCTVL)				19	6.3
Latvian Social Democratic Workers' Party (LSDSP)	1.6	4.6	12.8	4	3.5

Figure 11.28 General elections in Latvia, 1992–2006

Source: National Electoral Commission Electoral Database, Latvia, available online at: www.cvk.lv/cgi-bin/wdbcgiw/base/saeima9.GalRezS9.vis (accessed 5 June 2010)

2006 elections it formed a coalition with the Centre Party (LZS) and the Green Party (LZP). The New Era Party (JL) is also a conservative party that focuses on combating political corruption. In this sense, there have been tensions with other parties, because of its intransigent demands in this field.

The parties Harmony Centre and For Human Rights in United Latvia are parties of the Russian minorities that try to take part in political life, although are so far excluded from mainstream politics. They represent about one-fifth of the electorate, which in the end shows the dissatisfaction of part of the population with the present state of affairs. The Latvian party system is far from consolidated. The share of the vote is quite fragmented, personalisation of politics prevents a strengthening of party organisation, and the conflict between the large Russian minority and the Latvian population prevents a moderation of politics in the country (Figure 11.28).

The Estonian party system has made considerable progress since 2000. Some parties that seem to dominate politics from election to election are gradually emerging, two of them being important for the stability of the party system. On the one hand, there is the Reform Party (RE), which has been a part of most coalition governments since the mid 1990s. It is a liberal party, emphasising the free market economy and low taxation, and it has been instrumental in shaping the economic order in Estonia (Arter, 1996). On the other hand, the Agrarian–Liberal Centre Party is more socially inclined and Euro-sceptic. In the 2004 referendum, leader Edgar Savisaar imposed a 'no' position on the party, which led to dissent and people leaving the party (Pettai, 2005: 1006–7). Nevertheless, both parties have become important stable actors in the emerging Estonian party system. In 2003, a new conservative party emerged called Res Publica that was able to win the elections with over 24 per cent of the vote. It formed a coalition government with the Reform Party and the People's Union, but decided to leave the coalition in 2005, when Justice minister Kent Martti Vaher was forced to resign over his intention to introduce quotas for charges on corruption brought by prosecutors against local governments officials. As a protest, the whole party withdrew from the coalition (Pettai, 2006: 1096–7).

On the left, the Social Democratic Party has been getting stronger in terms of votes received. It became part of the coalition government of Prime Minister Andrus Ansip from the Reform Party, which also included the Pro Patria and Respublica Party. Last, but not least, the Greens were able to achieve representation in the 2007 general elections. The Estonian party system is less polarised, and both the Centre Party and the Reform Party, despite differences, work pragmatically together if necessary, both being at the centre – for example, between 2005 and 2007 after the breakdown of the coalition with the Pro Patria and Respublica Party. Meanwhile, the party system has been reduced to six parties, which clearly represents a considerable rationalisation, if we compare with the Latvian case. Last but not least, Estonia managed better the relationship and integration of the large Russian ethnic minority, in spite of occasional tensions with Moscow regarding symbolic politics. There are no parties representing the large Russian minority. The highly personalised electoral system devised by the prominent American–Estonian political scientist Rein Taagepera contributes to a strong relationship between political personalities and politicians at constituency level. This is reinforced by the small size of the country (Figure 11.29).

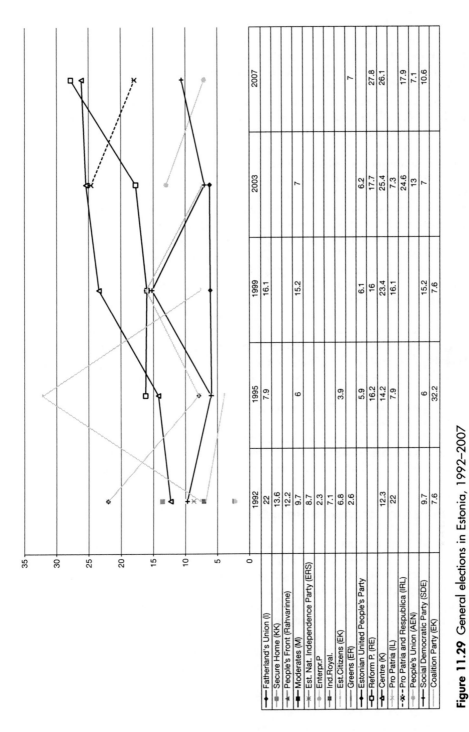

	1992	1995	1999	2003	2007
Fatherland's Union (I)	22	7.9	16.1		
Secure Home (KK)	13.6				
People's Front (Rahvarinne)	12.2				
Moderates (M)	9.7	6	15.2	7	
Est. Nat. Independence Party (ERS)	8.7				
Enterpr.P	2.3				
Ind.Royal.	7.1				
Est.Citizens (EK)	6.8	3.9			
Greens (ER)	2.6				7
Estonian United People's Party		5.9	6.1	6.2	
Reform P. (RE)		16.2	16	17.7	27.8
Centre (K)	12.3	14.2	23.4	25.4	26.1
Pro Patria (IL)	22	7.9	16.1	7.3	17.9
Pro Patria and Respublica (IRL)				24.6	17.9
People's Union (AEN)				13	7.1
Social Democratic Party (SDE)	9.7	6	15.2	7	10.6
Coalition Party (EK)	7.6	32.2	7.6	7	

Figure 11.29 General elections in Estonia, 1992–2007

Source: Estonian National Electoral Commission, electoral database, available online at: www.vvk.ee/index.php?id=11522 (accessed 5 June 2010)

In contrast to Latvia and Estonia, the Lithuanian party system was quite stable in the 1990s, but began to fragment considerably in the new millennium. Apart from the sudden appearance of the populist Labour Party in 2004, many of the parties had to deal with factionalism resulting in the formation of new parties. The electoral system forces parties to create coalitions on the left and right, in order to be able to move to the second round in the uni-nominal constituency part. After the general elections of 2008, a centre-right coalition was established under the leadership of the Christian democrats including the centrist National Revival Party and the conservative liberals (LRLS). In terms of realignment, the 2008 elections led to the collapse of the populist Labour Party and the strengthening of the more traditional social democrats (former communists) (LSDP). In spite of the high level of volatility and fragmentation, the left–right axis is leading to two main groups of parties on the left and right. On the left, the social democrats have now been the dominant party and have survived the challenge of the populist Labour Party set up by Russian-born millionaire Viktor Uspaskish.

According to Algis Krupavicius, the Lithuanian party system was on the path to stability between 1992 and 2000. Two main parties emerged on the left and right that contributed to the structuring of the party system: Homeland Union (TS), the Christian Democrats (LDKP) and the two social democratic parties (LDDP and LSDP). However, in 2000 the National Union–Social Liberals (NS-SL), under charismatic leader Arturas Pasaukas, were able to win 20 per cent of the vote, leading to a political earthquake. Four years later, the populist Labour Party emerged as the winner with almost 30 per cent of the vote. The high level of volatility is a result of the dissatisfaction of the population with the performance of the political system. This protest vote is easily attracted by populist parties with ready solutions (Krupavicius, 2005: 1094–5).

However, in the 2008 elections the share of the vote of these parties collapsed. It may be an indication of the high level of volatility of the party system. One right-wing conservative party is Order and Justice (TT), which has, so far, been sidelined by the other parties owing to its radical ideology in many issues. It has strong populist tendencies, but still has considerable electoral support (Figure 11.30).

The south-eastern model: Bulgaria and Romania

The south-eastern pattern of party systems is characterised by strong social democratic parties that emerged out of the former communist parties. As a reaction, liberal anti-communist umbrella parties emerged, which were able to attract the more conservative vote. In many ways, party fragmentation has declined over time and a left-wing and right-wing block emerged in both countries. In spite of this, there is still a high level of volatility (Tables 11.22 and 11.23).

In Bulgaria, the socialists are the strongest party since the 2005 elections. It is a very pragmatic party, which emphasises the expansion of the welfare state, as well as embracing a regulated market economy. Originally, the main opposition party was the Union of Democratic Forces, but this was replaced by the Movement for Stability and Progress (NDSV) led by Simeon II, the former King of Bulgaria in the elections of 2001. That year, the NBS II/NDSV achieved 42.7 per cent of the vote and was able to build a minority government that implemented major

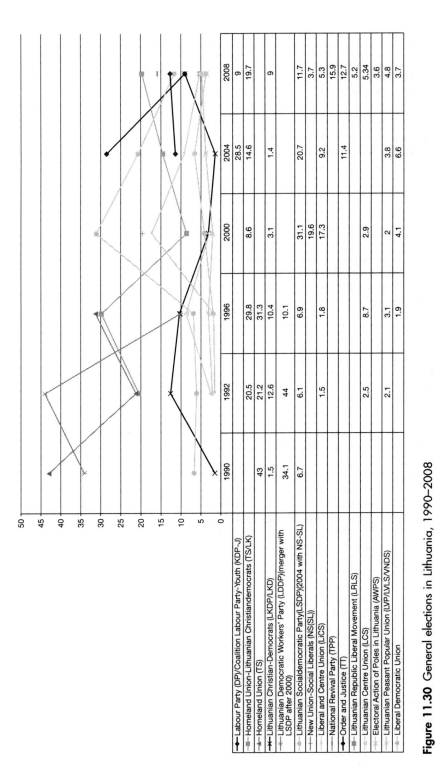

	1990	1992	1996	2000	2004	2008
Labour Party (DPI)/Coalition Labour Party-Youth (KDP-J)						9
Homeland Union–Lithuanian Christiandemocrats (TS/LK)		20.5	29.8	8.6	28.5	19.7
Homeland Union (TS)		21.2	31.3		14.6	9
Lithuanian Christian-Democrats (LKDP/LKD)	1.5	12.6	10.4	3.1	1.4	
Lithuanian Democratic Workers' Party (LDDP)(merger with LSDP after 2000)	34.1	44	10.1			
Lithuanian Socialdemocratic Party(LSDP)(2004 with NS-SL)	6.7	6.1	6.9	31.1	20.7	11.7
New Union–Social Liberals (NS(SL))				19.6		3.7
Liberal and Centre Union (LiCS)		1.5	1.8	17.3	9.2	5.3
National Revival Party (TPP)						15.9
Order and Justice (TT)					11.4	12.7
Lithuanian Republic Liberal Movement (LRLS)						5.2
Lithuanian Centre Union (LCS)		2.5	8.7	2.9		5.34
Electoral Action of Poles in Lithuania (AWPS)						3.6
Lithuanian Peasant Popular Union (LVP/LVLS/VNDS)		2.1	3.1	2	3.8	4.8
Liberal Democratic Union			1.9	4.1	6.6	3.7

Figure 11.30 General elections in Lithuania, 1990–2008

Source: Lewis, 2003: 64; Central Electoral Commission of the Republic of Lithuania, electoral database, available online at: www.vrk.lt/en/pirmaspuslapis/previouselections/sorted-by-the-type.html (accessed 5 June 2010)

Table 11.22 Electoral systems for the lower chambers in Bulgaria and Romania, 2008

Country	Electoral system	Constituency seats	Threshold (%)
Bulgaria (240 seats)	*Before July 2009:* Closed party lists elected by D'Hondt system	*Before July 2009:* 240 seats elected in 31 multi-member constituencies	4
	After July 2009: Mixed system: simple majority and proportional representation using Hare-Niemeyer electoral system	*After July 2009:* 31 single-member constituencies elected by first-past-the-post system 209 seats elected in multi-member constituencies	
Romania (334 seats)	*Until 2008:* D'Hondt proportional representation; closed list	*Until 2008:* 332 multi-member constituencies 2 reserved for minorities	5
	Since 2008: Mixed member electoral system Mixed member electoral system Rest of seats decided nationally, but allocated at district level	*Since 2008:* 315 multi-member constituencies Rest of seats distributed nationally, but allocated at district level	

Source: Interparliamentary Union, Parline database, available online at: www.ipu.org (accessed 4 June 2008)

Table 11.23 Political parties in Bulgaria and Romania, 2008

	Social Democrats	Christian Democrats/ Conservatives	Liberals	Nationalists/ extreme right	Other
Bulgaria	Bălgarska Socialističeska Partija (BSP) Bulgarian Socialist Party	Grajdani za Evropejsko Razvitie na Bulgaria (GERB) Citizens for European Development of Bulgaria Săjuz na Demokratični Sili (SDS) Union of Democratic Forces Demokrati za Silna Bulgarija (DSB) Democrats for a Strong Bulgaria	Nacionalno Dvizenie za Stabilnost i Vazhod (NDSV) National Movement for Stability and Progress	Nacionalen Săjuz Ataka (ATAKA) National Union Attack	Dvizenie za Prava i Svobodi (DPS) Movement for Rights and Freedoms (Turkish minority)
Romania	Partidul Social-Democrat (PSD) Social Democratic Party	Partidul Democrat Liberal (PDL) Democratic Liberal Party Partidul Conservator (PC) Conservative Party	Partidul National Liberal (PNL) National Liberal Party	Partidul România Mare (PRM) Great Romania Party	Uniunea Democrată Maghiară din România (UDMR) Democratic Alliance of Hungarians in Romania

Source: Author

liberalisation policies, leading to an improvement of the Bulgarian economy, but also to a deterioration of living conditions of the poorer parts of the population. Therefore, in the elections of 2005, the party lost half of the share of the vote, and the Bulgarian socialists were able to almost double their share. Owing to the imminent accession to the EU, the Bulgarian socialists formed a coalition with NBS/NDSV. Meanwhile, a new political party emerged before the 2007 European elections in Bulgaria and was able to further reduce the share of the vote of NBS/NDSV. The Citizens for European Development of Bulgaria got 21.7 per cent and became the largest party slightly ahead of the socialists with an almost equal share of the vote. NBSII/NDSV got only 6.47 per cent of the vote, behind the Turkish minority party Movements for Rights and Freedom (DPS) and the populist, far-right Attack. The polarisation between the DPS (which represents the Turkish minority in Bulgaria) and the aggressive nationalist, xenophobic Attack (which is rising in popularity, receiving 8.2 per cent of the vote in the 2005 elections) is proving poblematic for Bulgarian politics. This was at least partly a result of the low turnout, which was below 30 per cent. Nevertheless, it shows the high level of volatility that still exists within the Bulgarian party system (Figure 11.31). In the 2009 general election, new party GERB won and formed a minority government supported by Attack and other smaller conservative parties. The NBSII/NDSV declined to 2.9 per cent and lost representation in parliament.

In Romania, a two-party system between the former reform communists, now social democrats (PSD), and the liberals is emerging. In spite of the split of the liberals into two parties in 2006, the national liberals were not able to repeat their success in 2004 and have now been replaced by the breakaway liberal democrats. In spite of this, the party system has become more stabilised. The new liberal democrats have merged with the Democratic Party. The social democrats have been very important from the beginning and they could rely on substantial support, in spite of being associated with the former regime, or probably because of this fact. The minorities are well-represented in the Romanian party system, particularly the Hungarian minority (UDMR). The far-right Party of Great Romania particularly targets the minorities and has a strong following, although it suffered serious losses in the last elections.

Governments in Romania have become more stable over time. Between 2004 and 2008, the liberals were in power, but the elections of 2008 led to a coalition between the social democrats and the liberal democrats.

In March 2008, the Romanian parliament approved a change of the proportional electoral system to a mixed one, comprising one part of single-member constituencies elected by a plurality system and one part of multi-member constituencies by a proportional representation system. This will, of course, change the nature of party politics in Romania. One of the main reasons for this change was the intention to make elected MPs more accountable and more directly linked to the constituency. It is too early to assess whether this will produce a change of party system (*International Herald Tribune*, 4 March 2008) (Figure 11.32).

Party system consolidation in the Balkans

In comparison to the Central and Eastern European countries, the Balkans are still in the early process of consolidation, with most party systems still in the making.

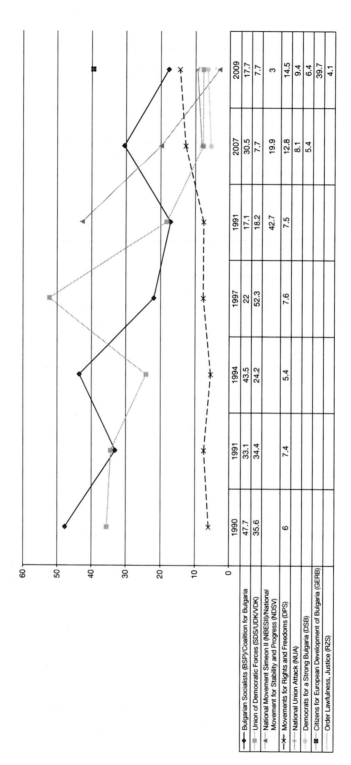

	1990	1991	1994	1997	1991	2007	2009
Bulgarian Socialists (BSP)/Coalition for Bulgaria	47.7	33.1	43.5	22	17.1	30.5	17.7
Union of Democratic Forces (SDS/UDK/VDK)	35.6	34.4	24.2	52.3	18.2	7.7	7.7
National Movement Simeon II (NBESII)/National Movement for Stability and Progress (NDSV)					42.7	19.9	3
Movements for Rights and Freedoms (DPS)	6	7.4	5.4	7.6	7.5	12.8	14.5
National Union Attack (NUA)						8.1	9.4
Democrats for a Strong Bulgaria (DSB)						5.4	6.4
Citizens for European Development of Bulgaria (GERB)							39.7
Order Lawfulness, Justice (RZS)							4.1

Figure 11.31 General elections in Bulgaria, 1990–2009

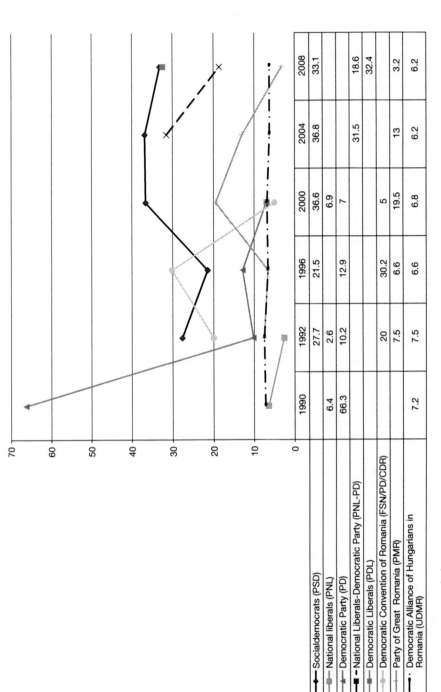

	1990	1992	1996	2000	2004	2008
Socialdemocrats (PSD)		27.7	21.5	36.6	36.8	33.1
National liberals (PNL)	6.4	2.6		6.9		
Democratic Party (PD)	66.3	10.2	12.9	7		
National Liberals–Democratic Party (PNL-PD)					31.5	18.6
Democratic Liberals (PDL)						32.4
Democratic Convention of Romania (FSN/PD/CDR)		20	30.2	5		
Party of Great Romania (PMR)		7.5	6.6	19.5	13	3.2
Democratic Alliance of Hungarians in Romania (UDMR)	7.2	7.5	6.6	6.8	6.2	6.2

Figure 11.32 General elections in Romania, 1990–2008

Source: Lewis, 2003: 65; Gabanyi, 2010: 653–4

The legacy of nationalism is still quite strong in Serbia, Bosnia-Herzegovina and Macedonia. In Serbia, democratisation began to set in only after Slobodan Milosevic was sent to The Hague in 2002. The main cleavage is between the parties who want to join the European Union as soon as possible, of which the Democratic Party is dominant, and the nationalist parties, particularly the Serbian Radical Party with almost 30 per cent, who regard Kosovo as an integral part of Serbia. In this sense, the party system is still fragmented, volatile and polarised between two irreconcilable blocks.

A genuine Croatian party system began to emerge only after the death of charismatic leader Franjo Tudjman in 2000. Although the party system was still fragmented, two parties emerged as the dominant ones: the moderate conservative Croatian Democratic Union (HDZ) and the Social Democrats (SDH); each one has been able to achieve between 20 and 35 per cent of the vote. Two smaller parties are the Croatian People's Party–Liberal Democrats (HNS) and the agrarian Croatian Peasants' Party (HSS). Moderation of politics has contributed to an improvement of the economy and reform efforts of successive Croatian governments.

More problematic has been the situation in Bosnia-Herzegovina. After more than one decade of international supervision and political engineering, there is no political party that is able to transcend the national divide. The Republika Srpska is alienated from the overall process and continues to remain separated from the Bosnian-Croatian Federation (*The Economist*, 6 November 2008). The party system shows similarities to the Belgian case – the party families having Bosnian, Croatian and Serbian branches. This means that the party system continues to be highly fragmented. In 2006, the strongest party was the Serbian Social Democratic Party with about a 20 per cent share of the vote. The inter-ethnic Party for Bosnia and Herzegovina got 15.5 per cent of the vote and may remain the main hope for the future.

In Macedonia, the party system is becoming more consolidated. After the 2008 elections, the Democratic Party for Macedonian National Unity (VMRO–DPMNE) remains the strongest party of the party system with almost 50 per cent of the vote, while the second largest is the Social Democratic Union of Macedonia (SDSM). The Albanian minority is represented by two small parties, the Democratic Union for Integration (BDI) and the Democratic Party for Albanians (PDSH) with 12.8 and 8.2 per cent respectively. There is a strong rivalry between the two parties, particularly in view of taking part in any coalition government.

Similarly, in Montenegro the Social Democratic Party dominates the political system with a 40–50 per cent share of the vote.

In Albania, the party system is again extremely fragmented. The national conservative Republican Party (PR) was the strongest political group with 20 per cent of the vote in the general elections of 2006. However, this is a splinter party of the Democratic Party, which, in the 2002 elections, got 36.7 per cent of the vote. The second largest party is the Social Democrats with 12.7 per cent. Apart from these two parties, there are still ten parties in parliament with a share of the vote below 10 per cent. One way to resolve this fragmentation would be to raise the threshold from the current 2.5 per cent to 5 per cent – this would certainly contribute to some rationalisation.

In sum, the Balkan party systems are probably still the least consolidated. Apart from the late development, other reasons for this relate to the ethnic composition of the respective countries. The most problematic party system is probably that of Kosovo and Bosnia-Herzegovina, largely because of the polarisation between the different ethnic groups and the respective political parties.

Multilevel electoral arenas

One characteristic of contemporary European politics is that political parties do not act in just one electoral area, but in multiple ones. As already mentioned, there are national general elections and local elections, but for some countries (for example, Spain, Germany, Belgium, France, the United Kingdom, Italy, Austria and, increasingly, the Czech Republic, Slovakia and Poland) there are also regional elections. There is now an intertwined dynamic between the different levels of elections within the national territories. Furthermore, political parties also have to campaign for elections to the European Parliament, which have taken place every five years since 1979. One problem of European elections is that they are still characterised by national campaigns. The European issues are not as salient as national issues. This has been changing over time, but factors such as the organisation of national and European elections at the same time leads to a nationalisation of politics. Another factor is that elections take place on different days, not just on a single day. For example, the UK and the Netherlands organise their elections on Thursdays, most other countries on Sundays. In spite of the fact that all EU member countries have to use proportional representation systems, they differ from country to country (Hix, 2005: 192–6). The most important obstacle to a Europeanisation of elections is probably the fact that nobody knows what the European Parliament does. Media reporting on the European Parliament at national level has been at a low level, with the result that European elections are regarded by most voters as second-order (or even third-order) elections after regional and local elections. Low turnout at European elections is particularly widespread in Central and Eastern European countries (Figures 11.33 and 11.34).

The European Parliament elections bring together all the party families that exist in Europe. Many new political parties in Central and Eastern Europe had to decide to which of the EP parliamentary groups they wanted to belong. There are seven parliamentary groups, of which the European People's Party (EPP) is the largest. This party includes Christian democrats, conservatives and some liberals. The second largest but more cohesive is the Party of European Socialists, which clearly has strong relations to the Socialist International. Many communist parties of Central and Eastern Europe transformed themselves into social democratic parties and joined the Party of European Socialists. The third largest group is the European Liberal Democratic and Reform (ELDR) group comprising mainly the liberal parties. Furthermore, on the left there is the European United Left–Nordic Green Left (EUL–NGL), which comprises the communists, some new left parties and some of the more left-wing greens from Nordic Europe. On the right, there is the European Conservative Party, which comprises Euro-sceptic and national-conservative parties, as well as the Independence/Democracy group (ID), which is even more strongly Euro-sceptic and comprises the Danish, British, French, Dutch and Polish Euro-sceptics (Hix and Lord, 1997; Hix, 2005: 186–92) (see Tables 11.24 and 11.25).

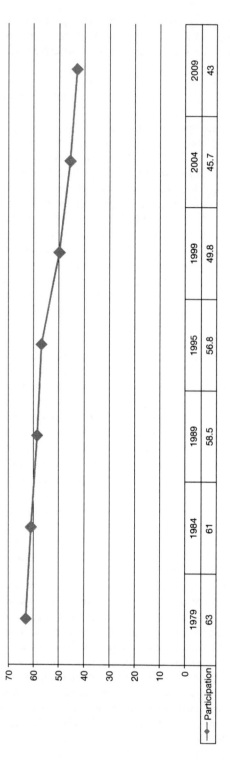

	1979	1984	1989	1995	1999	2004	2009
Participation	63	61	58.5	56.8	49.8	45.7	43

Figure 11.33 Turnout in European Parliament elections, 1979–2009

Source: European Parliament database, available online at: www.europarl.eu (accessed 5 June 2010)

Figure 11.34 Turnout at the European Parliament elections, 2009, according to member states

Although most of the populations of the member states don't know a lot about the European Parliament, their competences and importance have increased considerably over time. After the Treaties of the European Union, Amsterdam and Nice the European Parliament co-decides legislation with the Council of Ministers of the European Union. The standing committees of the European Parliament have become central in this process of legislation making. More than 90 per cent of the legislation is approved consensually between the two institutions – only a very small amount of legislative bills lead to some controversy (see Chapter 4).

In sum, the European electoral arena further reinforces the framing of national politics towards a limited number of party families that have achieved representation in the European Parliament. In this sense, dissemination and cooperation within the parliamentary groups have made political parties more Europeanised. Thus, even the more Euro-sceptic parties have learned from each other through the European arena and adjusted their strategies accordingly. This means that Euro-sceptic movements themselves are Europeanised movements even

Table 11.24 Distribution of seats of the 2004 European Parliament elections, according to countries and parliamentary groups

	EPP–ED	PES	ELDR	Greens	EUL–NGL	UEN	ID	NI	Total
Belgium	6	7	6	2				3	24
Bulgaria	5	5	5					3	18
Czech Republic	14	2			6		1	1	24
Denmark	1	5	4	1	1	1	1		14
Germany	49	23	7	13	7				99
Estonia	1	3	2						6
Ireland	5	1	1		1	4	1		13
Greece	11	8			4		1		24
Spain	24	24	2	3	1				54
France	18	31	10	6	3		3	7	78
Italy	24	17	12	2	7	13		3	78
Cyprus	3		1		2				6
Latvia	3		1	1		4			9
Lithuania	2	2	7			2			13
Luxembourg	3	1	1	1					6
Hungary	13	9	2						24
Malta	2	3							5
Netherlands	7	7	5	4	2		2		27
Austria	6	7	1	2				2	18
Poland	15	9	6			20	3	1	54
Portugal	9	12			3				24
Romania	18	8	6	1					33
Slovenia	4	1	2						7
Slovakia	8	3						3	14
Finland	4	3	5	1	1				14
Sweden	6	5	3	1	2	2	2		19
United Kingdom	27	19	11	5	1		8	7	78
	288	**215**	**100**	**43**	**41**	**44**	**22**	**30**	**783**

Source: European Parliament, website www.europarl.eu (accessed 23 December 2008)

if they do not acknowledge it. The highest level of Europeanisation can probably be found among the EPP–ED, PES, ELDR and the Greens. More resistance has come from the EUL–NGL, the UEN and particularly the ID (Figure 11.35).

Conclusions: the intertwinedness of electoral and party systems

The most important decision that the political elites from different political parties have to agree, either during the constitutional settlement or later in periods of

Table 11.25 Distribution of seats of the 2009 European Parliament elections, according to countries and parliamentary groups

	EPP	S&D	ALDE	Greens	ECR	GUE/NGL	EFD	N/A	Total
Belgium	5	5	5	4	1	0		2	22
Bulgaria	6	4	5	0	0	0	0	2	17
Czech Republic	2	7	0	0	9	4			22
Denmark	1	4	3	2	0	1	2	0	13
Germany	42	23	12	14	0	8	0	0	99
Estonia	1	1	3	1	0	0	0	0	6
Ireland	4	3	4	0	0	1	0	0	12
Greece	8	8	0	1	0	3	2	0	22
Spain	23	21	2	2	0	1	0	1	50
France	29	14	6	14	0	5	1	3	72
Italy	35	21	7	0	0	0	9	0	72
Cyprus	2	2	0	0	0	2	0	0	6
Latvia	3	1	1	1	1	1	0	0	9
Lithuania	4	3	2	0	1	0	2	0	12
Luxembourg	3	1	1	1	0	0	0	0	6
Hungary	14	4	0	0	1	0	0	3	22
Malta	2	3	0	0	0	0	0	0	5
Netherlands	5	3	6	3	1	2	1	4	25
Austria	6	4	0	2	0	0	0	5	17
Poland	28	7	0	0	15	0	0	0	50
Portugal	10	7	0	0	0	5	0	0	22
Romania	14	11	5	0	0	0	0	3	33
Slovenia	3	2	2	0	0	0	0	0	7
Slovakia	6	5	1	0	0	0	1	0	13
Finland	4	2	4	2	0	0	1	0	13
Sweden	5	5	4	3	0	1	0	0	18
United Kingdom	0	13	11	5	25	1	13	4	72
	265	184	84	55	54	35	32	27	736

Source: European Parliament, website www.europarl.eu (accessed 5 August 2009) (more detailed information on the elections in the member-states can be found there)

revision of the constitution, is probably the way members of parliament, of regional assemblies and local authorities should be elected. Different electoral systems may lead to different party systems, which will then shape national politics towards a more majoritarian or consensual style of politics. The United Kingdom and France adopted plurality systems that lead to a polarisation between left and right and the formation of two parties or blocks. This polarisation shapes their national politics. In the Netherlands, the generous proportional representation system with a threshold of 0.67 per cent of the vote, allows for many parties to be represented in parliament: at any point of time since the 1970s there have been ten or more parties in the Dutch Parliament. None of the parties is able to achieve absolute

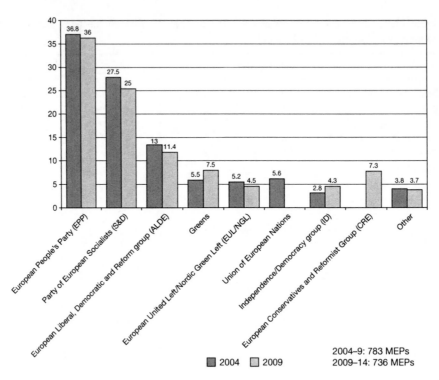

Figure 11.35 European Parliament elections, 2004 and 2009, according to share of seats

majorities, so that the party with the strongest votes has to form coalitions with other parties. In Germany, the mixed electoral system allows the voter to cast two votes, one for a constituency seat based on the simple plurality system and one for a proportional list. The end result is a fairly balanced result from all the parties that achieve the 5 per cent threshold. All these electoral systems are shaped by tradition (UK), but also by electoral engineering in order to achieve more stability (France, Germany).

While most West European party systems are adjusting to social and economic changes in their respective national arenas, the Southern European and Central and Eastern European party systems are latecomers to the club of European democracies. Central and Eastern European party systems in particular are still facing a high level of volatility and fragmentation. The most extreme cases can be found in the Baltic states and in Poland.

The party systems in the Balkans are still problematic and are characterised by strong nationalist parties, such as those in Serbia and Bosnia-Herzegovina, for example.

In sum, in spite of a high level of diversity across Europe, there are strong tendencies towards a convergence of party systems. In this respect, the European Parliament plays an important socialising role in pushing towards more professionalised and stable parties in Southern Europe and Central and Eastern Europe.

Suggested reading

Electoral systems

Farrell, David M. (2000), *Electoral Systems: A Comparative Introduction*. Basingstoke: Palgrave.

Farrell, D., M. Mackerras, I. McAllister (1996), Designing Electoral Institutions: Varieties of STV Systems, *Political Studies*, 44: 24–43.

Gallagher, Michael (1997), Electoral Systems and Voting Behaviour. In: Martin Rhodes, Paul Heywood and Vincent Wright (eds), *Developments in West European Politics*. Basingstoke: Macmillan, pp. 114–30.

International Institute for Democracy and Electoral Assistance (IDEA) (2009), website with excellent database on electoral systems in the world and turnout at www.idea.int.

Soberg, Matthew Shugart and Martin P. Wattenberg (eds) (2001), *Mixed-Member Electoral Systems*. Oxford: Oxford University Press.

Party systems and elections

Bartolini, Stefano (2000), *The Political Mobilization of the European Left, 1860–1980: The Class Cleavage*. Cambridge: Cambridge University Press.

Bartolini, Stefano and Peter Mair (1990), *Identity, Competition and Electoral Volatility: The Stabilisation of European Electorates 1885–1985*. Cambridge: Cambridge University Press.

Broughton, David and Mark Donovan (eds) (1999), *Changing Party Systems in Western Europe*. London: Pinter.

Caramani, Daniele (2004), *The Nationalization of Politics: The Formation of National Electorates and Party Systems in Western Europe*. Cambridge: Cambridge University Press.

Kitschelt, Herbert (1997), European Party System: Continuity and Change. In: Martin Rhodes, Paul Heywood and Vincent Wright (eds), *Developments in West European Politics*. Basingstoke: Macmillan, pp. 131–50.

Lewis, Paul G. (2003), *Political Parties in Post-Communist Eastern Europe*. London: Routledge.

Lipset, Seymour Martin and Stein Rokkan (1967), Cleavage Structures, Party Systems and Voter Alignments: An Introduction. In: Seymour Martin Lipset and Stein Rokkan (eds), *Party Systems and Voter Alignments: Cross National Perspectives*. New York: The Free Press, pp. 1–64.

Mair, Peter (1997), *Party System Change. Approaches and Interpretations*. Oxford: Oxford University Press.

Olson, David M. (1998), Party Formation and Party System Consolidation in the New Democracies of Central Europe, *Political Studies*, 46(3): 432–64.

Pennings, Paul and Jan-Erik Lane (eds) (1998), *Comparing Party System Change*. London: Routledge.

Sartori, Giovanni (2005), *Parties and Party Systems: A Framework for Analysis*. Colchester: ECPR Press (first published in 1976 by Cambridge University Press).

Electronic journals

Electoral Studies
Excellent for national election reports.

West European Politics
Excellent on party systems and national election reports.

Party Politics
Excellent on party systems.

European Journal of Political Research
Excellent yearbook: at the end of each year issues 7–8 hold national reports of all countries of the European Union and other OECD countries; also excellent database of elections since 1993.

Federal and Regional Studies
Excellent source for regional elections particularly Spain, Belgium, Germany, Austria and UK.

Websites

International Institute for Democracy and Electoral Assistance (IDEA) (2009), website with excellent database on electoral systems in the world and turnout at: www.idea.int (accessed 25 August 2009).

Interparliamentary Union (IPU) (2009), database with archive on elections and electoral systems attached to the file of each country at: www.ipu.org (accessed 25 August 2009).

Parties and Elections in Europe (2009), database on elections of all European countries at: www.parties-and-elections.de/ (accessed 25 August 2009).

QUESTIONS FOR REVISION

- What main factors should one take into account when designing an electoral system? Discuss, using examples from at least two countries in Europe.
- Compare the main features of the German and British electoral systems.
- How stable are the party systems in the Netherlands and France?
- How consolidated are the party systems in Hungary and Poland?
- What are the prospects for the emergence of a European party system in the long run?

Interest groups and systems of interest intermediation

- Patterns of interest intermediation and industrial relations at national level
  - From rigid to regulatory neo-corporatism
  - Tamed pluralism in Europe
  - Southern Europe: the weak state and weak interest groups
  - New democracies in Central and Eastern Europe
- Towards a multilevel system of interest intermediation
- Conclusions: from national systems of interest intermediation to a multilevel EU governance system

SUMMARY OF CHAPTER 12

This chapter deals with interest groups and the systems of interest intermediation across Europe. Interest groups and systems of interest intermediation have experienced major changes in the transition from industrial to the post-industrial society.

Both the employers' and employees' organisations have had to make major changes to their internal structures and external strategies in order to deal with the changing environment.

In Europe, two main systems of interest intermediation can be identified. First, there is a well-regulated inclusive system, called **neocorporatism**, in which social partners work with the government. The main outcomes of neo-corporatism are long-term tripartite agreements in the economic and social fields. Although, until the 1970s, this neo-corporatist system gave substantial power to both employers' and workers' organisations, today both groups are facing a decline in both membership and in their influence in society. However, a variant of neo-corporatism, which is less interventionist but more regulatory in its aim, continues to be dominant. Austria can be regarded as a good example in this respect.

The second system of interest intermediation provides for less-regulated competition between interest groups, in which lobbying becomes a major way to gain influence over policy-making. This less-regulated system of interest intermediation is called **pluralism.** The country where pluralism is strongest is probably the UK, but even the UK is more regulated than the United States, the pluralist country *par excellence*.

New forms of interest intermediation based on policy networks and other governance relationships have started to emerge and complement these two traditional systems of interest intermediation.

In contrast to the United States, interest groups have a closer relationship to national governments in Europe. The European integration process has highlighted that a European social model of capitalism is inherent in all member states. This European social model includes a continuing consultation and, in some cases, consultation with the relevant economic and social partners regarding economic, labour and social policy issues. The tripartite social dialogue is one of the elements of this European model of industrial relations. The three partners are the main business organisations, the trade unions and the government (representing the state). This has now become part of the industrial relations pattern of the European Union. Social partners, businesses and trade union organisations have become central to the implementation of policies relating to European integration. Each member state of the EU has to implement a 'growth and stability pact' with its national social partners so that the criteria of the Maastricht Treaty relating to the Economic and Monetary Union (particularly with regard to inflation control, budget deficit and public debt) are observed, and difficult reforms can be undertaken. This tripartite social dialogue is common in many other areas, such as vocational training policies, long-term economic policies and even central wage bargaining for public sector employees.

Europe is also characterised by dense civil societies that allow participation of the population in different issues. However, there are major differences among the countries. In the West European and Nordic countries there is an extremely well-developed civil society, however this is not the case in Southern Europe and Central and Eastern Europe. The longevity of authoritarianism and, in some cases, totalitarianism (in Romania, for example) in these countries has led to a late development of civil society, which is still lagging behind that of most West European and Nordic countries.

Last, but not least, there is the emergence of an organised European civil society at supranational level, with several Euro groups emerging in the 1980s and 1990s.

The main economic interest groups in European countries are the trade union confederations and the business and/or employers' organisations. Moreover, there are more specialised interest groups for agriculture, crafts and other sectors. Apart from the fact that globalisation and Europeanisation have put both employees' and employers' organisations under pressure, there is also now the need for organisations to be present at different levels of the EU multilevel governance system. While trade unions face the prospect of declining membership and transformation of their approach (from ideological to professional economic service), business organisations have to adjust to Europeanisation and globalisation and offer attractive service packages to their members.

Before we can turn to the European level, however, it is important to find the main patterns of interest intermediation and industrial relations at the national level.

Patterns of interest intermediation and industrial relations at national level

Europeanisation and globalisation are transforming national patterns of interest intermediation and industrial relations. Figure 12.1 shows four groups of countries and their respective patterns of adjustment.

Figure 12.1 Patterns of interest intermediation in Europe

From rigid to regulatory neo-corporatism

The negative experiences of capitalism in the inter-war period and the subsequent Second World War gave a major incentive to move away from an uncontrolled non-regulated capitalism. This meant that the pure pluralistic system of interest intermediation that was dominant in the US was not adopted by most European countries. Instead, pluralism was tamed through the cooperation between state institutions and economic interest groups' organisations. After 1945, economic interest groups in most European democracies had an important role to play in shaping economic and social policy. One of the main reasons was the fact that trade union confederations and social democratic parties became fairly strong and were able to impose welfare policies on business enterprises. Instead of complete imposition, government, business and trade union organisations negotiated compromises in order to combine competitiveness and social cohesion. However, this settlement was different in each country. Some countries accommodated pluralism more easily than others. A strong involvement of the traditional social partners in economic and labour market policy was labelled as 'neo-corporatism' or 'tri-partite', but there were differences between the countries in this respect as well. 'Corporatism' was part of the economic philosophy of social Catholicism developed in the nineteenth and early twentieth centuries that advocated a harmonious cooperation between interest groups and was against the socialist/communist 'class struggle' between employers and workers, and was also against the 'pluralist', 'non-regulated' approach of pure capitalism. It was an idealisation of the guild system of the Middle Ages in which regulatory frameworks created security for the different craftsmen and artisans and conflicts were resolved peacefully. It was presented as a third way between capitalism and socialism. Instead of separated interest groups, the different branches were organised into hierarchical and patriarchal vertical syndicates. Corporatism was later adopted by Italian fascism and copied by other authoritarian regimes, such as those in Austria, Portugal and Spain. 'Neo-corporatism' was a revival of such arrangements, although in a democratic and capitalist context. The 'tri-partite' or 'neo-corporatist' approach became important in countries with strong unified trade union confederations and business organisations, such as Sweden, Denmark, Norway, the Netherlands, Belgium and Austria. Alan Siaroff defines neo-corporatism as follows:

> [Within] an advanced industrial society and democratic polity, the co-ordinated, co-operative, and systematic management of the national economy by the state, the centralised unions, employers, (these latter two co-operating directly in industry), presumably to the relative benefit of all three actors.
>
> (Siaroff, 1999: 177)

This means that, for the ideal type of neo-corporatist mode of interest inter-mediation, particular conditions had to apply – conditions that could only be found in certain countries, for example Austria, the Netherlands, Belgium, Sweden, Denmark, Finland and Norway. Many countries, such as the United Kingdom, France, Germany and Italy, had neo-corporatist elements in their systems of interest intermediation, but were generally more pluralist.

According to Alan Siaroff (1999), neo-corporatist systems of intermediation experienced their peak between 1945 and the mid 1970s. This was also the culmination of industrial society, in which manufacturing dominated the gross domestic product and the employment structure. This led to a high level of unionisation density, which led to the emergence of a system of interest intermediation. Normally, trade union confederations had a strong ideological relationship with the main parties, leading to an intertwined relationship between political and socioeconomic structures. This became popular in small, open economies, such as those of Sweden, Denmark, Finland, Norway, the Netherlands, Belgium, Luxembourg and Austria (see Table 12.1).

However, since the 1970s, the generous welfare systems and working conditions in these neo-corporatist small states began to lose competitiveness, and were required to reform their economic and social systems. Welfare states could no longer grow because the respective economies were not able to finance them. Instead, reforms were undertaken to link welfare policies to labour market activation policies. This 'workfare' approach required most open economies to reduce labour costs that were previously imposed by legislation agreed through tripartite arrangements. Across the EU, this approach has been called 'flexicurity' and assumes that the majority of people of working age will have five or six jobs during their lifetime. This means that, instead of job security, the focus should be on employability and lifelong training, in order for people to be able to find employment. In short, 'flexicurity' means flexibility of labour markets, supported by a linked and generous welfare state. However, the asymmetrical quality and extension of services in national welfare states was still a major problem in this approach. 'Flexicurity' was designed for the Nordic countries, particularly for Denmark, which have quite different labour markets and welfare states from the weaker countries of Southern Europe and Central and Eastern Europe.

According to Franz Traxler (2004), social partners, particularly trade unions, needed to become more flexible in their approach towards the labour market and social policies. Traxler identified a cross-national transformation of neo-corporatism from a rigid interventionist to a light neo-corporatist approach. According to Traxler, this process started in the 1970s and is now leading to the restructuring of the system of intermediation, particularly in terms of wage regulation (Traxler, 2004: 576). This is also confirmed by a study of Philippe Schmitter and Jürgen Grote called *The Corporatist Sysiphus*. As the title of the study shows, Schmitter and Grote spoke of a renewed emergence of neo-corporatism in the 1990s, particularly as a result of the European integration process. However, both authors recognised that the rigid interventionist neo-corporatism, in which the state was dominant, was being replaced by a regulatory neo-corporatism that relied on voluntary bipartite agreements with support from the state. Furthermore, this regulatory neo-corporatism was designed to 'flexibilise' labour markets and make the economies concerned more competitive (Schmitter and Grote, 1997:5–12).

A look at the individual countries known to have a strong neo-corporatist legacy clearly confirms the theses of both Franz Traxler and of Philippe Schmitter and Jürgen Grote (Figures 12.2 and 12.3).

Sweden has been highlighted as probably the most traditional neo-corporatist country – the strong Trade Union Confederation (Landsorganisatione, LO), founded in 1898, now has 1.7 million members and the Swedish Enterprises

Table 12.1 The main features of the ideal type of neo-corporatism

Aspects	Description
Structural features	• a high degree of unionisation; • few unions grouped into highly institutionalised peak confederations • a business community dominated by large export-oriented firms, with a relatively powerful and centralised employer's federation • highly centralised wage bargaining • works councils in the main industrial firms and co-determination in key industries • a centralised, powerful, and active state involved at least moderately in the economy
Functional roles	• a central – and joint – role for labour and business in such policies as training, education, and social programmes, often implemented through tripartite boards or agencies • inclusion of social partners in economic and budgetary policy
Behavioural patterns	• tripartite shared economic and social consensus • mutual recognition of labour and business organisation as social partners with resulting patterns of cooperation • long-term outlook shared by both business and trade union organisations • low levels of strike activity • voluntary, bargained income policies • independence of decision-making of key actors
Favourable contexts	• a certain blurring of the public sector/private sector distinction • small open economy, neutral, and spending low on defence policies, profited from post-Second World War hegemony of the US • consensual, consociational tradtion(Lijphart), not majoritarian one • dominance of social democratic party • high level of social expenditure • successful economic performance in productivity, export competitiveness and maintenance of full employment

Source: Summarised from Siaroff, 1999: 177–9

Association (Svenskt Näringsliv) was re-founded in 2001 with this new name, although it had existed since 1902 under the name of Swedish Arbeiterverband (Svenska arbetergivarföreningen, SAF). The Svenskt Näringsliv comprises 50 organisations with 54,000 members and 1.5 million employees. Both remain central to the consensual style of politics with a culture of consultation and integration of relevant interest groups. The most important event leading to the establishment

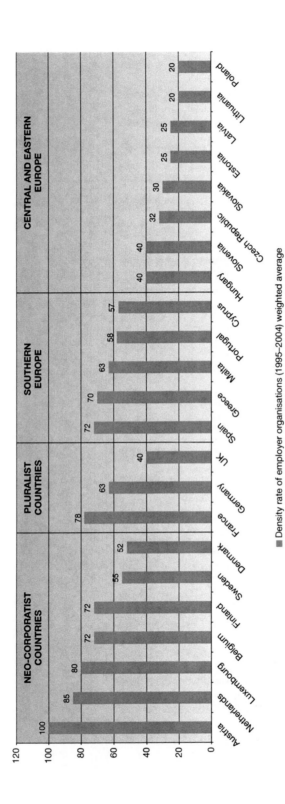

■ Density rate of employer organisations (1995–2004) weighted average

Figure 12.2 The density rate of employer organisations, 1995–2004, weighted average

Source: European Foundation for the Improvement of Living Conditions, 2007: 12

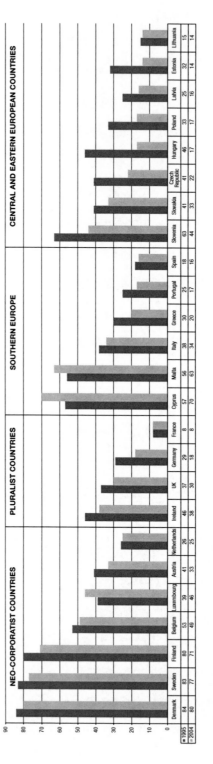

Figure 12.3 Net trade union density, 1995–2004, according to group of countries

Source: European Foundation for the Improvement of Living Conditions, 2007: 6

of the neo-corporatist system was probably the Saltjöbaden Agreement of 1938 between the main LO and SAF. The agreement was a trade-off that allowed the Swedish enterprises to rationalise and adjust to the crisis in exchange for a stronger welfare state provided mainly by the state to the workers.

The Swedish model reached its peak between 1960 and the late 1980s, following which Sweden had to deal with a major recession. Throughout the 1960s the whole neo-corporatist network was formalised (Götz, 2001: 382–3). Although globalisation and Europeanisation are transforming the Swedish model, particularly as a result of the growing importance of lobbying by many enterprises (Götz, 2001: 384), the system of interest intermediation has been rather resilient. However, the overall assessment has been somewhat mixed. According to a study by Torsten Svensson and Perola Öberg (2005), the Swedish networks among the different groups, particularly the business and employees' organisations, have not changed very much since the reforms of the early 1990s. There are still strong institutional structures that retain a lighter version of neo-corporatism. The traditional institutions of Swedish neo-corporatism, such as the symbolic Labour Court (Arbetsmarknadsdomstolen) and the Conciliators' Office, are still important in setting the standards of neo-corporatist cooperation, but some of the more powerful bargaining institutions may have lost in importance (Svensson and Öberg, 2005: 1088–9). Svensson and Öberg are adamant that very little has actually changed. The main organisations of labour and business continue to fulfil an important coordinating role in their networks, acting as a bridge to other networks. Although there has been a moderate withdrawal of the state since the early 1990s, the patterns of decision-making remain similar (Svensson and Öberg, 2005: 1089–91).

A more critical view is presented by Johannes Lindvall and Joakim Sebring (2005), who assert that Swedish corporatism has declined considerably since the 1990s, at a greater rate than in other, smaller democracies, particularly Denmark. Such dismantling started during the economic crisis of the Swedish economy in the late 1980s and the debate about possible EU membership. By 1991, the Swedish Employers' Confederation decided to withdraw from all the boards of all government agencies, something that had institutionalised character in Sweden. As a result of this unilateral withdrawal, the Swedish right-centre government had to exclude the trade union representatives from the government agencies as well, in order to preserve its neutrality (Lindvall and Sebring, 2005: 1058). This also meant a decline in consultation with the social partners, although consultation remains an important part of the Swedish culture of interest intermediation. According to Lindvall and Sebring, there has been a reduced influence on the part of the social partners, as well as reduced consultation, in policies addressing the labour market, immigration and pensions (Lindvall, Sebring, 2005: 1060–9).

Similar systems of interest intermediation were established in Denmark, Norway and Finland. Denmark was probably the country that adjusted best to the new challenges of globalisation and Europeanisation. In the Global Competitiveness Index for the year 2009–10 of the World Economic Forum, it is one of the most competitive economies, being ranked fifth (the previous year it was ranked third, coming after the United States and Switzerland) (World Economic Forum, 2010: 13–14). According to John L. Campbell and Ove K. Pedersen (2007), the Danish state was able to become more flexible and adjust to the new realities. One particular transformation was the decentralisation of the system of industrial relations. Tripartite framework agreements are still important at national level, but there has been growing flexibility and decentralisation to specific wage bargaining at company level.

There is also strong cooperation between trade unions and businesses. In this sense, the role of neo-corporatism has become more flexible and decentralised, while, at the same time, successive governments have directed their whole policy-making process towards labour market activation policies (Campbell and Pedersen, 2007; Due *et al.*, 1995: 145).

Neo-corporatism in Finland has been dominated by the trade union con-federations, which strategically want to preserve some kind of centralised wage bargaining. However, the collapse of the Soviet Union led to a substantial increase in unemployment in the 1990s, which gave a stronger bargaining position to the employers' organisations. The neo-corporatist system of intermediation, which was established after the Second World War, is slowly giving way to more flexible forms of system intermediation (Lappalainen and Siisäinen, 2001: 116–20).

In Norway, the neo-corporatist mode of interest intermediation was also quite dominant. According to Tom Christensen, over 3,000 interest groups are still formally involved in a vast network of government agencies (Christensen, 2005: 727). The two main interest groups are the Norwegian Trade Union Confederation (Landesorganisationen) and the Norwegian Employers' Organisation (Norges Arbeidsgiverforening, NAF). After decades of expansion of the formalised network of neo-corporatist agencies and boards, a crisis of the system began to emerge. Globalisation and Europeanisation played a particularly strong role in the rethinking of the Norwegian model. However, in comparison to Sweden and Denmark, the neo-corporatist mode of interest intermediation has been fairly resilient (Rothholz, 2001).

The Dutch neo-corporatist system of interest intermediation contributed to political and economic stability throughout the 1950s and 1960s. In the same way as in the Nordic countries, cooperation between interest groups goes back to the inter-war period. After the Second World War, neo-corporatist institutions were founded and expanded. At the centre is the Social and Economic Council (Sociaal en Economische Raad, SER), in which all relevant interest groups are represented, particularly employers' and employees' organisations. One particular feature of the Dutch system is that the trade union confederations were split along subcultural lines. There were the Catholic (Nederlands Katholieke Vakverbond, NKV), the Protestant Christian democratic (Christelijk Nationaal Vakverbond, CNV) and the socialist (Nederlands Verbond van Vakbewegingen, NVV) trade union con-federations, in which over 40 per cent of workers were organised. The Catholic and socialist confederations merged into the Dutch Trade Union Federation (Federatie Nederlandse Vakbeweging, FNV) in 1976. The business organisations were more unified. Between 1945 and 1970, there was a strong integration and consultation of these main social partners. However, the economic and social crisis of the 1970s led to major reforms by the Dutch coalition government of Christian democrats and liberals from 1982 to 1992. One of the main tasks was to work closely with the business and workers' confederations in order to achieve support for very difficult austerity measures. The main problem was that the Dutch economy was losing competitiveness and therefore its generous welfare state could no longer be financed. The 'Wassenaar agreement', which was reached by the social partners in 1982, transformed a centralised neo-corporatist system into a decentralised flexible one. Tripartite negotiations with heavy intervention of the state were replaced by bipartite ones between the social partners and a retreat of the state from the economy. The Dutch 'Polder-model' was referred to as an example of the capacity of neo-corporatist systems of interest intermediation to adjust to new realities, but keeping the basic principles of negotiated bargained principles carried by the main interest groups. Parallel to an increase in efficiency of the economic sector, the government strengthened the labour market activation policies (Hemerijck, 1995; Kleinfeld, 2001).

The 'purple coalition' government (between the Labour Party and the Liberals between 1992 and 2002) and the Christian Democratic and Liberal coalition government (after 2002, under Jan-Peter Balkenende) continued on the path of reform, despite strong protests against rationalisation measures and redundancies. The public sector was particularly affected by substantial cuts of personnel in public services. The density of unionisation declined to 25 per cent in 2007 and the main Dutch Trade Union Confederation (FNV) was challenged by internet-based, low-cost, sectoral trade unions that offered the same services for less money (Grünell, 2003; 2005; 2007; 2008). According to official figures of the FNV and CNV, the former comprised 50 unions and 1.5 million members, while the latter consisted of 11 unions and 350,000 members (FNV, 2008; CNV, 2008).

Belgium was also characterised by a rigid neo-corporatist system of interest intermediation, which made it possible for the state to strongly intervene in the economy between 1945 and 1973. As in the Netherlands, pillarisation of the Christian democratic, socialist and liberal subcultures led to the establishment of three main trade union confederations. Until the mid 1970s, the socialist General Federation of Labour of Belgium (Algemeen Vaksverbond/Federation General du Travail de Belgique, ABVV/FGTB) was the strongest movement with 44 per cent of all unionised workers in trade union elections, followed by the Christian Democratic General Christian Trade Union Confederation (Algemeen Christenlijk Vaksverbond/Confederation des syndicats chrétiens en Belgique, ACV/CSC) with 43 per cent. The General Confederation of Liberal Trade Unions of Belgium (Algemene Centrale der Liberale Vakbonden van België/Centrale Génerale des Syndicats Liberaux de Belgique, ACLVB/CGSLB) was quite small and got 6 per cent of the vote in the mid 1970s. The dominance of the socialist trade union confederation that existed until the mid 1970s was gradually replaced by that of the Christian democratic trade union confederation. One of the main reasons is that the majority of the population now live in Flanders, which is a Christian democratic stronghold (Hooghe, M., 2001: 34). In the 2004 trade union elections, 'social elections', which decide about the composition of the works' council in Belgium, reconfirmed the dominance of ACV–CSV, with 52.3 per cent of the works' council and 53.9 per cent in work safety committees, followed by the socialist ABVV–FGTB with 35.5 and 36 per cent respectively (Lovens, 2004).

In spite of federalisation, trade union confederations in Wallonia and Flanders still work closely together and in comparison to the political parties landscape, they are nationally organised. The decline of the political parties has eroded the intertwined relationship of the trade union movement with politics, which was one of the main characteristics of Belgium. Belgian trade unionism has one of the highest organisational levels in Europe. The main reason seems to be that unemployment benefits are administered by the trade union confederations, so the working population tends to remain attached to one of the confederations, even if they become unemployed. This also means that, in comparison to other countries, the unemployed remain part of the trade union movement (Hooghe, M., 2001: 36). The Belgian Employers' Organisation (Verbond van Belgische Ondernemingen/ Federation des Employeurs de Belgique, VBO/FEB) is the main social partner of the trade union confederations. Both are represented in a wide network of state-sponsored government boards, committees and agencies at national, sectoral and company level. Nationally, there is the Central Economic Development Board and the Central Board for Industry and Trade for economic, industrial and trade policy. Moreover, social issues are dealt with in the Central Labour Board and health safety issues in the Central Health and Safety Board. In comparison to other countries Belgian neo-corporatism has been resilient; however, the federalisation process is already creating major differences between the Flemish and Walloon parts. While Flanders is moving towards a more globalised and internationalised economy with flexible social partners supporting processes of competitiveness and social cohesion, such transformation has been lagging behind in Wallonia, in which trade unionism remains partly traditional.

In Austria, the negative experiences of the inter-war period, which led to the establishment of an authoritarian regime (1934–38) by the Christian Social Party and, later, occupation by Nazi Germany, contributed to a more consensual approach to politics and the economy. Furthermore, until 1955, Austria was occupied by Allied troops and therefore was not a free country. The State Treaty (*Staatsvertrag*) of 1955 finally led to its independence. One pillar of the Austrian Second Republic became the informal but well-entrenched social partnership (*Sozialpartnerschaft*) founded in 1957, which led to the establishment of a network of committees to bargain wages centrally and shape national economic policy. The large Austrian Trade Union Confederation (Österreichischer Gewerkschaftsbund, ÖGB), and the Austrian Association of Enterpreneurs (Vereinigung der Österreichischen Industriellen, VÖI; now known as Industriellenvereinigung, IV), and the Labour, Industry and Agriculture Chamber, which historically goes back to the nineteenth century, were all involved in this decision-making process, which was not covered by the constitution (Tálos, 2006: 426–8). This integration of the social partners still exists today, but because of a decline of trade union membership, the growing liberalisation of the economy resulting from the implementation of the single market policies, and the last wave of globalisation, the foundations of such cooperation, since the 1980s, have been gradually eroded. The dynamics of European integration have sidelined social partnerships, which led over the decades to a network of relationships that could be described as clientelism, patronage and partly political corruption. The controversial governmental coalition between 2000 and 2006, which was condemned by the Council of Ministers of the European Union, contributed to a dismantling of such clientelistic and patronage networks and pushed forward an agenda of liberalisation and decartelisation of Austrian politics. During this 'black–blue' (*schwarz–blau*) coalition between the People's Party and the Freedom Party, social partnerships lost importance, particularly in terms of consultation and decision-making processes (Tálos, 2005; Karlhofer and Tálos, 2006: 109–14).

Tamed pluralism in Europe

Pluralism in a democratic setting thus refers to 'free competition between a plurality of organised interests and supportive relations between groups and government'. In its ideal form it is a decentralised, unrestricted system (Newton and van Deth, 2006: 173–4) (see Table 12.2).

Traditionally, the United Kingdom followed a largely pluralist tradition, although there were influences from the rest of Europe that led to the adoption of neo-corporatist structures in the 1960s and 1970s. The most concrete example is the creation of the National Economic Development Council (NEDC) in 1962 and its expansion to the regions and other areas (these regional councils were known as 'the Neddies'). These were tripartite councils in which the social partners were able to shape economic policy and regional development. Such a neo-corporatist approach was used by the Labour Party in particular. In 1974 the Manpower Services Commission was created, although it was replaced in 1987 by more decentralised structures. Its main aim was to design labour market policies, particularly in the area of youth training. Other tripartite bodies were the Health and Safety Commission in 1975 and the still important Advisory, Conciliation and Arbitration Service (ACAS) in 1976. The latter has been used to solve major industrial disputes in the public sector. It included trade union representatives from the Trade Union Congress (TUC) and the Confederation of Business and Industry (Kavanagh, 2001: 193–4). However the expansion of neo-corporatism came to an abrupt halt after the Winter of Discontent in 1978–79, during which trade union confederations almost brought the country to a standstill because of their strike

Table 12.2 The main features of the ideal type of pluralism

Aspects	Description
Structural features	1 Very unrestricted, decentralised system 2 Trade union movement fragmented and competitive 3 Business organisation movement fragmented and competitve 4 Interest groups compete for influence in the political system
Functional roles	1 No clear functional roles for interest groups
Behavioural patterns	1 Competitive behaviour between interest groups 2 Lobbying
Favourable contexts	1 Stronger differentiation between public and private 2 Open economy 3 Competitive environment 4 Majoritarian type of democracy 5 Limited level of social expenditure 6 Competitiveness through high level of de-regulation of market

Source: Author's own compilation

activity. After Margaret Thatcher came to power in 1979, she completely changed the system of interest intermediation to one of pluralism. While the period between 1945 and 1979 was referred to as a period of 'organised capitalism' because of the inclusion of social partners, the 1980s are often referred to as a period of 'disorganised capitalism' (Johnston, 1993: 129).

Thatcherite liberalisation policies bypassed any consultation with social partners. Some interest groups that had considerable authority in the economy and society lost their power in the battle against Prime Minister Margaret Thatcher (Moran, 1989: 280–92). For example, the National Union of Mineworkers, under the leadership of Arthur Scargill, lost its battle with Margaret Thatcher's government in 1983–84, because they pursued antagonistic adversarial strategies (Moran, 1989: 292–3). Thatcher's drive towards pluralism had considerable influence on policies concerning the Single European Market as well as in the member states. Many of the reforms in France, Germany, Spain, Italy and other countries were influenced by the Thatcherite approach; however, none of these reform efforts had quite the same level of radicalism. In spite of the pluralistic tendencies in the UK, the opportunities to influence legislative processes are more 'framed' than one would expect. When interest groups lobby for specific legislation, there will be a long process of consultation, frequently leading to a Green Paper. Following this, a bill will be drafted and interest groups will have an opportunity to influence the process by lobbying backbenchers and civil servants. After the bill has been approved, interest groups still have the opportunity to influence the implementation process. Moreover, there are 'insider' and 'outsider' interest groups. Insider interest groups, such as the Howard League for Penal Reform or the National Farmers' Union, have special access to the Department of Justice and the Department of Agriculture respectively. The trade-off is that such interest groups have to follow a moderate code of conduct and be able to compromise on legislation in order to preserve their long-term influence. Outsider interest groups have no interest in belonging to an inner circle in this way. They often use radical, uncompromising strategies to achieve their aims. Some interest groups may use direct action or even terrorist tactics in order to publicise their issues. Two specific groups are 'Fathers-4-Justice' and 'Greenpeace', which both organise direct action in order to publicise their issues. In terms of terror tactics, the animal protection groups should be singled out. In some cases, these groups do not refrain from harassing people in order to prevent or stop the establishment of laboratories, mainly for the pharmaceutical industry, that use animals for their drugs trials. One such group is the Animal Liberation Movement which, according to their website, claim to be involved in bomb attacks against a £20 million laboratory established at Oxford University (*The Guardian*, 29 October 2008).

Thatcherism contributed to a move of the UK towards a more Americanised pluralist system and lobbying has grown over the past three decades. There are over 60 lobbying firms in the UK trying to gain influence over legislation. However, in 1994–95 a commission under Lord Nolan was established that created a code of conduct with specific, strict guidelines for MPs. Apart from full declaration of all their business interests, MPs are forbidden to influence legislation on behalf of any group (Jones, 2007a: 208–9).

After the New Labour Party came to power in 1997, Prime Minister Tony Blair made it clear that the government would keep equidistant from both the CBI and TUC. Therefore, in spite of a strong historical legacy binding the Labour Party to the trade union movement, there has been a move towards a more pragmatic, less ideological approach to industrial relations. This all fits with the process of the professionalisation of socioeconomic interest groups and the separation of certain interests from politics (Jones, 2007a: 275–6).

Although the Republic of Ireland was strongly influenced by the British legacy, the smallness of the country has led to the establishment of neo-corporatist structures within an overwhelmingly pluralist system of industrial relations. The culmination of such neo-corporatism was between 1959 and 1982, particularly in terms of wage bargaining at a central level in the tripartite National Wage Agreement. Furthermore, social partners are regularly consulted in the National Economic and Social Council (Elvert, 2001: 201, 207). Trade unionism in Ireland emulated the British model by creating the Irish Trade Union Congress (ITUC) in the 1930s. However, a major split happened in 1944 that led to the walk-out of eighteen trade unions and to the foundation of the Irish Congress of Trade Unions (ICTU). On the employers' side, there was the Irish Business and Employers Organisation (IBEC), which was re-founded in 1993, when the confederation of Irish industries and the Federal Union of Employers merged together. Other important business organisations were the Construction Industry Federation (CIF), which profited enormously from the booming 1990s, and the Irish Bankers' Federation (IBF) (Elvert, 2001: 205–10). Neo-corporatism becomes important in periods of crisis of the Irish economy, such as, for example, during the 1980s. This consensual approach to politics is facilitated by the smallness of the country (Elvert, 2001: 218–19) (Figure 12.4, Table 12.3).

The French model of industrial relations is difficult to classify, largely because of its strong *étatist* tradition. The role of the state in the economy has been a major factor since the beginning of the Fifth Republic. This means that a strong national economy is regarded as part of the overall identity of the country and that the unity of the country should prevail above particularistic interest groups. According to Alistair Cole, the French system of interest intermediation cannot be referred to as either pluralistic nor neo-corporatist. However, it has elements of the two embedded in the political system. The *étatist* political culture of the country does not allow pluralism to dominate, nor neo-corporatism. Traditionally, the agricultural sector and their associations have been strongly involved in national policy-making. Neo-corporatist structures were detected there. Furthermore, the *grands corps* of public administration have been instrumental in building neo-corporatist structures in their specific fields (Cole, 1998: 202–3).

Another characteristic of the French model is that trade union confederations are among the weakest in Europe. In 2004, only 8.8 per cent of workers were unionised in one of the five peak organisations. Trade union confederations are ideologically split. The General Confederation of Labour (Confederation General du Travail, CGT) is communist, and known for being less compromising, frequently rejecting participation in tripartite committees. The French Democratic Confederation of Labour (Confederation Française Démocratique du Travail, CFDT) originated from the Christian democratic trade union confederations, but, in the 1970s, took on the objective of creating a more secular, less ideological organisation that was close to the Socialist Party, yet would maintain an equal distance from all political parties. The Workers' Force (Force Ouvrière, FO) is dominated

Figure 12.4 Systems of interest intermediation in Europe 2010

by smaller groups, such as the Trotskyite left, and was a splinter group of the communist CGT in 1947. The French Confederation of Christian Workers (Confederation Française des Travailleurs Chrétiens, CFTC), founded in 1919, preserves the traditions of Christian democratic trade unionism. Finally, the more specialised General Confederation of Cadres (Confédération Général de l'Encadrement–Confédération Générale de Cadres, CGE–CGC), founded in 1944, represents most professions of the new middle classes in the services sector, as well as engineers and other technicians. The regularly held works council elections confirmed this fragmented pattern of representation. In 2003, the CFDT got 22.6 per cent, the communist CGT 22.1 per cent, CGT–FO 12.7 per cent, the CGE–CGC 6.6 per cent and the Christian democratic CFTC 6 per cent (Dufour, 2005).

The employers' organisations are divided according to sizes of enterprise and sectoral membership. The former National Council of the French Employers (Conseil National du Patronat Français, CNPF) has been known since 1998 as the Movement of French Enterprises (Movement des Entrepreneurs Français, MEDEF) and it represents mainly the larger business organisations in France. However, this

Table 12.3 The placement of countries according to a neo-corporatism–pluralism continuum

Dominance of neo-corporatism			Dominance of pluralism		
Strongly corporatist	Moderately to strongly corporatist	Moderately corporatist	Pluralism with some strong corporatism	Pluralism with some weak corporatism	Pluralist
Austria Sweden Norway	Netherlands Denmark Germany (West)	Finland Belgium Luxembourg	Ireland UK (1962–1979) Italy Unified Germany (after 1989) France Portugal Spain Greece	Central and Eastern European countries	USA Canada UK (1980s, 1990s)

Source: Simplified and amended from Siaroff, 1999: 184; this is based on the perceptions of different authors and is, therefore, an inter-subjective assessment. Germany and the UK are this author's own assessment

fact is really just a simplification. In reality, the MEDEF represents 70 per cent of firms with fewer than fifty employees (Woll, 2006: 496). The General Confederation of Small and Medium Sized Enterprises and Real Employers (Confédération Général des Petites et Moyennes Enterprises et du Patronat Réel, CGPME) represents the smaller and medium-sized enterprises, while the National Union of Liberal Professions (Union National des Professions Libérales, UNAPL), founded in 1977, is the association for the liberal professions (a diverse group, comprising physicians, pharmacists, lawyers, high-ranking technical staff, and university and school teachers – all highly educated with ethical and professional standards). Finally, there is the Crafts Union (Union Professionelle Artisanale, UPA), which was founded in 1977. These organisations are the officially recognised business confederations, and are able to take part in policy-making. There are also the chambers of commerce and industry that comprise all enterprises for a particular region (having compulsory membership). There is a tendency for firms to have double and triple membership in order to achieve the maximum level of influence in relation to the government (Woll, 2006: 496). This means that the representation of business enterprises is a fairly complex, intertwined set of multiple affiliations, including the compulsory chambers at local and regional level (Woll, 2006: 497–8).

In terms of representation for tripartite organisations, those listed above are the main official organisations, although there are other smaller employees' and employers' organisations. The weak membership numbers of French associations can be related to the strong individualism of French people as well as a state that distrusts organised interest groups, fearing they may present a challenge to the unity of the country. An important consultative forum is the Economic and Social Committee (Conseil Economique et Social, CES), in which all major interest groups are represented. However, collective bargaining (despite its coverage of over 90 per cent) and tripartite negotiations have both been rather weak. Between 1983 and the late 1990s, there has been a radical shift from a centralised system of industrial relations to a decentralised one at the level of the individual firm (Woll, 2006: 502–3).

French exceptionalism has been eroding since the early 1980s. Apart from globalisation, Europeanisation has been central to this process. The socialist policies of liberalisation after 1983 marked the beginning of a transformation of French capitalism. The internationalisation of the economy was pursued across all sectors of the economy, particularly at regional level. In a comparative study about the impact of Europeanisation on capitalism in the UK, Germany and France, Vivien Schmidt (2002) found that the more radical transformational changes were taking place in France, while, despite the Thatcherite revolution, British reforms did not lead to a change in the way capitalism worked in the country. Germany simply absorbed most of the pressure from the EU, but this did not lead to any substantial changes. France has moved from a 'state-led' to a 'state-enhanced' capitalism since the early 1980s, allowing the market to regulate the economy. This has had a major impact on the system of industrial relations, which is now less dirigiste (Schmidt, 2002: 202–4).

Like most other EU member states, French interest groups now work in a multilevel setting and have abandoned purely nationally oriented strategies of influence. The French state is also interested in adjusting to Europeanisation processes, so there has been a substantial shift in France towards pluralism, accompanied by a simultaneous withdrawal of the state. French interest groups are now embedded in supranational Euro groups. Their own financial resources remain weak, as do those of the employers' organisations (Quittkat, 2006: 222–30). There has been a flexibilisation and decentralisation of structures of interest groups, in particular MEDEF. The Europeanisation process has led to a different relationship with the state, which has been relatively keen to keep a good relationship with business organisations. This has led to major protests in society, which would like to see greater distance between the state on the one hand and trade unions and business organisations on the other (Woll, 2006: 490–1).

Although Germany is categorised here as dominated by a pluralist system of interest intermediation, a political culture of neo-corporatism has also been shaping the relationship between interest groups and the state. The main economic partners in Germany are the German Trade Union Confederation (Deutsche Gewerkschaftsbund, DGB), which comprises one of the largest and most powerful trade unions, IG-Metall, and Vereinte Dienstleistungsgewerkschaft (ver.di), for employees in different service sectors. Following the unification of the country, both the DGB's membership and its influence have declined steeply. And, as a result, the representation of the working population has also been declining (Rudzio, 2006: 65–6). In addition, independent trade union confederations related to specific professions have emerged and also many trade unions have sometimes large numbers of members who have retired or are unemployed. On the employers' side, there is the Federation of German Employers (Bund der deutschen Arbeitgeberverbände, BDA) and the Federation of German Industry (Bund der deutschen Industrie, BDI). Because no party is able to win an outright majority in parliament, the German style of politics has moved towards consensual bargaining. The German model was considerably influenced by neo-corporatism as practised by its neighbours in west Central Europe. Gerhard Lehmbruch found there was an historical legacy going back to the Peace of Westphalia, after the Thirty Years War, which made possible more cooperative and consensual politics (Lehmbruch, 1996: 4; Lehmbruch, 2002: 183). This means that the social partners are involved in a myriad of tripartite boards and committees where they actively take part in policy-making and/or advise the government. The heydays of neo-corporatism were in the 1960s, but since then the neo-corporatist network has been eroding. The Konzertierte Aktion (concerted action) between 1967 and 1976 was an important Keynesian neo-corporatist institution, devised to give greater macroeconomic and labour market policy stability to West Germany. A law for growth and stability provided the framework for this integration. The social partners were integrated in long-term economic policies. Moreover, the co-determination legislation of 1972 and 1976 led to strong industrial democracy in most enterprises in Germany. However, in 1976 the trade union confederations left the Konzertierte Aktion. According to Wolfgang Streeck and Anke Hassel (2003), the German state had the ability to co-opt important interest groups of civil society into important positions of the political and economic systems of Germany, forcing them to act responsibly. Wolfgang Streeck and Anke Hassel explain as follows:

> The high art of government in West Germany was to turn social organisations with a high level of guaranteed autonomy and independent power into agents of publicly licensed self-government, in the context of a negotiated public order within which the state was just a participant among others. Where this was successful, social autonomy was transformed into delegated public responsibility, and organised interest groups became quasi-public agencies more competent and legitimate in governing their constituents than state agencies.
>
> (Streeck and Hassel, 2003: 103)

After 1982, Chancellor Helmut Kohl was very keen to reduce the power of unions and push through liberalisation policies, particularly in the labour market. However, the unification process led to a return to neo-corporatist cooperation with the social partners. Such cooperation lasted until 1995. Afterwards the Helmut Kohl government was under pressure from the small- and medium-sized enterprises (*Mittelstand*) to reduce labour costs and to reform the labour market (Streeck and Hassel, 2003: 109–13). The decline of membership among trade unions, growing unemployment and the erosion of centralised wage tariff bargaining led to calls for greater liberalisation and pluralism. Also industrial democracy became less relevant owing to the decline of people engaged in or represented by the works council (Streeck and Hassel, 2003: 112–13).

According to Wolfgang Rudzio, in the mid 1990s there were still 189 committees and 174 supervisory boards in which the social partners were involved. Moreover, social partners have a right in the process of appointing judges to the social and labour courts (Rudzio, 2006: 82).

After coming to power, Chancellor Gerhard Schröder created a neo-corporatist institution called Alliance for Jobs and Training (Bündnis für die Arbeit), which was intended to reduce the high level of unemployment, create new jobs and enhance the competitiveness of the German economy. However, after the adoption of the Hartz reform in 2002, the trade union confederation left the committee as a protest against it (Streeck and Hassel, 2003: 114–20; Kemmerling and Bruttel, 2006).

Switzerland shows many similarities to Germany, not least because of its consensual style of politics. Although it has been categorised as a pluralist system of intermediation, Switzerland also has a network of light neo-corporatist institutions, in which the main social partners are represented (Linder, 2005: 122–5). Although social partnership and neo-corporatist structures exist at federal and cantonal levels, Switzerland has to be categorised as a pluralist country. Such categorisation has become even more valid with the pressures coming from globalisation and Europeanisation. After the creation of a dense intertwined system of interest intermediation with many public–private institutions (*Politikverflechtung*), since the 1990s one can observe a disintegration of such structures (*Entflechtung*) in order to improve the competitiveness of the Swiss economy (Linder, 2005: 304).

The main trade union confederation, the Swiss Federation of Trade Unions (Schweizerischer Gewerkschaftsbund/Federation Syndicale Suisse, SGB/FSS) and the Christian democratic-dominated Travailsuisse comprise a low number of unionised workers. Switzerland has one of the lowest trade union membership density rates, along with France and Spain. The neo-corporatist network is therefore biased towards the employers' organisations, which have a substantially higher grade of organisation: the Federation of Swiss Employers (Schweizerischer Arbeitgeberverband/Union Patronale Suisse, SAV/UPS), Economiesuisse as the consolidated federation of enterprises, the crafts federation (Schweizerische Gewerbeverband/ Union Suisse des arts et metiers, SGB/USAM), the Swiss farmers' confederation (Suisse des paysans, SBV–USB), Schweizerischer Bauernverband-Union and the Swiss Association of Bankers (Schweizerische Bankiervereinigung/Association Suisse de Banquiers, ABV/ASB). Switzerland has always been a country with a strong civil society, particularly in the social and economic sectors. Since the economic crisis of the late 1930s, economic and social partners have been integrated in economic policy-making that is enshrined in the constitution. This means that the legislative process has now integrated a pre-parliamentary stage in which consultation of relevant interest groups has become an integral part. The pre-parliamentary decision-making process can last a considerable amount of time; however, it will be built on a strong consensus (Linder, 2005: 305–6). There is a general willingness of the government to listen to interest groups, because they may recur to direct democracy through referendums, which may embarrass the government (Linder, 2005:111).

In sum, in comparison to the US, European pluralism has tendencies towards neo-corporatism and, apart from the UK, most other pluralist systems of interest intermediation are tamed by neo-corporatist elements.

Southern Europe: the weak state and weak interest groups

The Southern European systems of interest intermediation share some similarities. The weak state and the weak economy, with the exception of northern Italy, are factors that have shaped the way interest intermediation is undertaken in Southern European countries. Clientelism and patronage have played a role in all four countries (Sapelli, 1995; Magone, 2003a; Schmitter, 1995). However, Europeanisation has led to a 'hollowing out and simultaneous hardening of the state' in Italy, but also in the other Southern European countries that have reduced the power of such clientelistic and patronage tendencies (Della Sala, 1997).

David Hine characterised Italy as 'bargained pluralism' shortly before the Tangentopoli affair erupted in 1992. This means that it is a pluralist system characterised by many negotiated settlements and informal networks (Hine, 1993: 1–10). One characteristic of Italy and other Southern European countries is that they are dualistic in nature. The weak state just controls part of the economy, and a substantial part of economic transactions are undertaken in the informal sector (approximately one-fifth). Moreover, both trade union confederations and business organisations are extremely fragmented, the former in ideological terms and the latter sectorally or according to the size of the enterprises, in much the same way as in France. There are three main trade union confederations: the former communist General Confederation of Italian Workers (Confederazione Generale Italiana del Lavoro, CGIL), the Christian democratic Italian Confederation of Workers' Trade Unions (Confederazione dei Sindacati dei Lavoratori, CISL) and the socialist Union of Italian Workers (Unione dei Lavoratori Italiani, UIL). On the employers' side, the Confederation of Industry (CONFINDUSTRIA) is probably the most important, but there are also confederations for trade organisations (CONFCOMERCIO), for agriculture (CONFAGRICOLTURA) and for crafts (CONFARTIGIANATO). The strong presence of the state in the economy until 1992 was a major factor leading to Tangentopoli. Many business organisations paid kickbacks to Christian Democracy, the dominant party of the political and party system, to get contracts for tenders issued by public sector firms. Many of these kickbacks were used for illicit party financing or even personal enrichment (Guzzini, 1994). Since 1992, there has been a process of hollowing out of the state as a result of the pressures stemming from Europeanisation, particularly the Economic and Monetary Union (EMU) (Della Sala, 1997). In spite of the change of context, both trade union confederations and business organisations are still highly fragmented and therefore financially constrained in terms of shaping political processes.

According to Oscar Molina and Martin Rhodes (2007), Europeanisation played a major role in pushing social partners to work together in the 1990s. In 1992, the automatic adjustment of wages to rising inflation (*scala mobile*), which had been introduced in the 1970s, was abolished and, in 1996, a pact for employment (*patto per il lavoro*) was also agreed. The wish of the political elite, backed by a Europhile population, to take part in the Economic and Monetary Union led to cooperation between the social partners between 1992 and 1998. The Patto de Natale (Pact of Christmas) during the centre-left coalition government of Prime Minister Romano Prodi was an important instrument in stabilising the system of interest intermediation after Tangentopoli. Also, during the second Berlusconi government (2001–6), the social partners signed a pact for Italy (Patto per Italia) that concentrated on labour market reform based on a White Book presented by Marco Biagi, which also encompassed pension reform. In spite of the murder of Marco Biagi by the Red Brigades in 2003, the social partners were supportive of the Biagi law in 2003. The new social pact led to some flexibilisation of industrial relations at the level of the firm. However, the weak state is confronted with weak trade union confederations and weak business organisations. This means that difficulties of implementation emerged throughout this period (Molina and Rhodes, 2007: 810–16).

In spite of these changes, Italy is still lagging behind in terms of reforms towards a more efficient system of industrial relations. The labour market has about

10 per cent of people working in the informal sector in the north, and this figure increases to 20 per cent in the centre and 30–35 per cent in the south (Molina and Rhodes, 2007: 822). Although macroeconomic stability has been achieved, the micro-economic flexibilisation is still outstanding, jeopardising the competitiveness of the economy. Apart from the demographic change that affects all European countries, there is a specific north–south problem in terms of asymmetrical development. In 2004, the north and middle of Italy had a GDP per capita of 118 per cent of the Italy average, while the south had just 67.8 per cent. Moreover, there is a lagging behind in terms of new information and telecommunications technologies, and also a lower investment in research and development than in the northern countries. Moreover, the budget deficit and public debt continue to be problematic issues in the Italian case (Drüke, 2004: 22–5).

All the other Southern European countries – Portugal, Spain and Greece – are characterised by even weaker states and respective interest groups. All of them are engaged in substantial reforms in order to flexibilise the labour market and the economy. However, all three countries have weak economies with fairly low research and development investment. This means they are extremely dependent on foreign direct investment. This leads to a situation where the state is not only weak, but it also has to deal with a weak economy, which, in times of crisis or asymmetrical shocks, is less able than more advanced economies to deal with difficult situations.

In Spain, the Workers' Committees (Comisiones Obreras, CCOO) and the General Union of Workers (Union General de los Trabajadores, UGT) are the main trade union confederations. Spain has the lowest unionisation rate of the European Union after France, with 15–18 per cent of the working population being members. In contrast, the Spanish Confederation for Business Enterprises (Confederación Española de Organizaciones Empresariales, CEOE) was able to integrate with the Confederation for Small and Medium Sized Enterprises (Confederación Española de Pequeñas y Medianas Empresas, CEPYME). CEOE has been a reliable social partner since 1977 (Brinkmann, 2001).

Europeanisation has played a major role in pushing all three countries towards the European social model by better integrating the social partners in the decision-making process. In Spain, in 1991, the Economic and Social Council (Consejo Economico y Social, CES) was created. Social pacts, such as the 'Moncloa pacts' during the democratic transition in 1978, have been used extensively in Spain since then. The socialist government under Felipe Gonzalez used social pacts in order to flexibilise the labour market and economy; however, in 1988, both main trade union confederations became more critical and antagonistic in relation to the policies of the government. A return to social pacts happened during the first Aznar government between 1996 and 2000. This was supported by a substantial improvement in the economy (Royo, 2001; Chari, 2001; Molina, 2006; 2007). Social pacts have also been used by Prime Minister José Luis Zapatero, who is very keen to increase the competitiveness of the Spanish economy. Considerable efforts have been made to improve the research and development record of the government (Magone, 2009a: 323–7).

In Portugal, a Permanent Council for Social Concertation (Conselho Permanente de Concertação Social, CPCS) was established in 1984, and became the central body for negotiation of public sector workers' wages. Later, in 1994 it became part of the consultative Economic and Social Council (Conselho Economico e Social, CES). In a similar way to Spain, Portuguese governments were engaged in establishing social pacts with the social partners. However, the communist-led General Confederation of Portuguese Workers (Confederação Geral dos Trabalhadores Portugueses, CGTP) has so far been uncompromising on many issues, while the socialist/social democrat General Union of Workers (União Geral dos Trabalhadores, UGT) has been more conciliatory and supportive of government efforts to integrate the social partners. The most important employers' organisation is the Confederation of Portuguese Industry (Confederação da Industria Portuguesa, CIP), founded in 1974, which works closely with the Portuguese Association of Industry (Associação da Industria Portuguesa/Confederação Empresarial, AIP/CE), founded in 1837, and the Enterpreneurial Association of Portugal (Associação Empresarial Portuguesa, AEP), founded in 1845, both in Oporto (Magone, 2001a: 114–59).

Finally, the Greek system of interest intermediation has been dominated by the main trade union confederation, the Confederation of Labour (GSEE), which comprises all trade union federations. The Confederation of Public Servants (ADEDY), which was fairly close to New Democracy, is in the process of merging with GSEE. GSEE had a close relationship with the socialist party (PASOK), particularly during the Papandreou governments of the 1980s. However, trade union membership has been declining steeply in Greece. In 2004, only 20 per cent of the working population was a member of a trade union. In this sense, the business organisations such as the Federation of Greek industries (SEB), the National Confederation of Greek Commerce (ESEE) and the General Confederation of Professional Craftsmen and Small Manufacturers of Greece (GSEBEE) have gained in influence and importance over time. Over 70 per cent of business organisations are organised (EIRO, 2008). However, according to Dimitris Tsarouhas (2008), both trade union confederations and employees' organisations have been fragmented at the top of the hierarchy. Trade unionism in Greece is still characterised by ideological fragmentation, as in other Southern European countries, in spite of the unitary nature of GSEE. A particular problem is the high level of independence of the more than 7,000 primary unions (Lavdas, 2005: 302; Tsarouhas, 2008: 357–8).

As in Portugal and Spain, Europeanisation has been a major factor in creating social dialogue institutions in Greece. A network of social dialogue institutions, such as the tripartite Economic and Social Committee (OKE), founded in 1994 and emulating the European level institution, the National Employment Council (NEC), the Fund for Employment and Vocational Training (LAEK) and the Hellenic Institute for Occupational Health and Safety (ELINYAE), are examples of such institutional proliferation. The NEC became central to national wage bargaining between social partners supported by the government. Social pacts have also been used since 1997 as a support for membership of Economic and Monetary Union. However, these policies were not properly coordinated. There have been lots of initiatives, but they were not overarched by a more long-term strategy of growth and stability. There were changes to the highly conflictive pattern of industrial relations up to the late 1980s, in which clientelism and patronage networks of the main political parties with interest groups played an important role (Tsarouhas, 2008: 357–9). One major problem has been what Kostas Lavdas labels 'disjointed corporatism', which comprises the lack of a tradition of social dialogue and tripartism, and the fragmentation of interest groups, allowing an asymmetrical development of neo-corporatist arrangements. The European integration process based on 'competitive' corporatism further complicates the stalled process of social dialogue (Lavdas, 2001; 2005: 306–11).

In conclusion, the Southern European countries are characterised by a weak state, a weak economy and weak interest groups. In spite of Europeanisation of the system of interest intermediation, a culture of clientelism and patronage, and of the weak state, continues to prevail.

New democracies in Central and Eastern Europe

After forty years of a communist state or socialist regime, most Central and Eastern European countries are still creating systems of interest intermediation that are compatible with a liberal market economy, Europeanisation and globalisation. Such a task is difficult, because business organisations are still weak and membership density in trade unions remains low.

The accession process to the EU has also imposed economic criteria on the Central and Eastern European countries. Moreover, a framework for the implementation of such economic criteria was exported to the Central and Eastern European countries. The tripartite social dialogue has been institutionalised and expanded in all Central and Eastern European countries. This proliferation of new tripartite social dialogue institutions has led to a better integration of employers' and employees' representative organisations (Comité Économique Sociale Européen, 2002: 137–49). However, the high level of fragmentation in some countries has created problems of representativeness. Moreover, economic and social problems have been major challenges to these new institutions. In most countries, systems of interest intermediation are still work in progress, although slowly the new rationale is being integrated into economic and social policies.

The most consolidated system of interest intermediation is probably that of Slovenia, which was able to establish a tradition of social partnership that has become a model for other Central and Eastern European countries. The country was able to follow a path-dependent development that had its origins in the former Yugoslav system of interest intermediation (Grdesic, 2008: 135–8). The tradition of industrial democracy in former Yugoslavia played a major role in facilitating the transition to a free market economy. However, one should not generalise this – Croatia and Serbia are still struggling to build a credible system of interest intermediation after the Franjo Tudjman and the Slobodan Milosevic authoritarian periods of the 1990s (Grdesic, 2008: 139–47). From early on, Slovenian social partners were integrated in the decision-making process. Therefore, collective bargaining covers 100 per cent of workers. Moreover, the degree of bargaining centralisation is 43 per cent, much higher than the EU average of 34 per cent. Another positive fact is that the workplace representation – because of Yugoslavia's historical legacy – achieves 64 per cent in comparison to 53 per cent of the EU average (EIRO, 2008). The Slovenian constitution defines the upper chamber, the National Council, as a corporatist chamber of vested interests, which is reasonably rare in Europe and can only be found in the Irish Senate. This means that both employers' and employees' organisations and other interest groups are able to shape the legislative process. Moreover, an Economic and Social Council was established in 1994 with consultative powers. Although the employees' representatives are still fragmented, Slovenia, with 44 per cent, still has one of the highest membership densities of the Central and Eastern European countries. This applies to employers' organisations as well, which have a membership density of 40 per cent.

Among the Central European countries, Slovakia emerges as having the best organised labour movement. The membership density is about 30–35 per cent, which is fairly high among these new democracies, and the business organisations have an organisation level of 60 per cent, covering 30 per cent of employees. An Economic and Social Partnership Council has ensured a tripartite social dialogue since the late 1990s, but especially since 2004. However, social pacts have so far been rare since the late 1990s (EIRO, 2008).

In the Czech Republic, a Council for Economic and Social Agreement was established in 1997; however, interest groups remain weak. The main trade union confederation is the Trade Union Association of Bohemia, Moravia and Silesia (Odborové sdružení Čech, Moravy a Slezska, OS ČMS) founded in 1991. There are other smaller trade union confederations; however, membership density has been decreasing fast, from 46 per cent in 1995 to 22 per cent in 2004 (EIRO, 2008). There are two main business organisations: the Confederation of Industry of the Czech Republic (Svaz průmyslu a dopravy ČR, SPČR) and the Confederation of Employers' and Entrepreneurs' Associations of the Czech Republic (Konfederace zaměstnavatelskych a podnikatelskych svazů ČR, KZPS ČR). Overall they represent only one-third of all enterprises.

In Hungary, there are nine employers' organisations and several trade union confederations active in tripartite bargaining committees. Among them is the tripartite National Interest Reconciliation Council (Országos Érdekegyeztetö Tanács, OÉT) and the Economic and Social Committee (Szociális és Gazdasági Tanács, GSZT). However, the fragmentation of both trade unions and business organisations has been a major factor undermining a more stable regime. Trade union membership density declined from 19.5 per cent in 2001 to 16 per cent in 2004 (EIRO, 2008). During the Viktor Orbán government (1998–2002), there were tensions between the interest groups, particularly trade union confederations and the government. The recent difficult economic situation in Hungary, reinforced by the global financial crisis, has also led to increased strike activity and problems in the social dialogue related to employment legislation (Neumann et al., 2008).

The employees' as well as the employers' organisations in Poland are fairly fragmented. There are four main organisations representing either the employers or the employees. There was a steep decline of trade union membership of over 70 per cent between 1993 and 2003 (Mrozowicki and Van Hootegem, 2008: 198). In 2004, membership density in trade unions was 14–17 per cent and the trend was declining. According to Adam Mrozowicki and Geert van Hootegem, the causes of this decline are not only structural, but also a result of the impact of social and economic change on the individual lives of workers. The new capitalist reality leads to a new, very insecure context, to which different individuals adapt with different strategies. Some of them contribute to the establishment of a new trade union confederation, others try to re-establish the old one, and some simply attempt to get by on a daily basis. This research is important for ascertaining how trade union strategies can best be adjusted to the needs of their members (Mrozowki and Van Hootegem, 2008:

204–13). Therefore, a younger generation of trade unionists is very keen to move away from an ideological approach and towards a more professionalised economic trade unionism servicing their constituencies (Ost, 2002: 43–6). Tripartite social dialogue institutions are the tripartite Commission for Social and Economic Affairs and the regionalised voivodeship social dialogue commissions, which have existed since 2001 (EIRO, 2008).

All Baltic countries are still constructing their system of interest intermediation. There are tripartite social dialogue institutions in Lithuania (Tripartite National Council), Estonia (Economic and Social Council) and Latvia (Tripartite Cooperation Council) that were founded in the 1990s and further expanded and improved before accession to the EU in 2004. While Lithuania and Estonia have very fragmented trade union movement and business organisations, with several representatives, reinforced by low membership levels, Latvia only recognises as official representative organisations the Free Trade Union Confederation of Latvia (Latvijas Brīvo Arodbiedrību savienība, LBAS), and the Latvian employers' confederation (Latvijas Darba Devēju konfederācija, LDDK). The membership density of the LBAS is low. Membership density in all three countries is between 17 and 20 per cent and is declining. Coverage of collective bargained agreements covers a very small number of employees (EIRO, 2008).

In the eastern Balkans, Romania is still characterised by a high level of fragmentation both on the employees' representation side, with five trade union confederations, and on the employers' side, with eleven business confederations. There have been talks to merge four of the five trade union confederations into the General Confederation of Labour (Confederaţia Generală a Muncii, CGM). There have also been international attempts to unify and merge employers' organisations into one – in particular, by the International Employers' Organisation, who tried this in December 1995 but failed. A second attempt was undertaken between 1997 and 1999, also without success. Finally, in 2004, a new umbrella organisation was established called the Alliance of Employers' Confederations of Romania (Alianta Confederatilor Patronale din România, ACPR) comprising seven of the business confederations representing mainly domestic firms. However, the other four business confederations are in the process of negotiating an alternative umbrella organisation. Moreover, membership density in trade unions declined from 90 per cent in the early 1990s to 30–35 per cent in 2006. The membership density of business organisations also remains low (Trif, 2008: 471). The main tripartite body in Romania is the Economic and Social Council (Consiliul Economic şi Social, CES). Although Romania implemented most of the EU social acquis, there are still major problems in the labour market, such as people working in more than one job to make ends meet, sometimes working 80 hours a week, or the discrimination against certain groups, such as the Gypsy minority of the Roma. Structures were created, such as the National Agency of the Roma, to improve the situation over the long term.

Similarly, Bulgaria is still both creating and consolidating its system of interest intermediation. As in Romania, there are still problems of consolidation through mergers on the side of both employees' and employers' organisations. The system of collective bargaining is still incomplete and most agreements have been achieved through tripartite negotiations; however, there is some movement, albeit slow, towards bipartite bargaining structures between the social partners.

Towards a multilevel system of interest intermediation

Since the mid 1980s, the European social dialogue has gained new prominence, particularly as a result of the initiatives of Jacques Delors who was president of the European Commission between 1985 and 1995. The 'Val Duchesse' social dialogue started in 1985 and consisted of the main representatives of the European Trade Union Confederation (ETUC): the Union of Industrial and Employers' Confederations of Europe (UNICE), which changed its name in May 2007 to BUSINESSEUROPE, the European Centre of Enterprises with Public Participation (CEEP), the European Associaton of Craft, Small and Medium-Sized Enterprises (UAPME), the Council of European Professional and Managerial Staff (EURO-CADRES), and the European Confederation of Executives and Managerial Staff (CEC). There is a social dialogue committee (SDC) that meets three to four times a year and consists of sixty-four members (thirty-two employers' representatives and thirty-two employees' representatives). This is supported by workshops and seminars. If the social partners decide to enter negotiations, a mediator is appointed to oversee the process. Any results have to be approved by the SDC. Finally, there are social dialogue summits chaired by the European Commission to discuss long-term objectives and strategies (European Commission, 2009; Table 12.4).

Several other organisations joined the social dialogue afterwards. The social dialogue was enshrined in the Single European Act (SEA), ratified in 1987, and the social partners were able to agree on a social protocol that allowed them to develop framework legislation, which, if approved by them, would then be transposed automatically into European law. This social protocol was attached to the Treaty of the European Union (Maastricht Treaty) in 1993. It was not fully integrated into the Treaty of the European Union, because the UK government rejected its endorsement. The main reason was that the British Conservative government under Prime Minister John Major feared that this would lead to higher social costs. However, when the British Labour Party came to power in 1997, the new British government under Prime Minister Tony Blair subscribed to the social protocol, so that it could be enshrined in the Amsterdam Treaty, ratified in 1999 (Magone, 2001b: 51–77; Dølvik, 1999; Nadel and Lindley, 1998).

Although the number of agreements between the social partners has been low, they have created the first signs of what Gerda Falkner calls 'Eurocorporatism'. This means that social partners try consensually to bargain agreements for the whole of Europe (for corporatism, see pp. 488–90). So far, Europe-wide agreements have been quite scarce. Three main agreements have been signed and ratified so far – the Parental Leave Directive (1995), the Part-Time Directive (1997), and Fixed Term Work (1999) (Falkner, 1996a; 1996b; 2007: 281–3). This means that the member states have to monitor this minimalist legislation agreed under article 139(2) of the Nice Treaty relating to minimal standards. Furthermore, social partners can agree autonomous agreements among themselves that they themselves are in charge of monitoring across the EU (see Table 12.5).

Although this 'multilevel system of industrial relations' is still in its early stages, it is already making a considerable difference to national politics. The Lisbon Strategy, declared in 2000, sought to transform the EU into the most competitive, knowledge-based economy in the world by 2010, and has become the rationale behind this drive for systemic integration and convergence of policy-making styles.

Table 12.4 The main social partners in social dialogue at supranational level

Organisation	Constituency	Foundation year	Organisation
European Trade Union Confederation (ETUC)	Workers, employees	1973	82 national organisations from 36 countries, 11 European industry federations comprising more than 60 million members
BUSINESSEUROPE (former UNICE)	Employers	1958	41 employers' associations from 34 countries, representing 20 million businesses
European Centre of Enterprises with Public Participation and of Enterprises of General Economic Interest (CEEP)	Employers' association for public sector entities (local transport, energy, water ports), networked businesses and, in some countries, local authorities	1961	National sections in 17 countries
European Association of Craft, Small and Medium Sized Enterprises (UEAPME)	European crafts, trades and small businesses	1979	44 member organisations (national cross-sectoral small- and medium-sized enterprises, federation branches) in 26 countries, representing 11 million businesses across Europe and comprising 50 million staff
EUROCADRES	Professional and managerial staff representing all branches of industry, public and private services and administrative departments	1993	46 organisations in 46 countries comprising more than 5 million staff
European Confederation of Executives and Managerial Staff (CEC)	Professional, managerial and executive staff	1989	European branch federations and 17 national organisations comprising 15 million staff in 14 EU countries

Source: European Commission (2009), DG Employment, Social Affairs and Equal Opportunities, Social Dialogue webpage http://ec.europa.eu/employment_social/social_dialogue/typology_en.htm (accessed 29 January 2009)

Table 12.5 The types of agreements established in the context of the social dialogue, 2009

Type of agreement	Approved agreements
Agreements implemented by Council decision Implemented by Council decision, monitored by the Commission	• Framework agreement on parental leave, 1995 • Framework agreement on part-time work, 1997 • Framework agreement on fixed-term work, 1999 • European agreement on the organisation of working time of seafarers, 1998 • European agreement on the organisation of working time of mobile workers in civil aviation, 2000 • European agreement on certain aspects of the working conditions of mobile workers assigned to interoperable cross-border services, 2004 • Agreement on certain aspects of the working conditions of railway mobile workers assigned to interoperable cross-border services, 2007
Autonomous agreements implemented by the procedures and practices specific to management and labour and the member states Implementation and monitoring by the social partners	• Framework agreement on telework, 2002 • Framework agreement on work-related, stress, 2004 • Agreement on the European licence for drivers carrying out a cross-border interoperability service, 2004 • Agreement on Workers' Health Protection through the Good Handling and Use of Crystalline Silica and Products containing it • Framework agreement on harassment and violence at work

Source: European Commission (2009), DG Employment, Social Affairs and Equal Opportunities, Social Dialogue webpage http://ec.europa.eu/employment_social/social_dialogue/typology_en.htm (accessed 29 January 2009)

The open method of coordination (OMC), which allows for a voluntary mid-term to long-term convergence of policies, requires a strong input on the parts of the social partners in order to achieve maximum consensus. This is also the reason why social pacts have become central instruments in the policy-making process across the EU (Hamann and Kelly, 2007) (see Box 12.1).

The supranational level has also become a preferred arena for many Euro groups and lobbying firms that emerged in the 1980s. This organised civil society consists of many Euro groups, such as BUSINESSEUROPE, ETUC, CEEP and the UAPME. Moreover, there is a growing importance attached to business consultancies working for clients at the European level. According to Christian Lahusen there were 285 such firms employing 5,777 workers in 2000 (Lahusen, 2002: 701). Justin Greenwood estimates that 1,450 interest groups formally addressed EU institutions at the beginning of the millennium. Two-thirds would have been

---

Box 12.1 The European Economic and Social Committee (EESC)

The European Economic and Social Committee includes all relevant national social partners and important representatives of civil society. According to the size of the population each country appoints their representatives to the EESC. The EESC is organised in three groups. The first group consists of the national employers' organisations, the second group is the employees' and workers' organisations and the third group comprises relevant organisations from civil society. There have been criticisms that this 'industrial society' organisation of the EESC is outdated, and that a new structure, taking into account the services sector and transnational corporations should be developed. The decision-making process is consensual – it avoids partisan positions. The EESC has merely consultative powers; however, the European Commission is obliged to follow up the opinions of the EESC and to report on whether they have been included in legislation. Regular reports are issued by the European Commission showing a detailed follow-up of opinions and deliberations undertaken by the EESC and taken over or not by the European Commission. The EESC had a major crisis of identity after the creation of the Committee of the Regions and Local Authorities. However, it relaunched itself as the bridge between civil society and the European institutions. Since then, it has gained more visibility, particularly in exporting the European social model to Central and Eastern European countries (Magone, 1999; 2005). The Committee consists of 344 national representatives appointed by national governments. It has the same number of members and allocation according to countries as the Committee of the Regions.

Member states	Members of CoR
France, Germany, Italy and the United Kingdom	24
Poland and Spain	21
Romania	15
Austria, Belgium, Bulgaria, Czech Republic, Greece, Hungary, the Netherlands, Portugal and Sweden	12
Denmark, Finland, Ireland, Lithuania and Slovakia	9
Estonia, Latvia and Slovenia	7
Cyprus and Luxembourg	6
Malta	5

---

business interest groups, 20 per cent public interest groups, 11 per cent professional interest groups and 3 per cent trade union interest groups. Moreover, the number of individual lobbyists may be between 10,000 and 30,000 (although probably closer to the first figure) (Greenwood, 2003: 9; see also Eising, 2001). Many national associations are also present at supranational level, most of them organised in Euro groups such as ETUC, BUSINESSEUROPE and CEEP.

The estimates of lobbyist activity in Brussels made by the non-governmental organisation Lobbycontrol and the Alliance for Lobbying Transparency and Ethics Regulation (ALTER-EU) are much higher. According to Lobbycontrol, the number of lobbyists is estimated at 15,000 and they have stepped up their lobbying strategies (*Der Spiegel*, 16 October 2007). In the 1980s such strategy was still not regulated at European level, however, since then, we have seen more regulation, particularly in the European Parliament and European Commission. A code of conduct for lobbyists tames the industry, so that the American model of pluralism can be avoided. In spite of these initiatives, there are still major problems in the full control of lobbyism in the EU. ALTER-EU reported that out of only 20 per cent of the estimated 2,600 interest groups based in Brussels (estimated in the year 2000, the actual number may be higher and rate of registration lower) are registered in the voluntary register of the Commission, which has existed since June 2008. Controls of lobbyism are still very weak. The majority of lobbying firms, law firms and consultancies are still not resisted and most of the registered interest groups are large companies. ALTER-EU proposes that registration is made compulsory and the criteria of declaration should be stricter (ALTER-EU, 2009a; 2010a).

Gary Marks (1996) and his team have characterised the multilevel governance system as a 'multiple crack' structure of opportunities for interest groups, meaning the 'strategic exploitation of multiple points of access' at European, national and subnational levels in order to shape legislation in favour of interests (Marks *et al.*, 1996: 45). Such a multilevel structure of opportunities with different access points was used by all Euro groups, as well as by institutional actors such as offices of subnational regions based in Brussels. The number of regional offices increased considerably from 2 in the 1980s to 244 in 2002 (Smets, 1998: 328; Magone, 2003c: 12; Badiello, 2004: 328).

Conclusions: from national systems of interest intermediation to a multilevel EU governance system

The flexibilisation of industrial relations across the European Union is leading to a paradigm shift from rigid structures of interest intermediation, of which the interventionist Keynesian neo-corporatism of the 1960s and 1970s is a good example, to a governance model that allows closer cooperation between the public and private sectors. Instead of the dominance of the tripartite mode of interest intermediation, there is a growing reliance on bipartite governance regimes in different policy fields (self-regulation of social partners with hardly any participation of state actors). Private governance based on codes of conduct and benchmarking may be used in particular industries, such as the pharmaceutical industry, and also for decentralised company-level agreements. This also means that interest groups will have to adopt a more professional approach to particular problems and overcome ideological bias and strategies.

Although still in its early stages, the EU is moving towards a multilevel governance system in which the social partners will be central for many policies. There is an increasing involvement of the social partners at all levels of the multilevel governance system. This has also become a central piece of the European social model of capitalism. In spite of the convergence and systemic integration, there are still major differences between the European countries. Some have advanced considerably towards the new paradigmatic approach to industrial relations, while others are still lagging behind. This shows that the development towards this multilevel system of interest intermediation is quite asymmetrical and may well take a long time to become reality.

Suggested reading

General comparative books

Crouch, Colin (1994), *Industrial Relations and European State Traditions*. Oxford: Oxford University Press.

Visser, Jelle and Joris van Ruysseveldt (1996), *Industrial Relations in Europe: Traditions and Transitions*. London: Sage.

Industrial relations

European Foundation for the Improvement of Living Conditions (2009), *Developments in Industrial Relations in Europe 2008*. Luxembourg: Office of the Official Publications of the European Communities. (Electronically available: www.eurofound.europa.eu/pubdocs/2009/40/en/1/EF0940EN.pdf.)

Hammann, Kerstin and John Kelly (2007), Party Politics and the Re-emergence of Social Pacts in Western Europe, *Comparative Political Studies*, 40(8): 971–94.

Schmitter, Philippe (2008), The Changing Politics of Organised Interests, *West European Politics*, 31(1): 195–210.

Schmitter, Philippe C. and Jürgen Grote (1997), *The Corporatist Sysiphus: Past, Present and Future*. Florence: EUI Working Papers, SPS 97/4.

Siaroff, Alan (1999), Corporatism in 24 Industrial Democracies. Meaning and Measurement, *European Journal of Political Research*, 36: 175–205.

Traxler, Franz (2004), The Metamorphoses of Corporatism: From Classical to Lean Patterns, *European Journal of Political Research*, 43(4): 571–98.

European integration and industrial relations

Falkner, Gerda (1996a), The Maastricht Protocol on Social Policy: Theory and Practice, *Journal of European Social Policy*, 6(1): 1–16.

—— (1996b), European Works Councils and the Maastricht Social Agreement: Towards a New Social Policy? *Journal of European Public Policy*, 3(2): 192–208.

—— (2007), The EU's Social Dimension. In: Michelle Cini (ed.), *European Union Politics*. Oxford: Oxford University Press, pp. 271–86.

Marginson, Paul (2006), Europeanization and Regime Competition: Industrial Relations and EU Enlargement, *Industrielle Beziehungen*, 13(2): 97–117.

Marginson, Paul and Keith Sisson (2002), European Integration and Industrial Relations: A Case of Convergence *and* Divergence? *Journal of Common Market Studies*, 40(4): 671–92.

Euro groups and Euro-lobbying

Alliance for Transparency of Lobbying and Ethics Regulation (2009), The Commission's Lobbying Register One Year On: Success or Failure. Brussels: ALTER-EU. (Electronically available: www.alter-eu.org/en/system/files/publications/register-assessment-after-one-year.pdf accessed 25 August 2009.)

Bouwen, Pieter (2004), The Logic of Access to the European Parliament. Business Lobbying in the Committee on Economic and Monetary Affairs, *Journal of Common Market Studies*, 42(3): 473–95.

Bouwen, Pieter (2002), Corporate Lobbying in the European Union: The Logic of Access, *Journal of European Public Policy*, 9(3): 365–90.

Bouwen, Pieter and Margaret McCown (2007), Lobbying vs Litigation: Political and Legal Strategies of Interest Representation in the European Union, *Journal of European Public Policy*, 14(3): 422–43.

Greenwood, Justin (2003), *Organized Interests in the European Union*. Basingstoke: Palgrave.

Electronic journals

European Journal of Industrial Relations. (Excellent articles on industrial relations in East and West.)

Transfer. (Scientific journal of the European Trade Union Institute dedicated to the study of trade unions and industrial relations.)

Websites

Alliance for Lobbying Transparency and Ethics Regulation (ALTER-EU) (2009): excellent critical website monitoring lobbying at EU level at: www.alter-eu.org/ (accessed 25 August 2009).

European Foundation for the Improvement of Living Conditions (EUROFOUND) (2009): excellent database on different aspects including industrial relations at: www.eurofound. europa.eu (accessed 25 August 2009).

European Industrial Relations Observatory (EIRO) (2009), database with excellent reports on the situation of industrial relations in each European country at: www.eurofound. europa.eu/eiro/ (accessed 25 August 2009).

European Industrial Relations Observatory (EIRO) (2009), European Industrial Relations Dictionary at: www.eurofound.europa.eu/areas/industrialrelations/dictionary/index.htm (accessed 25 August 2009).

QUESTIONS FOR REVISION

- What are the main features of neo-corporatism? Discuss, using examples from at least two European countries.
- What are the main features of pluralism? Discuss, using examples from at least two European countries.
- Assess the consolidation of interest intermediation systems in Central and Eastern Europe. Discuss, using examples from at least two countries.
- Are we moving towards a European system of industrial relations?
- What positive and negative aspects can you identify in Euro-lobbying?

Convergence of national policy styles: the role of the European Union

SUMMARY OF CHAPTER 13

This chapter deals with the growing importance of the European Union in shaping the policy-making processes of the national states. Although the member states still have considerable control over most of its policies, international and European standards, benchmarking and good practice have led to a convergence of national policy styles. One can speak of a **growing Europeanisation of national policy making** (see Chapter 3).

In this chapter, we will concentrate on four policy areas that have become largely Europeanised, meaning that the supranational institutions of the EU have gained considerable influence over the outcome. These are:

- economic and monetary policy
- environmental policy
- European regional policy
- from welfare to workfare policy (employment and social policies).

Some policy areas, such as taxation, education, health, employment and social policy, remain under the control of member states. However, this control is increasingly subject to benchmarking and good practice, which are set mainly by the Organisation for Economic Cooperation and Development (OECD) and the European Union. In the education sector, the OECD regularly publishes a ranking of the quality of education in the member states: the PISA (Programme for International Student Assessment) study. This leads to policy changes towards the styles used by the best-performing countries. Such benchmarking and good practice must be adopted by all the European countries.

Similarly, in employment policy the European Union developed the open method of coordination, a soft mode of governance, in order to achieve a long-term **European Employment Strategy (EES)**. This was increasingly integrated in the overall Lisbon Strategy to create the most competitive knowledge-based economy in the world by 2010. This aim was not achieved, but at least the dynamics have been introduced to achieve this at a later date.

Members of the **Economic and Monetary Union (EMU)** are subject to the policies of the European Central Bank. This means that monetary policy is no longer in the hands of national governments – a typical practice of national sovereignty – and economic policy is increasingly a collective effort.

Slowly, national policy-making is being shaped and constrained by multilevel governance.

Introduction

In the previous chapter on interest groups and systems of interest intermediation, several national policy styles were recognised relating to the way in which they integrated relevant groups of society. On the one hand, the neo-corporatist policy style was more usual in the Nordic countries, the Netherlands, Belgium,

Luxembourg and Austria, while on the other, the pluralist style was more usual in the United Kingdom. In between, several countries had a more or less pluralist system with some neo-corporatist practices. National policy styles matter, because the more inclusive the process of decision-making is, the more long term the outcome, particularly in crucial policy areas such as economic, welfare and education policy. The more partisan and competitive are the relationships between governments and interest groups, the more the danger is that at the next elections a new party may re-negotiate or even unilaterally change policies. In this sense, today most policies are preceded by a long process of consultation and cooperation with interest groups, civil society and parliament. However, in the past twenty-five years, the European integration process has superseded nationally inspired policies in many areas. The growing impact of top-down 'Europeanisation' has changed policy-making processes at national level (see Chapter 4). There are still differences, but the European integration process is expanding into more and more areas. For the first time in the Lisbon Treaty, a clear distribution of competences between member states and the supranational level was enshrined (see Box 13.1).

In the following pages, we discuss some of these policies, which are either the exclusive competence of the European Union, or in which the supranational institutions have considerable influence.

The growing importance of European public policy

All member states of the European Union are under considerable pressure at the supranational level to implement policies designed to make them more compatible with the emerging Single European Market (SEM). After the enlargement of the European Union in 2004 and the integration of Bulgaria and Romania, the EU had a market of 493 million citizens (2006). The completion of the SEM remains probably the most important task for the European Union to achieve. The SEM is based on four main freedoms: freedom of movement, freedom of goods, freedom of capital and freedom of services. Since 1985, all member states have been engaged in an accelerated process of European integration that has led to the establishment of several policy regimes in order to transform national economies into a large market. A crucial factor in the creation of the SEM is Economic and Monetary Union, which started after the adoption of the Treaty of the European Union in 1993 and led to the introduction of the euro in twelve countries in 2002. Meanwhile, there are sixteen countries that have adopted the euro, among them two Central and Eastern European countries, Slovenia (2008) and Slovakia (2009). Such accelerated European integration was only possible because of the engagement of the former President of the European Commission, Jacques Delors, who relaunched the European Union as a major player in the world between 1985 and 1995. Mark A. Pollack speaks of the growing competence of the European Commission throughout the decade when Jacques Delors was in charge (Pollack, 1994). Such incrementalism of new policy areas came to an abrupt end after Delors's presidency. His successors had to deal mainly with the consolidation of the new policy areas. In 2000, Pollack assessed that after Delors's presidency the growing competence came to an end (Pollack, 2000). This means that in the past

> **Box 13.1 The catalogue of competences of the EU and the member states according to the Lisbon Treaty (in force since 1 December 2009)**
>
> For the first time, the Constitutional Treaty (not ratified owing to rejection in referendums in France and the Netherlands in 2005) and its renegotiated downgraded version, the Treaty of Lisbon, have enshrined in the consolidated version (section on the functioning of the EU) a clear catalogue of the competences assigned to the EU, those to be shared by the EU and the member states, and those of the member states, though strongly influenced in terms of further development by the EU. If a policy is not mentioned, it belongs automatically to a member state.
>
> | EU exclusive competences (powers) | EU competences shared with member states | Member states' competences, but with strong EU support input |
> |---|---|---|
> | • Customs union
• Competition rules for the functioning of the internal market
• Monetary policy for member states in the eurozone
• The conservation of marine biological resources under the common fisheries policy
• Common commercial policy
• Conclusion of international agreements if necessary | • Internal market
• Social policy, for the aspects defined in the Treaty
• Economic, social and territorial cohesion
• Agriculture and fisheries, excluding the conservation of marine biological resources
• Environment
• Consumer protection
• Transport
• Trans-European networks
• Energy
• Area of freedom, security and justice
• Common safety concerns in public health matters | • Protection and improvement of human health
• Industry
• Culture
• Tourism
• Education, vocational training, youth and sport
• Civil protection
• Administrative cooperation |

two decades the relationship between the supranational, national and subnational level has changed considerably. Policy-making across EU member states and beyond, particularly in the Balkans, has become similar. The rationale of European public policy is now linked to the overarching aim of the Lisbon Strategy issued in 2000, which aimed to make the European Union the most competitive knowledge-based economy in the world by 2010. Although the EU will not achieve this by 2010, the accelerated nature of the process has helped it to come closer to this ambitious aim. 'European public policy' did not exist before 1985. The European integration process was stagnating and policy-making was firm in the hands of the national governments before 1985. The European Commission presidency of Jacques Delors changed all that, and created a new rationale for the European integration process. While before 1985 nationally oriented, short-term projects were used to improve the situation in a particular country, after this date the whole approach was oriented towards European integration and based on long-term planning. The establishment of one particular policy such as the European regional policy led eventually to the emergence of other policies, such as environmental and employment policies. The best example of this long-term planning was the Single European Market programme (1985), which was shaped by the British Commissioner Lord Cockfield and contributed to the development of parallel policies. According to Christopher Ross, the European Commission referred to this as the 'Russian dolls' approach:

> François Lamoureux, Pascal Lamy's second in command during the Maastricht period, summarised the Delors team's approach as a 'Russian doll' strategy. 'You take the first doll apart', he said, 'and then, inside it is another one, which leads you to another and so on . . . until it is too late to turn back.' The Russian doll metaphor implied iterated episodes of strategic action to seize upon openings in the political opportunity structure, resource accumulation through success, and reinvestment of these resources in new actions to capitalise on new opportunities. There was a certain 'double or nothing' dimension to the next stage after 1987. The basic approach remained the same, but there was to be a significant change in direction. The White Paper and Single European Act sought to use the Community's traditional trade-market orientations. With the move to Russian dolls the Community shifted its targeting subtly towards state-building.
>
> (Ross, 1995: 39)

This shift from market-oriented policies towards state-building ones has also been recognised by other authors such as Simon Hix (2005), Vivien Schmidt (2006) and Stefano Bartolini (2005).

While Simon Hix defines the European Union as a political system, but not a state (Hix, 2005: 2–9), Vivien Schmidt calls it a regional state, meaning a regional–continental union of nation-states, 'in which the creative tension between the Union and its member states ensures both ever-increasing regional integration and ever-continuing national differentiation' (Schmidt, 2006: 9).

Although it is quite difficult to reach an exact definition of what the European Union is at the moment, the dynamic process of European integration is contributing to some kind of future-oriented polity that overcomes the indivisibility of national sovereignty of nation-states and transforms into a regime of 'shared sovereignty' or 'post-sovereignty' within the Euro-polity (Schmidt, 2006: 14–16). William Wallace calls it 'governance without statehood', which is characterised by 'post-sovereign politics', meaning that 'it spills across state boundaries, penetrating deep into previously domestic aspects of national politics and administration'.

Interference in each others' internal affairs has become an important part of this post-sovereign politics. It means, also, that national governments remain actors in the EU multilevel governance system, but not the only ones. The supranational institutions play a major role in moderating and framing policy-making at national level (Wallace, 2005: 493–4).

In a globalised world, nation-states have to find alternative ways of preserving their influence. The growing cooperation at European and international level is strengthening the position of the EU worldwide. According to Mario Telò, the future of the European Union will depend on whether it is able to make its European social model of capitalism the dominant paradigm across the world (Telò, 2005: 170). Such a model of capitalism has become central to the Lisbon Strategy, which wants the EU to become the most competitive knowledge-based economy in the world by 2010. Jeremy Rifkin has already contrasted the decaying American model with the emerging European one, which is based on environmentally friendly policies and social cohesion (Rifkin, 2004). President Barack Obama's election in the United States in 2008 has already given voice to many of the ideas of the European socioeconomic model, particularly in terms of investing in environmentally friendly, renewable energy sources in order to reduce dependency on oil (*Der Spiegelonline*, 25 January 2009).

In the past two decades, the European Union has emerged as a new model for world politics. The policy-making process has become sophisticated and complex, involving the supranational, national and subnational levels. Moreover, many of the powers of the member states were transferred to European Union institutions such as the Economic and Monetary Union – for example, environmental policy, competition policy and, of course, trade policy.

Although the EU annual budget is roughly €133 billion, which is about 1 per cent of the gross national income (GNI) of the EU, this is substantial in comparison to the budget of the 1970s, when it was below €10 billion (Laffan and Lindner, 2005: 193–5). However, the member states have set the ceiling of the EU budget at 1.24 of the EU's GNI, so that, for the near future, no major increases are foreseen. There are three main sources of revenue:

1   *Traditional own sources*: coming mainly from charges on imported goods from non-EU countries, €17.3 bn; 15 per cent.
2   *VAT-based revenues transferred from member states*: €17.8 billion; 15 per cent;
3   *Resource based on gross national income (GNI)*: uniform percentage rate of 0.67 per cent which each member state needs to pay, based on their GNI, €80 billion; 69 per cent (European Commission, 2009).

The Delors period led to a substantial growth in the budget by doubling it twice in 1988 and 1992, known as the Delors Package 1 and 2. As already mentioned, in 1988 the member states agreed to the financial projections of the EU for several years ahead. Meanwhile, there were four multi-annual programming budgetary packages, for the periods 1988–93, 1994–99, 2000–7 and 2007–13. These negotiations led to considerable tensions between the rich countries, such as Germany, the United Kingdom, the Netherlands and Sweden, which are net payers, and the poor countries, such as Portugal, Spain, Greece, Ireland, Poland and the

Czech Republic, which are net receivers. The most famous case was probably that of British Prime Minister Margaret Thatcher in several Council meetings between 1979 and 1984, during which she demanded her 'money back', and which led to a rebate of the UK contribution (Baldwin and Wyplosz, 2004: 64). Such a cleavage between the two groups of countries has become more prominent since 1999 and reached a peak during the British presidency in the Brussels Council meeting of 16–17 December 2005. It led to a compromise that resulted in the budget being frozen. Prime Minister Tony Blair had to sacrifice some of the British rebate in order to achieve a compromise. The supportive and generous role of Chancellor Angela Merkel on behalf of Germany should also be mentioned in this context. Her ability to seek a compromise was a major factor that led to the successful conclusion of the budget negotiations (Magone, 2009b: 199–201).

Most of this funding was used to create more economic and social cohesion across the EU territory, so that it became a level playing field for all the member states. Financial transfers come from different funds. Structural policies are financed through the European Regional Development Fund (ERDF), social cohesion and employment policies through the European Social Fund (ESF), and the Common Agricultural Policy (CAP) through the European Agricultural Guarantee and Guidance Fund (EAGGF).

The member states that profited most are in Southern Europe and Central and Eastern Europe. According to Brigid Laffan and Johannes Lindner, in 2002, net transfers from the EU budget were 2.39 per cent of GNI for Greece, 2.14 per cent for Portugal, 1.29 per cent for Spain and 1.29 per cent for Ireland, known as the 'cohesion countries', before the enlargement to Central and Eastern Europe (Laffan and Lindner, 2005: 193).

Most spending now goes on regional development, research and innovation, which are linked to the Lisbon Strategy. These policies have been integrated as part of the 'sustainable growth' strategy of the European Union. The continuing high expenditure of the Common Agricultural Policy has been criticised by developing countries across the world, because it undermines the competitiveness of their products. Although former Commissioner Franz Fischler was able to achieve a reform of the CAP and Common Fisheries Policy, which envisages a reduction in subsidies until 2013, this is still the single largest expenditure item of the budget; 42 per cent of the budget is spent on an average 3–4 per cent of the population. Other policy areas are still underfunded, particularly the external policies of the EU (Figure 13.1).

Europeanisation and policy convergence in EU member states

Europeanisation processes (see Chapter 4) are taking place in all member states, and European policy-making is a crucial aspect in this respect. Member states have to agree to policies framed at European level. This leads to the effects of convergence, which may be reinforced by policy diffusion and transfers (for a more detailed breakdown see Knill, 2005: 765–8). Apart from the hard instruments of European policy-making, there are also the soft modes of governance, such as benchmarking, best practice or the open method of coordination (OMC) (Caporaso and Wittenbrink, 2006). Depending on the policy area, there is a stronger, more

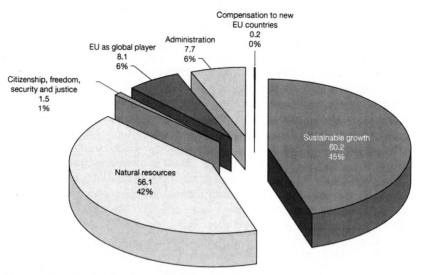

Figure 13.1 The distribution of the annual budget, 2009, according to policy areas, in absolute numbers and share of total

formalised input by the European institutions with regular controls, while in other areas (such as education, social or employment policies), which are still national competences, there is considerable use of the soft modes of governance. Through the regular monitoring of policy-making in individual countries and its reflection at supranational level in different committees, policy learning has become an integral part of the overall Europeanisation and convergence processes.

Economic and monetary policy: towards the stabilisation state

Apart from the single European market programme, Economic and Monetary Union has so far been the most salient policy in the European Union. Such a process started in the 1970s, particularly the Werner plan that had to be shelved owing to the economic crisis and instability of currencies. In spite of this, the members of the European Union joined the European Monetary System (EMS). At the heart of the EMS was the exchange-rate mechanism established in March 1979, consisting of Germany, the Benelux countries, Denmark, France, Ireland and Italy. However, the UK did not join the ERM. After joining the European Community, Portugal and Spain joined the EMS in the 1980s, which contributed to the consolidation of the EMS. Moreover, the UK joined in 1990, but in 1992 had to leave again owing to speculation about its currency. In 1988, after the Hanover Council and during the German presidency, the member states set Jacques Delors the task of developing a plan for Economic and Monetary Union. He headed a committee consisting mainly of bankers who prepared a report advocating that the EMU should be implemented in three stages. The first stage envisaged a period of convergence of economic and monetary policies. In the second stage the European Central Institute was founded, later to be called the European Central Bank. In the third stage the single currency would be implemented over a four-year period. The whole process started after the adoption of the Treaty of the European Union. Germany and the Bundesbank imposed some strict criteria, which were enshrined in the national growth and stability pacts agreed in June 1997 in the Amsterdam 'European Council' (public deficit should not be more than 3 per cent of gross domestic product (GDP), and public debt should be below 60 per cent of GDP), in order to avoid the inflationary tendencies of the new currency (McNamara, 2005: 143–7).

After 1993, one of the most important topics was the capacity of countries to adopt the euro in the third stage. Owing to the weakness of macroeconomic policies in Southern Europe, many economists expected that these countries would not be able to meet the criteria and move to the third stage of EMU. Many economists envisaged the emergence of a two-speed Europe, in which the Southern European countries would only join later (Dinan, 2004: 248). In reality, all Southern European countries became members of the Euro group in the first wave of countries. Portugal, Spain, Italy and Greece adopted strict policies in order to achieve membership of the euro in the first wave. After a report of the European Commission and confirmation by the European Council in Brussels in May 1998, eleven countries were given a green light to move to the third stage and adopt the euro. Among the eleven countries, Italy used extraordinary means, such as extra taxation, to achieve the third stage. It was the Romano Prodi government between 1996 and 1998 that introduced severe macroeconomic policies in order to reach the third stage of the EMU. Although the strict Maastricht criteria were the foundations for the selection of countries for the third stage, in reality the decision was merely political, owing to the fact that some countries such as Belgium and Italy had a public debt above the prescribed 60 per cent of GDP. Greece was the country that had most difficulty in achieving convergence, and was only allowed to join in 2001. Nevertheless, it joined the third stage with a public debt deficit similar to those of Belgium and Italy.

This political decision was also a result of the Euro-scepticism of the Nordic countries and the UK, with the UK deciding not to join because of the Euro-sceptic majority of the country. However, Prime Minister Tony Blair was a major supporter of the euro and tried to set up a campaign for joining the euro. In spite of these efforts, the vast majority of the population did not want to give up the pound. The Conservative Party, under the leadership of William Hague, used the slogan 'save the pound' in the 2001 legislative elections, but European issues remained secondary to the preoccupations of British citizens. In Denmark, in a referendum on 28 September 2000, 53 per cent of voters rejected joining the euro, although the Danish krone remained pegged to the euro. Currently, the majority of the population wants to join the euro, so that possibly there will be a second referendum to enable Denmark to become a member. Nevertheless, the rejection of the Treaty of Lisbon in the Irish referendum created some hesitation about conducting such a referendum by former prime minister Anders Føgh Rasmussen (*The Economist*, 14 August 2008).

In Sweden, the referendum on the euro on 14 September 2003 was clearer than the Danish vote – 56.2 per cent of voters rejected joining the euro, while just 41.8 per cent were supportive (*The Economist*, 18 September 2003). This means that the Swedish 'no vote' camp was quite strong, making it difficult for the government to organise a second referendum in the short or middle term. This course of events led to the dominance of Southern European countries, the Benelux, Germany and France in this unique project. Finland is the only exception from the Northern countries. After enlargement, a further four countries joined the euro: Malta, Cyprus, Slovenia and Slovakia.

Membership of the Euro group also required a strong observation of the growth and stability pacts attached to the adoption of the new currency. Each member of the Euro group was obliged to draft growth and stability pacts and negotiate them with their social partners. This was essential in order to keep inflation low and strengthen the stability of the eurozone. The overwhelming rationale is laid out in the Broad Economic Policy Guidelines agreed by the members of the Euro group. This economic governance established codes of conduct, benchmarking and best practice in several areas such as budget accounting, in order to harmonise the national practices into a European one. The Economic and Financial Committee and the Economic Policy Committee framed best practices and benchmarking through policy documents (Magone, 2006a: 189). This whole process of structuring macroeconomic policies has so far been undertaken informally and through soft coordination. The growth in complexity may cause problems for coordination, so that probably more formal structures will be necessary in the long run (Collignon, 2004; Puetter, 2004).

The very rigid growth and stability pacts created major problems for some countries. These asymmetrical shocks struck early in Portugal in 2002. The European Commission had to open excessive budgetary deficit procedures against Portugal, forcing the incoming government under Prime Minister José Manuel Durão Barroso (2002–4) to make substantial cuts in the public sector. The consequence was the deterioration of the weak Portuguese economy owing to a severe recession and the decline of tax revenues. In early 2003, the Portuguese economy was contracting (Magone, 2005: 46–8). Soon after Portugal's financial difficulties, Greece (2005) and, later on, France and Germany, also had excessive budgetary deficits and many small countries wanted the European Commission to start an excessive budgetary deficit procedure against the respective countries. However, France and Germany were able to rally a group of countries against the rigid growth and stability pact, which became a burden in a period of low growth. The strong influential position of France and Germany in the Council of Ministers led to the reform of the growth and stability pacts by introducing more flexibility and a long-term sustainable approach (*The Economist*, 29 November 2003; Maher and Hodson, 2004; Heipertz and Verdun, 2004). In March 2005, France and Germany were able to achieve more flexibility in the growth and stability pacts. This is quite ironic, because it was Germany and France that had first asked for strict, rigid criteria to force smaller countries with a problematic fiscal discipline record to be streamlined. Since then, growth and stability pacts are drawn for several years in order to achieve long-term sustainability through Stability and Convergence Programmes (SCP) (McNamara, 2005: 155–7). According to the report of the European Commission on the public finances of the member states in 2008, many member states fall short of reporting on the quality of public finances according to the form and contents required in codes of conduct in this area (European Commission, 2008a: 3).

In 2010, all member states were engaged in Stability and Convergence Programmes, which had already been in place for many years, and, owing to the financial crisis, were supposed to last beyond 2013. In some cases, such as Greece for example, the danger of defaulting on the payment of their public debt was a major problem affecting the Euro area. Although every country has problems with their public finances, some countries are at a greater risk of not achieving the sustainability of their public finances than other countries. Such sustainability is dependent on the efficiency of the agreed stability and convergence programmes. Table 13.1 shows that the European Commission monitors regularly the level of risk in losing the sustainability of public finances owing to commitments such as pensions and the lack of reform of a particular sector.

Table 13.1 The sustainability of public finances, 2007

	Problems	Countries
High-risk countries	• Age-related expenditure over long run • High level of public debt (Greece) • Medium-term objectives not achieved (Hungary, Czech Republic, Greece)	• Czech Republic • Cyprus (euro) • Greece (euro) • Hungary • Slovenia (euro)
Medium-risk countries	• Age-related expenditure (Netherlands) • Deterioration of structural balance (Spain, Ireland)	• Belgium (euro) • Germany (euro) • Ireland (euro) • Spain (euro) • France (euro) • Italy (euro) • Luxembourg (euro) • Malta (euro) • Netherlands (euro) • Portugal (euro) • Slovakia (euro) • United Kingdom
Low-risk countries	• Running large surpluses • Reducing debt • Accumulating assets • Comprehensive cost-saving pension reforms	• Denmark • Estonia • Latvia • Lithuania • Austria (euro) • Poland • Finland (euro) • Sweden

Source: European Commission, 2008a: 66–7

Although the single currency was only introduced six years ago, it has so far been a great success. Internationally, it is gaining new markets and adoption of the currency by more countries owing to the weakness of the US dollar and the American economy. Moreover, the recent global financial crisis related to the subprime mortgages scandal that originated in the United States and affected the whole world, led also to the decline of the British economy and the pound, which was a model for the European continent. Slowly, the euro gained a considerable reputation owing to the policies of the European Central Bank (ECB). Indeed, the ECB worked closely with the national central banks to preserve high levels of short-term liquidity through the granting of loans, which the respective enterprises had to pay back within a week, or in some cases after some months, with low interest. Collaterals are used to minimise the risk. Indeed, president Jean Claude Trichet was able to announce that the ECB was quite busy in the second half of 2008 negotiating and organising such loans. It was able to make windfalls on this borrowing, thus strengthening even more the reputation of the ECB in crisis management (*Börsenzeitung*, 30 December 2008). However, the eurozone is still characterised by low levels of growth. Further reforms will be needed to further integrate national economies into the single European market and increase the competitiveness of the region.

Although the cooperation and coordination mechanisms between the member states are still in the making, the global financial crisis has confirmed the importance of creating supranational supportive institutions based on 'post-national' or 'shared' sovereignty. Such economic and monetary regimes have contributed to stability in the eurozone, while countries outside it have had more difficulties, such as the United Kingdom and Iceland. Iceland submitted a membership application in June 2009, which was favourably supported by the EU institutions. Negotiations will start soon, although the whole process will be fairly smooth, owing to the fact that Iceland is already a member of the European Economic Area (EEA), and has therefore implemented most of the directives in parallel with the EU member states.

Kenneth Dyson characterises the EMU within the EU as part of the emerging 'stabilisation state', particularly in economic policies (Dyson, 2000: 657). He asserts as follows:

> What emerges is a picture of an EMU policy community bound together by a sound money paradigm and of the privileged role of EU central bankers within that community as the bearers and beneficiaries of that paradigm. Just as the construction of the single European market centralised the regulatory function at the EU level, so EMU has centralised the economic stabilisation function at the EU level. Seen in technocratic terms, the EU is no longer just a regulatory state. It is an emergent stabilisation state, dedicated to improving the economic efficiency of Europe by establishing and safeguarding economic stability. This small, exclusive EMU policy community continues to define the meaning and boundaries of the EU as a stabilisation state.
>
> (Dyson, 2000: 657)

In this sense, EMU has strengthened stability across the European Union and showed some resilience and resistance against the dangers of the recent financial crisis.

The regular Eurobarometer survey confirms that the vast majority of the population in the euro countries supports the single currency. Each country dealt with the single European currency in a different way. In most West European countries, the single European currency is well supported and the economy has adjusted to the new conditions. This contrasts heavily with Portugal, Spain, Greece and Italy where the euro has a lower level of support (see Figure 13.2). The main reason for this is the economic situation in these countries, particularly Portugal and Greece, which have had to deal with excessive budgetary deficits and cut public spending substantially. This has had a considerable impact on the economic prospects of these countries.

In sum, although there is plenty of scope for improvement, the EMU has to be considered as a great success and will contribute to the long-term dynamics towards the Single European Market.

Environmental policy: a crucial piece of the European model of capitalism

Although incidental environmental policy-making existed before the adoption of the SEA in 1987, of which the car emissions directive of the early 1980s was regarded as a milestone, only since then has environmental policy been an integrated part of all other policies. The recognition that the environment was seriously deteriorating and that this was to a large extent man-made led to an upgrading of environmental policy. The SEA allowed for qualified majority voting for relevant environmental policy areas. Such centrality of environmental policy became even more prominent in the Treaty of the European Union (1993) and the Treaty of Amsterdam (1999). This means that in the past three decades the European Union has become an active actor in global and European environmental policy. An environmentally friendly economy has become part of the Lisbon Strategy. This should be coordinated with the social dimension of the SEM and the objectives towards the most advanced knowledge-based economy. Since the 1970s, the EC/EU has been pushing for more awareness of the environment through Environmental Action Programmes (EAP), of which there are six. The fifth EAP focused on environmental education and the sixth on four main areas of policy-making: Climate Change, Nature and Bio-Diversity, Environment and Health, and Resources and Waste. The latter focus on a few policy areas in order to avoid dispersal and apply a more strategic approach towards environmental policy-making.

The number of directives, decisions and regulations on the environment have increased considerably over the past three decades. While in the 1960s and 1970s there were mainly one or two pieces of EC/EU legislation per year on the environment, this increased to over twenty in the 1980s, over forty in the 1990s and over eighty between 2000 and 2004. Afterwards, this declined to below forty (Lenschow, 2005: 308). Although directives have been the most numerous pieces of legislation adopted up to now, the role of decisions and regulations has increased over time. Much of this regulatory legislation had to be adopted by the new member states. According to Liliana Andonova, Central and Eastern European countries had to adopt 250 directives, decisions and regulations that were the costliest part

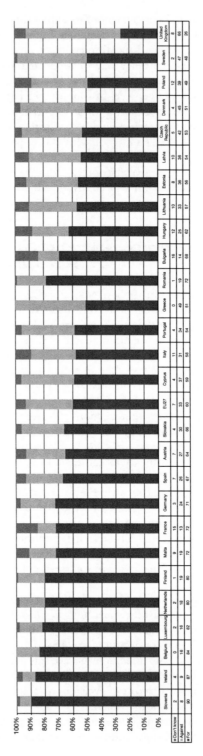

Figure 13.2 Support for the Single European Currency, March–May 2008

Source: Eurobarometer, 69, conducted March–May 2008, published November 2008, first results

of the *acquis communautaire*. They had to start from scratch owing to the neglect of environmental concerns by the former communist leaderships (Andonova, 2005: 135).

Since 1985, there has been a general policy-making thrust across Europe to integrate environmental policy in all other policies, so that more sustainability can be achieved. Between 1983 and 1987, the former Norwegian prime minister Grø Brundtlandt chaired a World Commission on Environment and Development of the United Nations on the relationship between further economic development and the environment. The report 'Our Common Future' introduced the concept of sustainable development, meaning that economic development must take into account the protection of the environment. Economic development must also be sustainable, which means that natural resources should be used with a view to renewing them. The concept of 'sustainable development' was contrasted against the concept of 'exponential growth' that dominated industrial countries until the 1970s (United Nations, 2010).

In 1992, the United Nations organised a conference on the environment and development in Rio de Janeiro that led to major discussions and first agreements on various environmental issues, including biodiversity and global climate change. This confirmed the urgency of environmental issues across the world. Global Climate Change became one of the most important single issues. The Intergovernmental Panel on Climate Change (IPCC), founded by the World Meteorological Organisation (WMO) and the United Nations, monitored and developed scenarios on the causes and consequences of global climate change. In 2008, the IPCC celebrated its twentieth anniversary. In this context, the EU and its member states have become leaders in developing policies to control carbon emissions and move towards sustainable development policies. Central to this global network on environmental policies is the protocol attached to the United Nations Convention on Climate Change (UNCC), known as the Kyoto protocol.

The European Union was required to reduce carbon emissions by 8 per cent between 2008 and 2012, and was referred to as the only regional integration organisation alongside 183 countries that ratified the Treaty. The United States remains the only country that signed the Treaty, but did not ratify it. Nevertheless, the change of administration from George W. Bush to Barack Obama may now lead to ratification, depending how much support there is from both Houses. The member states of the EU are legally bound by a burden-sharing agreement that sets individual emissions targets for each country. The new member states that joined the EU after 2004 have individual targets from 6 to 8 per cent. Considerable cuts were undertaken by Germany that reduced levels by 18.3 per cent (as a result of the major restructuring of East Germany after unification), by the United Kingdom (12 per cent through moving from coal to gas), and by Luxembourg (44.2 per cent as a result of restructuring of the steel industry). However, many early gains between 1990 and 2000 were lost in the first years of the millennium and ten countries have difficulties in meeting the set targets.

The Kyoto agreement uses three market-based flexible mechanisms to implement carbon emission reductions. The most well known is the Emissions Trading Scheme, which the EU created for the Single European Market. This allows firms to trade emission allowances among themselves in order to offset any burden to the overall targets. This is complemented by two more mechanisms, the joint implementation mechanism and the clean development mechanism. The former allows firms to count carbon emissions curbing projects that are undertaken in countries that have targets, the latter in countries that have no targets, towards the overall emissions target. The EU has been keen to combine all these mechanisms into a single system of carbon emissions reduction. However, the first years of ETS were not very efficient because the prices for emission allowances were too low, resulting in speculation that destroyed the rationale of these mechanisms. Therefore, until 2020, a change in the system is being implemented that includes the adoption of a single EU cap on emissions instead of the current twenty-seven caps. Moreover, the free allocation of emissions allowances will be partially auctioned in 2012 and fully auctioned by 2020. At least one-fifth of the revenue from this new system will be used by member states to reinvest in technologies to deal with climate change (European Commission 2008b; Albrecht and Arts, 2005).

Environmental policy includes requirements to increase energy from renewable sources such as wind and water. All the EU-27 have a target of 21 per cent by 2010; however, in 2005, such energy sources stood still at 14 per cent. The highest increases from renewable energy sources can be found in the new member states, particularly Romania. Parallel to this, energy intensity per unit of gross domestic product has decreased considerably since 1990. The EU-27 performs better than the USA, but is still behind Japan. Particularly, the fisheries sector is under considerable pressure owing to the strict quotas imposed by the common fisheries policy. Sustainable organic farming has become an important policy in order to change the way food is produced; however, there are still major variations in such production among the member states (European Commission, 2008c).

Although the European Union is a global leader in environmental policy initiatives, there are still major differences between the regions and countries of this regional supranational organisation. Tanja Börzel developed the labels of 'leaders' and 'laggards' to characterise the quality of the implementation of environmental directives. The conventional wisdom is to regard the Southern European and Central and Eastern European countries as laggards, and the West and Northern Europeans as leaders. However, according to Tanja Börzel, the picture is more mixed, particularly when the Northern and Southern European countries are compared. In some policy areas, the Southern European countries may be leaders and others laggards; the same applies to Northern countries. Börzel compared Germany and Spain in particular, and showed that there are not only differences between the two countries, but across policy areas. Germany, like Spain, had major difficulties implementing the Environmental Impact Assessment (EIA) that must be undertaken for all major projects, and includes consultation of the population (Börzel, 2000: 155–8; Börzel, 2002).

One particular aspect of environmental policy-making is the administrative capacity of not only legal, but also real implementation of European environmental policy. In this respect, in spite of improvements, the Southern European countries remain laggards in relation to the Nordic and other West European countries (Weale et al., 1996; Pridham and Magone, 2006). Italy has had the most difficulties in keeping pace with the dynamics of European environmental politics. However, this is a pattern that can be found with most other EU policies. The administrative problems are still difficult to solve – the record has improved, but not enough to catch up with the leaders or even middle-ranking countries

(Giuliani, 2001: 62). Figure 13.3 shows that Italy infringes European policy more than any other country. It is followed by Spain, in second place. Greece and Portugal are also among the worst offenders, but are now closer to the middle-ranking countries. France, the United Kingdom and Ireland are also high-ranking offenders, while the Nordic countries – Denmark, Sweden and Finland – infringe regulations the least.

As already mentioned, the Central and Eastern European countries were thoroughly screened before becoming members of the European Union. Most of the required legislation was implemented with the support of the European Union and other international organisations. Compliance with environmental policy was central to their prospects for joining the EU. The main reason was that the planned economies neglected environmental issues, so that the environmental dimension became part of the restructuring process. This meant that policy-making in these Central and Eastern European countries was framed and constrained by the benchmarks and standards set up by the international community. However, it is still too early to make an assessment of how environmental policy will remain central to these economies (Andonova, 2005: 141–55). For the moment, the level of infringements remains low, but only time will tell whether this will remain the case.

Less encouraging are the prevalent attitude patterns in Central and Eastern Europe. According to Ronald Inglehart and Christian Welzel, a silent cultural revolution has existed from the 'survival values' of industrial societies to the 'self-expressive values' of post-industrial ones across the world. The former are called materialists, because their lifestyle is dominated by consumerism, and the latter are called post-materialists, because they tend to emphasise the protection of the environment and the development of a more sustainable, moderate lifestyle (Inglehart and Welzel, 2005).

According to Eurobarometer data conducted between March and May 2008, only Sweden and the Netherlands have more pure post-materialists than materialists. All the other EU countries have stronger materialist subcultures than post-materialist ones. The largest group comprises those with both materialist and post-materialist values. However, based on the size of the post-materialist group in each country, we can organise the countries into three main groups – the predominantly materialist group, the predominantly mixed group, and those with a strong tendency towards post-materialism (based on data from Figure 13.4 and Table 13.2).

The predominantly materialist group comprises a few countries that still have a very small group of post-materialists (below 5 per cent) and a large materialist group. This includes Romania, Bulgaria, Portugal, Latvia and Lithuania. The predominantly mixed group – the largest group – includes countries with between 5 and 10 per cent post-materialists. The third group, representing between 10 and 23 per cent of the population, holds those countries inclined towards post-materialism. The Nordic countries, the Netherlands, Germany, the UK, the Czech Republic and Luxembourg are the representatives of this group.

This shows that environmental issues are becoming more important in European societies and therefore support for environmental policies that are linked to transnational and international efforts are supported by the respective national populations. This naturally strengthens the position of the EU at international level.

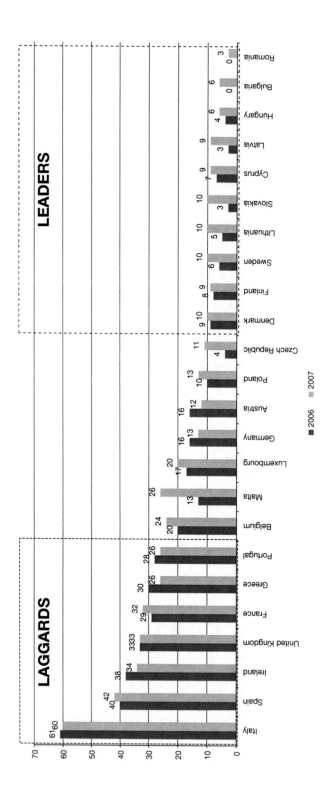

Figure 13.3 Environment infringements, 2006 and 2007

Note: Cases of infringements under article 226 of the EC Treaty referred by the European Commission to the European Court of Justice (ECJ) and judged by the ECJ as such, it envisages financial penalties.

Source: European Commission, DG Environment, available online at: http://ec.europa.eu/environment/legal/law/statistics.htm (accessed 3 January 2009)

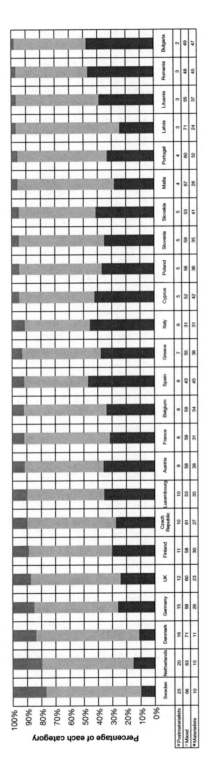

Figure 13.4 Materialists and post-materialists in the EU member states, 2008

Source: Eurobarometer, 69, November 2008 first results, field research conducted March–May 2008: 1. Values of Europeans: 69

	Sweden	Netherlands	Denmark	Germany	UK	Finland	Czech Republic	Luxembourg	Austria	France	Belgium	Spain	Greece	Italy	Cyprus	Poland	Slovenia	Slovakia	Malta	Portugal	Latvia	Lithuania	Romania	Bulgaria
Postmaterialists	23	20	16	15	12	11	10	10	9	8	8	8	7	6	5	5	5	5	4	4	3	3	3	2
Mixed	66	63	71	59	60	58	61	53	58	59	58	43	55	31	52	56	59	53	67	60	71	55	48	49
Materialists	10	15	11	26	23	30	27	35	38	31	34	45	38	31	42	38	35	41	28	32	24	37	45	47

Table 13.2 The categorisation of cultural patterns in EU member states, according to Inglehart's materialist–post-materialism continuum

Predominantly materialist	Predominantly mixed	Strong tendency towards post-materialism
• Portugal	• Austria	• Sweden
• Latvia	• France	• Netherlands
• Lithuania	• Belgium	• Denmark
• Romania	• Spain	• Germany
• Bulgaria	• Greece	• UK
	• Italy	• Finland
	• Cyprus	• Czech Republic
	• Poland	• Luxembourg
	• Slovenia	
	• Slovakia	

Source: Author's own categorisation based on Figure 13.4 data

However, one has to take into account the asymmetrical development of post-materialism across Europe. Some countries, such as Portugal, Romania, Bulgaria, Latvia and Lithuania, have large segments of the population that are still struggling to make ends meet, so that 'survival values' are still more important than 'self-expressive values' (see Chapter 3). There has also been a decline in post-materialist subcultures in each country since 2005. One of the main reasons seems to be the worsening economic situation. In spite of this, there is ground for optimism that post-materialism will gain more importance in the future.

European regional policy: the impact of structural funds

One of the most important EU policies became known as the European regional policy, which today comprises more than 45 per cent of the annual budget, if taken together with other smaller policies, all of which are designed to improve the competitiveness and socioeconomic cohesion of the European economy. The structural funds were introduced in order to help the poorer and less-developed countries of the EC/EU to prepare themselves by means of accelerated investment in infrastructures and human resources for the forthcoming Single European Market, which was scheduled to start on 1 January 1993. The structural funds became an important innovative policy area that contributed to a change in the dynamics of European integration. Before 1985, European regional policy was incidental and controlled by national governments. The new approach was dominated by the SEM rationale in which both competitiveness and socioeconomic cohesion were to be important aspects. In this sense, the structural policies of the Delors European Commission fitted into the European model of capitalism that regarded competitiveness and socioeconomic cohesion as complementary. A dispute between competing forms of neo-liberal and regulated capitalism was resolved by bringing the two together. According to a seminal study by Liesbet Hooghe, one of the main reasons is that, in terms of governance image, most European Commission top officials were inclined towards a social and regulated market economy, and only a minority was for a neo-liberal model (Hooghe and Keating, 1994; Hooghe, 1998; 2001).

The structural policies were negotiated between the national government and the European Commission, and a common support framework was agreed between the specific national governments.

The doubling of the budget achieved by the Delors Commission in 1988 and 1992 allowed for an extensive Europe-wide programme of European regional policy. Multi-annual programming allowed for the development of larger projects, particularly major infrastructures in the less-developed regions. The Southern European countries – particularly Portugal, Spain, Greece and the southern part of Italy – were the big winners of those new structural policies. Ireland also became part of what became known as the 'cohesion countries'. In 1992, an additional fund for larger national projects, the Cohesion Fund, further reinforced this financial transfer to the cohesion countries and other less-developed regions.

Between 1988 and 2013, there have so far been four multi-annual programmes for regional cohesion funded by structural funds. After a doubling of funding for regional cohesion in the first two packages up to 1999, funding remained at the same level, in spite of the fact that the EU has enlarged since 1988 from twelve to twenty-seven countries. The Central and Eastern European countries that joined the EU after 2004 received much less in terms of gross domestic product per capita than the cohesion countries.

Moreover, the European Commission learned fast from mistakes committed during the implementation of a multi-annual programme and reinforced its accountability and control mechanisms. Last but not least, the five–six objectives that existed until 1999 were reduced to three in the agenda 2000 prepared by the European Commission in order to adjust the EU to the enlargement. The main reason was that too many objectives were leading to a dispersal of funding. After 2000, there were only three objectives – for less-developed regions, for regions affected by industrial decline, and for rural development. In 2005–6, the three objectives were changed again to convergence (81.7 per cent including the Cohesion Fund), regional competitiveness and employment objectives (21.3 per cent) and territorial cooperation (2.4 per cent). This meant that the structural funds became increasingly integrated with the objectives of the Lisbon Strategy (Magone, 2006b: 208–14; Bourne, 2007: 298–9) (see Figure 13.5).

It is estimated that for the period 2004–6, Poland received €67 per person, Hungary €49 and the Czech Republic €29; in contrast, in 2000, Greece received €437 per person and Portugal €211 (Rupnik, 2004: 38). For the period 2007–13, 20 per cent of the total funds was allocated to Poland, but this is a slightly lower share per multi-annual programme than the 22.5 per cent that Spain, which has almost the same size population, received between 1988 and 2006 (see Table 13.3).

One particular important aspect of the allocation of funding was the partnership between supranational, national and subnational authorities. Partnership allowed for the European regions to become more involved in the policy-making process and sometimes to bypass the national government as main gatekeeper. Moreover, the allocation of funding not only comprised a European contribution that was substantial for these cohesion countries, but also a national

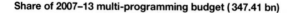

Share of 2007–13 multi-programming budget (347.41 bn)

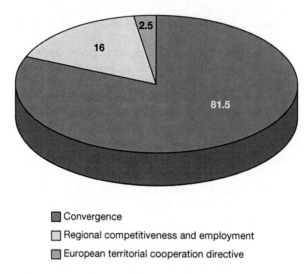

■ Convergence
□ Regional competitiveness and employment
■ European territorial cooperation directive

Figure 13.5 Indicative allocation of the structural funds, according to objectives for the the period 2007–13

Source: European Commission, Building a Union of Modern Attractive and Dynamic Regions, available online at: www.europa.eu (accessed 4 January 2009)

contribution that would match most of the rest of the funding and one from the private sector. The latter was a major problem for the new democracies of Southern Europe, Portugal, Spain and Greece, which had weak market economies and respective weak business enterprises, and had to subsidise domestic firms to take part in projects. However, most firms lacked the expertise to develop projects for submission. This meant that many projects in the industrial sector were put forward by larger transnational corporations. Such a problem may also be experienced in Central and Eastern Europe, in which domestic business enterprises are still quite weak, in order to invest in new projects.

Most of the funding was invested in new infrastructures such as roads and railways, but also bridges and other transport projects. Spain soon became the main recipient of the structural funds. The emerging regionalisation of the country throughout the 1980s and 1990s allowed for a stronger input of the autonomous communities. Although central government was and remains the main gatekeeper, regional governments were well integrated in the whole decision-making process. This contrasted heavily with Portugal and Greece, which remained centralised and without a proper upgrading of the role of regional actors. Civil society in all three countries remained weak and contributed only sporadically to the whole process of the implementation of the structural funds. Portugal and Greece used a top-down approach in relation to the implementation of the regional cohesion funds, which was highly centralised and defined in the respective national capitals without a genuine consultation of regional civil society actors. Although the Spanish political system is one of the most decentralised of the European Union and their regional governments have been better integrated, the national government has

Table 13.3 An indicative allocation of structural funds by member states for the period 2007–13 (million euro)

Country	Allocation (million euro)	Percentage of total sum
Belgium	2,258	0.6
Bulgaria	6,853	1.2
Czech Republic	26,692	7.7
Denmark	613	0.2
Germany	26,340	7.6
Estonia	3,456	1
Ireland	901	0.3
Greece	20,420	5.9
Spain	35,217	10.1
France	14,319	4.1
Italy	28,812	8.3
Cyprus	640	0.2
Latvia	4,620	1.3
Lithuania	6,885	2
Luxembourg	65	0.02
Hungary	25,307	7.3
Malta	855	0.3
Netherlands	1,907	0.6
Austria	1,461	0.4
Poland	67,284	19.4
Portugal	21,511	6.2
Romania	19,668	5.7
Slovenia	4,205	12.1
Slovakia	11,588	3.3
Finland	1,716	0.49
Sweden	1,891	0.5
United Kingdom	10,613	3.1
Inter-regional/Network cooperation	445	0.1
Technical assistance	868	0.3
Total	347,410	100

Source: European Commission, leaflet 'Building a union of modern attractive and dynamic regions' website www.europa.eu (accessed 4 January 2009)

remained the main gatekeeper and civil society continues to be weak (Magone, 2003a: 250–8).

In comparison to Southern Europe, Ireland emerged at the end of the 1990s as a positive model of structural funds. Ireland invested less in infrastructures, but more in human resources and research and development. The booming Irish economy was able to attract foreign direct investment from the United States, particularly in the research and development sector, which was combined with further programmes of the structural funds. Such economic growth strategy was possible because of the language of the country, the better-trained people, the low-taxation regime for business enterprises, and the culture of networking in this small country, all of which made possible the identification of the main problems of particular communities (Barry *et al.*, 2001; Mullally, 2004).

One negative aspect of the structural funds is that in spite of generous investment in the less-developed regions, there has been no convergence between the rich and poor regions within a specific country. On the contrary, in some countries, for example Spain, the gap between rich and poor regions has widened, with the result that the structural centre-periphery gap of development has remained, despite considerable investment. This is reinforced by weak social capital capabilities in the poorer regions. According to David Bailey and Lisa de Propris, one of the main reasons may have been the lack of preparedness and administrative resources for these less developed regions to take advantage of the structural funds. It takes some time for regional and national actors to adjust to the EU multilevel governance system that includes the principle of partnership, subsidiarity and solidarity. Sometimes all cultures of policy-making have to change accordingly in order to achieve maximum effect (Bailey and Propris, 2002: 419–23).

In spite of this lack of progress, there was some convergence between member states. Spain is expected to be a net payer by the end of the 2007–13 period, because it will have an average EU GDP per capital of over 100 per cent (Magone, 2009a: 339).

Ireland became one of the richest economies of the European Union at the beginning of the new millennium. In this sense, regional internal divergence has been offset by national convergence within the European territory. Moreover, more generally, there is the issue of policy-learning as well overcoming the earlier cycles of policy-making and implementation. The best example is Italy. According to Martin Bull and Joerg Baudner, the structural funds contributed to a change of rationale in the southern regions of Italy. A new virtuous policy cycle replaced a negative vicious one, in which Europeanised elites wanted to make the best out of the structural funds. However, the authors clearly show that at least a decade was needed to inculcate a new modus operandi (Bull and Baudner, 2004: 1064–73). Such policy learning effects over time could also be observed in Portugal and Greece (Magone, 2004: 215–39; Paraskevopoulos, 2005).

It is expected that in the 2007–13 period the structural funds will amount to 5–6 per cent of the gross domestic product of Central and Eastern European countries, 2 per cent of Greece and Portugal, 1 per cent of East Germany and 0.7 per cent of Spain. All this has cumulative effects on the performance of the European economy as a whole (Bradley, 2006: 193–7). Although the structural funds are a small amount divided among so many countries, it clearly has an important strategic effect owing to its multi-annual programming and integration in overall EU economic strategies such as the Lisbon Strategy (Figure 13.6).

From welfare to workfare states: the growing importance of flexicurity

One of the reasons why the SEM became so important for the prospects of the European economy was the fact that during the 1980s, all European countries in Western Europe had to deal with the rise of unemployment. After the decades of

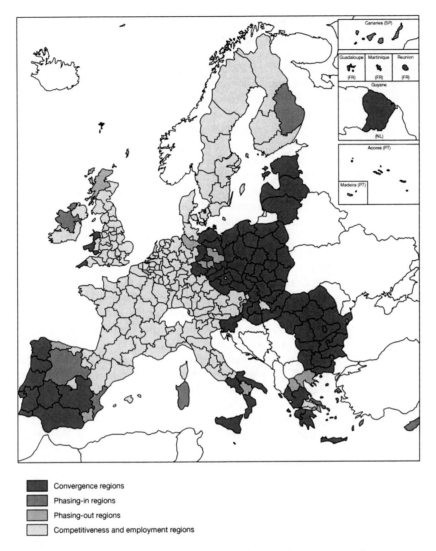

Convergence regions

Phasing-in regions

Phasing-out regions

Competitiveness and employment regions

Figure 13.6 Structural funds, 2007–13, according to objectives 1 and 2
Source: European Commission, available online at: www.europa.eu (accessed 29 January 2009)

full employment (less than 3 per cent unemployment) – the 1960s and 1970s – the 1980s became years of economic recession. The European Commission commissioned the Cecchini report on the potentials of the SEM. The report forecast the long-term creation of a substantial number of jobs through economies of scale and higher labour, capital, goods and services mobility, which clearly showed considerable gains for all member states if the internal market was fully implemented (Cecchini *et al.*, 1988) This rationale legitimised the stronger role of the European Commission under Jacques Delors to push forward most of the new policies that were designed to implement and frame the SEM.

Until the late 1970s, welfare states were designed to redistribute the accumulated wealth of the country, so that low-income social groups were able to improve their quality of life and also their life chances, particularly for the subsequent generation. Generous benefits for family, housing, education and social policy contributed to a more egalitarian society. Such redistributive policies were reasonably generous in the Nordic countries, continental Europe and the UK, but less so in Southern Europe.

During the 1980s, the European Commission pushed forward the concept of 'employability', meaning that, today, more important than a secure job is the ability to change jobs and careers when necessary, particularly through upgrading qualifications and continuous lifelong learning. Such a dynamic and flexible approach to employment has been labelled by the European Commission 'flexicurity' (influenced by the successful Danish model). This means that European labour markets should become more flexible, particularly by reducing the dismissal costs and other costly rigid regulations, and create instead strong welfare states that would support people when they become unemployed and need retraining in order to be competitive in the labour market. Denmark leads the world in terms of the best conditions for doing business, along with Singapore, Finland, Canada and Switzerland. However, flexicurity can only be partly exported to other countries, because it evolves over time and is concerned with specific Danish long-term choices. Mentalities have to change before flexicurity can work well in other countries (*The Economist*, 7 September 2006; 10 July 2008).

According to Gösta Esping Andersen, three worlds of welfare capitalism existed at the end of the 1970s. The Nordic/social democratic, the continental/conservative and the Anglo-Saxon welfare states (Esping-Andersen, 1990).

The Nordic/social democratic welfare state was the most generous and funded through the general taxation system. It envisaged flexible labour markets, supported by strong redistributive welfare states. In spite of changes in the 1990s, all these welfare states kept the same characteristics. Such welfare states can be found in Sweden, Denmark, Finland, Norway and Iceland. They all resemble the Danish/Swedish model of a generous welfare state, but with flexible labour markets.

The continental/conservative welfare state dates back to the nineteenth century. First beginnings can be located in Germany during the second empire under the chancellorship of Otto von Bismarck. The first social legislation was established during the 1870s and 1880s. It was financed through the voluntary contributions of employers and employees. The rationale for the expansion of social legislation, which Bismarck had established with the support of the Catholic Centre party, was to block the rise of the Social Democratic Party. Since then, the continental/conservative model has expanded considerably. During the 1960s, the West German model became the most generous welfare state in Western Europe. This was achieved because the economy was booming and full employment contributed to the funding of the welfare system. However, in the 1970s and 1980s the expanding welfare state began to create major problems for the German economy, which was facing major competition from abroad and was characterised by stagflation (economic stagnation and increased inflation.) Costs spiralled, not least because of the number of people dependent on benefits (Czada, 2005: 167–72). Shortly before unification, and even more so after unification, two-thirds of the population were living well and one-third were struggling or living in poverty, leading to tensions within society (Mangen, 1992: 225). The major reforms undertaken by Helmut Kohl in the 1980s and 1990s tended to treat the symptoms and not the problem as such. A major reform of the labour market and pensions system only took place in the new millennium under Chancellor Gerhard Schröder. The Agenda 2010 was linked to the Lisbon Strategy. Welfare policies became linked to employment. If a benefit receiver refused to take a job offered by the new federal agency of employment, they would suffer considerable cuts in their benefits. All this represented a very quick shift from redistributive welfare policies towards competitive workfare ones (Czada, 2005: 175–89; Kemmerling and Bruttel, 2006).

The pure Anglo-Saxon welfare state was to be found in the United States, which was characterised by the workfare policies that are now being implemented throughout Europe, but without the higher level of security given by a true welfare state. In Europe, only Ireland and the United Kingdom would qualify as welfare states, but until the 1970s both countries were following the European model of the welfare state. However, in the UK, after 1979, Prime Minister Margaret Thatcher changed the British welfare state, moving it towards the Anglo-Saxon model. In the United Kingdom, throughout the 1980s and 1990s, policies were designed to reform and reduce the welfare state. However, a radical change was too risky, so that most of the changes that have taken place since 1979 have been piecemeal, although always involving a reduction of state involvement. Prime Ministers Tony Blair and Gordon Brown continued on this path of 'flexicurity', but without matching the generous level of support known in the Scandinavian countries (Parry, 1987: 203–9; Moran, 2007).

Although Esping-Andersen has been criticised for his rigid typology, particularly owing to the evolution of the UK from the social democratic to Anglo-Saxon type, it remains an important contribution to the study of welfare states. Maurizio Ferrera, Anton Hemerijk and Martin Rhodes added a fourth and fifth welfare state type in Southern, Central and Eastern Europe respectively. These are latecomers to the European families of welfare states and in comparison to the previous three models even weaker in terms of social benefits. They are hybrid types with some elements of the Bismarckian social insurance model, and some elements of the British Beveridgean and social democratic model (particularly in the health sector). However, social benefits are extremely low in comparison to the those paid in other welfare systems (Ferrera et al., 2000; Ferrera, 2005; 2008).

Figure 13.7 illustrates the level of social expenditure in each country and region. This clearly shows a cleavage of countries with generous welfare states in Western and Northern Europe, the Nordic and continental/conservative welfare systems, and Southern, Central and Eastern Europe with extremely weak welfare systems. In between are the Anglo-Saxon countries. This, of course, remains a major problem for the flexicurity model. It may work in the Nordic countries, and perhaps in the continental/conservative welfare systems, but it will be difficult to implement it in the European periphery of Southern, Central and Eastern Europe. Many social budgets are constrained by a lack of reform in the pensions' sector. As a result of the declining birth rates across Europe and the increasing elderly population (an important electoral constituency in all EU countries), most European economies will have major difficulties in coping with the rising costs of a welfare system. Apart from the fact that in many European countries people will have to work

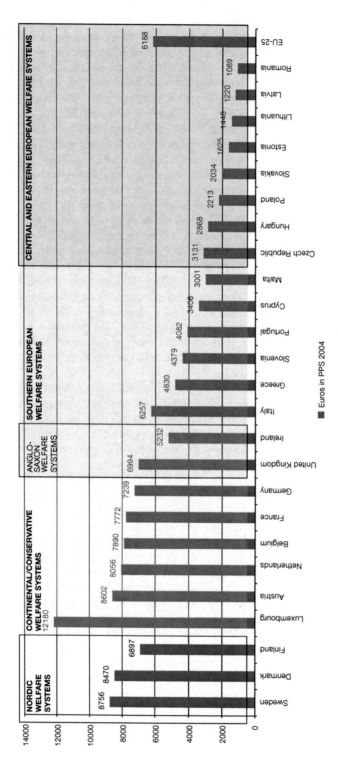

Figure 13.7 Social expenditure in the member states of the European Union, according to regions (in euros, in power purchasing standard (PPS))

Source: Author's own categorisation, based on data from European Commission, 2008d: 138

longer before they are entitled to a pension, there is also the urgent need to think more positively about immigration and respective integration policies. This challenge is already there, but will continue to increase over the next few decades. Already, the burden of paying an old age pension is the single largest item in the EU-25 average social expenditure (see Figure 13.8).

All EU member states are now part of the European Lisbon Strategy that links employment policies to other policy areas. This integrated approach aimed at implementing the Lisbon Strategy, namely to create the most competitive knowledge-based economy in the world. In terms of employment, the Lisbon Strategy wanted to achieve:

- overall employment rate of 70 per cent in 2010 (67 per cent in 2005);
- a female employment rate of 60 per cent in 2010 (57 per cent in 2005);
- an employment rate for older workers (aged 55–64) in 2010 of 50 per cent.

While the Nordic countries and the United Kingdom were able to meet the targets with no major difficulty owing to their flexible labour markets, other countries, in particular Germany, Italy, France and Spain, had to make major reforms in

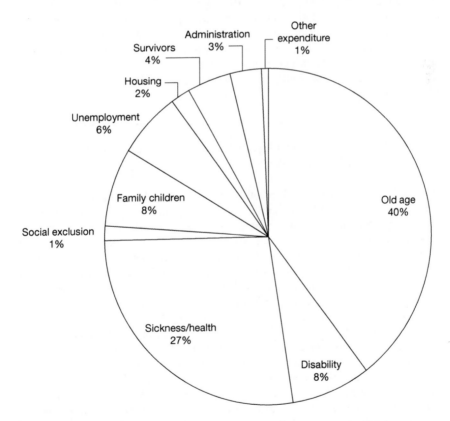

Figure 13.8 The structure of social protection expenditure in EU-25, 2004
Source: European Commission, 2008d: 142

order to open up the economy and allow increased flexibility. The global financial crisis of 2008 has led to major revisions of these targets, as a result of the difficulties being faced by some countries' economies (in particular those of Hungary, Portugal, Greece and Italy). At the beginning of 2009, unemployment was rising fast in all European countries, particularly in the United Kingdom and Spain (see Boxes 13.2 and 13.3).

In Germany, the Hartz reform of 2002 has improved the employment situation there. The tougher unemployment benefit regime and the restructuring of employment agencies has contributed to a flexibilisation of the system. However, some aspects of the Hartz reform have contributed to more poverty and to the rise of a large low-paid economy that reached over 22 per cent in 2007 (Kummerling and Bruttel, 2006; Dietz and Walwei, 2007). Similar tendencies were registered even earlier in the United Kingdom. Reform of the labour markets has proved to be difficult in France and Italy (Smith, 2004: 183–95; Drüke, 2004: 23). Italy, in particular, still has to deal with the imbalances of unemployment in the north and south of the country. The most successful story, at least before the global financial crisis of 2008, was that of the Spanish economy, which in the 1980s had record unemployment of one-fifth of the population, while at the end of 2007, it had fallen to about 7–8 per cent. Most of this expansion of the labour market was achieved through the flexibilisation of labour laws, particularly by making it easier to dismiss employees and using temporary employment to a greater extent (Magone, 2009a: 309). However, the structurally weak economy led to a return to the high figures of unemployment, which reached 3 million people (14 per cent) in mid 2009, resulting in the complete loss of those earlier successes (*The Economist*, 1 January 2009).

Box 13.2 The European Employment Strategy (EES) and the Open Method of Coordination (OMC)

One of the most important and innovative instruments of the EES is the open method of coordination (OMC) that is based on reports and monitoring by the member states on progress made on set targets towards 'flexicurity' (*flexible* labour markets and *strong* welfare states with strong employment activation policies to bring people back to work). This process of transnational employment monitoring started in 1998. In spite of major efforts by all countries involved in the original approach based on annual national employment plans that responded to feedback from the Employment Committee, slow progress was registered in reaching the targets in the mid-term review of 2005 (European Commission, 2007a).

The new approach towards flexicurity was based on mid-term three-year national reform plans with annual progress reports. All countries became involved in restructuring and adjusting their welfare systems towards the new paradigm of flexicurity. Among other measures is the decision to expand considerably the number of available nurseries for children under three years old across the European Union, so that more women can go to work (Borrás and Jacobsson, 2004; Rhodes, 2005: 290–300; López-Santana, 2006; Ferrera, 2008).

Box 13.3 The Lisbon Strategy and varieties of 'flexicurity'

In the extraordinary European Council of Lisbon in March 2000, member states agreed to the Lisbon Strategy, which envisages the transformation of the EU into the most competitive knowledge-based economy in the world by 2010. At the centre of this strategy is a considerable increase in research and development (R&D) and the flexibilisation of labour markets in order to increase the activity rates across the EU. The set target was to achieve an average activity rate of 70 per cent among the male population and 60 per cent among the female population. The flexibilisation of labour markets should be accompanied by strong welfare states focusing predominantly on activation policies. The Lisbon Strategy and the employment targets will not be achieved by 2010, but they have at least set the dynamics necessary to achieve it in the next decade. The Lisbon Strategy has become very complex, now covering most areas of policy-making.

The model known as 'flexicurity' was borrowed from the Danish experience. However, it became clear that the Nordic model is expensive and requires considerable investment in people by the state. This predisposition of the state to create support mechanisms for people out of work is less widespread in Southern Europe and Central and Eastern Europe. This means that there are varieties of flexicurity. In the Nordic countries, flexicurity has shown strong results owing to their tradition, while such flexicurity is less successful in the Southern European and Central and Eastern European countries, which have structurally weak economies. Between these extremes are most of the other European countries, including the Benelux, Germany and Austria. The UK labour market is flexible, but activation policies are not as strong as in the Nordic countries (Eurofound, 2007).

Another important feature of the social reality in Europe is that some countries have a simultaneous unequal income distribution and/or low incomes. These differences create different opportunities in the different countries. The convergence of lifestyles will be difficult to achieve, needing to be addressed by long-term policies. People are also at risk of sliding into the poverty trap in the high inequality countries – this is particularly true for Poland, Lithuania, Latvia and Estonia, which are facing major difficulties in this respect. According to European Commission data, 44 per cent of all people living on less than €5 a day live in Poland. Although the situation in Portugal is slightly better, it belongs more to the Central and Eastern European pattern than to Western Europe because of the low wages earned by the vast majority of the population who are mostly unqualified (European Commission, 2008d: 9) (see Table 13.4 and Figure 13.9).

In sum, the SEM is framing workfare policies across the European Union. The social dimension remains important, but is subordinate to employment policies. This means that since the early 1980s a major shift has taken place in Europe from welfare states with redistributive policies to workfare states with social policies to keep and enhance people in the labour market.

Table 13.4 Inequality and income levels in the European Union, 2005

	Low income countries (below EU average of €14,000)	High income countries (above EU average of €14,000)
Low inequality (0–5 times difference of income between lowest and highest earner)	*Below €5,000:* Hungary Slovakia Czech Republic *Above €5,000 and below €10,000:* Malta Slovenia Cyprus	Sweden Finland Denmark Belgium Netherlands France Germany
High inequality (5–10 times difference of income between lowest and highest earner)	*Below €5,000:* Lithuania Latvia Poland Estonia *Above €5,0000 and below €10,000:* Portugal Greece	UK Ireland Italy Spain

Source: European Commission, 2008: 145, median annual equivalised disposable income in euros

Conclusions: the Europeanisation of national public policy

Although there are still major differences between the European countries, the rationale of the SEM is pushing national political systems towards integration into a pan-European system. The process towards transnational European policy-making began during the European Commission under Jacques Delors between 1985 and 1995. His visionary leadership led to the establishment of the SEM and adjacent policies, such as the Economic and Monetary Union, European Regional Policy and employment policies. Since then, member states have integrated their national policies into the rationale of the Lisbon Strategy, formulated in 2000. The main aim of the Lisbon Strategy was to transform the European Union into the most competitive knowledge-based economy in the world by 2010. In 2005, the whole process towards fulfilling the Lisbon Strategy became more integrated through national reform plans. It is possible that some of the targets of the Lisbon Strategy may be met, although others will not. In spite of this, it is already an outstanding achievement to bring all European countries to work together and move in the same direction.

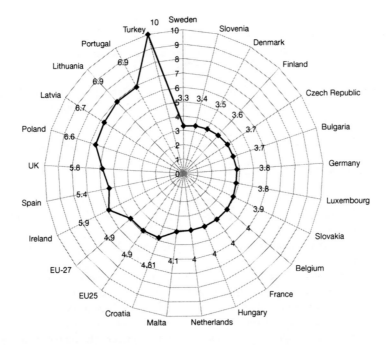

Figure 13.9 Income inequality in Europe, 2004–5
Source: European Commission, 2008d: 145

Suggested reading

Bulmer, Simon and Christian Lequesne (eds) (2005), *The Member-States of the European Union.* Oxford: Oxford University Press.

Schimmelfennig, Frank and Ulrich Sedelmeier (eds) (2005), *Europeanization of Central and Eastern Europe.* Ithaca, NY: Cornell University Press.

Schmidt, Vivien (2005), *Democracy in Europe: The EU and National Institutions.* Oxford: Oxford University Press.

Electronic journals

Journal of Common Market Studies

Journal of European Public Policy

West European Politics

Websites

European Commission (2009): several Directorates-General specialised in different policies at: www.europa.eu (accessed 25 August 2009).

Organization for Economic Cooperation and Development (OECD) (2009): lots of comparative information on policy performance of all members of the organisation at: www.oecd.org

---

QUESTIONS FOR REVISION

- What freedom of manoeuvre do national governments still have within Economic and Monetary Union? Discuss, using examples from at least two countries.
- What major reforms of the welfare system have there been in Germany and the UK?
- Which main factors contributed to the Europeanisation and internationalisation of the environmental policy of European countries?
- Assess the impact of the European Employment Strategy on member states of the European Union. Discuss, using examples from at least two countries.
- Have the European Union structural funds contributed to the convergence of the economies of Southern Europe and Central and Eastern Europe? Discuss, using examples from at least two countries.

Chapter 14

The intertwinedness of national and European foreign policy

- Patterns of national foreign policy
  - The foreign policies of the larger member states: the UK, France, Germany, Italy, Spain and Poland
  - The foreign policies of the small states
  - The foreign policies of the neutral states: Sweden, Austria, Finland, Switzerland and Ireland
- The consolidation of the Common Foreign and Security Policy (CFSP)
  - The objectives of the CFSP/ESDP and the Petersberg tasks
  - The institutions of the CFSP
  - The instruments of European foreign policy: slowly closing the expectations–capabilities gap
- Securing the borders of the European Union: the emergence of the European neighbourhood policy
  - The Euro–Mediterranean partnership: a stagnating project
  - The strategic partnership between the EU and Russia
- The European Union and the wider world
- Conclusions: towards global continental–regional governance

SUMMARY OF CHAPTER 14

Since the early 1970s, there has been a transition from a system of international relations in which states with pure realist aims dominated the global system to a global governance system in which states are working collectively in order to enhance a collective security across the world.

In this chapter, we analyse the priorities of member states' national policies and look at their increasing willingness to pull resources together at the European Union level in order to have greater influence over global issues, such as environmental policy, trade policy and political security issues.

Although national foreign policies are not likely to be replaced by a European foreign and security policy, an intertwined cooperation is a very likely outcome.

The chapter shows that there is a growing shift in resources from the national to the supranational level in order to increase the ability of the EU to respond to crisis situations. A 'militarisation' of the Common Foreign and Security Policy/European Defence and Security Policy (CFSP/ESDP) has taken place over the past decade in order to improve the cooperation of member states in international missions.

One of the major transformations of European politics has been the growing cooperation between the member states in defence and foreign policy. Such close integration of national polities towards common policies would not have been possible before 1945. This process is far from complete, and one may even assert that we are still at the beginning of the potential for a common foreign and security policy. It is useful to distinguish between the cold war period in which Western Europe and Central and Eastern Europe were divided along the Iron Curtain and each part was allied to one of the two superpowers: the United States and Russia. This period lasted until the Fall of the Berlin Wall on 9 November 1989 and was characterised by a dominance of the American and the Soviet hegemony respectively. After 1989, the European Union began to fill the vacuum left by the Soviet Union, but it had to share this with the member states. Germany, in particular, was able to overcome its semi-sovereign nature and slowly develop its own national foreign policy. This chapter will deal more with the period after 1989.

Patterns of national foreign policy

The foreign policies of the larger member states: the UK, France, Germany, Italy, Spain and Poland

One major problem for the continuing integration is that particularly the larger member states do not want to give up on their separate foreign policy capacities. The UK and France are probably the two countries with the most distinctive foreign policies. A large part of the identity of these two large European countries comes from their permanent seats in the United Nations Security Council, along with the United States, China and Russia. Moreover, the UK and France are the only two nuclear powers in Europe. In addition, they can both rely on large English-speaking and French-speaking cultural and, to some degree, political communities, which were created during the colonial period and with whom ties of friendship were established after decolonisation. After the Second World War (1939–45), the colonies of the British Empire became independent. However, the vast majority of the new countries kept close ties with the United Kingdom through the Commonwealth organisation, which was founded in 1960.

The Commonwealth is bound by a common colonial legacy and remains a resource of cultural like-mindedness for the fifty-five independent members, which contributes to the uniqueness, the self-understanding and identity of British foreign policy.

The UK works closely with the United States in order to preserve some international influence in global affairs. This 'special relationship' became particularly important after 1945, when the UK became a smaller country following the decolonisation process.

The culmination of such cooperation was during the 'Thatcher years', 1979–89, largely because of the strong personal relationship with US president Ronald Reagan. Both were extremely anti-communist and had a common purpose in the wish to reduce or constrain the power of the Soviet Union (Young, 1997: 208–12). Prime Minister John Major was not able to replicate this close cooperation with either Presidents George Bush or Bill Clinton. There was major hope that the election of New Labour in 1997 would lead to a change of British foreign policy. Prime Minister Tony Blair had a more positive, less realist 'state interest' view of the world. He had a very good relationship with Bill Clinton, and he shared many of the American goals. The collapse of the Soviet Union in 1991 had enabled the establishment of a new world order based on human rights and global democratic governance. Issues such as illegal or non-transparent arms sales were condemned by Foreign Secretary Robin Cook. However, Cook's 'ethical foreign policy' came to an end during the second Blair government (2001–5) (Jones and Byrd (2007: 714–22). The new foreign minister was Jack Straw who followed Blairite guidelines and was reasonably pragmatic in the execution of his job. The test case was the Iraq War in 2003. Allegedly, much of the information on which the reasons for the invasion of Iraq were based were wrong. This had to do partly with the 'group-think' of intelligence services (whereby no one dares to question the information available), and partly the result of their own decisions made by the American and British leaders. The Iraq War damaged the standing of British foreign policy in the world considerably. The use of false information led to some credibility problems of the British intelligence services and ultimately the Foreign Office (Jones and Byrd, 2007: 729–33).

Gordon Brown's foreign policy was less controversial and more low profile. There is also a growing acknowledgment that Britain has to work with other European players. Cooperation with France increased considerably in 2007 and 2008 as a result of the global financial crisis. It also seems that former Prime Minister Gordon Brown was fairly active in behind-the-scenes diplomacy. Moreover, the financial crisis presented Prime Minister Brown with an opportunity to play a pivotal role as a bridge between Europe and the United States. He worked with other European leaders towards a reform of international financial institutions (*The Economist*, 22 January 2009). In spite of this, the decline of both the British pound and the British economy has undermined, at least partly, the basis for a national foreign policy.

A good example of this is in the armed forces, who have been involved in two wars – Iraq and Afghanistan – leading to a considerable overstretching of resources. Defence spending in terms of GDP declined from 4 per cent in 1990 to 2.6 per cent in 2006. This contrasts heavily with the USA, which spent 4 per cent in 2006. In the past two years, British troops have been withdrawing from Iraq in order to deploy more troops in Afghanistan. However, financial and human resources and shortage of equipment have made any military task more difficult (*The Economist*, 29 January 2009) (see Figure 14.1).

France also has a distinctive foreign policy, which is more distant from that of the United States, although President Nicolas Sarkozy has tried to achieve better relations with the United States since his election in 2007. However, the period before and after the second Iraq War of March 2003 showed that traditionally France takes a more pacifist position in relation to the solution of conflicts than the United States and the United Kingdom. France has also created the Organisation of the Francophony (Organisation de la Francophonie), which was founded in 1970 and consists of fifty-six member states, including European members such as Belgium, Luxembourg, Bulgaria, Romania, Macedonia, Greece, Albania, Switzerland, Monaco and Cyprus. Moreover, further European observers are Poland, the Czech Republic, Slovakia, Hungary, Austria, Slovenia, Croatia, Serbia, Ukraine, Moldavia, Latvia and Lithuania. Although the organisation concentrates on cultural exchanges, it clearly also has a political mission: the promotion of the French language and culture across the world. The expansion of membership to the Central and Eastern European countries clearly shows that the centre of French foreign policy is Europe (Organisation Internationale de la Francophonie, 2009). The European Union originated from a French proposal by Jean Monnet, carried out by French Foreign Minister Robert Schuman. Since then, France has probably been one of the most active members of the EC/EU in order to achieve more European integration. At the centre of this European foreign policy is the Franco–German cooperation, which is extremely well established and has gained recently greater importance as a result of the Lisbon Treaty as well as the global financial crisis of

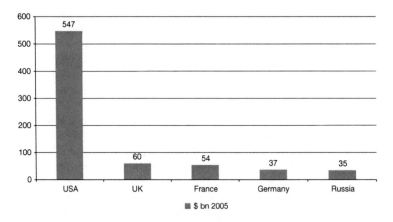

Figure 14.1 Defence spending in selected G8 countries, 2005

Source: Graph based on data from SIPRI, quoted in *The Economist*, 29 January 2009, printed edition

2008–9. The expansion of Francophonie to the Central and Eastern European countries reflects the intention of French foreign policy to have more allies in Europe after expansion.

Another region that remains important for France is Africa and the Middle East. The vast majority of countries of Francophonie are in Africa. This is the reason for the engagement of French troops, normally within United Nations contingents, for peacekeeping purposes. A good example is the successful military engagement in the Democratic Republic of Congo. There are currently 17,000 troops in the Democratic Republic of Congo operating as part of the UN MONUC Mission, most of them coming from India and Pakistan (BBC News, 21 November 2008).

An extremely controversial project was that developed by President Nicolas Sarkozy. During the French presidency of the European Union in the second half of 2008, Sarkozy proposed the establishment of a Mediterranean Union that would comprise the countries of North Africa, the Middle East and the European countries located in the region. This project of a Mediterranean Union was not originally supported by Germany, so Sarkozy had to downgrade the project. One of the main reasons was that it was seen as a project competing with the EU policy of the Euro–Mediterranean partnership, known as the 'Barcelona process', which began in 1995. Sarkozy had to change the proposal from 'Mediterranean Union', which was designed just for the countries of the region, to 'Union for the Mediterranean', which clearly comprised all EU member states and the Mediterranean countries. In total, the Union for the Mediterranean comprises forty-three countries, and Barcelona will be the main seat of the organisation. The original proposal was directed towards Turkey, as an alternative to EU membership, but this was rejected by the Turkish government, so that now it is only a stepping stone towards membership (*International Herald Tribune*, 10 May 2007; BBC News, 13 July 2008; European Commission, 2008).

No other European country has the same standing in world affairs as the UK and France. The permanent seats of both countries in the United Nations Security Council have been most important for their role in world affairs. Germany tried to achieve a permanent seat in the United Nations, but was not supported by the United States. Germany also tried to launch a bid with Brazil, Japan and India in January 2004, known as the 'G4', but the United States was only willing to support Japan. Foreign Minister Joschka Fischer interpreted this as a punishment by the US, because the German government did not support the Iraq War (*Deutsche Welle*, 8 January 2004; 17 July 2004; 20 August 2004; 20 September 2004; 9 June 2005). In spite of this, there is a major transformation of German foreign policy before and after the Fall of the Berlin Wall. The semi-sovereign status of Germany until 1989 clearly contributed to a low-key approach to foreign policy in West Germany. The constraints of the cold war prevented both East and West Germany from becoming too active and prominent internationally. In this context, the statesman-like role of Foreign Minister Hans-Dietrich Genscher between 1982 and 1992 should be highlighted. He was instrumental, through his *Ostpolitik* (Eastern policy), in reducing the tensions between both East and West Germany, and he played a major role in the detente policy during the late phase of the cold war.

After the unification, it was some years before a more self-confident Germany began to play an international role. This also included the deployment of German troops outside the country for peacekeeping operations. The Kosovo War led to major discussions within the red–green coalition of Gerhard Schröder about whether Germany should take part in it. Foreign Minister Joschka Fischer had major difficulties in getting approval from the Green Party. Support for the war in Afghanistan was also difficult, but after the 9/11 attacks it was possible to get a majority for such action in the Bundestag. However, the Iraq War reached the limits of what German foreign and defence policy was willing to accept from the US (Conradt, 2001: 274–8). The opposition to the Iraq War of March 2002 was widespread in Germany as in other European countries. The evidence presented by the US was not enough to warrant war against Iraq. In this regard, a Franco–German united front clearly led to the still existing split in Europe between Europeanists, who want to upgrade European foreign and security policy, and Atlanticists who want a continuing close relationship to the United States.

Although Chancellor Angela Merkel shifted German foreign policy closer to that of the US after the deterioration of relations during the Schröder years, the European arena also remains the main field of action for her government. The coalition government with the social democrats has contributed to a moderate foreign policy.

Spain, Italy, Poland and Romania can be considered as large countries, but they have not been able to develop strong or influential foreign policies. The lack of ambition and resources are important factors in this restricted world-view. Italy has been particularly sidelined in global terms. After the authoritarian expansionist foreign policy of the fascist regime under Benito Mussolini, Italian foreign policy did not adopt a leadership role. On the contrary, the high level of governmental instability, economic underdevelopment, at least until the end of the 1960s, and the cold war led to a subaltern position for Italy (Missiroli, 2000: 87–90). The growing importance of Common Foreign and Security Policy was endorsed by Italian foreign policy, even if this meant upsetting transatlantic relations. The Berlusconi governments have committed to stronger support for American foreign policy, particularly during the Iraq War. Italy sent troops to Iraq, and only after the return of a left-wing coalition government to power were they withdrawn. In early March 2005, an incident in Iraq had a negative impact on US–Italian relations. The journalist Giuliana Sgrena, who was held hostage in Iraq and freed after negotiations with the Italian government who paid a ransom, was almost killed by American soldiers when her car was heading towards Baghdad airport. Her bodyguard, from the secret service, was killed by the American soldiers. The US interpretation of the incident as simply an accident was not accepted by the journalist and the Italian government asked for an investigation to find out what happened. After this incident, the relationship between the two countries deteriorated slightly (*Der Spiegel*, 3 July 2005)

Spanish foreign policy has been more ambitious than Italian foreign policy. Soon after the end of the authoritarian dictatorship of General Franco, there was an attempt to build a new foreign policy. In spite of weak human and material resources, Spanish foreign policy was able to gain more visibility in the 1980s. In the same way as the UK and France, Spain concentrated on strengthening ties with the new democracies of Central and South America. Prime Minister Felipe Gonzalez was very keen to export the Spanish model of democratic transition, but also to create new markets for the Spanish economy (Story, 1995). The common language was a major advantage. In the 1990s, the Iberoamerican Community of Nations

(Comunidad Iberoamericana de Naciones) was established after substantial diplomatic efforts by the Spanish government under Prime Minister Felipe Gonzalez. Although the organisation is fairly informal and has very few institutional structures, it has been an important forum for discussing common issues and creating benchmarking and exchange of best practice. Spain was quite successful in integrating both Portugal and Brazil and making it a territorially comprehensive region. After several years of fruitless efforts, Felipe Gonzalez was able to launch the Euro–Mediterranean Partnership in November 1995 during the Spanish presidency of the European Union. Meanwhile, the Euro–Mediterranean Partnership has been in place for more than a decade (Magone, 2009a: 407–9). In spite of its mixed results, it contributed to some more cooperation between the northern and southern parts of the Mediterranean. Even French President Sarkozy's project of a Mediterranean Union (later a Union for the Mediterranean) was not able to replace this process (see above).

Both the government of José Maria Aznar (1996–2004) and that of José Luis Zapatero (from 2004) have been ambitious in foreign policy matters. Former Prime Minister José Maria Aznar linked his government's ambitions to a stronger commitment to the transatlantic partnership. An important moment for the visibility of Spain was when it supported the Iraq War, alongside American President George W. Bush and British Prime Minister Tony Blair. Spain was one of the non-permanent members of the UN Security Council and a strong ally of the UK and the US in pushing through resolution 1441 in 2002. However, the three countries failed to get a second resolution allowing the use of military force shortly before the Iraq War. The government of Prime Minister Aznar contributed with troops for Iraq, although the vast majority of the population were opposed to it. This strong support for the United States led to tensions with French president Jacques Chirac and German Chancellor Gerhard Schröder. Only after Aznar had stepped down as prime minister was Spanish foreign policy returned to a more pro-European approach, similar to that during the Gonzalez years. Zapatero developed the idea of an 'Alliance of Civilisations' in 2004, which was supported by Turkey and led to the establishment of a UN-sponsored organisation of the same name, headed by former Portuguese President Jorge Sampaio (Barreñada, 2006).

In comparison to these countries, the foreign policies of Poland and Romania have so far not been very visible. One reason was the long period of dependency on the Soviet Union that lasted until 1989. In this period, an independent Polish or Romanian foreign policy was not possible. Afterwards, both countries were engaged in a process of accession to the EU, which was quite time-consuming. It meant that the European dimension was important for both countries in this respect. In 2003 and 2004, shortly before and soon after joining the EU, Polish European foreign policy was fairly active, with the aim of achieving the same amount of votes in the Constitutional Treaty as was agreed in the Nice Treaty; however, in the end the Polish government had to agree to a compromise brokered partly by the Spanish government under Prime Minister Zapatero. In 2005 Poland was very keen to gain as much as possible from the financial perspectives (EU budgetary negotiations) that were negotiated during the year and agreed finally in the Brussels Council in December during the British presidency. For Poland, having close ties to the United States, particularly through NATO, is very important because Poland has a border with Russia. In this context, it is easy to see why the Polish government signed a treaty with the United States about the deployment of ten interceptor missiles in Poland in August 2008, shortly after the Georgia crisis erupted. This missile defence was directed against Iran, not Russia. However, the Russians regarded this as a stepping-up of the arms race and a return to the cold war. At the same time, the Polish president, Lech Kacynsky, was also trying to create a common front against Russia with other countries with borders with Russia, such as Estonia, Lithuania and the Ukraine (*The Times*, 15 August 2008; 20 August 2008). After 2007, Prime Minister Donald Tusk pursued a more pro-European and moderate foreign policy.

Romania's foreign policy is less confrontational. The development towards an EU Common Foreign and Security policy is regarded as an important paradigm change in Romanian foreign policy. It wants to play a full part in the European integration process. Romania is interested in achieving stability in the Black Sea through its organisations including the Black Sea Forum, in the western Balkans and the Caucasus, particularly Georgia. Its main priority is probably the relationship to the Republic of Moldova, which is Romanian-speaking (Ministry of Foreign Affairs, Romania, 2008). After 2007, Prime Minister Donald Tusk pursued a more pro-European and moderate foreign policy.

In conclusion, although all larger countries have consistent national foreign policies, only the UK, France, Germany and Spain have more global ambitions; Poland and Romania are still developing a national foreign policy and it will take some time until they become more salient. In the summer of 2008, the Georgia conflict reignited some solidarity between the countries of Central and Eastern Europe, because of the long legacy of Soviet dominance.

The foreign policies of the small states

National foreign policies of small countries are gradually becoming identical to the Common Foreign and Security Policy. The lack of human and material resources plays a major role in this development. The presidency of the European Union for half a year has been a major opportunity for small states to shape policy at global level. The role of the EU presidency to set new strategic aims and also to organise a range of bilateral and multilateral meetings puts a particular country in the limelight. Countries such as Austria, Belgium, Sweden, Finland, Luxembourg, Portugal and the Netherlands that have a long diplomatic tradition can play a major role in intermediating in conflicts or finding solutions to particular problems. The consensual nature of policy-making at EU level is particularly adjusted to the needs and possibilities of small states.

In the first half of 2008, Slovenia took over the presidency of the European Union. This was the first new member state after the 2004 enlargement to take over the presidency. Its main task was to consolidate the existing policies and push forward the ratification process of the Lisbon Treaty. Moreover, it focused on advancing the process of European integration of the western Balkans (EurActiv, 13 December 2007). According to an assessment by Slovenian president Daniel Tuerk in the European Discussion Forum in Prague on 9 December 2008, presidencies can be very difficult. The Slovenian presidency had to deal with the recognition of Kosovo's independence, which led to divisions inside Europe, and it also had to deal with a conflict between Colombia and Ecuador during the Euro–Latin American summit (*Prague Daily Monitor*, 10 December 2009). The Slovenian president expressed these thoughts in Prague, because the Czech Republic was about to take over the presidency in the first half of 2009. Most of the small states are integrated into NATO and the European Security and Defence Policy. This facilitates working together as a result of the like-mindedness of the foreign and security community that they represent. However, the new Lisbon Treaty has not changed much about the six-monthly rotating presidency, in spite of the appointment of President Herman van Rompuy. Both the six-monthly rotating presidency and the new president will work together in giving continuity to the work of the Council of the European Union. For small states, in particular, the six-monthly rotating presidency is an opportunity to project the country internationally. This is not the place to review the foreign policies of each of the small countries. It is sufficient to discuss two countries that diverge slightly from the mainstream.

The first country to be discussed is Portugal. Until 1974, Portuguese foreign policy was able to count on a large colonial Empire. However, since the 1960s, liberation movements in Mozambique, Angola and Guinea-Bissau have created major problems for the authoritarian regime. During democratic transition in 1974–75, Portugal carried out a rapid decolonisation process, which led to the establishment of new independent countries in Africa. The only case that did not work out well was East Timor, which was occupied by Indonesian troops. The new democratic regime developed a new foreign policy. One of the main objectives was to achieve the independence of East Timor through peaceful means. Accession to the EC/EU allowed Portugal to put even greater pressure on the international community to put the East Timor issue on the agenda. At last, at the beginning of the new millennium, following the use of disproportionate force by the Indonesian troops against the Timorese civilian population, the UN intervened and East Timor became a UN protectorate. Finally, in 2002, East Timor became an independent country. In spite of continuing problems, Portugal regards the independence of East Timor as a major achievement for Portuguese diplomacy (Magone, 2004: 256–8).

Another major achievement was the creation of the Community of Portuguese Speaking Countries (Comunidade de Paises de Lingua Portuguesa, CPLP) in 1995. The CPLP consists of Angola, Mozambique, Guinea-Bissau, Cape Verde and Islands, São Tomé e Principe, Brazil and Portugal. The support of Brazil, in particular, is regarded as very positive by Portugal. This CPLP follows the pattern of similar projects, such as the Commonwealth and the Francophonie (see pp. 555–6), which intend to promote cooperation between countries with a common historical and cultural legacy. However, all these countries within the CPLP, apart from Brazil and Portugal, are fairly poor, underdeveloped countries, so that in terms of human and material resources the organisation is weak. Nevertheless, the future prospects are bright. The end of war in Angola may contribute to a substantial improvement of the economic situation there and in other parts of the CPLP (Magone, 2004: 251–6).

The second country to be discussed here is Belgium. This small country moved towards federal structures in 1993, and since then there has been a growing affirmation of the two main parts of the country, not only in distinctive national policies, but also in foreign policy. Flanders and Wallonia are allowed to develop their own foreign policies, which have the same importance as national foreign policy. The only caveat is that the national level has *primus inter pares* status in relation to the coordination of the three policies (Bursens, 2002).

This is why Wallonia is increasing its efforts to build linkages with the Francophone community across the world. Several bilateral and multilateral agreements exist with Francophone African nations and Quebec (Lecours, 2002).

Flemish foreign policy has focused particularly on European countries. It has good relations with its neighbouring countries, especially with the Netherlands, largely because of linguistic and cultural ties. However, Flemish foreign policy has been fairly pragmatic, emphasising economic interests particularly. Flemish foreign policy concentrates very much on the new markets of Central and Eastern Europe. The Višegrad group (the Czech Republic, Hungary, Poland and Slovakia) and the Baltic states have been the main partners in this cooperation. Apart from economic cooperation, Flanders works closely with international institutions in order to improve environmental records, education and training (Vanden Berghe *et al.*, 2003: 3–11).

In a semi-official foreign policy mission statement written by Geert Bourgeois, the then minister for administrative affairs, foreign policy, media and tourism, the main mission was stated as follows:

> Flemish foreign and development policy will put Flanders on the world map and bring the world to Flanders. By participating in European decision making and developing bilateral and multilateral relationships, Flanders will participate actively in the international decision making process and in other forms of cooperation in the world community.
>
> (Bourgeois, 2004: 8)

One problem that is emerging is that 'Belgium' as an identity is beginning to be replaced by either Flanders or Wallonia. In the whole policy document, 'Belgium' appears only twice in relation to intra-Belgian coordination and the place of the Flemish representation in the Belgian permanent representation in Brussels (Bourgeois, 2004: 10, 32). This new architecture of Belgian foreign policy entails that Belgium's votes in the EU Council are divided between the different subnational entities of the country, so that national coordination is important if Belgium is to speak with one voice.

Subnational foreign policy, also known as paradiplomacy, has grown over the past twenty years and is becoming part of the European reality. The difference between the Belgian case and other countries, such as Spain, Germany, Austria, the UK and Italy, is that the two regions of Belgium are equal in status to the national government, something that is not possible in other countries (Keating, 1999a,b; Olivetti, 2004; Magone 2007c). Cross-border and transregional projects are leading to an 'internal European foreign policy', which is contributing to further integration at subnational level. The Euroregio MaasRhine may be quoted as an example in this respect. It was already set up in the 1970s and comprises regions from France, both parts of Belgium and Germany. Meanwhile, there are sixty-three cross-border projects, including third countries outside the EU such as Morocco, the Balkans and Russia, thirteen transnational programmes, four interregional programmes and two coordinating and information exchange programmes (European Commission, 2009).

The foreign policies of the neutral states: Sweden, Austria, Finland, Switzerland and Ireland

The neutral countries in Europe are a special case. During the cold war some countries remained neutral in relation to the alignments of the cold war, aligning themselves with neither the West nor the East. Traditionally, Switzerland and Sweden have been neutral countries.

Sweden has been neutral since 1812, following a bad experience during the Napoleonic Wars, when they lost a substantial amount of territory, most notably Finland to Russia. Swedish neutrality has been fairly pragmatic. It led to the establishment of an arms industry to defend the country. After joining the EU in 1995, there has been growing cooperation of Sweden with NATO and within a common foreign and security policy. Sweden is taking part in the Nordic Battlegroup, one of the two reaction forces of the EU. A point now being considered is whether Sweden along with Finland should reinforce its participation in the Response Force of NATO. This means that Sweden is becoming more integrated into European structures, and neutrality is becoming subordinate to the Europeanisation process (Ministry of Foreign Affairs, Sweden, 2008: 4). Sweden is probably one of the most generous countries with regard to development aid to developing countries, and this characteristic remains very important to Sweden. It also plays an important role as an intermediator. Like all other Nordic countries, Sweden's main objective is to create peaceful solutions to conflicts. Peace studies is a trademark of the Nordic countries, which contrasts heavily with security studies in the UK and the United States.

After the collapse of the Soviet Union in 1991, Finland moved towards a Europeanised foreign policy, which, pragmatically, is subordinate to the European integration process. Finnish neutrality is still relevant, but it is increasingly interpreted through a European lens. The perception of the European Union as a 'force for good' strongly motivates Sweden and Finland. According to Tapio Raunio and Teija Tiilikainen, the Finnish political elites had no difficulties becoming more integrated in the Common Foreign and Security Policy (CFSP). Neutrality and military non-alignment were interpreted through the lens of European integration. The membership of Finland in the EU and its military operations should be regarded as positive, because of its overall aim of preserving peace in Europe and the world. According to Raunio and Tiilikainen, there has also been a growing acceptance of transatlantic cooperation with the US, as a kind of balance to the nuclear arsenal of Russia (Raunio and Tiilikainen, 2003: 129–45).

A similar sense of pragmatism led Austrian political elites to embrace the Common Foreign and Security Policy. Neutrality was important for Austria during the cold war and was probably one of the major reasons it was able to obtain independence in 1955. However, after joining the EU in 1995, Austria had almost no problems in adjusting to the new reality of the Common Foreign and Security Policy. Neutrality was not regarded as a good enough solution to the problem of security. Integration in many peace-building institutions such as Partnership for Peace linked to NATO were actively sought by the Austrian government (Phinnemore, 2000: 209–11).

In Ireland, the adjustment towards the Common Foreign and Security Policy has been slow. There has been resistance to taking part in any military activities, unless led or organised by the United Nations. Irish troops are stationed in Kosovo, and the unilateral proclamation of independence in Kosovo led to a major debate about the whole neutrality question, because Ireland was supporting and Russia opposing independence. In effect, this meant Ireland was taking sides and abandoning neutrality. Overall, this balancing act has become more difficult for Irish politicians because of the growing involvement with the Common Foreign and Security Policy and, hence, the consequences (Tonra, 2000: 228; *The Guardian*, 15 February 2008). Fears about the loss of neutrality under the new Lisbon Treaty were also presented by the Euro-sceptic camp during the referendum campaign.

In comparison with other countries, neutrality is very much part of the Swiss identity. In contrast to all the other neutral countries, Switzerland is *not* a member of the EU. Switzerland has been neutral since 1527 and its neutrality has been framing Swiss foreign policy since then. The most important aspect of neutrality is that it does not allow taking part in armed conflict. In spite of being a neutral country, Switzerland can, if so decided by parliament, take part in UN humanitarian or military interventions. However, Swiss humanitarian missions are allowed in armed conflict. Switzerland participates in the Partnership for Peace programme of NATO, because it does not require the country to abandon neutrality or join armed conflict. Switzerland only joined the United Nations in 2002, when a majority of 54.3 per cent endorsed it in a referendum (Federal Department of Foreign Affairs, 2007; Department of Defence, Civil Protection and Sports, 2004).

In conclusion, neutral countries have to adjust their status to the reality around them. In the end, security is central to a neutral status. Many countries, such as Sweden, Finland and Austria, have had to rethink their neutrality as a result of the growing complexity of the security architecture in Europe.

The consolidation of the Common Foreign and Security Policy (CFSP)

Since the 1970s, the EC/EU developed a 'second pillar', which became known as the Common Foreign and Security Policy (CFSP). This policy was enshrined in the Treaty of the European Union, ratified in 1993. It had its origins in what became known as European Political Cooperation (EPC), which had existed since the 1970s and was restricted to issuing common statements of the EC about contemporary events. EPC was enshrined in the Single European Act (SEA). The upgrading of EPC to CFSP did not lead to major differences, if only because of the lack of resources attached to it. The European countries had serious difficulties in joining together and creating the necessary institutional framework for the CFSP. The lack of initiative of the EU and its member states during the Kosovo War led to the United States taking a more active role, albeit through NATO. The bombardment of Serbia – mainly by American and British bombers, leading finally to an agreement between the Serbian leader Slobodan Milosevic and NATO – put the EU under pressure to increase its capabilities in order to fulfil expectations. The Treaty of Amsterdam strengthened the CFSP, giving it institutions in the military realm and, moreover, the new figure of the High Representative of Common Foreign and Security Policy. The leadership role played by Javier Solana during the Kosovo War as NATO secretary-general led to his appointment as High

Representative of Common Foreign and Security Policy. The Nice Treaty further consolidated the CFSP. Since 1999, there has been a considerable effort to create the necessary structures for an efficient CFSP. The Council of the European Union became the focus point for a stronger involvement of the military in the new infrastructure (Howorth, 2005: 183–8) (Box 14.1).

This thrust for institutionalisation of the CFSP was a slow one, but nonetheless an important one. The EU needed to respond to the critics about a gap in the capabilities of its normal instruments of foreign policy and the expectations of the world towards this new superpower still in the making (Hill, 1998: 23). In spite of major efforts, this gap is far from being closed.

Another problem of the CFSP was the lack of integration of the different countries. It is still characterised by a variable geometry, with some countries being considerably involved, such as France, Britain and Germany, and others marginalised, such as the neutral countries referred to in the previous section. According to

---

Box 14.1 From European political cooperation to the Common Foreign and Security Policy

The European Union only slowly developed the mechanisms to move towards both a common position in foreign policy and the development of a common defence policy. The origins go back to European Political Cooperation (EPC), established informally in the 1970s. This was based on a network of both diplomats and the different ministries of foreign affairs. It was finally formalised in the Single European Act of 1987, by which time the network of officials had become fairly complex. In 1993, the Common Foreign and Security Policy was finally agreed, and it became the second pillar of the Treaty of the European Union in 1999. Later, the Treaty of Amsterdam in 1999 created the High Representative for Common and Foreign and Security Policy (known as 'Mr or Mrs CFSP').

The limits of EPC and, later, the CFSP were shown during the Balkan wars in Bosnia-Herzegovina (1991–95) and in Kosovo (1999). The EU was unable to act as one to try to solve the problems. Moreover, there were no resources and no capabilities to launch a sustained war in the air. The EU was dependent on US capabilities. This traumatic experience led to the 'militarisation' of the EU through the development of a European Security and Defence Policy (ESDP) (which had already been decided in Saint Malo in 1998).

From 1999, former NATO Secretary-General Javier Solana, in his capacity as the first 'Mr CFSP', substantially upgraded the military capabilities of the EU. Today, in 2010, the Council of the European Union has not only a civilian but also a military face, which coordinates most of the military and civilian actions of the European Union across the world.

On 1 December 2009, Javier Solana was replaced by Baroness Catherine Ashton. The title was changed slightly to 'High Representative of the Union of Foreign Affairs and Security Policy'. The new Treaty of Lisbon has substantially upgraded the role of the High Representative, who oversees the EU diplomatic services, coordinates EU foreign and security policy, and is vice-president of the European Commission.

Michael Smith, such differences are exaggerated, because the second pillar is no longer dominated by an intergovernmental logic, but rather by a transgovernmental one. According to him, several socialisation processes led to the creation of a solid policy community that frames cooperation, not in national, but in transnational and even supranational terms. This has been a slow process, having started in the 1980s, but one that is growing towards transgovernmentalism (Smith, 2004: 236).

The enlargement to Central and Eastern Europe has also strengthened issues related to security in the European Union. Most Central and Eastern European countries are still traumatised from the long period of dominance by the Soviet Union. Although Russia today does not have the same capacity as the Soviet Union, mixed messages (for example, the relationship with Estonia and Latvia, where there are large Russian minorities, the Georgia conflict during August 2008, and the gas dispute with Ukraine during January 2009) have reinforced the quest for stronger cooperation between European countries. For most Central and Eastern European countries NATO and transatlantic cooperation are crucial for their perceived security. The process of integration into NATO and the EU were interlinked for the Central and Eastern European countries (Schimmelfennig, 2003).

It is difficult to define the nature of the European Union, particularly in its Common Foreign and Security Policy. Most authors tend to portray the EU as a 'normative power', i.e. one that is setting new standards in international relations. This means that the EU is spearheading a development from realist 'state interest'-based international relations to a multilevel global governance system, of which the EU is the most advanced regional organisation (Magone, 2006a; Telò, 2005). The 'normative power' or 'civilian power' approach has been particularly emphasised by Ian Manners. The EU is defined as a civilian power interested in building sustainable peace across the world. It takes into account democracy and human rights in order to achieve these aims. At the centre is the freedom from fear and want. According to him, since 2003 there has been an emphasis on the militarisation of the CFSP, which is supported by the High Representative Javier Solana. This militarisation of the 'normative power' concept has also been used by the arms industry to lobby towards a European military–industrial complex. Indeed, in 2005, the European Defence Agency was created, which is in charge of procurement of armament for the emerging European military capabilities. Such militarisation has also been reinforced by the Institute of Security Studies based in Brussels and consisting of a network of national research institutes dedicated to security (Manners, 2006:189–93; Sjursen, 2006).

One element of this militarisation was the first European Security Strategy issued on 12 December 2003 under the title 'A Secure Europe in a Better World'. The key threats mentioned in the document were terrorism, the proliferation of weapons of mass destruction, regional conflicts, state failure and organised crime (Council of the European Union, 2003: 3–4). The document also emphasises the importance of working according to the UN Charter and with the US (Council of the European Union, 2003: 9, 13). In December 2008, a five-year review of implementation of the European Security Strategy was undertaken. Most of the identified security problems remained thus five years later. However, new security problems were presented such as cyberterrorism, energy security (particularly in the case of Russia and the Middle East) and global climate change (Council of the European Union, 2008a).

It is fair to say that High Representative Javier Solana has been responding to the criticism that the EU only has 'soft power'. On the other hand, Joseph Nye has criticised the US for having too much 'hard' military power, and for being weak in 'soft power', relating to diplomatic means and civilian reconstruction, of which the EU has plenty. Nye is pleading for a more balanced approach with both hard and soft power instruments (Nye, 2004).

In conclusion, the EU is still building its foreign policy and security capabilities in order to meet expectations, and this means that there is a continuing gap that may eventually be closed in the next decade.

The objectives of the CFSP/ESDP and the Petersberg tasks

The 'civilian' or 'normative' power of the European Union is also constrained by its commitment to close cooperation with the United Nations. Multilateralism and the centrality of the UN for the establishment of a more peaceful world, based on democracy, human rights and the rule of law are part of the self-understanding of the Common Foreign and Security Policy. The EU is committed to a strategic partnership with the UN in order to improve the quality of life for the world's population (European Commission, 2003a; United Nations, 2006b). The main objectives of the EU in relation to the Common Foreign and Security Policy are:

1   to safeguard the common values, fundamental interests, independence and integrity of the Union;
2   to strengthen the security of the Union;
3   to preserve peace and strengthen international security;
4   to promote international cooperation, and to develop and consolidate democracy and the rule of law, and
5   respect for human rights and fundamental freedoms.
                    (Council of Ministers of the European Union, 2010)

In spite of the militarisation of the European Security and Defence Policy (ESDP), and the European Security Strategy of 2003, the Petersberg tasks have so far been the main areas of engagement of the European Union. The Petersberg Declaration of June 1992 assigned several tasks to the West European Union (WEU), which, after the Treaty of Amsterdam, was incorporated into the European Union. The Petersberg tasks were also taken over by the ESDP. This means that apart from the common defence structures, the EU is engaged in humanitarian and rescue missions, peacekeeping missions, and tasks in which military forces are deployed for crisis management or peace-making efforts. Since 2003, the EU has been involved in nineteen missions of civilian, military or mixed nature between January 2003 and June 2008 (Wallace, W., 2005: 443).

The institutions of the CFSP

In the past fifteen years the CFSP has become a complex network of institutions. As already mentioned, the Treaty of Amsterdam and after the Kosovo War the Treaty of Nice created the structures necessary for a military dimension of the CFSP.

Although the political and strategic direction is developed and articulated at General Affairs and External Relations Council level, and in major issues at European Council level, with considerable input from the Directorate-General External Relations, of which Directorate A is dedicated to the CFSP, new security and military institutions were established in order to achieve a faster reaction to crisis situations. One of the major changes is that the function of the Secretary-General of the Council has now merged with that of the High Representative of the Common Foreign and Security Policy. In this respect, the High Representative, at the moment former NATO Secretary-General Javier Solana, is accountable to the Council. He is supported by a deputy secretary-general who concentrates his/her work on Council secretariat matters, while the Secretary-General/High Representative dedicates most of his/her time to external relations, but also to security/military issues of the CFSP.

Like other policies, external relations and security are also integrated in the traditional Council decision-making process that consists of many working groups. In this field, the Political and Security Committee (PSC) consisting of ambassadorial level representatives of the member states that are part of the CFSP, prepares all the work for the Council of Ministers. Everything goes through the proper Committee of Permanent Representatives I and/or II before it reaches the Council for General Affairs and External Relations. The PSC is advised by the Military Committee (EUMC) which consists of permanent representatives of the Defence chiefs of the member states. It is the highest military body and provides the PSC with advice on military matters within the European Union. This is supported by a Military Staff Committee (EUMS) consisting of ten military and security experts seconded by the member states with the tasks of early warning, situation assessment and strategic planning. For concrete operations there are several headquarters across Europe that can be used to coordinate multinational EU operations such as those in Paris and Potsdam. However, since July 2007 there has also been an EU Operations Centre (EU Ops Centre) in Brussels that is manned by eight officers, but in case of an operation can provide the infrastructure for 89 officers. The EU Ops Centre and other headquarters are used for smaller missions of up to 2,000 troops. A civilian–military cell (Civ–Mil) within the EU military staff has also been established in order to coordinate mixed civilian and military operations (Council of the European Union, 2009) (Figure 14.2).

There is also strong military cooperation with NATO, particularly in the use of assets for EU missions, as happened in the operations CONCORDIA in Macedonia and ARTEMIS in the Democratic Republic of Congo. Permanent arrangements were decided in a Brussels European Council in March 2003 that became known as 'Berlin-Plus' because it makes references to a meeting of the NATO Council in Berlin in 1996. The permanent arrangement allows for a close strategic partnership between the two organisations. They complement each other – ESDP does not replace NATO. There is now a permanent EU-Cell in the NATO Supreme Headquarters of the Allied Powers Europe (SHAPE). However, NATO allows the EU to develop its own capabilities and military and civilian structures to undertake actions without NATO involvement (Council of the European Union, 2009) (Figure 14.3).

On the civilian side, the PSC is also advised by a Committee for Civilian Aspects on Crisis Management (CIVCOM) that works closely with the Civilian

COUNCIL OF THE EUROPEAN UNION

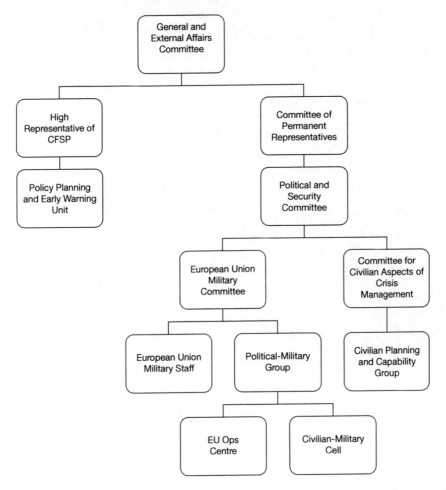

Figure 14.2 The institutional framework of the Common Foreign and Security Policy/ The European Security and Defence Policy (CFSP/ESDP), 2009

Planning and Conduct Capability group (CPCC). The latter, which was established in August 2007, develops strategic plans and conducts all civilian operations under ESDP. CPCC is an important coordination body for ESDP operations, something that has been missing so far. It consists of sixty members, half of whom are experts, the other half seconded civil servants such as police officers as well as rule of law, procurement logistics and finance officers. In July 2008, CPCC was in charge of 3,000 men and women working in three continents. CPCC functions as an upper level to the Head of Commission and allows for better coordination with the military side of any ESDP operation. Since 1 May 2008, the head of the CPCC has been Dutch diplomat Kees Kloupenhouwer (ESDP Newsletter, 6 July 2008: 24–5).

Figure 14.3 The intertwined membership of NATO and the EU

The ESDP is supported by three main agencies, which were also created in comparatively recently and are therefore still work in progress. The most important is probably the European Defence Agency, which was founded in 2004 and aims to promote the establishment of a European armaments industry, which should considerably improve the ESDP's military capabilities. It is supported by twenty-six member states (Denmark was the only EU country not to join the agency). The EDA has linkages to its predecessor, the Organisation for Joint Cooperation in Armament (Organisation Conjointe de Coopération en matière d'Armement, OCCAR), which comprised countries with strong armaments industries: Belgium, France, the UK, Germany, Italy and Spain. The whole process of cooperation started in 1993 between France and Germany, and this led, in 2001, to the creation of OCCAR.

The second agency is the Institute for Security Studies (ISS) based in Paris, which is linked to top national think-tanks in all member states. The ISS provides research and in-depth studies to the ESDP officers and the general academic community.

The third agency is the European Union Satellite Centre (EUSC), which provides geospatial intelligence (GEOINT) information to the ESDP planning units. It is based in Torrejón, near Madrid.

The structures of ESDP are gradually being set up. In the past decade, a myriad of new bodies attached to the Council of the European Union have emerged, with the purpose of improving the logistical and operational capabilities of the European Union. The Treaty of Lisbon has merged the present position of high representative with that of the commissioner for external relations and thereby created a 'foreign minister' of the European Union without using this title. Newly appointed Baroness Catherine Ashton heads the Council of General and External Affairs and is vice-president of the European Commission, although appointed by the Council (Article 9D and 9E of the Treaty of Lisbon).

The instruments of European foreign policy: slowly closing the expectations–capabilities gap

Institution-building has been accompanied by capability-building measures. These efforts have been made on the civilian side, as well as the military, although the emphasis has been on the latter.

On the civilian side, several headline goals led to the establishment of civilian capabilities to be deployed in crisis regions. In the European Council of Feira during the Portuguese presidency in June 2000 four areas were prioritised that are still the main areas of intervention of the European Union:

1 the police
2 strengthening of the rule of law
3 strengthening civilian administration
4 civil protection.

Member states have pledged to provide 5,761 police officers for advisory, training and replacement operations. Moreover, 1,400 of those officers can be deployed within thirty days. Importantly, 631 prosecutors, judges and prison officers, who can be deployed to strengthen the rule of law, have also been pledged. There are also 565 staff who can be deployed at short notice for civilian administration tasks. So far there are 579 civil protection experts and 4,445 staff for intervention teams. Finally, monitoring missions will now be able to count on 505 personnel. Measures were also undertaken to improve the offices of EU Special Representatives (Council of European Union, June 2008).

Until now there have been nineteen civilian missions, of which eight have been completed and eleven are still ongoing. Most of these missions are involved in advising, training and replacing police forces and rebuilding the rule of law institutions (see Tables 14.1 and 14.2).

Table 14.1 Ongoing EU civilian operations, January 2009

Region	Country	Mission	Objective	Personnel involved
Western Balkans	Bosnia-Herzegovina (January 2006–)	EU Police Mission (EUPM)	Police Training	166 international police, 35 international civilian staff and 200 local staff
	Kosovo (2008–)	European Union Rule of Law Mission (EULEX)	Building a sustainable and functional rule of law system	1,900 international staff
Ukraine–Moldova	Ukraine–Moldova (2005–9)	European Union Border Assistance (Moldova and Ukraine Border Mission)	Security and organisation of the border between Ukraine and Moldova, particularly in relation to the Russian breakaway Transdniestrian region	200
Middle East	Palestinian Authority (30 November 2005)	EU Border Assistance Mission (EUBAM)	Monitoring of all operations at the border crossing point	27 staff
	Palestinian Authority (1 January 2006–)	EU Police Mission (EUPOL COPPS)	Establishment of sustainable and effective policing arrangement	26 EU staff and 5 local staff
	Iraq 1 July 2005– 30 June 2009)	Integrated Rule of Law Mission (EUJUST LEX)	Integrated training in the fields of management and criminal investigation	1,483 judges
Africa	Democratic Republic of Congo (July 2007–)	EU Police Mission (EUPOL RD CONGP)	Assistance for reform efforts of Congolese national police and possible interfaces with justice system	39
	Democratic Republic of Congo (8 June 2005– mid 2007	Reform of Security Sector (EUSEC DR Congo)	Reform of the country's security sector	
Asia	Afghanistan	EU Police Mission (EUPOL Afghanistan)	Contribution to sustainable and effective civil policing	230

Source: Author's own compilation, based on data from the Council of the European Union, June 2008: 4–7; database available online, Council of Ministers of European Union: www.consilium.europa.eu (accessed 11 January 2009)

Table 14.2 Completed EU civilian operations, January 2009

Region	Country	Mission	Objective	Personnel involved
Western Balkans	FYRO Macedonia (15 December 2003–14 December 2005)	EU Police Mission (EUPOL PROXIMA)	Monitoring, mentoring and advising the country's police in order to fight organised crime and promote European policing standards	200
	FYRO Macedonia 15 December 2005–15 June 2006)	EU Police Advisory Team (EUPAT)	Support of development of an efficient and professional police service based on European standards of policing	30 police advisers
South Caucasus	Georgia (July 2004–July 2005)	EU Rule of Law Mission (EUJUST THEMIS)	Addressing urgent challenges in the criminal justice system	
Africa	Sudan/Darfur (July 2005– December 2007)	Support to African Union's AMIS II	Monitoring of humanitarian ceasefire agreement between rebel movements and the Sudanese government civilian component: provided training to police officers	31 civilians, 20 military
Asia	Indonesia (Aceh) (15 August 2005– 15 December 2006)	Aceh Monitoring Mission	Monitoring the implementation of various aspects of the peace agreement	36 monitoring staff

Source: Author's own compilation, based on data from the Council of the European Union, June 2008: 4–7; database available online, Council of Ministers of European Union: www.consilium. europa.eu (accessed 11 January 2009)

The military part of the CFSP is still a work in progress. After a commitment to establishing a 60,000 strong force in 2003, the goalpost has been shifting, or perhaps getting a more concrete definition. In the same year, the French, the British and the Germans developed the concept of a 'battlegroup', characterised by a minimalist structure, to conduct operations. The battlegroups would be rapid reaction forces of up to 1,500 soldiers each and would be framed regionally or nationally. Other countries would be able to participate as well. In 2006, two battlegroups were ready for action and several other battlegroups were being established across Europe. For example, the Nordic battlegroup includes Sweden,

Finland, Norway, Estonia and Ireland, and a south-eastern European battlegroup (HELBROC) comprises Greece, Cyprus, Bulgaria and Romania. The only purely national battlegroups were established by France, the UK, Italy and Spain (Council of European Union, 2008b; Military Capability Commitment Conference, 2004; website of the Council of the European Union, 2010) (Figure 14.4).

Although the EU and NATO have formed a 'capability group', there is a major thrust by European policy-makers to acquire considerable military capabilities, particularly transportation vehicles and large transport aircraft, in order to become more flexible and less dependent on NATO. All this is still work in progress and will take some time to achieve greater independence in the deployment and sustainability of troops abroad.

According to the European Defence Agency (EDA), most defence equipment procurement is national, and just a fraction is cooperative among EU members. For example, in 2007, 78.8 per cent of defence equipment procurement was national, and just 18.9 per cent cooperative among EU member states. The remainder was cooperative, but involved individual member states dealing with non-EU members. In terms of absolute numbers, €2.178 billion were spent for national capacities, and just €347 million for cooperative European projects (EDA, 2008: 13–14). The share for research and development projects declines to 13.3 per cent for collaborative European projects, while 83.3 goes to national ones (EDA, 2008: 15). This means

Figure 14.4 Variable geometry in European security

Table 14.3 Ongoing EU military missions, January 2009

Region	Country	Mission	Objective	Personnel involved
Western Balkans	Bosnia-Herzegovina 2004–)	Peacekeeping forces (EUFOR ALTHEA)	EU military and stabilisation tasks EU special representative present	2,500
Africa	Guinea-Bissau (2008–)	Advisory and assistance team for security reform (EU SSR Guinea-Bissau)	Advice and assistance team for reform of security sector in Guinea-Bissau	39
	Democratic Republic of Congo (2007–)	Advisory and assistance team for security reform (EUSEC DR Congo)	Advisory and training of security forces	39
	Chad (2008–9)	Peacekeeping mission (EUFOR Tchad/RCA)	Military bridging operation	3,700
	Somalia (8 December 2008–)	Mission against pirates (NAVFOR Somalia)	Policing of the waters on the coast of Somalia and protection of ship transport in the region	6 frigates, 3 patrol aircrafts and 1,200 troops

Source: Database available online, Council of Ministers of European Union: www.consilium.europa.eu (accessed 11 January 2009)

Table 14.4 Completed EU military missions, January 2009

Region	Country	Mission	Objective	Personnel involved
Western Balkans	FYRO Macedonia 2003–	Peacekeeping mission (CONCORDIA)	Stabilisation of security in the country	
Africa	Sudan/Darfur (2005–6)	Supporting peacekeeping mission of African Union (AMIS II)	Support activities for African Union engagement	31 civilians, 20 military
	Democratic Republic of Congo (2003)	Peacekeeping mission (ARTEMIS) situation in Bunia	Stabilisation of security and humanitarian	1,800
	Democratic Republic of Congo (2006–)	Peacekeeping mission (EUFOR Congo)	Support for UN during the elections in the country	2,300

Source: Database available online, Council of Ministers of European Union: www.consilium.europa.eu (accessed 11 January 2009)

that the EU is still falling below the benchmarks of 30 per cent for European collaborative procurement and of 20 per cent for research and development (EDA, 2008: 21). Moreover, national governments together have a total military force of 1.84 million personnel, but only 77,900 are deployed for national or European missions, that is just 4.2 per cent (EDA, 2008: 16–17).

In spite of the expectations and capabilities gap, it seems that the mentality of policy-makers in Brussels has become more bolder and more strategic. This can be seen, for example, in the engagement of the EU along the coast of Somalia, where pirates have been attacking ships. The NAVFOR Somalia, started on 8 December 2008, has added to the credibility of the ESDP. Although it has not solved the problem, it has certainly created greater security in Somalian waters. However, the military on the ground are aware that they are understaffed and poorly resourced. The area is simply too large for the few frigates and air patrol aircraft operating there (*International Herald Tribune*, 8 December 2008) (Tables 14.3 and 14.4).

Securing the borders of the European Union: the emergence of the European neighbourhood policy

The Central and Eastern European enlargement has created a Single European Market (SEM) of almost 500 million citizens. However, it has become clear that such an SEM can only work properly if the neighbours of the European Union have a similar mentality. The European Neighbourhood Policy (ENP) was established shortly before Central and Eastern European enlargement in a document on 'Wider Europe' in March 2003 and finally defined in a document called 'European Neighbourhood Policy' in May 2004. (European Commission, 2003; European Commission, 2004). Although economic integration and trade are the main aspects of the ENP, a political and security dimension, the latter linked to the European Security Strategy formulated in 2003, are also important. The ENP targets the Maghreb, Mashreq, the Middle East, Ukraine, Moldova, the Caucasus and Russia. In total there are sixteen countries taking part in the ENP (see Table 14.5).

The ENP is designed for those neighbouring countries that are not members of the European Union, but remain close to the regional governance system. The ENP wants to strengthen the political and economic integration of these countries into a larger area beyond the borders of the European Union. The ENP requires from its members the adoption of democratic values, protection of human rights, rule of law and the adoption of, or at least harmonisation towards, the *acquis communautaire*, meaning the over 1,800 pages of European law that all member states have to transpose into national law before they join the European Union. The building of civil society capability is also an important aspect of the European Neighbourhood Policy. Bilateral agreements with the respective countries lead to an agreed ENP Action Plan. The ENP is supported by a financial ENP Instrument (ENPI) that finances cross-border projects, and mobility and other programmes related to the overall process of integration. There has been a reform of funding taking place. Before the ENP, each region had its own programmes such as TACIS for Russia and the former Republics of the Soviet Union and MEDA for the Mediterranean countries. Since 2007, all these programmes have been replaced by the more flexible ENPI which amounts to €12 billion for the period 2007–13.

Table 14.5 Participants in the European Neighbourhood Policy (ENP)

Country	Population (millions) 2005	Gross national income (GNI)/ per capita (US$) 2005
Eastern borders		
Armenia	3.016	1,450
Azerbaijan	8.388	1,240
Belarus	9.776	2,760
Georgia	4.474	1,320
Moldova	4.206	930
Ukraine	47.075	1,520
Southern borders		
Algeria	32.854	2,730
Egypt	74.033	1,260
Israel	6.924	18,580
Jordan	5.473	2,460
Lebanon	3.577	6,770
Libya	5.853	5,530
Morocco	30.168	1,740
Palestinian Authority	3.626	1,230
Syria	19.043	1,380
Tunisia	10.029	2,880
EU-27 (GDP average)	493	22,232

Source: Author's own compilation, based on *Der Fischer Weltalmanach, 2008. Zahlen, Daten, Fakten* (Frankfurt a. M.: Fischer Verlag, 2007)

Although this is an overall increase of 35 per cent in relation to the previous, more fragmented, funding system, the number of countries is quite large, so it will be difficult to make a strong impact. It should be compared with the structural funds for the members of the EU, which amount to €347.41 billion over a six-year period. The ENP should be interpreted as a strategic project intended to increase the security of the European Union on its borders. There are individual country programmes as well as regional cooperation programmes among the southern and eastern neighbours. Apart from the fact that most democracies in the Mediterranean are quite illiberal, as well as showing high levels of corruption, the economic development level is still low, so such integration will take some time before becoming reality. Similar political and economic problems exist in relation to the Ukraine, Armenia, Azerbaijan, Georgia and, particularly, Belarus (see Table 14.5 and Figure 14.4). All this shows that the ENP still has problems that can only be solved in a long-term perspective. In spite of the nature of the democracies and political regimes in these countries, the ENP remains an important strategic policy area, with the clear intention of maintaining good relations with its neighbours and supporting the democratisation and economic liberalisation processes in these regions. Security issues, such as uncontrolled immigration, terrorism and energy security, can be solved much more easily if there are open channels between the EU and its more problematic neighbours.

577

The Euro-Mediterranean partnership: a stagnating project

One of the important achievements of Spanish foreign policy was to push forward the project of a Euro-Mediterranean partnership between the EU countries and the countries of the southern Mediterranean. The southern Mediterranean members of the Euro-Mediterranean Partnership are identical to the southern members in the European Neighbourhood Policy. The Euro-Mediterranean partnership was started at the Barcelona conference during the Spanish presidency under the chairmanship of Prime Minister Felipe Gonzalez in November 1995. This new approach to the Mediterranean policy followed the model of the Conference for Security and Cooperation in Europe that was established in 1973, and has become an Organisation since 1995. It focuses its work in three main fields – politico-military, economic–environmental and the human dimension. The Euro-Mediterranean Partnership also focuses on three areas: the political, the economic–financial and the cultural areas. Between 1995 and 2007, €16 billion were spent on the Euro-Mediterranean Partnership. One problem was that most of the countries were not able to absorb the funding available. Most of this was as a result of the lack of a project culture and obstructive bureaucratic structures. However, between 2000 and 2006 the situation improved considerably. In spite of this, one has to acknowledge that this is a fairly difficult field for the European Union because of the differences in administrative cultures and the weakness of a civil society. After a decade, the general assessment was that the whole project was stagnating. The agenda of the European Union has changed towards counter-terrorism measures since the 9/11 attacks, and the southern neighbours felt that they were being used by this changed rationale of the EU. This became quite evident during the tenth anniversary meeting in Barcelona under the British presidency, which was attended only by low-key officials from the southern Mediterranean, and most of the high-ranking representatives kept away (Gillespie, 2006: 277).

In the second half of 2008, French President Nicolas Sarkozy wanted to upgrade the Euro-Mediterranean Partnership by creating a Mediterranean Union of the northern and southern Mediterranean countries. However, resistance by German Chancellor Angela Merkel and other member states led to the downgrading of the project to a 'Union for the Mediterranean' with its seat in Barcelona. The new 'Union for the Mediterranean' is complementary to the Barcelona process and it is difficult to assess whether it will change the nature of the project at all. ENP and the Union for the Mediterranean have contributed to some confusion about the project, which is now embedded in an overall European Union foreign policy strategy, and is no longer just a development project.

The strategic partnership between the EU and Russia

Originally the European Union wanted Russia to be a participant of the European Neighbourhood Policy. Indeed, financial support for Russia comes from the ENPI. However, Russia rejected such a proposal, because the relations between the two are qualitatively different. The European Union has therefore developed a strategic partnership with Russia that leads to cooperation in several areas such as international terrorism, international crime and the reduction and non-proliferation of weapons of mass destruction. Tensions between the EU and Russia emerged during the Georgia conflict in August 2008 and the gas dispute with Ukraine in December 2008–January 2009. In both cases the EU has played an important role in dissuading the tensions between these countries. There is growing concern of some Central and Eastern European countries about the renewed self-confidence of Russia, particularly during the Georgia conflict. Poland and the Czech Republic are taking part in the US sponsored and funded missile shield programme, which is designed to protect against potential nuclear strikes by North Korea or Iran. Russia has been very critical of the intentions of the US in deploying interception missiles close to the border with Russia.

Another issue of conflict has been NATO membership of Central and Eastern European countries. The Partnership for Peace arrangement created a forum to integrate Russia in a European security and cooperation regime. However, the wish of Georgia to join NATO and respective support of the USA has created more tensions with Russia.

The strategic partnership established in 1994 covers several common spaces: economic issues and the environment; freedom, security and justice; external security; and research and education, including cultural aspects. While between 1991 and 2006, €2.7 billion were spent on supporting the EU–Russia cooperation programmes in the common spaces, this amount diminished considerably afterwards and is now targeted to specific projects. A renewal of the strategic partnership started in June 2008, but was interrupted by the Georgia conflict. However, during the twenty-second EU–Russia meeting in Nice in 2009, chaired by the French EU presidency, the Georgia conflict, pan-European security such as the missile deployment by the United States (and, later, Russia in response), and enhanced economic cooperation were discussed. The overall results were positive, contributing to a lowering of tensions between the EU and Russia (French Presidency, 2009). Moreover, the gas dispute between Russia and Ukraine was also solved by the Gas Coordination Group that was founded in 2006 to deal with such occasions. The Gas Coordination Group will monitor the transfer of gas through the Ukraine. When Russia cut off gas supplies in January 2009, many countries in the eastern and western Balkans were not able to get any gas in below freezing temperatures. The EU was keen to emphasise the importance of being a reliable partner and fulfilling contractual obligations (European Commission, IP 09/24,9 January 2009).

The European Union and the wider world

Although the ENP is a very important external policy of the EU, in the past two decades the engagement of this regional organisation in other parts of the world has increased considerably.

The most important partnership is, of course, the transatlantic cooperation between the European Union and the USA. This is a long-standing cooperation that has led to the establishment of a myriad of institutions and forums for policy implementation and discussion of major issues, respectively. Since 9/11 counter-terrorism cooperation has increased considerably, and security issues gained particular relevance when it was found out that most of the perpetrators of the terrorist attacks in the United States came from Europe, particularly Germany and

Spain. Although the EU was divided about the Iraq War of 2003, cooperation in the fight against terrorism never ceased throughout the period and beyond.

At the centre of this cooperation are, of course, economic relations. The 'New Transatlantic Agenda', which started in 1995, is geared towards closer cooperation between the EU and the US. The platform includes intergovernmental, trans-governmental and transnational elements. The most important aspect is probably the attempt to achieve harmonisation in regulatory practices, which has become important since the international financial crisis, and mutual recognition of standards. One major problem seems to be cooperation at civil society level which has been only partially successful. In spite of this, many commentators want a revival of an already stagnating 'New Transatlantic Agenda' (Liebert, 2006; Pollack, 2005; Marsh and Mackenstein, 2005: 110–16).

Since the 1970s, the EC/EU has kept an open dialogue with China. This has been quite difficult because of the nature of the regime, a one-party non-democratic state, but also because of certain erratic Chinese policies that led to the violation of human rights, such as, for example, the brutal crushing of the Tiananmen protests in 1989. Today, many human rights violations, including the use of the death penalty, are still criticised by the EU and its member states. In spite of this, EU–China relations have improved over time. China is now one of the largest markets in the world and the EC/EU is interested in strengthening economic relations with this emerging superpower. Annual meetings have been taking place between the EU and China since 1998 (Marsh and Mackenstein, 2005: 203–8).

The EU also established a multilateral forum. Known as the Europe–Asia meetings, they started in 1996 and include all ten member states of the Association for Southeast Asian Nations (ASEAN), South Korea, China, Japan and the EU-Member states – in total forty countries, comprising more than half of the population of the world. They meet regularly every two years. It is an informal gathering in order to discuss the problems of Asia and the EU.

The EU also has strong relations with the Latin American countries, and is presently engaged in several regional integration projects with them. Since 1991, the EU has supported the Mercosur, the common market of the southern cone comprising Brazil, Argentina, Paraguay, Uruguay and Venezuela. Meanwhile, the EU and Mercosur want to establish a transatlantic free trade area. However, such efforts have been quite difficult. There have been disagreements between the two sides that have not yet been bridged (Doctor, 2007). The EU also has relations with the Andean Community comprising Colombia, Ecuador, Peru and Bolivia. A 'strategic alliance' with the region has been established that may lead in the long term to a transatlantic free trade area. Similar negotiations are taking place with the Caribbean Community, comprising fifteen members. The plan envisages that the Caribbean Community members adopt a single currency (*International Herald Tribune*, 29 November 2008).

The EU is also engaged in Africa. It has been cooperating with the African Union over the Darfur crisis and other areas of conflict. Moreover, it supports the different regional integration projects, such as the South African Development Community. For decades, the EU had a development agreement with the new states that emerged out of European decolonisation. The Lomé Agreement, comprising countries from Africa, the Caribbean and the Pacific, is being replaced by regional 'Economic Partnership Agreements', which are designed to create regional development communities.

All this shows that national foreign policies are gradually being replaced by multilateral approaches spearheaded by the European Union. The EU governance model is being exported to other regions of the world, particularly in the southern hemisphere. This sometimes clashes, particularly in Latin America, with American projects such as the Free Trade Area of Americas. Some countries use this competition between the United States and the EU to their advantage, the best example being Brazil, one of the leaders of the Mercosur project (Magone, 2006; 2009c).

Conclusions: towards global continental–regional governance

Traditional foreign policy based on 'national interest' is being replaced by a more multilateral global governance approach. The EU member states are working closely together to establish multilateral structures in order to meet the challenges of an increasingly globalised world. Some larger countries such as the UK and France still pursue some national interests that are distinctive from the overall common foreign and security policy of the European Union. However, such possible areas of national interest are shrinking, while multilateral cooperation in solving problems is becoming more important. This became evident in the deployment of troops in Buni (Democratic Republic of Congo) in 2003, Bosnia-Herzegovina, Macedonia and Kosovo. Multilateral cooperation based on United Nations mandates allows risks to be shared and national expectations lowered.

In the past decade, there has been a 'militarisation' of the common foreign and security policy. This was a consequence of the weak performance of European countries during the Kosovo War. The dangers of genocide in many conflicts around the world and the growing threat of international terrorism, proliferation of weapons of mass destruction, and energy security have led to a stepping up of the EU's rhetoric with military and civilian capabilities. In spite of the progress made, there is still a long way to go.

Finally, in the past two decades the EU has developed strategy papers to deal with all regions of the world. Multilateral agreements and forums are increasingly shaping the relationships between the EU and other parts of the world. The rationale of the EU remains a more peaceful and democratic world, often known as 'democratic peace', under the auspices and leadership of the United Nations. As such, the EU represents a new form of global politics and all member states are engaged in pushing forward its values.

Suggested reading

Important articles on the Common Foreign and Security Policy (CFSP)

Hill, Christopher (1998), Closing the Capabilities–Expectations Gap? In: John Peterson and Helene Sjursen (eds), *A Common Foreign Policy for Europe?* London: Routledge, pp. 18–38.

Manners, Ian (2006), Normative Power Europe Reconsidered: Beyond the Crossroads, *Journal of European Public Policy*,13(2): 182–99.

General books on national foreign policy

Manners, Ian and Richard G. Whitman (eds) (2000), *The Foreign Policies of European Union Member States*. Manchester: Manchester University Press.

General books on the international relations of the European Union

Bretherton, Charlotte and John Vogler (2005), *The European Union as a Global Actor*. Second edition. London: Routledge.

Hill, Christopher and Michael Smith (2005), *The International Relations of the European Union*. Oxford: Oxford University Press.

Marsh, Steve and Hans Mackenstein (2005), *The International Relations of the European Union*. Harlow: Pearson-Longman.

Smith, Karen E. (2003), *European Union Foreign Policy in a Changing World*. Cambridge: Polity Press.

Further reading

Doctor, Mahrukh (2007), Why Bother with Interregionalism? Negotiations for a European Union–Mercosur Agreement, *Journal of Common Market Studies*, 45(2): 281–314.

Magone, José M. (2006), *The New World Architecture: The Role of the European Union in the Making of Global Governance*. New Brunswick, NJ: Transaction.

—— (2009b), Europe and Global Governance. In: Chris Rumford (ed.), *Sage Handbook of European Studies*. London: Sage, pp. 277–94.

Pollack, Mark A. (2005), The New Transatlantic Agenda at Ten: Reflections on an Experiment in International Governance, *Journal of Common Market Studies*, 43(5) 899–919.

Smith, Michael E. (2004), *Europe's Foreign and Security Policy: The Institutionalization of Cooperation*. Cambridge: Cambridge University Press.

Telò, M. (2005) *Europe: A Civilian Power? European Union, Global Governance, World Order*. Basingstoke: Palgrave.

Vasconcelos, Álvaro (2009), What Ambitions for European Defence for 2020? Paris: EUISS. Electronically available at: www.iss.europa.eu/uploads/media/What_ambitions_for_European_defence_in_2020.pdf (accessed 26 August 2009).

Electronic journals

European Journal of International Relations

European Security

International Organisation

Journal of European Public Policy

Journal of Common Market Studies

Websites

Council of the European Union(2009): information on Common Foreign and Security Policy at: www.consilium.europa.eu (accessed 26 August 2009).

European Commission (2009): directorate-general external relations at: http://ec.europa.eu/external_relations/index_en.htm (accessed 26 August 2009).

European Defence Agency (2009): information on defence capabilities of the EU at: www.eda.europa.eu (accessed 26 August 2006).

European Union Institute of Security Studies (EU-ISS) (2009): main European Union think-tank on CFSP, coordinating national counterparts; relevant articles, books and documents can be downloaded for research at www.iss.europa.eu (accessed 26 August 2009).

QUESTIONS FOR REVISION

- How important is national foreign policy in the context of the Common Foreign and Security Policy? Discuss, using examples from at least two countries.
- What are the problems of the European Defence and Security Policy?
- How important is the North Atlantic Treaty Organisation (NATO) today for the security of Europe?
- How relevant are the external policies of the European Union in the global governance system?
- What main challenges face the EU in its European Neighbourhood Policy (ENP)?

Chapter 15

Conclusions: reinventing Europe

- Learning from each other: diversity and convergence of European politics
- Mediatisation and electoral markets in Europe
- A multi-level governance system: European, national, regional and local
- Flexible means of communication: positive and critical issues of e-government and e-democracy
- Towards multicultural societies? The challenge of immigration
- The unification of the continent as an historical milestone: towards a region of democratic peace and stability
- Conclusions: the rise of post-sovereign European politics

Learning from each other: diversity and convergence of European politics

One particular characteristic of European politics is the number of states that exist across the continent. Most of these states are small, but there are also larger states such as Germany, the United Kingdom, France and Italy. There are also medium-sized countries such as Spain, Poland and Romania. The diversity of political systems also shows that national path-dependency has been important for all these countries. The French semi-presidential system was established because the Fourth Republic was not stable and efficient enough; since it was proclaimed in 1958, French politics has become more predictable and stable. The Napoleonic political culture played a major role in shaping the figure of the president in France. Furthermore, the French model was taken over by many other countries, such as Portugal, Poland, Romania, Bulgaria, Lithuania and Slovakia. However, each country has created a different balance between institutions. This means that institutional transfer is constantly taking place between the different countries, but each country adjusts the transferred institutions to their own national political cultures. Hungary for example emulated many of the German institutions, particularly the model of a Chancellor democracy, however the electoral system has led to a majoritarian type of democracy, instead of the consensual style prevalent in Germany.

One particular element of European politics is institutional transfer within a region. The Nordic countries are a good example in this respect. There has been permanent institutional transfer between all five Nordic countries, so that they now look very similar. Although Finland is a semi-presidential democracy, the Nordic institutional transfer contributed to the establishment of similar institutions in the judiciary and in the legislature, so that the political systems have become very alike. In Chapter 6 it was possible to see how the judiciary of all these countries converged to a Nordic model; this has also been visible among the countries with romanic languages, which overwhelmingly adopted the Napoleonic Code.

Another important aspect of institutional transfer has been among party systems. The established party families, which found their highest expressions in the European political party federations in the European parliament, have contributed to the stabilisation of many party systems in Southern, Central and Eastern Europe. The panoply of political parties is increasingly framed by traditional party families. New political parties have difficulty in staying outside the existing groups in the European Parliament. If they are not part of a parliamentary group, they are sidelined from important decision-making processes. Europeanisation of party politics has become an important aspect of contemporary European politics.

Mediatisation and electoral markets in Europe

Contemporary European politics is increasingly dominated by the media. The permanent media campaign has become an important feature of how politics is communicated to the public. The importance of 'spin doctors', electoral strategists, media managers and focus groups is changing the nature of representation in European politics. The marketisation of politics has transformed the way political parties conduct elections. The end of the mass party and its replacement by the cartel party has created a more economistic approach to politics. Indeed, we can speak of a political economy of electoral politics. Political parties are engaged in product marketing, so that now representation is constructed through the market and the media. This is an inversion of the representation process, which used to be more of a bottom-up, social movement. Such manipulation of representation can be observed particularly in Southern Europe and Central and Eastern Europe. The best example is the creation of the firm–party Forza Italia by Silvio Berlusconi in 1994. Berlusconi was able to use the knowledge of his business empire to create a new party and used product marketing strategies to achieve victory in the March 1994 elections. Since then, Italian politics has become much more Americanised and bipolarised between the left and the right. The model was followed by other countries – in the UK (Tony Blair and New Labour), France (Nicolas Sarkozy and the Union for the People's Movement, UMP) and Germany (Gerhard Schröder and the German Social Democratic Party, SPD).

This also means that political and electoral campaigns have led to a spiralling of costs. In spite of generous public funding in many European countries, there is still a need to raise even more money from private donors, creating problems of accountability and transparency. The dangers of political corruption, clientelism and patronage then become very real. Political corruption is still a major problem in Central and Eastern European countries, and, at least partly, is related to party politics. The Tangentopoli affair in Italy in 1993 highlighted the dangers of systemic corruption over four decades. The Helmut Kohl affair, when he refused to disclose all the transactions of a DM 2 million secret fund to a committee in the Bundestag between 1999 and 2002 is a good example. In France, the Elf scandal involved foreign minister Roland Dumas who was convicted, but then acquitted by a Higher Court, because he was not aware that his mistress had given him presents sponsored by Elf (*The Guardian*, 13 November 2003).

This political economy of electoral campaigns also led to the 'Cash for Honours' affair in 2006–7 in the United Kingdom. Many private donors allegedly made donations or loaned money to the Labour Party with very low interest rates (close to zero) in return for future Honours (lordships). Also allegedly, this had been a common practice of all the UK political parties. Prime Minister Tony Blair was interviewed twice by the London Metropolitan Police. In the end, the investigation was closed, with nobody being prosecuted.

This means that a 'crisis of representation' related to partyocracy in many European countries is leading to the emergence of left-wing and right-wing populist parties across Europe. Even the Netherlands, one of the countries where political parties have the highest scores in terms of trust, has seen the emergence of populist parties (for example, Pim Fortuyn List (2002–7) and, more recently, the Party of Freedom (Partij van Vrijheid, PvV) of Geert Wilders, who is against an 'Islamisation of Europe' and the 'European super-state'). Such a populist backlash can be found, for example, in Austria, where, in the 2008 legislative elections, one-third of the population voted for the right-wing Populist Freedom Party (FPÖ) and the Alliance for the Future of Austria (BZÖ).

A multilevel governance system: European, national, regional and local

Another aspect of European politics is that the traditional sovereign nation-state has been replaced by an integrated cooperative post-sovereign state within a multilevel governance system. The 'post-sovereign' state, as defined by William Wallace, works together with other states to resolve concrete problems (see Chapter 10). The European integration process led to the establishment of a European Union political system that includes not only national and supranational levels, but also subnational and global levels. This means that, since the 1980s, there has been a growth in the complexity of the way politics is run. The post-sovereign state operates in a globalised world, in which many policy areas are shared with other countries. This creates a high level of global and European interdependency that limits the possibilities for individual countries to move alone in most policy areas. Among these policy areas are the environment, global trade arrangements and security issues. Moreover, at subnational level regions and local authorities have become more self-confident and develop international networks or engage in cross-border cooperation. Some regions, such as Flanders, Wallonia, Catalonia and Scotland regard themselves as stateless nations. They have developed their own paradiplomacy parallel to the national governments.

The multilevel governance system is also a new structure of opportunities for non-governmental organisations (NGOs) and civil society associations. Many NGOs have become global players and tend to use the different levels to influence policy. In the European Union, the supranational level has seen an increase of Euro groups. This means that there has been a growing politicisation of the European integration process (Marks and Steenbergen, 2004).

Flexible means of communication: positive and critical issues of e-government and e-democracy

This growth of complexity has made the analysis of European politics more interesting, but also more challenging. The nation-state as such is only one of many actors that have emerged since the early 1980s. A thorough analysis needs to take into account all other levels and the interactions between three kinds of actors: political institutions, private economic and civil society actors. Governance is characterised by a high level of dynamics and flexibility that contrasts heavily with the rigid nation-state of the 1950s and 1960s. One of the reasons for this flexibility is that there is a continuing process of adjustment to new globalised and Europeanised realities. This also means that the institutions of national political systems have become more flexible. The new mobile technologies and, of course, the internet have changed our understanding of the state. e-Government and e-democracy have become new tools in the way democratic governments create a direct link to citizens.

There are also other more critical issues that may emerge from this increasing use of the new technologies. The 'Big Brother' state, as described in George Orwell's *1984*, may yet become a reality. Digital televisions create an interactive platform that can lead to a better service for the customer, but also to greater control by the state and large private corporations. The high number of surveillance cameras in European countries is important to preserve security, but could also lead to the surveillance state and all its negative implications.

Towards multicultural societies? The challenge of immigration

In spite of the social differences, lifestyles have converged across Europe. We cannot speak of a European society, but the cultural traits of most European countries are fairly similar. Social stratification has become comparable across all countries. The dominance of the services sector, a declining industrial sector and a very small, but efficient agricultural sector are the characteristics of the main employment sectors in Europe. However, there are still substantial differences between Western and Eastern Europe. Poland and Romania, for example, still have very large agricultural sectors. In spite of this, European integration will certainly lead to a decrease in the number of people working in the agricultural sector.

Since the early 1950s, Western Europe has experienced several immigration waves. Today we have multicultural societies in most Western European countries. Many children of immigrants have become integrated in the new societies and become citizens of the country. This multiculturalism if socially integrated is a source of wealth and diversity for the country and society. All northern countries have a very multicultural outlook, probably strongest in the UK, France and the Netherlands.

Meanwhile, the Southern European countries, which were emigration countries, have become new targets for immigrants. The population of Spain has been growing considerably, at least partly because of the number of immigrants that have come to the country since the early 1990s.

Overall, immigration has increased considerably in the same period. The main reason is that we now have global immigration movements from the southern hemisphere to the northern one, and from east to west. All this leads to new challenges for European societies. The decline of populations in most countries is leading to a necessary rethinking about immigration. Apart from more coordination between EU member states in relation to immigration policy, integration today also requires a European dimension, because most immigrants, like most European citizens, have to be more mobile in the context of an emerging single European market.

The unification of the continent as an historical milestone: towards a region of democratic peace and stability

In the past millennium, the European nations went to war with each other and concentrated their energies in trying to achieve supremacy over their neighbours. Such national behaviour started to change after 1945, after two 'European' civil wars in 1914–18 and 1939–45. The division of Europe soon afterwards contributed to a change of mentalities among European political elites. Such diffusion of behaviour was reinforced by the democratic nature of regimes in most European countries. The Franco–German reconciliation in the early 1950s must be regarded as the beginning of such a change of mentality. The creation of the European Communities in the 1950s allowed a new Europe based on democratic peace to be established. In spite of the cold war, which was dominated by the United States and Russia, Europeans on both sides of the Iron Curtain contributed to this unification process. The legendary Ostpolitik of Hans-Dietrich Genscher towards East Germany and Poland cannot be underestimated. It created conditions for dialogue, in spite of the differences of regimes. Václav Havel's heroic fight for democracy and human rights as a member of the Charta 77, along with other dissidents in Czechoslovakia, was a further contribution to the European integration process. The Solidarity protest movement in Poland in the 1980s contributed immensely to the change from an authoritarian dictatorship under General Jaruzelski to a semi-presidential democracy. The Iron Curtain began to be porous on the border between Austria and Hungary in 1989. Many East Germans fled the country through Hungary and Austria and moved to West Germany. Finally, on 9 November 1989 the Fall of the Berlin Wall ended the division of Europe. West and East became part of a new era in Europe and European integration became a central process.

However, war still continued to shape the continent. In 1991, the Balkan wars erupted and confirmed that divisive nationalisms were still creating wars in Europe. The wars lasted until 1999. Since then nationalist and ethnic divisions have continued to prevail in the Balkans. The United Nations, with a strong contribution from NATO and the EU, sent peacekeeping forces and civilian reconstruction teams to improve the situation in these countries. From the former Yugoslav states, only Slovenia was able to escape the atrocities of war and move peacefully towards European integration. In spite of this positive example, in the massacre of Srebrenica in 1995 by Bosnian-Serbs against Bosniaks allegedly carried out by Radko Mladić, over 8,000 Bosnian men and boys were killed on 11–13 July 1995. This was characterised by the United Nations as genocide and awakened memories of the Holocaust against the Jewish population by the National Socialist regime during the Second World War and the Rwanda genocide against the Tutsis perpetrated by the Hutus in April–July 1994. This atrocious event was even more shocking because peacekeepers did not intervene and allowed the massacre to take place. Most of these soldiers were Dutch, so the Dutch government, after a damaging report, decided to resign before the end of the legislature on 15 April 2002 (BBC News, 16 April 2002). Today, Bosnia-Herzegovina still exists as a country because of the presence of the international community. The mistrust between Bosnian-Serbs, Bosniaks and Bosnian-Croats has prevented reconciliation. All institutions are controlled, or at least monitored, by the High Representative for Bosnia-Herzegovina who is also the Special Representative of the EU. The Serbian Republic (Republika Srpska) remains outside the federation as an autonomous entity.

The growing tension between Serbia and the Albanian Kosovo Liberation Army (KLA) in 1999 led again to the intervention of the international community through NATO. The bombardment of Serbia created the conditions for a settlement, in which the international peacekeeping forces could be deployed. In February 2008, almost a decade after the conflict, Kosovo was recognised as an independent country by the US, most European countries (apart from Spain, Greece, Romania, Slovakia, Cyprus and Bosnia-Herzegovina), and some countries in Latin America, Africa and Asia. However, Russia and China, partly because of their own centre-periphery relations, did not recognise its independence. Kosovo continues to be a major divisive issue in Serbia, where the Europeanists want to move on and focus their energies on becoming part of the European Union, while the nationalists regard Kosovo as part of Serbia and remain intransigent.

In spite of these negative events of contemporary European politics, the overall thrust has so far been towards peace. In 2004, after a decade of democratisation, liberalisation and restructuring of economy, politics and society a major enlargement eastwards, comprising ten countries and the Mediterranean islands of Malta and Cyprus, took place. It is changing the nature of European politics. In 2007, Bulgaria and Romania also joined the European Union. And the waiting list has three further candidate countries, Croatia, Macedonia and Turkey. The EU will focus first on the Balkans, before it considers whether to intensify the process of the integration of Turkey.

The proposed membership of Turkey has, so far, been a divisive issue in Europe. The supporters claim that the European Union would set an example of cosmopolitanism by integrating a largely Muslim country, which is oriented towards the West and has participated actively in European fora over the past six decades. Moreover, Turkey has a large market of over 72 million people. And, as a political actor, it would certainly be an asset to the European Union when dealing with conflicts in the Middle East.

The sceptics regarding the eventual membership of Turkey refer to the fact that it would be too costly to integrate the country, because of the lower level of development of regions in the eastern part of the country. Moreover, there are still many outstanding problems in Turkish democracy, such as human rights issues. Furthermore, some refer to the religion issue and tend to follow a loose or more concrete vision of Europe as a Christian Christian community (Giscard D'Estaing). Last, but not least, Turkey would also change some of the security aspects of the European Union. The most important aspect is probably the fight of the Turkish military against the Kurdish separatist group, the PKK (during 2008, the Turkish army crossed the border into Iraq to fight against the PKK) and it should be borne in mind that the Turkish government is extremely worried about the possibility of an independent Kurdish state in the north of Iraq.

Turkey's membership is opposed particularly in France and Austria, and both countries intend to conduct a referendum on it after all negotiations have been undertaken. This is a further hurdle that is affecting the process of Turkish integration into the EU.

This leads us to the question of where the borders of the European Union are or should be. The Ukraine and Georgia seem to be keen to become members. In North Africa, Morocco has twice submitted an application for membership. The European Union is divided on this issue; there are some countries that want to continue enlargement, for example as the United Kingdom, Spain, Italy, Sweden and Poland, and others who would like it to come to a halt, for example France, the Netherlands and Austria. The European Council of 14–15 December 2006 during the Finnish presidency led to a new workable strategy towards enlargement. However, any further enlargement will depend on a further reform of the institutions, so that more members can be accommodated (Magone, 2008: 201). This probably means the need to create greater efficiencies in the decision-making processes, particularly in political and economic decisions. As a result of the crisis in the eurozone, particularly in Greece, economic governance will become a crucial area of reform for a future revision of the Treaty of Lisbon.

In spite of these divisions over strategy, the European Union has become a region of democratic peace and stability. The upgrading of the Common Foreign and Security Policy is also leading to the expansion of such democratic peace and stability to other parts of the world. The EU–UN strategic partnership has created a framework for humanitarian intervention by the European Union. The growing militarisation of the CFSP project has been a necessary upgrade in order to enforce peace agreements and support civilian operations (see Chapter 11). This region of democratic peace and stability is supported by other organisations, such as the intergovernmental Council of Europe and the Organisation for Security and Cooperation in Europe (OSCE).

Conclusions: the rise of post-sovereign European politics

The European integration process since 1985 has transformed European politics towards a multilevel governance system. The erosion of national sovereignty has exerted major pressure on the move towards post-sovereign regimes of cooperation. Therefore, national politics is now intertwined with supranational European and global politics. We can observe this globalised and Europeanised politics in the processes of institutional transfer, mediatisation and marketisation of electoral markets and party politics, the use of flexible ways of communication, and the growing cooperation in immigration and integration policies. The financial crisis of 2008–9, created by the United States, is a further challenge for the European socioeconomic model. A successful path through this crisis will strengthen the credibility of European politics and although these difficulties are certainly challenges, they are also to be seen as opportunities for Europe to reinvent itself.

References

Ågh, Attila (1996), Democratic Parliamentarianism in Hungary: The First Parliament (1990–94) and the Entry of the Second Parliament. In: David M. Olson and Philip Norton (eds), *The New Parliaments of Central and Eastern Europe*. London: Frank Cass, pp. 16–39.

—— (1998a), *The Politics of Central Europe*. London: Sage.

—— (1998b), The End of the Beginning: The Partial Consolidation of East Central European Parties and Party Systems. In: Paul Pennings and Jan-Erik Lane (eds), *Comparing Party System Change*. London: Routledge, pp. 202–16.

—— (2003), *Anticipatory and Adaptive Europeanization in Hungary*. Budapest: Hungarian Centre for Democracy Studies.

—— (2006), *Eastern Enlargement and the Future of the EU27: EU Foreign Policy in a Global World*. Budapest: 'Together Europe' Research Centre of the Hungarian Academy of Sciences.

—— (2007), The Role of ECE Parliaments in EU Integration. In: Ronald Holzhacker and Erik Albaek (eds), *Democratic Governance and European Integration: Linking Societal and State Processes of Democracy*. Cheltenham: Edward Elgar, pp. 249–67.

Aguiar, Joaquim (1985a), Partidos, estruturas patrimonialistas e poder funcional: A crise da legitimidade, *Análise Social*, 21: 759–83.

—— (1985b), Portugal: The Hidden Fluidity in an Ultra-Stable Party System. In: *Conflict and Change in Modern Portugal 1974–1984*. Walter C. Opello and Eduardo de Sousa Ferreira (eds). Lisbon: Teorema, pp. 101–26.

—— (1986), *O Pós-Salazarismo. 1974–1984*. Lisbon: Dom Quixote.

Albertazzi, Daniele and Duncan McDonnell (2005), The Lega Nord in the Second Berlusconi Government: In a League of Its Own, *West European Politics*, 28(5): 952–72.

Albrecht, Johan and Bas Arts (2005), Climate Policy Convergence in Europe: An Assessment Based on National Communications to the UNFCC, *Journal of European Public Policy*, 12(5): 885–902.

Alford, Robert (1964), *Party and Society: The Anglo-American Democracies*. London: John Murray.

Alliance for Lobbying Transparency and Ethics Regulation in the EU (ALTER-EU) (2009), The Commission's Lobby Register One Year On: Success or Failure? Brussels: ALTER-EU. Posted on website at: www.alter-eu.org/sites/default/files/documents/register-assessment-after-one-year.pdf (accessed 10 March 2010).

—— (2010), Which lobby firms are on the European Commission's Register of Interest Representatives, which ones are not? Posted on website at: www.alter-eu.org/sites/default/files/documents/eu-lobby-firms-registration.pdf (accessed 12 March 2010).

Altendorfer, Otto (2000), Wahlkampf in Deutschland. In: *Handbuch Der Moderne Medienwahllkampf: Professionelles Wahlmanagement unter Einsatz neuer Medien, Strategien und Psychologien*. Eichstätt: Media Plus Verlag, pp. 65–76.

—— Heinrich Wiedemann and Hermann Mayer (2000), *Handbuch Der Moderne Medienwahllkampf. Professionelles Wahlmanagement unter Einsatz neuer Medien, Strategien und Psychologien*. Eichstätt: Media Plus Verlag.

Altunişik, Meliha Benli and Özlem Tür (2005), *Turkey: Challenges of Continuity and Change*. London: Routledge.

Anderson, M.S. (1963), *Europe in the Eighteenth Century 1713–1783*. London: Longman.

Andeweg, Rudy and Galen Irwin (2002), *The Politics and Governance in the Netherlands*. Basingstoke: Palgrave.

Andonova, Liliane B. (2005), The Europeanization of Environmental Policy in Central and Eastern Europe. In: Frank Schimmelfennig and Ulrich Sedelmeier (eds), *The Europeanization of Central and Eastern Europe*. Ithaca, NY: Cornell University Press, pp. 135–55.

Angelov, Goran (2008), Trial and Error Experience: Local Self-Governance in Macedonia. In: Zdravko Zlopaka (ed.), *Block by Block. It's Good to Build Well. Models of Organisation of Local Self-Governance*. Banja Luka: Enterprise Development Agency, pp. 124–77.

Arco Latino (2008), available online at: www.arcolatino.org/en (accessed 10 October 2008).

Arendsen, Ger (2003), *Paises Baixos: El Panorama Canviant del Govern Local*. Col-lécio Món Local 8. Barcelona: Universitat Autonoma de Barcelona – Institut de Ciencies Politiques i Socials.

Armingeon, Klaus (2001a), Institutionalising the Swiss Welfare State. *West European Politics*, 24(2): 145–68.

—— (2001b), Schweiz: Das Zusammenspiel von langer demokratischer Tradition, direkter Demokratie, Föderalismus und Korporatismus. In: Werner Reutter and Peter Rütters (eds), *Verbände und Verbandssysteme in Westeuropa*. Opladen: Leske & Budrich, pp. 405–26.

—— (2006), Probleme des Übergangs vom Korporatismus zum Pluralismus. In: Ferdinand Karlhofer and Emmerich Tálos (eds), *Sozialpartnerschaft: Österreichische und Europäische Perspektiven*. Wien: LIT, pp. 135–58.

Arter, David (1996), *Parties and Democracy in the Post-Soviet Republics: The Case of Estonia*. Aldershot: Ashgate.

—— (1999), *Scandinavian Politics Today*. Manchester: Manchester University Press.

—— (2001), Regionalization in the European Peripheries: The Cases of Northern Norway and Finnish Lapland, *Regional and Federal Studies*, 11(2): 94–114.

—— (ed.) (2007), *Comparing and Classifying Legislatures*. London: Frank Cass.

Assemblée Nationale (2002–7), *Recueil des Statistiques XIIeme Legislature*. Annual reports (pdf), available online at: www.assemblee-nationale.fr (accessed 25 January 2009).

Assembly of European Regions (AER) (2008), available online at: www.aer.eu (accessed 10 October 2008).

Association of European Border Regions (AEBR) (2008), available online at: www.aebr.net/ (accessed 10 October 2008).

Auel, Katrin (2007), Adapting to Europe: Strategic Europeanization of National Parliaments. In: Ronald Holzhacker and Erik Albaek (eds), *Democratic Governance and European Integration: Linking Societal and State Processes of Democracy*. Cheltenham: Edward Elgar, pp. 157–89.

Auffermann, Burkhard (2009), Das politische System Finnlands. In:Wolfgang Ismayr (ed.), *Die politischen Systeme Westeuropas*. Opladen: Leske & Budrich, pp. 183–216.

Aylott, Nicholas (1999), The Swedish Social Democratic Party. In: Robert Ladrech and Philippe Marlière (eds), *Social Democratic Parties in the European Union: History, Organization, Policies*. Basingstoke: Palgrave, pp. 189–203.

—— (2005), 'President Persson': How Did Sweden Get Him? In: Thomas Poguntke and Paul Webb (eds), *The Presidentialization of Politics: A Comparative Study of Modern Democracies*. Oxford: Oxford University Press, pp. 176–98.

Bach, Maurizio (1995), *Die Bürokratisierung Europas: Verwaltungseliten, Experten und Politische Legitimation in Europa*. Frankfurt a. M.: Campus 1999.

Bäck, Henry (2007), *Suécia: les autoritats del nivell regional abocades a l'abolició o al renaixement*. Col-lecció Estudis. Serie Govern Local 4. Barcelona: Universitat Autonoma de Barcelona – Institut de Ciencies Politiques i Socials.

Badiello, Lorenza (2004), La Representación Regional en Bruselas: Evolución, Funciones y Perspectivas. In: Francesc Morata (ed.), *Gobernanza multinivel en la Unión Europea*. Valencia: Tirant lo Blanch, pp. 327–68.

Bahro, Horst, Bernhard H. Bayerlein and Ernst Veser (1998), Duverger's Concept: Semi-presidential Government Revisited, *European Journal of Political Research*, 34: 201–24.

Bailey, David and Lisa Propris (2002), The 1988 Reform of the Structural Funds: Entitlement or Empowerment? *Journal of European Public Policy*, 9(3): 408–28.

Baldersheim, Harald and Anne Lise Fimreite (2005), Norwegian Centre–Periphery Relations in Flux: Abolition or Reconstruction of Regional Governance, *West European Politics*, 28(4): 764–80.

Baldini, Gianfranco and Salvatore Vassallo (2001), Le regioni alla ricerca di una nuova identità istituzionale. In: Mario Caciagli and Alan Zuckerman (eds), *Politica in Italia. I Fatti dell'Anno e le Interpretazioni. Edizione 2001*. Bologna: il Mulino, pp. 127–45.

Baldwin, Richard and Charles Wyplosz (2004), *The Economics of European Integration*. London: McGraw-Hill.

Balme, Richard (1998a), The French Region as a Space for Public Policy. In: Patrick le Galès and Christian Lequesne (eds), *Regions in Europe*. London: Routledge, pp. 166–98.

—— (1998b), Las condicionees de la acción colectiva regional. In: Francisco Letamenda (ed.), *Nacionalidades y regiones en la Unión Europea*. Madrid: Fundamentos, pp. 69–91.

Bardi, Luciano (2007), Electoral Change and its Impact on the Party System in Italy, *West European Politics*, 30(4): 711–32.

Barreñada, Isaias (2006), Alliance of Civilizations, Spanish Public Diplomacy and Cosmo-politan Proposal, *Mediterranean Politics*, 11(1): 99–104.

Barry, Frank, John Bradley and Aoife Hannan (2001), The Single Market, the Structural Funds and Ireland's Recent Economic Growth, *Journal of Common Market Studies*, 39(3): 537–52.

Bartolini, Stefano (2000), *The Political Mobilization of the European Left, 1860–1980: The Class Cleavage*. Cambridge: Cambridge University Press.

—— (2005), *Restructuring Europe. Centre Formation, System Building, and Political Structuring between the Nation State and the European Union*. Oxford: Oxford University Press.

—— and Peter Mair (1990), *Identity, Competition and Electoral Volatility. The Stabilisation of European Electorates 1885–1985*. Cambridge: Cambridge University Press.

Basabe Lloréns, Felipe and Maria Teresa Gonzalez Escudero (2001), The Parliament of Spain: Slowly Moving onto the European Union. In: Andreas Maurer and Wolfgang Wessels (eds), *National Parliaments on their Ways to Europe: Losers or Latecomers?* Baden-Baden: Nomos Verlag, pp. 199–221.

Baukloh, Anja (2001), Portugal: Vom autoritären Korporatismus zum demokratischen Pluralismus. In: Werner Reutter and Peter Rütters (eds), *Verbände und Verbands-systeme in Westeuropa*. Opladen: Leske & Budrich, pp. 355–79.

Bauman, Zygmunt (2001), *The Individualised Society*. London: Sage.

Baun, Michael and Dan Marek (2006), Regional Policy and Decentralization in the Czech Republic, *Regional and Federal Studies*, 16(4): 409–28.

BBC News (2009), available online at: www.bbc.co.uk (accessed 11 January 2009).

Behnen, Michael (2002), Bürgerliche Revolution und Reichsgründung (1848–71). In: Martin Vogt (ed.), *Deutsche Geschichte – Von den Anfängen zur Gegenwart*. Frankfurt a. M.: Fischer, pp. 451–516.

Bell, John (2006), *Judiciaries within Europe: A Comparative Review*. Cambridge: Cambridge University Press.

Benz, Arthur (1998), German Regions in the European Union. From Joint Policy-Making to Multi-Level Governance. In: Patrick Le Galès and Christian Lequesne (eds), *Regions in Europe*. London: Routledge, pp. 111–29.

—— (2000), Two Types of Multi-Level Governance: Intergovernmental Relations in German and EU Regional Policy, *Regional and Federal Studies*, 10(3): 21–44.

Bélanger, Eric and Kees Aarts (2006), Explaining the Rise of the LPF: Issues, Discontent, and the 2002 Dutch Election, *Acta Politica*, 41(1): 4–20.

Bell, Daniel (1962), *The End of Ideology: On the Exhaustion of Political Ideas in the Fifties*. London: Collier Books.

Bell, David S. (2000), *Parties and Democracy in France: Parties under Presidentialism*. Aldershot: Ashgate.

Bellamy, Richard (ed.) (2006), *Constitutionalism and Democracy*. Dartmouth: Ashgate.

—— and Dario Castiglione (eds) (1996), Constitutionalism in Transformation: European and Theoretical Perspectives, special issue of *Political Studies Association*, 44(3).

Benoit, Kenneth (2003), Evaluating Hungary's Mixed Electoral System. In: Matthew Soberg Shugart and Martin P. Wattenberg (eds), *Mixed-Member Electoral Systems*. Oxford: Oxford University Press, pp. 477–93.

Bergman, Torbjörn (1993), Formation Rules and Minority Governments, *European Journal of Political Research*, 23: 55–66.

—— and Thomas Larue (2004), The regime parlamentaire en Suéde. In: Olivier Costa, Eric Kerrouche and Paul Magnette (eds), *Vers un renouveau du parlamentarisme en Europe?* Bruxelles: Éditions Université Libre de Bruxelles, pp. 231–54.

Better Regulation (2007), *Bodies in Ireland with Regulatory Powers. As of February 2007*. Paper posted on Irish Better Regulation website www.betterregulation.ie/eng/index. asp?docID = 97 (accessed 14 August 2008).

Beyers, Jan and Guido Dierickx (1998), The Working Groups of the Council of the European Union: Supranational or Intergovernmental Negotiations? *Journal of Common Market Studies*, 36(3): 289–317.

Bezes, Philippe (2001), Defensive vs. Offensive Approaches to Administrative Reform in France (1988–97): The Leadership Dilemmas of French Prime Ministers, *Governance: An International Journal of Policy and Administration*, 14(1): 99–132.

Bideleux, Robert and Ian Jeffries (2007a), *A History of Eastern Europe: Crisis and Change*. London: Routledge.

—— and —— (2007b), *The Balkans: A Post-Communist History*. London: Routledge.

Bindi Calussi, Federiga and Stefano B. Grassi (2001), The Parliament of Italy: From Benevolent Player to Active Player. In: Andreas Maurer and Wolfgang Wessels (eds), *National Parliaments on their Way to Europe: Losers or Latecomers?* Baden-Baden: Nomos Verlag, pp. 269–99.

Blatter, Joachim, Matthias Kreutzer, Michaela Rentl and Jan Thiele (2008), The Foreign Relations of European Regions: Competences and Strategies, *West European Politics*, 31(3): 464–90.

Blondel, Jean (1995), *Comparative Government: An Introduction*. London: Prentice Hall.

—— (2001a), Cabinets in Post-Communist East-Central Europe and in the Balkans. In: Jean Blondel and Ferdinand Müller-Rommel (eds), *Cabinets in Eastern Europe*. Basingstoke: Palgrave, pp. 1–14.

—— (2001b), Macedonia. In: Jean Blondel and Ferdinand Müller-Rommel (eds), *Cabinets in Eastern Europe*. Basingstoke: Palgrave, pp. 152–61.

—— and S.A. Andreev (2001), Bulgaria. In: Jean Blondel and Ferdinand Müller-Rommel (eds), *Cabinets in Eastern Europe*. Basingstoke: Palgrave, pp. 131–41.

—— and L. Chiodi (2001), Albania. In: Jean Blondel and Ferdinand Müller-Rommel (eds), *Cabinets in Eastern Europe*. Basingstoke: Palgrave, pp. 142–51.

—— and M. Cotta (eds) (2001), *The Nature of Party Government*. Basingstoke: Palgrave.

—— and S. Matteucci (2001), Moldova. In: Jean Blondel, Ferdinand Müller-Rommel (eds), *Cabinets in Eastern Europe*. Basingstoke: Palgrave, pp. 120–30.

—— and Ferdinand Müller-Rommel (2001), Poland. In: Jean Blondel and Ferdinand Müller-Rommel (eds), *Cabinets in Eastern Europe*. Basingstoke: Palgrave, pp. 50–61.

—— and I. Penescu (2001), Romania. In: Jean Blondel and Ferdinand Müller-Rommel (eds), *Cabinets in Eastern Europe*. Basingstoke: Palgrave, pp. 109–19.

—— and F. Privitera (2001), Serbia and the New Yugoslavia. In: Jean Blondel and Ferdinand Müller-Rommel (eds), *Cabinets in Eastern Europe*. Basingstoke: Palgrave, pp. 184–92.

—— and S. Selo-Sabic (2001a), Croatia. In: Jean Blondel and Ferdinand Müller-Rommel (eds), *Cabinets in Eastern Europe*. Basingstoke: Palgrave, pp. 162–72.

—— and —— (2001b), Bosnia-Herzegovina. In Jean Blondel and Ferdinand Müller-Rommel (eds), *Cabinets in Eastern Europe*. Basingstoke: Palgrave, pp. 173–83.

Blümel, Barbara and Christine Neuhold (2001), The Parliament of Austria: A Large Potential with Little Implications. In: Andreas Maurer and Wolfgang Wessels (eds), *National Parliaments on their Ways to Europe: Losers or Latecomers?* Baden-Baden: Nomos Verlag, pp. 313–36.

Boeckh, Katin and Ekkehard Völkl (2007), *Ukraine: Von der Roten zur Orangenen Revolution*. Regensburg: Verlag Friedrich Pustet.

Bogdanor, Vernon (ed.) (1988), *Constitutions in Democratic Politics*. Aldershot: Gower.

—— (1999), *Devolution in the United Kingdom*. Oxford: Oxford University Press.

Bolleyer, Nicole (2006), Intergovernmental Arrangements in Spanish and Swiss Federalism: The Impact of Power-Concentrating and Power-Sharing Executives on Intergovernmental Institutionalization, *Regional and Federal Studies*, 16(4): 385–408.

Borrás, Susana and Kerstin Jacobsson (2004), The Open Method of Coordination and New Governance Patterns in the EU, *Journal of European Public Policy*, 11(2): 185–208.

Börzel, Tanja (2000), Why There Is No Southern Problem: On Environmental Leaders and Laggards in the EU, *Journal of European Public Policy*, 7(1): 141–62.

—— (2001), Non-Compliance in the European Union. Pathology or Statistical Artefact? *Journal of European Public Policy*, 8(5): 803–24.

—— (2002), *States and Regions in the European Union: Institutional Adaptation in Germany and Spain*. Cambridge: Cambridge University Press.

—— (2005), Europeanization: How the European Union Interacts with Its Member States. In: Simon Bulmer and Christian Lequesne (eds), *The Member States of the European Union*. Oxford: Oxford Uiversity Press, pp. 25–44.

—— and Thomas Risse (2000), *When Europe Hits Home: Europeanization and Domestic Change*. European University Institute, working papers, no. 56.

—— and —— (2003), Conceptualizing the Domestic Impact of Europe. In: Kevin Featherstone and Claudio M. Radaelli (eds), *The Politics of Europeanization*. Oxford: Oxford University Press, pp. 57–80.

Bourdieu, Pierre (1989), *La Noblesse d'État. Grandes Écoles et esprit de corps*. Paris: Minuit.

Bourgeois, Geert (2004), *Buitenlands Beleid en Internationale Samenwerking. Beleidsnota 2004–2009*. Vlaams minister van Bestuurszaken, Buitenlands Beleid, Media en Toerisme, posted on the website of the Ministry of Foreign Affairs as the main policy document http://iv.vlaanderen.be/nlapps/docs/default.asp?fid = 233 (accessed 6 September 2009).

Bourne, Angela K. (2007), Regional Europe. In: Michelle Cini (ed.), *European Union Politics*. Oxford: Oxford University Press, pp. 287–303.

Bouwen, Pieter (2002), Corporate Lobbying in the European Union: The Logic of Access, *Journal of European Public Policy*, June, 9(3): 365–90.

—— (2004), The Logic of Access to the European Parliament. Business Lobbying in the Committee on Economic and Monetary Affairs, *Journal of Common Market Studies*, 42(3): 473–95.

—— and M. McCown (2007), Lobbying vs. Litigation: Political and Legal Strategies of Interest Representation in the European Union, *Journal of European Public Policy*, 14(3): 422–43.

Bradley, John (2006), Evaluating the Impact of European Union Cohesion Policy in Less Developed Countries and Regions, *Regional Studies*, 40(2): 189–99.

Brans, Marleen and Annie Hondeghem (1999), The Senior Civil Service in Belgium. In: Edward C. Page and Vincent Wright (eds), *Bureaucratic Elites in Western European States: A Comparative Analysis of Top Officials*. Oxford: Oxford University Press, pp. 121–46.

—— Christiaan de Visscher and Diederik Vancoppenolle (2006), Administrative Reform in Belgium: Maintenance or Modernisation? *West European Politics*, 29(5): 979–98.

Bréchon, Pierre (2000), Religious Voting in a Secular France. In: David Broughton and Hans-Martien ten Napel (eds), *Religion and Mass Electoral Behaviour in Europe*. London: Routledge, pp. 97–117.

Bretherton, Charlotte and John Vogler (2005), *The European Union as a Global Actor*. Second edition. London: Routledge.

Brinkmann, Sören (2001), Spanien: der lange Weg in die Zivilgesellschaft. In: Werner Reutter and Peter Rütters (eds), *Verbände und Verbandssysteme in Westeuropa*. Opladen: Leske & Budrich, pp. 427–51.

Brinton, Crane (1934), *A Decade of Revolution 1789–1799*. New York: Harper & Brothers.

—— (1952), *The Anatomy of Revolution*. New York: Prentice-Hall.

British Telecom (2004), *The Digital Divide in 2025*. London: BT.

Broughton, David and M. Donoval (1999), *Comparing Party Systems in Western Europe*. London: Pinter.

Bruno, Isabelle, Sophie Jacquot and Lou Mandin (2006), Europeanization Through its Instrumentation: Benchmarking, Mainstreaming and the Open Method of Coordination . . . Toolbox or Pandora's Box, *Journal of European Public Policy*, 13(4): 519–36.

Brusis, Martin (2002), Between EU Requirements, Competitive Politics and National Traditions: Re-creating Regions in the Accession Countries of Central and Eastern Europe, *Governance*, 15(4): 531–59.

—— (2005), Between EU Requirements, Competitive Politics and National Traditions: Re-creating Regions in the Accession Countries of Central and Eastern Europe, *Governance: An International Journal of Public Administration and Institutions*, 15(4): 531–59.

—— and Vesselin Dimitrov (2001), Executive Configuration and Fiscal, *Policy*, 8(6): 888–910.

Brzezinski, Zbigniew (1965), *The Soviet Block: Unity and Conflict*. Cambridge, MA: Harvard University Press.

Bull, Hedley (2003), *The Anarchical Society: A Study of Order in World Politics*. Basingstoke: Palgrave.

Bull, Martin and Joerg Baudner (2004), Europeanization and Italian Policy for the Mezzogiorno, *Journal of European Public Policy*, 11(6): 1058–76.

—— and P. Heywood (1994), (eds), *West European Communist Parties after the Revolution of 1989*. Basingstoke: Macmillan.

—— and James Newell (2005), *Italian Politics*. Cambridge: Polity Press.

—— and Gianfranco Pasquino (2007), A Long Quest in Vain: Institutional Reforms in Italy, *West European Politics*, 30(4): 670–91.

Bullmann, Udo (ed.) (1993), *Die Politik der dritten Ebene: Regionen im Europa der Union*. Baden-Baden: Nomos Verlagsgesselschaft.

Bulmer, Simon and C. Lequesne (eds) (2005), *The Member-States of the European Union*. Oxford: Oxford University Press.

Bundesamt für Justiz (2006), *Zahl der Richter, Staatsanwälte und Vertreter des öffentlichen Interesses in der Rechtspflege der Bundesrepublik Deutschland am 31. Dezember 2006*. Pdf document posted on website of Bundesministerium für Justiz at: www.bmj.de (accessed 14 September 2008).

—— (2008), *Gerichte des Bundes und der Länder am 1. Januar 2008 (ohne Dienst-und Ehrengerichtsbarkeit)*. Pdf document posted on website of Bundesministerium für Justiz at: www.bmj.de (accessed 14 September 2008).

Bundeskanzleramt Österreich (2006), *Das Personal des Bundes in Zahlen*. Wien: Bundeskanzleramt.

Bundesministerium des Innern (BMI) (2007), *Der öffentliche Dienst in Deutschland. Ein Überblick*. Berlin: BMI.

Bundesministerium für Justiz (2007), *The Austrian Judicial System. Institutions – Agencies – Services*. Vienna: Bundesministerium für Justiz.

Bundestag (2009), Online Database of Bundestag GESTA, statistical summary posted on website at: http://dip.bundestag.de/ (accessed 25 January 2009).

Burch, Martin (1988), The United Kingdom. In: Jean Blondel and Ferdinand Mueller-Rommel (eds), *Cabinets in Western Europe*. Basingstoke: Macmillan, pp. 17–32.

Burnham, June and Moshe Maor (1995), Converging Administrative Systems: Recruitment and Training in EU Member States. *Journal of European Public Policy*, 2(2): 185–204.

Bursens, Peter (2002), How Multi-Level are IGCs? The Belgium Federation and the 2000 Conference, *Regional and Federal Studies*, 12(3): 181–204.

Busch, Per-Olof and Helge Jörgens (2005), The International Sources of Policy Convergence: Explaining the Spread of Environmental Innovations, *Journal of European Public Policy*, 12: 860–84.

Caciagli, Mario (2006), *Regioni d'Europa. Devoluzioni, regionalismi, integrazione europea*. Bologna: il Mulino.

Campbell, David F.J. and Christian Schaller (eds) (2002), *Demokratiequalität in Österreich. Zustand und Entwicklungsperspektiven*. Opladen: Leske & Budrich.

—— Karin Liebhart, Renate Martinsen, Christian Schaller and Andreas Schedler (eds) (2006), *Die Qualität der österreichischen Demokratie. Versuch einer Annäherung*. Wien: Manz.

Campbell, John L. and Ove K. Pedersen (2007), The Varieties of Capitalism and Hybrid Success Denmark in the Global Economy, *Comparative Political Studies*, 40(3): 307–32.

Campmany, Juan (2005), *El Efecto ZP. 1.000 dias de campaña a la Moncloa*. Barcelona: Planeta.

Capano, Gilberto and Marco Giuliani (2003), The Italian Parliament: In Search of a New Role? In: Cristina Leston Bandeira (ed.), *Southern European Parliaments in Democracy*, special issue of *Journal of Legislative Studies*, 9(2): 8–34.

Capo Giol, Jordi (2003), The Spanish Parliament: The New Rules of the Game. In: Cristina Leston Bandeira (ed.), *Southern European Parliaments in Democracy*, special issue of *Journal of Legislative Studies*, 9(2): 85–106.

Caporaso, James and Joergen Wittenbrink (2006), The New Modes of Governance and Political Authority in Europe, *Journal of European Public Policy*, 13(4): 471–80.

Caramani, Daniele (2004), *The Nationalization of Politics: The Formation of National Electorates and Party Systems in Western Europe*. Cambridge: Cambridge University Press.

Carapeto, Carlos and Fátima Fonseca (2005), *Administração Pública. Modernização, Qualidade e Inovação*. Lisbon: Edições Silabo.

Cardona, Francisco and Thomas Dannequin (2010), *Can Civil Service Reforms Last? The European Union's 5th Enlargement and Future Policy Orientations*. Sigma working paper. Paris: OECD.

Carr, Raymond (1999), *España, 1808–1975*. Barcelona: Ariel.

Cassese, Sabino (1999), Italy's Senior Civil Service: An Ossified World. In: Edward C. Page and Vincent Wright (eds), *Bureaucratic Elites in Western European States: A Comparative Analysis of Top Officials*. Oxford: Oxford University Press, pp. 55–64.

—— (2003), The Age of Administrative Reform. In: Jack Hayward and Anand Menon (eds), *Governing Europe*. Oxford: Oxford University Press, pp. 128–38.

Castells, Manuel (2000), *The Power of Identity. Volume II of The Information Age: Economy, Society and Culture*. London: Blackwell.

Cecchini, P., M. Catinat and A. Jacquemin (1988), *The European Challenge 1992: The Benefits of a Single Market*. Aldershot: Wildwood House.

Cerny, Philippe (1990), *The Changing Architecture of Politics. Structure, Agency and the Future of the State*. London: Sage.

Chan, Kenneth and Ka-Lok Chan (2000), The Religious Base of Politics in Post-Communist Poland. In: David Broughton and Hans-Martien ten Napel (eds), *Religion and Mass Electoral Behaviour in Europe*. London: Routledge, pp. 176–97.

Chandler, J.A. (eds) (2000), *Comparative Public Administration*. London: Routledge.

Chari, Raj (2001), The EU 'Dimensions' in Economic Policy Making at the Domestic Level: Evidence from Labour Market Reform in Spain, *South European Society and Politics*, 6(1): 51–74.

Christelijk Nationaal Vakverbond (CNV) (2008), Christian National Trade Union Confederation from Protestant Christian Democratic Trade Subculture website at: www.cnv.nl (accessed 28 December 2008).

Christensen, Tom (2005), The Norwegian State Transformed? *West European Politics*, 28(4): 721–39.

Christiansen, Peter Munk, Asbjørn Sonne Nørgaard and Niels Chr. Sidenius (2001), Verbände und Korporatismus auf Dänisch. In: Werner Reutter and Peter Rütters (eds), *Verbände und Verbandssysteme in Westeuropa*. Opladen: Leske & Budrich, pp. 51–74.

Christiansen, Thomas (1997), Tensions of European Governance: Politicized Bureaucracy and Multiple Accountability in the European Commission, *Journal of European Public Policy*, 4(1): 73–90.

—— and Mark Gray (2004), The European Commission in a Period of Change: A New Administration for a New European Union? *Eipascope*, 2004 (3): 20–4.

—— and Knud Jørgensen (2000), Transnational Governance 'Above' and 'Below' the State: The Changing Nature of Borders in the New Europe, *Regional and Federal Studies*, 10(2): 62–77.

Chubb, Basil (1992), *The Government and Politics of Ireland*. London: Longman.

Church, Clive (2004), The Swiss Elections of October 2003: Two Steps to System Change? *West European Politics*, 27(3): 518–34.

—— (2008), The Swiss Elections of 21 October 2007: Consensus Fights Back, *West European Politics*, 31(3): 608–23.

Ciampani, Andrea and Davide Clari (2005), *Il Movimento Sindacale Transfrontaliero nella Governance Interregionale Europea. Il CSI Piemonte, Rhône-Alpes, Valle d'Aosta nella storia dell' integrazione europea*. Torino: Transalp.

Clogg, Richard (1998), *A Concise History of Greece*. Cambridge: Cambridge University Press.

Coakley, John (2000), The Foundations of Statehood. In: John Coakley and Michael Gallagher (eds), *Politics in the Republic of Ireland*. Third edition. London: Routledge, pp. 1–31.

Cobban, Alfred (1963), *A History of Modern France. Volume 2: 1799-1945*. Harmonds-worth: Penguin Books.

Cole, Alistair (1998), *French Politics and Society*. Hemel Hempstead: Prentice-Hall.

—— and Glyn Jones (2005), Reshaping the State: Administrative Reform and New Public Management in France, *Governance: An International Journal of Administration and Institutions*,18(4): 567–88.

Collignon, Stefan (2004), Is Europe Going Far Enough? Reflections on EU's Economic Governance, *Journal of European Public Policy*, 11(5): 909–25.

Collins, Neil and Mary O'Shea (2000),The Republic of Ireland. In: J.A.Chandler (ed.), *Comparative Public Administration*. London: Routledge, pp. 98–125.

Comité Economique et Sociale Européen (2002), *La societé civile organisée en Pologne, Republique tchéque, Slovakie et Hongrie*. Brussels: CES.

Commonwealth Secretariat (2009), website at: www.thecommonwealth.org (accessed 9 January 2009).

Conference of Peripheral and Maritime Regions (CPMR) (2008), website at: www.crpm.org/ (accessed 10 October 2008).

Connolly, Eileen and Eunan O'Halpin (2000), The Government and the Governmental System. In: John Coakley and Michael Gallagher (eds), *Politics in the Republic of Ireland*. London: Routledge, pp. 249–70.

Conradt, David P. (2001), *The German Polity*. Seventh edition. New York: Longman.

Consiglio Superiore de la Magistratura (2008), *The Italian Judicial System*. Rome: Consiglio Superiore de la Magistratura.

Corbett, Richard, Francis J. Jacobs and Michael Shackleton (2007), *The European Parliament*. London: John Harper Publishers.

Corte-Real, Isabel (2000), Administrative Reform in Portugal. In: Isabel Corte-Real, Koen Nomden, Michael Kelly and Franck Petiteville (eds), *Administrations in Transitions*. Maastricht: European Institute of Public Administration, pp. 1–26.

Cotta, Maurizio (1994), The Rise and Fall of the 'Centrality' of the Italian Parliament: Transformation of the Executive-Legislative Subsystem after the Second World War. In: Gary W. Copeland and Samuel C. Patterson (eds), *Parliaments in the Modern World: Changing Institutions*. Ann Arbor, MI: University of Michigan Press, pp. 59–84.

—— and Luca Verzichelli (2007), *Political Institutions in Italy*. Oxford: Oxford University Press.

Council for European Municipalities and Regions (CEMR) (2008), website at: www.ccre.org/ (accessed 10 October 2008).

Council of the European Union (2003), *A Secure Europe in a Better World. European Security Strategy*. Brussels, 13 December 2003.

—— (2008a), *European Security and Defence Policy.The Civilian Aspects of Crisis Management*. June 2008.

—— (2008b), *European Security and Defence Policy. Development of European Military Capabilities*. September 2008.

—— (2009), online database on ESDP structures and operations at: www.consilium.eu (accessed 9 January 2009).

Council of Ministers of the European Union (2010), 'Promoting Prosperity and Preserving Peace – The Council's Role in External Relations', html file posted on website at: www.consilium.europa.eu/showPage.aspx?id=248 (accessed 26 April 2010).

Courts Service (2005), *Sustaining the Momentum. Strategic Plan 2005–8*. Dublin: Courts Service.

Cowles, M.G., J. Caporaso and T. Risse (eds) (2001), *Transforming Europe. Europeanization and Domestic Change*. Ithaca, NY: Cornell University Press.

Cram, Laura (1997), *Policy-Making in the EU. Conceptual Lenses and the Integration Process*. London: Routledge.

—— (2001), Whither the Commission? Reform, Renewal and Issue Attention, *Journal of European Public Policy*, 8(5): 770–86.

Crampton, R. J. (2002), *The Balkans Since the Second World War*. London: Longman.

Crouch, Colin (1994), *Industrial Relations and European State Traditions*. Oxford: Oxford University Press.

Crowther, William and Steven D. Roper (1996), A Comparative Analysis of Institutional Development in the Romanian and Moldovan Legislatures. In: David M. Olson and Philip Norton (eds), *The New Parliaments of Central and Eastern Europe*. London: Frank Cass, pp. 133–60.

Czada, Roland (2005), Social Policy: Crisis and Transformation. In: Simon Green and William E. Paterson (eds), *Governance in Contemporary Germany*. Cambridge: Cambridge University Press, pp. 165–89

Dahme, Heinz-Jürgen (2008), Krise der öffentlichen Kassen und des Sozialstaats, *Aus Politik und Zeitgeschichte*, 12–13: 10–16.

Dalton, Russell J. (2002), Political Cleavages, Issues, and Electoral Change. In: Lawrence Le Duc, Richard G. Niemi and Pippa Norris (eds), *Comparing Democracies 2. New Challenges in the Study of Elections and Voting 2*. London: Sage, pp. 198–209.

Damgaard, Erik and Henrik Jensen (2006), Assessing Strengths and Weaknesses in Legislatures: The Case of Denmark, *Journal of Legislative Studies*, 12(3–4): 426–42.

Daniels, Philip (1999), Italy: Rupture and Regeneration? In: David Broughton and Mark Donovan (eds), *Changing Party Systems in Western Europe*. London: Pinter, pp. 71–95.

Dargie, Charlotte and Rachel Locke (1999), The British Senior Civil Service. In: Edward C. Page and Vincent Wright (eds), *Bureaucratic Elites in Western European States. A Comparative Analysis of Top Officials*. Oxford: Oxford University Press, pp. 78–204.

Davies, Norman (1998), *Europe: A History*. London: Pimlico.

Davis, R.H.C. (1988), *A History of Medieval Europe. From Constantine to Saint Louis*. London: Longman.

De Cecco, Marcello (2007), Italy's Dysfunctional Political Economy, *West European Politics*, 30(4): 763–83.

De Grand, Alexander (2004), The Legacy of Nationalism. In: Stanislao Pugliese (ed.), *Fascism, Anti-Fascism and Resistance in Italy*. Lanham, MD: Rowman & Littlefield, pp. 37–40.

Dehousse, Renaud (2003), Comitology: Who Watches the Watchmen? *Journal of European Public Policy*, 10(5): 798–813.

Della Porta, Donatella (2001a), A Judge's Revolution? Political Corruption and the Judiciary in Italy, *European Journal for Political Research*, 39: 1–21.

—— (2001b), *I partiti politici*. Bologna: il Mulino.

—— (2003), *I new global.Chi sono e cosa vogliono I critici della globalizzazione*. Bologna: il Mulino.

—— and Alberto Vanucci (1999), *Un Paese Anormale. Come la classe politica ha perso l'occasione di Mani Pulite*. Roma-Bari: Editori Laterza.

Della Sala, Vincent (1997), Hollowing Out and Hardening the State: European Integration and the Italian Economy, *West European Politics*, 20(1): 14–33.

—— (1998), The Relationship between the Italian Parliament and Government. In: Philip Norton (ed.), *Parliaments and Governments in Western Europe*. London: Frank Cass, pp. 73–93.

Delwit, Pascal (1999), Ecolo: les défis du 'plus grand' des partis verts en Europe. In: Pascal Delwit and Jean-Michel de Waele (eds), *Les Partis verts en Europe*. Brussels: Éditions Complexe, pp. 113–38.

—— (2003), *Composition, Decomposition et Recomposition du paysage politique en Belgique*. Brussels: Éditions Labor.

Den Boer, Monica and William Wallace (2000), Justice and Home Affairs. In: Helen Wallace and William Wallace (eds), *Policy-Making in the European Union*. Fourth edition. Oxford: Oxford University Press, pp. 523–42.

Department of Defence, Civil Protection and Sports and Department of Foreign Affairs – Switzerland (2004), *Swiss Neutrality*. Bern.

Department of Justice, Equality and Law Reform (2005), Strategy Statement 2005–7. Dublin: Department of Justice, Equality and Reform.

—— (2008), *Annual Report 2007*. Dublin: Department of Justice, Equality and Reform.

Department of the Taoiseach (2004), *Regulating Better. A Government White Paper Setting Out Six Principles of Better Regulation*. Dublin: Stationery Office.

Derlien, Hans-Ulrich (2003), Mandarins or Managers? The Bureaucratic Elite in Bonn 1970 to 1987 and Beyond, *Governance: An International Journal of Public Administration and Institutions*, 16(3): 401–23.

Derlien, Hans-Ulrich, Stefan Franck, Silke Heinemann and Stefan Lock (eds) (2005), *The German Public Service. Structure and Statistics*.Verwaltungswissenschaftliche Beiträge 35, Bamberg: Universität Bamberg.

De Winter, Lieven (1998), Parliaments and Governments in Belgium: Pioneers of Partyocracy. In: Philip Norton (ed.), *Parliaments and Governments in Western Europe*. London: Frank Cass, pp. 97–122.

—— and Joan Marcet i Morera (2000), Liberalism and Liberal Parties in the European Union. In: Lieven de Winter, Joan Marcet, Alastair H. Thomas, Ferdinand Müller-Rommel, Ruud A. Koole and Gérard Grunberg (eds), *Liberalism and Liberal Parties in the European Union*. Barcelona: Institut de Ciencies Politiques i Socials, pp. 13–23.

—— Donatella della Porta and Kris Deschouwer (1996), Comparing Similar Countries: Italy and Belgium. In: Kris Deschouwer, Lieven de Winter and Donatella della Porta (eds), *Partitocracies between Crises and Reforms: The Cases of Italy and Belgium*, special issue of *Res Publica*, 2: 215–36.

—— Marc Swyngedouw and Patrick Dumont, (2006), Party System(s) and Electoral Behaviour in Belgium: From Stability to Balkanisation, *West European Politics*, 29(5): 933–56.

—— Arco Timmermans and Patrick Dumont (2000), Belgium: On Government Agreements, Evangelists, Followers, and Heretics. In: Wolfgang C. Muller and Kaare Strom (eds), *Coalition Governments in Western Europe*. Oxford: Oxford University Press, pp. 300–55.

Dhimitri, Albana, Belinda Ikonomi and Majlinda Dhuka (2007), Regional Development Policy Performance in Albania. In: *Challenge of Regional Development in South East Europe/Strategies for Financing and Service Delivery*. Budapest: Fiscal Decentralization Initiative for Central and Eastern Europe, published online at: http://lgi.osi.hu/publications_datasheet.php?id = 368 (accessed 10 October 2008).

Diamanti, Ilvo (1996), The Northern League: From Regional Party to Party of Government. In: Stephen Gundle and Simon Parker (eds), *The New Italian Republic. From the Fall of the Berlin Wall to Berlusconi*. London: Routledge, pp. 113–29.

Dierickx, Guido (2003), Senior Civil Servants and Bureaucratic Change in Belgium, *Governance: An International Journal of Policy, Administrations and Institutions*, 16(3): 321–48.

Dietz, Martin and Ulrich Walwei (2007), Hartz IV: Reform der Reform? *Aus Politik und Zeitgeschichte*, 51–52 (17): 31–8.

Dimitrakopoulos, Dionnyssis G. (2001), Learning and Steering: Changing Implementation Patterns and the Greek Central Government, *Journal of European Public Policy*, 8(4): 604–22.

Dimitrova, Antoaneta (2005), Europeanization and Civil Service Reform in Central and Eastern Europe. In: Frank Schimmelpfennig and Ulrich Sedelmeier (eds), *The Europeanization of Central and Eastern Europe*. Ithaca, NY: Cornell University Press, pp. 71–90.

Dinan, Desmond (2004), *Europe Recast: A History of the European Union*. Basingstoke: Palgrave.

Direction de l'Administration Générale et de l'Équipement (2007), *Annuaire statistique de la Justice*. Paris: Direction de l'Administration générale et de l'Équipement.

Di Scala, Spencer (1995), *Italy: From Revolution to Republic, 1700 to the Present*. Boulder, CO: Westview Press.

Di Virgilio, Aldo (2005), Francia: le molte risorse del primo ministro. In: Gianfranco Pasquino (ed.), *Capi di governo*. Bologna: il Mulino, pp. 41–72.

Doctor, Mahrukh (2007), Why Bother with Interregionalism? Negotiations for a European Union-Mercosur Agreement, *Journal of Common Market Studies*, 45(2): 281–314.

Dølvik, Jon Erik (1999), *An Emerging Island? ETUC, Social Dialogue and the Europeanization of the Trade Unions in the 1990s*. Brussels: European Trade Union Institute.

Domstol (2008), website of the Norwegian Courts service at: www.domstol.no (accessed 17 September 2008).

Domstolsstyrelsen (2008), website of the Danish Courts service at: www.domstol.dk (accessed 17 September 2008).

Domstolsverket (2008), *Domstolstatistics.Court Statistics. Official Statistics of Sweden 2007*. Stockholm: Domstolsverket.

Donovan, Mark (1999), Italy: A Dramatic Case of Secularisation? In: David Broughton and Hans-Martien ten Napel (eds), *Religion and Mass Electoral Behaviour in Europe*. London: Routledge, pp. 140–56.

—— (2008), Il centro-destra: conflitti, unità e mobilitazione permanente. In: Mark Donovan and Paolo Onofri (eds), *Politica in Italia .I Fatti dell'Anno e le Interpretazioni. Edizione 2008*. Bologna: il Mulino, pp. 87–108.

Dorey, Peter (2004), Le Parlement en Grande-Bretagne. In: Olivier Costa, Eric Kerrouche and Paul Magnette (eds), *Vers un renouveau du parlementarisme en Europe?* Bruxelles: Éditions Université Libre de Bruxelles, pp. 107–30.

Dorn, Walter L. (1963), *Competition for Empire. 1740–1763*. New York: Harper & Row.

D'Orta, Carlo (2003), *What Future for the European Administrative Space?* Maastricht: EIPA working paper 2003, 5.

Drucker, Peter (2001), The Next Society: A Survey of the Near Future. *The Economist*, 3 November.

Drüke, Helmut (2004), Europas Stiefel drückt und zwickt. Grundprobleme der Wirtschaft Italiens, *Aus Politik und Zeitgeschichte*, 35–36: 18–25.

Due, Jesper, Jorgen Steen Petersen, Lars Kjerulf and Carsten Stroby (1995), Adjusting the Danish Model: Towards Centralised Decentralisation. In: Colin Crouch and Franz Traxler (eds), *Organised Industrial Relations in Europe: What Future?* Aldershot: Avebury, pp. 121–50.

Dufour, Christian (2005), 2003 Works Council Election Results and New Worker Representation Rules for SMEs. Posted on the EIROLINE database at: www.eurofound.europa.eu (accessed 31 December 2008), ID: FR0510103F of 27 October 2008.

Duggan, Christopher (1994), *A Concise History of Italy*. Cambridge: Cambridge University Press.

Düllfer, Jost (2002), Deutschland als Kaiserreich(1871–1918). In: Martin Vogt (ed.), *Deutsche Geschichte: Von den Anfängen bis zur Gegenwart*. Frankfurt a. M.: Fische, pp. 517–615.

Dumont, Patrick and Lieven de Winter (2000), Luxembourg: Stable Coalitions in a Pivotal Party System. In: Wolfgang C. Müller and Kaare Strøm (eds), *Coalition Governments in Western Europe*. Oxford: Oxford University Press, pp. 399–432.

—— and Philippe Poirier (2005), Luxembourg. In: *Political Data Yearbook*, special issue of *European Journal of Political Research*, 44(7–8): 1102–18.

Dunleavy, Patrick and R.A.W. Rhodes (1989), Government Beyond Whitehall. In: Henry Drucker, Patrick Dunleavy, Andrew Gamble and Gillian Peele (eds), *Developments in British Politics 2*. Basingstoke: Macmillan, pp. 107–43.

603

Dutch Presidency of the European Union (2004), 43rd Meeting of Directors-General Responsible for Public Administrative Reform.

Duverger, Maurice (1970), *Institutions et Droit Constitutionel*. Eleventh edition. Paris: Presses Universitaires de France.

Dyson, Kenneth (2000), EMU as 'Europeanization': Convergence, Diversity and Contingency, *Journal of Common Market Studies*, 38(4): 645–66.

—— and Kevin Featherstone (1996), Italy and EMU as 'Vincolo Esterno;: Empowering the Technocrats and Transforming the State, *South European Society and Politics*, 1(2): 272–99.

Ebbinghaus, Bernhard and Jelle Visser (1997), Der Wandel der Arbeitsbeziehungen im westeuropäischen Vergleich. In: Stefan Hradil and Stefan Immerfall (eds), *Die westeuropäischen Gesellschaften im Vergleich*. Opladen: Leske & Budrich, pp. 333–76.

Ehn, Peter, Magnus Isberg, Claes Linde and Gunnar Wallin (2003), Swedish Bureaucracy in an Era of Change. *Governance: An International Journal of Policy, Administration and Institutions*, 16(3): 429–58

Eisfeld, Rainer (1984), *Sozialistischer Pluralismus in Europa. Ansätze und Scheitern am Beispiel Portugal*. Köln: Verlag Wissenschaft und Politik.

Eising, Rainer (2001), Interessenvermittlung in der Europäischen Union. In: Werner Reutter and Peter Rütters (eds), *Verbände und Verbandssysteme in Westeuropa*. Opladen: Leske & Budrich, pp. 453–76.

Elgie, Robert (2000), Political Leadership: The President and the Taoiseach. In: John Coakley and Michael Gallagher (eds), *Politics in the Republic of Ireland*. London: Routledge, pp. 232–48.

—— (ed.) (2001), *Divided Government in Comparative Perspective*. Oxford: Oxford University Press.

—— (2003), *Political Institutions in Contemporary France*. Oxford: Oxford University Press.

Elias, Norbert (1976), *Über den Prozeß der Zivilisation* (2 volumes). Frankfurt a. M.: Suhrkamp.

Elster, Jon, Claus Offe and Ulrich K. Preuss (1998), *Institutional Design in Post-Communist Societies. Rebuilding the Ship at Sea*. Cambridge: Cambridge University Press.

Elvert, Jürgen (2001), Irland: Korporativismus aus Tradition. In: Werner Reutter and Peter Rütters (eds), *Verbände und Verbandssysteme in Westeuropa*. Opladen: Leske & Budrich, pp. 197–220.

Engels, Friedrich (1974), *The Condition of the Working Class in England*. Frogmore: Panther.

Enyedi, Zsolt (2000), Religious and Clerical Polarisation in Hungary. In: David Broughton and Hans-Martien ten Napel (eds), *Religion and Mass Electoral Behaviour in Europe*. London: Routledge, pp. 157–75.

Eriksen, Svein (1988), Norway. In: Jean Blondel and Ferdinand Müller-Rommel (eds), *Cabinets in Western Europe*. Basingstoke: Macmillan, pp. 183–96.

Erk, Jan (2005), From Vlaams Blok to Vlaamse Belang. The Belgian Far Right Renames Itself, *West European Politics*, 8(3): 493–502.

Esping-Andersen, Gösta (1985), *Politics against Markets: The Social Democratic Road to Power*. Princeton, NJ: Princeton University Press.

—— (1990), *The Three Worlds of Welfare Capitalism*. Princeton, NJ: Princeton University Press.

—— (1995), Post-Industrial Class Structures: An Analytical Framework. In: Gösta Esping-Andersen (ed.), *Changing Classes. Stratification and Mobility in Post-Industrial Societies*. London: Sage, pp. 7–31.

—— Zina Assimakopoulou and Kees van Kersbergen (1995), Trends in Contemporary Class Structuration: A Six-Nation Comparison. In: Gösta Esping-Andersen (ed.), *Changing Classes. Stratification and Mobility in Post-Industrial Societies*. London: Sage, pp. 32–57.

Etherington, John and Ana-Mar Fernandez (2006), Political Parties in Catalonia. In: David Hanley and John Loughlin (eds), *Political Parties in Spain*. Cardiff: University of Wales, pp. 74–107.

EUREGIO MaasRhine (2008), website at: www.euregio-mr.org/emr_site/index.php (accessed 10 October 2008).

European Anti-Fraud Office (2008), website at: http://ec.europa.eu/anti_fraud/index_en.html (accessed 17 September 2008).

European Commission (2000), Reforming the Commission. A White Paper. Brussels, 1 March COM (2000), 200 final (2 volumes).

—— (2001), *Building an Effective Partnership with the United Nations in the Fields of Development and Humanitarian Affairs*. Communication from the Commission to the Council and the European Parliament. Brussels, 2.5.2001, COM (2001), 231 final.

—— (2003a), *The European Union and the United Nations: The Choice of Multilateralism. Communication of the Commission to the Council and the European Parliament*, Brussels, 10.9.2003, COM (2003) 526 final.

—— (2003b), *Wider Europe – Neighbourhood: A New Framework for Relations with our Eastern and Southern Neighbours*. Brussels, 11 March 2003, COM (2000), 104 final.

—— (2004), *European Neighbourhood Policy. Strategy Paper*. Brussels, 12 May 2004, COM (2004), 373 final.

—— (2006a), *Questions and Answers on Emissions Trading and National Allocation Plans for 2008 to 2012*. Memo/06/452. Brussels, 29 November 2006.

—— (2006b), *On Strengthening the European Neighbourhood Policy*. Brussels, 4 December 2006, COM (2006), 726 final.

—— (2007a), Ten Years of European Employment Strategy. Luxembourg: Office of the Official Publications of the European Communities.

—— (2007b), *Working Together: The European Neighbourhood Policy*. Luxembourg: Office of the Official Publications of the European Communities.

—— (2007c), *Report of the Commission on the Working Committees during 2006*. Brussels, 20 December 2007, SEC (2007) 1713.

—— (2007d), *Employment in Europe 2007*. Luxembourg: Office of the Official Publications of the European Communities.

—— (2008a), Public Finances in EMU-2008. *European Economy*, X. Posted on DG Economic and Financial Affairs of European Commission at: http://ec.europa.eu/economy_finance/publications/publication_summary12834_en.htm (accessed 8 January 2008).

—— (2008b), *EU against Climate Change. Leading Global Action to 2020 and Beyond*. Luxembourg: Office of the Official Publications of the European Communities.

—— (2008c), *EU Environment-related Indicators 2008*. Brussels: European Commission.

—— (2008d), *Social Situation in the European Union 2007*. Luxembourg: Office of the Official Publications of the European Communities.

—— (2008e), *Barcelona Process: Union for the Mediterranean*. Brussels, 20 May 2008 COM (2008), 319 final.

—— (2009), EU Budget 2009, DG Financial Programming and Budget, http://ec.europa.eu/budget/index_en.htm (accessed 2 January 2009).

—— (2010), website at: www.europa.eu (accessed 19 June 2010).

—— (n.d.), *The European Neighbourhood Policy*. Leaflet.

European Defence Agency (2008), *Defence Data 2007*. Luxembourg: Office of the Official Publications of the European Communities.

European Economic and Social Committee (EESC) (2009), *The EESC: A Bridge Between Europe and European Civil Society*. Luxembourg: Office of the Official Publications of the European Communities.

European Foundation for Improvement of Living Conditions (EUROFOUND) (2007), *Varieties of Flexicurity: Reflections on Key Elements of Flexibility and Security*. Background paper EF/07/21 Dublin: EUROFOUND.

European Industrial Relations Observatory (2003), Annual Review for the Netherlands, available online at: www.eiro.eurofound.eu.int9 (accessed 30 March 2005).

European Industrial Relations Observatory (EIRO) (2008), European Industrial Relations Dictionary, available online at: www.eurofound.europa.eu (accessed 28 December 2008).

European Institute for Public Administration (2001), *Annual Report 2000.* Maastricht: EIPA.

—— (2003), *Study on the Use of the Common Assessment Framework in European Administrations,* Synthesis paper prepared for the 41st meeting of directors-general of public administration. Rome, December.

—— (2005), *Study on the Use of the Common Assessment Framework in European Public Administrations. 2nd European CAF Event.* Luxembourg 1–2 June 2005. Maastricht: EIPA, November.

Europol (2010), website of Europol at: www.europol.eu (accessed 19 April 2010).

Eythórsson, Grétar Thór and Detlef Jahn (2009), Das politische System Islands. In: Wolfgang Ismayr (ed.), *Die politischen Systeme Westeuropas.* Opladen: Leske & Budrich, pp. 195–218.

Evans, Anne and Gordon Evans (2001), Improving Government Decision-Making Systems in Lithuania and Latvia, *Journal of European Public Policy,* 8(6): 833–59.

Everson, Michelle (1998), Administering Europe? *Journal of Common Market Studies,* 36(2): 195–215.

Falkner, Gerda (1996a), The Maastricht Protocol on Social Policy: Theory and Practice. *Journal of European Social Policy,* 6(1): 1–16.

—— (1996b), European Works Councils and the Maastricht Social Agreement: Towards a New Social Policy? *Journal of European Public Policy,* 3(2): 192–208.

—— (2007), The EU's Social Dimension. In: Michelle Cini (ed.), *European Union Politics.* Oxford: Oxford University Press, pp. 271–86.

Farrell, David M. (1999), Ireland: A Party System Transformed? In: David Broughton and Mark Donovan (eds), *Changing Party Systems in Western Europe.* London: Pinter, pp. 30–47.

—— (2000), *Electoral Systems. A Comparative Introduction.* Basingstoke: Palgrave.

—— Mackerras, M. and McAllister, I. (1996), Designing Electoral Institutions: Varieties of STV Systems, *Political Studies,* 44: 24–43.

Featherstone, Kevin (2005), Introduction: 'Modernisation' and the Structural Constraints of Greek Politics, *West European Politics,* 28(2): 223–41.

—— and C.M. Radaelli (eds) (2003), *The Politics of Europeanization.* Oxford: Oxford University Press.

—— Georgios Kazamias and Dimitris Papadimitriou (2001), The Limits of External Empowerment: EMU, Technocracy and the Reform of the Greek Pension System, *Political Studies,* 49(3): 462–80.

Federal Department of Foreign Affairs (2007), *Rapport de politique étrangère.* 15 June, posted on website of the Ministry at: www.eda.admin.ch/etc/media lib/downloads/edazen/doc/publi.Par.0169.File.tmp/Aussenpolitischer%20Bericht_Fr_070627.pdf (accessed 5 September 2009).

Federatie Nederlandse Vakbeweging (FNV) (2008), website of the Dutch Trade Union Federation at: www.fnv.nl (accessed 28 December 2008).

Ferguson, Niall (2003, 2007), *Empire. How Britain Made the Modern World.* London: Penguin.

Ferrera, Maurizio (1996), 'The Southern Model' of Welfare State in Social Europe, *Journal of European Social Policy,* 6(1): 17–37.

—— (2005), *The Boundaries of Welfare.European Integration and the New Spatial Politics of Social Protection.* Oxford: Oxford University Press.

—— (2008), The European Welfare State: Golden Achievements, Silver Achievements, *West European Politics,* 31(1): 82–107.

—— Anton Hemerijk and Martin Rhodes (2000), *O Futuro da Europa Social. Repensar o Trabalho e a Protecção Social na Nova Economia.* Lisbon: Celta.

Fielding, Steven (1997), Labour's Path to Power. In: Andrew Geddes and Jonathan Tongue (eds), *Labour's Landslide. The British General Election 1997.* Manchester: Manchester University Press, pp. 23–35.

Fiers, Stefaan and André Krouwel (2005), The Low Countries: From 'Prime Minister' to President–Minister. In: Thomas Poguntke and Paul Webb (eds), *The Presidentialization of Politics: A Comparative Study of Modern Democracies.* Oxford: Oxford University Press, pp. 269–88.

Finer, Hermann (1949), *Theory and Practice of Government.* London: Methuen.

Finer, Samuel E. (1970), *Comparative Government.* London: Penguin Press.

—— (1999), *The History of Government* (3 volumes). Oxford: Oxford University Press.

Fink-Hafner, Danica (2005), Slovenia. In: *Political Data Yearbook 2004,* special issue of *European Journal of Political Research,* 44(7–8): 1179–87.

—— (2007), Slovenia. In: *Political Data Yearbook 2006,* special issue of *European Journal of Political Research,* 46(7–8): 1107–13.

Fischer Verlag (2008), *Der Fischer Weltalmanach 2008. Zahlen-Daten-Fakten.* Frankfurt a. M.: Fischer Taschenbuch Verlag.

Fix, Elisabeth (1999), *Italiens Parteiensystem im Wandel. Von der Ersten zur Zweiten Republik.* Frankfurt, a. M.: Campus.

Flora, Peter (1999), Introduction and Interpretation. In: Peter Flora, with Stein Kuhnle and Derek Urwin (eds), *State Formation, Nation-Building and Mass Politics in Europe. The Theory of Stein Rokkan.* Oxford: Oxford University Press, pp. 1–91.

—— with Stein Kuhnle and Derek Urwin (eds) (1999), *State Formation, Nation-Building and Mass Politics in Europe. The Theory of Stein Rokkan.* Oxford: Oxford University Press.

Føllesdal, Andreas (2006), Political Consumerism as a Change and Challenge. In: Michele Micheletti, Andreas Føllesdal and Dietlind Stolle (eds), *Politics, Products, and Markets. Exploring Political Consumerism. Past and Present.* New Brunswick, NJ: Transaction, pp. 3–20.

Foundethakis, Penelope (2003), The Hellenic Parliament: The New Rules of the Game. In: Cristina Leston Bandeira (ed.), *Southern European Parliaments in Democracy,* special issue of *Journal of Legislative Studies,* 9(2): 85–106.

Four Motors (2008), website at: www.4motors.eu/ (accessed 10 October 2008).

Frain, Maritheresa (1995), Relações entre o Presidente e o primeiro ministro em Portugal: 1985–95, *Análise Social,* XXX, 133(4): 653–78.

Franciscis, Maria Elisabetta de and Rosella Zannini (1992), Judicial Policy-Making in Italy: Constitutional Court. In: Mary L. Volcansek (ed.), *Judicial Politics and Policy-Making in Western Europe,* special issue of *West European Politics,* 15(3): 68–79.

Franklin, Mark (1985), *The Decline of Class Voting in Britain. Changes in the Basis of Electoral Choice, 1964–1983.* Oxford: Clarendon Press.

Frei Demokratische Partei (FDP) (2007), *Geschichte, Aufbau, Gremien und Bundesgeschäftsstellen.* Berlin: FDP.

Freire, André, Marina Costa Lobo and Pedro Magalhães (eds), *Portugal a Votos. As eleições legislativas de 2002.* Lisbon: Instituto de Ciencias Sociais, pp. 35–85.

French Presidency of the European Union (2008), Main Results of the EU–Russia Summit, posted on website at: www.eu2008.fr/PFUE/lang/en/accueil/PFUE-11_2008/PFUE-14.11.2008/CR_Sommet_UE_Russie.html (accessed 26 April 2010).

Friedrich, Carl J. (1952), *The Age of Baroque, 1610–60.* New York: Harper & Row.

—— (1966), *Totalitarian Dictatorship and Democracy.* New York: Praeger.

Fry, Geoffrey K. (1989), Inside Whitehall. In: Henry Drucker, Patrick Dunleavy, Andrew Gamble and Gillian Peele (eds), *Developments in British Politics 2.* Basingstoke: Macmillan, pp. 88–106.

Furlong, Paul (1995), Political Catholicism and the Strange Death of the Christian Democrats. In: Stephen Gundle and Simon Parker (eds), *The New Italian Republic. From the Fall of the Berlin Wall to Berlusconi*. London: Routledge, pp. 59–71.

Gabanyi, Anneli Ute (2002), Das politische System Rumäniens. In: Wolfgang Ismayr (ed.), *Die politische Systeme Osteuropas*. Opladen: Leske & Budrich, pp. 525–62.

Gallagher, Michael (1997), Electoral Systems and Voting Behaviour. In: Martin Rhodes, Paul Heywood and Vincent Wright (eds), *Developments in West European Politics*. Basingstoke: Macmillan, pp. 114–30.

—— (2010a), The Oireachtas: Parliament and President. In: John Oakley and Michael Gallagher (eds), *Politics in the Republic of Ireland*. London: Routledge, pp. 198–229.

—— (2010b), The Changing Constitution. In: John Oakley and Michael Gallagher (eds), *Politics in the Republic of Ireland*. London: Routledge, pp. 73–108.

—— M. Laver and P. Mair (2007), *Representative Government in Modern Europe. Institutions, Politics and Governments*. Boston, MA: McGraw-Hill.

Ganshof, F.L. (1964), *Feudalism*. New York: Harper & Row.

Geisler, Alexander and Ulrich Sarcinelli (2002), Modernisierung von Wahlkämpfen und Modernisierung von Demokratie? In: Andreas Dörner and Ludgera Vogt (eds), *Wahlkämpfe. Betrachtungen über ein demokratisches Ritual*. Frankfurt a. M.: Suhrkamp, pp. 43–67.

General Council of the Judiciary (2007), *The Spanish Justice System. All the Facts*. Madrid: General Council of the Judiciary.

Gerth, H.H. and C. Wright Mills (eds) (1946), *Essays from Max Weber*. New York: Oxford University Press.

Giannetti, Daniela (2005), Irlanda: Chairman or Chief? In: Gianfranco Pasquino (ed.), *Capi di governo*. Bologna: il Mulino, pp. 130–53.

Gianniti, Luigi and Nicola Lupo (2004), Il governo in parlamento: la fuga verso la decretazione delegate non basta. In: Stefano Ceccanti and Salvatore Vassallo (eds), *Come chiudere la transizione? Cambiamento, apprendimento e addattamento nel sistema politico italiano*. Bologna: il Mulino, pp. 225–44.

Giddens, Anthony (1992), *Sociology*. Cambridge: Polity Press.

—— (1998), *The Third Way: The Renewal of Social Democracy*. Cambridge: Polity Press.

Gierke, Otto von (1996), *Political Theories of the Middle Ages*. Bristol: Thoemmes Press.

Gilbert, Mark (1999), Le leggi Bassanini: una tappa intermedia nella riforma del governo locale. In: David Hine and Salvatore Vassallo (eds), *Politica in Italia. I Fatti dell'Anno e le Interpretazioni. Edizione 99*. Bologna: il Mulino, pp. 161–80.

Gillespie, Richard (1999), *Spain and the Mediterranean: Developing a European Policy towards the South*. Basingstoke: Macmillan.

—— (2002), The Valencia Conference: Reinvigorating the Barcelona Process? *Mediterranean Politics*, 7(2): 105–14.

—— (2006), Onward But Not Upward: The Barcelona Conference of 2005, *Mediterranean Politics*, 11(2): 271–8.

Ginsborg, Paul (1990), *A History of Contemporary Italy, 1943–88*. Harmondsworth: Penguin.

Giuliani, Marco (2001), Europeanization and Italy: A Bottom-Up Process? In: Kevin Featherstone and George Kazamias (eds), *Europeanization and the Southern Periphery*. London: Frank Cass, pp. 47–72.

—— (2003), Europeanization in Comparative Perspective: Institutional Fit and National Adaptation. In: Kevin Featherstone and Claudio M. Radaelli (eds), *The Politics of Europeanization*. Oxford: Oxford University Press, pp. 134–55.

Goetz, Klaus H. (1999), Senior Officials in the German Federal Administration: Institutional Change and Positional Differentiation. In: Edward C. Page and Vincent Wright (eds), *Bureaucratic Elites in Western European States. A Comparative Analysis of Top Officials*. Oxford: Oxford University Press, pp. 147–77.

—— (2001), Making Sense of Post-Communist Central Administration: Modernization, Europeanization or Latinization? *Journal of European Public Policy*, 8(6): 1032–51.

—— (2005), The New Member-States and the EU: Responding to Europe. In: Simon Bulmer and Christian Lequesne (eds), *The Member States of the European Union*. Oxford: Oxford University Press, pp. 254–80.

Goetz, Klaus H. and Helmut Wollmann (2001), Governmentalizing Central Executives in Post-Communist Europe: A Four-Country Comparison, *Journal of European Public Policy*, 8(6): 864–87.

Goldsmith, Mike (2003), Variable Geometry, Multilevel Governance: European Integration and Subnational Government in the New Millennium. In: Kevin Featherstone and Claudio Radaelli (eds), *The Politics of Europeanization*. Oxford: Oxford University Press.

Götz, Norbert (2001), Schweden: Neokorporatismus und Netzwerkkultur. In: Werner Reutter and Peter Rütter (eds), *Verbände und Verbandssysteme in Westeuropa*. Opladen: Leske & Budrich, pp. 381–403.

Gozi, Sandro (2004), Regioni Europee e Processo decisionale dell'Unione: Quale Equilibrio? I Casi di Belgio, Spagna, Germania e Regno Unito. In: Alessandro Alfieri (ed.), *La Politica Estera delle Regioni*. Bologna: il Mulino, pp. 191–209.

Grabbe, Heather (2001), How does Europeanization Affect CEE Governance? Conditionality, Diffusion and Diversity, *Journal of European Public Policy*, 8(6): 1013–31.

Grande Region (2010), website of the Grande Region SaarLorLux at: www.granderegion. net/fr/grande-region/index.html (accessed 19 April 2010).

Grdesic, Marko (2008), Mapping the Paths of the Yugoslav Model: Labour Strength and Weakness in Slovenia, Croatia and Serbia, *European Journal of Industrial Relations*, 14(2): 133–51.

Green, V.H. (1974), *Renaissance and Reformation: A Survey of European History between 1450 and 1660*. London: Edward Arnold.

Green-Pedersen, Christoffer (2002), New Public Management Reforms of the Danish and Swedish Welfare States. The Role of Different Social Democratic Responses, *Governance. An International Journal of Public Administration and Institutions*, 15(2): 271–94.

—— and Lisbeth Hoffmann Thomsen (2005), Bloc Politics vs. Broad Cooperation? The Functioning of Danish Minority Parliamentarianism, *Journal of Legislative Studies*, 11(2): 153–69.

Greenwood, Justin (2003), *Interest Representation in the European Union*. Basingstoke: Palgrave.

Grigorescu, Alexandru (2006), The Corruption Eruption in East-Central Europe: The Increased Salience of Corruption and the Role of Intergovernmental Organisations, *East European Societies and Politics*, 20(3): 516–49.

Gross, Hermann and Walter Rotholz (1997), Das politische System Norwegens. In: Wolfgang Ismayr (ed.), *Die politischen Systeme Westeuropas*. Opladen: Leske & Budrich, pp. 129–62, 151–93.

Grossregion Saar-Lorraine-Luxembourg (2008), website at www.grossregion.net/ (accessed 10 October 2008).

Grünell, Marianne (2005), The Netherlands: Industrial Relations Developments in Europe 2004. Posted on Eiroline database at: www.eurofound.europa.eu (accessed 31 December 2008). ID: NL0501104F, 21 July 2005.

—— (2006), Internet-based Trade Union Established. Posted on Eiroline database at: www. eurofound.europa.eu (accessed 31 December 2008). ID: NL0604019I, 12 October 2006.

—— (2007), The Netherlands: Industrial Relations Developments 2006. Posted on Eiroline database at: www.eurofound.europa.eu9 accessed 31 December 2008). ID: NL0703019Q, 13 June 2007.

—— (2008), The Netherlands: Industrial Relations Developments in Europe 2007. Posted on Eiroline database at: www.eurofound.europa.eu (accessed 31 December 2008). ID: NL0803029Q, 23 September 2008.

—— and Robbert van het Kaar (2003), The Netherlands: Industrial Relations Developments in Europe 2002. Posted on Eiroline database at: www.eurofound.europa.eu (accessed 1 February 2009). ID: NL0301105F, posted on 1 April 2003.

Gualini, Enrico (2003), Challenges to Multi-Level Governance: Contradictions and Conflicts in the Europeanization of Italian Regional Policy, *Journal of European Public Policy*, 10(4): 616–36.

Guardia Civil (2010), List of Victims of Terrorism According to Terrorist Groups, posted on website at: www.guardiacivil.org/terrorismo/acciones/tabla_fallecidos_terrorismo_mir.pdf (accessed 19 April 2010).

Gunther, Richard (2002), As eleições portuguesas em perspective a comparada: partidos e comportamento eleitoral na Europa do Sul. In: *Portugal a Votos. As eleições legislativas de 2002*. Lisbon: Instituto de Ciencias Sociais, pp. 35–85.

—— and Jonathan Hopkin (2002), A Crisis of Institutionalization: The Collapse of the UCD in Spain. In: Richard Gunther, José Ramón Montero and Juan J. Linz (eds), *Political Parties: Old Concepts and New Challenges*. Oxford: Oxford University Press, pp. 191–230.

—— and J.R. Montero (2001), The Anchors of Partisanship: A Comparative Analysis of Voting Behavior in Four Southern European Democracies. In: P.N. Diamandouros and José Ramón Montero (eds), *Parties, Politics and Democracy in the New Southern Europe*. Baltimore, MD, and London: Johns Hopkins University Press, pp. 83–152.

—— J.R. Montero and J.J. Linz (eds) (2002), *Political Parties. Old Concepts and New Challenges*. Oxford: Oxford University Press.

Guzzini, Stefano (1994), La longue nuit de la Première République. L'implosion clientéliste en Italie, *Revue Française de Science Politique*, 44(6): 979–1013.

Győrffy, Dora (2006), Governance in a Low-Trust Environment: The Difficulties of Fiscal Adjustment in Hungary, *Europe-Asia Studies*, 58(2): 239–59.

Győri, Enikő (2004), The Role of the Hungarian National Assembly in EU Policy-Making after Accession to the Union. In: John O'Brennan and Tapio Raunio (eds), *National Parliaments within the European Union. From 'Victims' of Integration to Competitive Actors?* London: Routledge, pp. 220–40.

Hacek, Miro (2006), The Relationship between Civil Servants and Politicians in a Post-Communist Country: A Case of Slovenia, *Public Administration*, 84(1): 165–84.

Haller, Max (1997), Klassenstruktur und Arbeitslosigkeit – Die Entwicklung zwischen 1960 und 1990. In: Stefan Hradil and Stefan Immerfall (eds), *Die westeuropäischen Gesellschaften im Vergleich*. Opladen: Leske & Budrich, pp. 377–428.

Halperin, Ernst (1957), *Der siegreiche Ketzer. Titos Kampf gegen Stalin*. Köln: Politik und Wirtschaft.

Hammann, Kerstin and John Kelly (2007), Party Politics and the Reemergence of Social Pacts in Western Europe, *Comparative Political Studies*, 40(8): 971–94.

Hammerschmid, Gerhard and Renate E. Meyer (2005), New Public Management in Austria: Local Variation on a Global Theme? *Public Administration*, 83(3): 709–33.

Hanley, David (1996), Introduction: Christian Democracy as a Political Phenomenon. In: David Hanley (ed.), *Christian Democracy in Europe: A Comparative Perspective*. London: Continuum.

Harvey, J. and L. Bather (1982), *The British Constitution and Politics*. Fifth edition. Basingstoke: Macmillan.

Harvie, Christopher (1994), *The Rise of Regional Europe*. London: Routledge.

Hassel, Anke (2005), Policy- und Machtinteressen in Sozialpakten in Europa. In: Ferdinand Karlhofer and Emmerich Tálos (eds), *Sozialpartnerschaft. Österreichische und Europäische Perspektiven*. Wien: LIT, pp. 109–33.

Haughton, Tim and Darina Malová (2007), Emerging Patterns of EU Membership: Drawing Lessons from Slovakia's First Two Years as a Member State, *Politics*, 27(2): 69–136.

Hayden, Robert M. (2005), 'Democracy without a Demos?' The Bosnian Constitutional Experiment and the Intentional Construction of Non-functioning States, *East European Politics and Societies*, 19(2): 226–59.

Hayward, Jack E.S. (1987), *Governing France: The One and Indivisible Republic*. London: Weidenfeld & Nicolson.

—— and A. Menon (eds) (2003), *Governing Europe*. Oxford: Oxford University Press.

Hegeland, Hans (2001), The Parliament of Sweden: A Successful Adapter in the European Arena. In: Andreas Maurer and Wolfgang Wessels (eds), *National Parliaments on their Ways to Europe: Losers or Latecomers?* Baden-Baden: Nomos Verlag, pp. 377–94.

Heidar, Knut (1995), Norway, *European Journal for Political Research*, 28(3/4): 446–7.

Heipertz, Martin and Amy Verdun (2004), The Dog That Would Never Bite? What Can We Learn from the Origins of the Stability and Growth Pact, *Journal of European Public Policy*, 11(5): 765–80.

Helms, Ludger (2008), *Parliamentary Opposition in New and Old Democracies*. London: Frank Cass, special issue of *Journal of Legislative Studies*, 13(14).

Hemerijck, Anton C. (1995), Corporatist Immobility in the Netherlands. In: Colin Crouch and Franz Traxler (eds), *Organized Industrial Relations in Europe: What Future?* Aldershot: Avebury, pp. 189–216.

Hendriks, Frank (2001), Polder Politics in the Netherlands: The 'Viscous State' Revisited. In: Frank Hendriks and Theo A.J. Toonen (eds), *Polder Politics: The Re-invention of Consensus Democracy in the Netherlands*. Aldershot: Ashgate, pp. 21–40.

Hentze, Margot (1939), *Pre-Fascist Italy: The Rise and Fall of the Parliamentary Regime*. London: George Allen & Unwin.

Her Majesty's Court Service (HMCS) (2006), *Business Strategy*. London: HMCS.

—— (2008), *2007/8 Annual Report and Account*. London: HMCS.

Hervé Guillorel (1981), France: Religion, Periphery, State and Nation-Building. In: Per Torsvik (ed.), *Mobilization, Centre-Periphery Structures and Nation-Building. A Volume in Commemoration of Stein Rokkan*. Bergen: Universitetsforlaget, pp. 390–428.

Hespanha, Pedro, Alcina Monteiro, A. Cardoso Ferreira, Fernanda Rodrigues, M. Helena Nunes, M. José Hespanha, Rosa Madeira, Rudy van den Hoven and Silvia Portugal (2000), *Entre of Estado e o Mercado. As fragilidades das instituicoes de proteccao social em Portugal*. Coimbra: Quarteto.

Hill, Christopher (1998), Closing the Capabilities–Expectations Gap? In: John Peterson and Helene Sjursen (eds), *A Common Foreign Policy for Europe?* London: Routledge, pp. 18–38.

—— and Michael Smith (2005), *The International Relations of the European Union*. Oxford: Oxford University Press.

Hine, David (1993), *Governing Italy: The Politics of Bargained Pluralism*. Oxford: Oxford University Press.

Hirczy de Miño, Wolfgang and John C. Lane, (1999), Malta: STV in a Two-Party System. In: Shaun Bowler and Bernard Grofman (eds), *Elections in Australia, Ireland and Malta under the Single Transferable Vote: Reflections on an Embedded Institution*. Ann Arbor, MI: University of Michigan Press, pp. 178–204.

Hix, Simon (2005), *The Political System of the European Union*. Second edition. Basingstoke: Palgrave.

—— and Christopher Lord (1997), *Political Parties in the European Union*. Basingstoke: Palgrave.

—— Abdul G. Noury and Gérard Roland (2007), *Democratic Politics in the European Parliament*. Cambridge: Cambridge University Press.

Hlepas, Nikolaus-Komninos (2005), *Grécia: La Democratització a través de la Descentralització?* Col·lecció Món Local 14. Barcelona: Universitat Autonoma de Barcelona – Institut de Ciencies Politiques i Socials.

Hobsbawn, E.J. (1964), *The Age of Revolution, 1789–1848*. London: Cardinal.

—— (1984), *The Age of Capital, 1848–1975*. Meridian Classic.

—— (1987), *The Age of Empire, 1875–1914*. London: Weidenfeld & Nicolson.

—— (1994), *The Age of Extremes. The Short Twentieth Century, 1914–1991*. London: Abacus.

—— (2000), *Nations and Nationalism since 1780. Programme, Myth, Reality*. Cambridge: Cambridge University Press

Hocking, Brian (2004), Patrullar por la 'frontera': La condición de actors de los gobiernos no centrales. In: Francesc Morata (ed.), *Gobernanza multinivel en la Unión Europea*. Valencia: Tirant lo Blanch.

Hoensch, Jörg K. (1989), *A History of Modern Hungary, 1867–1986*. London: Longman.

Hoetjes, Ben J.S. (2001), The Parliament of the Netherlands and the European Union: Early Starter, Slow Mover. In: Andreas Maurer and Wolfgang Wessels (eds), *National Parliaments on their Ways to Europe: Losers or Latecomers?* Baden-Baden: Nomos Verlag, pp. 337–58.

Hohn, Charlotte (1997), Bevölkerungsentwicklung und demographische Herausforderung. In: Stefan Hradil and Stefan Immerfall (eds), *Die westeuropäischen Gesellschaften im Vergleich*. Opladen: Leske & Budrich, pp. 71–95.

Holmes, Leslie (2003), Political Corruption in Central and Eastern Europe. In: Martin J. Bull and James L. Newell (eds), *Corruption in Contemporary Politics*. Basingstoke: Palgrave, pp. 193–206.

Holmes, Michael (1999), The Irish Labour Party. In: Robert Ladrech and Philippe Marlière (eds), *Social Democratic Parties in the European Union. History, Organization, Policies*. Basingstoke: Palgrave, pp. 123–32.

Holsti, K.J. (2000), Governance without Government: Polyarchy in Nineteenth Century European International Politics. In: James N. Rosenau and Ernst-Otto Czempiel (eds.), *Governance Without Government: Order and Change in World Politics*. Cambridge: Cambridge University Press, pp. 30–57.

Holzhacker, Ronald and E. Albaek (eds) (2007), *Democratic Governance and European Integration. Linking Societal and State Processes of Democracy*. Cheltenham: Edward Elgar.

Hooghe, Liesbet (1994), The Dynamics of Constitution-Building in Belgium. In: Patrick Dunleavy and J. Stanyer (eds), *Contemporary Political Studies*. Belfast: Political Studies Association, pp. 314–24.

—— (1998), EU Cohesion Policy and Competitive Models of Capitalism, *Journal of Common Market Studies*, 36(4): 457–77.

—— (2001), *The European Commission and the Integration of Europe. Images of Governance*. Cambridge: Cambridge University Press.

—— and Michael Keating (1994), The Politics of European Union Regional Policy, *Journal of European Public Policy*, 1(3): 367–93.

Hooghe, Marc (2001), Stabilität und Wandel neokorporatistischer Interessenvermittlung. In: Werner Reutter and Peter Rütters (eds), *Verbände und Verbandssysteme in Westeuropa*. Opladen: Leske & Budrich, pp. 31–49.

Hopflinger, Francois (1997), Haushalts- und Familienstrukturen im intereuropäischen Vergleich. In: Stefan Hradil and Stefan Immerfall (eds), *Die westeuropäischen Gesellschaften im Vergleich*. Opladen: Leske & Budrich, pp. 97–138.

Hopkin, Jonathan (1999), Political Parties in a Young Democracy. In: David Broughton and Mark Donovan (eds), *Changing Party Systems in Western Europe*. London: Pinter, pp. 207–31.

—— (2005), From Census to Competition: The Changing Nature of Democracy in the Spanish Transition. In: Sebastian Balfour (ed.), *Contemporary Politics of Spain*. Basingstoke: Palgrave, pp. 6–26.

House of Lords (2001–7), Public Bill Sessional Statistics for Session. Annual reports, posted on website of House of Lords at: www.publications.parliament.uk/pa/ld/billstat.htm (accessed 25 January 2009).

Howarth, David and Peter Loedel (2004), The ECB and the Stability Pact: Policeman and Judge? *Journal of European Public Policy*, 11(5): 832–53.

Howorth, Jolyon (2005), From Security to Defence: The Evolution of the CFSP. In: Christopher Hill and Michael Smith (eds), *International Relations and the European Union*. Oxford: Oxford University Press, pp. 179–204.

Hudson, Christine (2005), Regional Development Partnerships in Sweden: Putting the Government Back in Governance? *Regional and Federal Studies*, 15(3): 311–27.

Huizinga, Johan (1955), *The Waning of the Middle Ages: A Study of the Forms of Life, Thought, and Art in France and the Netherlands in the Fourteenth and Fifteenth Centuries*. Harmondsworth: Penguin.

Hungarian Parliament (2007), website at: www.mkogy.hu/angol/angol.htm (accessed 15 July).

Huntington, Samuel (1991), *The Third Wave: Democratization in the Late Twentieth Century*. Norman, OK: University of Oklahoma Press.

ICT and Government Advisory Committee (2001), *Citizen and Government in the Information Society. The Need for Institutional Innovation*. The Hague: Ministry of Interior and Kingdom Relations, p. 39.

Ignazi, Piero (1997), New Challenges: Postmaterialism and the Extreme Right. In: M. Rhodes, P. Heywood and V. Wright (eds), *Developments in West European Politics*. Basingstoke: Macmillan, pp. 300–19.

Illner, Michael and Zdenka Vajdova (2006), *El govern territorial a la República Txeca després de la transformació del sistema*. Barcelona: Universitat Autonoma de Barcelona – Institut de Ciencies Politiques i Socials.

Ilonski, Gabriella (2001), The Second Parliament as Seen by MPs. In: Attila Ágh and Sándor Kurtán (eds), *Democratization and Europeanization in Hungary: The Second Parliament 1994–1998*. Budapest: The Hungarian Centre for Democracy Studies, pp. 135–49.

—— (2007), From Minimal to Subordinate: A Final Verdict? The Hungarian Parliament 1990–2002, *Journal of Legislative Studies*, 13(1): 38–58.

Immerfall, Stefan (1995), *Einführung in den europäischen Gesellschaftsvergleich. Ansätze, Problemstellungen, Befunde*. Passau: Wissenschaftsverlag Richard Rothe.

—— (1997), Soziale Integration in den westeuropäischen Gesellschaften: Werte, Mitgliedschaft und Netzwerke. In: Stefan Hradil and Stefan Immerfall (eds), *Die westeuropäischen Gesellschaften im Vergleich*. Opladen: Leske & Budrich, pp. 139–73.

Inglehart, Ronald (1977), *The Silent Revolution: Changing Values and Political Styles*. Princeton, NJ: Princeton University Press.

—— (1996), *Modernization and Postmodernization: Cultural, Economic and Political Change in 43 Societies*. Princeton, NJ: Princeton University Press.

—— (2008), Changing Values among Western Publics from 1970 to 2006, *West European Politics*, 31(1): 130–146.

—— and Christian Welzel (2005), *Modernization, Cultural Change and Democracy: The Human Development Sequence*. Cambridge: Cambridge University Press.

International Constitutional Law (2010), at: www.servat.unibe.ch/icl/ (accessed 25 June 2010).

International Herald Tribune online (2009), website at: www.iht.com (accessed 11 January 2009).

International Parliamentary Union (2010), Parline database at: www.ipu.org/parline-e/parlinesearch.asp (accessed 12 April 2010).

Iokamidis, P.C. (2001), The Europeanization of Greece: An Overall Assessment. In: Kevin Featherstone and George Kazamias (eds), *Europeanization and the Southern Periphery*. London: Frank Cass, pp. 73–94.

REFERENCES

Irish Presidency of the Council of the European Union (2004), 42nd Meeting of Directors-General responsible for Public Administration, Resolutions, Dublin, 27–28 May.

Ismayr, Wolfgang (ed.) (2002), *Die politischen Systeme Osteuropas*. Opladen: Leske & Budrich.

—— (2010), Die politischen Systeme Osteuropas im Vergleich. In: Wolfgang Ismayr (ed.), *Die politischen Systeme Osteuropas*. Opladen: Leske & Budrich, pp. 9–79.

Israel, Jonathan I. (1998), *The Dutch Republic: Its Rise, Greatness, and Fall 1477–1806*. Oxford: Oxford University Press.

Italian Presidency of the Council of the European Union (2003), 11th Meeting of European Ministers Responsible for Public Administration, Rome. 1 December, Resolutions. Rome.

Jackiewicz, Irena and Zbigniew Jackiewicz (1996), The Polish Parliament in Transition: In Search of a Model. In: Attila Ágh and Gabriella Ilonski (eds), *Parliaments and Organized Interests: The Second Steps*. Budapest: Hungarian Centre for Democracy Studies, pp. 365–79.

Jacoby, Wade (2001), Tutors and Pupils: International Organizations, Central European Elites, and Western Models, *Governance: An International Journal of Policy and Administration*, 14(2): 169–200.

—— (2005), External Incentives and Lesson-Drawing in Regional Policy and Health Care. In: Frank Schimmelpfennig and Ulrich Sedelmeier (eds), *The Europeanization of Central and Eastern Europe*. Ithaca, NY: Cornell University Press, pp. 91–111.

Jakubowski, Alex (2005), Die Jamaika Koalition. ARD Berlin (tagesthemen, 22:30 Uhr, 19.09.2005), at: www.ard.de (accessed 18 December 2008).

Jalali, Carlos (2002), As mesmas clivagens de sempre? Velhas clivagens e novos valores no comportamento eleitoral português. In: André Freire, Marina Costa Lobo and Pedro Magalhães (eds), *Portugal a Votos. As eleições legislativas de 2002*. Lisboa: Instituto de Ciencias Sociais 2004, pp. 87–124

—— (2007), *Partidos e Democracia em Portugal 1974–2005*. Lisboa: Instituto de Ciências Sociais.

Jamieson, Alison (1998), *The Anti-Mafia: The Fight Against Organised Crime*. Basingstoke: Palgrave.

Jansen, Peter (2001), Frankreich: Verbände-eine Rechnung mit vielen Unbekannten. In: Werner Reutter and Peter Rütters (eds), *Verbände und Verbandssysteme in Westeuropa*. Opladen: Leske & Budrich, pp. 125–50.

Jasiewicz, Krzysztof and Agnieszka Jasiewicz-Betkiewicz (2006), Poland. In: Richard Katz and Ingrid van Biezen (eds), *European Data Yearbook 2005*, special issue of *European Journal of Political Research*, 45(7–8): 1231–46.

Jeffery, Charlie (ed.) (1997), *The Regional Dimension in the European Union: Towards a Third Level in Europe*. London: Frank Cass.

Jensen, Hanne Nexø and Tim Knudsen (1999), Senior Officials and Danish Central Administration: From Bureaucrats to Policy Professionals and Managers. In: Edward C. Page and Vincent Wright (eds), *Bureaucratic Elites in Western European States: A Comparative Analysis of Top Officials*. Oxford: Oxford University Press, pp. 229–48.

Jensen, Henrik (2007), A Model for the Strictest Scrutiny? The Danish European Affairs Committee in a Party Group Perspective. In: Ronald Holzhacker and Erik Albaek (eds), *Democratic Governance and European Integration: Linking Societal and State Processes of Democracy*. Cheltenham: Edward Elgar, pp. 207–28.

Jensen, Lotte, Asbjørn Sonne Nørgaard and Eva Sørensen, The Future of Public Administration in Denmark: Projections, Prospects and High Hopes, *Public Administration*, 8(1): 127–39.

Jessop, Bob (2002), *The Future of the Capitalist State*. Cambridge: Polity Press.

Johnston, R.J. (1993), The Rise and Decline of the Corporate Welfare State: A Comparative Analysis in Global Context. In: Peter J. Taylor (ed.), *Political Geography of the Twentieth Century: A Global Analysis*. London: Belhaven Press, pp. 117–70.

Jones, Bill (2007a), Pressure Groups. In: Bill Jones, Dennis Kavanagh, Michael Moran and Philip Norton (eds), *Politics UK*. Sixth edition. Edinburgh: Pearson-Longman, pp. 249–79.

—— (2007b), Devolution. In: Bill Jones, Dennis Kavanagh, Michael Moran and Philip Norton (eds), *Politics UK*. Harlow: Pearson Education, pp. 321–46.

—— and Peter Bird (2007), British Defence and Foreign Policy under the Blair Government. In: Bill Jones, Dennis Kavanagh, Michael Moran and Philip Norton, *Politics UK*. Harlow: Pearson Education, pp. 713–27.

Joppke, Christian (2007), Beyond National Models: Civic Integration Policies for Immigrants in Western Europe, *West European Politics*, 30(1): 1–22.

Jordan, Andrew, Roy Brouwer and Emma Noble (1999), Innovative and Responsive? A Longitudinal Analysis of the Speed of EU Environmental Policy-Making, 1967–97, *Journal of European Public Policy*, 6(3): 376–98.

Kälin, Walter (2002), Justiz. In: Ulrich Klöti, Peter Knoepfel, Hans-Peter Kriesi, Wolf Linder and Yannis Papadopoulos (eds), *Handbuch der Schweizer Politik*. Zürich: Neue Züricher Verlag, pp. 187–208.

Kamen, Henry (2000), *Early Modern European Society*. London: Routledge.

Kapsis, Ilias (2007), The Courts of the European Union. In: Michelle Cini (ed.), *European Union Politics*. Oxford: Oxford University Press, pp. 188–201.

Karasimeonov, Georgi (1996), The Legislature in Post-Communist Bulgaria. In: David M. Olson and Philip Norton (eds), *The New Parliaments of Central and Eastern Europe*. London: Frank Cass, pp. 40–59.

Karlhofer, Ferdinand (2001), Österreich: Zwischen Korporatismus und Zivilgesellschaft. In: Werner Reutter and Peter Rütters (eds), *Verbände und Verbandssysteme in West-europa*. Opladen: Leske & Budrich, pp. 336–54.

—— and Emmerich Tálos (2006), Sozialpartnerschaft am Abstieg. In: Emmerich Tálos (ed.), *Schwarz-Blau. Eine Bilanz des 'Neu-Regierens'*. Wien: Lit Verlag, pp. 102–16.

Karvonen, Lauri (1996), Christian Parties in Scandinavia: Victory over the Windmills. In: David Hanley (ed.), *Christian Democracy in Europe: A Comparative Perspective*. London: Pinter, pp. 121–41.

Kassim, Hussein, B. Guy Peters and Vincent Wright (eds) (2000), *The National Co-ordination of EU Policy: The Domestic Level*. Oxford: Oxford University Press.

—— (2003), Meeting the Demands of EU Membership: The Europeanization of National Administrative Systems. In: Kevin Featherstone and Claudio Radaelli (eds), *The Politics of Europeanization*. Oxford: Oxford University Press, pp. 83–111.

——, Anand Menon, B. Guy Peters and Vincent Wright (eds) (2001), *The National Co-ordination of EU Policy: The European Level*. Oxford: Oxford University Press.

Kask, Peet (1996), Institutional Development of the Parliament in Estonia. In: David M. Olson and Philip Norton (eds), *The New Parliaments of Central and Eastern Europe*. London: Frank Cass, pp. 193–212.

Katz, Richard (2003), Reforming the Italian Electoral Law, 1993. In: Matthew Soberg Shugart and Martin P. Wattenberg (eds), *Mixed-Member Electoral Systems*. Oxford: Oxford University Press, pp. 96–122.

—— and Peter Mair (1992), The Membership of Political Parties in Western Democracies, *European Journal of Political Research*, 22: 329–45.

—— and —— (1995), Changing Models of Party Organization and Party Democracy, *Party Politics*, 1(1): 5–28.

—— and —— (2002), The Ascendancy of the Party in Public Office: Party Organizational Change in Twentieth-Century Democracies. In: Richard Gunther, José Ramón Montero and Juan J. Linz (eds), *Political Parties. Old Concepts and New Challenges*. Oxford: Oxford University Press, pp. 113–35.

Kavanagh, Dennis (2001), *British Politics. Continuities and Change*. Oxford: Oxford University Press.

Keating, Michael (1998), *The New Regionalism in Western Europe: Territorial Restructuring and Political Change*. Cheltenham: Edward Elgar.

—— (1999a), Regions and International Affairs: Motives, Opportunities and Strategies. In: F. Aldecoa and M. Keating (eds), *Paradiplomacy in Action: The Foreign Relations of Subnational Governments*, special issue of *Regional and Federal Studies*, 9(1):1–16.

—— (1999b), 'Regional and International Affairs: Motives, Opportunities and Strategies', in Francisco Aldecoa and Michael Keating (eds), *Paradiplomacy in Action: The Foreign Relations of Subnational Governments*, aspecial issue of *Regional and Federal Studies*, 9(1): 1–16.

—— (ed.) (2005), *Regions and Regionalism*. Cheltenham: Edward Elgar.

—— (2006), Nationalist Parties in Galicia. In: David Hanley and John Loughlin (eds), *Spanish Political Parties*. Cardiff: University of Wales Press, pp. 142–57.

—— (2008), Thirty Years of Territorial Politics, *West European Politics*, 31(1): 60–81.

—— and John Loughlin (eds) (1997), *The Political Economy of Regionalism*. London: Frank Cass.

Keesbergen, Kees van (1996), The Distinctiveness of Christian Democracy. In: David Hanley (ed.), *Christian Democracy in Europe: A Comparative Perspective*. London: Pinter, pp. 31–47.

—— (1999), The Dutch Labour Party. In: Robert Ladrech and PhilippeMarlière (eds), *Social Democratic Parties in the European Union: History, Organization, Policies*. Basingstoke: Palgrave, pp. 155–65.

Kemmerling, Achim and Oliver Bruttel (2006), 'New Politics' in German Labour Market Policy? The Implications of the recent Hartz IV Reforms for the German Welfare State, *West European Politics*, 29(1): 90–112.

Kern, Robert W. (1974), *Liberals, Reformers and Caciques in Restoration Spain (1875–1909)*. Albuquerque, NM: University of New Mexico Press.

Kerrouche, Eric (2006), The French Assemblée Nationale: The Case of a Weak Legislature? *Journal of Legislative Studies*, 12(3–4): 336–65.

Kessler, Marie-Christine (n.d.), Les esprits des corps dans les grands corps de l'État en France. Posted on website of Centre d'Études et de Recherches de Science Administrative (CNRSA) at : www.cersa.cnrs.fr/spip.php?article53 (accessed 14 August 2008).

Kingdom, John (2000), Britain. In: J.A. Chandler (ed.), *Comparative Public Administration*. London: Routledge, pp. 14–49.

Kirby, David (2006), *A Concise History of Finland*. Cambridge: Cambridge University Press.

Kirchheimer, Otto (1965), Der Wandel des westeuropäischen Parteiensystems, *Politische Vierteljahresschrift*, 6: 20–41.

Kitschelt, Herbert (1995a), A Silent Revolution in Europe? In: Jack Hayward and Edward C. Page (eds), *Governing the New Europe*. Cambridge: Polity Press, pp. 123–65.

—— (1995b), *The Transformation of European Social Democracy*. Cambridge: Cambridge University Press.

—— (1997), European Party System: Continuity and Change. In: Martin Rhodes, Paul Heywood and Vincent Wright (eds), *Developments in West European Politics*. Basingstoke: Macmillan, pp. 131–50.

Kleinfeld, Ralf (2001), Niederlande: Verbände, Konkordanzdemokratie und Versäulung. In: Werner Reutter and Peter Rütters (eds), *Verbände und Verbandssysteme in Westeuropa*. Opladen: Leske & Budrich, pp. 287–312.

Klingemann, Hans-Dieter (1999), Kontinuität und Veränderung des deutschen Parteiensystems, 1949–1998. In: Max Kaase and Günther Schmid (eds), *Eine lernende Demokratie. 50 Jahre Bundesrepublik Deutschland*. Berlin: Edition Sigma, pp. 115–28.

Knapp, Andrew and Vincent Wright (2001), *The Government and Politics of France*. London: Routledge.

Knill, Christoph (2001), *The Europeanization of National Administrations: Patterns of Institutional Change and Persistence*. Cambridge: Cambridge University Press.

REFERENCES

—— (2005), Introduction: Cross-National Policy Convergence: Concepts, Approaches and Explanatory Factors, *Journal of European Public Policy*, 12(5): 764–74.

—— and Dork Lehmkuhl (2002), The National Impact of European Union Regulatory Policy: Three Europeanization Mechanisms, *European Journal of Political Research*, 41: 255–80.

Koenigsberger, H.G. (1987), *Medieval Europe 400–1500*. London: Longman.

Koller, Christophe, Ivar Trippolini and Sylvie Traimond (eds) (2006), *Statistischer Überblick zu den Kantonalen Verwaltungen und Behörden*. Bern: Idheap/Badac.

Koole, Ruud (2000), Fukuyama's Paradise? Liberal Parties in the Netherlands. In: Lieven de Winter, Joan Marcet, Alastair H. Thomas, Ferdinand Müller-Rommel, Ruud A. Koole and Gérard Grunberg (eds), *Liberalism and Liberal Parties in the European Union*. Barcelona: Institut de Ciencies Politiques i Socials, pp. 119–39.

Kopajtich-Škrlec (2008), Bit by Bit – But Where To? Local Self-Governance in Croatia. In: Zdravko Zlopaka (ed.), *Block by Block. It's Good to Build Well. Models of Organisation of Local Self-Governance*. Banja Luka: Enterprise Development Agency, pp. 78–123.

Kopecek, Lubomir (2007), The Far Right in Europe. A Summary of Attempts to Define the Concept, Analyze Its Identity, and Compare the Western European and Central European Far Right, *Central European Political Studies Review*, IX(4): 280–93.

Kopeinig, Margaretha and Christoph Kotanko (2000), *Eine europàische Affäre. Der Weisen-Bericht und die Sanktionen gegen Österreich*. Wien: Czernin Verlag.

Körösényi, András (2002), Das politische System Ungarns. In: Wolfgang Ismayr (ed.), *Die politischen Systeme Osteuropas*. Opladen: Leske & Budrich, pp. 309–53.

—— Gábor G. Fodor and Jürgen Dieringer (2010), Das politische System Ungarns. In: Wolfgang Ismayr (ed.), *Die politischen System Osteuropas*. 3., aktualisierte und erweiterte Auflage. Wiesbaden: Verlag für Sozialwissenschaften, pp. 357–417.

Kotchegura, Alexander (2008), *Civil Service Reform in Postcommunist Countries: The Case of the Russian Federation and the Czech Republic*. Leiden: Leiden University Press.

Kreppel, Amie (2002), *The European Parliament and a Supranational Party System: A Study in Institutional Development*. Cambridge: Cambridge University Press.

Krupavicius, Algis (2008), Lithuania. In: Richard Katz and Ingrid van Biezen (ed.) *European Data Yearbook 2005*, special issue of *European Journal of Political Research*, 47(7–8): 1048–59.

Kuhnle, Stein (1981), Emigration, Democratization and the Rise of the European Welfare States. In: Per Torsvik (ed.), *Mobilization, Centre-Periphery Structures and Nation-Building: A Volume in Commemoration of Stein Rokkan*. Bergen: Universitetsforlaget, pp. 501–23.

Kuhry, Bob and Evert Pommer (2004), Public Sector Performance. In: Bob Kuhry (ed.), *Public Sector Performance: An International Comparison of Education Health Care, Law and Order and Public Administration*. The Hague: Social and Cultural Planning), pp. 271–92.

—— and—— (2007), Public Sector Performance. An International Comparison. Mimeographed document, published as *Publication 2007/1* on Social Cultural Planning website at: www.scp.nl; this version is on www.irspm2007.org/Fullpaper/PT_Metrics_Kuhry%20Pommer.pdf (accessed 13 August 2008).

Kukorelli, István (2001), The Parliamentary Cycle of 1994–98: The Parliament of the Two-Thirds Majority. In: Attila Ágh and Sándor Kurtán (eds), *Democratization and Europeanization in Hungary: The Second Parliament 1994–1998*. Budapest: The Hungarian Centre for Democracy Studies, pp. 33–44.

Kysela, Jan (n.d.), Bicameralism in the Czech Republic: Reasons, Functions, Perspectives, posted on Czech Senate website at: www.senat.cz/zajimavosti/bikameralismus-eng.php?ke_dni=&O= (accessed 12 April 2010).

Ladler, Andreas (2005), Das Schweizer Parteiensystem und seine Parteien. In: Ulrich Klöti, Peter Knoepfel, Hanspeter Kriesi, Wolf Linder and Yannis Papadopoulos (eds), *Handbuch der Schweizer Politik*. Zurich: Verlag Neue Zürcher Zeitung, pp. 211–58.

Ladrech, Robert (1994), Europeanization of Domestic Politics and Institutions: The Case of France, *Journal of Common Market Studies*, 32(1): 69–88.

—— (2010), *The Europeanization of National Politics*. Basingstoke: Palgrave.

—— and P. Marlière (eds) (1999), *Social Democratic Parties in the European Union. History, Organization, Policies*. Basingstoke: Palgrave.

Laffan, Brigid (2001), The Parliament of Ireland: A Passive Adapter Coming from the Cold. In: Andreas Maurer and Wolfgang Wessels (eds), *National Parliaments on their Ways to Europe: Losers or Latecomers?* Baden-Baden: Nomos Verlag, pp. 251–68.

—— and Johannes Lindner (2005), The Budget. In: Helen Wallace, William Wallace and Mark Pollack (eds), *Policy-Making in the European Union*. Oxford: Oxford University Press, pp. 191–212.

Lahusen, Christian (2002), Commercial Consultancies in the European Union: The Shape and Structure of Professional Interest Intermediation, *Journal of European Public Policy*, 9(5): 695–714.

Landfried, Christine (1992), Judicial Policy-Making in Germany: The Federal Constitutional Court. In: Mary L. Volcansek (ed.), *Judicial Politics and Policy-Making in Western Europe*, special issue of *West European Politics*, 15(3): 50–67.

Landmann, Todd (2003), *Issues and Methods in Comparative Politics: An Introduction*. London: Routledge.

Lane, Thomas (2002), Lithuania: Stepping Westward. In: David J. Smith, Artis Pabriks, Aldis Purs and Thomas Lane, *The Baltic States: Estonia, Latvia and Lithuania*. London: Routledge.

Lange, Ulrich (2002), Deutschland im Zeitalter der Reichsreform, der kirchlichen Erneuerung und der Glaubenskampfe (1495–1648). In: Martin Vogt (ed.), *Deutsche Geschichte. Von den Anfangen bis zur Gegenwart*. Frankfurt a. M.: Fischer, pp. 144–216.

Lanzilotta, Linda (2007), *Evolution and Transformation of Italian Federalism*. European Institute, London School of Economics, London, 12 March.

LaPalombara, Joseph (1964), *Interest Groups in Italian Politics*. Princeton, NJ: Princeton University Press.

Lappalainen, Pertti and Martti Siisiäinen (2001), Freiwillige Vereinigungen in der Gesellschaft und Gewerkschaften im politischen System. In: Werner Reutter and Peter Rütters (eds), *Verbände und Verbandssysteme in Westeuropa*. Opladen: Leske & Budrich, pp. 103–23.

Laursen, Finn (2001), The Danish Folketing and the European Affairs Committee: Strong Players in the National Policy Cycle. In: Andreas Maurer and Wolfgang Wessels (eds), *National Parliaments on their Ways to Europe: Losers or Latecomers?* Baden-Baden: Nomos Verlag, pp. 99–115.

Lavdas, Kostas (2001), Griechenland: Verbände und Politik. In: Werner Reutter and Peter Rütters (eds), *Verbände und Verbandssysteme in Westeuropa*. Opladen: Leske & Budrich, pp. 151–68.

—— (2005), Interest Groups in Disjointed Corporatism: Social Dialogue in Greece and European 'Competitive Corporatism', *West European Politics*, 28(2): 297–316.

Lavenex, Sandra and William Wallace (2005), Justice and Home Affairs. In: Helen Wallace, William Wallace and Mark A. Pollack (eds), *Policy-Making in the European Union*. Fifth edition. Oxford: Oxford University Press, pp. 457–80.

Lazar, Marc (2008), La Nascita del Partito Democratico. In: Mark Donovan and Paolo Onofri (eds), *Politica in Italia. I Fatti dell'Anno e le Interpretazioni. Edizione 2008*. Bologna: il Mulino, pp. 87–108.

Łazowski, Adam (2007), The Polish Parliament and EU Affairs: An Effective Actor or an Accidental Hero? In: John O'Brennan and Tapio Raunio (eds), *National Parliaments within the European Union. From 'Victims' of Integration to Competitive Actors?* London: Routledge, pp. 203–19.

Lecours, A. (2002), Paradiplomacy: Reflections on the Foreign Policy and International Relations of Regions, *International Negotiation*, 7(1): 91–114.

Lees-Marshment, Jennifer (2004), *The Political Marketing Revolution: Transforming the Government of the UK*. Manchester: Manchester University Press.

Lehmbruch, Gerhard (1996), Die korporative Verhandlungsdemokratie, *Swiss Political Science Review*, 2(4): 1–41.

—— (2002), Quasi-Consociationalism in German Politics: Negotiated Democracy and the Legacy of the Westphalian Peace. In: Jurg Steiner and Thomas Ertman (eds), *Consociationalism and Corporatism in Western Europe: Still the Politics of Accommodation?* special issue of *Acta Politica*, 2, in *Acta Politica*, 37: 175–93.

Leiße, Olaf (2006), Rumänien und Bulgarien vor dem EU Eintritt. In: *Aus Politik und Zeitgeschichte*, 27(3): 6–12.

Lenschow, Andrea (2005), Environmental Policy. In: Helen Wallace, William Wallace and Mark Pollack (eds), *Policy-Making in the European Union*. Oxford: Oxford University Press, pp. 305–27.

Leonardi, Robert and Douglas Wertman (1989), *Italian Christian Democracy: The Politics of Dominance*. Basingstoke: Palgrave.

Leston-Bandeira, Cristina (2004), *From Legislation to Legitimation*. London: Routledge.

—— and André Freire (2003), Internalising the Lessons of Stable Democracy: The Portuguese Parliament. In: Cristina Leston-Bandeira (ed.), *Southern European Parliaments in Democracy*, special issue of *Journal of Legislative Studies*, 9(2): 56–84.

Letamendia, Francisco (2006), Basque Political Parties. In: David Hanley and John Loughlin (eds), *Spanish Political Parties*. Cardiff: University of Wales Press, pp. 142–57.

Leton, André and André Miroir (1999), *Les conflits communautaires en Belgique*. Paris: Presses Universitaires de France.

Lewis, Jeffrey (1998), Is the 'Hard Bargaining' Image of the Council Misleading? The Committee of Permanent Representatives and the Local Elections Directive, *Journal of Common Market Studies*, 36(4): 479–504.

—— (2007), The Council of Ministers. In: Michelle Cini (ed.), *European Union Politics*. Oxford: Oxford University Press, pp. 154–73.

Lewis, Paul G. (2003), *Political Parties in Post-Communist Eastern Europe*. London: Routledge.

Liebert, Ulrike (2006), *Renewing the Transatlantic Agenda: Predicaments and Preconditions*. Paper presented at the ECSA World Conference, Global Jean Monnet Conference 'Europe's Challenge in a Globalised World', Brussels, 23–24 November 2006.

Liegl, Barbara and Wolfgang C. Müller (1999), Senior Officials in Austria. In: Edward C. Page and Vincent Wright (eds), *Bureaucratic Elites in Western European States: A Comparative Analysis of Top Officials*. Oxford: Oxford University Press, pp. 90–120.

Lijphart, Arend (1975), *The Politics of Accommodation: Pluralism and Democracy in the Netherlands*. Berkeley, CA: University of California Press.

—— (1984), *Democracies: Patterns of Majoritarian and Consensus Government in Twenty-One Countries*. New Haven, CT: Yale University Press.

—— (1999), *Patterns of Democracy: Government Forms and Performance in Thirty-Six Countries*. New Haven, CT: Yale University Press 1999.

Linder, Wolf (2005), *Schweizerische Demokratie. Institutionen, Prozesse, Perspektiven*. Bern: Haupt.

Lindvall, Johannes and Joakim Sebring (2005), Policy Reform and the Decline of Corporatism in Sweden, *West European Politics*, 28(5): 1057–74.

Linek, Lukáš and Zdenka Mansfeldova (2007), The Parliament of the Czech Republic 1993–2004, *Journal of Legislative Studies*, 13(1): 12–37.

Lippert, Barbara (2003), Von Kopenhagen bis Kopenhagen: Eine erste Bilanz der EU – Erweiterungsperspektive, *Aus Politik und Zeitgeschichte*, 1–2: 7–15.

—— Gaby Umbach and Wolfgang Wessels (2001), Europeanization of CEE Executives: EU Membership Negotiations as a Shaping Power, *Journal of European Public Policy*, 8(6): 980–1012.

Lipset, Seymour Martin (2001), The Americanization of the European Left, *Journal of Democracy*, 12(2): 74–87.

—— and Stein Rokkan (1967), Cleavage Structures, Party Systems and Voter Alignments: An Introduction. In: Seymour Martin Lipset and Stein Rokkan (eds), *Party Systems and Voter Alignments: Cross National Perspectives*. New York: The Free Press, pp. 1–64.

Lobo, Marina Costa (2005), The Presidentialization of Portuguese Democracy? In: Thomas Poguntke and Paul Webb (eds), *The Presidentialization of Politics: A Comparative Study of Modern Democracies*. Oxford: Oxford University Press, pp. 269–88.

López Calvo, José (1996), *Organización y Funcionamiento del Gobierno*. Madrid: Tecnos.

López-Santana, Mariely (2006), The Domestic Implications of European Soft Law: Framing and Transmitting Change in Employment Policy, *Journal of European Employment Policy*, 13(4): 481–99.

Loughlin, John (1998), La autonomia en Europa occidental: Un Estudio comparado. In: Francisco Letamendia (ed.), *Nacionalidades y Regiones en la Unión Europea*. Madrid: Editorial Fundamentos, pp. 109–59.

—— (2000), Regional Autonomy and State Paradigm Shifts in Western Europe, *Regional and Federal Studies*, 10(2):10–34.

—— (ed.) (2004), *Subnational Democracy in the European Union*. Oxford: Oxford University Press.

—— (2009), The 'Hybrid' State: Reconfiguring Territorial Governance in Western Europe, *Perspectives on European Politics and Society*, 10(1): 51–68.

Lovens, Pierre François (2004), Social Elections Bring Little Change in Union Support. Posted on Eiroline database at: www.eurofound.europa.eu (accessed 28 December 2008). ID: BE0406301N, 9 June 2004.

Lucardie, Paul and Hans-Martien ten Napel (1994), Between Confessionalism and Liberal Conservatism: The Christian Democratic Parties of Belgium and the Netherlands. In: David Hanley (ed.), *Christian Democracy in Europe: A Comparative Perspective*. London: Pinter, pp. 51–70.

Lukšič, Igor (2002), Das politische System Sloweniens. In: Wolfgang Ismayr (ed.), *Die Politischen Systeme Osteuropas*. Opladen: Leske & Budrich, pp. 603–38.

Luther, Kurt Richard (2006), Strategien und (Fehl-)verhalten: Die Freiheitlichen und die Regierungen Schüssel I und Schüssel II. In: Emmerich Tálos (ed.), *Schwarz-Blau. Eine Bilanz des 'Neu-Regierens'*. Wien: Lit, pp. 19–37.

Luxembourg Presidency of the European Union (2005a), 44th Meeting of Directors-General Responsible for Public Administration, Resolutions. Mondorf-les-Bains, 9–10 June 2005.

—— (2005b), 12th Meeting of European Ministers Responsible for Public Administration, Resolutions. Mondorf-les-Bains, 8 June 2005.

—— (2005c), Information on the Structure of the Civil and Public Services of the EU Member States and Applicant Countries. Luxembourg.

—— (2006), Mid-term Programme 2006–7 for Cooperation between the Directors-General Responsible for Public Administration in the EU Member States. Luxembourg, 9 May 2006.

Lyrintzis, Christos (1984), Political Parties in Post-Junta Greece: A Case of 'Bureaucratic Clientelism'? In: Geoffrey Pridham (ed.), *The New Mediterranean Democracies*. London: Frank Cass, pp. 99–118.

—— (2005), The Changing Party System: Stable Democracy, Contested 'Modernisation', *West European Politics*, 28(2): 242–59.

Määttä, Seppo (2004), 'The Lisbon Strategy and Strategy Focused Public Administration'. European Institute for Public Administration, 28 October, unpublished document.

McCarthy, Patrick (1996), Forza Italia: The New Politics and Old Values of a Changing Italy. In: Stephen Gundle and Simon Parker (eds), *The New Italian Republic: From the Fall of the Berlin Wall to Berlusconi*. London: Routledge, pp. 130–46.

McGann, Anthony J. and Herbert Kitschelt, The Radical Right in the Alps: Evolution of Support for the Swiss SVP and Austrian FPÖ, *Party Politics*, 11: 147–71.

Mackie, Tom (1995), Parties and Elections. In: Jack Hayward and Edward C. Page (eds), *Governing the New Europe*. Cambridge: Polity Press, pp. 166–95.

McManus-Czubinska, Clare, William L. Miller, Radosław Markowski and Jacek Wasilewski (2004), When Does Turnout Matter? The Case of Poland, *Europe-Asia Studies*, 56(3): 401–20.

McNamara, R. Kathleen (2005), Economic and Monetary Union. Innovation and Challenges for the Euro. In: Helen Wallace, William Wallace and Mark Pollack (eds), *Policy-Making in the European Union*. Oxford: Oxford University Press, pp. 141–60.

Madeley, John (2000), Reading the Runes. The Religious Factor in Scandinavian Electoral Politics. In: David Broughton and Hans-Martien ten Napel (eds), *Religion and Mass Electoral Behaviour in Europe*. London: Routledge, pp. 28–43.

Magalhães, Pedro C., Carlo Guarnieri and Yorgos Kaminis (2006), Democratic Consolidation, Judicial Reform, and the Judicialization of Politics in Southern Europe. In: Richard Gunther, P. Nikiforos Diamandouros and Dimitri A. Sotiropoulos (eds), *Democracy and the New State in the New Southern Europe*. Oxford: Oxford University Press, pp. 138–96.

Magnette, Paul (2004), Le parlementarisme dans une démocratie de compromis: reflexions sur le cas belge. In: Olivier Costa, Eric Kerrouche and Paul Magnette (eds), *Vers un renouveau du parlementarisme en Europe?* Bruxelles: Éditions Université Libre de Bruxelles, pp. 91–106.

Magone, José M. (1997), *European Portugal: The Difficult Road to Sustainable Democracy*. Basingstoke: Macmillan.

—— (1998), The Logics of Party System Change in Southern Europe. In: Paul Pennings and Jan-Erik Lane (eds), *Comparing Party System Change*. London: Routledge, pp. 217–40.

—— (1999), La construzione di una società civile europea: legami a più livelli tra comitati economici e sociali. In: Antonio Varsori (ed.), *Il Comitato Economico e Sociale nella construzione europea*. Venice: Marsilio 2000, pp. 222–42.

—— (2000), Portugal. In: Hans Keman and Peter Mair (eds), *Political Data Yearbook 2000*, special issue of *European Journal of Political Research*, 38(3–4): 499–510.

—— (2001a), The Transformation of the Portuguese Political System: European Regional Policy and Democratization in a Small EU Member State. In: Kevin Featherstone and George Kazamias(eds), *Europeanization and the Southern Periphery*. London: Frank Cass, pp. 119–40.

—— (2001b), *Iberian Trade Unionism: Democratization Under the Impact of the European Union*. New Brunswick, NJ: Transaction.

—— (2003a) *The Politics of Southern Europe: Integration into the European Union*. Westport, CT: Praeger.

—— (2003b) *Economic and Social Dynamics and Community Institutions in an Enlarged Europe*. Institut d'études européennes, Université catholique de Louvain, Document no. 31, February.

—— (2003c), The Third Level of European Integration: New and Old Insights. In: José Magone (ed.), *Regional Institutions and Governance in the European Union*. Westport, CT: Praeger, pp. 1–30.

—— (2004), *The Developing Place of Portugal in the European Union*. New Brunswick, NJ: Transaction.

—— (2005), The Economic and Social Committee and Social Europe: The Structuring of European Civil Society. In: Antonio Varsori and Laura Leonardi (eds), *Lo spazio sociale europeo. Atti del convegno internazionale di studi, Fiesole (Firenze), 10–11 ottobre*. Florence: University of Florence Press.

—— (2006a), *The New World Architecture: The Role of the European Union in the Making of Global Governance*. New Brunswick, NJ: Transaction.

—— (2006b), The Rise and Fall of the Centre-Right Coalition Government in Portugal (2002–5), *Lusotopie*, XIII: 39–59.

—— (2007a), The Southern European Pattern of Parliamentary Scrutiny of EU Legislation: Emulating the French Model. In: Ronald Holzhacker and Erik Albaek (eds), *Democratic Governance and European Integration. Linking Societal and State Processes of Democracy*. Cheltenham: Edward Elgar, pp. 229–48.

—— (2007b), Southern European National Parliaments and the European Union. An Inconsistent Reactive Revival. In: John O'Brennan and Tapio Raunio (eds), *National Parliaments within the European Union: From 'Victims' of Integration to Competitive Actors?* London: Routledge, pp. 116–31.

—— (2007c), Paradiplomacy Revisited: The Structure of Opportunities of Global Governance and Regional Actors. In: Mario Kölling, Stelios Stavridis and Natividad Fernández Sola (eds), *The International Relations of the Regions: Subnational Actors, Para-Diplomacy and Multi-Level Governance*. Zaragoza: University of Zaragoza, pp. 3–28.

—— (2008), Leaderless Enlargement? The Difficult Reform of the New Pan-European Political System. In: Jack Hayward (ed.), *Leaderless Europe*. Oxford: Oxford University Press, pp. 188–207.

—— (2009a), *Contemporary Spanish Politics*. Second edition. London: Routledge.

—— (2009b), Europe and Global Governance. In: Chris Rumford (ed.), *Sage Handbook of European Studies*. London: Sage, pp. 277–94.

Magyar Köztarsasag Bírosagai (2008), website of the Hungarian National Council of Justice at: www.birosag.hu (accessed 17 September 2008).

Maher, Imelda and Dermot Hodson (2004), Soft Law and Sanctions: Economic Policy Coordination and Reform of the Growth and Stability Pact, *Journal of European Public Policy*, 11(5): 798–813.

Mair, Peter (1993), Myths of Electoral Change and the Survival of Traditional Parties: The 1992 Stein Rokkan Lecture, *European Journal for Political Research*, 24: 121–33.

—— (1997), *Party System Change: Approaches and Interpretations*. Oxford: Oxford University Press.

—— and Ingrid van Biezen (2001), Party Membership in Twenty Democracies (1980–2000), *Party Politics*, 7(1): 5–21.

—— W.C. Müller and F. Plasser (1999), Veränderungen in den Wählermärkten: Herausforderungen für die Parteien und deren Antworten. In: P. Mair, W.C. Müller and F. Plasser (eds), *Parteien auf komplexen Wählermärkten.Reaktionsstrategien politischer Parteien in Westeuropa*. Wien: Zentrum für Angewandte Politikforschung, pp. 11–29.

—— —— and —— (eds) (2004), *Political Parties and Electoral Change: Party Responses to Electoral Markets*. London: Sage.

Malová, Darina (2001), Slovakia: From the Ambiguous Constitution to the Dominance of Informal Rules. In: Jan Zielonka (ed.), *Democratic Consolidation in Eastern Europe. Volume 1: Institutional Engineering*. Oxford: Oxford University Press, pp. 347–77.

—— and Dana Sivaková (1996a), The National Council of the Slovak Republic: Between Democratic Transition and National State-Building. In: David M. Olson and Philip Norton (eds), *The New Parliaments of Central and Eastern Europe*. London: Frank Cass, pp. 108–32.

—— and —— (1996b), The National Council of the Slovak Republic: The Development of a National Parliament. In: Attila Ágh and Gabriella Ilonski (eds), *Parliaments and*

Organized Interests: The Second Steps. Budapest: Hungarian Centre for Democracy Studies, pp. 342–64.

Mangen, Steen (1992), Social Policy: One State, Two-Tier Welfare. In: Gordon Smith, William E. Paterson, Peter H. Merkl and Stephen Padgett (eds), *Developments in German Politics*. Basingstoke: Macmillan, pp. 208–26.

Manko, Rafal (2007), Is the Socialist Legal Tradition 'Dead and Buried'? The Continuity of Certain Elements of Socialist Legal Culture in Polish Civil Procedure. In: Thomas Wilhelmsson, Elina Paunio and Annika Pohjolainen (eds), *Private Law and the Many Cultures of Europe*, Amsterdam: Kluwer Law, pp. 83–103.

Manners, Ian (2006), Normative Power Europe Reconsidered: Beyond the Crossroads, *Journal of European Public Policy*, 13(2): 182–99.

—— and Richard G. Whitman (eds) (2000), *The Foreign Policies of the Member-States of the European Union*. London: Pinter.

Marcussen, Martin (2005), Central Banks on the Move, *Journal of European Public Policy*, 12(5): 903–23.

Marginson, Paul and Keith Sisson (2002), European Integration and Industrial Relations: A Case of Convergence *and* Divergence? *Journal of Common Market Studies*, 40(4): 671–92.

Marks, Gary (1993), Structural Policy and Multilevel Governance in the EC. In: Alan W. Cafruny and Glenda G. Rosenthal (eds), *The State of the European Community. 2: The Maastricht Debates and Beyond*. London: Longman-Lynne Rienner Publishers, pp. 391–497.

—— and Ivan Llamazares (2006), Multilevel Governance and the Transformation of Regional Mobilization and Identity in Southern Europe, with Particular Attention to Catalonia and the Basque Country. In: Richard Gunther, P. Nikiforos Diamandouros and Dimitri A. Sotiropoulos (eds), *Democracy and the New State in the New Southern Europe*. Oxford: Oxford University Press, pp. 235–62.

—— and Marco R. Steenbergen (eds) (2004), *European Integration and Political Conflict*. Cambridge: Cambridge University Press.

—— Richard Haesly and Heather Mbaye (2002), What do Subnational Offices Think They Are Doing in Brussels, *Regional and Federal Studies*, 12(3): 1–24.

—— Francois Nielsen, Leonard Ray and Jane Salk (1996), Competencies, Cracks and Conflicts: Regional Mobilization in the European Union. In: Gary Marks, Fritz W. Scharpf, Philippe C. Schmitter and Wolfgang Streeck (eds), *Governance in the European Union*. London: Sage, pp. 40–63.

Marlière, Philippe (1998), Introduction: European Social Democracy. In: Robert Ladrech and Philippe Marlière (eds), *Social Democratic Parties in the European Union: History, Organization, Policies*. Basingstoke: Palgrave, pp. 1–15.

Marsh, Steve and Hans Mackenstein (2005), *The International Relations of the European Union*. Harlow: Pearson-Longman.

Massari, Oreste (2005), Gran Bretagna: verso la presidenzializzazione? In: Gianfranco Pasquino (ed.), *Capi di governo*. Bologna: il Mulino, pp. 109–27.

Mateju, Petr, Blanka Rehakova and Geoffrey Evans (1999), The Emergence of Class Politics and Class Voting in Postcommunist Russia. In: Geoffrey Evans (ed.) *The End of Class Politics? Class Voting in Comparative Perspective*. Oxford: Oxford University Press, pp. 231–53.

Mateus, Rui, (1996), *Contos Proibidos: Memórias para um PS Desconhecido*. Lisbon: Dom Quixote.

Mau, Steffen and Roland Verwiebe (2009), *Die Sozialstruktur Europas*. Konstanz: UVK–UTB Verlag.

Maurer, Andreas (2003), Die Methode des Konvents – ein Modell deliberativer Demokratie? *Integration*, 25(2): 130–40.

—— and Wolfgang Wessels (2001), National Parliaments after Amsterdam: From Slow Adapters to National Players. In: Andreas Maurer and Wolfgang Wessels (eds), *National Parliaments on their Ways to Europe: Losers or Latecomers?* Baden-Baden: Nomos Verlagsgesellschaft, pp. 425–75.

—— Jürgen Mittag and Wolfgang Wessels (2000), Theoretical Perspectives on Administrative Interaction in the European Union. In: Thomas Christiansen and Emil Kirchner (eds), *Committee Governance in the European Union.* Manchester: Manchester University Press, pp. 23–44.

Maxwell, Kenneth (1995), *The Making of Portuguese Democracy.* Cambridge: Cambridge University Press.

Mazower, Marc (1998), *Dark Continent. Europe's Twentieth Century.* London: Penguin.

Meadows, Dennis L. (1972), *The Limits of Growth.* New York: Universe Books.

Meinecke, Friedrich (1998), *Macchiavellism: The Doctrine of Raison d'État and its Place in Modern History.* New Brunswick, NJ: Transaction.

Meny, Yves and Andrew Knapp (1998), *Government and Politics in Western Europe: Britain, France, Italy and Germany.* Third edition. Oxford: Oxford University Press.

Merkel, Wolfgang (1993), *Ende der Sozialdemokratie? Wählerentwicklung, Machtressourcen und Regierungspolitik im westeuropäischen Vergleich.* Frankfurt a. M.: Campus.

—— (1996), Institutionalisierung und Konsolidierung der Demokratien in Osteuropa. In: E. Sandschneider and D. Segert (eds), *Systemwechsel 2, Die Institutionalisierung der Demokratie.* Opladen: Leske & Budrich, pp. 73–112.

Merlingen, Michael, Cas Mudde and Ulrich Sedelmeier (2001), The Right and the Righteous? European Norms, Domestic Politics and the Sanctions against Austria, *Journal of Common Market Studies,* 38(1): 59–77 (particularly pp. 71–2).

Meyer-Sahling and Jan-Hinrik (2001), Getting on Track: Civil Service Reform in Post-Communist Hungary. In: *Journal of European Public Policy,* December, 8(6): 960–79.

—— (2005),The Institutionalization of Political Discretion in Post-Communist Civil Service Systems: Case of Hungary, *Public Administration,* 84(3): 693–716.

Mezey, M. (1979), *Comparative Legislatures.* Durham, NC: Duke University Press.

Michalka, Wolfgang (2002), Das Dritte Reich(1933–45). In: Martin Vogt (ed.), *Deutsche Geschichte: Von den Anfängen bis zur Gegenwart.* Frankfurt a. M.: Fischer, pp. 694–775.

Micheletti, Michele, Andreas Føllesdal and Dietling Stolle (2006), Introduction. In: Michele Micheletti, Andreas Føllesdal and Dietlind Stolle (eds), *Politics, Products,and Markets: Exploring Political Consumerism. Past and Present.* New Brunswick, NJ: Transaction, pp. ix–xvi.

Michels, Robert (1999), *Political Parties: A Sociological Study of the Oligarchical Tendencies of Modern Democracy.* New Brunswick, NJ: Transaction.

Miguet, Arnaut (2004), Political Corruption and Party Funding in Western Europe: An Overview. London School of Economics April. Report prepared for Transparency International, Expert Meeting on Political Finance Regulations, Athens 2002. Posted on website at: www.transparency.org (accessed 15 January 2009).

Military Capabilities Commitment Conference (2004), Declaration on European Military Capabilities. Posted on the website of the Council of the European Union at: www. council.eu (accessed 7 January 2008).

Miller, William L., Åse B. Grodeland and Tatyana Y. Koshechkina (2001), *A Culture of Corruption. Coping with Government in Postcommunist Europe.* Budapest: Central European University Press.

Milward, Alan S.(1992), *The European Rescue of the Nation-State.* London: Routledge.

Ministère de la fonction publique et de la Réforme Administrative (MFPRA) (2007), *Rapport d'activité 2006.* Luxembourg: MFPRA.

Ministère de Justice (France) (2008), website at: www.justice.gouv.fr/index.php?rubrique = 10054&ssrubrique = 10303 (accessed 2 September 2008).

Ministère de la Justice (Luxembourg) (2008), *Rapport d'Activité 2007*. Luxembourg: Ministère de la Justice.

Ministerie van Justitie (Netherlands) (2008), website of Dutch Ministry of Justice at: www.justitie.nl (accessed 13 September 2008).

Ministério da Justiça (Portugal) (2001), *Estatisticas da Justiça 2000*. Lisbon: Ministério da Justiça.

Ministry of Foreign Affairs (Romania) (2008), *Report on Romania's Foreign Policy, 2005–8*. Bucharest: Ministry of Foreign Affairs.

Ministry of Foreign Affairs (Sweden) (2008), Foreign Policy Statement 2008, posted on website of Ministry at: www.sweden.gov.se/sb/d/10276#item97835 (accessed 5 September 2009).

Ministry of the Interior (Estonia) (2005), *Local Government in Estonia*. Talinn: Ministry of the Interior.

Ministry of the Interior of Estonia (2005), *Local Government in Estonia*. Talinn: Ministry of the Interior, Department of Local Government, posted on website of Ministry of Interior at: www.siseministeerium.ee/public/LGinEstonia2005_20070322090339.pdf (accessed 19 April 2010).

Ministry of the Interior and Kingdom Relations (Netherlands) (2006), Kabinetsvisie 'Andere Overheid' at: www.MinBZK.nl (accessed 28 March 2006).

Ministry of Justice (United Kingdom) (2007), *Judicial and Court Statistics 2006 Presented to Parliament by the Secretary of State for Justice and Lord Chancellor by Command of Her Majesty the Queen*. London: Crown Publications.

—— (2008), website of the Ministry of Justice at: www.justice.gov.uk (accessed 13 September 2008).

Ministry of Regional Development (Czech Republic) (2001), *Discovering the Regions of the Czech Republic*. Prague: Ministry of Regional Development.

Missiroli, Antonio (2000), Italy. In: Ian Manners and Richard G. Whitman (eds), *The Foreign Policies of the European Union Member States*. Manchester: Manchester University Press, pp. 87–104.

Molas, Isidre (2001), Partis Nationalists:Autonomie et clans in Corse.Working paper no. 181. Barcelona: Institut de Ciencies Politiques i Socials.

Molina, Óscar (2006), Trade Union Strategies and Change in Neo-Corporatist Concertation: A New Century of Political Exchange? *West European Politics*, 29(4): 640–64.

—— (2007), State and Regulation of Industrial Relations in Spain: Old Wine in a New Governance Bottle? *South European Society and Politics*, 12(4): 461–79.

—— and Rhodes, Martin (2007), Industrial Relations and the Welfare State in Italy: Assessing the Potential of Negotiated Change, *West European Politics*, 30(4): 803–29.

Molina Álvarez de Cienfuegos, Ignacio (1999), Spain: Still the Primacy of Corporatism? In: Edward C. Page and Vincent Wright (eds), *Bureaucratic Elites in Western European States: A Comparative Analysis of Top Officials*. Oxford: Oxford University Press, pp. 32–54.

Montero, José Ramón (1998), Sobre las preferencias electorales en España: Fragmentación y polarización (1977–93). In: Pilar del Castillo (ed.), *Comportamiento politico y electoral*. Madrid: CIS, pp. 51–124.

—— and Kerman Calvo (2000), Spain. An Elusive Cleavage? In: David Broughton and Hans-Martien ten Napel (eds), *Religion and Mass Electoral Behaviour in Europe*. London: Routledge, pp. 118–39.

—— and —— (2005), Valores y Religiosidad. In: Mariano Torcal Loriente, Laura Morales Diez de Ulzurrun and Santiago Pérez-Nievas Montiel (eds), *España: sociedad y politica en perspectiva comparada*. Valencia: Tirant lo Blanch, pp. 147–70.

Montgomery, Kathleen (2006), Politics of Hungary. In: Gabriel A. Almond, Russell J. Dalton, G. Bingham Powell Jr. and Kaare Strøm (eds), *European Politics Today*. New York: Pearson Longman, pp. 403–56.

Moran, Michael (1989), Industrial Relations. In: Henry Drucker, Patrick Dunleavy, Andrew Gamble and Gillian Peele eds), *Developments in British Politics*. Basingstoke: Macmillan, pp. 279–94.

—— (2007), Social Policy. In: Bill Jones, Dennis Kavanagh, Michael Moran and Philip Norton (eds), *Politics UK*. Harlow: Pearson Longman, pp. 679–94.

Morgado, Maria José and José Vegar (2003), O *inimigo sem rosto. Fraude e Corrupção em Portugal*. Lisbon: Dom Quixote.

Mörth, Ulrika (2003), Europeanization as Interpretation, Translation and Editing of Public Policies. In: Kevin Featherstone and Claudio M. Radaelli (eds), *The Politics of Europeanization*. Oxford: Oxford University Press, pp. 160–78.

Mouritzen, Poul Erik (2004), *Dinamarca. El Govern Local: Preparat Per A La Reforma?* Col-leció Món Local 10. Barcelona: Universitat Autonoma de Barcelona – Institut de Ciencies Politiques i Socials.

Mrozowicki, Adam and Geert van Hoetegem (2008), Unionism and Workers' Strategies in Capitalist Transformation: The Polish Case Considered, *European Journal of Industrial Relations*, 14(2): 197–206.

Mudde, Cas (2004), The Populist Zeitgeist, *Government and Opposition*, 39(4): 542–63.

Mullally, Gerard (2004), Shakespeare, Structural Funds and the Irish Experience. *Innovation*, 17(1): 1351–610.

Muller, Walter (1999), Class Cleavages in Party Preferences in Germany – Old and New. In: Geoffrey Evans (ed.) *The End of Class Politics? Class Voting in Comparative Perspective*. Oxford: Oxford University Press, pp. 137–80.

Müller, Wolfgang C. (1996), Die Organisation der SPÖ, 1945–95. In: Wolfgang Maderthaner and Wolfgang C. Müller (eds), *Die Organisation der Österreichischen Sozialdemokratie 1889–1995*. Wien: Löcker Verlag, pp. 195–356.

—— (2000), Austria: Tight Coalitions and Stable Government. In: Wolfgang C. Müller and Kaare Strom (eds), *Coalition Governments in Western Europe*. Oxford: Oxford University Press, pp. 86–125.

—— (2006a), Regierung und Kabinettsystem. In: Herbert Dachs, Peter Gerlich, Herbert Gottweis, Helmut Kramer, Volker Lauber, Wolfgang C. Müller and Emmerich Tálos (eds), *Politik in Österreich.Das Handbuch*. Wien: Manz, pp. 168–87.

—— (2006b), Die Österreichische Volkspartei. In: Herbert Dachs, Peter Gerlich, Herbert Gottweis, Helmut Kramer, Volkmar Lauber, Wolfgang C. Müller and Emmerich Tálos (eds), *Politik in Österreich. Das Handbuch*. Wien: Manz, pp. 341–63.

—— Kaare Strøm and Torbjörn Bergman (eds) (2003), *Delegation and Accountability in Parliamentary Democracies*. Oxford: Oxford University Press.

Müller-Rommel, Ferdinand (2000), The F.D.P: Small, But Beautiful. In: Lieven de Winter, Joan Marcet, Alastair H. Thomas, Ferdinand Müller-Rommel, Ruud A. Koole and Gérard Grunberg (eds), *Liberalism and Liberal Parties in the European Union*. Barcelona: Institut de Ciencies Politiques i Socials, pp. 85–118.

—— (2001), Cabinets in Post-Communist East-Central Europe and the Balkans: Empirical Findings and Research Agenda. In: Jean Blondel and Ferdinand Müller-Rommel (eds), *Cabinets in Eastern Europe*. Basingstoke: Palgrave, pp. 193–201.

—— and Slavko Gaber (2001), Slovenia. In: Jean Blondel and Ferdinand Müller-Rommel (eds), *Cabinets in Eastern Europe*. Basingstoke: Palgrave, pp. 95–105.

—— and Ole Hersted Hansen (2001), Lithuania. In: Jean Blondel and Ferdinand Müller-Rommel (eds), *Cabinets in Eastern Europe*. Basingstoke: Palgrave, pp. 40–9.

—— and Gabriella Ilonski (2001), Hungary. In: Jean Blondel and Ferdinand Müller-Rommel (eds), *Cabinets in Eastern Europe*. Basingstoke: Palgrave, pp. 84–94

—— and Darina Malova (2001), Slovakia. In: Jean Blondel and Ferdinand Müller-Rommel (eds), *Cabinets in Eastern Europe*. Basingstoke: Palgrave, pp. 73–83.

—— and Zdenka Mansfeldová (2001), Czech Republic. In: Jean Blondel and Ferdinand Müller-Rommel (eds), *Cabinets in Eastern Europe*. Basingstoke: Palgrave, pp. 62–72.

—— and Ole Nørgaard (2001), Latvia. In: Jean Blondel and Ferdinand Müller-Rommel (eds), *Cabinets in Eastern Europe*. Basingstoke: Palgrave, pp. 29–39.

—— and Ferdinand Georg Sootla (2001), Estonia. In: Jean Blondel and Ferdinand Müller-Rommel (eds), *Cabinets in Eastern Europe*. Basingstoke: Palgrave, pp. 17–38.

Nadel, Henri and Robert Lindley (eds) (1998), *Les rélations socials en Europe. Économie et Institutions*. Paris: L'Harmattan.

Nalewajko, Ewa and Wesołowski, Włodzimierz (2007), Five Terms of the Polish Parliament, *Journal of Legislative Studies*, 12(1): 59–82.

Nannestad, Peter (2009), Das politische System Dänemarks. In: Wolfgang Ismayr (ed.), *Die politischen Systeme Westeuropas*. Opladen: Leske & Budrich, pp. 65–106.

Narud, Hanne Marthe (2003), Norway: Professionalization – Party-Oriented and Constituency-Based. In: Jens Borchert and Jürgen Zeiss (eds), *The Political Class in Advanced Democracies: A Comparative Handbook*. Oxford: Oxford University Press, pp. 298–319.

—— and Kaare Strøm (2000), Norway: A Fragile Coalition Order. In: Wolfgang C. Muller and Kaare Strøm (eds), *Coalition Governments in Western Europe*. Oxford: Oxford University Press, pp. 158–91.

Neelen, G.H.J.M., M.R. Rutgers and M.E. Tuurenhout (2003), *De bestuurlijke kaart van Nederland. Het Openbaar Bestuur en zijn omgeving in national en international perspectief*. Bussum: Uitgeverij coutinho.

Neisser, Heinrich (1997), Verwaltung. In: Herbert Dachs, Peter Gerlich, Herbert Gottweis, Franz Horner, Helmut Kramer, Volkmar Lauber, Wolfgang C. Muller and Emmerich Tálos (eds), *Handbuch des Politischen Systems Österreichs. Die Zweite Republik*. Wien: Manz, pp. 148–61.

—— (2006), Verwaltung. In: Herbert Dachs, Peter Gerlich, Herbert Gottweis, Helmut Kramer, Volkmar Lauber, Wolfgang Müller and Emmerich Tálos (eds), *Politik in Österreich. Das Handbuch*. Wien: Manz, pp. 201–12.

Nelken, David (1996), Stopping the Judges. In: Mario Caciagli and David I. Kertzer (eds), *Italian Politics: The Stalled Transition*. Boulder, CO: Westview Press, pp. 187–204.

—— (2003), Political Corruption in the European Union. In: Martin J. Bull and James L. Newell (eds), *Corruption in Contemporary Politics*. Basingstoke: Macmillan, pp. 220–33.

Neumann, László, András Tóth and Erzsébet Berki (2008), Hungary: Industrial Relations Development in Europe. Posted on EIROLINE database at: www.eurofound.europa.eu (accessed 28 December 2008). ID: HU0803029Q, 23 September 2008.

Newell, James L. (2006), Characterising the Italian Parliament: Legislative Change in Longitudinal Perspective, *Journal of Legislative Studies*, 12(3–4): 386–403.

Newman, Bruce I. (1999), *The Mass Marketing of Politics: Democracy in an Age of Manufactured Images*. London: Sage.

Newton, Kenneth and Jan W. Van Deth (2006), *Foundations of Comparative Politics*. Cambridge: Cambridge University Press.

Nicolacopoulos, Ilias (2005), Elections and Voters 1974–2004. Old Cleavages and New Issues, *West European Politics*, 28(2): 260–78.

Nieuwbeerta, Paul and Nan Dirk De Graaf (1999), Traditional Class Voting in 20 Postwar Societies. In: Geoffrey Evans (ed.), *The End of Class Politics? Class Voting in Comparative Perspective*. Oxford: Oxford University Press, pp. 23–56.

—— and W. Ultee (1999), Class Voting in Western Industrialized Countries: 1945–90: Systematizing and Testing Explanations, *European Journal for Political Research*, 35(1): 123–60.

Nikolov, Marjan (2006), Country Report: Local Borrowing in Romania. In: Marjan Nikolov (ed.), *The Future of Local Government Finance: Cases Studies of Romania, Bulgaria and Macedonia*. Skopje: Centre for Economic Analysis, pp. 5–37.

Nikolova, Pavlina (2007), Bulgarian Subnational Authorities on the Road in the EU. In: Mario Kölling, Stelios Stavridis and Natividad Fernández Sola (eds), *The International Relations of the Regions: Subnational Actors, Para-Diplomacy and Multi-Level Governance*. Zaragoza: University of Zaragoza, pp. 237–55.

Nomden, Koen (2000), Administrative Modernisation in the Netherlands. In: Isabel Corte-Real, Koen Nomden, Michael Kelly and Franck Petiteville (eds), *Administrations in Transitions*. Maastricht: European Institute of Public Administration, pp. 27–59.

Norris, Pippa (1997), Introduction: The Rise of Postmodern Political Communications? In: Pippa Norris (ed.), *Politics and the Press: The News Media and Their Influences*. Boulder, CO: Lynne Rienner, pp. 1–17.

—— (2001), The Twilight of Westminster? Electoral Reform and its Consequences, *Political Studies*, 49(5): 877–900.

Norton, Philip (1998a), Introduction: The Institution of Parliaments. In: Philip Norton (ed.), *Parliaments and Governments in Western Europe*. London: Frank Cass, pp. 1–15.

—— (1998b), Old Institution, New Institutionalism? Parliament and Government in the UK. In: Philip Norton (ed.), *Parliaments and Governments in Western Europe*. London: Frank Cass, pp. 17–43.

—— and D.M. Olson (eds) (2007), Post-Communist and Post-Soviet Legislatures, special issue of *Journal of Legislative Studies*, 13(1).

Norwegian Ministry of Government Administration and Reform (2007), *Pocket Statistics on Government Employees*. Oslo: Norwegian Ministry of Government Administration and Reform.

Nousiainen, Jaakko (1988), Finland. In: Jean Blondel and Ferdinand Müller-Rommel (eds), *Cabinets in Western Europe*. Basingstoke: Macmillan, pp. 213–33.

Nugent, Neill (2004), *European Union Enlargement*. Basingstoke: Palgrave.

Nunes da Silva, Carlos (2002), Local and Regional Government: Continuity and Innovation in Local Government. In: Stephen Syrett (ed.), *Contemporary Portugal. Dimensions of Economic and Political Change*. Aldershot: Ashgate, pp. 197–220.

—— (2004), *Portugal: Sistema de govern local*. Col·leció Món Local 11. Barcelona: Universitat Autonoma de Barcelona – Institut de Ciencies Politiques i Socials.

Nye, Joseph S. (2004), *Soft Power: The Means to Success in World Politics*. New York: Public Affairs.

O'Brennan, John and Tapio Raunio (2007), Introduction. Deparlamentarization and European Integration. In: John O'Brennan and Tapio Raunio (eds), *National Parliaments within the European Union. From 'Victims' of Integration to Competitive Actors?* London: Routledge, pp. 1–26.

O'Halpin, Eunan (1998), A Changing Relationship? Parliament and Government in Ireland. In: Philip Norton (ed.), *Parliaments and Governments in Western Europe*. London: Frank Cass, pp. 123–41.

Oliveira, Mónica D., José M. Magone and Joao A. Pereira (2005), Non-Decision Making and Inertia in Portuguese Health Policy, special issue, Legacies and Latitude in European Health Policy. In: *Journal of Health Politics, Policy and Law*, 30(1–2): 211–30.

Oliveira Marques, A.H. (1983), *Historia de Portugal. 2: Do Renascimento ás Revoluções Liberais*. Lisbon: Palas Editores.

Olivetti, Marco (2004), 'Il Potere Estero delle Regioni', in Alessandro Alfieri (ed.), *La Politica Estera delle Regioni*. Bologna: il Mulino, pp. 17–54.

Olsen, Johan P. (2002a), The Many Faces of Europeanization. In: *Journal of Common Market Studies*, 40(5): 921–52.

—— (2002b), Reforming European Institutions of Governance. In: *Journal of Common Market Studies*, 40(4): 581–602.

—— (2003), Towards a European Administrative Space? In: *Journal of European Public Policy*, 10(4): 506–31.

Olson, David M. (1998), Party Formation and Party System Consolidation in the New Democracies of Central Europe. In: *Political Studies*, 46(3): 432–64.

—— and Philip Norton (1996), Legislatures in Democratic Transition. In: David M. Olson and Philip Norton (eds), *The New Parliaments of Central and Eastern Europe*. London: Frank Cass, pp. 1–15.

Oñate, Pablo (2003), Parliament and Citizenship in a Triangular Relationship, 1982–2000. In: Cristina Leston-Bandeira (ed.), *Southern European Parliaments in Democracy*, special issue of *Journal of Legislative Studies*, 9(2): 130–50.

Opitz, Maximilian (2009), Zwischen Minderheiten und Machtpolitik. In: *Aus Politik und Zeitgeschichte*, 13(23): 25–31.

Organisation Internationale de la Francophonie (2009), website at: www.francophonie.org (accessed 9 January 2009).

Oschlies, Wolf (2003), Das politische System of Bosnien-Herzegovinas. In: Wolfgang Ismayr (ed.), *Die politischen Systemen Osteuropas*. Opladen: Leske & Budrich.

Ost, David (2002), The Weaknesses of Strong Social Movements: Models of Unionism in the East European Context, *European Journal of Industrial Relations*, 8(1): 33–51.

Overbeek, Henk (1991), *Global Capitalism and National Decline: The Thatcher Decade in Perspective*. London: Unwin Hyman.

Owen, Barry (2000), France. In: J.A. Chandler (ed.), *Comparative Public Administration*. London: Routledge, pp. 50–74.

Pabriks, Artis and Aldis Purs (2002), Latvia. The Challenges of Change. In: David J. Smith, Artis Pabriks, Aldis Purs and Thomas Lane, *The Baltic States. Estonia, Latvia and Lithuania*. London: Routledge.

Page, Edward C. (1995), Administering Europe. In: Jack Hayward and Edward C. Page (eds), *Governing the New Europe*. Cambridge: Polity Press, pp. 257–85.

Pagoulatos, George (2005), The Politics of Privatisation: Redrawing the Public–Private Boundary, *West European Politics*, 28(2): 358–80.

Pallaver, Günther (2005), Austria: La centralità del canciliere. In: Gianfranco Pasquino (ed.), *Capi di governo*. Bologna: il Mulino, pp. 13–40.

Panebianco, Angelo (1988), *Political Parties: Organization and Power*. Cambridge: Cambridge University Press.

Paoli, Letizia (2007), Mafia and Organised Crime in Italy: The Unacknowledged Successes of Law Enforcement, *West European Politics*, 30(4): 854–80.

Paraskevopoulos, Christos J. (2005), Developing Infrastructure as a Learning Process in Greece, *West European Politics*, 28(2): 445–70.

Parry, Richard (1987), Social Policy. In: Henry Drucker, Patrick Dunleavy, Andrew Gamble and Gillian Peele (eds), *Developments in British Politics 2*. Revised version. Basingstoke: Macmillan, pp. 197–222.

Parti Socialiste (2009), website at: www.ps.fr (accessed 16 January 2009).

Pasquino, Gianfranco (1995), Italy: A Democratic Regime under Reform. In: Josep Colomer (ed.), *Political Institutions in Europe*. London: Routledge, pp. 138–69.

Pasquinucci, Daniele and Luca Verzichelli (2004), *Elezioni europee e classe politica sovra-nazionale 1979–2004*. Bologna: il Mulino.

Pčolinsky, Vladimir and Antónia Štensová (2007), Slovak Parliamentary Elections 2006, *Central European Political Studies Review*, IX(2–3): 102–13.

Pedersen, Karina and Tim Knudsen (2005), Denmark: Presidentialization in a Consensual Democracy. In: Thomas Poguntke and Paul Webb (eds), *The Presidentialization of Politics: A Comparative Study of Modern Democracies*. Oxford: Oxford University Press, pp. 159–75.

Pedersen, Mogens N. (1979), The Dynamics of European Party System Systems: Changing Patterns of Electoral Volatility, *European Journal of Political Research*, 7(1): 1–26.

Pelinka, Anton and Sieglinde Rosenberger (2003), *Österreichische Politik. Grundlagen, Strukturen, Trends*. Wien: WUV.

Pellikaan, Huib, Tom van der Meer and Sarah de Lange (2003), The Road from a Depoliticized to a Centrifugal Democracy, *Acta Politica*, 38(1): 23–49.

Pennings, Paul and Jan-Erik Lane (eds) (1998), *Comparing Party System Change*. London: Routledge.

Pernthaler, Peter and Peter Hilpold (2000), Sanktionen als Instrument der Politikkontrolle-der Fall Österreich, *Integration*, 23(2): 105–10

Peters, Guy B. (2003), Dismantling and Rebuilding the Weberian State. In: Jack Hayward and Anand Menon (eds), *Governing Europe*. Oxford: Oxford University Press, pp. 113–27.

Pettai, Vello (2001), Estonia: Positive and Negative Institutional Engineering. In: Jan Zielonka (ed.), *Democratic Consolidation in Eastern Europe. 1: Institutional Engineering*. Oxford: Oxford University Press, pp. 111–39.

—— (2005), Estonia. In: Ingrid van Biezen and Richard Katz (eds), *Political Data Yearbook*, special issue of *European Journal of Political Research*, 44(7–8): 1002–7.

—— (2006), Estonia. In: Ingrid van Biezen and Richard S. Katz (eds), *Political Data Yearbook*, special issue of *European Journal of Political Research*, 44(7–8): 1094–100.

—— and Ülle Madise (2006), The Baltic Parliaments: Legislative Performance from Independence to EU Accession, *Journal of Legislative Studies*, 12(3–4): 291–310.

Phinnemore, David (2000), Austria. In: Ian Manners and Richard G. Whitman (eds), *The Foreign Policies of European Union Member States*. Manchester: Manchester University Press, pp. 204–23.

Pierre, Jon and Peter Ehn (1999), The Welfare State Managers: Senior Civil Servants in Sweden. In: Edward C. Page and Vincent Wright (eds), *Bureaucratic Elites in Western European States. A Comparative Analysis of Top Officials*. Oxford: Oxford University Press, pp. 249–65.

Pinto, António Costa and André Freire (2005). *O Poder dos Presidentes. A República Portuguesa em Debate*. Lisbon: Campo da Comunicação.

Piqani, Darinka (2007), Constitutional Courts in Central and Eastern Europe and their Attitude towards European Integration, *European Journal of Legal Studies*, 1(2): 1–22. Online publication at: www.ejls.eu (accessed 4 August 2010).

Plöhn, Jürgen (2001), Interessengruppen um Zeichen von Traditionen, sozialem Wandel und politischen Reformen. Werner Reutter and Peter Rütters (eds), *Verbände und Verbandssysteme in Westeuropa*. Opladen: Leske & Budrich, pp. 171–96.

Ploštajner, Zlata (2008), Small and Smaller – What Is the Smallest? Local Self-Governance in Slovenia. In: Zdravko Zlopaka (ed.), *Block by Block. It's Good to Build Well. Models of Organisation of Local Self-Governance*. Banja Luka: Enterprise Development Agency, pp. 36–77.

Poguntke, Thomas (2005), A Presidentializing Party State? The Federal Republic of Germany. In: Thomas Poguntke and Paul Webb (eds), *The Presidentialization of Politics. A Comparative Study of Modern Democracies*. Oxford: Oxford University Press.

—— and Paul Webb (2005), The Presidentialization of Politics in Democratic Societies: A Framework for Analysis. In: Thomas Poguntke and Paul Webb (eds), *The Presidentialization of Politics. A Comparative Study of Modern Democracies*. Oxford: Oxford University Press, pp. 1–25.

Polanyi, Karl (1944), *The Great Transformation*. New York, Toronto: Rinehart.

Poli, Davide (2005), Svezia: piu poteri ma piu competitori? In: Gianfranco Pasquino (ed.), *Capi di governo*. Bologna: il Mulino, pp. 281–309.

Pollack, Mark (1994), Creeping Competence: The Expanding Agenda of the European Community, *Journal of Public Policy*, 14(2): 95–140.

—— (2000), The End of Creeping Competence? EU Policy Making Since Maastricht, *Journal of Common Market Studies*, 38(3): 519–38.

—— (2004), *The Engines of European Integration: Delegation, Agency, Agenda Setting in the EU*. Oxford: Oxford University Press.

—— (2005), The New Transatlantic Agenda at Ten: Reflections on an Experiment in International Governance, *Journal of Common Market Studies*, 43(5): 899–919.

Pollitt, Christopher and Geert Bouckaert (2004), *Public Management Reform. A Comparative Analysis*. Oxford: Oxford University Press.

Polsby, Nelson (1968), The Institutionalisation of the US House of Representatives, *American Political Science Review*, 62: 144–68.

Pridham, Geoffrey (ed.) (1985), *The New Mediterranean Democracies: Regime Transitions in Spain, Greece and Portugal*. London: Frank Cass.

—— and José Magone, (2006), The Environment, Socioeconomic Transformation, Political Change in the New Southern Europe. In: Richard Gunther, P. Nikiforos Diamandouros and Dimitri A. Sotiropoulos (eds), *Democracy and the State in the New Southern Europe*. Oxford: Oxford University Press, pp. 263–304.

—— and Susannah Verney (1991), The Coalitions of 1989–90 in Greece: Inter-party Relations and Democratic Consolidation, *West European Politics*, 14(4): 42–69.

Programa de Reestruturação da Administração Central do Estado (PRACE) (2006), *Modelo de Reestruturação da Administração Central do Estado*. Lisbon: March 2004; pdf document posted on Ministry of Finance website (Portugal): www.min-financas.pt (accessed 4 August 2010).

Puetter, Uwe (2004), Governing Informally: The Role of the Eurogroup in EMU and the Stability and Growth Pact, *Journal of European Public Policy*, 11(5): 845–70.

Putnam, D. Robert, with Bob Leonardi and Rafaella Y. Nanetti (1994), *Making Democracy Work. Civic Traditions in Modern Italy*. Princeton, NJ: Princeton University Press.

Quaglia, Lucia, Fabrizio de Francesco and Claudio M. Radaelli (2008), Committee Governance and Socialization in the European Union, *Journal of European Public Policy*, 15(1): 155–66.

Quinlivan, Aodh (2006), *El govern local a la Republica d'Irlanda*. Col-leció Món Local 20. Barcelona: Universitat Autonoma de Barcelona – Institut de Ciencies Politiques i Socials

Quittkat, Christine (2006), *Europäisierung der Interessenvermittlung. Französische Wirtschaftsverbände zwischen Beständigkeit und Wandel*. Wiesbaden: Verlag für Sozialwissenschaften.

Radaelli, Claudio M. (1999), The Public Policy of the European Union: Whither Politics of Expertise? *Journal of European Public Policy*, 6(5): 757–74.

—— (2003), The Europeanization of Public Policy. In: Kevin Featherstone and Claudio M. Radaelli (eds), *The Politics of Europeanization*. Oxford: Oxford University Press, pp. 27–56.

Rae, Douglas (1967), *The Political Consequences of Electoral Laws*. New Haven, CT: Yale University Press.

Ramió, Carles (2001), Las Administraciones Públicas. In: Manuel Alcántara and Antonia Martínez (eds), *Política y Gobierno en España*. Valencia: Tirant lo Blanch, pp. 531–59.

Ramiro Fernandez, Luis (2003), Electoral Incentives and Organizational Limits: The Evolution of the Communist Party (PCE) and the United Left (IU), *Political Science Debates*, 1: 9–39.

Ramón, Ricard (2004), El Comité de las Regiones: El Largo Camino Hacia la Institucionalización de la Europa Multinivel. In: Francesc Morata (ed.), *Gobernanza multinivel en la Unión Europea*. Valencia: Tirant lo Blanch, pp. 285–325.

Raunio, Tapio and Teija Tiilikainen (2003), *Finland in the European Union*. London: Frank Cass.

Recchi, Ettore and Luca Verzichelli (2003), Italy: The Homeland of the Political Class. In: Jens Borchert and Jürgen Zeiss (eds), *The Political Class in Advanced Democracies. A Comparative Handbook*. Oxford: Oxford University Press, pp. 223–44.

Regeringskansliet (2007a), *Facts and Figures: Swedish Government Offices.Yearbook 2007*. Stockholm: Regeringskansliet.

—— (2007b), *The Swedish Judicial System. A Brief Presentation*. Stockholm: Regeringskansliet.

Reiterer, Albert F. (2003), *Gesellschaft in Österreich. Struktur und Sozialer Wandel im globalen Vergleich.* Wien: WUV.

Republique Française (1999), Ministère de la function publique de la reforme d'État et de la decentralisation. *Rapport annuel de relations internationals et de la cooperation administrative 1988–99.* Paris: MFPRED.

Reschová, Janica and Jindriska Syllová (1996a), The Legislature of the Czech Republic. In: David M. Olson and Philip Norton (eds), *The New Parliaments of Central and Eastern Europe.* London: Frank Cass, pp. 92–107.

—— and —— (1996b), The Legislature of the Czech Republic. In: Attila Ágh and Gabriella Ilonski (eds), *Parliaments and Organized Interests: The Second Steps.* Budapest: Hungarian Centre for Democracy Studies, pp. 322–41.

Reutter, Werner (2001a), Einleitung: Korporatismus, Pluralismus und Demokratie. In: Werner Reutter and Peter Rütters (eds), *Verbände und Verbandssysteme in Westeuropa.* Opladen: Leske & Budrich, pp. 9–30.

—— (2001b), Verbände zwischen Pluralismus, Korporatismus und Lobbyismus. In: Werner Reutter and Peter Rütters (eds), *Verbände und Verbandssysteme in Westeuropa.* Opladen: Leske & Budrich, pp. 75–101.

Rhodes, Martin (2005), Employment Policy. In: Helen Wallace, William Wallace and Mark Pollack (eds), *Policy-Making in the European Union.* Oxford: Oxford University Press, pp. 279–304.

Rhodes, R.A.W. (1996), The New Governance: Governing without Government, *Political Studies*, 44(4): 652–67.

—— (1997), *Understanding Governance: Policy Networks, Governance, Reflexivity and Accountability.* Buckingham: Open University Press.

—— (2003), What is New About Governance and Why Does It Matter? In: Jack Hayward and Anand Menon (eds), *Governing Europe.* Oxford: Oxford University Press, pp. 61–73.

Riedel, Sabine (2002), Das politische System Bulgariens. In: Wolfgang Ismayr (ed.), *Die politische Systeme of Osteuropas.* Opladen: Leske & Budrich, pp. 563–602.

Rifkin, Jeremy (2004), *The European Dream: How Europe's Vision of the Future is Quietly Eclipsing the American Dream.* Cambridge: Polity Press.

Rihoux, Benoit (1999), La transformation inachevée d'un 'parti-mouvement' en un parti de pouvoir. In: Pascal Delwit and Jean-Michel de Waele (eds), *Les Partis verts en Europe.* Brussels: Editions Complexe, pp. 139–64.

Ringdal, Kristen and Kjell Hines (1999), Changes in Class Voting in Norway 1957–89. In: Geoffrey Evans (ed.) *The End of Class Politics? Class Voting in Comparative Perspective.* Oxford: Oxford University Press, pp. 181–202.

Roberts, Geoffrey K. (2000), The Ever-Shallower Cleavage: Religion and Electoral Politics in Germany. In: David Broughton and Hans-Martien ten Napel (eds), *Religion and Mass Electoral Behaviour in Europe.* London: Routledge, pp. 61–74.

Rokkan, Stein (1980), Eine Familie von Modellen für die vergleichende Geschichte Europas. In: *Zeitschrift für Soziologie*, 9: 118–28.

—— (1999). In: Peter Flora, with Stein Kuhnle and Derek Urwin (eds), *State Formation, Nation-Building and Mass Politics in Europe. The Theory of Stein Rokkan.* Oxford: Oxford University Press.

—— and Derek W. Urwin (1983), *Economy, Territory and Identity: Politics of West European Peripheries.* London: Sage.

Roller, Elisa (2002), Reforming the Senate? Mission Impossible, *West European Politics*, 25(4): 69–92.

Rose, Lawrence E. (2006), *Noruega: El govern local en la cruilla.* Col-léció Món Local 17. Barcelona: Universitat Autonoma de Barcelona – Institut de Ciencies Politiques i Socials.

Rose, Richard (1995), Dynamics of Democratic Regimes. In: Jack Hayward and Ed Page (eds), *Governing the New Europe.* Oxford: Oxford University Press, pp. 67–92.

—— (2006), Politics in England. In: Gabriel A. Almond, Russell J. Dalton, G. Bingham Powell Jr and Kaare Strøm (eds), *European Politics Today*. New York: Pearson Longman, pp. 84–133.

Rosenau, James N. (2000), Governance, Order and Change in World Politics. In: James N. Rosenau and Ernst Otto Czempiel (eds), *Governance Without Government: Order and Change in World Politics*. Cambridge: Cambridge University Press, pp. 1–29.

Ross, Cameron (ed.) (2004), *Russian Politics under Putin*. Manchester: Manchester University Press.

Ross, Christopher (1995), *Jacques Delors and European Integration*. Cambridge: Polity Press.

Rószás, Arpád (2004), Regional Policy in Hungary: Institutional Preparations for EU Accession. In: Attila Ågh (ed.), *Europeanization and Regionalization: Hungary's Accession*. Budapest: Hungarian Centre for Democracy Studies, pp. 78–112.

Rothholz, Walter (2001), Norwegen: Korporatismus und die politische Kultur des Wohlfahrtstaates. In: Werner Reutter and Peter Rütters (eds), *Verbände und Verbandssysteme in Westeuropa*. Opladen: Leske & Budrich, pp. 313–34.

Rouban, Luc (1999), The Senior Civil Service in France. In: Edward C. Page and Vincent Wright (eds), *Bureaucratic Elites in Western European States: A Comparative Analysis of Top Officials*. Oxford: Oxford University Press, pp. 65–89.

Royo, Sebastian (2001), The Collapse of Social Concertation and the Failure of Socialist Economic Policies in Spain, *South European Society and Politics*, 6(1): 27–50.

Rudé, George (1980), *Revolutionary Europe: 1783–1815*. Glasgow: Fontana.

Rudzio, Wolfgang (2006), *Das politische System der Bundesrepublik Deutschland. 7. Aktualisierte und erweiterte Auflage*. Wiesbaden: Verlag der Sozialwissenschaften.

Rupnik, Jacques (2004), Élites et opinions publiques européennes face à un moment historique pour l'Europe. In: Jacques Rupnik (ed.), *Les Européens face à l'élargissement. Perceptions, acteurs, enjeux*. Paris: Presses de Sciences Po, pp. 11–45.

Ruzza, Carlo E. and Oliver Schmidtke (1996), Towards a Modern Right: Alleanza Nazionale and the 'Italian Revolution'. In: Stephen Gundle and Simon Parker (eds.), *The New Italian Republic: From the Fall of the Berlin Wall to Berlusconi*. London: Routledge, pp. 147–58.

Rydgren, Jens (2004), Explaining the Emergence of Radical Right-Wing Populist Parties: The Case of Denmark. In: *West European Politics*, 27(3): 474–502.

Sá, Jorge A., Vasconcellos Miguel Frasquilho, Watson Wyatt Limited and cooperation of Margarida da Pitta Garcia and Carla Gonçalves (2001), *Portugal Europeu?* Lisbon: Vida Económica.

Saalfeld, Thomas (1998), The German Bundestag: Influence and Accountability in a Complex Environment. In: Philip Norton (ed.), *Parliaments and Governments in Western Europe*. London: Frank Cass, pp. 44–72.

—— (2000), Germany: Stable Parties, Chancellor Democracy, and the Art of Informal Democracy. In: Wolfgang C. Müller and Kaare Strøm (eds), *Coalition Governments in Western Europe*. Oxford: Oxford University Press, pp. 32–85.

—— (2004), Party Identification and the Social Bases of Voting Behaviour in the 2002 Bundestag Elections. In: *German Politics*, 13(2): 170–200.

Sadurski, Wojciech (2008), 'Solange chapter 3': Constitutional Courts in Central and Eastern Europe – Democracy – European Union, *European Law Journal*, 14(1): 1–35.

Salomone, William A. (1960), *Italy in the Giolittian Era: Italian Democracy in the Making 1990–1914*. Philadelphia, PA: University of Pennsylvania Press.

Sandberg, Siv (2005), *El govern local a Finlandia*. Col·lecció Món Local 16. Barcelona: Universitat Autonoma de Barcelona – Institut de Ciencies Socials.

Sanford, George (2001), *Democratic Government in Poland. Constitutional Politics Since 1989*. Basingstoke: Palgrave.

Sapelli, Giulio (1995), *Southern Europe since 1945: Tradition and Modernity in Portugal, Spain, Italy, Greece and Turkey*. London, New York: Longman.

Sartori, Giovanni (2005), *Parties and Party Systems. A Framework for Analysis*. Colchester: ECPR Press (first published in 1976 by Cambridge University Press).

Sassoon, Donald (1997), *One Hundred Years of Socialism. The West European Left in the Twentieth Century*. London: Fontana Press.

Scarrow, Susan (2003), Germany: The Mixed-Member System as a Political Compromise. In: Matthew Soberg Shugart and Martin P. Wattenberg (eds), *Mixed-Member Electoral Systems*. Oxford: Oxford University Press, pp. 55–69.

Schaap, Linze (2003), Government or Governance in the Rotterdam Region? In: José M. Magone (ed.), *Regional Institutions and Governance in the European Union*. Westport, CT: Praeger, pp. 153–71.

Schaeffer, Robert K. (1982), The Standardization of Time and Space. In: Edward Friedman (ed.) *Ascent and Decline in the World System* (5: Political Economy of the World-Systems Annuals). Beverly Hills, CA: Sage, pp. 76–9.

Scharpf, Fritz W. (1999), The Viability of Advanced Welfare States in the International Economy: Vulnerabilities and Options, *Journal of European Public Policy*, 7(2): 190–228.

—— (2002), The European Social Model. Coping with the Challenges of Diversity. In: *Journal of Common Market Studies*, 40(4): 846–70.

Schefbeck, Günther (2006), Das Parlament. In: Herbert Dachs, Peter Gerlich, Herbert Gottweis, Helmut Kramer, Volker Lauber, Wolfgang C. Müller and Emmerich Tálos (eds), *Politik in Österreich.Das Handbuch*. Wien: Manz, pp. 139–67.

Scherpereel, John A. (2004), Renewing the Socialist Past or Moving Toward the European Administrative Space? Inside Czech and Slovak Ministries. In: *Administration and Society*, 36(5): 553–93.

Schiemann, John W. (2004), Hungary: The Emergence of Chancellor Democracy. In: *Journal of Legislative Studies*, 10(2–3): 128–41.

Schimmelfennig, Frank (2003), *The EU, NATO and the Integration of Europe. Rules and Rhetoric*. Cambridge: Cambridge University Press.

—— and U. Sedelmeier (eds) (2005), *Europeanization of Central and Eastern Europe*. Ithaca, NY: Cornell University Press.

Schmidt, Vivien (2002), *Democracy in Europe: The EU and National Institutions*. Oxford: Oxford University Press.

—— (2005), *The Future of European Capitalism*. Oxford: Oxford University Press.

Schmidt-Neke, Michael (2002), Das politische Systeme Albaniens. In: Wolfgang Ismayr (ed.), *Die politischen Systeme Osteuropas*. Opladen: Leske & Budrich, pp. 767–806.

Schmitter, Philippe C. (1995), Organized Interests and Democratic Consolidation in Southern Europe. In: Richard Gunther, P. Nikiforos Diamandouros and Hans-Jürgen Puhle (eds), *The Politics of Democratic Consolidation: Southern Europe in Comparative Perspective*. Baltimore, MD: Johns Hopkins University Press, pp. 284–314.

—— and Jürgen Grote (1997), *The Corporatist Sysiphus: Past, Present and Future*. Florence: EUI working papers, SPS 97/4.

Schout, Adriaan and Kees Bastmeijer (2003), The Next Phase in the Europeanization of National Ministries: Preparing EU Dialogues, *Eipascope*, 1: 12–21.

Schröder, Konrad (1993), Many Languages, One World. In: Monica Shelley and Margaret Winck (eds), *What is Europe? 2: Aspects of European Diversity*. London: Routledge, pp. 13–64.

Seawright, David (1999), A Confessional Cleavage Resurrected? The Denominational Vote in Britain. In: David Broughton and Hans-Martien ten Napel (eds), *Religion and Mass Electoral Behaviour in Europe*. London: Routledge, pp. 44–60.

Seisselberg, Jörg (1996), Conditions of Success and Political Problems of a Media-Mediated Personality-Party: The Case of Forza Italia, *West European Politics*, 19(4): 715–43.

Service Publique Federal Justice (SPF) (2008a), *Justice en chiffres 2008*. Brussels: SPF Justice.

—— (2008b), *La justice en Belgique*. Brussels: SPF Justice.

Siaroff, Alan (1999), Corporatism in 24 Industrial Democracies: Meaning and Measurement, *European Journal of Political Research*, 36: 175–205.

Silberman, Bernard S. (1993), *Cages of Reason: The Rise of the Rational State in France, Japan, the United States and Great Britain*. Chicago, IL: Chicago University Press.

Simon, Maurice D. (1996), Institutional Development of Poland's Post-Communist Sejm: A Comparative Analysis. In: David M. Olson and Philip Norton (eds), *The New Parliaments of Central and Eastern Europe*. London: Frank Cass, pp. 60–81.

Sjursen, Helene (2006), The EU as a 'Normative' Power: How Can This Be? *Journal of European Public Policy*, 13(2): 235–51.

Slovenian Presidency of EU (2008), 50th Meeting of Directors-General Responsible for Public Administration, Brdo 28 and 29 May 2008. Conclusions on the Future of EUPAN, posted on website of European Public Administration Network (EUPAN) at: www.eupan.eu (accessed 12 April 2010).

Smets, Isabelle (1998), Les Régions se Mobilisent – Quel 'Lobby Regional' a Bruxelles? In: Paul Claeys, Corinne Gobin, Isabelle Smets and Pascaline Winand (eds), *Lobbying, Pluralism and European Integration*. Brussels: European Interuniversity Press, pp. 50–66.

Smith, David J. (2002), Estonia: Independence and European Integration. In: David J. Smith, Artis Pabriks, Aldis Purs and Thomas Lane (eds), *The Baltic States: Estonia, Latvia and Lithuania*. London: Routledge.

Smith, Gordon (1976), *The Politics of Western Europe*. London: Heinemann.

Smith, Karen E. (2003), *European Union Foreign Policy in a Changing World*. Cambridge: Polity Press.

Smith, Michael E. (2004), *Europe's Foreign and Security Policy: The Institutionalization of Cooperation*. Cambridge: Cambridge University Press.

Smith, Timothy B. (2004), *France in Crisis: Welfare, Inequality and Globalization since 1980*. Cambridge: Cambridge University Press.

Socialdemokraterna (2001), Party Programme of the Social Democratic Party. Adopted by the Party Congress in Västerås, 6 November 2001, posted on website of Swedish Social Democratic Party at: www.socialdemokraterna.se/upload/Internationellt/Other%20Languages/party_program_english.pdf (accessed 14 April 2010).

Soeffner, Hans-Georg and Dirk Tänzler (2002), Medienwahlkämpfe-Hochzeiten ritueller Politikinszenierung. In: Andreas Dörner and Ludgera Vogt (eds), Wahlkämpfe. *Betrachtungen über ein demokratisches Ritual*. Frankfurt a. M.: Suhrkamp, pp. 92–114.

Soper, J. Christopher and Joel S. Fetzer (2003), Explaining the Accommodation of Muslim Religious Practices in France, Britain and Germany, *French Politics*, 1: 39–59.

Sotiropoulos, Dimitri (1999), A Description of the Greek Higher Civil Service. In: Edward C. Page and Vincent Wright (eds), *Bureaucratic Elites in Western European States: A Comparative Analysis of Top Officials*. Oxford: Oxford University Press, pp. 13–54.

—— (2004), Southern European Public Bureaucracies in Comparative Perspective, *West European Politics*, 24(3): 405–22.

—— (2006), Old Problems and New Challenges: The Enduring and Changing Functions of Southern European State Bureaucracies. In: Richard Gunther, P. Nikiforos Diamandouros and Dimitri A. Sotiropoulos (eds), *Democracy and the State in the New Southern Europe*. Oxford: Oxford University Press, pp. 197–234.

Sozialdemokratische Partei Deutschlands (2008), website at: www.spd.de (accessed 22 December 2008).

Sousa, Luis de (2001), Political Parties and Corruption in Portugal, *West European Politics*, 24(1): 157–80.

Spanou, Calliope (1996), Penelope's Suitors: Administrative Modernisation and Party Competition in Greece, *West European Politics*, 19(1): 97–124.

Spence, David (2000), Plus ça change, plus c'est la même chose? Attempting to Reform the Commission, *Journal of European Public Policy*, 7(1): 1–25.

Spence, R.F. (2000), Italy. In: J.A.Chandler (ed.), *Comparative Public Administration*. London: Routledge, pp. 126–47.

Sprudzs, Adolf (2001), Rebuilding Democracy in Latvia: Overcoming a Dual Legacy. In: Jan Zielonka (ed.), *Democratic Consolidation in Eastern Europe. 1: Institutional Engineering*. Oxford: Oxford University Press, pp. 139–64.

Sprungk, Carina (2007), The French Assemblée Nationale and the German Bundestag in the European Union: Towards Convergence in the 'Old' Europe? In: John O'Brennan and Tapio Raunio (eds), *National Parliaments within the Enlarged European Union. From 'Victims' of Integration to Competitive Actors?* London: Routledge, pp. 132–62.

Staes, Patrick and Nick Thjis (2005a), Quality Management on the European Agenda, *Eipascope*, 1: 33–41 (particularly p. 37).

—— and —— (2005b), Report on the State of Affairs of the Common Assessment Framework (CAF) after Five Years, *Eipascope*, 3: 41–9.

Stone, Alec (1992), Where Judicial Politics Are Legislative Politics: The French Constitutional Council. In: Mary L. Volcansek (ed.), *Judicial Politics and Policy-Making in Western Europe*, special issue of *West European Politics*, 15(3): 29–49.

Stone Sweet, Alec (2000), *Governing With Judges: Constitutional Politics in Europe*. Oxford: Oxford University Press.

Storey, Hugh (1995), Human Rights and the New Europe: Experience and Experiment, *Political Studies*, XLIII: 131–51.

Story, Jonathan (1995), Spain's External Relations Redefined: 1875–1989. In: Richard Gillespie, Fernando Rodrigo and Jonathan Story (eds), *Democratic Spain: Reshaping External Relations in a Changing World*. London: Routledge, pp. 30–49.

Stoykova, Pavlina (2007), Parliamentary Involvement in the EU Accession Process: The Bulgarian Experience. In: John O'Brennan and Tapio Raunio (eds), *National Parliaments within the European Union. From 'Victims' of Integration to Competitive Actors?* London: Routledge, pp. 255–71.

Strandberg, Urban (2006), Introduction: Historical and Theoretical Perspectives on Scandinavian Political Systems, *Journal of European Public Policy*, 13(4): 537–50.

Streeck, Wolfgang and Anke Hassel (2003), The Crumbling Pillars of Social Partnership, *West European Politics*, 26(4): 101–24.

Sundberg, Jan (2004), Finland. In: *Political Data Yearbook 2003*, special issue of *European Journal of Political Research*, 43(7–8): 1000–5.

Svallfors, Stefan (1999), The Class Politics of Swedish Welfare Policies. In: Geoffrey Evans (ed.), *The End of Class Politics? Class Voting in Comparative Perspective*. Oxford: Oxford University Press, pp. 203–28.

Svensson, Torsten and Perola Öberg (2005), How are Coordinated Market Economies Coordinated? Evidence from Sweden, *West European Politics*, 28(5): 1075–1100.

Swenden, Wilfried and Theo Maarten Jans (2006), Will It Stay or Will It Go? Federalism and the Sustainability of Belgium, *West European Politics*, 29(5): 877–94.

Swianiewicz, Pawel (2006), Polónia. *El Govern Local a Polónia: La Transició de l'Estat Centralitzat Autoritari al Sistema d'Autogovern*. Col·leció Món Local 21. Barcelona: Universitat Autonoma de Barcelona – Institut de Ciencies Politiques i Socials.

Szomolányi, Soňa and Grigorij Mezeznikov (1997), Das Parteiensystem der Slowakei. In: Dieter Segert, Richard Stöss and Oskar Niedermayer (eds), *Parteiensysteme in Postkommunistischen Gesellschaften Osteuropas*. Opladen: Westdeutscher Verlag, pp. 135–56.

Szukala, Andrea and Olivier Rozenberg (2001),The French Parliament and the EU: Progressive Assertion and Strategic Investment. In: Andreas Maurer and Wolfgang Wessels (eds), *National Parliaments on their Ways to Europe: Losers or Latecomers?* Baden-Baden: Nomos Verlagsgesellschaft, pp. 223–48.

Taggart, Paul (1995), New Populist Parties in Western Europe, *West European Politics*, 18(1): 34–51.

—— (1998), A Touchstone of Dissent: Euroscepticism in Contemporary European Party Systems, *European Journal for Political Research*, 33: 363–88 (particularly pp. 365–6).

—— (2000), *Populism*. Buckingham: Open University Press.

—— (2004), Populism and Representative Politics in Contemporary Europe, *Journal of Political Ideologies*, 9(3): 269–88.

—— and Alecs Szcerbiak (2004), Contemporary Euroscepticism in the Party Systems of the European Union Candidate States of Central and Eastern Europe, *European Journal of Political Research*, 43(1): 1–28.

Talmon, J.L. (1955), *The Origins of Totalitarian Democracy*. London: Secker & Warburg.

Tálos, Emmerich (2005), Vom Vorzeige-zum Auslaufmodell? Österreichs Sozialpartnerschaft 1945 bis 2005. In: Ferdinand Karlhofer and Emmerich Tálos (eds), *Sozialpartnerschaft. Österreichische und Europäische Perspektiven*. Wien: LIT, pp. 185–209.

—— (2006), Sozialpartnerschaft: Austrokorporatismus am Ende? In: Herbert Dachs, Peter Gerlich, Herbert Gottweis, Helmut Kramer, Volkmar Lauber, Wolfgang C. Müller and Emmerich Talos (eds), *Politik in Österreich: Das Handbuch*. Wien: Manzsche Verlag, pp. 425–42.

Taras, Ray (2006), Politics in Poland. In: Gabriel A. Almond, Russell J. Dalton, G. Bingham Powell Jr. and Kaare Strøm (eds), *European Politics Today*. New York: Pearson Longman, pp. 349–401.

Telò, Mario (2005), *Europe: A Civilian Power? European Union, Global Governance, World Order*. Basingstoke: Palgrave.

ten Napel, Hans-Martien (1999), The Netherlands: Resilience Amidst Change. In: David Broughton and Mark Donovan (eds), *Changing Party Systems in Western Europe*. London: Pinter, pp. 163–82.

Thoenig, Jean-Claude (2005), Territorial Administration and Political Control: Decentralization in France, *Public Administration*, 83(3): 685–708.

Thomas, Alasdair H. (2000), The Liberal Democrats in Britain. In: Lieven de Winter, Joan Marcet, Alastair H. Thomas, Ferdinand Müller-Rommel, Ruud A. Koole and Gérard Grunberg (eds), *Liberalism and Liberal Parties in the European Union*. Barcelona: Institut de Ciencies Politiques i Socials, pp. 27–81.

Thomassen, Jacques and Rudy B. Andeweg (2004), Beyond Collective Representation: Individual Members of Parliament and Interest Representation in the Netherlands, *Journal of Legislative Studies*, 10(4): 47–69.

Thomson, David (1972), *Europe Since Napoleon*. Harmondsworth: Penguin.

Thoonen, Theo A.J. (1998), Provinces vs Urban Centres: Current Developments, Background and Evaluation of Regionalisation in the Netherlands. In: Patrick Le Galés and Christian Lequesne (eds), *Regions in Europe*. London and New York: Routledge, pp. 130–49.

Tilly, Charles (1981), Sinews of War. In: Per Torsvik (ed.), *Mobilization, Centre-Periphery Structures and Nation-Building. A Volume in Commemoration of Stein Rokkan*. Bergen: Universitetsforlaget, pp. 108–26.

—— (1990), *Coercion, Capital, and European States*, AD 990–1990. Oxford: Basil Blackwell.

Timmins, Graham (2000), Germany. In: J.A. Chandler (ed.), *Comparative Public Administration*. London: Routledge, pp. 75–97.

Tömmel, Ingeborg (1998), Transformation of Governance: The European Commission's Strategy for Creating a 'Europe of the Regions', *Regional and Federal Studies*, 8(2): 52–80.

Tongue, Jonathan (2007), Northern Ireland. In: Bill Jones, Dennis Kavanagh, Michael Moran and Philip Norton (eds), *Politics UK*. Harlow: Pearson Education, pp. 767–76.

Tonra, Ben (2000), Denmark and Ireland. In: Ian Manners and Richard G. Whitman (eds), *The Foreign Policies of European Union Member States*. Manchester: Manchester University Press, pp. 224–42.

Traxler, Franz (2004), The Metamorphoses of Corporatism: From Classical to Lean Patterns, *European Journal of Political Research*, 43(4): 571–98.

Trentini, Marco and Massimo Angelo Zanetti (2001), Italien: Verbände zwischen Abhängigkeit vom politischen System und Autonomiebestrebungen. In: Werner Reutter and Peter Rütters (eds), *Verbände und Verbandssysteme in Westeuropa*. Opladen: Leske & Budrich, pp. 221–40.

Trif, Aurora (2008), Opportunities and Challenges of EU Accession. Industrial Relations in Romania, *European Journal of Industrial Relations*, 14(4): 461–78.

Tsarouhas, Dimitri (2008), Social Partnership in Greece: Is There a Europeanization Effect? *Comparative Political Studies*, 14(3): 347–65.

Tsoukalis, Loukas (2005), Managing Interdependence: The EU in the World Economy. In: Christopher Hill and Michael Smith (eds), *International Relations and the European Union*. Oxford: Oxford University Press, pp. 225–46.

Tuchman, Barbara (1962), *Guns of August*. New York: Macmillan.

Učakar, Karl (2006), Die Sozialdemokratische Partei Österreichs. In: Herbert Gottweis, Helmut Kramer, Volkmar Lauber, Wolfgang C. Müller and Emmerich Tálos (eds), *Politik in Österreich.Das Handbuch*. Wien: Manz, pp. 322–40.

Uçarer, Ernek M. (2007), Justice and Home Affairs. In: Michelle Cini (ed.), *European Union Politics*. Oxford: Oxford University Press, pp. 304–19.

Ulam, Adam (1998), *The Bolsheviks.The Intellectual and Political History of the Triumph of Communism in Russia*. Cambridge, MA: Harvard University Press.

United Nations (1988), Report of the World Commission on Environment and Development: Our Common Future Transmitted to the General Assembly as an Annex to Document A/42/427 – Development and International Co-operation: Environment. Available online at: www.un-documents.net/wced-ocf.htm (accessed 2 January 2008).

—— (2006a), *The Swiss Confederation: Public Administration.Country Profile*. Website of the UN Department of Economic and Social Affairs at: http://unpan1.un.org/intradoc/groups/public/documents/UN/UNPAN023324.pdf (accessed 14 August 2008).

—— (2006b), *The Partnership Between the UN and the EU. The United Nations and the European Commission Working Together in Development and Humanitarian Cooperation*. Brussels: United Nations System in Brussels.

—— (2006c), Grand Duchy of Luxembourg. Public Administration Country Profile. May 2006. Posted on website of the United Nations at: http://unpan1.un.org/intradoc/groups/public/documents/un/unpan023316.pdf (accessed 12 April 2010).

—— (2010), Report of the World Commission on Environment and Development: Our Common Future, Transmitted to the General Assembly as an Annex to Document A/42/427 – Development and International Co-operation: Environment. Available online at: www.un-documents.net/wced-ocf.htm (accessed 26 April 2010).

van Biezen, Ingrid (2003), *Political Parties in New Democracies*. Basingstoke: Palgrave.

Vanden Berghe, Yves, Maarten Van Alstein and Lina Neeb (2004), *Flemish Foreign Policy with Regard to Central and Eastern Europe (1992–2003)*. United Nations University, Comparative Regional Integration Studies, occasional paper O-2004-3.

Van der Meer, Frits and Theo A.J. Thoonen (2005), Competency Management and Civil Service Professionalism in Dutch Central Government, *Public Administration*, 8(4): 839–52.

Vandevivere, Claire (2001), The Federal Parliament of Belgium: Between Wishes, Rules and Practice. In: Andreas Maurer and Wolfgang Wessels (eds), *National Parliaments on their Ways to Europe: Losers or Latecomers?* Baden-Baden: Nomos Verlag, pp. 77–98.

Van Holsteyn, Joop J.M. and Galen A. Irwin (2000), The Bells Toll No More. The Declining Influence of Religion on Voting Behaviour in the Netherlands. In: David Broughton and Hans-Martien ten Napel (eds), *Religion and Mass Electoral Behaviour in Europe*. London: Routledge, pp. 75–96.

—— G. A. Irwin and J.M. den Ridder (2003), In the Eye of the Beholder: The Perception of the List Pim Fortuyn and the Parliamentary Elections of May 2002, *Acta Politica*, 38(1): 69–87.

Van Kersbergen, Kees (1999), The Dutch Labour Party. In: Robert Ladrech and Philip Marlière (eds), *Social Democratic Parties in the European Union: History, Organization, Policies*. Basingstoke: Palgrave, pp. 155–165.

Van Praag, Philip (2003), The Winners and Losers in a Turbulent Political Year, *Acta Politica*, 38(1): 5–22.

Vasconcelos, Álvaro (2009), *What Ambitions for European Defence for 2020?* Paris: EUISS Available online at www.iss.europa.eu/uploads/media/What_ambitions_for_European_ defence_in _2020.pdf (accessed 26 August 2009).

Vatter, Adrian (2002), *Kantonale Demokratien im Vergleich. Entstehungsgründe, Interaktionen und Wirkungen politischer Institutionen in den Schweizer Kantonen*. Opladen: Leske & Budrich.

Vehar, Primoz (2007), The National Assembly of the Republic Slovenia and EU Affairs and after Accession. In: John O'Brennan and Tapio Raunio (eds), *National Parliaments within the European Union. From 'Victims' of Integration to Competitive Actors?* London: Routledge, pp. 241–54.

Verfassungsgerichtshof (2008), website of Austrian Constitutional Court at: www.vfgh.gv.at (accessed 17 September 2008).

Verzichelli, Luca (1995), The New Members of Parliament. In: Richard S. Katz and Piero Ignazi (eds), *Italian Politics: The Year of the Tycoon*. Boulder, CO: Westview Press, pp. 115–34.

—— (2003), Much Ado about Something? Parliamentary Politics in Italy Amid the Rhetoric of Majority Rule and an Uncertain Party System, *Journal of Legislative Studies*, 9(3): 35–55.

—— (2004), Le parlement italien est-il encore une institution central? Le renouveau de la démocratie parlementaire en Italie. In: Olivier Costa, Eric Kerrouche and Paul Magnette (eds), *Vers un renouveau du parlementarisme en Europe?* (Bruxelles: Éditions Université Libre de Bruxelles, pp. 131–58.

Visser, Jelle and J. van Ruysseveldt (1996), *Industrial Relations in Europe. Traditions and Transitions*. London: Sage.

Vocelka, Karl (2002), *Geschichte Österreichs. Kultur-Gesellschaft-Politik*. München: Wilhelm Heyne.

Vodička, Karel (2005), *Das politische System Tchechiens. Lehrbuch*. Wiesbaden: Verlag für Sozialwissenschaften.

Vogt, Martin (2002), Deutschland von der Bonner 'Wende' zu den Problemen der Einheit (1982–96). In: Martin Vogt (ed.), *Deutsche Geschichte. Von den Anfängen bis zur Gegenwart*. Frankfurt a. M.: Fischer, pp. 888–970.

Volcansek, Mary L. (1992), Judges, Courts and Policy-Making in Western Europe. In: Mary L. Volcansek (ed.), *Judicial Politics and Policy-Making in Western Europe*, special issue of *West European Politics*, 15(3): 1–8.

von Beyme, Klaus (1984), *Parteien in westlichen Demokratien*. München: Piper.

—— (1996), Party Leadership and Change in Party Systems: Towards a Postmodern Party State? *Government and Opposition*, 31(2): 135–59.

von Thadden, Rudolf and Anna Hofmann (eds) (2005), *Populismus in Europa-Krise der Demokratie?* Göttingen: Wallstein Verlag.

Wagner, Richard (2006), Autistische Nachbarn, *Aus Politik und Zeitgeschichte*, 27(3): 3–6.

Wallace, Helen (2005), An Institutional Anatomy and Five Policy Methods. In: Helen Wallace, William Wallace and Mark A. Pollack (eds), *Policy-Making in the European Union*. Oxford: Oxford University Press, pp. 49–90.

Wallace, William (2005), Post-Sovereign Governance: The EU as a Partial Polity. In: Helen Wallace, William Wallace and Mark A. Pollack (eds), *Policy-Making in the European Union*. Oxford: Oxford University Press, pp. 483–503.

Wallerstein, Immanuel (1974), *The Modern World System. 1: Capitalist Agriculture and the Origins of the European World-Economy in the Sixteenth Century*. New York and San Francisco, CA: Academic Press.

Waschkuhn, Arno and Anita Bestler (1999), Das politische System Maltas. In: Wolfgang Ismayr (ed.), *Die politischen Systeme Westeuropas*. Opladen: Leske & Budrich, pp. 673–95.

Weale, Albert, Geoffrey Pridham, Andrea Williams and Martin Porter (1996), Environmental Administration in Six European States: Secular Convergence and National Distinctiveness? *Public Administration*, 74(2): 255–74.

Weber, Eugen, (1977), *Peasants into Frenchmen: The Modernization of Rural France 1870–1914*. London: Chatto & Windus.

Weber, Max (1934), *Die Protestantische Ethik und der Geist des Kapitalismus*. Tübingen: J.C.B. Mohr.

Webster, Christian (1968), *The Croce and the Fasces. Christian Democracy and Fascism in Italy*. London: Hollis & Carter.

Wegs, J. Roberts and Robert Ladrech (2006), *Europe Since 1945: A Concise History*. Basingstoke: Palgrave.

Welan, Manfred (2000), *Regierungsbildung insbesondere 1999/2000*. Diskussionspapier 80-R-2000, February. Wien: Universität für Bodenkultur-Institut für Politik, Wirtschaft und Recht.

Wessels, Wolfgang (2002), Der Konvent: Modelle für eine innovative Integrationsmethode, *Integration*, 25(2): 83–98,

—— (2008), *Das politische System der Europäischen Union*. Wiesbaden: Verlag der Sozialwissenschaften.

—— Andreas Maurer and Jürgen Mittag (2003), The European Union and Member-States Analysing Two Arenas Over Time. In: Wolfgang Wessels, Andreas Maurer and Jürgen Mittag (eds), *Fifteen Into One? The European Union and Its Member States*. Manchester: Manchester University Press, pp. 3–28.

Wilhelmsson, Thomas, E. Paunio and A. Pohjolainen (eds) (2007), *Private Law and the Many Cultures of Europe*. Amsterdam: Kluwer Law.

Willemsen, Heinz (2002), Das politische System Makedoniens. In: Wolfgang Ismayr (ed.), *Die politischen Systeme Osteuropas*. Opladen: Leske & Budrich, pp. 731–66.

Williams, E.N. (1999), *The Ancien Regime in Europe: Government and Society in the Major States. 1648–1789*. London: Pimlico.

Wisse, Ewa (2006), *Promoting Democracy: An International Exploration of Implementation and Policy Practice*. The Hague: Ministry of the Interior and Kingdom Relations, pp. 109–10.

Witte, Els, Jan Craeybeckx and Alan Meynen (2000), *Political History of Belgium: From 1830 Onwards*. Brussels: VUB, University Press.

Woll, Cornelia (2006), National Business Associations Under Stress: Lessons from the French Case, *West European Politics*, 29(3): 489–512.

Wollmann, Hellmut (1996), Institutionenbildung in Ostdeutschland: Neubau, Umbau und 'schöpferische Zerstörung'. In: Max Kaase, Andreas Eisen, Oscar W. Gabriel, Oskar Niedermayer and Hellmut Wollmann (eds), *Politisches System: Band 3 of Berichte zum sozialen und politischen Wandel in Ostdeutschland*. Opladen: Leske & Budrich, pp. 47–153.

World Economic Forum (2010), Global Competitiveness Report 2009–10. Geneva: World Economic Forum.

Wright, Vincent (2001), *The Government and Politics of France*. Fourth edition. London: Routledge.

Yannis, Nicos (2004), Greece: On New European Tracks, *South European Society and Politics*, 9(1): 121–41.

Yates, Jacqueline (2000), Sweden. In: J.A. Chandler (ed.), *Comparative Public Administration*. London: Routledge, pp. 148–72.

Young, John W. (1997), *Britain and the World in the Twentieth Century*. London: Arnold.

Zajc, Drago (1996), Legislative Developments in a New Democracy: The Case of Slovenia. In: Attila Ágh and Gabriella Ilonski (eds), *Parliaments and Organized Interests: The Second Steps*. Budapest: Hungarian Centre for Democracy Studies, pp. 380–94.

—— (2007), Slovenia's National Assembly 1990–2004, *Journal of Legislative Studies*, 13(1): 83–98.

Zervakis, Peter (2002), Das politische System Griechenlands. In: Wolfgang Ismayr (ed.), *Die politischen Systeme Westeuropas*. Opladen: Leske & Budrich, pp. 687–730.

—— and Gustav Auernheimer (2002), Das politische Systeme Zyperns. In: Wolfgang Ismayr (ed.), *Die politischen Systeme Osteuropas*. Opladen: Leske & Budrich, pp. 819–68.

—— and —— (2009), Das politische System Griechenlands. In: Wolfgang Ismayr (ed.), *Die politischen Systeme Westeuropas*. Opladen: Leske & Budrich, pp. 819–58.

—— and Tasos Costeas (2010), Das politische Systeme Zyperns. In: Wolfgang Ismayr (ed.), *Die politischen Systeme Osteuropas*. Opladen: Leske & Budrich, pp. 1097–1157.

Z'graggen, Heidi and Wolf Linder (2004), *Professionalisierung der Parlamente in internationalen Vergleich*. Studie im Auftrag der Parlamentsdienste der Schweizerischen Bundesversammlung. Bern: Institut für Politikwissenschaft. Posted on website of Swiss Parliament: www.parlament.ch (accessed 4 August 2010).

Ziemer, Klaus and Claudia Yvette Matthes (2010), Das politische System Polens. In: Wolfgang Ismayr (ed.), *Die politischen Systeme Osteuropas. 3. Aktualisierte und erweiterte Auflage*. Wiesbaden: Verlag Sozialwissenschaften, pp. 209–73.

Zlopaka, Zdravko (2008), It Won't Build By Itself. Local Self-Governance in Bosnia-Herzegovina. In: Zdravko Zlopaka (ed.), *Block by Block. It's Good To Build Well. Models of Organisation of Local Self-Governance*. Banja Luka: Enterprise Development Agency, pp. 179–206.

Zubek, Radoslaw (2001), A Core in Check: The Transformation of the Core Executive, *Journal of European Public Policy*, 8(6): 911–32.

Zwaan, Jaap W. De (1995), *The Permanent Representatives Committee: Its Role in European Union Decision-Making*. Amsterdam: Elsevier.

Index